LANDLORD AND PEASANT IN PERSIA

LANDLORD AND PEASANT IN PERSIA

A STUDY OF
LAND TENURE AND LAND REVENUE
ADMINISTRATION

BY

ANN K. S. LAMBTON
O.B.E., PH.D. (Lond.)
Reader in Persian in the University
of London

Issued under the auspices of the
Royal Institute of International Affairs

OXFORD UNIVERSITY PRESS
LONDON NEW YORK TORONTO
1953

Oxford University Press, Amen House, London E.C. 4
GLASGOW NEW YORK TORONTO MELBOURNE WELLINGTON
BOMBAY CALCUTTA MADRAS KARACHI CAPE TOWN IBADAN
Geoffrey Cumberlege, Publisher to the University

PRINTED IN GREAT BRITAIN
AT THE UNIVERSITY PRESS, OXFORD
BY CHARLES BATEY, PRINTER TO THE UNIVERSITY

AUTHOR'S PREFACE

THE object of the present work is to examine in broad outline the position of landlord and peasant in contemporary Persia and the historical factors out of which the existing situation has developed. The work thus falls into two parts: in Part I an attempt has been made to outline the history of land tenure and land revenue administration in Persia in Islamic times down to the grant of the Constitution in 1906. In Part II the situation during the period subsequent to that date is described.

The continuity of practice in many respects has been striking. Certain problems tend to recur, and there has been a similarity in the attitude of the governments of the day towards these problems, and towards the land-holding classes and the peasantry. Further, the attitude of the landlords towards the peasants, although modified by the conditions of the twentieth century, resembles in many respects that of the landlords of earlier times. In the field of husbandry also there has been little change. Much study still remains to be done in these various fields. Nevertheless, a useful purpose may be served by putting forward, even at this stage, the material which has been collected.

Part II consists of a description of the general position of the landlord and peasant in Persia primarily in its social and political aspects. It does not aim at a comprehensive examination of the economic position of the landlord and peasant. Reliable statistics upon which to base such an examination are lacking. In this part of the study I have confined myself to describing those areas of which I have personal knowledge. Although certain broad principles can be inferred from the evidence, it is not sufficient to form a basis for widespread generalizations.

Since this work is intended to be an introduction to the subject, although attention has been drawn to some of the difficulties with which the rural population is faced at the present day in Persia, no attempt has been made to suggest in detail the lines along which they might be solved.

The material for Part II was collected in Persia mainly between July 1948 and September 1949. I had, however, begun to study the problems concerned during earlier visits to Persia in 1936–7 and 1939–45. On all three occasions I travelled widely.

It remains for me to express my gratitude to the Royal Institute of International Affairs and to the Leverhulme Research Fellowship Committee who made grants towards the cost of my journey in 1948–9, and to the Governing Body of the School of Oriental and African Studies for their generosity in granting me leave of absence for the Session 1948–9 to enable me to visit Persia to collect material for this work.

It is my pleasant duty to express my gratitude to Sir Reader Bullard for reading through the manuscript and for his help, advice, and encouragement, not only during the actual preparation of the book in its final form, but also during the years 1939–45, in Tehrān. I am also much indebted to Dr Doreen Warriner and Sir Malcolm Darling, who kindly read through Part II and made valuable suggestions, to Professor Vesey-FitzGerald for his assistance in Chapter IX, to Professor P. Wittek for reading through Part I and for making valuable suggestions, to Sir Giles Squire for his advice, and to Mr A. C. Trott for permission to make use of his translation of the Civil Code. My debt to Professor H. A. R. Gibb is not simply for the time he generously gave to reading through Part I of the work, but goes far deeper. It was as one of his students at the School of Oriental Studies that my interest in this field was first aroused. Much of my knowledge was acquired under his guidance and has become part, as it were, of my stock-in-trade and I should like here to acknowledge my debt. It must, however, be made clear that in spite of the assistance which I have received from these and other quarters the responsibility for the views expressed in this work and for the many shortcomings which will doubtless be found in it is mine alone.

Thanks are also due to Miss H. Oliver of the Royal Institute of International Affairs for her help in preparing the manuscript for the press, to Mr N. C. Sainsbury for proof-reading, and to the Oxford University Press for their careful printing.

Lastly, it remains for me to express my gratitude to the Persian authorities, in particular to the Director and staff of the Library of the National Assembly, to the Director of the National Library, and to Ḥājjī Ḥusayn Āqā Malik, Ḥājjī Ḥusayn Āqā Nakhjavānī, and Ḥājjī Muḥammad Āqā Nakhjavānī for their generosity in placing their valuable libraries at my disposal, and to my many Persian friends, too numerous to be mentioned by name, for their unfailing kindness and help during my various journeys.

August 1951

CONTENTS

PART I

PART II

ABBREVIATIONS USED IN REFERENCES TO SOURCES[1]

Arch. d'hist. du droit orient.: *Archives d'histoire du droit oriental.*

A.K.: Muntakhab ud-Dīn Badī' al-Kātib al-Juvaynī, *'Atabat al-Katabat.*

B.M.: British Museum.

B.S.O.A.S. (*B.S.O.S.*): *Bulletin of the School of Oriental and African Studies.* (*Bulletin of the School of Oriental Studies.*)

Bibl. Geog. Arab.: *Bibliotheca Geographorum Arabicorum*, ed. M. J. de Goeje (Leyden).

Bu.: Bundārī, *Zubdat an-Nuṣrat wa Nukhbat al-'Uṣrat.*

E.I.: *Encyclopaedia of Islam.*

G.M.S.: Gibb Memorial Series.

I.A.: Ibn ul-Athīr, *al-Kāmil fī't-Ta'rīkh.*

I.K.: Ibn Khallikān, Biographical Dictionary.

J.N.E.: *Journal of Near Eastern Studies* (Chicago).

J.R.A.S.: *Journal of the Royal Asiatic Society* (London).

M.F.A.: Archives of the Ministry of Finance Secondary School, Tehrān.

M.R.: Rashīd ud-Dīn Faẓlullāh, *Makātībi Rashīdī.*

M.S.K.: *Majmū'ehyi Munsha'āti 'Ahdi Saljūqi va Khwārazmshāhīān va Avā'ili 'Ahdi Mughul.*

Munsha'āt: *Munsha'āt, being a Collection of Nādir Shāh's Farmāns.*

Proc. R.G.S.: *Proceedings of the Royal Geographical Society* (London).

R.E.I.: *Revue des études islamiques* (Paris).

R.M.M.: *Revue du monde musulman* (Paris).

S.N.: Niẓām ul-Mulk, *Sīāsat Nāmeh.*

Ṭab.: Ṭabarī, *Ta'rīkh ar-Rusūl wa'l-Mulūk* (*Annales quos scripsit Abu Djafar Mohammed ibn Djarir at-Tabari*).

T.G.: Rashīd ud-Dīn Faẓlullāh, *Tārīkhi Mubāraki Ghāzānī.*

T.M.: *Tadhkirat al-Mulūk.*

T.Q.: Ḥasan b. Muḥammad al-Qummī, *Tārīkhi Qumm.*

Z.D.M.G.: *Zeitschrift der deutschen morgenländischen Gesellschaft* (Leipzig)

[1] For details see the sections on Persian manuscript sources and Persian and Arabic printed and lithographic sources in the Bibliography, below, p. 411.

NOTE ON TRANSLITERATION

THE system of transliteration adopted is, with modifications, that adopted by the Royal Asiatic Society. This system was designed primarily with a view to transliterating Arabic words and consequently the transliteration is not specially adapted to the needs of Persian. Much that is Persian, however, is common to Arabic; especially was this the case in medieval times, and many technical terms have become familiar in the conventional transliteration. Consequently it has been considered preferable to maintain substantially the conventional transliteration; it has, however, been thought desirable to transliterate the letters ذ, ز, ض, and ظ, which are all pronounced alike in Persian, by the letter *z* (with various diacritical marks to distinguish the one from the other). Similarly, ث, س, and ص, which are pronounced in Persian alike, are represented by *s*, and differentiated by diacritical marks.

The system used in this work is not based on phonetic principles and if viewed from a phonetic standpoint will be seen to contain various inconsistencies. The letter *u* is used to represent a vowel approximating to the vowel in the English word *book*, and *ū* to represent the vowel approximating to the vowel in the English word *boot*. The letter *i* is used to represent a vowel approximating to the vowel in the English word *bed*, but when preceding the 'silent *h*', in a final position, although it is approximately the same as the vowel in the English word *bed*, the combination has been transliterated by *eh*, which differentiates it from a word such as ده *dih*, where the final *h* has its full value as a consonant. Where a relative adjective has been made out of a word ending in the 'silent *h*' this has been followed in the transcription by ', thus Ganjeh but Ganjeh'ī (a man of Ganjeh, etc.). Further, in certain Arabic words the conventional transcription of *a* has been retained for the final ه, thus Abū Ḥanīfa (and not Ḥanīfeh). Diacritic marks have not been used with the vowels in words which have been Anglicized, e.g. Samanid (for Sāmānid).

The following table gives the Arabic letters with the equivalents used in the Latin script. The conventional transcription, where this varies, is put in parenthesis.[1]

[1] In the text where the works of authors who wrote in Arabic are quoted, the conventional transcription has in some cases been used; thus the form Ibn Athīr has been used in preference to Ibn Aṣ̤īr. Certain words such as Ithna 'Asharīya have also been kept in their conventional form, since it is in this form that they are best known. Similarly, certain proper names have been retained in the form under which they have become generally known in England: thus Tehrān has

Arabic letter	Latin equivalent
ب	*b*
پ	*p*
ت	*t*
ث	*s̤* (*th*)
ج	*j*
چ	*ch* as the sound represented by *ch* in the English word *church*.
ح	*ḥ*
خ	*kh* as the sound represented by *ch* in the Scottish word *loch*.
د	*d*
ذ	*z̠* (*dh*)
ر	*r*
ز	*z*
ژ	*zh* as the sound represented by *j* in the French word *jour*.
س	*s*
ش	*sh*
ص	*ṣ*
ض	*ẓ* (*ḍ*)
ط	*ṭ*
ظ	*z̤*
ع	ʿ as the glottal stop between the words India Office.
غ	*gh* This represents a glottal fricative or plosive according to phonetic context. The sound does not occur in standard English. The same sound as the Perso-Arabic *ghayn* is said to be heard on Tyneside.
ف	*f*
ق	*q* see غ above.
ک	*k*
گ	*g*
ل	*l*
م	*m*
ن	*n* followed by *b* in the same word = *ṃ*.
و	where (1) a consonant = *v* (conventionally *w*); (2) preceded by خ in certain Persian words و is not pronounced and is represented by *w̱*; (3) a vowel = *ū*, approximating to the vowel in the English word *boot*; and (4) a diphthong = *ou* (conventionally *au* and *aw*) approximating to the diphthong in the English word *no*.[1]
ه	*h* where *h* in a final position represents the 'silent *h*' the preceding vowel is written *e*, the combination together being *eh* (conventionally *ah* or *a*), e.g. ميمه Maymeh.

been preferred to Tihrān. On the other hand, the forms Yazd, Mashhad, and Rasht have been preferred to the forms Yezd, Meshed, and Resht on the grounds that these forms are consistent with the system of transcription adopted, and more nearly represent the Persian pronunciation than the conventional forms.

[1] In a few instances *o* has been used to represent و as in Do Bandar.

Arabic letter	Latin equivalent	
ی		where (1) a consonant = *y*; (2) a vowel = *ī*, approximating to the vowel in the English word *bead*; (3) a diphthong = *ay* (conventionally *ai*) approximating to the diphthong in the English word *bay*; or = *ai*, approximating to the diphthong in the English word *by*;[1] and (4) the *iẓāfeh* after ا or و = *yi* (conventionally *i* or *-i*).

Hamzeh is represented by ʾ if in a medial or final position. If initial it is omitted in the transliteration.

ا	*ā*	as the vowel in the English word *bard*.
َ or *fatḥeh*	*a*	approximating to the vowel in the English word *bad* but slightly less rounded and more 'fronted'.
ِ *kisreh*	*i*	approximating to the vowel in the English word *bed*.
ُ *ẓammeh*	*u*	,, ,, ,, ,, ,, ,, *book*.

The *iẓāfeh* (conventionally represented by *i* or *-i*) is represented by *i* unless the word to which it is attached ends in a vowel or the 'silent *h*', in which case it is represented by *yi*.

The Arabic definite article is represented by *ul* or *al* unless it precedes a sun letter (ت, ث, د, ذ, ر, ز, س, ش, ص, ض, ط, ظ, or ن) in which case the *l* is assimilated to the sun letter; in certain circumstances if it follows *ū*, *ī*, or *ā* the vowel of the article is elided. Complete uniformity has not been observed in the transliteration of the Arabic definite article, owing to the fact that Persian usage requires *ul* (which is the nominative form) whereas Arabic usage varies according to grammatical context and the article is accordingly conventionally represented by *al*.

[1] Where ی is preceded by *fatḥeh* and has a *sukūn* it is transcribed *ay*, but where ی has a *tashdīd* and is preceded by *fatḥeh* it is transcribed *aiy*.

SOURCES

I

THE sources for the study of land tenure, rural organization, and the relations between the various classes holding or living on or from the land, fall into certain broadly defined categories according to the various aspects with which they deal. First is the legal theory as put forward by the jurists. The sources for this can be subdivided into three main groups: (1) those works dealing with the Sunnī theory—and Sunnism, it must be remembered, was the religion of the majority in Persia until Ṣafavid times; (2) the Shīʿī theory; and (3) the modern secular theory as put forward in the Fundamental Laws, the Civil Code, and modern legislation.[1] The Sunnī theory is put forward in the works of the early jurists of the various schools: Shaybānī and Abū Yūsuf for the Ḥanafīs, Shāfiʿī in his *Umm*, Bukhārī in his *Shurūṭ*, Ibn Māja in his *Ṣadaqāt*, Nasāʾī in his *Waṣāyā* and his *Iḥbās*, Ibn Saʿd in his *Ṭabaqāt*, ash-Shīrāzī in his *Tanbīh*, Yaḥyā b. Ādam in his *Kitāb al-Kharāj*, and Māwardī in his *Aḥkām as-Sulṭānīya*. Abū Yūsuf, al-Khaṣṣāf, and Yaḥyā b. Ādam in the early Abbasid period assembled the traditions and legal prescriptions concerning *kharāj*, while the work of Māwardī, which is of great importance, represents to some extent an attempt to reduce to uniformity the variety of practices which had grown up since the Islamic conquests and to reconcile these with the theory of the Qurʾān and the Traditions.

The Shīʿī sources vary somewhat according to the different Shīʿī sects, of which, for the purpose of this study, the Ithna ʿAsharī or Jaʿfarī is the most important. Muḥammad b. al-Ḥasan b. ʿAlī Abū Jaʿfar Ṭūsī, who died between 458/1065–6 and 460/1067–8, summed up the previous Shīʿī law in his *Kitāb al-Mabsūṭ* and *an-Nihāya fiʾl-Fiqh*. The *Sharāyiʿ al-Islām fī Masāʾil al-Ḥalāl waʾl Ḥarām* of Najm ud-Dīn Abuʾl Qāsim Jaʿfar b. ʿAlī Yaḥyā al-Muḥaqqiq al-Avval, who was born in Ḥilla in 602/1205–6 of a family of jurists, largely restated the work of Ṭūsī. The later Shīʿī sources of the Ṣafavid period add little to the earlier authorities. The early Shīʿī authorities are even more theoretical than the Sunnī authorities, since the Shīʿī, except for certain isolated instances such as the Zaydīs in the Caspian provinces and the Buyids, did not achieve political power in Persia until the Ṣafavid period, and there was thus no imperative need for them, as there was for the Sunnī jurists, to reconcile theory with practice.

Secondly, there are those sources which put forward the theory

[1] See Chs. VIII and IX.

of the philosophers. These are concerned not with the legal aspect, but with the relations of the different classes of the population, and more will be said of them in the following section.

Thirdly, there is the theory of the statesmen. The border-line between this class of work and the theory of the philosophers is not clearly marked, and to separate them is a somewhat artificial process. Perhaps the most famous of the works of the statesmen is the *Sīāsat Nāmeh* of Niẓām ul-Mulk, which is concerned essentially with practical administration. The author in his preface clearly states that the purpose of his work was to afford guidance to the ruler. What concerned Niẓām ul-Mulk was not the question of abstract justice or legal theory but what was likely to strengthen the ruling dynasty and, equally, what would weaken its position. Strong supporter though he was of orthodox Islām—whether for political or other reasons—he was realist enough to see that the departure from orthodox legal theory was such that there could be no return to legal theory unmodified by the practices which had grown up. He was concerned rather to regularize the existing position, and where possible he attempted to relate this to pre-Islamic Persian practice. Merging into the theory of the statesmen are literary works such as the *Qābūs Nāmeh* of ʿUnṣur ul-Maʿālī Kā'ūs b. Iskandar, and the *Naṣīḥat ul-Mulūk* of Ghazālī. Although couched in somewhat different form from the work of the statesmen, their ultimate purpose, which was the edification of the ruler and his descendants, is to some extent the same. Here also the concern of the writers is the actual welfare of the state. More will be said of these works also in the following section.

Fourthly, there are administrative handbooks compiled for the guidance of rulers and officials. This class merges into the third class but differs from it in that it aims at description rather than edification. One of the most important of these handbooks is the *Tadhkirat al-Mulūk* belonging to the Ṣafavid period.[1]

Fifthly, a considerable amount of incidental information is to be obtained from the Arab and Persian geographers. The works of the earlier geographers, dating from the third/ninth century, were compiled in the form of road books. In the fourth/tenth century the writing of systematic geographies starts and is supplemented by the works of travellers and pilgrims. For further information on the works of the geographers the reader is referred to *The Lands of the Eastern Caliphate* by G. Le Strange.[2]

Sixthly, there is the witness of historians to actual practice. Here, although the sources are seldom explicit on such mundane matters as land tenure and the relations of landlord and peasant,

[1] Ed. V. Minorsky (Gibb Memorial Series, 1943).
[2] Especially pp. 11 ff.

some information is to be obtained. The works of the historians can be divided into two broad categories: universal histories and local histories. Of the early histories The Book of Conquests (*Kitāb Futūḥ al-Buldān* of Balāẕurī, written in the middle of the third/ninth century, contains much useful information; to the Chronicles of Ṭabarī (224–310/839–923), known as the *Ta'rīkh ar-Rusūl wa'l Mulūk*, we are indebted for many details concerning Sasanian Persia. Ibn Miskawaih's *Tajārib al-Umam* gives a picture of conditions under the Buyids (*c.* 320–447/932–1055), while the *Tārīkhi Mubāraki Ghāzānī* of Rashīd ud-Dīn is invaluable for the reign of the Īlkhān Ghāzān Khān (694–703/1295–1304). The later historians, whether in the Ṣafavid or the Qājār period, unfortunately devoted little attention to the life of the people.

Among the local histories there are certain notable exceptions to the general lack of interest in social as opposed to political history. Outstanding is the *Tārīkhi Qumm*, which was composed originally in Arabic in the year 378/988–9, by Ḥasan b. Muḥammad b. Ḥasan Qummī. No copy of the original Arabic is known to exist, but a Persian translation of part of the work made in the year 805–6/1402–4 by Ḥasan b. ʿAlī b. Ḥasan b. ʿAbd al-Malik Qummī has come down to us.[1] This work contains much valuable material on fiscal and other matters; the author claims to have drawn upon official records and local histories, some of which are no longer extant. Various documents are quoted in the work concerning land revenue matters. The *Tārīkhi Bukhārā* of Narshakhī, also written originally in Arabic in the fourth/tenth century, and known to us only in a Persian recension of the sixth/twelfth century, the *Tārīkhi Rūyān* of Ouliā Ullāh Āmulī written in the eighth/fourteenth century, the *Tārīkhi Ṭabaristān va Rūyān va Māzandarān* of Ẓahīr ud-Dīn Marʿashī and the *Tārīkhi Jadīdi Yazd* of Aḥmad b. Ḥusayn, both written in the ninth/fifteenth century, and the *Shīrāz Nāmeh* of Aḥmad b. Abi'l Khayr Zarkūb, completed in 744/1343–4, all throw some light on local conditions. The local histories of the Qājār period are in this respect also far in advance of the general and dynastic histories. Among them especially deserving of mention are the *Fārs Nāmehyi Nāṣirī* of Fasā'ī (composed in the reign of Nāṣir ud-Dīn Shāh, 1848–96), the *Tārīkhi Tabrīz* of Lisān ul-Mulk Sipihr (written during the reign of Muẕaffar ud-Dīn Shāh, 1896–1907), and the *Tārīkhi Bakhtīārī* of Sardar Asʿad (Ḥājjī ʿAlī Qulī Khān), completed in 1333/1914–15.

Seventhly, there are original documents, royal *farmāns*, collections of state documents, *vaqf nāmehs*, government archives, and miscellaneous documents of various kinds, such as those dealing

[1] See my article, 'An Account of the *Tārīkhi Qumm*', *B.S.O.A.S.*, xii. 3 and 4.

with land sales and transfers of land. Of the first named there are examples scattered through the pages of the works of the historians and in literary collections. Notable examples are the edicts of Ghāzān Khān preserved in the *Tārīkhi Ghāzānī*, mentioned above. In the later histories numerous *farmāns* have been preserved, but the majority of them deal with political affairs rather than with the details of the administration. Of the literary collections, special mention should be made of the *Majmaʿ al-Inshā* of Īvāghlī Ḥaydar.[1] More important, perhaps, than the *farmāns* thus preserved in the works of the historians and others are the large collections in private hands. These are for the most part uncatalogued, and their contents often unknown. Many of the documents contained therein may be of little worth, but it is highly probable that a detailed examination of these private collections would bring to light much that is at present obscure in the general field of land tenure. Few *farmāns* relating to Mongol and Timurid times are known to survive. For the Āq Qoyunlū and Qarā Qoyunlū periods the sources are somewhat richer, while for the Ṣafavid period a large number of documents of different kinds exists. Coming to Qājār times the number of documents is greater, but the information to be obtained from them is perhaps scantier.

I have made use of a number of documents belonging to private collections. In this connexion I am especially indebted to Ḥājjī Muḥammad Āqā Nakhjavānī and Ḥājjī Ḥusayn Āqā Nakhjavānī for placing at my disposal a number of interesting documents in their possession. I was also fortunate in finding a number of documents on view in the Museum of the Faculty of Arts in the University of Tabrīz, and am indebted to the head of the University for his permission to make copies of these. Of great importance was a document belonging to Mr Muḥsin Ganjeh'ī.[2] I am also much indebted to Ḥājjī Mīrzā ʿAbdullāh Anṣārī of Iṣfahān for his generosity in allowing me to make a copy of *farmāns* in his possession,[3] and for his help in elucidating the meaning of some of the terms used in them.

Among the collections of state documents of primary importance for the Seljūq period is the unique manuscript known as the *ʿAtabat al-Katabat*. The original is in the National Library in Cairo.[4] A photostat of this exists in the National Library in Tehrān. The author or compiler of this collection was Muntakhab ud-Dīn Badīʿ al-Kātib al-Juvaynī.[5] The collection was made probably

[1] See C. Rieu, *Catalogue of Persian MSS. in the British Museum*, i. 389 *a*.

[2] See pp. 88 ff. [3] See pp. 102 ff.

[4] Special No. 19, General No. 6292; see *Catalogue of Persian MSS. in Khediv Library*, publ. 1306, p. 466.

[5] See *Lubb al-Albāb* of Awfī, i. 78–80, *Taʾrīkhi-Jahān-Gushā* of Juvaynī, ii. 9–10, and *Tazkireh* of Dawlatshāh Samarqandī, pp. 90–1.

between the years 538–48/1143–54 on the orders of Abu'l Fatḥ Nāṣir ud-Dīn Ṭāhir b. Fakhr al-Mulk al-Muẓaffar b. Niẓām al-Mulk, who was Sanjar's *vazīr* from Jumādī I 528 to Ẕu'l Ḥijja 548 (27 February 1134 to February–March 1154).[1] In addition to copies of state documents it contains a number of private letters, some of which appear to have been added to the collection after its original compilation.

In addition to the *'Atabat al-Katabat* there is a collection known as the *Munsha'āti 'Ahdi Saljūqī va Khwārazmshāhīān va Avā'ili 'Ahdi Mughūl*. The original is in the Asiatic Museum of the Academy of Sciences in Leningrad.[2] This contains a number of the same documents as are in the *'Atabat al-Katabat*, but has less information on agrarian matters.

In addition to these collections of state documents, our knowledge of the Khwārazmshāh and Mongol periods is supplemented by two collections, *at-Tavassul ila't-Tarassul* of Bahā ud-Dīn Muḥammad b. Mu'ayyad, and the *Makātībi Rashīdī*.[3] The former, though it deals mainly with Khwārazm and not with Persia proper, contains a good deal of valuable information. The latter consists mainly of letters from Rashīd ud-Dīn, the *vazīr* of the Īlkhān ruler Ghāzān Khān, and forms an important source for the period. Unfortunately, for the post-Mongol period we are less well served by collections of this kind.

Lastly, there are official records. There is no Public Record Office in Persia. In various libraries, notably the library of the National Assembly and the library of the Buyūtāti Salṭanatī, are preserved odd volumes of revenue rolls, but as far as I am aware there is no complete collection in existence which is available to the public. I was fortunate, however, in being able to use a series of official reports compiled between the years 1294/1877 and 1300/1883 preserved in the Archives of the Ministry of Finance Secondary School, which were made available to me through the Library of the National Assembly. For the western provinces of Persia on the borders of the former Ottoman Empire, in which they were from time to time incorporated, there are detailed records of the fiscal administration in the Turkish archives.[4] These I have not been able to consult. What existed under Turkish rule for these areas may have existed also under Persian rule, and it may be found that the somewhat haphazard appearance which the Persian scene

[1] See introduction by Mīrzā Muḥammad Khān Qazvīnī to the Tehrān photostat copy.

[2] See V. Rosen, *Les Manuscrits persans de l'Institut des Langues Orientales* (Petrograd, 1886), No. 26, pp. 146–59; see also preface by 'Abbās Iqbāl in his edition of the *Ḥadā'iq as-Sihr* of Rashīd ud-Dīn Vaṭvāṭ (Tehrān, 1308).

[3] Ed. Muḥammad Shafī' (Lahore, 1945).

[4] I am indebted to Professor B. Lewis for this information.

at all periods presents does not reflect the nature of Persian practice, but is due to the deficiencies of our sources. When we come to the present day, however, we are no better off than we are for the past. There are few published reports dealing with matters such as land ownership and kindred subjects. Various government departments publish from time to time statistical information, but the statistical data at present available are insufficient upon which to base any conclusions.[1] For this reason I have confined my observations in Part II for the most part to those areas of which I have personal experience. In these circumstances many of the conclusions reached in this work can be put forward only in the most tentative fashion.

II

Islamic jurisprudence has been described as essentially a science of classification. This tendency towards classification is not only found in juristic treatises but also runs through much of the philosophical and literary writings of the medieval Muslim world. Society is divided into groups or classes. That class upon which all other classes are superimposed is the peasantry, and the prosperity of the state is generally recognized to depend in the last resort upon the activities and well-being of the peasants. Consequently the authorities attach importance to the peasantry and to agriculture. The statesmen realized for the most part that the main revenues of the kingdom derived from the land and that if the condition of the peasantry was unduly depressed, the general level of prosperity would decline, and with it the revenue.

Reinforcing this essentially practical attitude was an ethical point of view deriving from two sources. On the one hand was the traditional Persian outlook, the mainspring of which is to be found in the Avesta (and goes back, therefore, to the period before the migration of the Avestan people into eastern Persia). The Avesta is unequivocal in its praise for the settled life of the peasant, the practice of agriculture, and the reclamation of waste-land.[2] Thus the Vendidad states: 'Creator of this material world, Thou Holy One! where . . . is the Earth mostly gladdened? Ahura Mazda answered: Wherever grain is most produced, O son of Spitama, Zarathustra, and grass and fruit-bearing trees; wherever arid land

[1] For example, the statistics published by the Department General of Agriculture for agricultural produce for the years 1309/1930–1 and 1310/1931–2 show the amount of crops grown in the different areas and the average price, the number of animals owned in each district and the trade in agricultural products and animals, and the number of villages and inhabitants. The figures for the two years differ considerably and probably reflect an imperfect statistical organization.

[2] See W. Geiger, *Civilization of the Eastern Iranians* (London, 1885–6), i. 12.

is changed into watered and marshy into dry land.'[1] The religion of Mazda, moreover, urged its followers to ceaseless activity in agriculture and bade them fight against sterility and barrenness, and to create in their place affluence and culture.[2] The prototype of the Persian King of Kings was Yima, whom Ahura Mazda describes as the Feeder, Protector, and Overseer of the world.[3] The function of the King of Kings was thus to provide whatever was necessary for the cultivation of the land, such as irrigation channels, and also to see to their upkeep, because by this means the provisions of the people could be assured.[4] Similarly, it was incumbent upon him to provide stores in a bad year. Further, with the treasure he amassed he was to provide needy cultivators with cattle and seed.[5] This belief that agriculture, and in particular the reclamation of waste-land and the planting of trees, is a praiseworthy action has to some extent persisted throughout Persian history, though it is perhaps seldom translated into action.

The second source from which the ethical point of view derives is Islām. The classical Islamic conception of the ruler was that he was the shepherd of his people. The people were regarded to some extent as a trust from God, and it was the duty of the ruler to ensure conditions in which the citizens had the widest scope for developing their moral nature by practising such religious and ethical duties as would fit them best for participation in the life hereafter. Since, moreover, the majority of the ruler's subjects were in most cases peasants and nomads, it is clear that he would be concerned with the general question of agriculture. A classical example of the ethical attitude towards office is the famous letter of the Commander of the Faithful ʿAlī to Mālik al-Ashtar on the latter's appointment over the *kharāj* in Egypt in the year 38/658–9.[6] Even in this document, however, the ethical aspect is not entirely divorced from the pragmatic; and Mālik al-Ashtar is instructed

> to give greater attention to the development of the land than to the collection of the *kharāj*, because it [*kharāj*] can only be obtained by the development of the land and whoever demands *kharāj* without developing the land ruins the country and destroys the people, and his work will last but a short time. If the people complain of the heaviness of taxation, or of some natural calamity, the interruption of irrigation, misfortune, or that the land has been changed by becoming waterlogged or parched, lighten their burden in such a way as you would expect would lead to the putting right of their affairs. You should not regard it as a burden to do anything which will lighten their burden. Verily it is a store

[1] Vendidad, iii. 4, quoted by Geiger, p. 209. [2] ibid. p. 204.
[3] Vendidad, ii. 12, quoted by F. Spiegel, *Eranische Altertumskunde* (Leipzig, 1871–8), iii. 637.
[4] Spiegel, iii. 637–8. [5] ibid. p. 636.
[6] ʿAlī b. Abī Ṭālib, *Nahj al-Balāgha* (Beirut, 1307), ii. 45–60.

which they will return to you in developing your district and in adorning your province. In addition, you will earn their excellent praise and pride in having spread justice among them. Further, you may count upon the surplus of food which you have caused them to store up on account of what you remitted to them, and on account of the confidence which you gave them, because of your justice towards them in your compassion for them. It may be that some event will take place such that you may have to ask their assistance and this they would bear with good grace, because a country which is flourishing can put up with whatever you impose upon it. The ruin of a country comes from the destitution of its people and the people are made destitute when the minds of their governors are concentrated on amassing wealth and when their tenure is insecure and when they do not take warning.[1]

It cannot be denied, however, that the ethical view tended to be relegated more and more to the background; the only time, or the most important time, when the individual peasant entered into direct relationship with the state was through the tax-collector, and it was with the peasant in his function as a tax-payer that the state came to be mainly concerned. In diplomas issued to officials and others there are exhortations to treat the people well, and in the pre-Mongol period frequent statements to the effect that they are a trust from God, but coupled with these pious addresses is the practical consideration that an impoverished peasantry will lead to a decrease in revenue and hence to the decline of the kingdom. A document contained in the collection known as *at-Tavassul ila 't-Tarassul* compiled by Bahā ud-Dīn Muḥammad b. Muʿayyad Baghdādī puts this view forward with some clarity. The document concerned is a diploma for the *miʿmār* of Khwārazm[2] and belongs to the latter half of the sixth century A.H. (twelfth century A.D.). The preamble reads as follows:

There are many foundations upon which rulership depends and innumerable matters of importance upon which kingship is contingent,

[1] ʿAlī b. Abī Ṭālib, *Nahj al-Balāgha*, ii. 52–3. cf. Najm ud-Dīn Rāzī's exposition of the duties of the *vazīr*: 'Let the *vazīr* be continually solicitous concerning the condition of the *amīrs*, prominent persons, the peasants and the military, so that he will provide the peasants with equipment . . . and will not lay heavy burdens upon them. This will be achieved when the *vazīr* strives to develop the material prosperity and agriculture of the country and when the calamitous characteristic of a desire to amass wealth does not appear in his nature. Let him not begin tyranny or make innovations, or keep the allowances of the military in arrears, because the peasants will be ruined and the soldiers without equipment. The ruin of the peasants will bring about the ruin of the country. The ruin of the country causes instability . . . therefore the *vazīr* must strive for the material prosperity of the kingdom and the peasants, the prominent persons and the military.' (*Mirṣād al-ʿIbād* (Tehrān, 1312), p. 268.)

[2] The title reads: 'This diploma was written for the *miʿmār* of Khwārazm.' In the phrase used, '*jihati miʿmārīyi vilāyati khwārazm*', *miʿmārī* might be taken as the equivalent of the modern *ʿumrān*, i.e. development, but in view of the phraseology in the document it seems to me more likely that *miʿmārī* is here rather a function to be exercised by an individual.

and manifest roads and paths[1] leading to the achievement of desires, and certain fundamental and derivative principles for the acquisition of wealth.[2] If these rules are put into operation along the right way and their beginnings and endings and their operation are considered by the eye of a wise man, then the castle of kingship will daily become more firmly established and more impregnable and the foundation of success will become hourly stronger and more exalted, and repose of mind from the clamour of tumult will at once be acquired. The most important principle and the strongest pillar of kingship, the observance of which is vital and solicitude for which is obligatory, and to which the words of the Prophet (who holds the reins of knowledge and breathes upon the gardens of truth), 'they demanded sustenance from the hidden things of the earth', exhort, is the cultivation, development, tilling, and husbandry of the province, because the affairs of the government of the world are made strong by cultivation and [agricultural] development, and the state of the kingdom depends upon husbandry: 'There is no kingdom without men, no men without money and no money without [agricultural] development.' If negligence and slackness are shown over cultivation and [agricultural] development, there will be a deficit and a decrease in the taxes of the *dīvān*, and if in the sphere of the *dīvān* there are straitened circumstances and the incoming sums decrease, the defraying of expenses becomes impossible and the wages necessary for the retinue [of the ruler] are not paid, and this causes a conflict of views and arouses desires, and coolness affects the sincerity of the intentions of his servants and resentment clouds the purity of mind of his supporters and thoughts of dispersal and a desire for ascendancy are formed in their hearts, and if steps are not taken by him to remedy that and reparation is not made—God forbid—kingship vanishes and the basis of the kingdom is destroyed.

It is therefore clear, as indicated in these words, that to show solicitude for [agricultural] development and to devote attention with every care to this matter, in keeping with the dictates of royal wisdom, is necessary and, in accordance with kingly sagacity, obligatory. But this matter can only be furthered and this important affair can only be advanced by a *miʿmār* who is adorned by a past record of capability and courage and distinguished by excellent conduct and admirable skill and whose illustrious acts are manifest and apparent upon the pages of history and whose memorable actions are clearly evident upon the face of time.[3]

After a general exhortation to the grantee to follow in the steps of his father (who had held the office before him) and to pursue righteousness, the document goes on

and let him reconcile the augmenting of the revenue with the ease of the peasants (*raʿīyat*), nay rather let him even consider care for the peasant to have precedence, because if the peasants are in a flourishing

[1] lit. chapters and sections.

[2] The *va* in the text after *vuṣūl* appears to be superfluous.

[3] *at-Tavassul ila't-Tavassul*, ed. by Aḥmad Bahmanyār (Tehrān, 1315), pp. 110–11.

condition and their desires centred on husbandry the revenue is collected in full and a good name laid up as treasure and the face of desire is made beautiful by the ornament of achievement in the best possible way. Let him follow the way of courtesy and good treatment in his dealings with the people and his peasants (*ra'āyā*) in general and with the tax-collectors (*'ummāl*), district tax-collectors (*mutaṣarrifān*), heads of villages,[1] and officials in particular, because the honour of this world coupled with a bad name is worth nothing. Let him strengthen all with his good care and great solicitude, and make them abundant in cultivation and [agricultural] development and in submission to [his] decree. Let him specially favour by his increased compassion, patronage, care and support whoever performs praiseworthy acts of service and increases development and cultivation, and let him consider it obligatory to show such a person different kinds of favours on our behalf so that we may make the garment of the days of that person adorned with the embroidery of honour and may single him out from among mankind by increase of favours and glory. 'We will reward those who do good like this' so that that person, seeing the effect of his excellent effort, shall be led to desire above all to increase [prosperity] and at the same time the desire of others [to emulate him] shall be excited. Let Shams ud-Dīn carry out whatever chastisement and correction he can administer himself in whatever way he considers [best] against whoever fails to fulfil the conditions necessary for development and cultivation or to exert effort, and against that person whose misfortune he [Shams ud-Dīn] attributes to negligence and neglect and who seeks excuses and pretexts to which to ascribe the occurrence of ruin and disorder; and if such a person is not brought to repentance by reproach and the censure of his error and shortcomings, and the scales are not removed [thereby] from his eyes, let him [Shams ud-Dīn] refer [the matter] to the Supreme Dīvān, may God exalt it, and let him appeal to our opinion, may God enlighten it, so that a reproof from us by way of repairing that shortcoming may be meted out by us to that delinquent, and we may appoint another who will follow a contrary course and will abandon the practice of falling short and follow the path of creating abundance. And if in making flourishing the tax-districts of the province and in making fruitful the projects which he deems necessary, he [Shams ud-Dīn] has need to refer to our opinion, let him consider it obligatory to seek the [requisite] information so that the sublime order, may God exalt it, may be put into execution without delay in accordance with the most illuminated opinion and the veil of doubt be lifted from before his vision.[2]

In conclusion the document states:

Let all the notables of the time from among the chosen, the famous, the *mutavallīs*, the district tax-collectors (*mutaṣarrifān*), the heads of districts (*ru'asā*), stewards (*vukalā*), heads of villages (*dihāqīn*) and officials

[1] The term used is *dihāqīn*. Coupled as it is with tax-collectors and officials (*kārkunān*), it seems likely that it is used in its earlier meaning of 'heads of villages' (see p. 13 below), or 'landowners', though by this period the term is also used to mean 'peasants'.

[2] *at-Tavassul ila't-Tarassul*, ed. by Aḥmad Bahmanyār, pp. 112–13.

(*karkunān*) and all the people of the province of Khwārazm, may God preserve them and protect it, consider the grantee, may God prolong his authority, as endowed with this great charge and entrusted with this very important affair . . . and let them refer to him that which concerns the development and cultivation of the province and make it known to the *dīvān* and cause it to reach our ear through him. . . .[1]

A somewhat similar attitude is to be found in the *Sīāsat Nāmeh* of Niẓām ul-Mulk, who urges care in the choice of tax-collectors and recommends that they should exercise tolerance towards the peasants.

Injunctions [he writes] must be given to tax-collectors (*'ummāl*) who are entrusted with a tax-district to treat well the people of God, may He be glorified and exalted, to take only that which is due, to demand it with civility and courtesy and to request nothing from the tax-payers until they begin to reap the harvest, because if they [the tax-collectors] demand [the tax] before it falls due, the peasants will suffer distress and they will be forced to sell the crop in advance for a song[2] and in that way they will be exterminated and dispersed. And if any one of the peasants is in difficulty and has need of draught oxen and seed, let them [the tax-collectors] give him a loan and relieve him, so that he may be able to maintain himself and not go into exile.[3]

Similarly, if there was any sign of decay in the affairs of the peasants or any tendency towards their dispersal in any district this was at once to be investigated.[4] From the anecdotes Niẓām ul-Mulk quotes in illustration of the points he makes, however, it is clear that the motive behind his exhortations to treat the peasants well was mainly the purely practical one of ensuring a full treasury and preventing the decay of the kingdom. At the same time the ethical point of view which regards the extension of cultivation as praiseworthy in itself is not entirely absent. In the first chapter, after expressing the view that God in every age singles out one of the people whom he endows with kingly virtues and to whom he relegates the affairs of the world, Niẓām ul-Mulk continues:

and he [i.e. the ruler] will accomplish whatever appertains to the material prosperity of the world such as the making of *qanāts*, the digging of major irrigation channels, the building of bridges over great rivers where roads meet, the development of villages and hamlets and the making of fortresses and the founding of new cities and exalted buildings and wonderful pavilions and hospices on the major roads. By such action his name will be remembered and he will receive the reward of that action in the next world and prayers for his well-being will be continually offered.[5]

Forming an intermediary class between the expositions of the

[1] ibid. p. 114. [2] ? *bi nīm diram.*
[3] *Sīāsat Nāmeh*, ed. C. Schefer (Paris, 1891–3), p. 18.
[4] ibid. p. 119. [5] ibid. p. 6.

statesmen on the one hand and the philosophers on the other are the manuals of education and edification composed for princes and rulers. These works represent, broadly speaking, the ethics of the official classes. Here again there is no specific theory of land or any systematic exposition of the position of the peasant. Emphasis is, on the whole, on political expediency rather than on ethical considerations. Kā'ūs b. Iskandar b. Qābūs, the author of the *Qābūs Nāmeh*, for example, writing for the instruction of his son, states

do not put a soldier in power over the peasants (*ra'īyat*) because the kingdom will not become flourishing without peasants, and as you look after the interests of the soldiers, so also look after the interests of the peasants, because the king is like the sun and it is not fitting that the sun should shine upon one and not upon the other, and, although the peasants can be reduced to obedience by the army, the army can also be maintained by the peasants, because revenue is provided by them. It is through justice that the peasants are made flourishing and well-to-do. Therefore do not permit injustice because the kingdom of just kings lasts long and grows old while the kingdom of the unjust soon disappears because justice brings prosperity and injustice ruin.[1]

In the theory of Kā'ūs b. Iskandar estates were valued for the revenue they afforded. Advising his son on the subject of the purchase of estates, he writes

When you have bought an estate (*ẓī'at*) strive continually to develop it. Daily undertake some new development so that you may continually obtain some new source of income. Do not rest from developing your estates because an estate is valuable for its revenue.[2]

Similarly, were his son to be a peasant (*dihqān*), this would demand that he should be continually occupied in developing his land so that he might enjoy the fruits thereof.[3]

Ghazālī, in addition to his many theological works, wrote also at least one work which can be classed among the manuals of instruction written for rulers and others, namely, the *Naṣīḥat ul-Mulūk*. The work is based on a metaphysical conception of the world, but the stories quoted by Ghazālī in illustration of his points are largely designed to show the concrete advantages in the practice of justice, without which, he believed, material prosperity could not be achieved. The true *sulṭān*, writes Ghazālī, was he who practised justice. Upon this depended the prosperity of the kingdom. If the king was just the world was prosperous and his flock (*ra'īyat*) in security.[4] Anūshīravān and various others of the

[1] *Qābūs Nāmeh*, p. 208.
[2] ibid. p. 107. [3] ibid. p. 214.
[4] *Naṣīḥat ul-Mulūk*, ed. Jalāl Humā'ī (Tehrān, 1315–17), p. 41.

pre-Islamic Persian kings are mentioned as having made the world prosperous and, continues Ghazālī,

the efforts of the kings to make the world prosperous were [made] because they knew that the greater the material prosperity the greater the extent of their rule and the more numerous their subjects, and they also knew the truth of the saying of the wise men that 'religion depends upon kingship, kingship upon the army, the army upon material possessions and material possessions and material prosperity upon justice'.[1]

Ruin and decay came, in the view of Ghazālī, on the one hand, from the weakness of the ruler and, on the other, from his tyranny: either resulted in straitened circumstances for the peasants.[2] He also warns, again for practical reasons, against the laying of unjust impositions upon the people, stating that such a practice was as if 'a person laid the foundations of a wall and built on these before they were dry: neither the wall nor its foundations would remain'.[3] Kings, ministers, and *kadkhudās* were to demand taxes at the proper time and in the proper way and as the interests of the kingdom demanded: nothing was to be taken from the poor, and the kings, ministers, and *kadkhudās* were to consider their position, rank, and worth to be bound up with the interests of the subjects, and to regard the interests of the latter as their own, so that they would acquire a good name in this world and pardon and acceptance in the next.[4]

Ghazālī in his *Kīmīā as-Saʿādat* also puts forward, from a somewhat different angle, certain considerations with regard to agriculture and husbandry and the ethical duties of those engaged therein. In a section devoted to justice in commercial and other transactions he states that 'a peasant who has food exercises full possession over this. He can sell it whenever he wishes. It is not obligatory upon him to sell it promptly, but it is preferable that he should not delay, and if he has an inner desire that prices shall rise [and holds it against this hope], this is blameworthy.'[5]

The theory of the philosophers is also based on religion. Naṣīr ud-Dīn Ṭūsī, who at the end of his life was in the service of the Mongol, Hūlāgū, wrote his famous philosophical work, the *Akhlāqi Nāṣirī*, before the fall of the caliphate. He presupposes a supreme ruler appointed by and directly responsible to God, and after discussing the nature of man and his need for co-operation and association he passes on to the question of the maintenance of equity among the members of the community. He resolves society into

[1] ibid. p. 48; cf. Masʿūdī, *Murūj az-Ẕahab*, ed. C. Barbier de Meynard and Pavet de Courteille (Paris, 1861–77), ii. 210.

[2] *Naṣīḥat ul-Mulūk*, p. 55.

[3] ibid. p. 71.

[4] ibid. p. 101.

[5] *Kīmīā as-Saʿādat* (Bombay, lithog.), p. 141.

four classes, each of which was to be kept in its appropriate place and within which each person was to be employed in that occupation to which he was best fitted: in this way, under the administration of the philosopher king, each would, in so far as the possibility lay within him, attain perfection. The first three orders of society were men of the pen, men of the sword, and merchant classes; the base of this hierarchical order was formed by 'husbandmen, such as agricultural labourers (*barzigarān*), and peasants (*dihāqīn*), those who plant trees and carry on agriculture, who prepare the food of all groups, and without whom the continued existence of anyone would be impossible'.[1]

The later philosophers were much influenced by Naṣīr ud-Dīn.[2] Many of them make a similar division of society into classes. Muḥammad b. Maḥmūd Āmulī in his compendium of sciences, known as the *Nafā'is ul-Funūn*, written in 735/1334–5, which, in so far as political theory is concerned, adds little or nothing to the work of Naṣīr ud-Dīn, states that 'agriculture is the best of natural occupations . . . and is the primary industry upon which the good order of the world and the perpetuation of the human race depend'.[3] Jalāl ud-Dīn Davvānī in his *Akhlāqi Jalālī* also closely follows Naṣīr ud-Dīn. He considers that temporal sovereignty consists in the maintenance of the classes in their appropriate places, in which case only will the state be balanced and its affairs regular.[4]

The philosophers, however, do not go into details concerning the relations of those engaged in agriculture with the members of other classes of the population, nor the conditions under which they would hope to see agriculture carried out. For this we must turn to the work of the famous Ṣūfī writer Najm ud-Dīn Rāzī, who died in 654/1256. In his *Mirṣād al-'Ibād min al-Mabda' ila' l-Mi'ād* he puts forward a comprehensive theory of society and discusses the relations of the different classes to one another. His concern is the spiritual progress (*sulūk*) of the various classes. The picture he gives is no doubt somewhat idealized but it is not without interest as an illustration of the attitude towards society prevailing among the leaders of contemporary Ṣūfī opinion, whose influence in moulding public opinion cannot be entirely neglected.

The section entitled 'On the spiritual progress of leaders,[5] land-

[1] pp. 180–1.

[2] Naṣīr ud-Dīn was himself much influenced by al-Fārābī's work, *al-Madīnat al-Fāḍila.*

[3] *Nafā'is ul-Funūn* (Tehrān, lithog.), ii. 159.

[4] Tr. W. F. Thompson, *Practical Philosophy of the Muhammadan People* (London, 1839), pp. 388–9.

[5] The word used is *ru'asā*, which means here perhaps those who hold land either as private property or as grantees, and enjoy authority over those living on the land.

owners,[1] and crop-sharing peasants' in the *Mirṣād al-'Ibād* reads as follows:

God most high said 'We supplied him who wished to till the next world with provisions in his tilling, and we took from him who wished to cultivate this world and from his possessions in the next world a portion', and the Prophet of God, upon him be blessing and peace, said 'Whoever cultivates crops or plants a tree, birds and beasts will not eat thereof but God will inscribe it in the register of his good acts'. And the Prophet, upon him be blessing and peace, said 'Seek provision in the hidden places of the earth'. Know that the word *rīāsat* [leadership] is derived from *ra'īs* [leader]. 'The leader of the people' means 'the head of the people'; the work of the 'head' is to oversee, to listen and to explain, and the duty [of the leaders] is to fulfil the conditions which we shall set forth.

Husbandry (*dihqanat*) or agriculture is a trade with God and is the best of all industries and trades when carried out as it is meant to be carried out. If anyone had been endowed with the eye of knowledge, he would see that it is a vicegerency from God in His capacity of the Provider of Food and if anyone engages in this work with perspicacity and vision, the good deriving therefrom is without limit and he will achieve high rank and honour. These persons [i.e. those engaged in agriculture] belong to three groups, and there are customs, conditions and principles proper to each group and those who observe them will attain to the rank of the faithful witnesses, the martyrs, the righteous, and the blessed. The first group are leaders (*ru'asā*) and landowners who own wealth and property and need crop-sharing peasants (*muzāra'ān*), helpers (*shāgirdān*), bailiffs (*mubāshirān*), and hired labourers (*muzdūrān*), who may engage on their behalf in agriculture and in the development of the land. The conditions and customs appropriate to their state are as follows: first let them not become presumptuous because of their wealth and property and let them not set their hearts on these things. Let them consider these things to be a loan and a trust in their hands and let them consider everything which exists as belonging to God because 'to God belongs the kingdom of the heavens and of the earth'. Let them not be in the bonds of a desire to amass, hoard, and increase goods and let them not look with contempt upon inferiors, helpers, and hired labourers, and in their leadership and crop-sharing agreements and husbandry let them consider the cultivation of the next world because 'this world is the field in which the next world is cultivated'. When one of them brings out seed from his storehouses let him do so with the intention of cultivating the harvest of the next world, not of this world, i.e. let him resolve that if God most high causes the seed to grow and a harvest is reaped therefrom he will make it lawful for whatever creature, human or otherwise, eats thereof, because the creation of God, whether man or beast, needs food, everyone not being able to practise this kind of husbandry, and let him engage in the service of God's creation for the satisfaction of God so that he may worship God by serving God's people. He must in no way

[1] The word used is *dihāqīn*, which also means peasant proprietors (see p. 3, n. 3 and p. 13 below), but its earlier sense of landowner would alone seem appropriate here.

practise injustice against the crop-sharing peasant, the bailiff, the helper, or the hired labourer and must pay their wages, and their share [of the crop] in full. When the harvest comes to hand on the sown fields and gardens, etc., and the taxable minimum is reached, let him first put aside that portion due by way of *zakāt* (alms tax), and place it apart from the rest of the harvest in a store-house and quickly distribute it to those who are entitled to *zakāt* in accordance with the decree of the *sharīʿa*, because if anything belonging to the portion due as *zakāt* gets mixed up with that which belongs to him his right to any of it becomes doubtful. And let him not be concerned to lay up store for the next year from that which remains. Let him rely upon God, for agriculture is itself the essence of reliance upon God, because where the harvest is concerned, one must hope for the favour and grace of God, since no created being has any share or strength in that matter: nourishing [the seed] in the earth and causing it to grow is the work of God—'verily God causes the corn-seed and the date-stone to split'—and the rain of mercy and the warmth of the sun are among His abundant treasures. He must always keep open house to travellers whether rich or poor and he must serve the people of God with a glad heart, good belief, and pure intention to the extent of his income and profit, and he must consider himself under an obligation [so to act]. If in some year his profit is small, or there is a dry year and rain does not come, he must not be heavy at heart or grieve for his daily bread, or show ingratitude to God by coveting and amassing wealth, and he must not in his heart and on his tongue disavow, or protest at, the acts of God, but he must consider that there is wisdom therein and must submit with contentment to whatever comes, knowing that daily bread is from God to whom belongs glory and power and saying 'in the heavens is your sustenance'. He must not fall short of that old woman, who said: 'An old woman looked out and saw her sown plot dried up and said, "both that which is new and that which is old, all food comes from thee. Do whatever thou wishest." '

Shaqīqi Balkhī used to say that if the sky should turn to iron and the earth to brass and if the sky should not rain and nothing should grow in the earth and all the people of the world were his family, he would not be in the slightest degree anxious. If the leader or the landowner exercises his function as leader or as landowner in this way and sows seed with this resolve and does not lay his burdens upon his partners, and plants trees in this spirit of sincerity and does not arbitrarily expropriate the water and lands of others and observes the commands and prohibitions of the *sharīʿa* and pays *ʿushr* (tithe) in this faith, ten good actions will be entered in the register of his good actions for every morsel and every grain and every fruit which reaches any man, bird, or animal from his belongings, estate, cultivated land or gardens, and each will be the means of propinquity [to God] and of [spiritual] advance. Indeed, if his resolve is to do this work for the people, good accrues to him for every grain and fruit which as the result of his labour reaches the people, even if the latter buy it. The great have said three hundred and sixty persons, sowers, reapers, carpenters, ironsmiths and other craftsmen, must work in order that a morsel of bread may be baked.

When from that one morsel of bread the food of one holy man of God is provided, God will forgive them all for the sake of that one holy man and will free them from the fire of hell.

The second group, bailiffs, village headmen (*kadkhudās*), and [landlords'] representatives, must preserve equality between the peasants (*raʿīyat*) and not give preference to the strong over the weak; they must not take bribes and must be the helpers of God; they must strengthen religion and the people of religion; they must keep the peasants (*raʿāyā*) in tranquillity and comfortable circumstances; and must exert great effort to prevent oppression from afflicting them; they must not covet the possessions, property, and belongings of the peasants (*raʿīyat*), but must be moderate and satisfied with little and must live honestly and keep themselves far from corrupt things; they must reprimand the corrupt and exhort the people to do that which is recommended and forbid them to do that which is forbidden. If they see presumption or corruption in one of the peasants (*raʿīyat*) let them punish him and bring him to repentance. Let them act in the appropriate manner and let them know that they will be called to account for whatever happens to them or to the peasants at the present time: 'Each one of you is a shepherd and each one of you is responsible for his flock.' Let them seek to win over the peasants (*raʿīyat*) by good words and let them give good promises and praise them [the peasants] for their good actions and prevent them from doing evil. Let them live honestly on that which belongs to them and keep themselves far from corruption. Let them look after travellers well and keep themselves far from haughtiness and pride. If they act in accordance with these conditions, God most high will requite them with goodness and [spiritual] advance for every act of devotion, charity, righteousness and kindness which was performed in the interests of the peasants (*raʿāyā*) in this world.

The third group are the crop-sharing peasants and paid labourers who carry on agriculture in the property of a third party. They must act with trustworthiness and in good faith and avoid perfidy and misappropriation and not show any lack of solicitude [for the interests of the other party]. They must practise uprightness and honesty in the absence of the leaders, village headmen, and landowners and in their presence, and must strive to preserve the possessions and estates of the latter; and they must exert themselves in developing [the land] and in husbandry. Let them not treat beasts of burden cruelly, place heavy loads upon them, work them very hard, or beat them much; God most high will ask them to answer at the resurrection for whatever they place upon them [beasts of burden] beyond their strength and He will exact justice and retribution for 'God is mighty and He is the avenger'. When they are engaged in cultivation and ploughing they must continually repeat the names of God and when the time of prayer comes round they must engage in prayer. Even if they cannot pray together, let them on no account leave out the prayers and let them perform the other conditions which have been mentioned.

Let none of these three groups consider itself in truth the agent or the cultivator. Let them consider such to be God in accordance with the phrase 'Did you cultivate it or did we', for hand and foot, sight and hearing, strength and power, landed estate or possessions, and flocks, land and water, seed and grain all belong to the Lord of Power. The crop-sharing peasant can broadcast the seed or plant the sapling but he cannot exert any power over the seed. That is the prerogative of God, who with the perfection of His power splits the seed in the earth and causes it to shoot and gradually destroys the seed in the earth and then after a while causes it to live again and to give fruit and to multiply a hundred-fold or seven hundred-fold or double that. Thus in reality the cultivator and the owner, the powerful one and the creator is God. He hides the food of his slaves in the corners of the earth. He brings it forth so that Muḥammad, upon him be peace, sends forth the people in search of it, saying 'Seek food in the hidden places of the earth.' Accordingly the crop-sharing peasant, the helper, the workman, the hired labourer, the bailiff, the village headman, the landowner,[1] and the leader of the people must consider themselves intermediaries and recognize God as the real cultivator and provider. They must hold abundant the provisions of God for the slaves [of God] so that they may be the vicegerents of God in His capacity as the giver of daily bread, and must adorn their day with those things which have been described, so that God most high may inscribe a good action in their registers for whatever reaches the people, animals, and birds by means of cultivation, and so that He may favour them with [spiritual] advance and propinquity, just as Muḥammad, upon him be peace, expressed the good news in the following words: 'whoever cultivates or plants trees, birds and beasts will not eat thereof but God will inscribe it in the register of his good acts.'[2]

Najm ud-Dīn is clearly writing from a somewhat different standpoint from the statesmen and the authors of the works written for the edification of princes on the one hand, and from the philosophers on the other hand. He is primarily concerned with the purpose of man's existence, and he considers it possible for man to fulfil his true end—the service of God and his creatures—by engaging in agriculture as in other occupations. The guiding motive of the statesmen and, to a large extent, of the authors of the works written for the edification of princes was, in contradistinction to Najm ud-Dīn, political expediency: their concern was solely, or mainly, to increase the revenue of the ruler, by which means they believed his dominion could be best assured. Care for the peasants was enjoined not mainly because this was in itself desirable, but because a failure to exercise such care would lead to a dispersal of the peasants and their disappearance would bring about decay in financial affairs, which in turn would cause the decline of the kingdom. The exposition of the philosophers is nearer to that of Najm ud-Dīn, but here also questions of temporal expediency are more prominent: the main emphasis is on the

[1] *dihqān va mālik.*

[2] *Mirṣād al-ʿIbād,* pp. 294–8.

maintenance of the orders of society in their appropriate places because only in this way could society be preserved.

The theory of Najm ud-Dīn includes much that is best in medieval Muslim civilization, and discloses a view of society which can be found from time to time both in earlier and in later ages. His attitude towards agriculture and those engaged therein was, however, seldom the dominant attitude. More often it was overlain on the one hand by the view which regarded land as a source of revenue, and on the other by the view which regarded society as a hierarchy and the peasants as simply and solely the providers of the sustenance of other classes. For the exponents of the former view only questions of expediency limited the exploitation of the land and those who worked on it: exploitation beyond a certain limit would result in the ruin of the land and the dispersal of the peasants. This to some extent was a safeguard, but with the practice of making short-term assignments of land and the buying of offices it largely ceased to be effective. The exponents of the hierarchical view of society at its best believed that each individual should hold that position for which his capacities best fitted him, but they were in practice more often concerned with the performance of duties by the peasants, while denying to them any rights for fear lest the hierarchy should be disturbed. This theory thus reinforced the conservative tendencies which were inherent in pre-Islamic Persian society and which have continued to exist in a modified form down to the present day.

Since going to press the *Sharaf Nāmeh* of 'Abdullāh Marwārīd has been published by H. R. Roemer (*Staatsschreiben der Timuridenzeit*, Wiesbaden, 1952). From documents for the office of *bukāvul* in a *madraseh* and a *khānqāh* (ff. 31b–32b) it is clear that the *bukāvul* was in charge of the commissariat arrangements of these institutions. In the late Īlkhān period he was, according to Roemer, a military official in charge, among other things, of the payment of the army and the distribution of booty (ibid., p. 156). A misunderstanding of this and other technical terms led me to mistranslate a passage concerning the military reforms of Ghāzān (see below, p. 89). The *īdājīs* were also officials attached to the commissariat of the army. The precise meaning of the passage in question is still not entirely clear to me, but the general sense appears to be that the allowances due to the army remained for the most part unpaid, because of the slackness and corruption of the various officials who were charged with their collection and distribution, and that Ghāzān, as part of his reform, forbade the *būkāvulān* to take presents (i.e. bribes or commissions).

INTRODUCTION

The Village

THE distribution of the rural population of Persia and the mode of life of the people has been governed by two major factors, namely, geographical conditions and political developments. Persia is a country with great variety in natural conditions. Broadly speaking, the area can be divided into five major regions: upland districts with unirrigated farming, such as parts of Āẕarbāyjān; other upland districts where oasis cultivation only is possible because of insufficient rainfall, such as Arāk and Iṣfahān; inland depressions such as Sīstān; and the two narrow lowland coastal belts, one in the north along the southern shores of the Caspian Sea, with its thick forest land and heavy rainfall, and the other along the northern shores of the Persian Gulf, with its oppressively hot climate and inhospitable hinterland. The greater part of Persia is situated on the plateau which falls away in the centre and east to the great central desert, an arid, uninhabited, untracked salt desert. The traveller entering Persia from the south or the north cannot fail to be impressed by the magnificent scenery as he mounts through steep mountain passes from the lowlands, whether he comes by way of the Pāytāq Pass from ʿIrāq or up the famous Pīri Zan and other passes from Bushire, or from the north over the various routes leading from the Caspian Sea, which pass first through thick forest and then cross the watershed of the Elburz.

On the plateau itself there is much variety of scenery, dominated almost always by near or distant peaks. The climate on the plateau is one of extremes, with hot summers and relatively cold winters. The annual rainfall, which is about 10 inches in the north-west, declines progressively towards the south-east.[1] There are clear skies for some nine months of the year. The clearness of the atmosphere gives a great range of vision and beauty of colouring. Types of cultivation include the typical oasis cultivation of the Iṣfahān area, which merges on the one hand into the areas on the borders of the central desert such as Yazd and Kirmān, and on the other either into the mountain regions where settlements are confined to the often narrow mountain valleys, or into the rolling uplands of the largely dry farming areas of Āẕarbāyjān, Kurdistān, and parts of Khurāsān, which in turn merge into the steppeland of Gurgān. The main crops grown on the plateau are wheat,

[1] B. A. Keen, *The Agricultural Development of the Middle East* (London, 1946), p. 6.

barley, millet, maize, lucerne, pulses of different kinds, cotton, tobacco, opium, fruit trees, and vines.

Although the geographical conditions of the five main regions vary considerably, they are all with the exception of the Caspian littoral subject to a greater or lesser degree to one limiting factor, namely, insufficient rainfall and lack of water, both in those areas where dry farming prevails and in those where irrigated farming is practised. Irrigation, indeed, is the great limiting factor to agricultural development in Persia, and in the irrigated farming areas has largely determined the type of husbandry which is practised. The availability of water has further largely determined the site of settlements and militated against the establishment of isolated farms. Further, where water has to be shared for irrigation, this fact has influenced the shape and distribution of the holdings. In the case of the mountain districts also natural conditions have decided the type of settlement, causing the villages to be concentrated in the mountain valleys. Certain areas of the country such as the steppelands of Gurgān, on the other hand, invite the tribes to adopt a semi-nomadic life with their herds. A similar habit is forced on the pastoral elements of the community in central and southern Persia since the hot lowlands of the south, while affording good pasture in early spring, are unable to support flocks in the summer and autumn; certain of the upland regions have a climate too severe in winter for the herds to remain without the provision of stabling and fodder.

The second major factor which influenced the distribution of population in early times was political developments. Unfortunately, we have little knowledge of the early Persian settlements. There seems little doubt, however, that in the earliest times for which we have any records the dominant type of settlement was the village. The nature of the country and the mode of its settlement by the Avestan people were such as to demand concentrated rather than dispersed settlements: only when in sufficient numbers could they defend themselves against hostile aborigines and protect themselves from wild animals. Further, the tribal nature of society in early times determined that the village made up of a clan should be the model settlement.[1]

In later times the advantages of concentration continued to outweigh its drawbacks: irrigation works could best be carried out as a corporate enterprise, while resistance to predatory elements, whether in the shape of nomadic tribes or of rival groups, and to extortion by government officials was only possible if sufficient numbers were banded together. Although there is little information concerning the structure of the village in pre-Islamic times, it

[1] See Geiger, *Civilization of Eastern Iranians*, i. 247.

is clear that a certain communal organization was in existence at the time of the Islamic conquest[1] or was created in the early centuries of Islamic rule, since the Muslims in many cases dealt with the conquered peoples in groups. It does not follow from this that the only type of organization was a communal one—indeed the presumption is to the contrary—but it is clear that government policy in the early centuries of Islamic rule fostered such communal organizations, since administrative convenience demanded that their relations should be with communities rather than with individuals. Another reason for their adopting such a policy cannot be excluded. One of their main interests was in the collection of revenue from the conquered lands, and this could only be achieved if a certain degree of prosperity prevailed. Agriculture could hardly flourish if the peasantry was discontented and overburdened. The early Muslims may well have been influenced by considerations of general agricultural prosperity to treat the village as a unit, realizing that if the peasant had some interest in his land and some degree of local self-government he would be more likely to cultivate it better. In any case, whatever the motive, the tendency in early Islamic times was for the village to be treated as a corporate unit, and this tendency continued down to the twentieth century A.D.[2] But although the fiscal system on the one hand favoured the survival of communal groupings, on the other hand it also brought about certain changes in the structure of village society. The tendency was for the burden of taxation to grow in the course of time, and this weighed most heavily upon the peasants and smaller landowners who had fewer economic reserves to tide them over bad times and less possibility of resisting unjust demands. This made them more dependent upon the relatively rich and the powerful, who therefore came to assume quite naturally a position of authority with regard to the tax-payers generally, both as their protectors *vis-à-vis* the government and as responsible for them towards the government. This resulted in the rise of a powerful class of landed proprietors, the depression of the small landowner into the lower ranks of society,[3]

[1] Thaʿālibī credits Āfarīdūn with a saying that there were five types of associate, among which were 'the cultivator in the private estate and the co-proprietor of a village' (*Histoire des Rois des Perses*, ed. H. Zotenberg (Paris, 1900), p. 41). The tradition related about Qubād and the peasant woman (see p. 15) suggests also that the early Muslims believed that in Sasanian times on some lands no intermediary was interposed between the king and the peasant.

[2] Taxation was imposed on a tax-district, then subdivided among the townships, after which it was partitioned among the villages, where it was finally laid upon the individual tax-payers.

[3] Significant of this is the change in meaning of the word *dihqān*. Under the Sasanians the *dihqāns* were a special class of landowner (see Ch. I). By the eleventh century A.D. the word appears sometimes as a technical term to designate a class of landowner and sometimes to denote what would appear to be

and the growth of a semi-servile rural population. This tendency was accentuated when the landowner proper was largely superseded, first by the revenue farmer and then, with the spread of the system of land assignments or *iqṭā'* from the fifth century A.H./eleventh century A.D. onwards, by the assignee. The decisive stage in this development was the settlement of the military on the land.[1] Finally, in the twentieth century, the assignees were retransformed into landowners.

The village in Persia has thus been from early times the unit which formed the basis of social life, and the group into which the population organized themselves for economic and political co-operation. This importance of the village as the unit in rural life has persisted through medieval times down to the present day. The isolated settlement is still the exception and not the rule. Where small farms or hamlets (known as *mazra'eh*) are founded they are in almost all cases attached to a parent village.[2]

The basis of the village is the peasant holding. This is reckoned in two main ways, by plough-land or by a share of water. The size of the former varies from area to area but the basic supposition is a series of uniform measurements. The term for this in most parts of Persia is *juft*. This means either a yoke of oxen or the amount of land which can be cultivated by a yoke of oxen. In east Persia the prevalent term for a plough-land and also for a yoke of oxen is *zouj*; in parts of Khurāsān this term also means a certain unit of water. In Khūzistān the local name for a plough-land is *khīsh*, which also means 'plough'. It is a noteworthy fact that this division of the village land into plough-lands is widely found in villages both in the landlord areas and in the peasant-proprietor areas. It

little more than a peasant proprietor. This is its meaning in the *Qābūs Nāmeh* (p. 214). Nāṣiri Khusrou, writing in the fifth/eleventh century, also uses the term to mean 'peasant' (see *Dīvān*, ed. Naṣrullāh Taqavī (Tehrān, 1304–7), p. 557). At the present day *dihqān* means peasant.

[1] See Ch. III.

[2] The reason for this in pre-Constitution times (i.e. before 1906) was partly, no doubt, convenience in fiscal administration. The hamlets were assessed with the parent village and the responsibility for the payment of the whole sum due rested upon the parent village. At the present day also these hamlets are regarded as belonging to the village near which they are situated, even if the ownership of the two is not in the same hands (see, for example, p. 268 below). The meaning of *mazra'eh* in Qājār times when used as a technical term was a place which paid a definite sum by way of taxation for water and land as part of the assessment of a province or of a village (*qarīeh*) (*Mir'āt al-Qāsān*, B.M. Or. 3603, f. 64a). By this undertaking it appears that the inhabitants were exempt from poll tax (*sarāneh*) and cattle tax (*mavāshī*), whereas the inhabitants of the village (or *qarīeh*) paid dues and taxes which included a land tax, water dues, cattle dues (*mavāshī*), a tax on sheep and goats (*marā'ī*), and a tax on weaving (*nassājī*) (ibid. f. 64a). The term *mazra'eh* appears to be used by Ḥamdullāh Mustoufī also to mean a hamlet or settlement attached to a parent village (see *Geographical Part of the Nuzhat-al-Qulūb*, ed. G. le Strange (G.M.S., 1919), p. 50).

is the typical basis of the village in Āẕarbāyjān, Kurdistān, Hamadān, Arāk, Iṣfahān, Fārs, Khūzistān, and Tehrān.[1] The equality of the shares into which the village land is divided is not strictly speaking quantitative, but takes into consideration also quality; that is to say the size and shape of the holdings may vary considerably; the common factor is that they are holdings such as one plough can normally cultivate. In certain landlord areas especially in east Persia a number of plough-teams work together and cultivate a varying number of plough-lands which are grouped together, but it is significant that the village land is in most cases nevertheless reckoned in *juft* or plough-lands. In other words the guiding principle of the division of the land both in landlord areas and in peasant-proprietor areas is equal apportionment. This tendency to equalize the shares is further reinforced in certain landlord areas by the periodic redistribution of the lots among the tenants. Although the units are normally considered to belong to the head of the family, they are expected to provide for the needs of the family group. One of the most important rights attaching to the *juft* or plough-land is the right to use the village pastures and to collect scrub for fuel in them. This right is highly significant and points to an original communal settlement, membership of which implied the right to a share in the arable land and water with an appendant pastoral right. The right to a share in the common pasture applies both to villages in peasant-proprietor areas and to those in landlord areas. In the latter the right is a customary one whereas in the former it is recognized by law, but in few cases is the landlord able to withhold this right from the village community.

From the general principle underlying the structure of the village it can perhaps be inferred that the original form of settlement was a communal one, and that individual rights derived from the superior right of the community. With the change in the social structure of the village which accompanied the growth of large landowners or assignees[2] the tradition of communal ownership was weakened, but on the other hand the tendency to keep the shares, which had been originally apportioned according to certain fixed proportions, equalized, had been reinforced from another source, namely, the equalitarian traditions of Islamic society. It may be questioned how far these developments deeply affected rural communities, especially in view of the fact that the Turkish military classes, who rose to power in the fourth/tenth century, were mainly centred in the towns and did not, as far as is known, usually live on

[1] There are exceptions to this, as in Khīr in Fārs, where each unit is composed of five men and four oxen, and in ʿAqīlī in Khūzistān, where each unit is composed of six men and four oxen. (See below, pp. 370–1.)

[2] See below, pp. 54 ff.

the estates assigned to them; and it may well be that the really decisive factor in maintaining the original structure of the village was the question of husbandry. The all-important factor in the situation was the plough-oxen, and the amount of land one man could cultivate was limited thereby. The landlord from the point of view of economic advantage had no interest in maintaining this system: indeed the substitution of plough-teams and the consolidation of holdings had on purely technical grounds much to recommend it. That the arrangement in plough-lands has nevertheless persisted down to the present day points to a strong tradition behind it, and suggests that (1) the communal village settlement and not the landlord settlement was the original type of settlement, and (2) the present form of ownership by large landlords which is the dominant form of tenure in Persia to-day has developed out of or been imposed upon an earlier communal form of settlement with equalized individual rights.

At the same time that the large landed estates began to develop out of or to be superimposed upon the earlier communal settlements, although the economic interests of the landlord inclined towards a consolidation of the holdings, there were other factors as well as custom which reinforced the communal tendency. For purposes of tax collection it was easier for the government to deal with the village communities as a whole; this appears to have been the case under the Sasanians and was largely true of the situation after the Islamic conquest when villages in some cases were assessed as a whole and the community made collectively responsible for the payment of the individual shares.[1] Further, with the spread of the custom of making land assignments, which was superimposed on the older basis, since the privileges of the assignees consisted not only in the right to collect the revenue but also in the levying of dues and services on the population, it was clearly more convenient for them to keep the allotment of dues proportionate to shares and holdings. This, too, was, no doubt, a powerful factor in preserving the traditional arrangement of the village. From the point of view of the landlord there was a further advantage in preserving the *juft* or plough-land as a unit, in that if the obligation to pay dues and perform labour service rested upon the plough-land, it would not be affected by the subdivision of a holding among co-heirs. The periodic redistribution of holdings which is carried out in some areas at the present day[2] derives in all probability not so much from an equalitarian tendency in society as from a desire on the part of the landlord to keep the allotment of dues proportionate to the shares and holdings, reinforced by a wish to prevent the tenant from getting a vested interest in his holding.

[1] See Chs. I and II.

[2] See Ch. XVI.

The second way in which the village holding is reckoned is by reference to a share in the water. This arrangement is typical of certain areas where cultivation is carried on mainly by spade, as in certain areas in the neighbourhood of Iṣfahān, and in mountain areas where water and the configuration of the land and not the capacity of the plough-oxen are of paramount importance. In such cases the available amount of water is normally divided into a varying number of shares of equal duration in time and apportioned to the land. The size and shape of the holdings tends to vary with the configuration of the land to a greater extent than in the case of the villages divided into *juft*. For the most part this type of division tends to be found in the peasant-proprietor areas rather than in landlord areas. That this should be so is probably due mainly to the fact that peasant proprietorship is at the present day confined largely to the mountain regions and to the less fertile regions where the main limiting factor is water and not plough-oxen.[1] With certain exceptions, when the village holdings are arranged in this way, periodic redistribution is not usual.[2]

In certain districts, notably in the neighbourhood of Yazd, the arrangement of the village does not conform to either of the types described above. Here the land and water are separately owned, and the size of the holdings is not roughly equalized by the capacity of the plough-oxen or by an equal share of the water, but depends rather upon the ability and enterprise of the individual peasant. In view of the insufficient nature of the evidence it is not possible to do more than conjecture the reasons for this, and to suggest that the special development of this area is to be explained by geographical conditions and the political consequences which followed therefrom. Yazd, situated as it is on the edge of the central desert, was neither strategically important nor agriculturally prosperous, and for this reason in Ṣafavid and Qājār times was to some extent outside those areas which were assigned and reassigned to military leaders and others. In areas which were assigned the status of the peasants was reduced from that of communal owners to tenants and the general tendency was for their position in the course of time to be still further depressed. If the peasantry in the Yazd area have retained or acquired a greater degree of independence and initiative it is probably due to the fact that they were less affected than peasants in other districts by the main trend of political events, and that the stimulus of their natural environment was such as to call forth extra powers of resistance.

Kirmān also at the present day presents certain peculiar features

[1] See Ch. XIV.

[2] Varzaqān in the Uzum Dil district of Āẕarbāyjān is an exception to this (see p. 310, n. 1).

in so far as the division of the village land is concerned. In this area the village land is divided into six shares or *dāng*, each of which comprises one-sixth of the village water supply together with the land watered thereby. In this case little trace remains of an earlier communal tradition. Here again the explanation is probably to be sought in geographical conditions. The methods of irrigation owing to the configuration of the ground are such that the settlement of the area may well have been carried out mainly by powerful leaders rather than by groups of joint settlers. Yāqūt records that in Kirmān, which under the Seljūqs of Kirmān had been in a flourishing condition, land was going out of cultivation when he wrote (i.e. in the seventh/thirteenth century).[1] The devastation brought about by Tīmūr at the close of the eighth/fourteenth century may well have accentuated this trend and destroyed the existing basis of village organization, and unfavourable natural conditions may have prevented its revival. In any case there are fewer traces of any communal organization in Kirmān than in most other parts of Persia.

Just as the site of the village was influenced by natural conditions, so its lay-out was largely dictated by considerations of security, i.e. by political conditions. Security from attack by raiders is in many parts of Persia of relatively recent establishment. In addition to sporadic raids, those areas situated on the routes between the main provincial centres have lain in the path of military conquerors and have been frequently fought over. Ordinary caution demanded that the villages in the plains should either be walled or at least should have some central point or walled enclosure into which the population could retire with their animals in times of emergency. For example, many of the villages in the plains to the north of Iṣfahān, such as Gaz (Jaz), are walled, and the entrance to the village is through narrow gates; similarly, the central part of Mūrchehkhw̱art comprises a fortress in which the villagers and their cattle have their quarters. The reasons for this are not far to seek. The district of Burkhw̱ār lay in the path of the Afghān invaders who attacked Iṣfahān, the capital of the day, at the close of the Ṣafavid period and sacked the surrounding country. Gaz was one of the few villages which managed to hold out and resist capture.

The hamlets attached to the villages in most areas tend to be walled for security both against encroachment by raiders and against the depredations of wild animals. These hamlets in fact often consist merely of a walled homestead or *qalʿeh* in which are quarters for the peasants and their animals with possibly a part reserved for the owner. In some cases, if conditions are favourable

[1] *Jacut's geographisches Wörterbuch*, ed. Wüstenfeld (Leipzig, 1866–73), iv. 264.

and the hamlet grows, the settlement spreads beyond the original walled enclosure.

For the most part the houses of the village, whether the latter is walled or not, tend to be clustered together. The central point of the village is the mosque (where there is one) and the village shop (if such exists). The larger villages in many cases have caravanserais, but these tend to be on the outskirts rather than in the centre of the village. The gardens in those villages which have gardens are usually found on the edge of the village rather than in it; the cultivated lands are situated in most cases round the village and farther afield, beyond them, are the village pastures. The shape and lay-out of the village and its lands, however, is naturally modified by the configuration of the land and the availability of water. For example, in the mountain valleys the need for a walled village is clearly less frequently felt since in many cases the village does not lie in the path of invading forces, or it may itself be situated in an impregnable position. Further, when built up against the valley wall it can hardly be surrounded by cultivated lands; these are likely rather to stretch out to one side of it or to be found higher up or lower down the valley wherever this broadens out and offers the possibility of cultivation.

The population of the villages consists variously of the landlords (unless these are absentees), those who work or own the units into which the village land is divided (who may be crop-sharing peasants, tenants, or peasant proprietors) agricultural labourers and squatters, artisans such as the carpenter and the blacksmith, officials such as the village headman, tradesmen such as the village shopkeeper, and members of the religious classes. All classes are not found in each village. For example, peasant proprietors are not normally found in the landlord villages, nor are there craftsmen, shopkeepers, or members of the religious classes in all villages. It is with the position of these various classes and their relation to each other, to the land and to the state that the following pages are mainly concerned.

PART I

CHAPTER I

ORIGINS: THE ARAB CONQUEST

THE history of Persia before the immigration of the Persian, or more properly speaking the Avestan, people is unknown to us apart from Elam and isolated references in Assyrian inscriptions.[1] The earliest records which we have of the Avestan people before their migration into east Persia disclose a standing opposition between the settled and the semi-settled element.[2] After their migration into east Persia fixed settlements formed the central point of their economic, religious, and political life; but the dichotomy between settled and semi-settled continued.[3] Society was patriarchal and based on the household (*nmāna-*) the village (*vis-*), the tribe (*zantu-*), and the country (*dahyu-*).[4] Gradually, as cultivation spread and fresh soil was won, certain families took considerable quantities of land into their possession.[5] The normal type of settlement was the village, single farms being the exception to the general rule in east Persia. The people were grouped in tribes and the village of a clan formed the model according to which the new settlements were arranged and managed. This type of settlement, as pointed out in the Introduction, was largely imposed upon them by circumstances. In the course of time leaders whose power and influence derived on the one hand from their tribes and on the other hand from their territorial possessions emerged, and by Achaemenid times played an important role.

In the western part of the Persian plateau and in Mesopotamia, some sort of service appears to have been attached to the land from early times. The normal way for the ruler to maintain his troops and pay his officials was to provide them with grants of land. Thus, the code of Hammurabi in arts. 36, 38, and 71 forbids the sale of *ilku* (i.e. land upon which there is royal service) by royal officers to whom it has been granted. Art. 38 forbids such title-holders to give *ilku* land for debt, and art. 71 prevents alienation of

[1] A. Christensen, 'Introduction bibliographique à l'histoire du droit de l'Iran ancien' (in *Archives d'histoire du droit oriental*, ii. 243).

[2] Geiger, *Civilization of Eastern Iranians*, i. 11 ff. The Avesta extols the settled life of the peasant and the careful tending of cattle and recognizes a religious merit in the cultivation of the soil, and in the reclaiming of land still lying waste, as also in the gradual promotion of cultivation (ibid. p. 12).

[3] ibid. p. 225.

[4] Christensen, *L'Iran sous les Sassanides* (Copenhagen, 1936), p. 13.

[5] Geiger, p. 247.

ilku land and compels the purchaser to return such land to the vendor.[1] Researches into real estate transactions in Nuzi (situated ten miles south-west of Kirkūk) in the second millennium B.C. have shown that all land belonged to the king, and was only held as a grant or fief by his subjects.

Legally, these subjects had possession but not ownership of the property entrusted to their care. In return for the use of this land each subject owed some type of service to the king, but he had no right to dispose of or transfer his property to any person other than a male relative of his immediate family. As the feudal practices declined and private ownership developed in fact if not in theory, a legal circumvention became necessary in order to facilitate the transfer of real estate between private persons. The method which lent itself most readily to a synthesis of the older legal concept with a newer legal practice was, it appears, a pseudo-adoption. With a few necessary additions and regulations, required by a sale contract although not needful in a real adoption, this new method seemed to satisfy all requirements. Property was thus bought and sold without offending the letter of the law.[2]

By this transaction the seller would adopt the buyer as his son and deed him with a specified parcel of property as an inheritance share. In return, the purchaser gave a *qîštu* or gift consisting of commodities totalling in value the price of the property.[3]

Various other transactions in land appear to have existed, including (1) *ditennūtu*, a loan secured by real estate given as collateral;[4] (2) *šupe'ŭltu*, exchange to consolidate scattered holdings.[5] In two texts referring to the former type of transaction it is stipulated that 'the *ilku* "feudal service" shall remain with the seller'.

The first Persian empire, that of the Achaemenids, rising about the year 550 B.C. on the ruins of the earlier empires centred in Mesopotamia, followed some, at least, of the feudal practices of its predecessors, and those provinces which had been the centre of ancient empires preserved in some measure their institutions after the Persian conquest.[6] Meanwhile, the King of Kings emerged as the head of the country and satraps as provincial governors replaced the heads of the tribes.[7] The satrap was the head of the administration of his province; he collected the taxes, controlled the local officials and the subject tribes and cities, and was the supreme

1 P. M. Purves, 'Commentary on Nuzi Real Property', *J.N.E.*, iv (April 1945), p. 75.

2 F. R. Steele, *Nuzi Real Estate Transactions* (Philadelphia, 1943), p. 15.

3 Purves, *J.N.E.*, iv, p. 69.

4 Steele, p. 47.

5 ibid. p. 53. See also H. H. Lewy, 'Système féodale et exploitation du domaine royal d'après les textes de Nuzi', *Arch. d'hist. du droit orient.*, iii, pp. 162–5.

6 See N. Adontz, 'L'Aspect iranien du servage', *Le Servage* (*Communications présentées à la Société Jean Bodin*, Réunions des 16, 17, et 18 Octobre 1936), pp. 136 ff.

7 Christensen, *L'Iran sous les Sassanides*, p. 15.

judge of the province. He was responsible for the safety of the roads and had to put down brigands and rebels. He was assisted by a council of Persians, to which provincials were also admitted, and was controlled by a royal secretary and by emissaries of the king. The regular army of the province and the fortresses were independent of him and commanded by royal officers. He was, however, allowed to have troops in his own service.[1] The revenues were paid in cash and kind. Every Persian able to bear arms was bound to serve the king, the great landowners on horseback and others on foot. The well-to-do who did not need to till their lands in person were pledged to appear in court as frequently as possible. Such of their children as proved their worth were called to high office and rewarded generally with grants of land. Further, numbers of Persians were dispatched to the provinces, settled there, and endowed with lands. These colonists formed the nucleus of the provincial military levy and composed the Persian council and household of the satraps.[2] The effect of this colonizing movement, which was a marked feature of the Achaemenid organization, was to broaden the basis of power of the great families, upon whose support the Achaemenids had relied in their rise to power; whereas originally they had drawn their power from Fārs whence they came, they subsequently derived it from large landed estates in all parts of the empire. With the decay of the Achaemenid empire the satraps enjoyed practical independence, especially as it became customary to appoint them as generals-in-chief of their army district, contrary to the original rule. Alexander, who overthrew the last Darius in 330 B.C., and the Seleucids appear to have continued Achaemenian institutions in their essentials,[3] but it was not till Parthian times when the Scythian nomads became the ruling race that pre-Islamic Persian feudalism achieved its full development. They (the Scythians) were invested with large landed property and formed the council of the king.[4] There were seven main families, who constituted the class of great vassals who raised their subjects for or against the ruler. Between them and the peasants was an intermediary class holding sub-fiefs. The link between these and the great feudatories was stronger than between the king and the great feudatories, between whom, according to the classical historians, there appears to have been a certain antagonism.[5] The empire was composed of vassal-kingdoms and provinces governed directly as satrapies.[6] Each satrapy had one or

[1] See art. on 'Satrap' in *Encyclopaedia Britannica* (11th ed.).
[2] ibid. art. on 'Persia'.
[3] Christensen, *L'Iran sous les Sassanides*, p. 14.
[4] See *Encyclopaedia Britannica*, art. on 'Parthia'.
[5] Christensen, pp. 16–17, 23.
[6] *Cambridge Ancient History*, ix. 590.

more ruling houses, whose heads were the feudal lords of many villages and cities. The Parthian army consisted of the retinues of the feudal lords; consequently it was natural that the Parthian kings should appoint the heads of powerful clans to be governors of their several countries, thus making the position of a satrap almost a hereditary office.[1] According to Rostovtzeff the most prominent feature of the economic and social life of the Parthian empire was 'the feudal structure of both social and economic life with the great feudatories leading, with the minor feudal lords holding cities and villages, with small free landowners cultivating their holdings and with bondmen working for both large and small landowners'.[2]

The main features of the feudal system of the Arsacids appear to have been inherited by the Sasanian dynasty which was founded in A.D. 226. The latter continued to rule in Persia until they were overthrown by the Muslim invaders. Although the sources for this period are still fragmentary and incomplete, this much is clear: that society was based largely on a profound belief in the sanctity of family ties, and that the laws were designed to preserve the family and landed estates and to maintain a clear distinction between the different classes of society, assigning to each its proper place in the social order.[3] The seven privileged families, one of which, the Sasanian, had become the royal family, still held their leading position.[4] Unfortunately we have no precise knowledge of the nature of the Sasanian feudal system. For example, it is not known what authority the royal government had in the fiefs, what immunities the feudal nobility enjoyed, or precisely what services were attached to the land. It is clear, however, that the feudal nobility had to pay taxes to the central government or the local governor or to both, and were obliged to perform military service.[5] As in earlier times it appears that the great feudatories held or owned lands in widely separated areas.[6] Next in the landed hierarchy after the feudal nobility were the heads of villages, known as *dihqāns*, who derived their power from a hereditary title to the local administration. They were an immensely important class, although the actual area of land they cultivated as the hereditary possession of their family was often small. They were the repre-

[1] ibid. xi. 114.
[2] ibid. p. 120.
[3] Christensen, pp. 329–30.
[4] ibid. pp. 98–9.
[5] ibid. p. 101.
[6] ibid. pp. 370–1. cf. the story of Anūshīravān and a governor of Āẕarbāyjān related by Niẕām ul-Mulk in the *Sīāsat Nāmeh*. This is not in itself evidence of conditions actually prevailing but it describes what was believed at a later period to have been Sasanian practice. The governor wanted to build a country house. An old woman who owned property where the governor wished to build refused to sell this and so he evicted her. She appealed to Anūshīravān, who sent to investigate the case and was told the governor in question owned houses, caravanserais, and landed estates in Khurāsān, ʿIrāq, Fārs, and Āẕarbāyjān (pp. 30 ff., also quoted by Christensen, pp. 370–1).

sentatives of the government *vis-à-vis* the peasants, and their principal function was to collect taxes; and, in the opinion of Christensen, it was due to their knowledge of the country and people that sufficient revenue was provided for the upkeep of a luxurious court and the cost of expensive wars—sums, indeed the equal of which the Arab conquerors were unable to raise.[1] The feudal nobility and the *dihqāns*, however, were not the only landowners. The priests also derived their influence in part from their territorial possessions.[2] During the reign of Anūshīravān (A.D. 531–78) after the overthrow of the Mazdakite rebellion the great nobility who had been organized by the king were docile and quiet. The lesser nobility, which passed its time on its lands occupied with the duties of local administration, lived in conditions of perhaps greater ease than the rest of the population. Christensen considers that the miseries of public and social life in general were probably less in the time of Anūshīravān than formerly.[3] The keynote to political and social life was nevertheless insecurity;[4] and none were safe from the capricious exercise of force by the strong against the weak.

The peasants were attached to the soil and under obligation to perform labour service and to serve as foot-soldiers. The law gave them little protection and when Hurmuzd IV urged the military not to commit violence against the peaceful population when on campaign, he probably had in mind the *dihqāns* and not the peasants. According to Ammianus Marcellinus, the nobility arrogated to themselves 'rights of life and death over the slaves and people'.[5]

Agriculture was the main source of revenue. The official at the head of the revenue collection was known as the *vastryoshansalar* (i.e. the head of the agriculturists). He was probably also concerned with the supervision of agriculture and irrigation,[6] for the control of which various regulations existed, including ones dealing with different sorts of canals, their upkeep and use, and the building of dykes and bridges, and other matters.[7] Considerable difficulty appears nevertheless to have been experienced in the collection of taxation, and arrears were common.[8]

[1] Christensen, p. 107.

[2] ibid. p. 112. There was a rigid division between the various classes or estates and between the nobility and the common people. In the *Tansar Nāmeh* there is a statement to the effect that the common people were forbidden to purchase real estate belonging to the nobles (ed. M. Mīnovī (Tehrān, 1311), p. 19).

[3] Christensen, p. 434.

[4] Agathias Scholasticus states 'the stronger oppressed the inferior and they exercised much cruelty and inhumanity among themselves' (quoted by Christensen, p. 434).

[5] xxiii, 6, 80, quoted by Christensen, p. 316.

[6] Christensen, p. 117.

[7] ibid. p. 316.

[8] The remission of arrears was a step sometimes taken by a ruler on his acces-

It appears that up to the reign of Qubād (d. A.D. 531) the land tax was assessed on the produce at varying rates according to the type of farming practised and the nature of the crops raised. During the reigns of Qubād and his son and successor Anūshīravān it was assessed by measurement of the land, except in the case of date palms and fruit trees, the tax on which was assessed according to the number of trees.[1] The story of the incidents leading up to the change in the method of assessment is related in substantially the same form by many early Islamic writers. According to this tradition Qubād when out hunting one day came to an orchard where a woman was making bread. Standing beside her was a child whom she kept restraining from taking some of the fruit. Qubād asked her why she did this. She replied that the fruit was shared between her and the king, and since neither the latter nor his tax-collector had yet divided it, it was not lawful for her children to take any of the fruit. Qubād is then alleged to have determined to abolish this custom and to assess the tax on the land instead of on the produce. Before he could carry out his determination he died. Anūshīravān, his son and successor, implemented his plan and imposed a land tax on the estates, arable lands, gardens, orchards, and vineyards throughout the country and imposed a poll tax exempting from it only a few persons.[2] Christensen believes that this reform in the taxation system was both a relief to the population and a benefit to the treasury. In later times it formed the basis of the assessment of the caliphs.[3]

sion in order to acquire popularity. For example, Bahrām V (Bahrām Gūr) ordered arrears to be cancelled on his accession (Christensen, p. 119). According to another tradition, Bahrām remitted the land tax for five years. This is alleged to have resulted in the people devoting themselves to pleasure and merriment so that the flourishing condition of the country was changed to ruin. Bahrām accordingly reimposed the land tax and made it obligatory on both cultivated and waste-land. The people were thus forced to cultivate the waste-land, and the yield of this became greater than that of the cultivated land. (*T.Q.*, p. 187.)

[1] According to Ṭabarī, Qubād began the measurement and Anūshīravān completed it (I, 2, 960). Grain paid 1 *dirham* per *jarīb*, vineyards 8 *dirhams* per *jarīb*, and trefoil 7 *dirhams* per *jarīb*; the rate for Persian date palms was 1 *dirham* per four trees, and for palms of inferior quality 1 *dirham* per six trees, and for olives 1 *dirham* per six trees. One to two *qafīz* in land were also paid per *jarīb* on grain land. The tax was paid in three instalments per annum (I, 2, 961–3). Masʿūdī gives a somewhat different account: according to him, Qubād fixed the rate in the Sawād for wheat and barley at 2 *dirhams* per *jarīb* (*Kitāb at-Tanbīh wa'l-Ischrāf*, ed. de Goeje (*Bibl. Geog. Arab.*), p. 39).

[2] *T.Q.*, p. 179. See also *Ṭab.*, I, 2, 960–3; Ibn Ḥauqal states that the tax was paid in the form of a share of the harvest in pre-Islamic times until the time of Qubād. The latter established the payment of fixed rents throughout the province of Fārs, payable when the granaries and threshing-floors were full (*Kitāb Ṣūrat al-Arẓ*, ed. J. H. Kramers (*Bibl. Geog. Arab.*), ii. 303–4).

[3] p. 361; Hamadānī is quoted by the *Tārīkhi Qumm* as stating that Qubād was the first person to measure the land and institute [land] registers, [to define] the boundaries of the lands and [to fix] the land tax, and that he instituted a *dīvāni*

According to another tradition Ardashīr b. Bābak, the founder of the Sasanian dynasty, was the first person to make the payment of land tax customary. A letter from a landowner in Nihāvand written to the scribes of Rukh ud-Douleh is quoted by the *Tārīkhi Qumm* to this effect. The writer maintains that the Persians considered this practice abominable and held that sharing (i.e. the assessment of the government tax by way of a fixed proportion of the crop) was more just.[1]

The Arab conquest of Persia in the seventh century A.D.[2] marks a major break in Persian history. Persia became part of the Muslim world and a new theory of state common to all Muslim territories was evolved. The change in matters of local administration, which remained in the hands of the indigenous population, was smaller. Many local customs continued to be observed under Muslim rule. The tax system, in spite of the efforts of the jurists to adapt it to the Islamic scheme, continued to resemble former Sasanian practice in many respects rather than to conform to the rules laid down by Muḥammad and those who guided the fortunes of the primitive Muslim community. In the course of time changes were brought about, but this movement of change was a two-fold one: on the one hand legal theory reacted upon and influenced the development of social and economic institutions, while on the other hand Islamic theory was modified by the attitude of mind and custom prevailing in the conquered territories. The process took some time to work out and there were many local variations. Ultimately, however, a new civilization was created, the unifying force of which was Islām.

There are indeed few aspects of Persian life where the influence of Islām cannot be traced. In so far as matters of land are concerned Islām has materially affected the conception and development of landed property and land tenure. Water and pasture were considered to belong to all Muslims in common.[3] The existence of private property was both recognized and approved of, and was held to be inviolable except when it was necessary to resort to

kharāj in Ḥulwān, which he called the *dīvāni ʿadl* (*T.Q.*, p. 180). It seems likely that the land registers continued to be kept there. When Muʿāwīah appointed an official in charge of land tax in Mesopotamia, the list of crown lands which had been in the possession of the Sasanian king and his family had to be procured from Ḥulwān (Ibn Wāẓiḥ, *Taʾrīkh*, ed. M. Th. Houtsma (Brill, 1883), ii. 258).

1 *T.Q.*, pp. 182–3.

2 The battles of Qādisīyeh in 16/637 and of Nihāvand in 21/642 were important stages in this conquest. The term Persia is used as a geographical term in the following pages, and not to denote a political entity. It was not till Ṣafavid times (see Ch. V) that Persia became a national state in the modern sense of the word and the term Persia came to denote a political as well as a geographical entity.

3 See Abū Yūsuf, p. 147. This is presumably a relic of desert communism.

expropriation for definite reasons, either legal, as in the case of a debtor, or because it was considered to be in the public interest, as when the state claimed the land for a fort or street or some other purpose.[1]

The speed and comparative ease of the Muslim conquest was in all probability in some measure due to the fact that Islām offered the mass of the people release from conditions of intolerable social inferiority, while the old system had little in it to rouse their loyalty or to make them feel that in opposing the invaders they were fighting for the preservation of a way of life which was conducive to their own well-being, or that in supporting their ruling class they were supporting those who were concerned for their well-being. In any case, whether the success of the Muslims is to be ascribed to military superiority, or to religious fervour, or to the weakness of the opposition because of political and social discontent and economic decay, or is to be attributed to all these factors, the conquest of Persia was accomplished with little difficulty.

The rapidity with which the Muslim conquests in general were carried out and their extent resulted in a wide divergence between theory and practice, and the measures adopted to deal with the administrative problems which arose in the conquered territories were often of an *ad hoc* nature. The work of the early jurists[2] is largely an attempt to fit these various solutions into the framework of the law. One of the main difficulties which confronted them was how to reconcile actual practice with Quranic precept, especially where the division of booty and land in the conquered territories was concerned, and to justify the payment of a higher rate of taxation than the canonical *ʿushr*, i.e. tithe, by Muslims and converts who were in possession of land in the conquered territories. According to the Qur'ān one-fifth of all booty was to be set aside for the prophet Muḥammad, and the remainder was to be divided among the combatants. With the extension of the Muslim conquests considerable modifications were made in the allocation of the booty. In Mesopotamia drained marshes and swamps, property

[1] This clearly provided a loophole by which expropriation could be carried out; justice was not always scrupulously observed in such matters.

[2] In the following pages Sunnī authorities will for the most part be quoted rather than Shīʿī. It was not till Ṣafavid times that Persia became Shīʿī (see Ch. V). Up to that time, although the Shīʿah were endemic in Persia they were never in a majority throughout the country. Sunnism was for the most part the religion of the governing classes, hence the importance of Sunnī rather than Shīʿī theory in the pre-Ṣafavid period. For a discussion of the influence of Islamic theory on the modern Civil Code, see Ch. IX. There are four main schools or rites of Sunnī theory: the Mālikī founded by Mālik b. Anas (97–179/715–95), the Ḥanafī, founded by Abū Ḥanīfa (d. 150/767), the Shāfiʿī, founded by ash-Shāfiʿī (150–204/767–820), and the Ḥanbalī, founded by Aḥmad b. Muḥammad b. Ḥanbal (164–241/780–855). Of these the Ḥanafīs and Shāfiʿīs were the most important in Persia.

belonging to fire-temples and post-houses, to princes and their wives and to those who fell in battle, and mills were exempted from the booty by most authorities, although some maintained that the estates belonging to the former royal house and the property of those falling in battle were not thus exempted.[1] These lands became in effect crown lands. Løkkegaard believes that in the fully developed conception of booty 'the State in all the subdued countries reserves for itself the absolute title to all land'.[2]

In an attempt to reduce to a system the variety of practices which grew up during the period of conquests, and the various measures taken to lessen the financial dislocation which was threatened on the one hand by the widespread acquisition of land in the conquered territories by the Muslims, and on the other by the conversion of the conquered peoples,[3] the jurists divided the lands conquered by the Muslims into three categories: (1) those conquered by force and abandoned by their inhabitants who had been killed or captured or who had fled, (2) lands acquired peacefully because their owners had abandoned them, and (3) lands coming into Muslim ownership by virtue of a treaty but remaining in the

[1] *Ṭab.*, I, 5, 2468; Abū Yūsuf, pp. 86–7.

[2] *Islamic Taxation in the Classic Period* (Copenhagen, 1950), p. 49. He states that there was a distinction between state domains known as *ṣavāfī*, which derived from that part of the booty which accrued to the leader of the community apart from that which was divided among the combatants, i.e. the one-fifth, and other lands, known as *fay'* land (which derived from the four-fifths). According to the Shīʿī theory of the Ithna ʿAsharī school as put forward by al-Muḥaqqiq (see Ch. IX), the modifications in the theory of booty were somewhat wider. According to his exposition the following categories of land were reserved for the *imām*, i.e. the successor of the Prophet: (1) lands acquired in any way other than by war, whether abandoned by their owners or voluntarily handed over to him; (2) lands untenanted and without owners, whether abandoned by their owners or land which was always untenanted, such as land from which the population had fled, beaches and shores of the sea, the summits of mountains, etc.; (3) the produce of such lands; (4) the produce of rivers and forests untenanted and without owners; and (5) after the conquest of enemy territory, all the effects, movable and immovable, of the conquered ruler, provided such goods had not been seized formerly from a Muslim, ally, or tributary, whose property they had been. (*Sharāyiʿ fī Masā'il al-Ḥilāl*, tr. A. Querry, *Droit musulman* (Paris, 1871–2), i. 179–80). All land conquered by force of arms became the property of the Muslim community as a whole and not only of the combatants. The administration of these lands belonged to the *imām* alone. Ownership of these lands could never be acquired by possession, and the transfer of these lands by sale, gift, or endowment was null and void. The *imām* only had the right to dispose of the usufruct of these lands to the public good, such as the protection of frontiers, holy war, the construction of bridges, etc. Dead lands similarly belonged to the *imām* (ibid. i. 337). See also Ch. IX.

[3] Wellhausen has pointed out how the original practice, namely, that Islām freed from all tributary obligation and that hence *kharāj* land became tax-free when acquired by an Arab Muslim or when the non-Arab became a Muslim, led to embarrassment. If, on the one hand, the amount of the tribute was reduced in proportion as those formerly liable became converted to Islām, the treasury suffered, while, on the other hand, if the sum due remained unchanged the community, since numbers had been lessened by conversion, was less able to bear the tax. (*Das arabische Reich und sein Sturz* (Berlin, 1927), pp. 173–4.)

possession of their original owners on condition they paid *kharāj*, or tribute. Concerning the disposal of lands in the first class there was some difference of opinion between the various schools. According to ash-Shāfiʿī such lands were treated as booty and divided among the conquerors, unless the latter renounced them, in which case they were immobilized for the public good. Mālik, on the other hand, did not permit their division among the captors but considered they belonged to the community, while according to Abū Hanīfa the *imām* (i.e. the caliph) could either divide them among the captors, in which case they paid *ʿushr*, or return them to their original owners and levy from them *kharāj*, or immobilize them for the benefit of the Muslim community; in the latter case the land, whether it was occupied by Muslims or by tributaries, became Muslim territory since the ownership of it belonged to the Muslims. Lands which were in the second category paid *kharāj*; this represented a *dominium* which had to be paid by whoever exploited them, Muslim or non-Muslim. Here again there was some difference of opinion among the authorities as to the nature of this payment. Such lands could not be sold or mortgaged. Lands in the third category were of two kinds: (*a*) those which were immobilized and continued to pay *kharāj* even if the occupiers were converted to Islām or if their occupation rights were transferred to Muslims, and (*b*) those which remained in the possession of their original owners who paid *kharāj*, but from which they were exempted on conversion. These lands could be sold or mortgaged.[1] In matters of detail in the case of these lands also there is some difference of opinion between the various schools.

In discussing the tax regimes to which the various regions were subject Māwardī, the famous Sunnī jurist, who died in 450/1058, considers that the Muslim conquests (i.e. land outside the sacred cities of Mecca and Medīna and the Ḥijāz) could be divided into four categories: (1) land the inhabitants of which in order to retain possession of the soil had become Muslims; (2) dead land reclaimed by Muslims; (3) land conquered by force and divided as booty among the conquerors; and (4) land the inhabitants of which had surrendered by virtue of a treaty. The first three categories paid *ʿushr*. Land in the fourth category constituted *fay'*[2] and paid *kharāj*. It was divided into (*a*) land the inhabitants of which renounced their rights of property under the terms of capitulation, and (*b*) land the inhabitants of which were accorded, by the terms of capitulation, rights of property. In the first instance the sale of the land was not permissible and the *kharāj* imposed on it represented a rent, from liability to which the inhabitants could not free them-

[1] Māwardī, *al-Aḥkām as-Sulṭānīya*, ed. Enger (Bonn, 1853), pp. 255–6.
[2] See above p. 18, n. 2.

selves by conversion; it was levied on both Muslims and tributaries (*ẕimmīs*). In the latter instance the sale of the land was permitted and the *kharāj* represented a poll tax which ceased to be due on conversion. In other words tributaries but not Muslims paid this *kharāj*.[1]

From the exposition of the jurists it follows that land in Persia after the Muslim conquest can be divided either according to the tax regime to which it was subject or according to ownership. In the first case land falls into two major categories, (1) *ʿushr* land and (2) *kharāj* land. Becker makes a distinction between these two types of land and holds that strictly speaking whereas *ʿushr* land can be owned as property, only the usufruct of *kharāj* land can be enjoyed.[2] According to the second mode of division land falls into four categories: (1) crown lands comprising in part the former crown lands of the Persian kings and in part lands conquered by force, (2) lands belonging to the community and administered by the *imām*, comprising cultivated lands which have no owner, (3) land held as private property (*a*) by Muslims, i.e. Arabs, comprising land which had been acquired by force, dead land which had been reclaimed, and land acquired by purchase (and inheritance), and (*b*) by non-Muslims, who had been confirmed in the full ownership of their land; and (4) land the ownership of which vested in the Muslim community, occupied by its original owners, i.e. non-Muslims, who exercised occupancy rights only. Lands in the first category were in some cases assigned to non-Muslims. For example, Ibn Wāẓiḥ states that Muʿāwīah, the Umayyad caliph (reg. 41–60/661–80), made the former Persian crown lands into crown lands and gave them as assignments to members of his house.[3] Land in the second category could not be sold. It appears also to have been assigned in some cases by the *imām* to Muslims.[4]

[1] Māwardī, p. 299. al-Muḥaqqiq gives a similar exposition concerning lands acquired by peace treaty. He states that these were left in the possession of their owners subject to the fulfilment of the conditions imposed by the *imām*. The owner remained free to exercise full rights of ownership and to dispose of his lands by all legal means. The lands could be sold to a Muslim and the charges and servitudes attaching to them became obligatory on the new owner. These last three statements applied only to those lands the owners of which had been confirmed by the *imām* in their exercise of the right of ownership. If in the peace treaty it was stipulated that the lands acquired became the property of the Muslim community, with authorization given to the original owners to remain provided they paid poll tax, the lands were subject to the same disposition as those acquired by force of arms, i.e. cultivated lands became the communal property of the Muslims and dead lands the property of the *imām*. When the population of a country embraced Islām their rights of property were confirmed and the land was exempted from all tax except *zakāt* (*Droit musulman*, i. 338).

[2] *Islamstudien* (Leipzig, 1924–32), i. 226.

[3] *Ta'rīkh*, ii. 277.

[4] Landed property in Qazvīn which had no owner was given in assignments to Muslims (P. Schwarz, *Iran im Mittelalter* (Leipzig, 1929–36), vii. 944).

In the course of time it seems likely that the actual ownership of land in this category tended to be usurped.

Although in theory the law made a clear distinction between these various categories of land, in practice the rigidity of the law was modified by the complexity of existing circumstances. Moreover, as time went on the confusion increased. The tendency grew for land in the second category to be assimilated on the one hand to land in the first category and for both to be looked upon as the private estates of the *imām*,[1] and on the other hand for land in the first two categories to be assimilated to land in the third category, becoming by usurpation private property. The rate of taxation paid by land in section (*b*) of the third category and land in the fourth category differed from the rate paid by land in section (*a*) of the third category, being *kharāj* in the former case and *ʿushr* in the latter, unless it was land acquired by purchase by Muslims, i.e. Arabs, from non-Muslims, in which case it continued to pay *kharāj* as it had when held by non-Muslims. In practice it appears that the Persian landowning class in large measure retained their lands and for some time their privileged status also,[2] even if in some cases in order to do so they placed themselves under the protection of some Muslim, which action enabled them to retain their lands on more favourable terms. Iṣṭakhrī, writing in the tenth century A.D., states:

> in Fārs there are estates the owners of which had placed themselves under the protection of great men in the entourage of the caliph in ʿIrāq, their estates being in the names of these great men and a quarter of the *kharāj* being remitted from them. But these estates remained in the effective possession of their original owners, who transmitted them by sale and inheritance.[3]

The exposition by jurists of the conquest of the Sawād, the area stretching from Ḥadītha near Mawṣil to Ābādān and from ʿUzhayb near Qādisīyeh to Ḥulwān, illustrates the divergence between theory and practice and the difficulty in which the early Muslims found themselves when faced with the necessity of reconciling theory with practice and rationalizing the precedents which had been established. The jurists differ both as to the nature of the conquest of the Sawād and the tax regime to which it became subject. According to the ʿIrāqī school it was conquered by force; nevertheless, ʿUmar did not divide it among the conquerors as booty, but left it instead in the hands of the original holders, making the land subject to *kharāj*. Abū Yūsuf (d. 182/798) relates in

1 cf. Wellhausen, pp. 171–2.

2 See Løkkegaard, pp. 171–2.

3 *Kitāb Masālik al-Mamālik*, ed. de Goeje (*Bibl. Geog. Arab.*), p. 158. See also Ibn Ḥauqal, ii. 303, and pp. 25–6 below.

some detail 'Umar's action in refusing to distribute the conquered territories among the conquerors[1] and concludes

> The decision taken by 'Umar to oppose partition among the conquerors of the conquered territories as soon as God had shown him the decisive passage of His holy book on this subject, was for him and his work a manifest action of divine protection, and a benefit for the Muslim community. His decision that *kharāj* should be paid so that the produce therefrom could be divided among the Muslims was beneficial for the whole community, because if it had not been immobilized to provide the pay and the sustenance of the military the frontier provinces would not have been populated, the troops would have been deprived of the necessary means of carrying on the holy war and the return of the infidels into their former possessions would have had to be feared, because these would have been found without defenders and mercenaries.[2]

According to Shāfi'ī the Sawād was conquered by force and divided among the conquerors, to whom it was given with full proprietory rights; subsequently 'Umar requested them to give it up, to which all except a few agreed; from these he had to buy their rights. The situation as far as the Muslims was concerned then became clear and he fixed *kharāj* on the land. There were, however, disagreements concerning the ultimate ownership of the land. Abū Sa'īd Iṣṭakhrī and many other Shāfi'īs after him consider that 'Umar immobilized the land for the benefit of the Muslim community, while leaving the land in the hands of its inhabitants in return for the payment of *kharāj*, which therefore represented a life-rent. The fact that the land could be transferred from one holder to another did not constitute a right of ownership of the soil but merely the ownership of plantations and buildings made after the conquest.[3] From this it would appear that the holders merely exercised occupancy rights and acquired certain other rights only in so far as they cultivated the land. Other Shāfi'īs, including Abu'l 'Abbās b. Surayj, consider that 'Umar, after having taken back the Sawād from those who had conquered it, sold it to the cultivators and peasants[4] for a price representing the *kharāj* which they would have to pay annually, holding that such a proceeding was permissible if the public interest so demanded; the conclusion of the contract in their view involved a transfer of ownership.[5]

When this exposition of the jurists is seen against the historical background, the dilemma both of the theorist and of the administrator becomes clearer. Whatever the theory and the actual nature of the conquest, the administration was in fact thrown into disorder because there were wholesale conversions of the conquered peoples

[1] pp. 37–43. [2] p. 43. [3] Māwardī, pp. 302–3.
[4] The text has *al-akarat wa'd-dihāqīn*, which I take to mean those who were actually cultivating the land. [5] Māwardī, p. 303.

who demanded that the privilege of the payment of *zakāt* instead of *kharāj* should be extended to them, and because Arab Muslims began to acquire *kharāj* land and to assume that this should be liable henceforward only to *ʿushr*. Ḥajjāj, the Umayyad governor of ʿIrāq (d. 95/713), in order to stop the loss which the treasury was suffering on account of these two tendencies is alleged to have decided that Arabs who from then on acquired *kharāj* land should pay *kharāj* on that land, and to have reimposed *kharāj* on those lands which had been transferred to Arabs and therefore ceased to pay *kharāj*. Similarly, he is said to have decreed that conversion should not release the conquered peoples from their obligation to pay *kharāj* as long as they remained in their villages and retained their lands. Further, he forbade them to emigrate and eventually brought back by force those who did emigrate. These measures caused a considerable outcry. ʿUmar II (99–101/717–20) sought the same object by somewhat different means. He sought to establish the view that *kharāj* land was first of all the joint property of the Muslims and, secondly, was in the joint possession of the communities found on it, to whom the Muslims had handed it over. These communities in return for the payment of tribute enjoyed the usufruct of the land. Separate lots could not therefore be taken away from the whole and could not become tax-free private estates by passing into Muslim ownership. He prohibited the selling of *kharāj* land to the Arabs as from the year 100/718–19. In the case of converts, their property was to revert to the village community to which they belonged. A convert might remain on his land as a lease-holder, or he might come into the town (which practice Ḥajjāj had forbidden). In fact, however, ʿUmar was unable to establish the principle of the inalienability of *kharāj* land. But later practice made a distinction between *kharāj* and *jizya* which had not existed before: the former came to be regarded only as affecting the land and had to be paid by Muslims and non-Muslims holding *kharāj* or tributary land, while the latter affected persons and was paid by non-Muslims only.[1]

Conditions, however, as pointed out above, were not uniform in the different provinces of the Arab empire. The practice in Khurāsān differed, for example, from the Sawād. There the last Umayyad governor, Naṣr b. Sayyār (appointed in 120/738), carried

[1] See D. C. Dennett, *Conversion and the Poll Tax in Early Islam* (Harvard, 1950), p. 9, for a discussion of the meaning of the terms *kharāj* and *jizya*. He maintains that '*kharāj* and *jizya* as synonymous terms meant not tribute but simply *tax* . . . for centuries the terms *kharāj* and *jizya* had the general meaning of *tax* as distinct from tribute, and that either could mean land or poll tax according to the modifying phrase which indicated whether it was a tax on lands or on heads or necks. Besides the general meaning, each of these words had a specific meaning: *kharāj* meant land tax, *jizya* poll tax. This specific meaning existed in early, as well as in later, times' (pp. 12–13).

out a reform in the fiscal administration, by which both Arabs and Persians were made to contribute to the land tax in proportion to their property while the poll tax was paid only by *ẕimmīs*. This development is also to be explained in the light of the peculiar circumstances prevailing in the province. Under the Sasanians, in addition to the land tax special trade and industrial taxes were levied, and everyone, except the privileged, paid a poll tax, graded according to income. When the Arabs conquered Khurāsān the local leaders in many cases capitulated by treaty, agreeing to pay a fixed sum annually. In so far as the individual tax-payer was concerned he continued to pay according to the Sasanian system. The local leaders collected the taxes as they pleased, and paid to the Arabs the agreed sum.[1] With the migration of Arab tribes to Khurāsān there was wide-scale conversion to Islām. The fact that this was not followed by a serious fiscal problem and that the sum due from the remaining non-Muslim communities did not prove a crushing burden in view of their dwindling numbers leads Dennett to deduce that 'local collectors were not very willing to release the converts from their taxes, or that the tribute was not at first very high or both',[2] and to explain the reform of Naṣr b. Sayyār in the following terms. The assessors and collectors of the land tax and poll tax, out of the proceeds of which the fixed sum due to the Arabs from the various districts was paid,

> were the native princes, acting in co-operation with the heads of the religious communities. The Arabs, following the rules elsewhere, had ordered these assessors to release converts of their poll taxes. This order had not been obeyed. A man named Bahrāmsīs, for example, assessed the taxes of the Magians, and when one of his people turned Muslim, Bahrāmsīs not only did not free him from his poll tax, but penalized him further, and to make his position invidious relaxed the taxation on the Magians. The son of Gregory (ibn Jarījūr) who assessed and collected the Christian taxes treated Christian renegades in the same manner, as did ʿAqībah the Jews. The result was that 30,000 Muslims were paying their poll taxes unjustly, while 80,000 unbelievers were getting off scot free. Moreover, these assessors were discriminating unjustly in the land tax, bearing down heavily on converts and letting their own people off lightly.[3]

This was the situation which Naṣr b. Sayyār set out to reform and as a result of his action the 30,000 Muslims were freed from the payment of poll tax and the 80,000 unbelievers made to pay. He further 'reclassified *kharāj* and put it in order. Then he assessed the tribute stipulated in the treaty of capitulation.'[3]

With the rise of the Abbasids in the eighth century A.D. various

[1] See Dennett, *Conversion and the Poll Tax in Early Islam*, pp. 116–18.
[2] ibid. p. 119.
[3] ibid. p. 126.

developments in the distribution of land can be observed. Crown lands, known as *savāfī*, appear to have greatly increased.[1] These, as stated above, derived in the first place from the one-fifth of the booty which was set aside for the Prophet and his successors. It seems clear that in the course of time the conception of crown lands underwent development, and it came to be tacitly assumed that the leader of the community, whether he was the caliph or a local ruler, might appropriate to himself wide areas of land.[2] In this it is probable the Muslims were influenced by the practice which had prevailed in the conquered lands, where large areas of the country had been the private estates of the former ruling family. In any case it was the practice both of the Umayyad and Abbasid caliphs, and later of the rulers of the minor dynasties which arose in different parts of Persia when the caliphate began to decline, to acquire by conquest, confiscation, or purchase large areas for themselves as crown lands. The negotiations between Hārūn ar-Rashīd (reg. 170–93/786–809) and the Ispahbud Vandād Hurmuzd, one of the local rulers of Ṭabaristān, is an illustration of the way such estates were sometimes acquired. According to one source Hārūn ar-Rashīd forced Vandād Hurmuzd to sell him valuable estates. The form this transaction took was that of a gift, but Hārūn sent Vandād in return 1 million *dirhams* and other presents.[3] The account given by Ẓahīr ud-Dīn Marʿashī in the *Tārīkhi Ṭabaristān* and by Oulīā Ullāh in the *Tārīkhi Rūyān* differs slightly. They state that Ma'mūn, Hārūn's son, wished to buy certain estates, which belonged to Vandād Hurmuzd. When Ma'mūn reached Ray, Vandād came to see him. The caliph's deputies told him he must sell these estates to the caliph. He refused, saying it was a foul action to sell property. Some days later Ma'mūn came to make a treaty with him and Vandād Hurmuzd having, according to our sources, no alternative, made Ma'mūn a present of 300 villages in the mountains and plains and wrote a deed of gift for them for him.[4]

There were other ways also in which the extent of crown lands was increased. In some cases the owners of land in the conquered territories transferred their property into crown lands, handing them over to the caliph of the day and sharing the proceeds with

[1] Schwarz, vii. 876.

[2] When Ṭāhir b. Muḥammad b. ʿAmr b. Laiṣ gave assignments to his army in Fārs in 289/901–2, he received a letter to the effect that the caliph wished to keep Fārs as his special hunting ground and as crown land (*Tārīkhi Sīstān* (Tehrān, 1314), p. 274).

[3] Ibn Isfandīār, *Tārīkhi Ṭabaristān*, ed. ʿAbbās Iqbāl (Tehrān, 1320), i, pt. i. 197–8.

[4] *Tārīkhi Ṭabaristān va Rūyān va Gīlān*, ed. B. Dorn, *Muhammedanische Quellen* (St. Petersburg, 1850–8), p. 160; Oulīā Ullāh Āmulī, *Tārīkhi Rūyān*, ed. ʿAbbās Khalīlī (Tehrān, 1313), p. 53.

him. Their purpose in so doing was to obtain protection from lawless elements or from unjust tax-collectors.[1] al-Balāẕurī quotes certain cases where this was done and states that the estates in question became part of the caliph's estates (*ẕīā'*); the former owners appear to have held them on a crop-sharing agreement.[2] Another similar case is that of the owners of estates in the Jibāl who are alleged to have been forced to hand over their estates to the caliph in the time of Mu'taẓid (reg. 279–89/892–902). The author of the *Tārīkhi Qumm* states that when this happened the estate was given back to its former owner on a life rent so that he should have the unimpeded right to whatever was not due by way of tax (*kharāj*) to the caliph, and he was freed from the payment made in lieu of performing labour service,[3] pasture tax, house tax and the dues paid to trusted men[4] and others, which were outside the regular assessment.[5] These cases would appear to be slightly different from the process described by Iṣṭakhrī (see p. 21 above) where it appears that effective ownership remained in the hands of the original owners.

Certain tax-free grants of land to individuals, mention of which is found in various sources, were presumably made out of crown lands or lands which the *imām* held on behalf of the community. Such grants were probably hereditary, but being gifts they were presumably revocable at any time during the lifetime of the grantee. Whenever the grant was not revoked it presumably passed, or was regranted at the death of the original grantee, to his heirs.[6] In some cases the tax was not remitted entirely but merely reduced, and the holder was allowed to pay this directly to the public treasury, i.e. not through the normal agency of the local

[1] In so far as the responsibility for the payment of the *kharāj* of a district was a collective one (see p. 41), there was another advantage to be gained by such a practice: namely, that the owner, by placing himself in a direct relationship with the government, would not be liable to pay a higher rate of taxation in order to make good the district quota when this by reason of defaulters fell short of the sum due.

[2] See al-Balāẕurī, *Kitāb Futūḥ al-Buldān*, ed. de Goeje (Brill, 1866), pp. 310–11; see also Løkkegaard, pp. 68–70. In a similar way landowners would place their estates under the protection of some powerful neighbour in order to obtain his protection. Balāẕurī also mentions that the people of Zanjān and of Qāqizān placed their estates under the protection of Qāsim b. Hārūn ar-Rashīd, the people of the latter place agreeing to pay him one-tenth for his protection (apart from the one-tenth due to the public treasury) (p. 323).

[3] The text reads *bahāyi kār*, the precise meaning of which is not clear. It represents possibly some kind of labour service or payment made in lieu of performing labour service.

[4] i.e. payments made to local officials and others.

[5] *T.Q.*, p. 187.

[6] To what extent such grants were subject to subdivision among the heirs of the original grantee in accordance with the Islamic law of inheritance is not clear. If they were transmitted by the original grantee by inheritance they were presumably subject to the ordinary laws of inheritance, but if they were technically regranted to one of his heirs subdivision will have been avoided.

tax-collector. In this way he was relieved of any control by the tax-collectors or alterations in the tax to which he was liable. These grants were known as *īghār*.[1] 'Alī b. 'Isā appears to have resumed or taken over the ownership of certain estates in the Īghārayn, i.e. a district comprising Marj and Karaj; these estates probably derived their name from the fact that they were originally tax-free grants or grants with a reduced rate of taxation. He is alleged to have ordered that food (i.e. an allowance) from the produce of the estate was to be given to whoever gave up his estate voluntarily. All taxes assessed by measurement to which the holder of an estate was (normally) liable were to be demanded from him, but he was not to be molested or troubled in any other way.[2]

There was lastly another form of crown lands in the shape of state reserves in which the caliph's flocks, remounts for the army, and animals used for the post, etc., were pastured.[3] The *Tārīkhi Qumm*, for example, mentions that pastures were reserved in every village in the neighbourhood of Nihāvand for the beasts of the caliph; the author also mentions their usurpation by one of the military leaders.[4]

Another form of land-holding which became of considerable importance later was *vaqf*. The underlying conception of *vaqf* land originally appears to have been that at the conquest the soil became the property of the conquerors, who, however, surrendered their rights voluntarily or on requital. The land then became *vaqf*, i.e. *res extra commercium*. The peasants acquired the usufruct (*manfa'a*) on payment of rent for the land, which was immobilized for the benefit of the entire Muslim community.[5] In fact the situation was more complicated. In later times the term *vaqf* was used mainly to designate land immobilized for the benefit of some charitable object. In theory such land was immobilized in perpetuity, but in practice it was subject to confiscation, as were other types of land. An early instance of such interference is the action of the Buyid 'Aẓud ud-Douleh (d. 372/982) who interfered with the *ouqāf* of the Sawād, appointing over them inspectors and comptrollers and paying their beneficiaries

[1] See Løkkegaard, p. 62; see also al-Khwārazmī, *Mafātīḥ al-'Ulūm*, ed. van Vloten (Leyden, 1895), p. 60.

[2] *T.Q.*, p. 187. See *Jacut's geographisches Wörterbuch*, ed. F. Wüstenfeld (Leipzig, 1866–73), i. 420, and Ibn Khurdādbeh, *Kitāb al-Masālik wa'l-Mamālik*, ed. de Goeje (*Bibl. Geog. Arab.* vi), p. 244.

[3] See Løkkegaard, pp. 20 ff. Balāẕurī, for example, mentions the pastures of the flocks of the Caliph al-Mahdī (reg. 158–69/775–85) in the neighbourhood of Hamadān and their usurpation (pp. 310–11).

[4] pp. 185–6. A similar practice existed in pre-Islamic Arabia, special areas known as *ḥimā* being allotted to the tribal leaders (see H. Lammens, *Berceau de l'Islam* (Rome, 1914), i. 60 ff.).

[5] See above, p. 19; see also Løkkegaard, pp. 55 ff.

a fixed wage.[1] Another similar case was the seizure by the Buyids of the estates which had been made into *ouqāf* by the Ashʿarī Arabs of Qumm for the benefit of the *imāms* (i.e. the descendants of ʿAlī who, according to the Shīʿī, succeeded him as the leader of the Muslim community) and their descendants.[2]

From the decline of the Abbasid Caliphate in the third/ninth century onwards one of the most important types of land-holding came to be the *iqṭāʿ*, which term covers both the assignment of land and its revenue. The origins of the *iqṭāʿ* go back to early Islamic times, but it was not till the rise of the Seljūqs in the fifth/eleventh century that this type of holding became the most important form of land-holding in the country.[3] In practice crown lands, together with all waste-land, dead lands, and swamps,[4] were assigned from the earliest times to the Arabs as heritable property liable to taxation, this type of assignment being known as *iqṭāʿ at-tamlīk*.[5] The jurists, who attempted to trace the origin of the custom back to the practice of the Prophet Muḥammad, laid down certain conditions for the making of such grants. Abū Yūsuf, for example, held that land could only be given with a permanent tenure, and subsequent caliphs could not dispossess the assignee or his heirs or anyone to whom the assignee had sold the land, unless the land was left fallow, in which case the holder lost his right to it.[6] The state, however, was not interested in juridical theory and was primarily concerned in collecting rent for these lands, and it let its domains, in spite of the jurists, also on a short or lifelong tenure, which assignments were known as *tuʿma*.[7] Merging into this type of tenure was the revenue farm. Land belonging to the village communities was assessed in a lump sum and in many cases farmed as was the revenue of whole provinces. The tax-farmer was very similar to the emphyteuticarius or the *muqṭaʿ* (i.e. the holder of an *iqṭāʿ*), since there was hardly any difference between the tax-farmer who could collect taxes by force and a private individual who, under state protection, was answerable for the taxes of the land he held as a tenant, hereditary or otherwise, from the state. The actual taxes in either case were paid by the

[1] Ibn Miskawaih, *Eclipse of the ʿAbbasid Caliphate*, ed. H. F. Amedroz and D. S. Margoliouth (Oxford, 1921), iii. 71. A large sum is said to have been realized by these measures and to have been expended on *iqṭāʿāt* (see below).

[2] *T.Q.*, p. 279. These were also, according to the *Tārīkhi Qumm*, made into *iqṭāʿ*.

[3] See Ch. III.

[4] Known collectively as *qaṭāʾī*.

[5] See also Løkkegaard, pp. 58 ff.

[6] pp. 90–2. ʿUmar is alleged to have said, 'if others come and cultivate land which has been left by its owner uncultivated for three years, the right of the former to it is preferable.'

[7] Becker emphasizes the similarity between this type of tenure and the Byzantine emphyteusis and considers it to be a revival or development of this system (*Islamstudien*, i. 220 ff.).

peasants: *muqṭaʿ* and tax-farmer were the middlemen between the peasant and the state.[1]

Writing in the fifth/eleventh century, Māwardī attempted to rationalize historic precedent. He recognized two types of *iqṭāʿ*, which he called *iqṭāʿ at-tamlīk* and *iqṭāʿ al-istighlāl* respectively, the former representing an assignment of land and the latter an assignment of its revenue. He held that it was legal to assign as *iqṭāʿ at-tamlīk* dead lands, dating from pre-Islamic or from Islamic times, and cultivated lands either in Islamic territory (the *dār ul-islām*) or in infidel territory (the *dār ul-ḥarb*). In the latter case lands could be assigned before conquest by the Muslims, the taking possession of them by the assignee being contingent upon their conquest. In so far as the assignment of revenue was concerned, Māwardī considered it legal to assign *kharāj* land and *ʿushr* land, and he considered members of the army to be among those to whom it was most fitting to make such assignments of the revenue of *kharāj* land, but he stipulates that such grants should not be hereditary.[2]

Māwardī was right to distinguish between these two types of *iqṭāʿ*, for it seems clear that two very different principles underlay their grant. In the case of the first-named, the *iqṭāʿ at-tamlīk*, in so far as this was an assignment made of uncultivated lands with possession conditional upon their cultivation, the object was clearly to promote cultivation and thereby to increase the revenue of the state. Different motives, however, led to the grant of the second type, the *iqṭāʿ al-istighlāl*. In this case the cultivation of the land was the concern of the conquered peasants who were liable to tribute, and the principal objects were first to assure deserving members of the community, and especially the seasoned fighters of Islām, of a sure means of livelihood, to pay them for their services and to encourage them to further deeds by the prospect of such reward; and secondly, the desire to maintain in the hands of a powerful military aristocracy dominion over the conquered peoples.[3]

It has been pointed out above that there was a tendency for crown lands and lands belonging to the community to be confused and also for both to become by usurpation private property. The grant of assignments of land led to a further confusion or assimila-

[1] ibid. i. 239.

[2] pp. 181–8. Ibn Jamāʿa (639–733/1241–1333) distinguishes three types of *iqṭāʿ*: the *iqṭāʿ at-tamlīk*, the *iqṭāʿ al-istighlāl*, and the *iqṭāʿ al-irfāq*. Under the last named he includes the assignment of mines (which Māwardī had included under *iqṭāʿ al-istighlāl*), of roads and markets. (*Islamica*, vi. 4. 374–83). His third category is thus really a farm (*iltizām*) scarcely differing in principle from the farming of tax-districts.

[3] P. A. von Tischendorf, *Das Lehnswesen in den moslemischen Staaten* (Leipzig, 1872), pp. 20, 21; cf. Balāẕurī, p. 127.

tion of one type of land to another, since in theory land assigned as *iqṭāʿ at-tamlīk* was regarded as heritable property and was at first scarcely distinguishable from private property. Later there were further developments in the *iqṭāʿ* system, after which it was mainly only by usurpation that *iqṭāʿ* land became converted into private property. These developments will be discussed more fully in Chapter III. It is sufficient to point out here that the practice of making assignments was not confined to the caliph. His governors assigned to their followers districts in the areas under their control. The local rulers followed a similar practice.[1]

[1] For example Ṭāhir b. Muḥammad b. ʿAmr b. Laiṣ gave many *iqṭāʿ* to his army in 289/901–2 (*Tārīkhi Sīstān*, p. 274). The Dāʿī Kabīr, who ruled in Ṭabaristān about the year 310/923, is reputed to have devoted one day of each week to the administration of landed estates and *iqṭāʿs* (Ibn Isfandiār, *Tārīkhi Ṭabaristān*, i, pt. i. 284), which suggests that in this area the *iqṭāʿ* system was part of the bureaucratic machinery of the state.

CHAPTER II

REVENUE ADMINISTRATION

It has been suggested that legal theory, although to some extent a rationalization of practice, nevertheless affected the development of institutions. There is another matter which profoundly affects the question of land tenures and the composition of the landowning classes, namely, the revenue administration. Certain types of tenure, such as the *iqṭāʿ al-istighlāl* (see p. 29), had their origin in practices connected with revenue farming and the distinction, as pointed out, between a revenue farmer and a *muqṭaʿ* or assignee was in practice often small. Further, both the revenue farmer and the *muqṭaʿ* tended in the course of time to be transformed into landowners. Other changes were also brought about in the composition of the landowning class as the result of practices in connexion with the revenue administration. When the finances of the state fell into an even more precarious condition than was usually the case, the rates of taxation were raised, so that in some cases such heavy economic pressure was put upon the inhabitants that the landowners sold their lands while the peasants often simply abandoned theirs.

It will not be out of place, therefore, to give some further details concerning the tax-regimes to which the various areas were subject. As in the case of the legal theory of land, the canon law laid down certain precepts. The believer paid an alms tax known as *ṣadaqa* or *zakāt* on his possessions (certain principles being laid down fixing the taxable minimum and the method of payment). When paid on land it was known as *ʿushr*, or tithe; hence the distinction between *ʿushr* land and *kharāj* land, which paid tax assessed in a variety of ways. In practice, as has been pointed out, the distinction between believer and unbeliever in matters of land-holding and land tax was in many cases abandoned and both paid rates of taxation which, in the case of the believer, were strictly speaking uncanonical. The origins of these taxes and the methods by which they were assessed must in many cases be sought in local custom which goes back to pre-Islamic times. Indeed for the most part the tax-regime of the Sasanian empire, in so far as it concerned the land, was taken over, and the task of the jurists in this case also was to rationalize historic precedent and to fit this into the framework of the law.

A considerable variety of practice existed in different parts of the empire, both as regards the actual rate of the land tax, the method by which it was assessed, and the way in which the amount due in kind was converted into money. The main factors affecting this question, according to the juristic theory, were the mode of conquest, geographical situation, manner of irrigation, nature of holding, type of cultivation, prices, and the quantity of the crop; in fact, however, local custom was in all probability the decisive factor.

The assessment was based upon a measurement of the land, or upon the extent of the crop, a fixed proportion being taken by way of tax, or by valuation, or by special regulation, or the tax-payers compounded for a certain sum. In contradistinction to *ṣadaqa* (*zakāt*), the rates of which were fixed, it was generally accepted that the *imām*, i.e. the leader of the Islamic community, could increase or decrease the rate of assessment of *kharāj* according to the taxable capacity of the payees. Further, he could levy the tax in cash or kind.[1] The case of the Sawād is often cited by the Muslim jurists as a model for the fixing of the rates of taxation, although they differ as to the actual rates of taxation to which it was subjected by the Caliph 'Umar (reg. 13–23/634–44).[2] According to one account the rate was fixed at 1 *dirham* and 1 *qafīz*[3] (in kind) per *jarīb*. According to another account the rates per *jarīb* were for vines 10 *dirhams*, for dates 8, for sugar-cane 6, for trefoil 5, for wheat 4, and for barley 2 *dirhams*.[4] Various other figures are given in different traditions.[5] There is also a difference of opinion whether waste-land was included in the assessment or omitted. In one account it is also added that 5 *dirhams* per *jarīb* of sesame, 3 *dirhams* for vegetables, such as leeks, onions, and garlic, etc., and 5 *dirhams* on cotton were levied.[6] From this it is clear that the Muslims took over substantially the tax system which they found in operation at the time of the conquest (see p. 15). This system by which taxes were assessed on the area of land held and levied in cash or in cash and kind, appears to have continued until the reign of the Abbasid al-Manṣūr. By that time it seems that changes in price level had occurred, so that the tax-payers had difficulty in raising the money to pay the taxes, and as a result the Sawād was becoming ruined. Accordingly a change was made in the method

1 Abū Yūsuf, p. 129.

2 See also Dennett, *Conversion and the Poll Tax in Early Islam*, pp. 14 ff., for a discussion of the tax administration of the Sawād under the Arabs.

3 i.e. $5\frac{1}{3}$ *riṭl* (Abū Yūsuf, p. 81).

4 Māwardī, p. 304.

5 See Ibn Khurdādbeh, p. 11; *T.Q.*, pp. 181–2; Abū Yūsuf, pp. 56–8; as-Sūlī, *Ādāb al-Kuttāb*, pp. 218; Balāẕurī, p. 269; Ibn Rustah, *Kitāb al-A'laq an-Nafīsa*, ed. de Goeje (*Bibl. Geog. Arab.*), p. 105. Abū Yūsuf, however, was of the opinion that wheat and barley ought to pay two-fifths of the crop if unirrigated and three-tenths if irrigated by *dālīeh* (a certain type of water-wheel), while dates, vines, fodder, and gardens ought to pay one-third, and summer crops one-quarter (p. 77).

6 *T.Q.*, p. 182.

of assessment and the tax was reckoned on the actual produce instead of on the land. The rates imposed appear to have been half the produce on unirrigated land, one-third on land irrigated by *dālīeh*, and a quarter on land irrigated by *dūlāb* (also a type of water-wheel). Date palms, vines, and fruit trees were counted and the tax fixed according to geographical position, the rate not to exceed half the produce.[1]

Fārs which had under the Sasanians been in the hands of the landed aristocracy preserved its 'feudal' character into Islamic times. As late as the fourth/tenth century it appears that the greater part of the province was still in the hands of the old landed proprietors.[2] Cultivated lands were subject to *kharāj* or *'ushr*. A pasture-tax (*marā'ī*) and a tax on mines at the rate of one-fifth and a water-tax were levied. *Kharāj* was assessed in three ways: the amount due being calculated on the basis of the extent of the area, i.e. by measurement (*masāḥat*), or on a basis of the actual produce (*muqāsameh*), i.e. a definite share of the crop was taken; or the assessment was fixed at a lump sum not specifically based either on measurement or on the actual produce (*muqāṭa'eh*), i.e. the holder or holders of the land compounded for a certain sum, which did not vary with the extent of the area sown or the crop.[3] In the case of measurement the area actually sown only was taken into account. Most of the province, according to Iṣṭakhrī, was assessed in this way. The rates varied in different parts of the province; the rate in Shīrāz was 190 *dirhams* per 1 large *jarīb* (i.e. three and two-thirds the small or ordinary *jarīb* of 60 *gaz* of 9 *qabẓeh*) on irrigated wheat or barley, 192 *dirhams* per *jarīb* of trees watered by streams, 237 *dirhams* per *jarīb* of irrigated trefoil or vegetables, 256⅔ *dirhams* per *jarīb* of irrigated cotton,[4] 1,425 *dirhams* per *jarīb* of vineyards. This was higher than in other districts of Fārs. The *kharāj* of Kuvār, for example, was two-thirds the rate of Shīrāz.[5] Unirrigated crops paid one-third the rate for crops irrigated by *qanāts*, crops watered by well paid two-thirds of the rate, and crops which received water once one-quarter; crops which received water

[1] Māwardī, p. 306. In the time of 'Aẓud ud-Douleh, the Būyid, 10 per cent was added to the original tax (*al-aṣl*). (Ibn Miskawaih, *Eclipse of the 'Abbasid Caliphate*, iii. 71.) See p. 15 above for the rates levied under the Sasanians.

[2] Similarly, at the end of the third/ninth century, Iṣfahān, especially the districts of Barā'ān and Burkhwār, was largely in the hands of Persian large landed proprietors (Ibn Wāẓiḥ, *Kitāb al-Buldān*, ed. Gaston Wiet (Cairo, 1937), pp. 76, 77).

[3] The *muqāṭa'eh* was thus a kind of farm. In so far as it freed the inhabitants of the area to some extent from the interference of the tax-collectors it was probably beneficial. It differs from the type of revenue farm where the right to farm the taxes of a district was put up to auction and sold to the highest bidder, which was a practice highly injurious to agricultural prosperity.

[4] Ibn Ḥauqal has 257⅔ *dirhams* (ii. 302).

[5] Iṣṭakhrī, p. 157; see also Ibn Ḥauqal, ii. 302.

twice were regarded as irrigated crops for purposes of taxation.[1] In Dārābjird, Arrajān,[2] and Shāpūr a variety of rates prevailed according to the quality of the land.[3] Vineyards and plantations were apparently exempt from land tax in Fārs until ʿAlī b. ʿĪsā b. al-Jarrāḥ imposed *kharāj* on them in all districts of Fārs in 302/914–15.

Where the assessment was by the *muqāsameh* method two practices prevailed. In the case of the nomad leaders who held documents from ʿAlī, ʿUmar, and other caliphs the rate was one-tenth, one-third, or one-quarter of the crop, as stipulated in the documents. Elsewhere the public treasury fixed the rate. Crown lands were assessed by *muqāsameh* or by contract (*muqāṭaʿeh*). The assessment in either case was paid in cash.[4] Muqaddasī states that fields which paid a fixed land tax paid 20 *dirhams* even when the land was barren.[5]

In the Qumm area the assessment was made by measurement. Between 189/804–5 and 303/915–16 it was measured eight times.[6] The period for which a settlement held good appears to have varied considerably. For example, Māh Baṣra (Dīnavar) was settled for ten years in 302/914–15. The Īghārayn (Marj and Karaj) on the other hand was settled for a period of three years in 297/909–10, but in fact the assessment remained in force for sixty years.[7]

Where a considerable variety of physical conditions was encountered in one tax district, as was the case, for example, in Qumm, a number of tax schedules were drawn up to meet local needs. According to the *Tārīkhi Qumm* there were seven such schedules, known as *vaẓīʿeh*, or *ṭisq*, in Qumm. The rates per *jarīb*[8] for the various crops according to these schedules were as shown in the table on p. 35.[9]

Crop-sharing peasants and persons belonging to the protected communities (i.e. *ẕimmīs*) paid a poll tax according to two different schedules: by the first they paid 24 *dirhams* per man and by the second 12 *dirhams*.[10]

The owners of flocks and bedouins were similarly assessed according to two schedules; paying either 12 *dirhams* per man or 6 *dirhams*.[11] Under the fourth schedule there is mention of a house

[1] Iṣṭakhrī, p. 157. Ibn Ḥauqal has a slightly different version: 'Melons, cucumbers, and beans watered by well pay two-thirds the *kharāj* rate; and if irrigated land receives water only once, the *sulṭān* takes one-quarter of the *kharāj*, but if water is given twice, the full rate is demanded' (ii. 302).

[2] This city no longer exists. Its site is near the modern Bihbahān.

[3] Iṣṭakhrī, pp. 157–8; Ibn Ḥauqal ii. 302–3.

[4] Iṣṭakhrī, p. 158; Ibn Ḥauqal ii. 302–3.

[5] *Kitāb Aḥsan at-Taqāsīm*, ed. de Goeje (*Bibl. Geog. Arab.*), p. 453.

[6] *T.Q.*, pp. 101–6.

[7] ibid. p. 186.

[8] Presumably of approximately 3,600 *gaz*.

[9] pp. 112–22.

[10] ibid. pp. 112–13, 120.

[11] ibid. p. 113.

Schedule
(in *dirhams*)

	1st	*2nd*	*3rd*	*4th*	*5th*	*6th*	*7th*
Wheat, Barley, Peas, Lentils	15⅙	13⅙	12⅙	15⅙	9⅙	6⅙	3⅙
Cotton	38	30	..	..	..	..	38 if irrigated by *qanāt** except in certain places where it was 30
Trees	38	..	..	..	..	..	38
Vineyards in flourishing condition†	50	32	..	..	..	..	32 except in three districts
Vineyards in bad condition	25	16	..	..	..	..	..
Pot herbs	25	15	..	..	..	..	..
Cucumber ground	25	15	..	..	..	..	25 except in three districts
Melon ground (*jālīz*)	25	..	..	[25‡]	..	..	25 except in three districts
Carrots	25	..	..	..	..	..	25
Turnips	25	15	..	..	..	..	25
Onions	25	..	..	..	..	..	25
Garlic	25	..	..	..	..	..	25
Leeks and other vegetables	25	..	..	..	..	..	25
Trefoil	30	15	..	15 except in three districts which paid 25	..	..	..
Millet	14	..	..	14	..	..	..
Sesame, Carroway	15	..	..	15	..	..	..
Saffron		..	..	..	..	..	62 except in three districts 42
Fenugreek, Clover	9⅙	..	..	9⅙	..	..	..
Fruit trees	5 p. *ṭāq*§	..	..	..	..	..	1 p. 10 trees
Pistachios, Olives	1 *dirham* p. 6 trees or 36 *ṭāqs*§	..	..	2 p. 6 trees	..	..	..
Vats of grape syrup	2 *dirhams* p. vat	..	..	2	..	..	..
Walnut trees (full grown)	1½	..	..	1½	..	..	1
Walnut trees (medium sized)	1	..	..	1	..	..	..
Walnut trees (young)	½	..	..	½	..	..	..
Water mills near the river	70	..	..	70, 25 or 12	..	..	15
Water mills in Qūhistān	25	12	..	25	..	..	..

* See p. 36, n. 2.

† The text has *kharāb* as opposed to *ābād* in the previous entry (p. 109). The meaning of *kharāb* here appears to be 'in bad condition' rather than 'ruined', i.e. out of production, since if the latter were the case there would be little reason for assessing them at half the rate of those which were in good condition.

‡ The tax on melon ground not watered by the river was one-third of a *jālīz* watered by the river.

§ i.e. a young tree which has no branches.

tax (or tax levied on the heads of families) at the rate of 12 *dirhams* and 6 *dirhams*.[1]

In Nihāvand the rates under the fourth tax schedule differed somewhat and were as follows:

[River] irrigated wheat, 6½ *dirhams* per *jarīb*
[River] irrigated barley, 4½ *dirhams*
[*Qanāt*] irrigated[2] wheat, 1½ *dirhams*
[*Qanāt*] irrigated barley, 1⅔ *dirhams*
Lentils, 2 *dirhams*
Peas, 4 *dirhams*
Fenugreek, ⅔ *dirham*
Clover, ⅓ *dirham*
Vineyards, 4 *dirhams* per irrigation canal
Sesame, 4 *dirhams*
Saffron, 30 *dirhams*
Millet 1½ *dirhams*
Cotton, 15 *dirhams*[3]

Similarly, estates belonging to Hamadān under the seventh tax schedule paid a slightly different rate, which was as follows:

Wheat and barley, 8⅓ *dirhams*
[*Qanāt*] irrigated[4] sown land, 3 *dirhams*
Different kinds of vegetables, 16 *dirhams*
Vineyards, 28 *dirhams*
Fenugreek and millet, 3⅙ *dirhams*
Saffron, 43⅓ *dirhams*
Peas and sesame, 10 *dirhams*
Fruit-bearing trees, 1 *dirham* per three trees
Saplings, 1 *dirham* per tree
Walnut trees, mature trees, 2 *dirhams*
Medium-sized trees, 1⅔ *dirhams*
Young trees, ⅔ *dirham*
Vats of grape syrup, 1 *dirham* per vat
Cotton, 62 *dirhams*
Mills, 30 *dirhams*[5]

[1] *T.Q.*, p. 120.

[2] The meaning of the phrase *gandum ke āb az zamīn kashad* is uncertain. It is probable that the phrase, which is used again on p. 121, means land irrigated by *qanāt*. The phrase *ke āb az bīkhi zamīn kashad* is used on pp. 120 and 121, apparently in the same sense, and in contradistinction to land which has been irrigated in some other way (*ke ānrā āb dādeh bāshand*). The latter presumably refers to land watered by river; the rates are in all cases higher, and this would lend support to the interpretation that the former phrase means land watered by *qanāts* and the latter land watered by rivers. On the other hand, in some of the districts in the neighbourhood of Kāshān a distinction is made at the present day between *qanāts* which draw their water from deep water-bearing strata and others which derive from surface water, and the phrase *ke āb az zamīn kashad* may refer to surface *qanāts*, the water of which in a dry year decreases.

[3] *T.Q.*, p. 120. [4] See note 2 above. [5] *T.Q.*, pp. 121–2.

Not many documents concerning the details of the administration remain. One such is preserved in the *Tārīkhi Qumm*.[1] It contains the instructions given to surveyors which the author of the *Tārīkhi Qumm* found in an old book in Qumm. It reads as follows:

The surveyor must not measure the river banks (*ṣuvar*) which are called in the dialect of Qumm *marz*, the *qanāts*,[2] irrigation channels (*anhār*), waste-land or uncultivated land. If such land is situated in the middle of cultivated land and has been included in the measurement he should deduct it afterwards from the total of the measurement. Further, if a crop has not grown because of pest, or if there is cotton, which has not taken root or has taken root but has not been given water, or the water to which it had a right has not reached it, the owner should be called upon to swear to the truth of his words and then his land should be compared with land which is like it and a valuation arrived at by analogy.

In the case of a canal on either side of which medium-sized trees are planted, whether they are upheld by a trellis, which is called in the dialect of Qumm *sābāṭ*, or not, the length of it should be measured, and the result multiplied by $\frac{1}{2}$ *gaz*. If the canal is planted on one side only, the length should be multiplied by $\frac{5}{12}$ *gaz*, and [the assessment] calculated in this way. This is the rate for trees along the edge of a canal also.

A vineyard or garden which has been planted four years, the centre of which has been planted, should be entered [in the register] under newly-created vineyards and half of what is imposed on fully-grown vineyards should be deducted [from the assessment] and entered. A vineyard which is called *muṭabbaq* [i.e. the vines of which are not trained on trellises] or in the idiom of the people of Qumm *ghayri sābāṭ* should, like the gardens and vineyards of Qumm, be measured. One-third should be omitted from the total on account of *qanāts* which are called in the dialect of Qumm *kūz*. A vineyard which is in bad condition[3] should be written off together with land fallen into decay. The vines in a vineyard, the interior of which has not been planted in rows, but the middle of which is planted irregularly, should be counted and reckoned at twenty-four medium-sized vines to a *qafīz*. Vegetables and fruit-bearing trees in vineyards should not be reckoned. He [the surveyor] should not be over-zealous but should content himself with assessing vines.

The trees in a garden which has been irregularly planted with different kinds of fruit trees, should be counted and thirty-six trees should be reckoned to a *qafīz*. A garden in which fruit trees are planted close together should not be measured or the trees counted.[4]

[1] The author of this work was in Qumm in the latter half of the fourth/tenth century.

[2] The term used is *savāqī*, which is presumably used here for *kārīz* or *qanāts* rather than for streams.

[3] See above, p. 35, n. † and p. 38. *Kharāb* here would seem to imply rather 'ruined'.

[4] The reason for this is not clear. The intention may be that a garden before

Trees which are not fruit-bearing, whether they are in rows or irregularly planted should not be reckoned or measured and no tax should be assessed on them.[1] A tree of four years' growth which has been planted should be included among new trees and not included in the assessment.

Land growing saffron which is in bad condition[2] should be assessed at half the rate of the *kharāj* of land which is in good condition.

Walnut trees and pistachio-nut trees should be entered separately in the register as mature, of medium growth, or young.

A tree on the side of an irrigation canal (*jūy*), or *qanāt*, or in a river bed should not be assessed or entered in the register.

On every 100 *jarīb* of grain, cotton, vines, saffron, or vegetables $16\frac{2}{3}$ *dirhams* is the due of the surveyor and *muʿābir*; 10 *dirhams* goes to the surveyor, and $6\frac{2}{3}$ *dirhams* to the *muʿābir*. The latter is the person whom the tax-collectors and governors send after the surveyors and valuers have measured [or valued] an area in order to see that the surveyors have not made a mistake or shown [undue] leniency. For every ten walnut trees 1 *dirham* is the due of the surveyors and valuers; for every water-mill in use $\frac{1}{2}$ *dirham*, and for every 10 *ẕimmīs*, the latter being Jews and Christians, 2 *dirhams* and for every 30 vats of grape syrup 1 *dirham*.

The surveyor must not come out of the sown plot (*kardū*) or garden until the cultivator (*barzīgar*) and owner's representative (*miʿmāri arbāb*) are present. After they have agreed to what has been fixed on the area, he must write it in their presence and then seal it with his seal and the owner of the land must also seal it; he must then transmit [the document] to the proper authorities.

When the *muʿābir* comes to a village which, although it is situated among places which have been measured, has been forgotten, this having become apparent after the assessment and valuation, he should take from it one-tenth of the *kharāj*. This is very auspicious and considered to be well-omened.

Townships and villages (*mavāẓiʿ*) which are brought into cultivation after the measurement and upon which no tax has been fixed shall be reckoned on the analogy of neighbouring villages.

Abū Bakr Muḥammad ibn Yaḥyā Ṣūlī wrote in his book that in order to make [a contract by] measurement between the owner of landed estates and the *sulṭān* [i.e. the caliph] a knowledge of multiplication and division was imperative. When the surveyor measures a piece of ground and estimates the length and breadth of it, he must multiply the length by the breadth or the breadth by the length. Also, it is incumbent upon them to know how much 60 *gaz* of land is in *ḥāshimīyeh ẕirāʿ*, the latter being equal to $1\frac{1}{3}$ *gaz*. The technical term among accountants for this quantity [of land] is *ashl*. One *ashl* is the equivalent of 10 *bāb*, and 1 *bāb*

it is in full production and before the trees have been thinned should not be subject to tax, or that gardens of this kind should be assessed by valuation or on the produce and not by measurement.

[1] The text has *māl bar ān vazʿ nakonad*, the usual meaning of which is 'no deduction on them should be made', but here the sense would appear to require 'no tax should be assessed on them'.

[2] *Kharāb*. See above, p. 35, n. † and p. 37.

equals 6 *gaz*; one *gaz* is the equivalent of 6 *qabẓeh* and 1 *qabẓeh* is 4 *angusht*; thus 1 *gaz* equals 24 *angusht*. The surveyor when measuring lands (*arāẓī*), open country (*ṣaḥārī*), and villages in order to assess the *sulṭān's* [i.e. the caliph's] revenue thereon can neglect *angusht* and *qabẓeh* and must not be too meticulous. My object in mentioning *angusht* and *qabẓeh* in this place is that since breadth and length were under discussion, what pertains to knowledge of the *ẓirā'* should be mentioned, so that it should be clear how many *angusht* make a *gaz*. My object is not that the surveyor should pay great attention to detail or that he should not pass over a *qabẓeh* or an *angusht*. On the contrary, he should not pay attention to these details but should prevent the [*sulṭān's*] revenue being wasted in other directions. Much experience has shown that the abandonment of these details has a beneficial effect on the revenue of the *sulṭān* and leads to its increase and causes the subjects to pray for his well-being, whereas being strict over the measurement and paying attention to [every] *qabẓeh* and *angusht* is the cause of ruin, disaster, and evil repute, and results in the misfortune of the *sulṭān* of the time and draws the curses of the people upon him.

To continue: when it is found that a piece of land measures by the *ḥāshimīyeh ẓirā'* 3,600 *gaz*, this is equivalent to 1 *jarīb*, and 1 *jarīb* equals 10 *qafīz* and 1 *qafīz* equals 360 *gaz* (1 *qafīz* equalling 10 *'ashīr* and 1 *'ashīr* 36 *gaz*). Thus it is clear that 1 *jarīb* equals 100 *'ashīr*. When they [the surveyors] want to measure a piece of land, let them first see how many *bāb* it is (1 *bāb*, as I have mentioned, being 6 *gaz*), then let them reckon every 10 *bāb* as 1 *ashl*. Any amount less than ten (*bāb*) is left as it is, and described as 1 *ashl* and so many *bāb*; any number less than six shall not be converted into the category above, and similarly anything less than six *gaz* shall be so left. For example in describing a piece of land, let them say it is so many *jarīb*, so many *qafīz*, so many *'ashīr*, so many *bāb*, and one-third or one-half or one-sixth of a *bāb*.

Hamadānī relates in his book that if a walnut tree has spread its roots, its condition being such that it is included in the assessment and its height is 1 *bāb*, it should be taken as fully mature. Abū Bakr ibn 'Abd ar-Raḥīm said when the trunk of a walnut tree is as thick round as a man the tree shall be regarded as mature (*khīār*) and the tax upon it is 2 *dirhams*. When the trunk measures two-thirds of a *bāb*, i.e. 4 *gaz*, but less than 1 *bāb*, the tree is not fully grown and the tax on it is $1\frac{1}{3}$ *dirhams*. When its trunk measures one-third of a *bāb* or more, but less than two-thirds of a *bāb*, it is known as *dūn* and is less mature; the tax due upon it is two-thirds *dirham*. When walnut trees have no branches they are known as *ṭāq* and for every 8 *ṭāq* 1 *dirham* is due.

Ibn Māsik has recorded that when Saymarī [Ṣaymarī?] measured Hamadān he did not measure almond trees, count them, or include them in the total. Similarly, service trees and medlars or fruit-trees such as pears and apricots [are not included], but nectarines and prunella are treated as *ṭāq*: for every 300 *ṭāq* 1 *dirham* is due.[1]

Quoting from the same source, the *Tārīkhi Qumm* gives an

[1] *T.Q.*, pp. 107–10.

account of some of the tricks practised by the peasants in order to deceive the surveyors. The author writes

Another trick is for a peasant to swear saying, 'I will take you to every piece of land which I have and show it to you', and then to take the surveyor, after having thus taken oath, through his lands but not to tell which his land is except where he considers it expedient. In this way he does not perjure himself because he takes the surveyor through all his lands and the latter has seen them all. If the surveyor takes an oath from the owner of an estate which he wants to measure to the effect that the owner will not deceive or trick the surveyor or leave out any side of that estate in the measurement and the owner takes [such] an oath saying, 'I will not dissimulate concerning the right of the *sulṭān* [i.e. the caliph]; if you oppress me I will dissimulate concerning that over which you commit injustice, but for the rest accept my word without taking an oath from me', then, in this case, if the owner of the estate acts deceitfully or dissimulates in leaving out [land] from the assessment, he is not blameworthy because the *sulṭān* [i.e. the caliph] has no right over his possessions, and he has not committed perjury because he has [merely] passed over part of the land over which the *sulṭān* [i.e. caliph] has no right.[1]

The instructions given [to surveyors] in the year 290/902–3 when a certain Ḥasan b. Muḥammad b. Baddāl ordered an assessment to be made in the Jibāl are also illustrative of current practice. The assessment was to be made in accordance with the exigencies of the time. Having given due consideration to these, the surveyors

ought to adjust the yardstick, the conversion rate, price levels and rates of interest according to the demands of the time and to remit and impose whatever [tax] was necessary, and having fixed the yardstick, they should take from each piece of cultivated land three pieces of land, good, bad, and medium, and should put them together and take one-third from each [piece and thus obtain the average]. They should separate the share of the cultivator and convert the remainder [at current prices]. They should [then] consider what remained after the expenses (*nafaqeh*) had been deducted; from this they should set aside a share for the landlord by way of rent for the land and spend whatever was necessary on public works and the wages of trusted persons and paid officials.[2]

These instructions apparently refer to lands the ownership of which had been surrendered to the caliph in return for some sort of occupation right.[3] From this it appears that the expenses in connexion with the cultivation of the land were not deducted from the peasant's share of the crop but were a charge on the landowner.[4]

The taxes were normally assessed in *dirhams*. In order to ascertain the actual liability of the tax-payer the sum due in *dirhams* was converted at a fixed rate into gold *dīnārs* and then reconverted into

[1] *T.Q.*, pp. 110–11.
[2] ibid. p. 187.
[3] See above, p. 26.
[4] cf. Ch. XVII.

currency *dīnārs*. The conversion was a complicated operation and by manipulation of the rates the final amount due in currency *dīnārs* could be increased or lowered. This operation was performed by middle-men or brokers known as *jahbaẕ*, for the remuneration of whom a certain proportion was added to the rate. Thus in 315/927–8 $\frac{5}{6}$ *dīnār* was added to the conversion rate in Qumm on account of Ibn Dā'ūd and the *jahbaẕ*, and in 317/929–30 $3\frac{1}{3}$ *dīnārs* for the *iqṭā'* of the son of Mahdī the *jahbaẕ* because of his negligence.[1] Between 287/900 and 305/917–18 the rate had risen from 17 *dīnārs* per 1,000 *dirhams* to 200 *dīnārs*; it was then lowered to 109 *dīnārs* in 340/951–2.[2]

The responsibility for the payment of the *kharāj* of any given district was a collective one, though the assessment was made on individuals.[3] In Qumm, for example, if anyone failed to pay the full tax on his land because of a bad yield, the deficit on his contract was in fact divided among the other payees of *kharāj*, the conversion rate being raised in order to make good the deficit.[4] Abu'l Ḥasan b. 'Abbād, the well-known Buyid *vazīr* who came to Qumm in 335/946–7, is reported to have disapproved of this practice and said that since every tax-collector who came to Qumm had transferred the *kharāj* of those who were unable to pay to the other payers of *kharāj*, affairs had reached such a pitch that all had become unable to pay and the town had become ruined. He accordingly lowered the conversion rate in 340/951–2, the rate being fixed as stated above, at 109 *dīnārs* per 1,000 *dirhams*.[5]

The *kharāj* was normally paid in instalments and the solar year was used for the purpose of tax collection. This practice was carried over from Sasanian times. The number of instalments, however, varied from time to time. Originally the first instalment fell due when the crops ripened. After the decline of the Sasanians the intercalary days were omitted, and as a result the first instalment in the course of time fell due before the crops ripened. To remedy this the caliph Mu'taẓid ordered the reinsertion of the intercalary days in 282/895–6[6] by which time they had been omitted for 240 years. The calendar was accordingly put back two months to the 1st Khurdād in the 184th year of the Yazdigirdī era.[7]

[1] *T.Q.*, pp. 142–3.

[2] See my article, 'An Account of the *Tārīkhi Qumm*', *B.S.O.A.S.*, xii. 3 and 4 (1948), p. 594. In Fārs *c.* 389/998–9 the conversion rate for the purpose of making assignments of revenue was fixed at 300 *dirhams* to the *dīnār* (see below p. 50).

[3] See also the documents quoted below, pp. 42 ff.

[4] *T.Q.*, p. 143. See also the documents quoted below, pp. 42 ff. on the *jahbaẕ*.

[5] *T.Q.*, pp. 143–4.

[6] The text has A.H. 182, which is clearly a misprint for A.H. 282.

[7] *T.Q.*, pp. 144–6; see also Ibn Jouzī, *al-Muntaẓam fi 't-Ta'rīkhi 'l-Mulūk* (Haydarabad, 1357–9), v. 149. Ṭabarī states that Mu'taẓid deferred the demand for the first instalment of *kharāj* in A.H. 282/895–6 to 11th Hazīrān (3rd ser., iv. 2143).

In so far as the *kharāj* was paid in kind it was collected on the threshing floor and the crops could not be moved until authorization had been received from the tax-collector.

The tax was remitted to the government through the agency of the *jahbaẕ*. The custom in Qumm was for the tax-payers to bring a *jahbaẕ* to the *dīvān*, where he gave an undertaking that the tax due from them would be collected in full and brought to the *dīvān*; they similarly gave a written undertaking to the tax-collectors that they were responsible for whatever came into his possession by way of taxes. The following is an example of such a contract:[1]

This is a document belonging to ʿAbdullāh ibn Jaʿfar, the Imām al-Muqtadirbillāh, the Commander of the Faithful, may God prolong his life, which was written for him by those of the *kharāj*-payers of the district of Qumm, both Arabs and Persians, who have signed the document and attested it to the effect that so-and-so son of so-and-so, the tax-collector of the Commander of the Faithful, who is in charge of the revenue collection, *kharāj* and the estates of Qumm for such and such a year and the arrears from former years, requested us to appoint a *jahbaẕ* to be responsible for the *kharāj* taxes and [the taxes of] the estates of Qumm and whatever goes with these two [kinds of tax] in Qumm. It was customary for us to do this, and it was incumbent upon us to appoint a *jahbaẕ* and also that we should guarantee him and the correctness of that for which he was responsible. Accordingly we have chosen so-and-so the *jahbaẕ* son of so-and-so for this purpose and we have appointed him as *jahbaẕ*. He will be responsible for collecting the taxes of this district for this tax year and the arrears of former years, and we stand surety for him and whatever he has to collect in our town for this year and the arrears for former years and subsequent years and whatever is incumbent upon that by way of additional levies[2] which it is customary to pay and whatever is or may become the due of the *jahbaẕ* for what he does as long as he holds the position of *jahbaẕ*. We requested so-and-so to be set up and to be empowered to take whatever *kharāj* taxes are collected and whatever goes with them in our town in this year and the arrears of former years and subsequent years and whatever is incumbent on that by way of additional levies which it is customary to pay and whatever is or may become the due of the *jahbaẕ* on what he collects from different taxes. Each of us severally stands surety for him and for what he is responsible and for what comes into his effective possession and we will produce it whenever we are requested to do so, and that sum will be deducted from the total sum incumbent upon him [the *jahbaẕ*]. Reliable and accepted information concerning what he [the *jahbaẕ*] collects from

[1] The text of this is given by the *Tārīkhi Qumm* (pp. 149–51) in Arabic (of which the above is a translation). A Persian translation is also given in the *Tārīkhi Qumm* but does not correspond exactly with the Arabic.

[2] *al-kusūr wa'l kifāya*. The precise meaning of these terms is not clear. The former is probably an additional levy for broken coins and the latter possibly some levy in connexion with the conversion from *dirhams* to *dīnārs*.

the additional levies is to be found in what the scribe of the daily registers in Qumm records in the daily registers for the *dīvān* concerning the revenue collected, and from the receipts (*barāt*) given to the tax-payers. For other taxes information can be got from the reports (*maḥārīm*) which are written every day and the dues of the *jahbaẕ*; and the dues of the *jahbaẕ* are as stated in the contract made with him, and concerning the deduction of his expenses [information can be obtained] from the authorizations sent to him by such and such a tax-collector for those. And so we have become surety to the Commander of the Faithful and to his tax-collector, so-and-so, and to his deputy for so-and-so son of so-and-so, the *jahbaẕ*, himself and for whatever he shall collect and that we shall bring this whenever such and such a tax-collector asks us to do so, whether night or day. And the *jahbaẕ* shall represent the tax-payer in whatever is incumbent upon him and he shall do so according to the conditions mentioned in this document. And if he does not do this as stipulated he will be dismissed in spite of all the dues which are stipulated for him in his office of *jahbaẕ*.

And all this is binding upon us, so that it will become possible for the Commander of the Faithful, his tax-collector and his deputy, to hold responsible all of us collectively and in groups or individually or with such and such a *jahbaẕ* and those under him. If one of us pays his share of the *kharāj* the remainder are not thereby absolved from responsibility until such and such a *jahbaẕ* has paid the full due of the Commander of the Faithful and whatever he should collect by way of taxes for that year and arrears for former years and subsequent years so long as we continue him in his office [as *jahbaẕ*]; and in this each of us is surety for his fellows and a guarantor for them according to this document. Those of us who are alive are surety for the dead, those of us who are present for the absent and the well-to-do for the poor, and none of us can be absolved except by the payment of that which we have guaranteed and which we have made incumbent upon ourselves. All those who signed and registered their names at the end of the document are witnesses to the validity of what is written in it. After whatever has been written in it has been read to them and they have attested their acceptance of it, they have made it incumbent upon themselves, being in a sober state and fit condition to undertake responsibility. [Dated] such and such a month of such and such a year.[1]

Another document which Aḥmad ibn Isḥāq Qummī Zaʿfarānī the *jahbaẕ* gave in his own name is quoted in the same source and reads as follows:

This is a document which Aḥmad ibn Isḥāq Qummī, whose house is in Qumm, has written for Abū ʿAbdallāh ibn Jaʿfar, the Imām al-Muqtadirbillāh, the Commander of the Faithful. This document is witness to the fact that when ʿAlī ibn Muḥammad ibn Sahl, the tax-collector of the Commander of the Faithful for the *kharāj* and the estates in the district of Qumm for the year 310/922–3 and arrears for former years, began to feel when he was collecting the *kharāj* tax from

[1] *T.Q.*, pp. 149–51.

those who were liable to it, that it would not be collected in full, and thought, in order to put this right, that he would entrust the affair to a *jahbaẕ* who should be responsible for the collection of all the *kharāj* taxes for this year, he demanded that they should appoint another *jahbaẕ* to collect the *kharāj* of the district of Qumm and the poll tax and that they should write 'We have appointed him and we are surety for him and for what comes into his possession'. Then all assembled to choose a *jahbaẕ* and to give to the Commander of the Faithful a written undertaking for his person and for the taxes. Then they required ʿAlī ibn Muḥammad [to affirm]:[1] 'Let him order that whatever had been collected by way of *kharāj* in this year be handed over to me so that I may obtain effective possession of it in full so that it may be authenticated and then transferred to the public treasury and the caliph or be expended on the expenses and allowances proper to it according to their orders and in payment of bills issued by ʿAlī ibn Muḥammad or his deputy. I also asked ʿAlī ibn Muḥammad to make me responsible for it and to entrust it to me, and to address himself to me for what the people of Qumm had chosen [i.e. had undertaken to pay] to him and to make me surety for this so that I may take steps to collect in full the *kharāj* for the year 310/922–3 and the arrears for former years, and so that I may hold the payers and those from whom *kharāj* is due to the payment of the proper dues and customs which are current and known among them, such as the paying and remitting of additional levies[2] due to the caliph and the wages of the *jahbaẕ* and dues for weighing according to the custom of former tax-collectors. I will not add anything to this and I will follow the way of former *jahbaẕ* with them and I will not permit any of them to waste anything in weighing and I will not deal with them except with justice and equity and by public contraction.[3] At whatever time or hour any of the *kharāj* taxes are paid to me, I will write them a receipt for that in the presence of the scribe of the daily register who has been chosen on behalf of the payers of *kharāj* to watch over the *jahbaẕān* and I will mention that moment and that day in that receipt [and] whatever may have been paid on whatever days of whatever month and the scribe of the daily register will register it, and when it has been written in detail, I will add it up, seal it and send it to the *dīvān* so that the totals of these twelve months tally exactly with the bills and the daily register and its details, and I will remit whatever of this sum is ordered to be remitted to the public treasury, and I will weigh it and I will not deduct from the caliph's revenue the wages of the weigher and assayer or other expenses; similarly the hire of the beasts of burden which carry the taxes to the public treasury, the advances in grain, the wages of the messengers and writers, and stipends and expenses shall not be deducted from the caliph's revenue; I will expend on this that which I shall take for the wages of the *jahbaẕ* and the dues of the weigher and weighing from the payers of *kharāj* in such a way

[1] This appears to be the meaning of the text.

[2] See above, p. 42, n. 2.

[3] *Bi muʿāmaleh.* The precise meaning of this term is not clear. It is met with frequently in documents belonging to later periods also. Løkkegaard (p. 94) states that it was used both 'of tenancy as well as of public contraction'.

that it will suffice for this purpose. Should there be a surplus from this, following the example of former *jahbaẕ* in the transfer of *kharāj* to the public treasury in the capital, I will pay this to the public treasury, together with whatever is surplus to the wages and other expenses connected with the *kharāj* in Qumm in the *kharāj* months of the year 310/922–3, at the end of the *kharāj* months of this year, after every stipend, expense and allowance which is incumbent upon me to pay, as it may have been upon other *jahbaẕ*, has been paid or to the wages of anyone who may have helped in the collection of those taxes, such as the scribe in whose hands are the accounts and the messenger who takes the taxes to the public treasury and certifies them, or [to the sum] allotted for the cost of paper and cloth [*kirbās*] for scrips and baskets and sacks and other allowances which amount to 1,300 *dīnārs*. I will pay all this which I have mentioned to the public treasury with 1,300 *dīnārs* as the wage of the *jahbaẕ*, so that I will pay whatever instalment is due month by month during these twelve months of the *kharāj* year 310/922–3, namely 180⅓ *dīnārs* a month, and I will not delay this payment or bring forward any pretext for failure to pay it and I will not act contrary to anything which is made incumbent upon me in this document such as living and dealing justly and equitably with the payers of *kharāj* and other tax-payers as was the custom of other *jahbaẕ*. Then he accepted [this] and answered me concerning what I had demanded of him and made me surety for the taxes and I became surety for them for the amount mentioned and stipulated in the document. My contract will not be fulfilled except by the payment of the instalments mentioned in the document and I attested to these sums myself in the month of Rabīʿ I 311/June–July 923.[1]

Great difficulties appear to have been experienced in the collection of taxes. This was due mainly to two factors: on the one hand the inability of the government to collect them from their more powerful subjects,[2] and on the other to over-taxation. Arrears were

[1] *T.Q.*, pp. 153–5.

[2] A peculiar device was adopted in Qumm to ensure that the revenue demand, which the tax-collectors had been unable to collect from the Arab owners of estates, was realized in full. Ten prominent men among the Arabs were made surety for the *kharāj* of Qumm, and an undertaking was taken from them in the name of the caliph and sealed; other tax-payers dealt with these men and not with the tax-collectors direct. If anyone defaulted on his *kharāj* these ten men would sell or mortgage his estate as circumstances demanded. This *kharāj* was known as *kharāj valad al-ab* (*T.Q.*, pp. 155–6). An example of such a contract is quoted by the *Tārīkhi Qumm* and reads as follows: 'This is a document belonging to such and such a Commander of the Faithful and the tax-collector so-and-so son of so-and-so in the district of Qumm, which so-and-so son of so-and-so and so-and-so son of so-and-so wrote for him to the effect that such and such a tax-collector requested that we should be made surety for the payment of the *kharāj* taxes of this district for such and such a year, the amount of which is so many thousand *dirhams*, and, at the rate of 17 *dirhams* to the currency *dīnār*, so many thousand currency *dīnārs*, in cash to the public treasury and of the proper weight, and that we should pay this revenue to the *jahbaẕ* set up for this purpose in the instalments fixed for the tax-payers of Qumm, namely in twelve different months, the first of which is Khurdād (May/June) of such and such a year, and the last Urdībihisht (April–May) of that year. We will pay to him every month

an item frequently appearing in the assessments. On occasion efforts were made to collect the full tax by force, and there are frequent references to disturbances arising on this account. In Qumm alone there were rebellions because of such attempts in 210/825–6 in the reign of Ma'mūn,[1] and again in the reigns of Mu'taṣim (218–27/833–42), Musta'īn (248–51/862–66), Mu'tamid (256–78, 870–92), and Mu'taẓid (279–89/892–902).[2]

The population no doubt did all they could to avoid the payment of taxation. For example the Arabs of Qumm were reputed to have expended much effort to this end. A number of ruses adopted by them, as described by Abū Muḥammad al-Ḥasan b. al-Ḥusayn b. 'Abdallāh b. Mahdī, the scribe, are quoted in the *Tārīkhi Qumm*. For instance they were alleged to teach their children,

> as hunting hawks were taught when young to seek prey, to default on the *kharāj*. They would take a switch, throw their small sons down and beat them, teaching them to say 'O God, O God, O master, consider my condition: in truth rust has attacked my grain and ruined it and the

whatever instalment may be due or whatever may be added to it by way of an additional tax (*takmileh*, i.e. an additional tax laid upon those who remained in a tax district to make good a deficit occurring because some had left the province or defaulted), deficits and supplementary dues (*tavābi' va lavāḥiq*), that we should not refrain from or put off their payment or cause disturbance or make any objection on any pretext whatever, that we should not hold back the tax of any month after it falls due and that we should not adduce at this time as an excuse any natural calamity or pest nor make a pretext of the drying-up of springs and underground irrigation channels (*kārīz*) or a decrease in cultivation or cheapness or low prices or dispute about this, or disorder in the affairs of the payer or the flight of one unable to pay or anything which causes disturbance in the revenue for which we are surety, and if part of the *kharāj* should be transferred from some of us to others the tax of that person shall be deducted from the total tax due from that person and added to the undertaking of that person among us to whom the tax was transferred. We accepted this and were made surety for it. Thus we became guarantors to the Commander of the Faithful and the tax-collector [in charge of it] and his deputy. It is a correct, valid, and binding guarantee on our side. Our undertaking under this guarantee is not redeemed, except by payment of it. Each of us is surety at this time for his companion as long as he is party to this guarantee and in this document each one of us, the living for the dead, the present for the absent, the rich for the poor, is surety, and the obligation of each of us is redeemed only by the payment of what we have guaranteed and we have ourselves concluded a contract with the Commander of the Faithful and his tax-collector and his deputy and have given an undertaking whether he desires to demand the revenue from us in a group or individually, that when one of us pays his share of the revenue, his obligation is not thereby redeemed with regard to the remainder of the shares of the others until the whole amount guaranteed has been paid. All the witnesses, whose names are mentioned in this document are witness to this and attest that they have accepted this, and have attested to it and signed it with their own hands and have registered their names at the end of the document. After whatever has been entered in this document had, as a precaution, been read to them word by word, they, with [full] knowledge, attested it and made it incumbent upon themselves, being in possession of their reason and in a sober and fit condition to undertake responsibility and this was in such and such a month of such and such a year' (pp. 157–8).

[1] *Ṭab.* ii, 2, 1092–3; Balāẓurī, p. 314; *T.Q.*, p. 163. [2] ibid. p. 163.

worm has got into my cotton land and eaten it and what remained locusts have devoured completely'.

The child would repeat these words as he was beaten, until he remembered them and could reproduce them at the appropriate moment. It appears that one of the reasons why the Arabs of Qumm were so intent upon reducing their *kharāj* was because of the heavy expenses they incurred in keeping up their state and because of their open-handedness which coupled with the demands of *kharāj* often reduced them to ruin.[1]

As against this, however, there is also little doubt that the assessments were usually severe. Various methods moreover were adopted in order to raise the assessment from time to time. The manipulation of conversion rates has already been mentioned. Another method of raising the assessment was to use a yardstick shorter than the regulation. It is alleged, for example, that Ḥasan Taḥtākh destroyed Nihāvand in this way. He reduced the length of its *gaz* and thereby increased the tax to $6\frac{5}{6}$ *dirhams* (per *jarīb*) whereas formerly it had been at most 4–5 *dirhams*.[2] It must not be supposed, moreover, that the tax-payer's liability ceased with the payment of *kharāj* and the extra dues or levies connected with it. Many other dues which had been current in Sasanian times continued to be paid. Edicts abolishing these were from time to time promulgated,[3] but the dues would usually be reimposed after a while. Although the central treasury seldom benefited from these, it proved virtually impossible to prevent their levy by provincial officials. Dues which had been levied at the Persian New Year and Mihragān (i.e. at the autumn solstice) under the Sasanians continued to be levied.[4] Further extraordinary levies were frequently made for some special purpose, such as to pay for a military expedition or to carry out some public work.[5]

In areas where the caliph's control was weaker and campaigning between rival governors and local leaders was a frequent occurrence, the tendency was for the population to be subject to frequent levies and much extortion. The *kharāj* would often be levied several times over in the same year by the rival leaders.[6]

[1] ibid., pp. 162–3.

[2] ibid. p. 185. Similarly, Abū 'Alī in the Book of Hamadān, for example, relates how Hārūn ar-Rashīd coming to Hamadān and finding it in a ruined condition was told that this was due to the extortion of the tax-collectors (ibid. p. 189).

[3] e.g. 'Umar II in a letter to 'Abd ul-Ḥamīd of Kūfeh forbade the levy of dues over and above tribute (Wellhausen, p. 189).

[4] ibid.

[5] For example in 283/896–7 4,000 *dīnārs* were collected from holders of *iqṭā's* and the owners of estates to pay for work on certain canals of the Euphrates (Ibn Jouzī, v. 162).

[6] e.g. Under Aḥmad b. Muḥammad b. Ous, who was appointed governor of Little Chālūs and Kālār by his father, who in turn had been appointed governor

Such conditions were clearly likely to affect agriculture adversely.[1] Insecurity, however, was not limited to the hazards of military conquest: the owners of estates had no security of tenure even in times of relative peace. The confiscation of property and capricious expropriation was a common occurrence. At times the transaction might be given a legal appearance in that it took the form of a sale, but it is quite clear that in many cases such sales were not entered into freely by both parties: the local ruler or governor when sufficiently strong could and often did compel the owner of an estate which he coveted to transfer this to him.[2]

Over-taxation and extortion and insecurity were undoubtedly the general rule. There were of course exceptions to this; certain governors made some effort to assure the prosperity of the areas under them. For example, Gardīzī alleges that ʿAbdullāh b. Ṭāhir (reg. 213–30/828–44) wrote to all his officials warning them to treat the cultivators of the province well and to strengthen those tillers of the soil who had become weak and to reinstate them in their

of Āmul, Rūyān, and Chālūs by Sulaymān b. ʿAbdallāh b. Ṭāhir, *kharāj* was levied three times, once for Muḥammad b. Ous, once for Aḥmad, and once for his *vazīr* Majūsī. Such was the tyranny of Aḥmad and his father that the people sold their estates and those who could migrated (Ibn Isfandīār, pp. 223–4). When Yaʿqūb b. Layṣ (reg. 254–65/868–78) invaded Ṭabaristān in A.D. 874, in an attempt to take that province from the Dāʿī, he levied two years' *kharāj* on the people of Rūyān, and the people as a result had nothing to eat. He also extorted two years' *kharāj* from the people in the plains of Girdābād (Oulīā Ullāh Āmulī, p. 70).

[1] An extreme example is the Caspian provinces where feuds and warfare between the local leaders and the caliph's governors were endemic. For instance, one of these local leaders, Mazyār, who had fled from Ṭabaristān to ʿIrāq, after accepting Islām was sent back to the mountain country as governor on behalf of the caliph Ma'mūn. He then threw off the caliph's yoke. He made fortified positions in the mountains and prevented the people from engaging in agriculture, making them, instead, do forced labour on moats and fortresses, and 'committed such tyranny and oppression as was never committed before or after him'. (Oulīā Ullāh Āmulī, p. 55.) Yaʿqūb b. Layṣ, also during his expedition to Rūyān, is said to have cut down the trees of the people and burnt their houses (ibid. p. 70). Under the Sayyids (i.e. the ʿAlids) in Ṭabaristān considerable changes in land ownership appear to have been brought about. When Ismāʿīl b. Aḥmad the Samanid came to Ṭabaristān in 288/900 he gave back to the real owners all the old *amlāk* of the notables of Ṭabaristān, which for fifty years the Sayyids and others had usurped. In addition, he restored the landed estates and real property of the subjects and the weak, and contented himself with the levy of *kharāj* once a year (Ibn Isfandīār, p. 259). In the Caspian provinces and the neighbourhood bodies of Daylamite robbers were a constant source of trouble and created conditions of insecurity (Oulīā Ullāh Āmulī, p. 71).

[2] To quote a few cases only: during the reign of Hārūn ar-Rashīd, Muḥammad b. Yaḥyā b. Khālid al-Barmakī and Mūsā, his brother, who were governors in Ṭabaristān, bought forcibly the estates of the landowners (Ibn Isfandīār, p. 190); Layṣ b. Fazl, appointed governor by Ma'mūn over Sīstān *c.* 199/814–15 bought estates in all places (in his governorate), as also did Muḥammad b. al-Ḥazīn al-Qousī, Ṭāhir b. al-Ḥusayn's governor in Sīstān in 206/821–2, and Ibrāhīm b. al-Ḥazīn, governor *c.* 230/844–5 (*Tārīkhi Sīstān*, pp. 176, 177, 190). When Aḥmad b. Ismāʿīl captured Muḥammad b. ʿAlī b. al-Laiṣ, *c.* 298/910–11, he 'gave back to the Muslims their goods and estates (*amlāk*)', which Muḥammad had presumably confiscated (ibid. p. 293).

positions 'because God causes us to be fed by their hands . . . and it is unlawful to treat them unjustly'.[1]

The broad general lines of land-holding, taxation, and administration in the eastern part of the caliphate during the seventh to the ninth centuries A.D. were as outlined above, but there were many local variations. Persia, it must be remembered, at this time was not a political entity. The country was split up into a number of provinces which formed part of the lands first of the Umayyad Caliphate and then of the Abbasid Caliphate. Certain areas for geographical and political reasons retained or developed special features, which have tended to persist to a greater or lesser extent down to modern times. Fārs, for example, as mentioned above, had certain special features. Other districts which in all probability also developed on slightly different lines from the other provinces were the Caspian provinces, Sīstān and Kurdistān.

The Disintegration of the Abbasid Empire

The rapid expansion of the Arab empire had put a certain strain upon its internal structure. By the tenth century A.D. this was becoming apparent in the breakdown in the economy of the lands of the Eastern Caliphate. Some new basis had to be found to replace the old gold economy. This basis was land. The stages by which this change in the basis of the economy of the area was brought about were gradual. The first phase ends with the emergence of the *iqṭā'* system, which was systematized during the Great Seljūq period, and was accompanied by a major change in the theory of land ownership.

With the growth of mercenary armies which replaced the citizen armies of early Islamic times, the problem of paying these armies became increasingly difficult.[2] At first soldiers and *amīrs* were assigned the rent of the land, either as a guarantee of their pay, or as part of their pay. Finally, when the rent began to come in with increasing irregularity, they were given the estates themselves.[3] In addition to and apart from these assignments to the soldiery the Turkish generals, as emphyteuticarii or *muqṭa'*, took over large landed properties, and, as tax-farmers, extensive districts. The sums due from them to the central treasury in these various capacities they frequently withheld, or only paid when compelled to do so by force.[4] The former type of assignment, i.e. that to the

[1] Gardīzī, *Zayn ul-Akhbār*, ed. Muḥammad Nāẓim (Berlin, Iranschāhr, 1928), p. 8.

[2] The character of the Turkish troops who largely composed these mercenary armies was also not such as to make for a peaceful and prosperous countryside (cf. Harley Walker, 'Jāḥiz on the Exploits of the Turks', *J.R.A.S.* (Oct. 1915), pp. 670–1, 678).

[3] *E.I.* art. on *iqṭā'*.

[4] Becker, *Islamstudien*, i. 241.

soldiery, grew out of the earlier and legally recognized assignments of *kharāj*, while the latter type was a development of the emphyteusis system, upon which were superimposed Turkish, and later Mongol, influences. The existence of large bands of soldiery had become already by the fourth/tenth century a menace to stable government and prosperity, but it was not till Buyid times that the full extent of this was seen. Muʿizz ud-Douleh (reg. 320–56/932–67) introduced the custom of quartering troops on the population and made a practice of giving lands to the troops, the result of which was to bring agriculture into a state of hopeless disorganization. These steps were taken partly in an attempt to solve the ever pressing problem of paying the army. Ibn Miskawaih states that

in 334/945–6 the Daylamites mutinied against Muʿizz ud-Douleh violently and indulged in fierce abuse and vituperation of him. He promised to remit their pay to them by a fixed term and was compelled to oppress the citizens and to extort money from improper sources. He assigned to his officers, his household, and his Turks the estates of the caliph, the estates of persons who had gone into hiding, i.e. those of Shīrzād, and the rights of the treasury on the estates of the people. Thus most of the Sawād became alienated from the treasury and inaccessible to the revenue officers . . . most of the *dīvāns* became superfluous . . . and all offices were united in one.[1]

In theory some sort of system by which assignments were granted appears to have been evolved, but the discrepancies between theory and practice were considerable. When Bahā ud-Douleh arrived in Fārs *c.* 389/999 the Daylamites of Fārs assembled in Shīrāz to discuss the question of assignments, what should be reclaimed, and what should be retained by the existing holders. It was settled that the original grants should be converted at the rate of 300 *dirhams* to the *dīnār*. What each man had as an original grant was then to be examined, and he was to be given out of what was in his possession what produced that yield at that rate; the remainder was to be resumed and the grants made at the end of Ṣamṣām ud-Douleh's reign declared null and void.[2] In Baghdād the standing army of ar-Rahīm, the Buyid, held *iqṭāʿs*. Ṭughril Beg in 447/1055–6 seized these from their holders and commanded them to find other means of subsistence.[3] It seems clear that the Buyids in fact caused considerable changes to be made in the actual ownership of land. According to Muqaddasī they took away from the ordinary people their houses and landed estates. Most of the people were forced against their will to emigrate.[4] Similarly,

[1] *Eclipse of the ʿAbbasid Caliphate*, ii. 96; see also *I.A.*, viii. 342.
[2] *Eclipse of the ʿAbbasid Caliphate*, iii. 327; see also pp. 165–6.
[3] *I.A.*, ix. 421.
[4] pp. 399–400. Bayhaqī relates that when Masʿūd b. Maḥmūd passed through

Aḥmad b. Abi'l Khayr Zarkūb in the *Shīrāz Nāmeh* writes: 'in the time of the Daylamites the affairs of the country were thrown into confusion. Disorders and acts of sedition followed one after another, so much that estates were forsaken and abandoned. From that time *iqṭā'*s appeared. Most of the land became state land (*dīvānī*). Before most of the lands were private property (*milk*).'[1] Similarly, in the *Tārīkhi Qumm* it is stated that when the Gīlānīs and Daylamites conquered Qumm they abolished the *dīvāni āb* and established *iqṭā'āt*.[2] Capricious expropriation was common not only in those provinces which the Buyids ruled but also in the other provinces of Persia. Misuse of power, not only by the rulers but by all who enjoyed power, was the rule, not the exception. Reference to complaints of usurpation are often met with in the sources.[3]

Meanwhile in the eastern provinces of the caliphate the Samanid dynasty had established itself in Transoxania in the early years of the third/ninth century. The Samanids originally drew their power from the local landowners.[4] Their military forces were in

Ray in 421/1030 on his way to Khurāsān after Maḥmūd's death, the people said, 'now we eat and sleep happily and are secure in our possessions and women folk and estates which was not the case in the time of the Daylamites'. (*Tārīkhi Bayhaqī*, ed. Ghanī & Fayyāẓ (Tehrān, 1324), p. 20.)

[1] p. 26. Similarly, in the Persian translation of Māfarūkhī mention is made of the decline in agriculture under the Buyid Mu'ayyid ud-Douleh after his conquest of Iṣfahān (B.M., Or. 10980, f. 24a). 'Aẓud ud-Douleh (d. 372/982) was a notable exception among Buyid rulers. He made an attempt to foster agricultural prosperity: he cleaned out blocked-up canals, built mills on them, mended holes in the dams, and settled bedouin from Fārs and Kirmān in dead lands. (Ibn Miskawaih, *Tajārib al-Umam*, ed. L. Caetani (Leyden, 1909–17), vi. 509 ff.).

[2] p. 53.

[3] One such instance, for example, is the case referred to Mas'ūd b. Maḥmūd when he held public audience in Nayshāpūr in 421/1030 by the *qāẓī* Sa'īd who alleged that tyranny had been committed against the Bū Mīkā'īlī family, an important local family to which he belonged, by the Ghaznavid official, Ḥasanak, and others. As a result of this they had been deprived of their estates, and the *ouqāf* of their fathers had been abolished, and the income therefrom withheld from the beneficiaries. He requested Mas'ūd, therefore, to make an order for the re-establishment of these *ouqāf* so that the usufruct might reach the beneficiaries. Mas'ūd ordered this to be done, but refused to give a decision concerning their private estates on the grounds that he did not know what his late father had decreed concerning these, and ordered the case to be referred to the *dīvān* for investigation. The Bū Mīkā'īlīs accordingly went to the *dīvān* and reported that the peasants, their (the Bū Mīkā'īlī) stewards, and the agricultural labourers had been seized and money extorted from them, and they had been reduced to extremities. Bū Sahl Zouzanī reported this to Mas'ūd who gave them back their estates. (Bayhaqī, pp. 40–1.)

[4] See W. Barthold, *Turkestan down to the Mongol Invasion*, 2nd ed. (London, 1928), p. 226. The Samanids were upholders of the forces of law and order. Agriculture appears to have flourished. Narshakhī states that under the Samanids the value of a *juft* (i.e. a plough-land) in the neighbourhood of Bukhārā was 4,000 *dirhams*; by the sixth/thirteenth century it had fallen in value, and because of the prevailing disorder no one wanted the land even for nothing (Narshakhī, *Tārīkhi Bukhārā*, ed. Mudarris Riẓavī (Tehrān, 1317), pp. 37–8). The value of

part formed of Turkish slave troops who also filled administrative posts. They had a fully developed bureaucratic system which included separate *dīvāns* for crown lands and *ouqāf*.[1] According to Niẓām ul-Mulk both the Samanids and their successors, the Ghaznavids, paid their officials in money but did not make land assignments to them.[2] There are, however, cases of estates being acquired by purchase by *ghulāms* who attained to the highest ranks.[3] In the course of time, power fell into the hands of the Turkish slaves with whom the Samanids filled their court, and one of these, Alptigīn, founded the Ghaznavid dynasty in 384/994, which succeeded to Samanid domains south of the Oxus, and largely took over the Samanid system of administration. It was into this area that the Seljūqs irrupted in the first half of the fifth/eleventh century.

the silver *dirham* had meanwhile fallen. In 220/835 it was equal to 85 *ghadrafī dirhams*, but in 522/1128 100 silver *dirhams* were only worth 70 *ghadrafī dirhams* (ibid. p. 44; but see Barthold, p. 204).

[1] Barthold, p. 229; Narshakhī, p. 31.

[2] *S.N.*, p. 92.

[3] Barthold, pp. 238–9.

CHAPTER III

THE *IQṬĀʿ* SYSTEM AND THE SELJŪQS

THE early years of the fifth century A.H., saw a major change in the social and political structure of the lands of the Eastern Caliphate. The military, largely as a result of the breakdown in the financial economy of the state, had been able to seize power and to divert the revenue from the state treasury into their own pockets as assignees (*muqṭaʿs*). They had no permanent interest in the land and were concerned in the main with squeezing in the shortest possible time as much as they could out of the land in their temporary possession. This had given rise to political and economic problems of considerable magnitude. The Buyids made no attempt to solve them. The result was anarchy. If a stable government was to be established, it was clearly imperative to find a solution to these problems; the Seljūq period sees an attempt to solve them not by a radically new solution, but by a regularization of the position of the *muqṭaʿ*, and by bringing order into the *iqṭāʿ* system, which was to be the dominant feature in the field of land tenure and land revenue administration for many years to come. The work of the Seljūqs is of importance because it decided the main lines along which the system was to develop, and this system lasted in its essentials through the Middle Ages down to the twentieth century.

The granting of assignments of land was not in itself an innovation. As shown in the previous chapter, the practice was not unknown in the early years of Islām, and jurists sought to show that later practices developed from these early precedents. While there would seem to be some basis for this, it must be remembered that the Islamic law-books represented the ideal and not actual practice. Conformity with the legal theory was abandoned in practice at an early stage—if it ever existed—and once abandoned there was little check on arbitrary action, and the system which grew up in many respects bore little resemblance to the exposition of the jurists. The *iqṭāʿ* system is sometimes spoken of as feudalism, but the circumstances in which the *iqṭāʿ* system became established and the causes which gave rise to it were different from those which prevailed in Western Europe when feudalism developed. The results were dissimilar, and it is misleading to talk of feudalism in the lands of the Eastern Caliphate, including Persia, unless it is first made clear that Islamic feudalism does not correspond to any of the various types of feudalism found in Western Europe. The element of mutual obligation inherent in the nexus of feudal tenure in Western Europe is notably absent.

In the view of Becker, the *muqṭaʿ* had originally no military duties, and it was only with the militarization of the state that the military, by abuse, penetrated into the already existing system of assignees.[1] In his view the *iqṭāʿ* system grew up as an administrative and bureaucratic system and changed into a military system as the result of an attempt to meet a military problem when the gold economy had broken down. It differed thus from Western European feudalism both in origin and in the fact that the *muqṭaʿ* had originally no military duties.[2] Poliak, however, disputes this and accounts for the difference in the development of the *iqṭāʿ* system in Muslim lands and feudalism in the West by the concentration in the Muslim world of assignees in cities, in contradistinction to their dispersal in castles in the West, this concentration being made possible by more highly developed monetary conditions and by the physical nature of the country.[3] His assertion that the assignees were concentrated in towns seems, broadly speaking, to be borne out by the available evidence, but the validity of his rejection of Becker's theory that the military penetrated into the *iqṭāʿ* system subsequently and by abuse seems more doubtful. The basis of the 'dominion' of the orthodox caliphs and the Umayyads was the 'citizen' army, and not till Abbasid times was this replaced by a mercenary army. That is to say, prior to this the dominant class was not the 'military' in the usual sense of the word (i.e. mercenaries), but those belonging to the conquering race, whose chief duty as citizens was to bear arms to defend and to extend the dominion of the community of the faithful. The Arabs, as the dominant class, probably considered it their privilege to receive the revenue, but in the early period of the Arab expansion, at least, the actual administration was left largely in the hands of the local officials who had served the former administrations. As the composition of the dominant class under the Abbasid caliphs changed, the new masters of the country appropriated to themselves such privileges as the former members of the dominant class had enjoyed, including the right to the revenue.

Further, in so far as the central power was insufficient to discharge its public duties it surrendered public rights to powerful individuals and inevitably considerable social changes accompanied this surrender. In the first place, as pointed out above, it was only the right to collect the revenue which was thus surrendered. Later,

[1] *Islamstudien*, i. 240.

[2] cf. W. H. Moreland, who clearly shows that the *iqṭāʿ* system of Mughal India was a bureaucratic and not a feudal organization (*The Agrarian System of Muslim India* (Cambridge, 1929), pp. 218–21).

[3] 'La Féodalité islamique', *R.E.I.*, 1936, x. 248.

as the weakness of the central power grew, the population were forced in order to preserve their property more and more to seek the patronage of the influential, and this in turn, since it increased the influence of the latter, reinforced the tendency to alienate to assignees not only the right to collect the revenue but also the land itself, and so the opportunities of the assignees to extend patronage grew still further. Finally, with the growth in the political and social power of the assignee the central power was forced on the one hand to defer to him more and more, and on the other the relations between him and the local population which had originated in a free agreement tended to become burdened with services. As a result the political and economic subjection to, and dependence upon, the assignee of the population settled on the land and the social differentiation between the military and the non-military classes tended to increase. There were, however, no doubt considerable local variations. While the peasants, except when driven by undue extortion to migrate, continued to cultivate the soil to which they were often virtually attached, the position of the landowners, as distinct from that of the peasants, was more directly affected by the relative power of those to whom the grants of revenue and land were made. In some cases they were possibly expropriated or driven by poverty to sell their property; in others they may have continued as the owners of the soil, with, in theory at least, full rights of alienation, paying their taxes direct to the *muqṭaʿ* together with any other dues the latter might choose to levy. Where those in possession of the land had been tenants on crown land (or land which had formerly belonged in common to the Muslim community), they became, in effect, tenants of the *muqṭaʿ* to whom the land was assigned. This broadly appears to have been the situation when the Seljūq migration in the fifth/eleventh century took place.

Towards the end of the fourth/tenth century, various tribes in Turkistān were in a state of unrest and showing a general tendency to move westwards. Among them were the Ghuzz. About the year 425/1033–4 a body of Seljūq Ghuzz crossed the Oxus into Khurāsān and asked permission of Masʿūd ibn Maḥmūd, the Ghaznavid, to live under his protection. The nature of this movement was that of a tribal migration: the Ghuzz were accompanied by their families and their flocks. As they increased in numbers and influence, the need for fresh pastures became ever more pressing. They began to harry the Ghaznavid forces; and while avoiding direct conflict with them, they occupied any places from which the Ghaznavids temporarily withdrew. The Seljūqs themselves were not originally leaders of the Ghuzz but as increasing, though not uninterrupted, success attended their forays and expeditions they were in due course transformed from shepherds into military conquerors, the final stage of this transition being marked by the battle of Dindinqān (431/1040). After this it remained for them to consolidate their conquests in Khurāsān and the neighbourhood and to continue their movement westwards.

The power of the Seljūqs during the period of expansion was based on the Turkomān tribes. Their background and customs belonged to the Central Asian steppe.[1] They were as little able as had been the Arabs before them to take over the direct administration of their conquests. In the first stage of the Seljūq migration, before their transformation from shepherds into military conquerors had been completed, the tendency was for the local rulers to look upon the various groups of Turkomāns as tribal auxiliaries, useful to them in their local struggles; and as such they probably received from the local rulers assignments in accordance with the prevailing custom of making grants of land to the *amīrs* and soldiers. Gradually, as the Seljūqs increased their power, and became themselves the rulers of a large empire, they reduced many of the former local rulers to the position of vassals and brought to an end the dominion of others. They also began themselves to assign large areas of the empire to their followers. In due course, after the initial period of expansion, the basis of their power began to alter, in the same way as the basis of the power of the caliphate had altered after the Arab expansion. The Seljūq government came to rely more and more on armies composed, not of Turkomāns, but of slaves and freedmen, who, as the dominant class, began to appropriate to themselves the privileges of the former ruling class, which included the collection of the revenue. Moreover, since these Turkish slaves and freedmen were in many cases carefully trained not only in the art of war, but also in administrative affairs, it was natural that they should take over, in a large measure, the administration of the country, and that they should, when their power increased, divert the revenue from the central treasury into their own pockets.

There were thus two major problems which the Seljūqs had to solve, both of which closely affected land tenure and land revenue administration: first, how to incorporate into the structure of their empire a large nomadic element, the basis of whose livelihood was the tending of flocks, and to whom the Seljūqs for family reasons were under special obligations;[2] and secondly, how to pay their

[1] It is important to remember, however, that the Seljūqs had become converted to or familiar with Islām in the time of their ancestor Seljūq (*I.A.*, ix. 322) and that after they became the rulers of an empire they showed considerable respect for orthodox Islām and Islamic institutions, this respect being dictated in part by political exigencies.

[2] *S.N.*, p. 94.

military forces. The failure to find a satisfactory solution to the first problem was one of the factors leading to the overthrow of the Great Seljūqs in the reign of Sanjar (511–52/1117–57). The methods adopted to solve the second problem, on the other hand, while not entirely successful, decided the general principles of military organization and administration which were to persist in Persia in a more or less modified form down to the Constitutional Revolution.

One of the important effects of the Seljūq migration was to introduce into western Asia a new element in the population, namely, the Turks.[1] Many of the Turkomāns moved on to Asia Minor and Syria, but large bodies of them were to be found all over the empire, though probably to a lesser extent in Ṭabaristān and Daylam, which was inaccessible country populated by a robust and hardy people, and in Fārs and Kurdistān, which were already populated by semi-nomadic groups. The entry into Persia of the Turkish elements which at the present day form the majority of the population in Āẕarbāyjān, Hamadān and the neighbourhood, and Gurgān, probably dates mainly from Seljūq times. The Seljūq family were themselves Turkomāns, and their leading military officials and provincial governors were mainly Turks[2] or Turkomāns. In official documents relating to the period Turks and non-Turks (*tājīks*) are usually both mentioned, which suggests that there was a clear division between these two elements, as there had been formerly between Arabs and non-Arabs or Persians (*'ajam*).[3]

The second major division of the population was between the nomads and settled, which in part cut across the division between Turk and non-Turk. The most important nomadic elements consisted of the Turkomāns. As the basis of the Seljūq power shifted from the Ghuzz Turks to slaves and freedmen, the position of the Turkomāns in relation to the rest of the population became less favourable. A document issued by the *dīvāni inshā'* of Sanjar appointing Inānj Balkā Ulūgh Jāndār Beg *shihneh* of the Turkomāns in Gurgān refers to them as being the most deserving of all classes.[4] In this document Inānj Balkā was instructed to treat the people well, not to institute new levies, and to give each leader, with his household and followers, his due and not to allow them to engage in violence. The Turkomān leaders of Gurgān and the neighbourhood were to refer to him their requests to the govern-

[1] In post-Seljūq times there were also influxes of Turks into Persia, notably under the Mongols. Some of the Turkish tribes of Fārs claim to have entered Persia in Mongol times.

[2] i.e. Turkish slaves or freedmen.

[3] See *A.K.*, ff. 31, 61, 82, 108, 110, 116, 118, 169.

[4] The reason for this was that the Turkomāns lived far from cities and consequently news of their afflictions took a long time to reach the court (*A.K.*, f. 158).

ment.[1] In some cases the nomads apparently were taxed by the central government at so much per tent.[2] To maintain stability on the borders of Khurāsān in face of pressure from the Ghuzz on the fringes of the empire was, however, the most difficult of the tribal problems which faced the central government. Towards the end of the Great Seljūq period the Ghuzz were increasing in numbers. Their relations with Sanjar are illustrative on the one hand of the standing opposition between the settled and the nomadic or semi-settled elements, and, on the other, of the difficulty of subjecting the nomads to control. These Ghuzz used to pay an annual tribute of 24,000 sheep to the *sulṭān*'s kitchen. This used to be collected by a *muḥaṣṣil* on behalf of Sanjar's *khwānsālār*, and the tyranny which the *sulṭān*'s entourage exercised in the collection of these dues was alleged to be excessive. According to the sources, a certain *muḥaṣṣil* used to haggle over the sheep they brought, saying he must have bigger and fatter ones;[3] in short the *sulṭān*'s officials used to treat the Ghuzz with great brutality, and to deprive the *kalāntars* of their goods. One day this *muḥaṣṣil* was killed by them. The *khwānsālār* was afraid to tell the *sulṭān* of this and, at first, paid the tribute due from the Ghuzz himself. Eventually he told Qumāj, governor of Balkh. Qumāj advised the *khwānsālār* to tell the *sulṭān* that a group of Ghuzz had transgressed the limits set to them, but that if the *sulṭān* would make Qumāj *shihneh* over them he would punish them and pay to the royal kitchen 30,000 sheep annually. The proposal was made. The *sulṭān* agreed and Qumāj was sent as *shihneh* to the Ghuzz, but they refused to submit to him on the grounds that they were the special subjects of the *sulṭān* and drove him out with contempt. Qumāj and his son then made an expedition against the Ghuzz and were defeated and killed. When news of this reached the court the *amīrs* agreed that such an action could not be condoned, and that if the Ghuzz were not punished their acts of hostility would increase, and accordingly they urged Sanjar to set out himself against them. The Ghuzz, learning of this, became apprehensive and sent a messenger accusing Qumāj of violating their women and children and offering to pay 100,000 *dīnārs* and 100 Turkish slaves if the *sulṭān* would forgive them. The *sulṭān* was prepared to agree, but the *amīrs* urged him to march against the Ghuzz, which he did. When he came near to them they sent their women and children in front and came forward in humility offering to give 7 *mann* of grain per household. The *sulṭān* again wanted to accept this offer and abandon the

[1] *A.K.*, ff. 156–60.

[2] Ibn ul-Athīr, *Histoire des Atabecs de Mosul*, tr. de Slane (in *Recueil des historiens des Croisades*, Paris, 1876), p. 91.

[3] According to ar-Rāvandī, he tried to obtain bribes from them also (*Rāḥat us-Ṣudūr wa Āyat us-Surūr*, ed. M. Iqbāl (G.M.S., 1921), p. 177).

expedition, but the *amīrs* prevented him. Battle was joined, and Sanjar was defeated and captured (548/1153–4).[1]

In addition to the tribal areas on the borders of Khurāsān there were also considerable tribal areas elsewhere, notably in Fārs. One of the most important of the tribal groups in Fārs was the Shabānkāreh, who gave repeated trouble to the Seljūqs and their governors.

Finally there was the division of the population into military and civil, which coincided largely with the first grouping, since the military were mainly Turks and the civil officials probably mainly non-Turks.[2]

Of the composition of the settled rural population there is not a great deal of information. Small landowners known as *dihqāns* continued to exist. They are referred to in the *'Atabat al-Katabat* as a definite class of the population.[3] The peasants are seldom mentioned. In a diploma for the tax-collector of Marv there is a reference to the peasants on the *sulṭān*'s estates (*barzīgarāni asbābi khāṣṣ*).[4] In a letter to a provincial governor (probably belonging to this period but undated) peasants and artisans are classed together as the third class, the first class being those who were loyal and served at Court and the second the seditious.[5]

In so far as the theory of land ownership is concerned, it would seem likely that the ideas of the steppe were to some extent superimposed upon the system existing in the conquered territories. This gave a new orientation to the theory of land, which did not reach its full development until Ṣafavid times, when it became imbued with Shī'ī absolutism. The main feature of the land administration of the Seljūqs, as stated above, was the *iqṭā'* system. In view of the new circumstances much of the old Islamic theory was no longer applicable. The country was no longer divided clearly into the *dār ul-islām* and the *dār ul-ḥarb*. Much of the campaigning of the period was within the empire itself, and the conquests of land were often made at the expense of Muslim or nominally Muslim holders. The *imām* was, moreover, no longer the spiritual and temporal leader of the community, nor was the latter one undivided body. Consequently, the rules for the

[1] Ḥāfiẓ Abrū, *Jughrāfīā* (MS. belonging to Ḥājjī Ḥusayn Malik in Tehrān), f. 220. Sanjar remained a prisoner in the hands of the Ghuzz for three years. See also ar-Rāvandī, pp. 177–9; Bundārī, *Zubdat an-Nuṣrat*, ed. M. T. Houtsma (Leyden, 1889), pp. 281–3; Ibn an-Niẓām al-Ḥusaynī, *al-'Urāẓa fi'l Ḥikāyat as-Saljūqīya*, ed. Süssheim (Leyden, 1909), pp. 101–4; Ḥamdullāh Mustoufī, *Ta'rīkh-i-Guzīda*, ed. E. G. Browne (G.M.S., 1913), pp. 460–1.

[2] Cf. *A.K.*, f. 108 where *sipāhī* and *ra'īyat* and f. 36 where *lashkarī* and *ra'īyat* are contrasted.

[3] ff. 104, 107; *M.S.K.*, f. 25b.

[4] *A. K.*, f. 131. cf. also, the use of the term *asbāb* in the phrase *har cheh dar ān vilāyat dīvāni khāṣṣrāst az mu'āmalāt va irtifā'āti asbāb va dīgar abvāb* . . . (ibid. f. 130). See also p. 70, n. 3.

[5] *M.S.K.*, f. 62a.

division of the booty and conquered territory were no longer applicable.

The Seljūq leaders were the leaders of their people but not originally territorial sovereigns.[1] They conceived of their rule, in all probability, as extending wherever their people roamed, and not, at first in any case, as being tied to, or confined to, any given area. In the steppe each tribe had its own grazing ground or *yurt*, over which the leader of the group, as the representative of the tribe, exercised dominion, probably allotting, in the case of the large tribes, specific pastures in it to the various sub-groups, though guided in this by tribal custom and limited by tribal tradition. This conception of the Seljūq family as the guardian of the tribe or group of tribes was in due course modified by the Persian ideal of an autocratic sovereign, which prevailed in the conquered territories, but the conception that the leadership of the group was vested in the Seljūq family persisted in a modified form throughout the period. The kingdom was conceived of as the personal estate of the ruling *khān*, held by him on behalf of his people, although he could dispose of it within certain limits as he wished. It became the established practice for him to assign different parts of the kingdom to minor members of his family, sons, brothers, and others.[2] These assignments were probably not intended to be of a permanent nature, but there arose a tendency for one branch of the family to regard certain districts as its own *iqṭāʿ*, as certain branches of the tribe had probably tended to hold, by tradition, certain particular *yurts* in the Central Asian steppe. These assignments did not carry with them any permanent rights: the *malik* merely held the area (as did the *muqṭaʿ* in other *iqṭāʿs*) at the will of the *sulṭān*, who could, and frequently did, revoke the assignment. To what extent the *malik* had jurisdiction over his *iqṭāʿ* to the exclusion of the *sulṭān* is not clear. The latter appears to have delegated to him certain functions in a given area, including presumably his rights over the land. In a diploma issued by Alp Arslān for one of his sons for possession of Gīlān and Khẉārazm, these districts were given to the *malik* as his own property (*milkīyat*). He was instructed to look after the interests of the people of those parts and to observe former rules in the collection of taxes. The people were also commanded to regard him as the owner (*mālik*) of those districts, and the officials of his *dīvān* were to consider him as in charge of those districts, and were ordered to pay their taxes in full without delay.[3]

[1] This leadership was not of old standing, but the result of military successes at the time when the Ghuzz moved into Transoxania and Khurāsān.

[2] They were known as *maliks* in contradistinction to the *sulṭān* or ruling *khān*.

[3] Īvāghlī Ḥaydar, *Nuskhehyi Jāmiʿeh Murāsilāt*, B.M. Add. 7688 f. 3a, b.

In a diploma for the governorship of Gurgān and the surrounding country issued by Sanjar's *dīvān* to the Seljūq *malik*, Masʿūd, the people of Gurgān, Ṭabaristān, Dihistān, Basṭām, and Dāmghān are ordered to pay taxes and *dīvān* dues to the *muqṭaʿs* and *mutaṣarrifs* on Masʿūd's decree.[1]

Niẓām ul-Mulk appears to have regarded the *sulṭān* as the sole owner of the soil.[2] In so doing it is possible that he is extending the theory of the ruling *khān* as the representative of the tribe to cover the position of the *sulṭān* as the ruler of a territorial empire over which he held proprietory rights. Or perhaps he was attempting to invest the theory of the steppe with the content of the theory of absolute ownership which he derived from Sasanian tradition. Another possibility cannot be ruled out, namely, that in asserting the paramountcy of the *sulṭān* he was attempting to protect the peasants from arbitrary exactions by the assignees.

The *iqṭāʿ* to members of the ruling family was not the only type of *iqṭāʿ*: there were also 'administrative' *iqṭāʿs*, 'military' *iqṭāʿs*, and *iqṭāʿs* granted as personal estates. The 'administrative' *iqṭāʿ* was in effect a provincial government and resembles the earlier assignments made by the Arabs and known as *tuʿma* (see p. 28). The traditional distinction between this type of *iqṭāʿ* and the 'military' *iqṭāʿ* which, as pointed out in Chapter II, derived from the *iqṭāʿ al-istighlāl*, was preserved, the latter not being hereditary except by usurpation. The distinction, however, tended to be obscured because the 'administrative' *iqṭāʿ* had by Seljūq times become militarized. Niẓām ul-Mulk probably brought about a general unification of the *iqṭāʿ* system, but it is with the 'administrative' *iqṭāʿ* that he is especially concerned. The old idea of the promotion of cultivation, underlying the grant of the original *iqṭāʿ at-tamlīk* is also found in the theory of Niẓām ul-Mulk. He states that if attention is drawn to the ruin and dispersal of the inhabitants of any district it must be at once investigated, and the condition of the *muqṭaʿ* and *ʿāmil* inquired into, in order to prevent the land becoming waste, the peasants becoming dispersed, and money being levied unjustly.[3]

The practice of giving 'administrative' *iqṭāʿs* to *amīrs* and others was common throughout the Seljūq period. Under the later *sulṭāns* the grant of such an *iqṭāʿ* tended to become merely an official recognition of the *de facto* possession of the district by an *amīr*. It was doubtless due to the inability of the later *sulṭāns* to control the *amīrs* that they often assigned to them each other's domains, in order to play one *amīr* off against another, or even assigned the same district simultaneously to two persons. Except where an *iqṭāʿ* was granted by way of acknowledgement of the con-

[1] *A.K.*, f. 42. [2] *S.N.*, p. 28. [3] ibid. p. 119.

quest of an area by an *amīr*, the *muqṭa'* had, generally speaking, to take possession of his *iqṭā'* by force. As the power of the *amīrs* grew, however, a hereditary tendency began to appear, and there are cases of *amīrs* who were able to ensure the succession of their sons or dependants after them. There are also cases recorded of the disposal of an *iqṭā'* by testament. It appears that the *iqṭā'*, other than the *iqṭā'* granted by way of a personal estate, was not subject to the ordinary laws of inheritance, and that it was transmitted undivided to one of the holder's heirs.

Originally the relation of the *muqṭa'* to the central government was probably mainly a financial one, but with the general militarization of the administration this financial obligation was largely replaced by a military one. The extent to which this was the case probably varied in different parts of the empire. While the 'administrative' *iqṭā'* appears to have been common in the central and western parts, in Khurāsān, under Sanjar, there seems to have been a closer control over the *iqṭā'* system and the areas granted were supposed to bring in certain definite sums of money in return for which the holder furnished the ruler with military contingents. A register appears to have been kept in the *dīvān* of the *iqṭā's* and the number of troops the *muqṭa's* were required to furnish. In a diploma issued by Sanjar's *dīvān* for the governorship of Gurgān to 'Aẓud ud-Dīn the latter was required to look carefully into the *iqṭā's*, to confirm men who were in service in their *iqṭā's* according to their former descriptions and to recover for the *dīvān* anything which had been fraudulently or without his or the *sulṭān's* permission incorporated into anyone's *iqṭā'*.[1] Mention of the record of *iqṭā's* kept in the *dīvān* is also made in other documents.[2] In some cases, however, the relation appears to have been a purely financial one: in a diploma issued by Sanjar's *dīvān* to the *ispahbud* Sirāj ud-Dīn, of Māzandarān, the officials of the *iqṭā'* office were ordered to write a diploma for 30,000 *nayshāpūrī dīnārs* in his favour, so that all officials entering the province of Māzandarān would consider exempt from taxation the *iqṭā'* of Sirāj ud-Dīn, and not take possession of it or consider interference [in it] lawful. The document makes it clear that this grant was in reward for his services on campaigns and at the Court.[3]

According to Ibn Khallikān, the *vazīr* in Seljūq times, whether of the *sulṭān* or of governors, was paid by an *iqṭā'* in the form of a grant of one-tenth of the produce of the soil.[4] This was clearly something rather different from either the 'administrative' or the

[1] *A.K.*, f. 631; *M.S.K.*, f. 2b.
[2] e.g., *A.K.*, f. 132.
[3] ibid. ff. 162–4.
[4] Ibn Khallikān, *Biographical Dictionary*, tr. from the Arabic by Baron M. G. de Slane (Paris, 1842–71), iii. 297.

'military' *iqṭāʿ*. Niẓām ul-Mulk and his friends were accused by Abu'l Maḥāsin b. Kamāl al-Mulk before Malikshāh of misappropriation of the state revenue. He admitted to taking one-tenth of Malikshāh's wealth, and alleged that he spent this upon the standing army, alms, gifts, and *ouqāf*.[1] Jamāl ud-Dīn al-Jawād al-Iṣfahānī, the *vazīr* first of Zangī and after him of his son Sayf ud-Dīn, also held an *iqṭāʿ* of this kind.[2] In addition, the *vazīr* also held various assignments of land; these differed from the 'military' and 'administrative' *iqṭāʿs* in that the holder was not under an obligation to furnish the *sulṭān* with troops. But this distinction was to some extent obscured by the fact that since the maintenance of private armies by important persons was the general rule, the produce of these assignments was probably largely spent on the upkeep of troops. The *muqṭaʿ* of this type of *iqṭāʿ* was clearly an absentee. Other officials were similarly paid by *iqṭāʿ*.[3]

The payment of the standing army and of the various *junds*, or local militia, was largely by assignments. Bundārī claims that Niẓām ul-Mulk introduced the practice of assigning *iqṭāʿs* to the soldiery. This, however, is hardly correct. The Seljūqs in so doing were in fact continuing the practice of the Buyids and others.[4] Bundārī goes on to state that Niẓām ul-Mulk, seeing the disorder of the country and the irregularity of the payment of taxes, assigned the country to the soldiery (*ajnād*), handing over to them its produce and the levy of taxes, the income from which they devoted to making the country prosperous.[5] What in fact seems to have been happening was that a unification of the 'military' assignment and the 'administrative' assignment was taking place. Some slight difference between the two, however, still persisted. In so far as the latter type was concerned the *amīrs*, when not on campaigns, lived on and administered directly their assignments, which were granted not only in reward for past services, but also in the hope of future services, whereas in the former case members of the standing army remained in service and merely received the produce of their assignments, which were grants for services actually being rendered at the time. The precise form in which payment was made is not clear: in the case of the soldiers it was probably in the form of a draft which would be cashed by a broker. Further, the *iqṭāʿs* of the standing army tended naturally to be smaller than those of the great *amīrs*, partly owing to the fact that the standing army remained with the *sulṭān* under his direct control, whereas

[1] *I.A.*, x. 84–5. [2] *I.K.*, iii. 297.

[3] See, for example, *M.S.K.*, ff. 29b–30a for a diploma for the office of *dādbeg* issued by Ṭughril b. Muḥammad's *dīvān*. [4] See pp. 49 ff.

[5] *Bu.*, p. 58. It appears that some 400,000 men were on the military rolls and received payment by *iqṭāʿ* or drafts on the revenue (see *S.N.*, p. 144; Ḥāfiẓ Abrū, *Jughrāfīā*, f. 178a).

the great *amīrs*, who were either sent to the provinces or went of their own accord, were often able to usurp the control of large areas. A hereditary tendency appeared in these 'military' assignments as it had in the 'administrative' assignments, but was not the normal practice under the Great Seljūqs. In the areas under the control of Sanjar, it appears that the *iqṭāʿs* held by the soldiers and officials in the provincial governments were held, in theory at least, from the royal *dīvān* and not, as was often the case in other areas, from the hand of the *muqṭaʿ* or provincial governor.[1]

In addition to the assignments to the individual members of the standing army, there were under Malikshāh a number of assignments throughout the country which were intended to provide for the needs of the army on campaigns.[2] Whether the *iqṭāʿ* represented a proportion of the crop which was levied on the local population for this purpose, kept in royal storehouses and used when required, or areas of land directly administered, the produce being used when necessary to supply the royal army, is not clear. Certain areas in districts assigned to the *amīrs* and *maliks* were similarly 'reserved' on occasion by the *sulṭān* in order better to maintain control over the *muqṭaʿ*.[3]

A different type of *iqṭāʿ* from those outlined above was the *iqṭāʿ* assigned as a personal estate; these were granted as a kind of gift. It is often difficult to distinguish them from other types, because the same person frequently held more than one type of *iqṭāʿ*. Such 'personal' *iqṭāʿs* were usually granted on a life-long or hereditary tenure—but, as other gifts, they were presumably, according to Islamic law, revocable during the lifetime of the grantee. Included in, or approximating to, this type of assignment were those *iqṭāʿs* granted to members of the religious classes (as distinct from those granted to religious 'officials' in lieu of salaries). The purpose of these 'personal' *iqṭāʿs* would seem to be to afford to the holder a means of livelihood, without imposing upon him any obligation. ʿAlā ud-Douleh Kālinjār when he surrendered Iṣfahān to Malikshāh is alleged to have said: 'I have no pretensions to the sultanate, but one must have a home. A small province is sufficient for me as my *iqṭāʿ*, where I can employ myself in prayer.'[4]

'Personal' *iqṭāʿs* probably also carried with them in certain cases exemptions from taxation. For example, the estates (*amlāk*) of

[1] See *A.K.*, ff. 42, 62–3, 132–3.

[2] See Rāvandī, p. 131; Ḥamdullāh Mustoufī, *Taʾrīkh-i-Guzīda*, p. 449; Ibn an-Niẓām al-Ḥusaynī, p. 60.

[3] Sanjar, when he reinstated Maḥmūd b. Muḥammad in 513/1119 as ruler of the western provinces of Persia, retained various places, including Ray, in the possession of his own *dīvān* (*I.A.*, x. 389).

[4] Aḥmad b. Ḥusayn, *Tārīkhi Jadīdi Yazd* (Yazd, 1317), p. 64.

Ẓīā' ud-Dīn who was appointed *qāẓī* of Astarābād by Sanjar were to be held exempt from taxation.[1]

Unlike the 'administrative' *iqṭāʿs*, which became hereditary only by usurpation and passed, when transmitted by inheritance or testament, to one person who became, or was designated by the holder as his heir, these 'personal' *iqṭāʿs* were presumably broken up by the Islamic laws of inheritance. On the death of the holder the estate would either be divided into separate lots, or the heirs would hold the estate jointly, in which case they would usually appoint one of their number to manage it on behalf of the joint holders. In so far as the estate became divided into separate units its transition into private property would have been facilitated.

That there was a distinction between *iqṭāʿ* and *milk*, (pl. *amlāk*), or private estates, is suggested by the statement of Ibn Balkhī that part of the meadow land and villages of Rūn in Fārs was *milk* and part *iqṭāʿ*.[2] It may be that when an *iqṭāʿ* granted as a 'personal' estate was passed on by inheritance to the original grantee's heirs it tended to become *milk* or private property. It is possible that whereas *milk*, or private property, was held with full proprietary rights, 'personal' *iqṭāʿs*, even when held on a hereditary tenure, were considered to be held at the ruler's will (even though he were not the original grantee), and were therefore subject to revocation whereas Islamic law on the contrary only allowed the revocation of a gift during the lifetime of the original grantee, and possibly that they required confirmation by each reigning *sulṭān*. On the other hand, since *amlāk* were not immune from confiscation, the difference in practice between a 'personal' *iqṭāʿ* and *milk* would appear to have been small. For example, it is stated that Barkyāruq's *vazīr* ʿAbd ul-Jalīl ad-Dihistānī took away estates (*amlāk*) from their owners and assigned them to others.[3]

Although the major part of the empire was alienated as *iqṭāʿ* from the direct control of the *sulṭān*, there were areas in different parts retained as crown lands, or as the private estates of the *sulṭān*. These were in some cases farmed by *amīrs* and others. Mention is made of such lands in Basṭām,[4] Ray,[5] Marv,[6] and Kūfeh.[7] Alp Arslān also appears to have held a number of private estates, some of which had been newly created. Apparently some of them were in the hands of the *amīrs*.[8] The estates of Īghārayn (see p. 27) appear moreover to have become the private estates of the Seljūq *sulṭāns*.[9]

[1] *A.K.*, f. 103.
[2] Ibn Balkhī, *Fārs-nāma*, ed. G. le Strange and R. A. Nicholson (G.M.S., 1921), pp. 124, 155.
[3] *Bu.*, p. 89.
[4] *A.K.*, f. 110.
[5] ibid. ff. 140, 143.
[6] ibid. f. 131.
[7] *I.A.*, x. 8.
[8] Niẓām ul-Mulk, *Nasāʾih Nāmeh*, f. 30b.
[9] Yāqūt, *Muʿjam al-Buldān*, i, 420.

In the theory of Niẓām ul-Mulk the rights of the *muqṭaʿ* over the population in his *iqṭāʿ* were only financial. He had no rights over the land or the cultivators, the ruler merely having delegated to him certain financial rights. Niẓām ul-Mulk states,

Let the assignees who have *iqṭāʿs* know that they have no authority over the peasants beyond this, that they should take the due amount which has been assigned to them from the peasants with civility, and that when they have taken that, the peasants shall be secure in their persons, and their money, wives, children, goods, and estates, and the *muqṭaʿs* have no claim over them. Let the *muqṭaʿs* know that the kingdom (*mulk*) and the subjects (*raʿīyat*), all belong to the *sulṭān*. The *muqṭaʿs* who are set over them and the governors (*vālīs*) are like *shihnehs* in relation to the subjects [i.e. peasants], as the king is to others [i.e. peasants not on assigned lands], so that the latter may be happy, and the *muqṭaʿ* may be safe from punishment and torment in the next world.[1]

Niẓām ul-Mulk further forbids the *muqṭaʿ* to prevent the peasants under him from coming to represent their case, threatening him with punishment and the cancellation of his *iqṭāʿ*.[2] That such a warning was necessary suggests that it may have been the common practice for *muqṭaʿs* to prevent the peasants from going to the court to obtain redress for their grievances. In practice, however, the powers exercised by the *muqṭaʿ* in the 'administrative' *iqṭāʿ* were often far wider than those envisaged by Niẓām ul-Mulk. In many cases he had complete control.

In so far as *iqṭāʿs* assigned in lieu of wages or as private estates were concerned, it appears that in some cases immunity from all interference by government officials was given. In a diploma issued from the *dīvān* of Ṭughril b. Muḥammad for a certain individual as *dādbeg* it is stated that the officials of the *dīvān* were not to enter or make claims on his *iqṭāʿs*.[3]

In practice the position of the peasants on assigned land appears to have varied considerably. Their freedom of movement was often restricted and they were frequently subjected to forced labour. A story is related about the treatment of the cultivators of Zangī and Ḥusām ud-Dīn Taymūrtāsh respectively which throws some light on the matter. Zangī on a certain occasion demanded from Ḥusām ud-Dīn the return of a number of cultivators who had left the city of Mawṣil for Mārdīn. Ḥusām ud-Dīn sent back an answer saying, 'We treat the cultivators well, and take one-tenth from them by way of a share of the grain crops and if you had done likewise they would not have left you.' Zangī sent back a message saying,

Tell your master, if you took one per cent it would be too much, for you

[1] *S.N.*, p. 28. [2] ibid.
[3] *M.S.K.*, f. 30 a.

are occupied with your pleasures in Mārdīn, but we, if we took two-thirds, it would be little in view of what we are charged with by way of holy war. But for me, it is long since your master had drunk water in security in Mārdīn, for the Franks would have taken it. If you do not return the cultivators, I will take every cultivator in Mārdīn to Mawṣil.

Ḥusām ud-Dīn then sent back the cultivators in question.[1]

There was in all probability a considerable area of *vaqf* land in the Seljūq empire, but it had not by any means reached the extent it later reached under the Ṣafavids.[2] A certain measure of control appears to have been exercised over *ouqāf* by the state, which was in keeping with the general religious policy of the Seljūqs, which was to bring the religious organization within the general framework of the state. In diplomas issued for governors from Sanjar's *dīvān*, the *mutavallīs* of *ouqāf* are placed under their jurisdiction, and the governor is charged with supervision of the expenditure of the income from endowments, and also with the conditions and administration of endowments.[3] A general supervision of *ouqāf* is, in a diploma issued by Sanjar's *dīvān*, entrusted to the *qāẓī* of the royal army. He was instructed to investigate their produce, reduce disorders in them, prevent usurpation of them, and cause their produce to be put to the use for which it was intended. The *mutavallīs* were instructed to give him full information and to pay the dues of his office.[4] At the same time there was also an office known as the *dīvāni ouqāf* in certain towns, which was in charge of the administration of *ouqāf* in that district. A diploma issued for the deputyship of the *dīvāni ouqāf*, also from Sanjar's *dīvān*, gives an idea of the extent of this supervision. A certain Ẓīā' ud-Dīn was appointed deputy to ʿAzīz ud-Dīn, who was the *mutavallī* of the *ouqāf* of Gurgān and the neighbourhood. He was to show clearly what the conditions (*aḥvāl*) of the *ouqāf* were, to investigate any disturbances in their affairs, to show praiseworthy effort in bringing them into a flourishing condition, to reclaim them, and to demand their produce. If there had been misappropriation (of *vaqf* property) or peculation, he was to put this right if he could and if not to refer it to the *dīvān*. The notables and well-known and reliable persons of the town of Gurgān and its districts among the *sayyids*, *qāẓīs*, *imāms*, heads (of districts, i.e. *ru'asā*), landowners (*dihāqīn*), deputies (*navvāb*) and *muqṭaʿs* were to strengthen him in his office and to surrender to him whatever appertained to his office as deputy of ʿAzīz ud-Dīn. They were to hide nothing from him, and they were to give attention to whatever he referred to the office of the *ra'īs* and the office of the *shihneh* and help him, and if he needed an assistant and a *shihneh* they were to designate someone,

[1] Ibn ul-Athīr, *Histoire des Atabecs de Mosul*, p. 141.
[2] See Ch. V. [3] *A.K.*, ff. 49, 57. [4] ibid. ff. 115–16.

and were to carry out in accordance with his request whatever concerned that office. All groups and Islamic rites were to give him a copy of their *ouqāf* and hide nothing so that they should not become subject to a disavowal and denial (of their claims) and they were to consider null and void all acts of aggression and possession to which ʿAzīz ud-Dīn did not agree and they were not to take possession (of any *ouqāf*) without his permission.[1]

The *dīvāni ouqāf*, however, did not administer all *ouqāf* directly; it is specifically stated in a diploma issued by Sanjar's *dīvān* for the office of *qāẓī* of Nouqān in the district of Ṭūs, which carried with it the office of *mutavallī* of (certain) *ouqāf*, that the *dīvāni ouqāf* should not interfere in these *ouqāf* or make any tax demands upon them.[2] Similarly Ẓahīr ud-Dīn, when he was appointed *mudarris* of the *madraseh* of Balkh and various other *madrasehs* and charged with teaching in the Sarsang mosque, was given full charge of their *ouqāf*.[3]

There appears to have been a tendency not only to usurp *ouqāf* and to divert their revenues to purposes other than those for which they were intended, but also for their material condition to decline. This is shown in the diploma granted to ʿAzīz ud-Dīn for the *ouqāf* of Gurgān issued by Sanjar's *dīvān*. This document, after a short preamble, refers to the disorders prevailing in the *ouqāf* of Gurgān and its dependencies and states that these would grow worse unless the *ouqāf* were entrusted to an able and reliable person. Accordingly ʿAzīz ud-Dīn was instructed to look into the conditions (*ahvāl*) of the *ouqāf*, call for the *vaqf nāmehs*, make known their past produce, for whom they had been constituted, and how their produce was expended. If those who were in possession acted in accordance with the conditions laid down by the founder and devoted the produce to the purpose for which it was intended, he was to confirm them in their positions, but otherwise to refer to the *dīvān*. In future every place which belonged to the *ouqāf* was to be entrusted to a God-fearing and reliable person, so that there should be no negligence in its administration, and it should be removed from peculation and misappropriation so that ʿAzīz ud-Dīn could devote its proceeds to charitable objects according to the conditions laid down by the settlors. He was to make the greatest efforts to make the *ouqāf* prosperous. Their proceeds were to be spent upon the proper objects 'with the cognizance of reliable persons of the *dīvāni ishrāf*'. He was to terminate the possession of those who devoured (the proceeds illegally), and to prevent aggression and seizure (of the *ouqāf*) by usurpers, and was to appoint officials and experienced administrators of good faith and conduct who would not practice oppression. The *muqṭaʿs*, *shihnehs*,

[1] *A.K.*, ff. 103–5. [2] ibid. f. 66. [3] ibid. f. 72.

ru'asā, *ʿummāl*, *dihāqīn*, and the notables among the *sayyids*, *imāms*, and *qāẓīs* were to obey this decree and provide him with all facilities, and to place under his authority the *ouqāf* of the city and its neighbourhood, in whatever district they were, whether in a ruined or flourishing condition, old or new; all classes and rites were to furnish him with a clear and detailed list of what *ouqāf* belonged to them. The deputies (*navvāb*), governors, *muqṭaʿs*, and *shihnehs* of the town and its districts were to respect and support ʿAzīz ud-Dīn and his deputies and not to interfere in anything which concerned the *dīvāni ouqāf*. All Turks and non-Turks, military and civil, were to respect this order and to surrender to the deputies of ʿAzīz ud-Dīn whatever appertained to that office and to pay their dues to ʿAzīz ud-Dīn's deputies, according to ancient custom.[1]

In addition to the various classes of lands discussed above it is clear that private property was also recognized by the Seljūqs, and comprised private property already in existence when they succeeded to the lands which formed part of their empire, property created by grants made by themselves, and property the ownership of which derived from occupation. The transmission of private property by testament and by sale was recognized. Tāj ud-Dīn Aḥmad ibn al-ʿAbbās when appointed *ra'īs* of Māzandarān and other districts was instructed to see that when landed property was transferred from one person to another it should be done in good faith. Further, he was to act with caution in affairs connected with property left by the dead; if a legatee was absent Tāj ud-Dīn was to hold the property for him until he returned. He was instructed generally to preserve the property of the Muslims. Title-deeds appear to have been held by the owners of estates. These were written by the *qāẓī's* office.[2]

There appears, however, to have been no orderly or regular system of land registration; the holders of land in many cases probably had some sort of title-deed in their possession, but there seems to have been no process for the transfer or cancellation of these when the property was transmitted from one holder to another. According to Rashīd ud-Dīn, Malikshāh forbade the hearing of land claims based on documents which were over thirty years old.[3] This decision, which was confirmed by the leading religious and juridical officials of the day, appears to have been based on practical considerations and a desire to prevent disturbances by the preferment of fraudulent claims.[4]

[1] *A.K.*, ff. 105–8; *M.S.K.*, ff. 24b–25a.

[2] Cf. *A.K.*, f. 24.

[3] *T.G.*, p. 241.

[4] The reason for Malikshāh's action is alleged to have been the fact that many old title-deeds were in the hands of the people, and these they would take to the *qāẓīs*, stir up trouble and establish [fraudulent] claims, and on this account the people were in difficulties. Malikshāh and Niẓām ul-Mulk accordingly

The tendency for the status of the population living on the land to be depressed has been pointed out, and also the growing differentiation between the military and non-military classes. The growth in patronage of the former gave added possibilities for extortion, and it is almost certainly the case that the population in general and the peasants in particular, whether on land assigned as *iqṭā's* under provincial governors, in crown lands, or in *vaqf* land, were subject to a considerable degree of extortion. The extent to which Niẓām ul-Mulk, for example, emphasizes the tendency of officials, provincial or otherwise, to oppress the population of the country the moment control was relaxed is striking. In most of the diplomas issued for *muqṭa's* or provincial officials the grantee is always urged to treat the population well and to protect them from undue extortion. For example, in a diploma for the governorship of Gurgān, Ṭabaristān, Dihistān, Basṭām, and Dāmghān issued by Sanjar to the Malik Mas'ūd, the latter was granted the produce of the plains, mountains, land, and sea, and given full powers; and was instructed to consider kindness and conciliation of the subjects as the main pillar in the government of the country. He was to exhort all the governors, *muqṭa's*, and officials to refrain from practising extortion against the subjects and to demand *kharāj*, *'ushr*, and *dīvān* dues as fixed, according to the law, and at the right time, and not to demand extra levies.[1]

In a diploma for the office of *ra'īs* of Māzandarān also issued by Sanjar's *dīvān*[2] the grantee Tāj ud-Dīn is instructed to be a just arbitrator and mediator between the officials and the people and not to allow the *mutaṣarrifs* and officials to oppress the people or the people to oppress one another, and as far as possible not to allow extraordinary demands and levies to be made. If some contingency made a levy expedient, it was to be levied justly; and equality in its levy was to be preserved among the people, the owners of private property, and those who had been assigned the right to collect their dues on the country.[3] He was not to place

issued an order to the effect that all claims based on title-deeds which had not been preferred for thirty years should not be heard. This was given to all the *muftīs* of Khurāsān, 'Irāq, and Baghdād so that a *fatvā* in accordance with the *sharī'a* should be issued and sent to the *dār ul-khilāfa* to be signed. Rashīd ud-Dīn alleged that the order still existed in his day and that copies of it were to be found in the provinces (ibid. pp. 237–8). Rashīd ud-Dīn implies that a similar practice was followed by other Seljūq *sulṭāns* (ibid. p. 230).

[1] *A.K.*, ff. 32–42. [2] ibid. ff. 52–60.

[3] *Arbābi asbāb*, The meaning of this term is uncertain. It is possible that it means those persons who had been given the right to collect direct from a given area the sums which were due to them or which had been allotted to them. The precise meaning of *asbāb* is not clear. In this series of documents it appears to be used for some sort of right or property in land. Cf. *Sabbaba 'alā* = to charge a payment on a fund or district. (Hilāl as-Sābī, *Historical Remains of Hilāl as-Sābī*, ed. H. F. Amedroz (Leyden, 1904), p. 62). See also above p. 59.

the burden of the strong on the weak, or to prefer the rich to the poor, but to treat all equally. He was, moreover, to exert himself in alleviating the conditions of the people.[1] The *ra'īs* and *zaʿīm* of the districts and villages were to obtain diplomas from his *dīvān* and were to pay their dues. All Sanjar's officials were to treat Tāj ud-Dīn with respect and to preserve immune from misfortunes and accidents (or extraordinary contributions) the administrators of properties (*vukalāyi asbāb*),[2] peasants and those living on landed estates (*mustaghallāt*).[3] In another diploma, also for the office of *ra'īs* of Māzandarān, the grantee is ordered to appoint a deputy in every city and quarter so that the affairs of the subjects may be conducted with justice, and to observe equal treatment between landlords (*arbāb*) and their partners (*shurakā*) in properties (*asbāb*),[4] and in private estates (*amlāk*) in the apportioning of extraordinary dues so that the strong should not oppress the weak or the rich the poor.[5] This seems to imply that the state exercised a general supervision over agreements between landowners and crop-sharing peasants. Similarly, in a diploma for the office of *ra'īs* of Sarakhs the grantee is ordered to see that all classes got their dues and rights according to their degrees and ranks. He was to strive to alleviate the condition of all and to lessen the imposition of the strong on the weak and the rich on the poor, and not to allow demands for dues and fodder to be made on the people for the pre-eminent and chosen among the army and local troops or holders of *dīvān* bills.[6] In diplomas for the *nā'ib* of Ray similar injunctions are found; in one the grantee is ordered to prevent the rich practising extortion on the poor or the soldiery on the subjects,[7] and in the other he is instructed to prevent the strong oppressing the weak.[8]

It appears that the affairs of the people were largely in charge of the *ra'īs* of a given area. In a diploma for the *ra'īs* of Basṭām it is stated that since the people of Basṭām had been subject for years to extraordinary demands and afflictions, the office of *ra'īs* of the town and district was granted to a certain Sharaf ud-Dīn in order to alleviate their lot.[9] He was entrusted with the interests of the subjects. He was to treat kindly those who had been frightened (scared away) and to abolish unseemly dues.[10]

In another diploma for the governorship of Gurgān issued by Sanjar's *dīvān* the grantee, ʿAlī ibn Aḥmad al-Kātib, is enjoined to urge every official to follow the path of justice, and to see that all

[1] *A.K.*, f. 55.
[2] Or possibly *vukalāyi asbāb* is used for *arbābi asbāb*. See note 3, p. 70.
[3] *A.K.*, f. 59; *mustaghallāt* can also mean real estate such as shops, baths, and caravanserais, in which sense it is almost exclusively used in modern times.
[4] See note 3, p. 70.
[5] *A.K.*, f. 47.
[6] ibid. f. 81.
[7] ibid. f. 87.
[8] ibid. f. 140.
[9] ibid. ff. 108–9.
[10] ibid. f. 109.

the subjects were free from the vexation and distress they had suffered in the past. He was to consider it his first duty to treat the subjects well, and to instruct the *muqṭaʿs*, *mutaṣarrifs*, and *vālīs* to exert themselves in so doing and neither to make extraordinary demands upon the people nor to impose new dues upon them.[1]

Similarly, in a diploma issued by Sanjar's *dīvān* for the office of *shihneh* of the Turkomāns the grantee, although his excellence was such that he needed no instructions, was 'according to custom' commanded to treat the subjects well.[2]

In the case of private estates, it appears that these were on occasion rented. In a diploma for the office of *qāẓī ul-quẓāt* of Astarābād issued to Ẓīā' ud-Dīn the local governor, *muqṭaʿs*, *mutaṣarrifs*, and officials were to hold immune the tenants of his property from improper dues and levies.[3]

Land tax (*kharāj* and *ʿushr*) in the directly administered area (which became smaller and smaller as more and more of the empire was alienated from the control of the central government in the form of *iqṭāʿs*) was collected by government tax-collectors. In the *iqṭāʿs* it was presumably collected by the *muqṭaʿ* or his representatives. It was probably collected both in cash and kind, the assessment being based on the amount of the crop. A good many areas also appear to have been put up to public contraction, this being the meaning of the term *muʿāmaleh* which is sometimes used together with *irtifāʿāt* in the sources, the latter meaning (tax levied by way of a share of) the produce.[4] There was a special *dīvāni muʿāmaleh va qismat*.[5] In theory land tax fell due after the harvest was reaped, but in practice it was probably often demanded before the harvest was ready. Niẓām ul-Mulk writes, 'The tax-collectors must be charged to treat well the people of God and only to take the due amount [from them in taxation] and also demand that with civility and courtesy.' He stresses the fact that the taxes were not to be demanded before they fell due, because this led to the ruin and dispersal of the peasants.[6] If the tax-collector took anything in excess from the subjects he was to be removed from office.[7]

[1] *A.K.*, ff. 133–4. [2] ibid. f. 159. [3] ibid. f. 103.

[4] ibid. ff. 92, 130. A significant phrase occurs in a letter in the same collection, which throws light on the meaning of *muʿāmaleh*: *az muʿāmaleh hīch chīz bi kas nadihand ki ʿāmili dīvān bi sari ān kār miāyad*, 'nothing is being given to anyone by way of public contraction because a tax-collector belonging to the *dīvān* is coming to be in charge of that affair' (f. 241).

[5] ibid. f. 51. This *dīvān* was presumably concerned with revenue derived from public contraction and possibly also with revenue paid in kind or reckoned in kind and subsequently converted into cash.

[6] *raʿāyā*. The modern meaning of this term is peasants. In classical Persian it is used for subjects in general as distinct from the ruling and military classes, but in view of the fact that the peasants were probably the main class of taxpayers, it can often be translated by 'peasants'.

[7] *S.N.*, p. 18.

Alp Arslān is said to have levied the land tax in two instalments.[1] Reductions were given on occasion in the event of some natural calamity.[2]

In addition to the land tax, innumerable dues and cesses were levied both by the central government and the *muqṭaʿ*. The nature of these varied. In some cases they were levied as regular taxes, in others as extraordinary taxes. The rates of the taxes appear to have been subject to variation. In the diplomas issued to governors, tax-collectors, or other officials concerned with the collection of taxation, the grantee is usually enjoined to levy the taxes only in accordance with the fixed rates and at the proper time and to protect the people under him from extraordinary levies.[3] One form of special levy was known as *ẓarībeh*[4] and possibly represented some sort of extra payment involved by converting the tax, which was assessed in *dīnārs*, into *dirhams* or currency *dīnārs*.[5] Another due was known as *ṭayyārāt*.[6] In addition to the levy of ordinary and extraordinary taxes, drafts were also in some cases made on the provinces. Thus Sanjar gave Ḥusayn Kurd, who had captured the *amīr* Qarājeh in battle near Hamadān *c.* 521/1127–8, a present of 10,000 *dīnārs* and a further 10,000 *dīnārs* on the province (*vilāyat*) of Zārim, and wrote a draft (*barāt*) therefor.[7] These drafts appear to have been in some cases collected directly from the peasants (see p. 75) and meant, therefore, that there was virtually no limit to the demands which might be made on the peasants.

From what has been stated above it will be seen that insecurity was the dominant note in the life of the people. The constant passage of armed forces through the country, petty wars among the *amīrs*, and the bands of unemployed soldiery and robbers who roamed the countryside can hardly have conduced to the well-being of the country population. In addition there was from time to time the manipulation of prices and the hoarding of goods to create artificial shortages as the inevitable concomitant of such con-

[1] Ṣadr ud-Dīn, *Akhbār 'ud-Dawlat 'is-Saljūqiyya*, ed. Muḥammad Iqbāl (Lahore, 1933), p. 30; *I.A.*, x. 51.

[2] Another letter demanding reduction of taxation is also preserved in the same collection. The writer states that there had been a crop failure in Juvayn as a result of hail. The people, unable to pay their *kharāj*, had been forced to borrow grain, and if the district was not to be deserted and the people destroyed, some reduction in their *kharāj* would have to be granted. (*A.K.*, ff. 302–3.)

[3] See *A.K.*, ff. 41, 47, 81, 117, 131, 134, 140, 142, 150.

[4] See ibid f. 110.

[5] This is the meaning of *ẓarībeh* in the *T.Q.* (see pp. 142–4). Whether it actually has this meaning in Seljūq times is not certain. In one document the phrase *ẓarā'ibi shahr* occurs (*A.K.*, f. 140), which suggests rather dues or tolls levied at the gates of towns.

[6] *A.K.*, ff. 110, 140, where the term *ṭayyārāt* follows *ẓarā'ib*; it may mean tolls levied at the gates of towns.

[7] Marʿashī, *Tārīkhi Ṭabaristān va Rūyān va Māzandarān*, ed. B. Dorn, p. 234.

ditions.[1] There were, of course, interludes: from time to time in various areas, if not throughout the whole empire, owing to the strength of the *sulṭān* or the local governor or *muqṭaʿ*, security was established for a period, and the people were able to follow their occupations in peace and relative prosperity. One such area is alleged to have been Marv during the reign of Sanjar when, according to Juvaynī, the landowners (*dihāqīn*) were exceedingly prosperous.[2] The general tendency of Turkish government, however, was no doubt towards oppression.[3]

The condition of the peasants in any given area depended primarily on the personality of the local officials to whom the central government had delegated authority. In theory, and to a limited extent in practice, the peasants had the possibility of demanding redress from the central government in the event of oppression. However, the practical difficulties in doing so were considerable. In the first place in many cases long distances had to be covered, and secondly the concentration of power locally in the hands of the governor or *muqṭaʿ* made it relatively easy for him to prevent such demands for redress being preferred. The ultimate remedy of the peasants when driven to desperation was emigration or, rather, flight. There are references to this in the sources from time to time. A letter preserved in the *ʿAtabat al-Katabat* shows, however, that it was possible for the local people to express their wishes to some extent. A certain Burhān ud-Dīn, writing to the governor of Nayshāpūr, expresses the hope of the people of some region in the neighbourhood that the *ḥākim* of that district would be reappointed. He states that the office of *ḥākim* was important to the people because the assessing of water rates and *kharāj* was in his hands. The office had been for two years in the hands of a certain Majd ud-Dīn Najm ul-Ḥukamā Abū Bakr, who had performed his duties with humility and piety. When the people of the district had heard that he was to be transferred, the notables and the common people had two or three times come to the writer and asked him to request their master in Nayshāpūr to renew his appointment as *ḥākim*.[4]

The difficulty of combining the need of the state to raise as much

[1] Tāj ud-Dīn when appointed *raʾīs* of Māzandarān by Sanjar was instructed to give no chance to hoarders to create such shortages. (*A.K.*, f. 56.)

[2] *Taʾrīkh-i-Jahān-Gushā*, ed. M. M. Qazvīnī (G.M.S., 1912–37), i. 119. See also Ḥāfiẓ Abrū, *Jughrāfīā*, f. 174 a.

[3] Ghazālī mentions the tyranny of the Turks and the general decay of morality under them. He ranks them together with tax-collectors and *sulṭāns* as tyrants whose wealth is unlawful. (*Kīmīā as-Saʿādat*, p. 155; cf. also pp. 134, 225.)

[4] *A.K.*, ff. 182–6. The letter is undated but probably refers to the period immediately before or just after the fall of Sanjar. Another letter in the same collection addressed to Burhān ud-Dīn, mentioning his absence from Nayshāpūr, is clearly written at the time of the invasion of Khurāsān by the Ghuzz (ff. 230–3).

revenue as possible and the desirability of ensuring the well-being of the subjects—and in Seljūq times there was in theory, at least, still some attention paid to this aspect—is illustrated by a letter also preserved in the *ʿAtabat al-Katabat*. The writer, addressing the *sulṭān*, states that he was engaged in the affairs of the *dīvān*. He sought to acquire on the one hand the satisfaction of the officials of the *dīvān* and on the other to preserve the (well-being of the) subjects, knowing that it was necessary to collect the *dīvān* dues and also that the well-being of the state lay in caring for the state of the poor. He hoped that by combining the interests of both, the *mutaṣarrifs* and *muḥaṣṣils* would be content, the revenue gradually collected, the well-being of the subjects assured, and those who had been scared away would return. In conclusion the writer states that he would report to the *dīvān* the condition of the peasants in the hope of justice and clemency being extended to them.[1]

Another letter in the same collection shows the constant uncertainty and insecurity which prevailed. The writer, addressing some prince (or official), after expressing his thanks for past and present favours states that the peasants had always been well known for their good husbandry.[2] They had been subject to distress and injury but had for some time been under the care of the prince to whom the letter was addressed. Under the shadow of his justice they were engaged in agriculture (*dihqanat*) and were getting on with the deputies of the governors and *muqṭaʿs* and passing their time as best they could. A certain Saʿd ud-Dīn Jamāl ul-Islām Aḥmad had now come to the district as *mustoufī* and the people were happy on that account. But the *dīvān* had ordered arrears of taxation and an increased rate to be collected. Saʿd ud-Dīn had collected the amount and paid it to the holders of drafts and the people had obeyed the order. They now feared lest another draft should be made upon them, and that since there was nothing there to collect, they would be forced to leave the district if a new demand was made. It was not fitting that such a district should be ruined. The writer states that he had reassured the people and was writing to the prince to say that if the wretched people were not treated with kindness they would flee the country.[3]

With the overthrow of the Great Seljūqs and the invasion of Khurāsān and the neighbourhood by new groups of Ghuzz, the condition of the settled people in that area deteriorated, the country was laid waste, and the settled population subjected to new inroads by the nomads.[4]

[1] ibid. ff. 250–2.

[2] Or 'the subjects for their good behaviour as subjects.'

[3] ibid. ff. 272–3.

[4] In a letter preserved in the *ʿAtabat al-Katabat*, probably written about this time, reference is made to the unsettled state of affairs. The writer complains of the ruinous state of the country, increasing differences among the people, and

To sum up, the Great Seljūq period marks an important period in the history of land tenure, both in theory and practice, in Persia. The Islamic theory was largely adapted to fit the new circumstances and, where it could not be adapted, relegated to the background. Among the Persian élite of the conquered territories the pre-Islamic conception of the absolute nature of the rule of the sovereign had survived the Islamic conquest (somewhat modified, no doubt, by Islamic theory). With the advent of the Seljūqs this conception of the autocratic sovereign was fused with the conception of the ruling *khān*, who came to be regarded in theory not only as the ruler of the people, but also as enjoying proprietary rights over the territory which he ruled, his powers being limited to a greater or lesser extent by Islamic tradition, i.e. by a belief in a supernatural power to which the *sulṭān* was responsible and under whom he ruled his people as a trust. But, in contradistinction to theory, *de facto* possession of land became (or continued to be) the most important factor in deciding the ownership of the land, as appears to have been recognized by Malikshāh, and, since military power was largely in the hands of the Turks, it was they who, as *de facto* holders, became the owners of vast areas of land. The composition of the landowning class was thus modified to a far greater extent than had been the case under the Arabs. In so far, however, as local administration and the relations between the landowner and the peasant were concerned, the traditional practices appear for the most part to have continued.

After the death of Sanjar, the Great Seljūq empire broke up into a number of succession states forming, broadly speaking, economic-political units. The theory of land and the life of the people in so far as rural organization was concerned probably did not differ much from the Great Seljūq period except in degree: greater or less prosperity and security of tenure depending upon the relative strength and justice of the local ruler and his officials.[1]

their emigration from the district. A group had been with him in Nayshāpūr. They had requested a reduction in their assessment. This had been refused. Since then further calamities, such as hail, untimely cold, the passing through the country of various armies, and the ruin of *kārīz* had afflicted them. He therefore pleads for a reduction in their assessment (ff. 235–40).

[1] Fārs, under the Atābeg Abū Bakr Zangī (557–71/1162–75), was relatively prosperous. Taxes, including *khums*, *suds*, and *ʿushr*, were levied by measurement and valuation on the land and its produce and on trees. There appears, however, to have been an attempt to increase the area held by the state, though not to deny altogether the existence of private property. Abū Bakr Zangī's *vazīr*, ʿImād ud-Dīn Mīrāṣī, made a new settlement, known as the *qānūni mīrāṣī*, and as a result all the estates (*amlāki nafīseh va ẓīāʿ va ʿaqār*) of the great men, *sayyids*, *ʿulamā*, and *qāẓīs*, gradually came into the hands of the officials of the *dīvān*. He appointed *sharīʿa* judges to look into the title-deeds of estates, and only confirmed those which had been in the possession of their owners for fifty years. Anything which had not been held for fifty years or more was confiscated to the *dīvān*. (Fasā'ī, *Fārs Nāmehyi Nāṣirī* (Tehrān, 1894–6), ii. 21.)

CHAPTER IV

THE MONGOLS AND THE BREAK WITH TRADITION

WITH the Mongol invasion of Persia in the thirteenth century the development which had begun with the Muslim conquest was interrupted. The Mongol period can be divided into three main phases: the period of expansion, when the dominant influence was the tradition of the steppe (as it had been during the period of Seljūq expansion); the Īlkhān period which saw the Persianization of the Mongols; and the period of decline. During the Īlkhān period there was an attempt—relatively successful for a time—to subordinate the tribal influence to settled government and, with the conversion of the dynasty under Ghāzān to Islām, an attempt to subordinate Mongol tradition to some extent to Islamic theory. As in the Seljūq period there were further modifications in the composition of the landowning class. Again, as under the Seljūqs, the most serious problems of the Mongols were the tribal and monetary problems, and their failure to solve these two problems was even greater than that of the Seljūqs, and had disastrous results on the agricultural prosperity of the country.[1]

The immediate effect of the Mongol invasion of Persia was widespread devastation and depopulation, and, owing to the massacre or flight of the inhabitants, much land became vacant; in the words of Juvaynī most of the populated and cultivated lands became dead or unclaimed land.[2] Fārs, which was at that time under the Salghārid dynasty (i.e. the Atābegs of Fārs), was a notable exception. It was spared devastation by the timely payment of tribute. The conquered lands were looked upon as the *yurt* of the Mongol ruling family, in which their flocks and those of their followers grazed: the conquered population was not regarded as having any rights *vis-à-vis* the Mongols. It does not appear, however, that in the early period the Mongols regarded themselves as the proprietary owners of the soil although as conquerors they no doubt considered the produce of the land as their right. In due course, however, as the Mongol leaders began to acquire land under proprietary title, by hereditary grant, occupation, and usurpation, land began to fall into the following classes: *yurt*, *dīvānī*, *īnjū*,[3]

[1] Among the tribes which still exist and are believed by tradition to have entered Persia in Mongol times are the Aynālū (Fasā'ī, ii. 309), the Bahārlū (ibid. p. 310), and the Qashqā'ī.

[2] *Ta'rīkh-i-Jahān-Gushā*, i. 118.

[3] See Barthold, 'İlhanlılar Devrinde Malî Vaziyet', *Türk hukuk ve iktisat tarihi mecmuası*, i (1931), pp. 150–2.

ouqāf,[1] and *milkī*. The first-named was nothing but a continuation of the practice of the steppe and did not originally imply proprietary rights over the soil.

Īnjū land was crown land, which was allotted to members of the ruling family; the revenue from it went to meet the expenses of the establishments of the ruler and members of the ruling family and was probably also expended on the upkeep of the army.[2] These lands, however, were not entirely immune from government levies (see p. 87). *Dīvānī* land was state land, but since the distinction between the state and the ruling family was not always clear, the difference between *dīvānī* and *īnjū* land was not always apparent. *Milkī* land was private property.

The extent of the several types of land-holding varied. All lands were subject to confiscation by the state and might at any time become *īnjū* land. Lands were not only confiscated by rulers; their officials also frequently confiscated the estates of their enemies and rivals. For example Rashīd ud-Dīn, the *vazīr* of Ghāzān Khān (reg. 1295–1304), ordered the confiscation to the *dīvān* of the estates of Sharaf ud-Dīn Muẓaffar[3] in the Yazd area. Sharaf ud-Dīn's son protested, and after a sojourn of two years at the royal court, received back the family estates from the *sulṭān*, who sent him to Maybud.[4] Some of the estates of Rashīd ud-Dīn himself also probably derived from confiscations (see below). Usurpation of lands by the powerful *amīrs* and officials became especially common when the power of the central government declined. This was the case particularly after the death of Abū Sa'īd (736/1335). A striking example is the case of Sharaf ud-Dīn Shāh Maḥmūd Īnjū, who had been overseer (*mubāshir*) of crown lands in Fārs. He usurped these and then established a virtually independent governorate.

The vicissitudes to which land was subject are illustrated by the following case. In the *vaqf nāmeh* of the landed property of the Īnjū *sayyids* of Fārs it is stated that a certain *sayyid* Abū Qatāda Zayd Aswad ibn Ibrāhīm ibn Muḥammad ibn Qāsim ibn Ibrāhīm Ṭabāṭabā was brought to Shīrāz from Mecca by 'Aẓud ud-Douleh the Daylamite in 352/963–4. 'Aẓud ud-Douleh gave him his daughter in marriage and made several estates in Fārs into *vaqf* for the male descendants of Zayd Aswad. In due course the estates

[1] Under Taqūdār Aḥmad (reg. 680–3/1281–4) the *shaykh* 'Abd ur-Raḥmān was appointed administrator-general of all *vaqf* in the kingdom and the order was given that their revenues should be devoted exclusively to the purposes for which they were founded (Vaṣṣāf, *Tārīkhi Vaṣṣāf* (lith. 1269), p. 114.

[2] See Barthold, p. 150, and Rashīd ud-Dīn, *Histoire des Mongols de la Perse*, ed. M. Quatremère (Paris, 1836), i. 130, n. 12.

[3] d. 713/1313. He was the father of Mubāriz ud-Dīn Muḥammad, who founded the Muẓaffarid dynasty of Fārs.

[4] Aḥmad b. Ḥusayn, p. 88.

of the Ṭabāṭabā'ī *sayyids* (as his descendants were known) in Fārs became numerous. After the Mongols conquered Fārs they confiscated these estates and they became *īnjū*, i.e. *khāliṣeh* of the *dīvān*. One of the Ṭabāṭabā'ī *sayyids*, Abu'l Mīāman Ḥasan, then went to Abāqā (663–80/1265–81), the ruler of the day, to try to get back his estates and those of his family. He was received with respect and given a *yarlīgh khānī* or royal order for a pension (*tarkhānī*). Some time passed but his affairs did not prosper. Then in the presence of reliable men of the state and the people of the *sharī'a* of the Prophet he transferred half his estates legally in the year 672/1273–4 to the Mongol prince Arghūn (son of Abāqā and grandson of Hūlāgū) and the other half, after the dues of his family had been deducted, to his eldest son, Qutb ud-Dīn Aḥmad. When Aḥmad, the son of Hūlāgū, succeeded his brother Abāqā (in 680/1281), Abu'l Mīāman remained with Arghūn in Khurāsān. Once more all the Ṭabāṭabā'ī estates in Shīrāz were made into *īnjū*, i.e. *khāliṣeh*, until Arghūn succeeded, when a royal *yarlīgh* was issued to the effect that half the Ṭabāṭabā'ī estates should be *īnjū* and half be handed over to Qutb ud-Dīn Aḥmad Ṭabāṭabā'ī. Nearly seventeen years elapsed between the time when Abu'l Mīāman Ḥasan went to the court of Abāqā and Arghūn to get back his estates and his return to Shīrāz. When news of Abu'l Mīāman's death reached Arghūn he ordered a *yarlīgh* to be issued to the effect that half the estates of the Ṭabāṭabā'ī *sayyids* of Shīrāz should be handed over to the possession of Sayyid Qutb ud-Dīn Aḥmad and the other half, which Abu'l Mīāman Ḥasan had given to Arghūn, should be handed over to Qutb ud-Dīn Aḥmad as *īnjū*. Since then the descendants of Qutb ud-Dīn have been known as the Īnjū *sayyids*.[1]

The Mongol leaders continued to own considerable flocks which annually migrated from summer to winter quarters. The royal flocks were under officials known as *qa'ānchīs*. No account appears to have been kept of their transactions, though Ghāzān made an attempt to remedy this.[2] The depredations of owners of flocks were a constant source of anxiety to the settled population in the neighbourhood of their pastures.[3] Not only did the Mongol princes and leaders own large flocks; their ministers also in some cases were the possessors of considerable flocks and herds. According to a letter sent with his will to Moulānā Ṣadr ud-Dīn Muḥam-

[1] Quoted by Fasā'ī, ii. 42. At the time when the *Fārs Nāmeh* was written, i.e. 1304/1886–7, the dignity and rank of the Īnjū *sayyids* had declined. Some of them were living on their hereditary estates and some were engaged in writing documents and title deeds in the *sharī'a* courts.

[2] *T.G.*, pp. 339–40.

[3] For example, Rashīd ud-Dīn in a letter to the people of Khūzistān reports that the *amīrs* of four hundred and the others who wintered their flocks in Mashkūk and Do Bandar had, out of contumaciousness, let their flocks into the crops in those areas (*M.R.*, p. 177).

mad Turkeh, Rashīd ud-Dīn owned 3,000 horses, mares, and other animals in Anatolia, Dīār Bakr, Tabrīz, Kirmān, and Shīrāz, 5,000 she-camels with the Arab tribes, and 5,000 other camels with the Khalaj. He also had 500 flocks of sheep and goats, each of 500 head, in Anatolia, Baghdād, Dīār Bakr, Shīrāz, Tabrīz, Iṣfahān, Māzandarān, Khurāsān, Luristān, and other provinces. Further, he had 10,000 head of cows in the hands of small landowners (*dihāqīn*) and the heads (*ru'asā*) of villages and townships.[1]

When the Mongols began to administer the country they imposed a number of taxes and levies. Among these were *qubchūr* (*qūbchūr*) and *qilān*: the former appears to have been a cattle-tax. The taxable minimum was 100 head and the rate at which the tax was levied 1 per cent.[2] Under Ghāzān Khān it was paid by villagers and by nomads. The villagers paid in two equal instalments, at the Nou Rūz and at the autumn solstice; in either case the tax had to be paid within twenty days. The nomads paid in one instalment at the Nou Rūz; the tax similarly had to be paid within twenty days.[3] The term *qubchūr* was also used to cover certain casual imposts.[4] The precise meaning of *qilān* is uncertain. Barthold takes it to be a tax on cultivated land and generally levied upon villages.[5] He quotes a *shikāyat nāmeh* of the period of the Central Asian ruler Tuqluq Tīmūr (1348–62/3) in which it is mentioned that under the old Mongol *khāns* no *qilān* tax was taken from *īnjū* gardens (or garden proprietors).[6] This would support the theory that it was some kind of tax levied on land, but is not in itself conclusive, nor are the other examples he quotes. Thus, for example, the *yarlīgh* of Ghāzān Khān to the effect that those who were under the protection of the hunters were from then onwards to be included among those who were subject to *qilān* gives no clear indication of the nature of the tax or levy.[7] From various references in the *Tārīkhi Ghāzānī* it would appear that the *qilān* tax was not a tax already established in the conquered territories of Persia and hence it seems unlikely that it was *kharāj* or land tax (though Radloff translates it thus).[8] Discussing the reign of Ghāzān Khān Rashīd ud-Dīn states that

he advised his *amīrs*, *yārghūchīs*, and *vazīrs* not immediately to accept

[1] *M.R.*, p. 235.

[2] It seems to have been used also in a general sense to denote a levy or tax (cf. Rashīd ud-Dīn, *Histoire des Mongols de la Perse*, p. 256, n. 83). It appears to be used in a general sense to mean levy or tax in Juvaynī, i. 22.

[3] *T.G.*, p. 264.

[4] See M. Mīnovī and V. Minorsky, 'Naṣīr al-Dīn Ṭūsī on Finance', *B.S.O.A.S.*, x. 784.

[5] op. cit. pp. 151–2.

[6] ibid. p. 151.

[7] See A. C. M. d'Ohsson, *Histoire des Mongols* (Hague, Amsterdam, 1834–5), v. 440.

[8] *Uigurische Sprachdenkmaeler*, No. 22, pp. 28–32 (quoted by Barthold).

the words of a group of persons who came before them to complain against some governor (*ḥākim*) or *mutaṣarrif*, because it might be that that group had not formerly given *qilān*, having shifted their burden on to others and that the governor [in question] had included them among those liable to *qilān*: such people would of course complain.[1]

Similarly, in a *yarlīgh* assigning *iqṭā*'s to the Mongol army it is stated: 'these *iqṭā*'s have been fixed for [settled on] those soldiers (*mardumi chirīk*) who are included in [are liable to] *qilān* and called up for service (*?kūch dihand*)'.[2] In another passage concerning Ghāzān Khān's prohibition of large dowries on the grounds that these prevented divorce, which was held in certain circumstances to be desirable in the interest of increasing the population, the text reads:

> If a man is doubtful concerning the friendship and agreement of a wife, he should be able to separate from her without any discussion, anxiety or hindrance. [It was desirable that] men should have children, and responsibility for the sustenance of these is upon the father. If the substance of the father is consumed by the dowry of his wife, whence, when he must undertake *qilān* or serve as a soldier, will the sustenance of his children and what is necessary for *qilān* and his work be provided?[3]

In the new assessment for Iṣfahān made under Rashīd ud-Dīn a tax on cultivated land is mentioned at the same time as exemption from *qilān*.[4] Similarly, in a letter from Rashīd ud-Dīn to the governor of Ahvāz and Shūshtar land tax is mentioned and also *qilān* for the *umarā* of the *khān* (see p. 95). From these passages it would seem that *qilān* is rather some sort of corvée for military service, agricultural labour, or public works.[5] Such a meaning, moreover, would not be contrary to the examples quoted by Barthold.

Local officials known as *bāsqāqs*, and sometimes appointed by the military commander, were charged with the collection of the revenue. In provinces where the government taxes were levied in kind, chiefly by valuation or as a definite share of the crop, the governors and tax-collectors were able to extort more than they should and to impose new dues. In most years they would demand the taxes in advance and when converting the share due in kind into cash so contrive the transaction that the loss fell upon the peasants and cultivators.[6] Further, the taxes were in many cases collected several times a year. Little, however, was remitted to the central treasury, which in spite of all kinds of impositions made on the people remained empty.

[1] *T.G.*, p. 180. [2] ibid. p. 308. [3] ibid. p. 324.
[4] See below, p. 94.
[5] In Kirmān at the present day *qalūn* (?= *qilān*) is used for *bīgārī*, i.e. corvée, and *qalūnī* for *bīgārī*, 'one who performs such labour'.
[6] *T.G.*, p. 267.

It appears that the revenues of the provinces were in some cases farmed, and that the revenue farmers extracted double the amount of the sum for which they had contracted but paid nothing into the treasury. As a result when money was needed for the army, the protection of the frontiers, or some public work, there was none in the treasury and it was necessary to have recourse to confiscations and to make extraordinary levies (*nimārī*) and to take advances from the people. Disorder and anarchy on that account prevailed in the kingdom and the army was weak and without equipment and provisions.[1] Officials of all kinds lived on the country. *Īlchīs* with their large trains as they passed through the country made all kinds of requisitions on the peasantry in spite of the fact that the government also levied taxes for their entertainment and had established post stations (*yām*) throughout the empire to provide for their needs. These *īlchīs* would be dispatched on the slightest pretext and were often accompanied by as many as 500 or 1,000 cavalry. They would stir up local disputes (in order to extract money for settling them) and would take the animals of the peasants, travellers, and others. They were held in great disrepute, and the decline in the countryside was largely brought about by the outrages they committed. Robbers would even pretend they were *īlchīs* and seize animals from the peasants and others on this pretext.[2] The royal hunters, of whom there were large numbers throughout the empire, were another source of oppression. They, too, lived on the country, and like the *īlchīs*, revenue officials and others would seize the peasants' mules and donkeys, a practice that was clearly disastrous to agricultural work.[3] Moreover, they caught the pigeons which were a valuable source of manure.[4]

Another custom which was contrary to the well-being of the peasants and the countryside in general was that of writing drafts upon provincial districts. This was no novelty: it was practised in Seljūq and pre-Seljūq times, but it had not reached the proportions to which it was carried in Mongol times. As financial disorder and official corruption increased and the general level of prosperity declined, it became more difficult to realize these drafts and it became customary to send military expeditions to collect the sums assigned in them. The writing of drafts on provincial districts was in itself, apart from the methods adopted to collect what was assigned, a fruitful source of peculation and extortion. The money and goods so collected would be shared between the officials passing through the districts and the local officials. Revenue was swallowed up in this way, and nothing remitted to the treasury.

In the same way the military were largely paid by drafts drawn

[1] *T.G.*, p. 258.
[2] ibid. pp. 270–4.
[3] ibid. pp. 341–3.
[4] ibid. p. 348.

upon the provinces. When the tax-collectors delayed in remitting these, the soldiery themselves used to go to the provinces and demand the payment of the drafts by force and make special levies of animals and fodder.[1]

Such was the extortion practised by officials that on the approach of the tax-collectors the peasants would leave their villages. Rashīd ud-Dīn relates that anyone visiting the villages of Yazd would not find a single person to speak to or from whom to inquire the way. The few persons who had remained in the villages would appoint watchmen. When warned of the approach of someone they would hide in the *kahrīz* (i.e. the underground water channels) or in the sand dunes. If any of the large landowners from Yazd went to see their villages, they would find them deserted.[2] He tells a story of a landowner who went to Fīrūzābād, one of the large villages of Yazd, to see if he could collect something from the yield of an estate which he had there. For three days he tried in vain to get hold of one of the *kadkhudās*. All he found were seventeen tax-collectors with bills and drafts on the place waiting there. They had taken a *dashtbān* and two peasants whom they had found in the fields, brought them into the middle of the village, where they had tied them up, and were beating them to induce them to produce food and to disclose the whereabouts of the other peasants.[3] The ruin of the country, indeed, was alleged never to have been equalled in any other time.[4] The peasants in many cases were in need of seed, but such were the straits to which they were reduced that even if the *dīvān* provided them with seed they used this (for food) and did not sow it.[5]

Lastly, public order was at a very low ebb. Large numbers of fugitive slaves and disaffected elements were roaming the countryside. They had an organized spy system and the local people were often forced to enter into league with them, in the hope of thereby escaping their depredations.[6]

Financial disorder and corruption were extreme when Ghāzān ascended the throne in 694/1295. He realized the difficulty of immediate reform and determined to go slowly. His first measure was to prohibit the writing of drafts on the peasants by the lower grades of tax-collectors (*mutaṣarrifs*). He ordered the *bītikchīs* (revenue officials) to go to the provinces and make a list of the property of all villages. It is claimed in a *yarlīgh* quoted by Rashīd ud-Dīn that as a result of this many places which had never before been registered were assessed.[7] Those in undisputed possession of *īnjū* land, *ouqāf* land, and hereditary grants were to

[1] ibid. pp. 300–1.
[2] ibid. p. 249.
[3] ibid. p. 251.
[4] ibid. p. 349.
[5] ibid. p. 346.
[6] ibid. pp. 277–9.
[7] ibid. p. 258.

be confirmed and the properties to be registered in their names. Thus, as in Seljūq times, in the interests of public order the person in possession was regarded as owner.

Bītikchīs, *maliks*, and *bāsqāqs* were forbidden under threat of punishment to write drafts on the land. One *bītikchī* was appointed to each province and made responsible to the *dīvān*. The revenue demand was to be paid in two instalments to an official known as the *ṣāḥib jamʿ*, one of whom was appointed to each province, and to be remitted to the central treasury. The tax was to be levied normally in cash and not in kind. Where the tax was paid in kind, the goods delivered by the peasants were to be taken to the bazaar and sold. Any contravention of this by officials was to be punished.[1] In some areas, such as Baghdād, land tax (*kharāj*) was to be paid in cash (*vujūh al-ʿayn*) when the summer crops were harvested. Regulations were made for the delivery of the quota on winter and summer crops in the *garmsīr* and the *sardsīr*. In the *garmsīr* the quota in wheat and barley etc. was to be transported at a fixed date by the owner to the state granary and handed over to a receiver within twenty days. In the *sardsīr*, winter and summer crops were similarly to be transported within a period of twenty days.[2]

Ever-increasing financial stringency is the keynote to the Īlkhān period prior to the reign of Ghāzān Khān. Not only were taxes levied several times over, but the taxes on the land were collected in advance. Thus Vaṣṣāf has a significant passage referring to the year 694/1295 which reads

> Since no money remained in the treasury because in that year in the course of eight months three rulers had succeeded to the throne and twice in the far corners of the empire there had been large military expeditions, inevitably demands for payments in advance (*taqdimeh*)[3] and extraordinary levies (*nimārī*) were made and *mavāshī* had been taken at the rate of 20 per cent in most of the tax districts, especially in Fārs.[4]

Further, Rashīd ud-Dīn states that prior to Ghāzān Khān

> even if the *mutaṣarrifs* did not write drafts on the revenue in favour of anyone at the end of the year when they presented their accounts the whole revenue had been dissipated and they had outstanding claims [i.e. the amount they collected was insufficient to meet the expenses of collection].[5]

[1] *T.G.*, pp. 253–4. When the peasants paid their taxes two further payments were taken from them known as *dah o nīm* and *ḥaqqi khazāneh*. Both were probably dues levied for the expenses of the tax-collectors, the former possibly being an additional levy of 10½ per cent on the harvest or on the amount due by way of tax.

[2] ibid. pp. 264–5.

[3] i.e. that which is taken in advance (Muḥammad b. Maḥmud Āmulī, *Nafā'is ul-Funūn* (Tehrān, lithog.), i. 88). In modern Kirmānī usage *taqdimeh* means an advance given to a peasant.

[4] *Tārīkhi Vaṣṣāf*, p. 326 (quoted by Barthold, op. cit. p. 155).

[5] *T.G.*, pp. 255–6; Barthold, op. cit. p. 157.

Rashīd ud-Dīn goes on to compare the conditions prevailing under Ghāzān Khān with the unsatisfactory state of affairs which had existed formerly:

at the present time the kingdom is flourishing. From the provinces a surplus remains from the harvest (*irtifāʿ*) in the hands of the *mutaṣarrifs* and last year's grain is held in the granaries so that it is not necessary to give it to the people by way of *ṭarḥ* and nor is it necessary to sell it with haste every year as soon as it ripens. Whereas formerly grain was pledged in advance before it had ripened, now the *dīvān* has one year's grain in the granaries and money in the treasury.[1]

It is not absolutely clear from this extract whether the government was forced to sell its share of the harvest in advance in order to obtain badly needed money or whether the tax demand being made in advance on the peasants they were forced to sell their grain on the stalk in order to meet these demands. Barthold takes it to mean that *ṭarḥ* was some sort of advance given to the peasant. It is possible that it was rather some sort of practice by which the government forced the peasants to buy its share of the harvest in advance at a fixed price. This would have been an additional way for the government to provide itself with badly needed cash.[2]

The habit of writing bills on the provinces and the extortion of governors was to some extent stopped. But it was found that the tendency towards extortion ran right through the hierarchy of officialdom and society in general, and that, in spite of Ghāzān's reforms, the *kadkhudās* and *ruʾasā* continued to levy more than they ought from the individual tax-payers. These officials were accordingly forced to send a detailed list of each tax-payer's liability to the *dīvān*. As a result revenues were alleged to have come in, civil and military expenses were paid, and the granaries were full.[3] In some cases drafts on the revenue, however, were still made for the payment of pensions and salaries.[4] Farming of the revenue also continued in a modified form. In a letter to the people of Khūzistān, Rashīd ud-Dīn informs them that Sirāj ud-Dīn Dizfūlī, the tax-collector, was to farm the province of Bayāt to the *ruʾasā* and *ṣudūr* of that place for a fixed sum and to use the produce thereof for the salaries of *amīrs* of four hundred provided they demanded their dues at harvest time.[5]

Detailed instructions were given in a *yarlīgh* to *bāsqāqs*, *mulūk*,

[1] *T.G.*, p. 256. Ḥamdullāh Mustoufī also alleges an increase in the prosperity of the country under Ghāzān Khān compared with the earlier Mongol period. He points out, however, that there had been a marked decline in the revenue since Seljūq times and even more since Sasanian times. (*Geographical Part of the Nuzhat-al-Qulūb*, p. 27.)

[2] See also p. 103, n. 3.

[3] *T.G.*, pp. 254–6.

[4] See, for example, *M.R.*, pp. 18–19, 42–3, 255, 262.

[5] ibid. p. 179.

navvāb, *mutaṣarrifs*, *quẓāt*, *sādāt*, *imāms*, *ṣudūr*, landowners (? *arbāb*), prominent persons, trusted persons, *ru'asā*, *kadkhudās*, peasants in general (*'umūmi ra'āyā*) and townspeople, as to how the people were to be informed of their liabilities, the method of collection, and the time-limit for the payment of their dues. One per cent extra was to be taken from those who procrastinated. Anyone who contravened the regulations was to receive seventy strokes.[1] Levies known as *tamghā* were to be paid according to different arrangements in the various provinces as set forth in notifications posted up in public places. No dues were to be increased or new dues imposed.[2]

These regulations appear to have been applied not only to land in the possession of the *dīvān* but also to land assigned to the Mongol princesses (*khavātīn*), princes, and *amīrs*, i.e. to *īnjū* land, to *iqṭā's* entrusted to the army (see below), and all lands on which were assigned the payment of allowances of whatever kind and which had consequently been entrusted to individuals, land disposed of by way of gift, and *ouqāf*.[3]

In certain provinces where the government dues were assessed on the produce, i.e. a definite share of the produce was taken by way of tax, or where they were assessed by valuation, notably in Baghdād and Fārs, conditions had been abnormally bad. The governors and tax-collectors used to levy all kinds of new dues and usually demanded the taxes in advance (*bi taqdimeh*), and often raised the conversion rates. Ghāzān Khān remedied this state of affairs so that the sums due were levied according to the assessment, and villages were given in perpetuity to the *qāẓīs* and *muqṭa's* on condition that they paid double the amount at which these places had formerly been assessed, though this amount had never in fact been paid.[4]

Ghāzān, presumably because he realized that insecurity of tenure was one of the reasons for the prevailing decay, attempted to secure the position of the peasants and the landowners in their title to the land by a series of measures. His conferment of proprietary rights where occupation was undisputed has already been mentioned (pp. 83-94). He further decreed that no disputed property was to be bought by the mothers, the widows,[5] the wives, children, daughters, or sons-in-law of *amīrs* of ten thousands, or *amīrs* of tens, hundreds, or thousands, Mongols, or *bītikchīs* of the great *dīvān*. *Qāẓīs*, 'Alids, religious leaders, *shaykhs*, and *ru'asā* were

[1] *T.G.*, pp. 257–63.

[2] ibid. pp. 262–3. *Tamghā* covered various kinds of *octroi* and also in some cases was used for a capital levy (see Mīnovī and Minorsky, *B.S.O.A.S.*, x. 781). See also Barthold, op. cit., pp. 153–5.

[3] *T.G.*, p. 266.

[4] ibid. p. 267.

[5] The reading of the text is doubtful.

not to write a title-deed in the name of a member of any of these groups when land was in dispute. The cost of a seal for orders written by a *qāẓī* on land was to be 19½ *dīnārs*. A special office was set up to record the sale of lands and mortgages.[1]

Injū lands were meanwhile assigned to the male heirs of princes by Ghāzān to obviate the need of making levies on the population for the upkeep of their households. These lands were separated from the *dīvān* and given over into the possession of the princes. All his own *injū* lands he made into a *vaqf* for his male children by his chief wife, and if she had no male issue they were to go to the sons of his other wives. At the time of the composition of the *Tārīkhi Ghāzānī* all the *injū* lands were alleged to have been in the hands of the *nā'ibs* (representatives or deputies) of Ghāzān's wives, and were well cultivated. When the army was in need of money, he ordered drafts to be made on them for 1 million *dīnārs*.[2] Two points are worthy of notice here. In the first place, it is not, by Islamic law, legal to constitute a *vaqf* for unborn children of the first generation.[3] Secondly, the grants were subject to demands for extraordinary levies.

According to the *yāsā* of Chinghīz Khān claims to land lapsed after thirty years if they were not preferred during that period. Under Malikshāh a similar practice had prevailed (p. 69). Ghāzān, as had Malikshāh before him, sought to give religious validity to this regulation and induced the *qāẓī* Fakhr ud-Dīn Harāt to write a decree to the effect that land claims would lapse after thirty years. Any *qāẓīs* disobeying it were threatened with dismissal. A *yarlīgh* to this effect was issued in Rajab 699/1300.[4] Its main object, as had been that of Malikshāh's decree, was to prevent dishonest persons making claims to lands to which they had no title, and to obviate the misuse of documents which, after sale or inheritance, had remained in or fallen into the hands of unauthorized persons. Old documents were to be annulled and new ones to be written in the *qāẓī's* office and on the sale of property, old documents were to be annulled, or in cases where only part of the property was sold, the necessary adjustments were to be made in the document.[5] The scribe who wrote the documents was to be paid at the rate of 1 *dirham* per 100 *dīnārs*. The *mudīr* who testified to a claim was to receive half a currency *dīnār*.[6] Instructions were given to the *qāẓīs* to decide land cases on the basis of equity and not according to the strict rules of evidence as laid down in the *sharīʿa*. Claims were to be carefully investigated with a view to preventing the establishment of false claims.

From a document concerning a case of disputed land ownership

[1] *T.G.*, pp. 219–20. [2] ibid. pp. 330–1. [3] See below, p. 231.
[4] *T.G.*, pp. 221–2. [5] ibid. p. 228. [6] ibid. pp. 228–9.

dated 791/1389 it would appear that the *qāẓīs* maintained some degree of independence in the decision of land cases. The document concerns a dispute over land in Kuhan Harzan[1] in Āẕarbāyjān. One of the parties to the dispute was Khwājeh Ghīāṣ ud-Dīn Muḥammad ibn Khwājeh Rashīd ad-Dīn Muḥammad, who had at some time or other been a *vazīr* and was, therefore, presumably a man of some influence. He and his brother Kamāl ud-Dīn Muḥammad had, according to the document, been involved for some time in a dispute over some land with the descendants of a certain Pīr Ayyūb and the peasants of Kuhan Harzan. Shihāb ʿAlī, the *qāẓī* of the *muʿaskar*, was ordered to investigate the case in accordance with the *sharīʿa*. Shihāb ʿAlī, therefore, had immediately summoned the *kadkhudās* of Kuhan Harzan, and the parties to the dispute had nominated their *vakīls*. The substance of the dispute was that 2 *dāng* of the lands of the estate in question had been usurped by Ghīāṣ ud-Dīn, and the other party demanded their return with compensation. Ghīāṣ ud-Dīn's *vakīls* demanded a delay to enable them to produce two legal witnesses and legal proof of their client's ownership. After two days two witnesses were brought who testified that 4 *dāng* of the estate were the property of Khwājeh Rashīd ud-Dīn Muḥammad Tabrīzī and the other 2 *dāng* had been bought by him from Pīr Ayyūb. The representatives acting for the sons of Rashīd ud-Dīn were unable to furnish documentary proof in support of this claim. The other party was then required to bring forward four persons to swear that Rashīd ud-Dīn Muḥammad had not bought 2 *dāng* of the property from their father. Four of the *kadkhudās* and elders of the village accordingly came forward and bore witness to this. A decision was then given in favour of the descendants of Pīr Ayyūb and the peasants of Kuhan Harzan, to the effect that

> 2 complete *dāng* of the 6 *dāng* of the fields (*arāẓī*) of the hamlets (*mazāriʿ*) of Alākī, which are held jointly and undivided (*mushāʿ*), are the right (*ḥaqq*) and property of the peasants (*raʿāyā*) of the township of Old Harzan, with absolute and full rights of possession. This right (*ḥaqq*) belongs to them, and the property (*milk*) belongs to them, and the estate (*ʿaqār*) belongs to them. They have full legal rights of ownership over it, and this [document] is a legal record of what occurred. Dated the last day of Rabīʿ II 791 [27 April 1389].[2]

Originally the Mongol army was formed by a compulsory levy on the people[3] and received no payment; a levy on horses, sheep, oxen, felt, and curds (*qurūt*), etc., was made on all who served for

[1] Now known as Harzandi ʿAtīq.

[2] This document belongs to Mr Muḥsin Ganjeh'ī, and was on view in the museum of the Faculty of Arts of Tabrīz University in September 1949.

[3] Juvaynī, i. 22–3.

the expenses of the camp and for the sustenance of any soldier who was poor. Subsequently a small allowance of provisions was given to those who served. Gradually their pay was increased. It was given chiefly in the form of drafts. As stated above, these drafts remained for the most part unpaid, and because of the difficulty the soldiers had in collecting their pay it became customary for them to sell their drafts to brokers (? *īdājīs*) at half their value. Ghāzān, after some four to five years, took steps to remedy this state of affairs. He ordered the proceeds of the requisitions on the land in favour of the soldiers to be put in store-houses at harvest time and entrusted to the *shihneh* or military governor of the province, who was to pay them and meet their bills in cash at the proper time. Further, the able-bodied peasants (? *būkāvulān*)[1] were not to be pressed into service, and special provisions and fodder were not to be requisitioned by the military. As a result of this, at least some of the bills were paid in cash by the *dīvān*.[2]

However, Ghāzān's reforms were not entirely successful, and in 703/1303–4 he decided, instead of issuing drafts to the soldiery, to transfer to them the land on which these drafts were made as their *iqṭā'*s, and to define their shares so that they would see these and consider them their own. The main reasons which had led him to take this step were that not more than 20 per cent of the drafts which were issued were paid. Secondly, when it went on an expedition the army disturbed the country through which it passed because the soldiers used to claim, whether rightly or wrongly, that they had nothing and must therefore live on the land, and they used to take the peasants' animals, alleging that their own beasts had died. In such circumstances it was not possible to equip an army quickly, or to raise money rapidly or easily to meet some sudden emergency. Thirdly, it appears that most of the soldiers desired to own estates and to practise agriculture.

Ghāzān accordingly came to the conclusion that if the military were provided with *iqṭā'*s they would both achieve their desires and also no longer be a drain on the treasury. Thus, broadly the same sequence of events is followed as in late Abbasid times, but the precise details of Ghāzān's system were rather different: the soldiers themselves became responsible for the cultivation, and the actual holdings appear to have been relatively small. What class of land was distributed to them in this way is not mentioned: presumably it was land taken over by the Mongols which had formerly been crown lands, or land which had fallen vacant because of the death or flight of its former owners. Ghāzān's grants raised a somewhat different problem from that raised by the grant of *iqṭā'*s by the

[1] Barthold translates 'overseers of food and drink' (*Turkestān down to the Mongol Invasion*, p. 382).

[2] *T.G.*, pp. 300–1.

Seljūqs. In the case of the 'administrative' and 'military' *iqṭā*'s of the Seljūqs the existing rights of the landowners were in some measure preserved, the *muqṭa*' being interposed between the *sulṭān* and the landowner and peasants. But in the case of Ghāzān's grants the Mongol soldier appears to have been interposed immediately between the government and the peasants, who were to pay their dues direct to the military instead of to the *dīvān*. The villages were assigned with the peasants who lived in them: any peasants who had left an area thus assigned during the previous thirty years were to be sent back. The assignees were not to accept peasants from other provinces, nor were they to transfer peasants from one village to another on the grounds that both villages were theirs.[1]

These *iqṭā*'s were assigned to the commanders of thousands, who in turn divided the land among the commanders of hundreds, who were charged with the detailed distribution of the individual *iqṭā*'. This distribution was then communicated to the central government. The land was to be divided by lot, and a share of good and waste-land was to be entered in the register against the name of each holder. One copy of this was to be held in the *dīvān* and one by the commanders of thousands; copies of the division made by the commanders of hundreds were to be held by them.[2] Dead lands in the areas assigned in this way were to be cultivated by the holders by the labour of captives and slaves. The whole produce was to go to the holders. If anyone else, moreover, put forward a claim to these dead lands (in the assigned areas) and substantiated it, 10 per cent of the produce was to be paid to the *dīvān*, the rest to be shared between the military who had cultivated the land and the owner.[3] A *bītikchī* was to be sent annually to see who had exerted himself in improving the cultivation of his holding and who had failed to do this. The former were to be singled out by a special mark of favour and the latter to be punished. These grants were not alienable by sale or gift. In the case of the death of the holder, a near relative could be appointed as his deputy. If he had no issue, one of his slaves would be appointed in his place and failing that someone else belonging to his hundred. In the case of misdemeanour land was transferred by the *amīr* from the holder to someone else and the transfer duly registered.[4]

The soldiers (*chirīk*) were not to incorporate neighbouring lands into their *iqṭā*'s, to make them into *yurt*, or to prevent persons using their pastures. No bills were to be written on these lands. The only obligation of the soldier was to pay 50 *manni tabrīz*[5] (?grain) to the royal *aṃbār*.[6]

[1] *T.G.*, pp. 305–6.
[2] ibid. pp. 307–8.
[3] ibid. p. 306.
[4] ibid. p. 308.
[5] See Appendix III.
[6] *T.G.*, p. 307.

Owing to the circumstances of the Mongol invasion and Mongol rule large areas in Persia and the neighbourhood had become dead lands, but there was a general reluctance to reclaim these because they were believed to be *dīvānī*, *īnjū*, or private lands.[1] Ghāzān in his efforts to increase the prosperity of the country and to bring these back into cultivation, classified them into three groups. First were those lands having water available which did not require much labour to be reclaimed. On these nothing was taken in the first year; in the second year one-third of the *dīvān* dues was paid, the remaining two-thirds going to the man who had reclaimed it, together with all other proceeds; and in the third year three-quarters of the *dīvān* dues was levied. Second were those lands where a moderate amount of labour was needed to provide water. In the first year nothing was paid on these; in the second year one-third of the *dīvān* dues, and in the third year two-thirds. Third were those lands to reclaim which a dam had to be constructed or a *kahrīz* (underground irrigation channel) repaired. Nothing was paid on these in the first year, one-third of the *dīvān* dues in the second year, and half in the third year. Anyone reclaiming dead land acquired thereby rights of ownership and rights of sale. Land tax was subsequently fixed on these lands by analogy (*qīās*), since the levy of land tax by valuation (*ḥarz*) or in the form of a share of the crop (*muqāsameh*) were to be abolished. A *dīvāni khāliṣeh* was set up to deal with dead lands which were *khāliṣeh*.[2] In those provinces where it had been formerly the custom to give one-tenth by valuation to the *dīvān*, dead lands privately owned when reclaimed paid the same rates as those set out above to the *dīvān*, unless the former owner reappeared, in which case half these rates went to him. Elsewhere where there had been no tax levied by valuation no tax was paid on the produce to the *dīvān*, the full rate as set out above going to the owner. In Mongol *yurts*, since it was unlikely the Mongols would allow the peasants access to cultivate the lands, dead lands were to be cultivated by their own slaves.[3] Dead lands were to be registered and registration renewed every two years by the *dīvāni khāliṣeh* for purposes of control.[4]

In order to relieve the peasants of the impositions of the *īlchīs*, Ghāzān reorganized the post (*yām*) and confined its use to official envoys. Each post-house was entrusted to an *amīr* who was allotted funds more than sufficient for its upkeep.[5] Hunting parties were then forbidden to live on the country or to use the post-horses.[6] Private individuals were forbidden to send *īlchīs*. An order was published to the effect that *īlchīs* were given all the money

[1] ibid. pp. 351–2.
[2] ibid. pp. 353–4.
[3] ibid. p. 355.
[4] ibid. p. 356.
[5] ibid. p. 274.
[6] ibid. p. 275.

they required for their journeys and were not to take anything from the country as they passed through. The fodder for their animals was provided by the state.[1]

To improve public order the provision of the *yāsā* of Chinghīz Khān obliging the members of a caravan to act together against robbers was reaffirmed, and to refrain from co-operation was made a crime.[2] The nearest garrison was bound, in the event of robbers appearing, to pursue them, and anyone aiding and abetting robbers was threatened with heavy punishment. Road guards (*rāhdār*) were established on the more dangerous roads. They were entitled to levy ½ *āqcheh* per four loaded quadrupeds or per two loaded camels. Nothing was to be levied on foodstuffs, grain, or unloaded beasts. It was alleged that these measures achieved their purpose.[3]

How far in general Ghāzān's efforts at reform were successful on a long-term view is doubtful. The moment control was relaxed there was a tendency to relapse into the old habits, and thus it was a constant struggle to restrain the officials from committing extortion against those under their power. This is clear from the letters of Rashīd ud-Dīn to his sons and others. In a letter to his son Jalāl ud-Dīn, the governor of Anatolia, he recommends his son to follow certain precepts. The twenty-fourth is a recommendation to return the estates of the weak, which usurping *bītikchīs* and powerful *navvāb* had seized and made into *dīvān* land.[4] Writing to Ṭakhṭākh Īnjū, governor of Shīrāz, he states that the people of Shīrāz had complained of his (Ṭakhṭākh's) levying irregular taxes. Reproving the *amīr*, he threatens him with punishment if he does not abandon his oppression and continues to trouble the people of that area by levying irregular taxes and *ṭayyārāti dīvānī*[5] without authorization. Rashīd ud-Dīn was meanwhile sending his son, Ibrāhīm, to Shīrāz to attend to affairs there. He was to take from the *mutaṣarrifs* and *bītikchīs* the accounts for past years and to tax the people according to the assessment (*qānūn*) fixed by the *dīvān*, to remit the tax to the treasury, so act that the people were at ease, and to return to anyone whatever had been taken unjustly.[6] In another letter, addressed to the officials and people of Sīvās, he states that reports had reached him that the revenue of the *ouqāf* of the *dār us-sayyāda* of Sīvās was not being put to its proper use, and the property was decaying. This is attributed to the tyranny

[1] *T.G.*, p. 276.

[2] ibid. p. 279.

[3] ibid. pp. 280–1.

[4] See *M.R.*, pp. 78–93.

[5] According to Naṣīr ud-Dīn Ṭūsī, this was revenue derived from four classes of property: 'property which escheats to the state, [property] belonging to the king, which has been appropriated by others, lost things, and the property of those who are absent.' (See Mīnovī and Minorsky, *B.S.O.A.S.*, x. 774.) The term would seem here to mean rather extraordinary levies or dues. See above p. 73, n. 6.

[6] *M.R.*, pp. 168–71.

of the *mutavallīs* and those in charge. They were to be replaced by better people. If the decline in the revenue of the endowments was due to the ruined condition of the villages, the *dīvān* revenue was to be devoted to making the villages populous; but if the decline was because of drafts and extraordinary levies, made by the *dīvān*, the endowments were to be exempted from such drafts and levies.[1]

At times Rashīd ud-Dīn had to remonstrate with his own sons. For example, in a letter to his son Maḥmūd, the governor (*ḥākim*) of Kirmān, he states that spies had informed him that Maḥmūd had committed oppression against the people of Bam, and that he had reduced them to extremities by levies made on the country for his own expenses and dues for the *dīvān*, repeated royal drafts, *qilān*,[2] taxes on flocks (*qubchūr*), levies for soldiers, and various extraordinary taxes. Accordingly for three years the district was to be exempt from *qilān*, *qubchūr*, *ṭayyārāt*,[3] and the *dīvān* dues of Kirmān and dues for the great court, so that ruined places and barren villages should be made populous. Further, seed, money for agricultural implements, and advances were to be given to the people from the produce of the Rashīdī estates in the district of Bam.[4]

In another letter, to his son ʿAbd ul-Mu'min, governor of Simnān, Dāmghān, and Khwār, Rashīd ud-Dīn mentions that the *qāẓī* of Simnān had told him that his villages and hamlets (*mazāriʿ*) in Simnān, Khwār, and Dāmghān had become ruined and barren because of the impositions, dues, and extraordinary levies of the *dīvān* and were lacking in seed and agricultural implements. Rashīd ud-Dīn accordingly ordered his son to make no drafts or demands on these estates and to exempt them from all *dīvān* dues.[5]

Injunctions to treat the peasants well are frequent in Rashīd ud-Dīn's letters. Probably this amounted to little more than a pious wish. For example, Sunqur Bāvurchī is enjoined to treat the small landowners (*dihāqīn*) and crop-sharing peasants (*muzāraʿān*) kindly and to collect the taxes in such a way that he would win for himself a good name.[6]

The general tendency throughout the period was for the incidence of taxation to be increased either by raising the rate or by the imposition of new levies. Ghāzān's attempts to control this tendency have already been referred to. The rates probably varied in the different provinces. New assessments were made from time to time. Writing to Moulānā Ṣadr ud-Dīn Muḥammad

[1] ibid. pp. 156–9.
[2] See above, pp. 80–1.
[3] See above, p. 92, n. 5.
[4] *M.R.*, pp. 10–12.
[5] ibid. pp. 27–9.
[6] ibid. p. 13. He was governor of Baṣra at the time.

Turkeh, Rashīd ud-Dīn, after referring to the poverty of the people of Iṣfahān, states that Khwājeh 'Alī Fīrūzānī had been sent to make a new assessment (*qānūn*) and to annul the old registers (*dafātir*) which had been current in the time of the 'oppressive Turks and *bītikchīs*'. It had been settled that the people of Iṣfahān should pay one-tenth on cultivated land (*mazrū'ī*), one-twentieth for *tamghā*, one-half *ṭassūj* per sheep or goat, one *ṭassūj* per ox (or cow), two *ṭassūj* per horse, and three *ṭassūj* per camel. The produce of orchards was to be carefully valued by the officials and the *kharāj* on it fixed. The estates of the people were to be exempt from extraordinary taxes, *qilān* and *qubchūr*, and whereas they formerly provided 1,000 mounted *chirīk*, they were only to give 500, and the wages and daily sustenance of these *chirīk* were to be a charge on the tax of Iṣfahān. Dues in wood, soap, fruit, cloth, and such like, which were levied in Iṣfahān were to be done away with entirely and expunged from the register. Instructions had been sent to all parts of the kingdom that a new assessment should be made after the fashion of Iṣfahān.[1]

It is unlikely, however, that uniformity of practice was in fact established. In another letter, after reproving his son Shihāb ud-Dīn, then governor (*ḥākim*) of Tustar (Shūshtar) and Ahvāz, for surrounding himself with an evil entourage, Rashīd ud-Dīn sets out a number of precepts for his guidance. Whether this letter precedes the letter quoted above is not clear because neither is dated. Precept No. 37 advises him to appoint well-to-do tax-collectors over the province of Khūzistān because such persons would not try to deprive the people of their goods. The persons appointed should moreover be just, trustworthy, able, and knowledgeable about the area, knowing where the original tax could be levied and whence extraordinary levies could be obtained.[2] The tax-collector should be chivalrous, protect the noble-born, provide for their means of sustenance and exempt their estates from taxation, and should content himself with the dues and assignment which were allotted to him by the *dīvān*.[3] No. 39 states that Rashīd ud-Dīn had exempted some of the *bulūk* of Tustar from *tamghā* and *nimār* (?). *Kharāj* was to be taken at the rate of 10 per cent in kind. Shihāb ud-Dīn was to continue to hold exempt those private estates which had been exempted. The *dīvān* taxes (*mināli dīvānī*)[4] were to be taken in kind at the rate of 6 *kharvār* per 10 *kharvār*, 4 *kharvār* being left with the peasant for seed and labour. This provision presumably refers to crown lands, and the *kharāj* to tax levied on private property. Cattle-tax (*mavāshī*), *qilān*,

[1] *M.R.*, pp. 32–4. [2] ibid. pp. 118–19. [3] ibid. p. 119.

[4] The term *mināl* is used at the present day for the share of the crop which the government takes from the holders of *khāliṣeh* and for the dues it levies on them.

and *chirīk* were to be levied on every *bulūk* apart from the exempted estates which are mentioned in the letter.[1] The taxes of Khūzistān are listed under the following heads: *tamghā*, *kharāji arbāb*, *māl va kharāji dīvānī*, *mavāshī*, *nimār va qappānī*, *nahāleh*, *chirīk*, and *qilān* for the *'umarā* of the *khān*. All the places mentioned were exempt under the heading *tamghā*. *Kharāji arbāb*, except in one case, was at the rate of 1 *jarīb* in 10 *jarīb*. *Māl va kharāji dīvānī* was everywhere 6 *jarīb* per 10. *Mavāshī* varied from 400 to 10,000 *dīnārs*. All except Havīzeh were exempt from *nimār* and *qappānī*, Havīzeh paying 1 *mann* per 10 *mann*. Two places paid 400 *dīnārs* and 1,000 *dīnārs* respectively under *nahāleh*. Under *chirīk* the numbers varied from 1 to 10, and under *qilān* the amounts ranged from 20 to 600 *dīnārs*.[2]

Over-taxation and extortion, corruption and misrule, decay and public disorder, however, were not the only aspects of the Mongol regime. Ghāzān, among the rulers, clearly tried to bring about reform, and officials and landowners such as Rashīd ud-Dīn did something to reclaim land and to increase productivity. It appears, for example, that a large part of Khūzistān belonged to him, having been, so he alleged, transferred to him legally (i.e. in accordance with the *sharī'a*). In a letter preserved in the *Makātībi Rashīdī* addressed to the people of Khūzistān, he announces the appointment of Sirāj ud-Dīn Dizfūlī as tax-collector for the area, and states that he was to summon the *mubāshirs*, and demand accounts for past years (nothing having been received for some time past). He was to treat the peasants kindly and to cause them to cultivate the land. Describing the former prosperity of Khūzistān, Rashīd ud-Dīn states that for five years he had been expending money and effort in making it prosperous. He had spent 70 *tūmāns* on the cost of dams,[3] agricultural implements, seed, and advances to the peasants, and 200 yoke of oxen had been put in to work the land in his property in Ahvāz over and above the units which were already worked by the peasants on a crop-sharing basis. Since most of the villages situated in Khūzistān had come into his possession, some having been bought and some, which had been barren, having been reclaimed by his efforts, his officials in the area had devoted most of the produce of the land to wages, the expenses of dams and the clearing of irrigation channels, advances to the peasants, the wages of the *dashtbān*, and to current and future expenses.[4]

[1] *M.R.*, p. 121.

[2] ibid. pp. 122–3. If *qilān* meant some kind of labour service, this sum was presumably levied in lieu of the performance of labour service.

[3] Or 'draught oxen'. The term *band* which is used in the text may mean 'dam', 'plough-land', or 'yoke of oxen'.

[4] *M.R.*, pp. 181–2.

The methods employed by Rashīd ud-Dīn to found new villages can be seen from his letters. In the letter quoted above he states that five pieces of land had been transferred to him by the owners. Sirāj ud-Dīn was to bring 500 date palms from Havīzeh to plant in them. He was to bring ten energetic and capable peasants to plant the trees and to make a settlement. He was to make a walled enclosure (*ḥiṣār*) for them in which they should live. He was to give them every year each a sum of 100 *ruknī dīnārs* and 1 *mann* of bread a day until the trees and palms bore fruit; after that he was to give them every year 1 *kharvār* of wheat and 1 *kharvār* of barley, and from the produce 3 *dīnārs* on every 10 *dīnārs*, and in kind 3 *mann* on every 10 *mann* for their labour.[1] In some cases, however, the labour for the making of these new villages was furnished by slaves or by men pressed into service. Thus, in a letter to his son Jalāl ud-Dīn, governor of Anatolia, Rashīd ud-Dīn states that he had founded five villages near Tabrīz. Four of these had been populated, each by forty persons, male and female. The fifth one had no peasants. Rashīd ud-Dīn accordingly asked his son to send him forty Anatolian slaves and slave girls to settle in and cultivate the village.[2] Similarly, in a letter to Sunqur Bāvurchī, his slave and governor of Baṣra, he asks that 200 slave boys and 200 slave girls—Indians, Abyssinians, Qairovīs, and different sorts of black slaves—should be bought for him from his personal funds and sent to Tabrīz for his property.[3]

A striking feature of the Mongol period is the great increase which appears to have taken place in the size of private estates and private fortunes. Under the Seljūqs large areas of land were under the control of the *muqṭa*ʿ*s* but these were in the nature of provincial governorates rather than private estates. But under the Mongols the civil officials acquired vast fortunes derived partly from, or at

[1] *M.R.*, p. 182.

[2] Quoted by Lisān ul-Mulk in *Tārīkh va Jughrāfīāyi Dār as-Salṭanehyi Tabrīz* (Tehrān, lithog., 1223), pp. 143–4.

[3] *M.R.*, p. 14. In another letter to Jalāl ud-Dīn he instructs him to dig a canal in the plain of Malāṭīyeh from the Shaṭṭi Furāt, and to found ten villages. The peasants for these villages were to be collected from the towns and provinces of Anatolia, Qinnisrīn, and ʿAwāṣim. They were to be provided with seed and agricultural implements, and were to be given advances. At the head of the canal on either side there were to be eight villages and at the end two villages (ibid. p. 246). In another letter he informs the governors (*ḥukkām*), *nā'ibs*, *qāẓīs*, *sayyids*, *ṣudūr*, *mutaṣarrifs*, peasants, people, and nomads of the province of Dīār Bakr and Dīār Rabīʿa that one Zakī ud-Dīn Masʿūd had been sent to make a new canal in the neighbourhood of Mawṣil and to found on either side of it walled villages. He was to collect peasants from the neighbourhood of the towns and frontier districts of Dīār Bakr, Dīār Rabīʿa, Greater Armenia, Lesser Armenia, and Anatolia, and give them seed, agricultural implements, and advances so that in ease and comfort they could engage in agriculture and make the places populous (ibid., p. 244). He was to take 20,000 excavators from these provinces to excavate the canals, to make dams, to build houses, and to make walls for the villages (ibid., p. 245).

any rate invested in, land. These lands, unless confiscated by the state or usurped by rivals, were transmitted by inheritance to the owner's heirs. The will of the great *vazīr* Rashīd ud-Dīn Fazlullāh gives a list of his property. This included: first the estates which he had bought in the *rub'i maskūn* (of Tabrīz)[1] and made populous. These he left in part as *ouqāf* for his male and female heirs and charitable purposes and in part as private property for his children and the *'ulamā*. Secondly, estates in (i.e. which had been part of?)[2] the crown lands (*amlāki khāṣṣeh*) and Ghāzānī lands (*zīā 'i ghāzānī*) which he had cultivated and watered and which belonged to him.[3] In this category were estates in various parts of the empire. Some of these he transmitted to his heirs, and some he constituted into *ouqāf*.[4] Since Rashīd ud-Dīn was able thus to transmit these estates to his heirs and to constitute them into *ouqāf*, it follows that he exercised full rights of ownership over them and therefore presumably had acquired them by grant, gift, or purchase.[5] His estates (*amlāk*) in Tūrān, some of which were the gift (*soyūrghāl*) of the *sulṭāns* and some of which had been bought by his stewards, the *a'yān* of which, because they were far away and not under the rule of the *sulṭāns* of Īrān, he had farmed for a definite sum, he made into *ouqāf* for his male and female issue. Similarly, his estates in Syria and the Yemen, 'some of which were the gift (*soyūrghāl*) of the Malik Nāṣir, ruler of Egypt and the gift (*soyūrghāl*) of the noble king, ruler of the Yemen, and some of which his stewards (*vakīls*) had bought according to the *sharī'a*, he made into *ouqāf* for the Ka'ba and Jerusalem. In Sind and India he also had estates some of which had been bought and some of which were the gift (*soyūrghāl*) of the *sulṭāns* of India. These were made into a *vaqf* for the *khānqāh* of Shihāb ud-Dīn 'Umar as-Suhravardī. His date palms, some of which had been bought and others planted by himself in the different provinces, amounted to 39,000 trees. Some were given as private property to his sons and others made into *ouqāf*. The orchards and vineyards which he possessed in the provinces are listed in another document, and had apparently been made into *ouqāf* for various charitable purposes.[6]

[1] This area, no longer inhabited, is known at the present day as the *rab'i rashīdī*.

[2] This is presumably the meaning of the text. The word used is *amlāk*, which normally means private estates over which the owner has full rights of ownership. If this is the sense of *amlāk* here, the text must mean that they had been formerly part of the crown lands and part of the private estates of Ghāzān Khān and had been transferred to Rashīd ud-Dīn. The text states quite clearly that they 'belonged to him' (Rashīd ud-Dīn).

[3] *M.R.*, pp. 224–5.

[4] ibid. pp. 225–32.

[5] For example, in the provinces of Shabānkāreh and Nayrīz he constituted 100 *fiddan* into *ouqāf* for the two *madraseh* of Shabānkāreh and the office of *mutavallī* (*M.R.*, p. 232). The centre of the province of Shabānkāreh was Īj.

[6] *M.R.*, pp. 233–4.

In addition to the flocks he owned[1] he appears to have owned large numbers of domestic fowl, which he presumably let out to the peasants on some sort of *ṭarāz* agreement.[2] These included 20,000 hens which were in the hands of the peasants (*ra'āyā*) of the villages of Tabrīz, Sulṭānīyeh, and Hamadān. Their produce was to be devoted to the sick. He left 10,000 geese and 10,000 duck which were in the possession of the people of the villages of Tabrīz and Marāgheh to his children. One thousand head of oxen and 1,000 head of asses he made into a *vaqf* for the transport of fruit, compost, manure, and stones, etc., for the Rashīdī quarter of Tabrīz and the orchards of Tabrīz which he had brought into cultivation, and entrusted these quadrupeds to the crop-sharing peasants (*muzāra'ān*) of the villages of Mihrānarūd, and the gardeners of Fatḥābād and Rashīdābād.[3]

Rashīd ud-Dīn, although perhaps the outstanding example of a wealthy official in this period, is not by any means an exceptional case. Ibn ut-Ṭiqṭaqī in 'Irāq grew rich on farming crown lands under Abāqā (663–80/1265–81).[4] The daily income of Shams ud-Dīn Muḥammad Juvaynī, the chief minister of Hūlāgū and after him of Abāqā and Takūdār (680–3/1281–4), was estimated at 10,000 *dīnārs*.[5]

The composition of the landowning class under the Mongols underwent considerable change. First were the members of the ruling class, i.e. Mongols, who held as assignees and as private landowners considerable areas of land. The hostility prevailing between these and the local population would appear to have been greater than that between the former ruling classes and the peasants. The statement mentioned above that the Mongols were to cultivate dead lands in their *yurts* by slaves because they would be unlikely to allow the peasants access is significant. Secondly, there were large land-holdings by prominent officials; it is possible that the *qāẓīs* also became an increasingly numerous element in the landowning class. Grants to them by Ghāzān have already been mentioned. If this policy was followed, it was of some importance, since the effect would have been to increase the community of interest between the *qāẓīs* as a class and the landowners; formerly they had formed an intermediate class between the common people and the upper class of officials (civil and military), and represented to some extent a relatively impartial centre to which the common people could appeal. Once their interest became bound up with the

[1] See above, p. 80. [2] See below, p. 351.
[3] *M.R.*, pp. 235–6.
[4] He was worsted in an intrigue against 'Alā ud-Dīn 'Aṭā Malik Juvaynī, the governor of Baghdād, and his goods, estates and property confiscated by the latter (Juvaynī, i. xxxi, xxxii).
[5] ibid. p. xlviii.

landowning class this ceased to be so.[1] Thirdly, there was the former landowning class. The extent to which it survived varied in the different areas. The dealings of government officials appear to have been mainly with the peasants, but this does not necessarily mean that the landowning class had disappeared, but rather that the government found it easier to collect taxation from the peasants than from the landowners, who were possibly largely absentees. In so far as the landowners were in fact absentees they probably collected their dues from the peasants in person once a year or sent bailiffs to collect these for them. This would appear to have been the practice of the landowner mentioned above (p. 83).

To recapitulate briefly, the Mongol period marks a further movement away from Islamic theory in spite of Ghāzān's attempt to give his reforms in land matters the sanction of the *sharīʿa*. It also sees an increase in large land-holdings and, on the whole, a decline in productivity and prosperity. The hostility between the peasantry and the ruling classes was heightened and the gulf between them widened, to an even greater extent than had been the case under the Seljūq Turks. Lastly, by the introduction of decrees or *yarlīgh* issued by the rulers concerning runaway peasants the force of law was given to practices which had formerly been sanctioned only by *ʿurf*, or custom, and the peasant became more effectively tied to the soil than had been the case formerly.

On the disintegration of the Mongol empire the various provinces tended to split up into geographical and economic areas, and a number of provincial governors and local leaders asserted their independence. The Caspian provinces, which had always proved difficult to incorporate into an empire centred on the plateau, were among the first to break away. Here probably even in Mongol times the life of the people had continued very much on traditional lines.[2] Yazd, under Sharaf ud-Dīn Muẓaffar b. Muḥammad b. Muẓaffar (d. 754/1353–4), was apparently prosperous. To quote from the *Tārīkhi Jadīdi Yazd*, 'The prosperity of the town and province reached such a degree that the peasants (*mardumi dihāqīn*) were not provided with the means of cultivation and they brought grain, cotton, and fruit to the town on horses and

[1] See also pp. 121 and 126.

[2] Labour service appears to have been a regular feature of local life. Marʿashī in the *Tārīkhi Ṭabaristān va Rūyān va Māzandarān* describes how Sayyid Fakhr ud-Dīn, who became *ra'īs* of Āmul in 763/1361–2, made his seat of government in the village of Vātāshān and built his government buildings in it with forced labour (*bīgārī*) (pp. 401–2). Marʿashī also states that it was the custom in spring for the governors (*ḥukkām*) of Māzandarān to mount their horses and go out for some ten days to see to the rice cultivation and to assemble the people and go to the forest regions which were fit for cultivation, clear them of trees, scrub, and thorn and make irrigation channels so that the agricultural labourers could sow rice and wheat for them (the landowners) (p. 413).

mules and wore silk and satin clothes and boiled fat hens in milk'.[1] The mere fact, however, that it is thought worth recording that the peasants were not provided by the landowners with the means of cultivation (i.e. agricultural implements, seed, and oxen) shows not so much the prosperity of the peasants as the low standard of living which was considered normal.

In most areas of the country, however, political leadership was changing hands relatively frequently; this probably meant that there were considerable changes also in land ownership. *Khāliṣeh* land was presumably taken over by whoever was temporarily dominant in any given area. It is probable that there was also a tendency to usurp *vaqf* land.[2]

In 782/1380 Tīmūr began a series of campaigns in Persia. Although he held the marches of the Iranic world against the nomadic hordes of Central Asia,[3] Tīmūr nevertheless drew his own support largely from nomadic or semi-nomadic tribes which lived on the produce of their flocks. As the Mongols had done before him, he allotted to his followers *yurts*. For example, in 804/1402 after consultation with his leading followers concerning their *yurts* in the *qishlāq* (winter quarters) he allotted to each a town and province.[4] How permanent these *yurts* were or what the relation of their holders was to the settled population is not clear.[5] Tīmūr's successors were unable to hold his conquests, although they retained their hold on north Persia for nearly a century. On the death of Shāhrukh, Tīmūr's son, in 850/1447

> the *amīrs* and princes went at each other's throats; each seized what he could from the treasury and the army and set out for some province or frontier district . . . and seized it. They practised tyranny and oppression, committed massacres, and coveted the wealth of the merchants, subjects, and peasants . . . decay set in in the provinces and the people were dispersed . . . famine and plague broke out throughout Persia.[6]

Insecurity became once more the dominant note. Constant campaigning took place; the armies passing to and fro lived on the

[1] Aḥmad b. Ḥusayn, p. 213.

[2] There is a reference in the *Tārīkhi Jadīdi Yazd* to *vaqf* land being enclosed: The Ḥājibī garden in the Yazd area, which had fallen into ruin after the death of the Atābeg Yūsuf Shāh, had been made into *khāliṣeh* by the Muẓaffarids; 'the brother of Shāh Yaḥyā (b.744/1343), Shāh Ḥusayn, made a wall round it, brought it into cultivation and took possession of it. On his death, it was divided among his effects and fell to a boy. It was subsequently made into a *vaqfi amvāt*, and the people each took a piece of land and enclosed it with a wall' (p. 195).

[3] See A. J. Toynbee, *Study of History*, iv. 491 ff.

[4] 'Abd ur-Razzāq b. Jalāl ad-Dīn Isḥāq Samarqandī, *Maṭla' as-Sa'dayn*, B.M. Add. 17928, f. 328a.

[5] Certain areas of the country were set aside as royal hunting grounds as, for example, the country round Sulṭānīyeh (cf. Aḥmad b. Ḥusayn, p. 243).

[6] Aḥmad b. Ḥusayn, pp. 8–9.

country, and conquerors wrote drafts on the country for their followers. On the approach of some new conqueror or victorious prince the people would disperse for fear of the demands which might be made upon them.[1] When Shāhrukh b. Tīmūr (807–50/1404–47) came to Iṣfahān he gave an amnesty to the people, so that demands for arrears should not be made upon the peasants and they should engage in agriculture.[2] On the other hand, when Muḥammad Sulṭān (d. 855/1451–2) came to Iṣfahān after the death of Shāhrukh, his *vazīr*, Shaykh ul-Islām Saʿd ud-Dīn Abi'l Khayr, fixed a special levy per household in Yazd and other provinces for the army to be collected by those holding bills which were drawn up in Iṣfahān.[3] These heavy exactions ruined the people. When this was reported to Muḥammad Sulṭān, he ordered that on no account was the additional tax of 1 *dīnār* to be unnecessarily imposed upon the peasants.[4]

Broadly speaking, however, the period between the decline of the Īlkhāns and the rise of the Ṣafavids brings little new in the field of land tenure and rural organization. But in so far as the government had moved away from the ideal of Islamic theory, so the tendency towards arbitrary action increased. Hinz, for example, points out that Uzun Ḥasan, of whose tax regime instituted between 1470 and 1477[5] we have detailed information, arbitrarily raised existing taxes and imposed new ones on the population. The incidence of taxation, however, varied considerably in the different tax districts.[6] The various demands made upon the rural population included dues levied on each plough-land, a tax levied on the produce varying from some 14 per cent to 20 per cent, and taxes on vineyards. The population were also required to furnish so many loads of firewood, fodder, etc., per annum by way of a pasture tax.[7] There were also a number of dues levied such as a percentage upon the harvest for certain local officials, a tax on mills, and various levies made on feast-days, etc.[8] The nomads paid a cattle-tax, as also did the peasants.[9] Such changes as there were in taxation were of degree rather than of a more fundamental nature. Minorsky indeed has remarked on 'the persistence of the administrative tradition' from the fourteenth to the seventeenth centuries A.D. He distinguishes between two main types of landholding: hereditary grants, known as *soyūrghāl*, carrying certain immunities, and *tuyūl*, the holders of which enjoyed the temporary

1 cf. ibid. pp. 243–4.
2 ibid. pp. 249–50.
3 ibid. p. 257.
4 ibid. pp. 266–7, *farʿi yak dīnār bar raʿāyā va muzāraʿīn qismat nakonand.*
5 See W. Hinz, 'Das Steuerwesen Ostanatoliens im 15. und 16. Jahrhundert', *Z.D.M.G.*, c. 1. (New Series vol. 25), 1950, pp. 177–201.
6 ibid. p. 179.
7 ibid. pp. 180–1.
8 ibid. pp. 181–2.
9 ibid. 181.

right to collect government taxes for their own benefit.[1] Both forms of grant can be traced back to Seljūq times, to the 'administrative' and the 'personal' *iqṭā'* respectively. It seems that in the intervening period between the fall of the Mongols and the rise of the Ṣafavids the distinction between these two types of *iqṭā'* had become less sharp and that there was a tendency for all types of assignment, whether known as *soyūrghāl*, *tuyūl*, or *iqṭā'*, to become unified and to represent grants of 'immunity' to the holders from all interference by government officials. Parallel with, or perhaps preceding, this development was a tendency to regard all land as subject to the exercise of full proprietary rights over it by the petty territorial princes, who were the *de facto* holders of the land. This conception began to supersede both the earlier Islamic theory, which regarded all land which had no owner as the property of all Muslims and permitted its alienation by the *imām* only in the interests of the community, and the theory of the steppe, which regarded the ruling *khān* as holding the land as the representative of his people.

From the documents which survive from the period some idea can be gained of the multiplicity of the dues which were levied on the land and its holders. In the *soyūrghāl* of Qāsim b. Jahāngīr quoted by Minorsky, exemption was given from thirty taxes and dues. Another document, dated 904/1498–9, in which the Amīr Alvand of the Qarā Qoyunlū conferred the village of Nahri Āmis near Gulpāyagān on Jalāl ud-Douleh Jābir, the *vazīr*, also illustrates the continuity of tradition.[2] From this document it would appear that *soyūrghāls*, although often described as 'permanent' and 'gifts in perpetuity', were in fact nothing of the sort, and deeds of re-investiture were required from time to time. In this document the governors (*ḥukkām*), tax-collectors (*'ummāl*), *kalāntars*, and *kadkhudās* of the province of Gulpāyagān were forbidden to make any demands, whether for regular taxes or extraordinary levies in Nahri Āmis. Nor were any drafts to be made upon the area. A new grant was not, moreover, to be demanded every year. The beneficiary was granted exemption from the following taxes and levies: *māl o jihāt* (ordinary taxes), *ikhrājāt* and *khārijīāt* (extraordinary levies), dues demanded by virtue of decree or otherwise (*'avāriẓāti ḥukmī va ghayri ḥukmī*), *'alafeh* (levies for the food of officials), *'ulūfeh* (levies for the fodder of the animals of officials),[3] *qunughlā* (levies for the entertainment of envoys and others), *bīgār* (forced labour), *shikār* (hunting tax), *ulāgh* (postal couriers or levies of animals for

[1] See 'A Soyūrghāl of Qāsim b. Jahāngīr Āq-Qoyunlū', *B.S.O.A.S.* ix. 4, p. 960.

[2] The original document is in the possession of Ḥājjī Mīrzā 'Abdullāh Anṣārī.

[3] cf. Rashīd ud-Dīn, *Histoire des Mongols de la Perse*, p. 369, n. 166.

the post), *ulām* (guides forced without pay into the service of an official to show him the way from one village to another),[1] *sāvarī* (presents), *sāchuq* (entertainment dues), *pīshkash* (presents), *zari chirīk va pīādeh* (levies for irregular cavalry and infantry), *mushtuluq* (levies made on special occasions such as the announcement of good news), *iḥdāṣ* (innovations), *kad va sar shumār* (? family tax and poll tax), *khāneh shumār* (house tax), *yāmbardār* (levies for the post), *dastandāz* (? perquisites, tips), *ʿīdī va nourūzī* (new year levies), *ḥaqq us-saʿīyi ʿummāl* (tax-collectors' perquisites), *ʿushr* (? tithe),[2] *rasm us-ṣadāreh* (commission for the *ṣadr*), *rasm ul-vizāreh* (commission for the *vazīr*), *ghalleh ṭarḥ*,[3] *ibtīāʿī* (? purchase tax), *ḥarz* (valuation), *masāḥat* (measurement), *rasm al-ḥarz va masāḥat* (commission for valuation and measurement), *iẓāfeh va tafāvuti tasʿīr* (? levies made to adjust the conversion rate), *taqabbul* (? some kind of levy made at the time of the agreement made by the tax-payer to pay the sum due as fixed by the tax-collector), [the taxes known as] *sad yak* (1 per cent), *sad do* (2 per cent), and *sad chahār* (4 per cent), the dues of the *dārūgheh*, *kalāntar*, assessor (*mumaiyiz*), and receiver (*ṣāḥib jamʿ*), *shīlān bahā* (levies made for assemblies on feast days), *sufreh bahā* (levies made for those who prepared banquets), *salāmāneh* (levies made for royal audiences and levies made on receipt of news of the ruler's well-being), *ikhrājāti qilāʿ va ṭavāyil va jouqehgāh* (levies made for the expenses of the upkeep of fortresses, royal stables, and royal hunting preserves), *murgh* (requisitions of domestic fowl), *gūsfand* (requisitions of sheep or goats), *qilān* (labour service), *qubchūr* (cattle tax), *yirghū* (levies for the investigation of crimes), *sarghū* (?) and other requisitions by the *dīvān* (*takālīfi dīvānī*) or royal demands (*muṭālibāti sulṭānī*), or whatever could be levied by way of taxation under any guise whatsoever. This list is rather more lengthy than the list of taxes from which exemption is granted in the *soyūrghāl* of Qāsim b. Jahāngīr Āq Qoyunlū. The majority, however, of the taxes and dues are mentioned in both documents.

The main burden of taxation fell on the peasants as before. Although exemption was granted to the holders of *soyūrghāls* from the payment of various dues to the *dīvān* there is no reason to suppose that the holder did not collect these or similar dues from the peasants on this land for his own benefit. The same probably

[1] See *Kurāsat al-Maʿī* (MS. in Majlis Library, Tehrān), ff. 610–11, for a note giving the meaning of *ulāgh* and *ulām* as stated above.

[2] This may refer to the one-tenth levied by certain officials as their perquisite and not to the old land tax of early Islamic times.

[3] The precise meaning of this term in Āq Qoyunlū times is not clear. Under Ẓill as-Sulṭān in the Iṣfahān area (in late Qājār times) it was the custom to dump grain from *khāliṣeh* lands on peasants and force them to buy this at a higher price than the current price. This practice was known as *ghalleh ṭarḥ*. See also p. 85.

applied to *vaqf* lands exempted from *dīvān* dues. In a document dated 893/1488 exemption from twenty-seven taxes and dues is granted to a *vaqf* property in Fārs.[1] Another document, a *farmān* dated Ẕu'l Qa'da 773/1372 issued in Tabrīz by the Jala'irid Sulṭān Aḥmad (son of Shaykh Uways) for Shaykh Ṣadr ud-Dīn Mūsā, the son of Shaykh Ṣafī ud-Dīn Ardabīlī, the ancestor of the Ṣafavids,[2] gives an indication of the kind of impositions to which the holders of estates, whether these were immobilized as *vaqf* or not, were subject. In this *farmān* the governors (*ḥukkām*), *nā'ibs*, *mutaṣarrifs*, and *bītikchīs* of Ardabīl and its dependencies and districts are forbidden to make any demands or write drafts on the places in the hands of his disciples since 'certain ancient tax exemptions enjoyed by the estates (*amlāk*) and *ouqāf* of his blessed retreat had been confirmed by virtue of a royal decree and [the right] to collect certain [other] taxes had been granted to his followers, so that his peasants (? *ra'āyā*) shall not be troubled'. The governors of Ardabīl were to consider his villages exempt and not to write drafts on them. *Amīrs* and travellers were not to alight at his house or the houses of his followers, and they were not to take their animals for the post.

Another document, from the *malik* Kayumārs b. Bīsitūn (807–57/1404–53) to the *mutavallī* of the shrine of Shaykh Majd ud-Dīn Gīlān al-Āmulī, after defining the limits of the *vaqf* property, grants exemption from *ulāgh*, *ulām*, *bīgār*, *qubchūrmeh*,[3] and *mavāshīyeh* on cattle and sheep, and from irregular taxes (*maks*) and other dues.[4]

[1] Quoted by Professor Minorsky in his article 'A Soyūrghāl of Qāsim b. Jahāngīr Āq-Qoyunlū' (referred to on p. 102).

[2] The original *farmān* is in the Bibl. Nationale, Paris. The text is quoted in article entitled 'Farmāni Sulṭān Aḥmadi Jalā'ir' (*Yādgār*, Āẕar 1323, pp. 25–9). Sulṭān Aḥmad held Ardabīl as a *soyūrghāl* from his father, Shaykh Uways, who ruled from 757/1356 to 777/1374. Aḥmad eventually succeeded his brother, Ḥusayn, as *sulṭān* in 784/1382.

[3] *Qubchūrmeh* is possibly a variant of *qubchūr*.

[4] *Kurāsat al-Ma'ī* (MS., Majlis Library), ff. 610–11; see the glossary for the meaning of these terms.

CHAPTER V

THE GROWTH OF ABSOLUTISM: THE ṢAFAVIDS

THE rise of the Ṣafavids in the sixteenth century A.D. marks the beginning of a new period in the history of Persia. Politically, it sees the emergence of Persia as a national state in the modern sense of the term,[1] and in religion, the adoption by Persia of the Ithna ʿAsharī (or the Jaʿfarī) version of Shiʿism as the official state religion. In the sphere of land tenure a new content was given to the forms which have been outlined in the previous chapters. The old institutions moulded by Islamic practice during the early centuries, and modified by the practice of the steppe in Seljūq times, were infused with new drive by the absolutism of Shiʿism. The conception of the Ṣafavid monarch differed from both that of the caliph and that of the ruling *khān*; no longer was the conception of society based even in part on the acceptance of the rough equality of the steppe or of government by means of a limited consultation among the more privileged members of the community. Outwardly there were resemblances, but in fact the conception of society was altogether more autocratic and arbitrary. The position of the ruler was reinforced by the theory of divine right.[2] Increased absolutism in religion affected the whole range of social and political life. In the field of land tenure the theory of the ruler as the sole landowner, already foreshadowed by Niẓām ul-Mulk, became more definite. Its practical application, however, was modified by circumstances. The inability of the Ṣafavids to provide themselves with adequate military forces once the basis of power had shifted from the tribes from whom they had originally derived their support led them, as the failure to pay their military forces had led their predecessors, to alienate large areas from the direct control of the state. At first drafts were made on the revenue for the military leaders, then the land itself was assigned, and finally it became, or tended to become, by usurpation, *de facto* private property. Although the theory that

[1] cf. Toynbee, *Study of History*, ii. 254.

[2] Significant is the difference in phraseology between documents granting *iqṭāʿs* or appointing officials to various offices in Seljūq times and similar documents in Ṣafavid times. In the former, in so far as the holder is urged to treat the subjects well, it is because they are a charge from God; in the latter it is in order that the subjects, being satisfied, should pray for the well-being of the ruler, not because he, being by nature sinful, is in need of their prayers, but because their function as citizens is no longer primarily to worship God but to glorify the ruler. The emphasis has changed. The ruler has become the central figure to the exclusion of all else.

ownership was vested in the ruler provided a convenient cover under which he could expropriate his subjects' lands, it would appear that the theory of the ruler as the sole landowner did not receive in practice complete and unqualified acceptance. The fact that Shāh 'Abbās himself felt it necessary to constitute his private estates into *ouqāf* in order to enable him to enjoy the income therefrom and yet to avoid the moral blame attaching to the use of wrongfully acquired property would seem to suggest that in practice private persons enjoyed full rights of ownership over land. If the ownership of all land had been vested in the ruler, there could have been no question of wrongfully acquired land, since the ruler could not have usurped what already belonged to him. The recognition of private property in effect is further corroborated by the fact that private persons also could constitute their lands into *ouqāf*, which they could not have done unless they exercised full rights of disposal over their property.

Professor Minorsky considers that the Ṣafavids were the direct successors of the Turkomān dynasties of the Black Sheep or Qarā Qoyunlū and the White Sheep or Āq Qoyunlū. 'Not improperly', he writes, 'the early Ṣafavid state may be considered as the third stage of the Turkomān dominion in Persia. The military force of Shāh Ismā'īl with which he defeated the Āq Qoyunlū Alvand and Murād was organized like that of his enemies on purely tribal principles.'[1] The great majority of Shāh Ismā'īl's supporters belonged to the tribes from Asia Minor, Syria, and Armenia mixed with the tribes detached from the rival Qarā Qoyunlū and Āq Qoyunlū. Under the Āq Qoyunlū and Qarā Qoyunlū an easterly movement had begun among the Turkomān tribes who in Seljūq times had moved into Armenia, Upper Mesopotamia, and Anatolia. This was continued under the early Ṣafavids. These Turkomān tribes were cattle-breeders and lived apart from the surrounding population. They migrated from winter to summer quarters. They were organized in clans and obeyed their own chieftains.[2] Thus, as with the Seljūqs and with the Mongols, there was a dichotomy between settled and semi-settled or nomadic, and between Persian and non-Persian. Similarly, as had been the case in Seljūq times, the Turkomāns proved an unstable basis upon which to rely. Already under Shāh Ṭahmāsp (930–84/1524–76) rivalries among the tribal groups and their unruly natures had endangered the existence of the state, and Shāh Ṭahmāsp had started to disband and disperse them.[3]

Under Ṭahmāsp most of the empire was indirectly administered. According to Alessandri, apart from the area kept by Ṭahmāsp and his sons, it was divided into fifty parts. The governors of these had

[1] *T.M.*, p. 30. [2] ibid. p. 188. [3] ibid. p. 30.

charge of 500–3,000 horsemen each which they had to keep and muster when required. In all they did not amount, in the view of Alessandri, to more than 60,000 cavalry, although the muster was on paper higher.[1]

The provincial governments resembled in many ways the old Seljūq 'administrative' *iqṭā'*s. They were alienated from the control of the central government and the provincial governor was under obligation, as had been the Seljūq *muqṭa'*, to provide military contingents. Chardin writes that the provincial governor was a petty prince in his province. He and his officers and the troops which he maintained consumed the greater part of the revenue; a part only, in the form of presents and certain dues, was given to the king. In the same way as the *shāh* received dues and contributions from the provincial governors, so the provincial governors received similar dues and contributions from those living within their governorates.[2] They were able to sub-assign the area under them and had complete control.[3]

There were, however, three officials appointed by the central government in each province. One of these, known as the *jānishīn*, was always in the provincial capital with the governor; the second was the *vazīr* or comptroller; and the third the *vāqi'eh nivīs*, whose duty consisted principally in reporting to the *shāh* all that occurred. These officials were there, in fact, to watch over the governor's actions and to oppose him should he undertake anything contrary to the interest of the state.[4]

By the time of Shāh 'Abbās (996–1038/1587–1629) a change in the basis of Ṣafavid power had taken place: he no longer depended, as had the earlier rulers, upon tribal contingents, but relied instead for support on new regiments recruited from non-tribal elements, chiefly Georgian and Armenian converts to Islam.[5] The creation of these new forces depending directly upon the *shāh* raised the problem of how they were to be paid. A solution was sought along the lines followed by former dynasties: that is to say the military, composed of regular troops maintained by the ruler, and the militia in the provinces, were paid by land assignments made from *khāṣṣeh* (i.e. *khāliṣeh* land). As in the case of the earlier military *iqṭā'*, the hereditary principle was recognized, and these assignments were transmitted by inheritance to the holder's male heirs unless they refused to carry arms. The provincial militia had to present themselves within twelve hours of receiving a call, and every year they had to take part in a review before a deputy from

[1] In *Italian Travels in Persia in the 15th and 16th Centuries*, Hakluyt Society, 1st ser., vol. 49, pp. 226–7.
[2] *Voyages du Chevalier Chardin*, ed. L. Langlès (Paris, 1811), v. 408.
[3] ibid. v. 380. [4] ibid. v. 257–8. [5] *T.M.*, pp. 30–1.

the court or the provincial governor.[1] In the case of the standing army the assignments were made to groups of soldiers and not to individuals,[2] in order to avoid the difficulty of collection by individual assignees. In some cases collection was made direct from the assignment, in others from the treasury. In the latter case, an official (known as a *taḥṣīldār*) deducted 5 per cent (by way of brokerage or commission) for assignments in the neighbourhood of Iṣfahān and 10 per cent for assignments elsewhere. The payment of these assignments by the *taḥṣīldār* was often held in arrears. It would appear, therefore, that in so far as the military forces under the direct control of the ruler increased relative to the contingents provided by the provincial governors, it was a necessary corollary that the extent of the land under the direct control of the ruler should increase to enable him to pay them.

For the rest, crown lands were alienated in part by temporary or life grants (see below) to officials and others, while in part they were retained under the administration of a comptroller who received the revenues on behalf of the *shāh*. Although Chardin states that the distinction between provinces and crown lands had been unknown before the reign of Shāh Ṣafī (A.D. 1629–42), it seems that in fact some broad general distinction was made between *dīvānī* (i.e. state) land and *khāṣṣ* (i.e. crown) land, though the division may have become sharper under Shāh Ṣafī. His *vazīr*, Sārū Taqī, had urged him to abandon his father's policy of maintaining governors in the provinces, thereby removing them from the control of the central government, a policy which had been forced upon him by his need of military contingents to enable him to carry on his wars. The *shāh* approved of this suggestion and Fārs, one of the most important provinces in view of size and riches, but one needing fewer troops since it was not a frontier province was resumed, as it were, by the central government, and an overseer placed in charge of its administration. Shāh ʿAbbās II (1052–77/1642–67), continuing his father, Shāh Ṣafī's, policy, abolished provincial governments in the interior of the kingdom wherever there was no danger of war, as in Qazvīn, Gīlān, Māzandarān, Yazd, Kirmān, Khurāsān, and Āẕarbāyjān. Whenever the danger of war occurred governors were re-appointed. Thus, at the beginning of the reign of Sulaymān (1077–1105/1667–94) when there was a threat from the Cossacks in the Caspian area, governors were appointed in Māzandarān and Gīlān. Similarly, the invasion of Khurāsān and Āẕarbāyjān by Turkomāns being feared, governors were appointed over these provinces also. When the danger was past the policy of Shāh Ṣafī was reverted to.

[1] Chardin, v. 298–9, 303–4.
[2] State guilds were also paid by group assignments. (Chardin, v. 423–4.)

Chardin goes on to say that the people objected to this policy on the grounds that it took money out of circulation, enriched only the king, and led to oppression by his officials and to military weakness.[1] Chardin believed that the reason why the oppression committed by the provincial governors was less than that committed by the comptrollers of the crown lands was, first, that it was in the interests of the governor that the province should be flourishing since it was in effect his private domain, whereas the interest of a comptroller lay in obtaining as much as he could under the pretext of collecting more for the *shāh*. Secondly, the governor had not to send so many presents to the court nor to increase the sum remitted annually to make his services valuable as the comptroller had to do. Thirdly, the *shāh* was less ready to put up with extortion committed by a governor than by a comptroller since the royal treasury did not benefit therefrom.[2]

Although, as stated in Chapter IV, a tendency towards a general unification of all types of assignment had already begun before Ṣafavid times, assignments still fell into certain broad general categories, all covered by the term *tuyūl*.

Certain features characteristic of the early *iqṭā' at-tamlīk* and the *iqṭā' al-istighlāl* can still be found in the Ṣafavid *tuyūl*. The old conception which had underlain the grant of the *iqṭā' at-tamlīk* in early times (see p. 29), namely, the promotion and fostering of cultivation of the land, can be discerned in certain grants (see below). In so far as full administrative powers were given to the grantee in his *tuyūl*, the resemblance is rather to the Seljūq 'administrative' *iqṭā'*, however. In return for the grant a military contingent had to be provided by the grantee. The following *farmān* dated Muḥarram 1110 (July–August 1698)[3] illustrates these points:

A decree, obeyed by all the world, is issued to this effect, that in view of the royal compassion for the *amīr* and governor (*ḥākim*) Lāchin Sulṭān, son of the late Shīr 'Alī Sulṭān Barādūst, the former governor (*ḥākim*) of Sumāy and Targivar, he has been appointed from the beginning of the 10th month of Tūshqān Il[4] to the amirate of the above mentioned district, and we have ordered him to be given whatever was the *tuyūl* of his late father, so that he may undertake, in a fitting manner, the above-mentioned affair and whatever pertains thereto. Let him show excellent efforts in the ordering of the army, the collection of revenue, and the cultivation of the districts of his *tuyūl*, and hold ready, as entered (against his name) in the *dīvān*, forty-seven men, fully equipped and armed, and let him so treat the soldiers, *kadkhudās* and peasants that all should be satisfied with his good treatment of them, and return thanks so that prayers for the well-being of the person of our

[1] v. 250–4, 276–7. [2] ibid. v. 279.
[3] *Farmān* in the possession of Ḥājjī Ḥusayn Āqā Nakhjavānī.
[4] The Year of the Hare.

blessed, successful, and illustrious prince (*navvāb*) shall be made. Let the elders (*rīsh safīdān*) and peasants of the above-mentioned districts consider the said person as their governor possessing full powers. Let them not contravene his words or what he considers advisable and let them consider necessary obedience and devotion to him. Let the great and noble *mustoufīs* of the Supreme Dīvān enter a record of this gift in the eternal register and prepare a *tuyūl nāmehcheh* with the necessary conditions and consider it valid.

The term *tuyūl* also covered assignments of land made to officials in lieu of salary. These assignments were of two kinds: either the land was attached in perpetuity to the office, important offices all having land attached to them for the payment of salaries, or the land was assigned by the accounts department annually.

Where the produce of an area assigned in lieu of salary fell short of the sum required, the overseer of the province provided what was missing. If, on the other hand, the assignment provided a surplus over and above the amount of the assignment, the surplus was, in theory, unless otherwise stated, remitted to the treasury.

The estimate of the revenues of the areas assigned went back, according to Chardin, to time immemorial. He alleges that the interests of the *shāh* were much neglected and that generally the assignments paid three to four times the estimated amount.[1] A report from a Venetian envoy dated 1578–9 takes a similar view. It states: 'There are an infinite number of villages and manors all assigned for the pay of the cavalry, the lowest pay of whom is 100 ducats each per annum, although they extract a much larger sum, they themselves having the land worked, and getting the triple out of it.'[2]

Lands thus assigned for the payment of salaries were not subject to the inspection of the *shāh's* officials. They were virtually, in the view of Chardin, the property of those to whom they were assigned. The grantees treated the inhabitants as they pleased.[3] Where the assignments were hereditary the inhabitants, in his view, were better treated than in any other land in Persia, because the holder, regarding the assignment as his private property in perpetuity, hoped to hold the office throughout his own lifetime and to transmit it to his children.[4]

The following document dated Ṣafar 1041 (September 1631) for the allotment of salary illustrates this type of grant:[5]

A royal decree was issued to the following effect: In accordance with the order of the late and venerable prince (*navvāb*) the position of *malik* and *rīsh safīd* of Arvaniq, which is one of the tax-districts of the

[1] Chardin, v. 417.
[2] *Chronicle of the Carmelites in Persia* (London, 1939), i. 52, n. 1.
[3] Chardin, v. 418.
[4] ibid. 419–20.
[5] *Farmān* in the possession of Ḥājjī Ḥusayn Āqā Nakhjavānī.

dār us-salṭaneh Tabrīz, was handed over to the sole care of the blessed *malik*, ʿAlā Beg Arvaniqī, so that he should undertake the above-mentioned charge and exert himself in whatever was necessary thereto, and, observing complete equality [of treatment] and justice between the peasants [subjects], should allow no unjust appropriations to be made. This order was dated Ẕu'l Qaʿda 1038 (June–July 1629) and was to the effect that since in accordance with the order of the sublime prince (*navvāb*) the position of *malik* of the above-mentioned district had been allotted in lieu of wages to the above-mentioned *malik* ʿAlā Beg, the peasants of the above-mentioned district were to consider him their *malik* and not to transgress what he ordered or considered expedient, and were to consider whatever was necessary for [appertained to] the above-mentioned charge, in accordance with ancient custom, as belonging to him, and were not to consider anyone as sharing [in it] with him, and were to consider the dues of the office of *malik*[1] which are customary according to the practice of the time of the late august and sublime *khāqān* and in the time of the august prince, as belonging to him and to pay these, and the *kalāntar* of the *dār us-salṭaneh* Tabrīz was not to interfere in the dues of the above-mentioned *malik*, and when appropriations were made, he was to assign in the name of the above-mentioned *malik*, whatever was the share (*rasad*) of the district of Arvaniq, so that he [the *malik*] could write notes of assignment on this which would be paid, district by district, and the *kadkhudās* were to meet these claims out of the produce of the property in question and to consider these notes of assignment valid through his signature and seal. Meanwhile the above-mentioned *malik* had represented that the *kalāntar* of Tabrīz did not give him authority as *malik* of the above-mentioned district and was preventing [him from collecting] his dues, and prior to this the peasants of the above-mentioned district had on receipt of an earlier order presented a petition to the effect that since the dues of the *malik* of the above-mentioned district were not separately mentioned in the register, if there were any dues in the ordinary assessment and the peasants had paid [these] to former *maliks*, the *malik* [i.e.] the above-mentioned ʿAlā Beg, should treat the peasants in the same way. Accordingly we order that the *kadkhudās* and peasants of the district of Arvaniq shall pay to him the dues of the *malik* as mentioned above in accordance with what was given to the *maliks* in the time of the late august *shāh* and the time of the world-conquering prince, and they are to consider the contents of the order of the late august prince and the order of our blessed prince which was issued in accordance with it as authentic from beginning to end, and they shall not engage in transactions of sale and purchase except subject to the order of the above-mentioned *malik*, and they shall consider whatever pertains to the above-mentioned charge as belonging to him. The duty of the above-mentioned *malik* is to follow such a path with the peasants so that they may be content with him and return thanks and so that he may be the cause of prayers for the well-being of our blessed prince. They are to consider it forbidden to demand a new decree every year. When the order

[1] *Rusūmi malikī*, or possibly *rusūmi milkī*, 'the dues from the property'.

(*parvānehcheh*) has been sealed by the royal seal they are to consider it valid. The *vakīls* of the *beglarbegī* of Āẕarbāyjān are to put it into effect. Dated Ṣafar A.H. 1041.

Chardin recognizes two other main classes of land, namely, *vaqf* land and estates in the possession of private persons. Many areas were constituted by the Ṣafavids into *ouqāf* for charitable purposes, especially for the benefit of Shīʿī shrines, notably the shrine of the Imām Riẕā in Mashhad and of his sister Fāṭimeh in Qumm. Some of these *vaqf* lands were endowments which had belonged to the Ṣafavid family before they became the rulers of Persia.[1] The greatest accession to lands of this class probably took place in the reign of Shāh ʿAbbās, in the year 1015/1606–7 or 1016/1607–8, when he decided to constitute all his private estates (*jamīʿi amlāk va raqabāti muktasabi khāṣṣehyi khẉud*), 'the just value of which was 100,000 *tūmāni shāhīyi ʿirāqī* and the produce of which after the deduction of the provision of what was needed for their cultivation was, using a medium conversion rate, nearly 7,000 *tūmāns*', together with various buildings in Iṣfahān and the neighbourhood into *ouqāf* for the twelve *imāms* and Muḥammad and Fāṭimeh, the wife of ʿAlī b. Abī Ṭālib. He vested the office of administrator in himself and thereafter in the reigning monarch. According to the terms of the *vaqf nāmeh*, drawn up by Shaykh Bahā ud-Dīn, the revenue of the *vaqf* was, after the deduction of the dues of the *mutavallī* (*ḥaqq ut-toulīyeh*), to be expended at the discretion of the *mutavallī* and according to the exigencies of the time.[2]

In addition to the increase in the area of *vaqf* land brought about

[1] In a manuscript described in the library of the shrine of the Imām Riẕā in Mashhad as the *Ṣulūk va Sijillāti Taymūrī* and known as the *Ṣarīḥ ul-Mulk* in the library of the Buyūtāti Salṭanatī in Tehrān, it is stated that in 1011 (1602–3) Shāh ʿAbbās sent Bahādur Khān to Balkh where he discovered a *vaqf nāmeh* in which Tīmūr had made certain endowments for the Ṣafavid family. The document gives a list of estates (*amlāk*), including properties in Iṣfahān, Hamadān, Ṭalish, and Ṭārim, which had been 'bought with legal gold and made into *ouqāf* for the male descendants of Sulṭān Khẉājeh ʿAlī.' The names of the leaders of various tribes, various *amīrs*, *kadkhudās*, and chiefs who had owned these estates, are added to the document with an acknowledgement that without any force or pressure being put upon them and in complete agreement and full possession of their faculties they had sold these estates. The date of this transaction is given as 806 (1403–4).

The document, after recording that the great *khāqān* had bought these places legally, states that he had vested the *toulīyat* of these estates in the male descendants of Sayyid ʿAlī Manṣūr b. Sayyid Jamāl ad-Dīn b. Sayyid ʿAlī Manṣūr b. Sayyid Jabrāʾīl al-Ḥusaynī. They were to collect the revenue annually and pay it to Khẉājeh ʿAlī b. Shaykh Ṣadr ad-Dīn Mūsā b. Sulṭān Shaykh Ṣafī ad-Dīn Isḥāq b. Sayyid Jabrāʿīl al-Ḥusaynī and his descendants.

Later *farmāns* belonging to Ṣafavid times granting various immunities to the *mutavallī* of the *ouqāf* of the Ṣafavid order in Ardabīl also exist. (See, for example, Ḥusayn b. Abdāl Zāhidī, *Silsilat an-Nasabi Ṣafavīyeh* (Berlin, Iranschāhr, 1924–5), pp. 104–5 and 108–10).

[2] Iskandar Beg, *Tārīkhi ʿĀlam-ārāyi ʿAbbāsī* (Tehrān, lithog., 1896–7), p. 536; see also Chardin, vi. 60.

by the action of the ruling house, there was also a tendency on the part of private owners to constitute their property into *vaqf*. The reason for this is, in part, to be sought in the fact that *vaqf* lands were not subject to the same extent to confiscation as were other lands, and by constituting their lands into *ouqāf*, landowners in some measure protected them; by vesting the office of *mutavallī* in themselves or their families they were nevertheless able to benefit from the major portion of the revenue, while paying a portion thereof to the charitable object, for the purpose of which the *vaqf* had nominally been made. Further, according to Chardin, many persons fearing the lands in their possession had been wrongfully acquired would constitute them into *vaqf*, hoping thereby to avoid any moral consequences which might result from the ownership of usurped property, while nevertheless continuing to enjoy in large measure the revenue thereof. Chardin is not altogether clear on the details of such a proceeding. He further declares that if wrongly acquired land was constituted into a *vaqf*, or so constituted under a false title, this title became valid after one year of uninterrupted possession, and could not thereafter be disputed.[1] The office of *mutavallī* of various of these *ouqāf*, such as those made for the Shīʿī shrines, appears to have been highly profitable. The tendency was for these offices to be concentrated in the hands of a few individuals who accumulated vast fortunes. Shāh ʿAbbās II redistributed these offices in an attempt to break up the large fortunes.[2]

A *farmān* dated Rabīʿ II 1073[3] (November–December 1662) concerning the payment of dues by peasants on *vaqf* land suggests that *vaqf* land was often let. The document concerns the Ghīā-ṣīyeh *ouqāf*,[4] some of which were charitable and others personal *ouqāf*, and illustrates the preference shown by the authorities for a crop-sharing agreement over a contract by which the peasants compounded for a lump sum. It reads as follows:

Since formerly the noble Kāmrān Beg, the *mutavallī* of the exalted Ghīāṣīyeh endowments had reported that the shares accruing to the *vaqf* from the Ghīāṣīyeh endowed properties, which are situated in every district, were fixed on the actual crop and amounted to one-tenth of the harvest, but the peasants of some of the districts of the above-mentioned Ghīāṣīyeh area which were charitable or personal *ouqāf*, had, as soon as an agreement had been made in former years between the *mutavallīs* and the peasants for a fixed rent, although they had accepted it, evaded the payment of the proper share, and since in accordance with an earlier

[1] Chardin, v. 381.
[2] ibid. vi. 63–5.
[3] In the possession of Ḥājjī Ḥusayn Āqā Nakhjavānī.
[4] These would appear to be the *ouqāf* created by Ghīāṣ ud-Dīn b. Rashīd ad-Dīn mainly in Āẕarbāyjān. In the document quoted below, the original *vaqf* was constituted in 734/1333–4.

royal order and a decree of the former *ṣadri dīvān* it had formerly been settled that the *kadkhudās* and peasants of the endowed properties of the Ghīāṣīyeh area, in view of the fact that the former rent and contract was legally abrogated by the death of the lessor and the lessees and the interests and well-being of the *vaqf* property so demanding, should pay the share in accordance with the actual crop (*hast o būd*), all the peasants (*zāri'ān*) are to pay their dues in accordance with the actual crop to the above-mentioned *mutavallī* and the manager (*mutaṣaddī*) of the *vaqf* property and the overseers (*nāẓirān*), and deliver the true share, in accordance with the practice of Āẓarbāyjān, especially the *dār us-salṭaneh* Tabrīz and the surrounding districts, to the *mutavallī*, the overseer, and manager so that they may act in accordance with the conditions laid down by the settlor of the endowment and the decree of the *dīvān us-ṣadāreh*, and they shall not take their stand upon the former contract or consider it valid. Meanwhile Kāmrān Beg had come to the exalted *dīvān us-ṣadāreh* and requested a confirmatory decree. Accordingly it was decided that the *kadkhudās* and peasants of the districts of the Ghīāṣīyeh endowed properties should act in the way which was formerly decided upon. It is the duty of the Shaykh ul-Islām and the official of the exalted *beglarbeg* and the illustrious *vazīr* of Āẓarbāyjān to give legal effect to this and not to allow any possibility of disobedience and contravention of the law or of the accounts of the peasants, and so act that the share accruing to the *vaqf* shall be paid in accordance with the actual crops. Let them show the greatest possible care in this matter and consider it their duty [to carry out this order].

Another *farmān*, dated 1101/1689,[1] concerns a similar dispute regarding the same property. It states that Muḥammad Rahīm, the *mutavallī* of the Ghīāṣīyeh property in the *dār us-salṭaneh* Tabrīz, had reported to the supreme *dīvān us-ṣadāreh* that in some of the *ouqāf* in the neighbourhood of Marand, including Shindvār in Arvaniq, contracts and leases had been concluded between the *mutavallīs* and the peasants, and the latter 'having accepted these, are not satisfied to pay according to the actual crops, and as a result a considerable loss was suffered by the administration of the *vaqf*, and the peasants were evading the payment of the proper share [to the *vaqf* authorities]'. He had demanded a decree and the *mustoufīs* of the *ouqāf* of the empire had confirmed that in the *vaqf* constituted in Muḥarram 734 (September–October 1333) the villages in question were part of the *vaqf*, and had given a statement of the dues according to the undertaking of the former *mutaṣaddīs*, Mir 'Ādil and Muḥammad Ibrāhīm. The peasants (*ra'āyā*) and cultivators (*zāri'īn*) were to accept the assessment or hand the area over to the bailiffs (*mubāshirs*) who would arrange for the cultivation directly and pay the salaries of those holding drafts. It was decided, therefore, that the peasants of the said *ouqāf* should

[1] In the possession of Ḥājjī Ḥusayn Āqā Nakhjavānī.

not base their position on any rent or contract which had been made at some time by a former *mutavallī*, but act as the well-being and interest of the property demanded and pay the proper share estimated on the actual crops in accordance with the custom prevailing in the province of Āẕarbāyjān, and especially in the *dār us-salṭaneh* Tabrīz and the neighbourhood, to the *mutavallī* and *mutaṣaddī* of the administration of the properties of the above-mentioned endowments who were to spend the proceeds of the *vaqf* as directed by the supreme *dīvān us-ṣadāreh*. The document ends:

> It is the duty of the *vakīls* of the victorious army commander and the exalted *beglarbeg* and the illustrious *vazīr* of Āẕarbāyjān to give legal effect [to this order] and not to give opportunity for disobedience and contravention of any item written above. Let them so act that the proper share accruing to the *vaqf* in accordance with the crops is paid to the *mubāshirs* of that property. If the peasants and cultivators of the above-mentioned districts have any legal plea or reasonable request, let them refer it to the *dīvān us-ṣadāreh* so that whatever is in accordance with the blessed *sharīʿa* and the proper assessment shall be fixed so that they shall act accordingly. Let them consider the greatest effort incumbent upon them in this matter and let them not demand a new decree every year.

In so far as estates in the hands of private individuals are concerned, Chardin maintains that these were held by their owners on a 99-years' lease. During this period the holders could settle and dispose of the land as they pleased. On the lapse of 99 years a new lease for the same period was issued on payment of one year's revenue. On some lands a small annual tribute per *jarīb* was also fixed.[1] In fact, however, private estates appear to have existed, and it may well be that Chardin was mistaken and that such leases applied only or mainly to *vaqf* land, the extent of which was very considerable at the time Chardin was writing. If this was the case the practice would be in keeping with the present-day custom of granting 99-year leases for *vaqf* land, owing to the fact that such land cannot technically be sold.[2]

Chardin also mentions that hereditary grants, known as *soyūrghāl*, were made out of *vaqf* land to eminent families among the religious classes. These grants passed from generation to generation by a kind of prescriptive right.[3] *Soyūrghāls* were not, however, confined to *vaqf* land or their recipients to members of the religious classes. They were also granted out of dead lands or crown lands[4] and usually carried with them certain immunities

[1] Chardin, v. 381–2. [2] See below, p. 233. [3] Chardin, vi. 65.

[4] A document granting a *soyūrghāl* to Iʿtimad ud-Douleh Muḥammad Beg, the *vazīr* of Shāh ʿAbbās, states that since he had said the water which he had

from taxation. The term *soyūrghāl* was further applied to money grants made from the revenue.[1] It appears that on death these grants, unless resumed by the state or usurped, which must frequently have been the case, were divided among the original grantee's legal heirs.[2] Further, although the original grant was frequently 'in perpetuity' and officials were prohibited from demanding a new order every year, it seems likely that on the death of the original grantee it may often have been necessary to obtain confirmation of the grant.[3]

To what extent the use of the term *soyūrghāl* is confined to grants, hereditary or otherwise, made to individuals as distinct from grants made in lieu of salary is not absolutely clear. A document issued by Shāh Ismā'īl to Khwājeh Kamāl Abu'l Fatḥ b. Khwājeh Jamāl ad-Douleh, the inspector (*mushrif*) of the royal treasury, and dated Ẕu'l Ḥijja 918 (February–March 1513) is interesting in that it grants immunity to the holder from any future demands on account of an increase in prosperity in the area.[4]

It allots 38,000 *tabrīzī dīnārs* as a *soyūrghāl* on the village of Vīst in the tax-district of Gulpāyagān to Khwājeh Kamāl ud-Dīn Abu'l Fatḥ. The *dīvān* dues of the area were to be remitted to the representatives (*vukalā*) of the beneficiary according to the current undertakings. The area was to be exempt from demands [by the government tax-collectors] for taxes (*māl o jihāt*), extraordinary levies (*ikhrājāt*), dues demanded by virtue of a decree or otherwise (*'avāriẓāti ḥukmī va ghayri ḥukmī*), *'alafeh*, *'ulūfeh*, *salāmī*, *sāvarī*, *pīshkash*, *chirīk*, and similarly the perquisites (*ḥaqq us-sa'ī*) of the tax-collectors (*'ummāl*), *ulāgh*, *ulām*, and other requisitions by the *dīvān* (*taklīfāti dīvānī*), royal demands (*muṭālibāti sulṭānī*), or whatever could be levied by way of taxation under any guise whatsoever.[5] Moreover, if by chance any increase in the revenue of the

obtained from a *qanāt* (in the neighbourhood of Iṣfahān) to irrigate certain lands might, when led into the Mubārak channel, be sufficient to reclaim the lands behind the Hazārjarīb, any dead lands which he reclaimed would be granted to him as a permanent hereditary *soyūrghāl* with exemption from taxation (MS. in possession of Dr Mihdī Bayānī, Tehrān). It may be, however, that this land was situated in land which had been constituted into *ouqāf* by one or other of the Ṣafavid monarchs.

[1] e.g. a *farmān* dated Ramaẓān 1047 (Jan.–Feb. 1638) quoted in a *farmān* of 1067 (1656–7), granting 20 per cent of the poll tax of the Armenians of the whole of Āẕarbāyjān, levied at the rate of 6 *dīnārs* per head, as a *soyūrghāl* to Mīr Ni'matullāh (MS. in the possession of Ḥājjī Muḥammad Āqā Nakhjavānī).

[2] As in the case of the *farmān* quoted in the preceding note.

[3] Although the grant mentioned in note 1 above was granted in perpetuity, nevertheless disputes broke out among the original heirs, and in a *farmān* dated Sha'bān 1115 (Dec. 1703–Jan. 1704) the grant is confirmed, and another *sayyid* was added to the list of beneficiaries. This *farmān* is in the possession of Ḥājjī Muḥammad Āqā Nakhjavānī.

[4] It is not clear whether the grant is by way of a gift or an assignment in lieu of salary. The original document is in the possession of Ḥājjī Mīrzā 'Abdullāh Anṣārī.

[5] For the meaning of these terms see the glossary.

area owing to increased cultivation took place, no increase was to be demanded from the grantee's representatives, nor was it to be included (in the assessment) by valuation or measurement.

A *farmān* of Sulṭān Ḥusayn dated 1120/1708 concerning a grant[1] to Mūsā Beg Qūllar Āqāsī, a former *beglarbegī* of Āẕarbāyjān of the hamlet (*mazraʿeh*) of Doulatābād and Khusrouābād in the district of Joushaqān, has a significant phrase, which states that these places had been given to him as a *soyūrghāl* by way of *iqṭāʿi tamlīk* (see p. 28) with its taxes and dues. The area had four disused *qanāts*. Some four years previously Mūsā Beg had brought two of them into use again and work on the other two to reclaim them was nearly finished. He further intended to make a *qanāt* in some dead land, and accordingly requested that the taxes and dues of the *dīvān* on the lands which would be watered by these *qanāts* should be granted to him as a hereditary *soyūrghāl* and that the government assessors should not increase the ordinary assessment of his *soyūrghāl* if they found production in these villages rose. In response to his request the document states that he was granted as a permanent and hereditary *soyūrghāl* the taxes and *dīvān* dues of the old *qanāts* and any *qanāts* which might be newly made in the area. The great *mustoufīs* of the *dīvān* were instructed to consider these as the *soyūrghāl* of him and his descendants and to remit from their joint assessment (*bunīcheh*) extraordinary provincial levies (*ikhrājāti mamlakatī*), extraordinary taxes, requisitions by the *dīvān* (*iṭlāqāti dīvān*), especially for foot-soldiers, presents (*pīshkash*), expenses of envoys, etc., and were on no account to write drafts on the area, and if the production of the area increased because of the coming into operation of new *qanāts* nothing extra was to be added to the original assessment. The governors (*ḥukkām*), *vazīrs*, *dārūghehs*, *tuyūldārs*, *mutaṣarrifs*, and other officials of the *dīvān* were on no account to write drafts on it or demand dues by way of *ʿulūfeh*, *ʿalafeh*, barley, straw, wood, domestic fowl, fodder, labour service (*bīgār*), hunting dues (*shikār*, or perhaps 'the provision of beaters'), *ṭarḥ*, *dastandāz*, *ulāgh*,[2] *kabk*,[3] roadguards (*qarāsūrān*), or other dues. On no account were they to molest the peasants and cultivators (*raʿāyā va barzigarān*), *muqannīs*,[4] or officials of Mūsā Beg, and any matters which came up for decision between the peasants of Mūsā Beg were to be referred to him: the governors (*ḥukkām*) and others were not to interfere. Twice in the document the words *bi dastūri aṣl* (original assessment) are used concerning the terms on which the

[1] I have seen a copy of this but not the original, which is said to be in Khusrouābād.

[2] For the meaning of these terms, see the glossary.

[3] i.e. partridges; cf. below, p. 334.

[4] i.e. those who make and repair *qanāts*.

soyūrghāl has been granted. This would appear to indicate clearly that a *soyūrghāl* did not necessarily confer immunity from all taxation. In this case it would seem that taxes according to some original assessment were still to be paid, but that immunity from extraordinary dues and increases in taxation was granted. The provision referring the decision of all disputes among the peasants to the grantee is further of considerable importance (see below).

It appears that exemption from taxation was also granted to individuals. These 'immunities' were 'personal' and did not attach to their lands as such, but in so far as they engaged in agriculture the lands were exempted. In a *farmān* dated 1079/1668–9[1] the Anṣārī family, a family of *sayyids*, were given permanent exemption from taxation wherever they might be, in Tabrīz or elsewhere. Accordingly, government officials were forbidden to levy any taxes or dues upon them. Any cultivation of the land or trade which they undertook was to be exempt. They were to be permanently exempt from taxation, dues and extra levies (*'avāriẓāt va ikhrājāt va ṣādirīāti* [*sic*] *dīvānī*), and provincial impositions (*taḥmīlāti vilāyatī*) such as *do 'ushr*, *dah yak*, and *ḥaddi mīāneh*, poll tax (*sar shumār*) and house tax (*khāneh shumār*), etc.

Dead lands belonged either to the state or to the *shāh*, according to the district in which they were situated. But since, according to Chardin, the *shāh* was the owner of all state property, he could declare them crown lands when he pleased, instead of their being disposed of by the governors of the provinces. If made into crown lands they were placed under overseers, who were receivers on behalf of the *shāh*. All land, therefore, which was not held or actually occupied and was not in a condition to be occupied, belonged to the *shāh* wherever it might be in the empire. If anyone wanted land to build a house in a place not actually occupied by anyone or for which no one could produce evidence of possession, the land was demanded of the governor and the overseer if it was state land, but if it was crown land, the demand had to be referred to the *shāh* or his officials in that province. Such grants as were obtained, according to Chardin, were made unconditionally or on condition of an annual payment. The grant was made for 99 years, according to the terms of the Civil Code, after the elapse of which a due had to be paid for the renewal of the lease for a similar term. If during the period the land was sold, the contracts had to be shown to the overseer and a small due paid, and the 99-years' grant renewed from that date.[2] If Chardin is right in stating that these grants applied to dead lands this would be strong evidence in support of the belief that ownership of the soil was vested in the *shāh*

[1] In the possession of Ḥājjī Ḥusayn Āqā Nakhjavānī.
[2] Chardin, v. 382–3.

alone. Moreover, if these grants really concerned 'dead lands', they represent a clear departure from the practice of Muslim law, whether Sunnī or Shīʿī. It is possible, however, that Chardin was mistaken on this point, and that such leases applied only to *vaqf* land, for the reason that full ownership of these lands could not technically be acquired.

The renting of property was in fact probably fairly common, especially in the case both of *vaqf* lands and crown lands. Tenants (*musta'jirān*) of the hamlets (*mazāriʿ*) of Mughānāt are mentioned in a document dated 966/1558–9[1] and of the Maḥāll of Iṣfahān in the *Tadhkirat al-Mulūk*. Another document dated 1041/1631–2, at the head of which is the seal of Shāh Ṣafī I,[2] concerns a complaint preferred by the tenant (*musta'jir*) of certain districts belonging to Arvaniq in the neighbourhood of Tabrīz, to the effect that the wages of a group of people had been wrongly charged to it by the *mustoufīs*. The plaintiff's plea that the areas in question had been made into *vaqf* by Muḥammad Beg and certified by the *dīvān* was upheld, and the document forbids that group of people in whose favour these drafts had been made to trouble the tenants (*musta'-jirīn*) of the area. The *beglarbegī* of the area was to give effect to this decision.

Crown lands directly administered were under the charge of the *vazīr* of the capital. His duty was to administer the *maḥālli khāṣṣeh* so that no place remained without the requisite oxen (? *bī nasaq*)[3] and without cultivation. He was to give whatever was necessary for cultivation by way of seed or advances to the peasants and tenants and to recover this at harvest time. He was to find peasants for every place in the crown lands which had lacked peasants and to promote its cultivation.

In the event of a crop failure [in crown lands] officials would be sent to the area concerned with the estimator of crops (*rayyāʿ*) and surveyor (*maṣṣāḥ*) to fix the estimate, and after the usual share of the peasant had been deducted the remainder would be collected by the *dīvān* and devoted to the payment of *dīvān* drafts.

Among the duties of the *vazīr* mentioned above was to collect the peasants, to increase cultivation, repair buildings and *qanāts*, and to protect the peasants from violence and oppression from any quarter.[4]

The *mustoufī* of Iṣfahān wrote drafts on and assigned the revenues and crops collected by the *vazīr* of Iṣfahān, and cleared the

1 Ḥusayn b. Abdāl Zāhidī, p. 105.
2 In the possession of Ḥājjī Ḥusayn Āqā Nakhjavānī.
3 Minorsky translates 'neglected'. I would suggest that it means without 'a cultivating unit', or *juft*. *Nasaq* is used at the present day in this sense in various areas, a village being divided into, or capable of carrying, so many *nasaqs*.
4 *T.M.*, ff. 72a–73a.

accounts of the peasants. In November, according to custom, the conversion rates (*tas'īr*) were fixed by the *'āmils* and officials, the peasants' accounts closed, and a final receipt given to them. At the same time the rolls of summons (*ṭavāmīri toujīh*) of men with donkeys (*mardi ulāghdār*), men with spades, etc., to be provided by the tax-payers were prepared.[1]

There appears also to have been a group of lands which was under a *vazīr* of the *sarkāri intiqālī*. These would seem to be *khāliṣeh* and *vaqf* lands which had been transferred or leased to individuals, since among the duties of this *vazīr* was to strive to increase cultivation and to repair buildings and *qanāts* in *khāliṣeh* and *vaqf* land, and to protect the payers [of rent?] so that no one should cause them violence. He was also charged with the administration of estates and cultivated lands, the care of gardens, real estate (*mustaghallāt*), mills, and *qanāts*. A statement sealed and attested by him of the condition of the crop of every district was to be submitted by the peasants and lessors. He was to provide from the revenue of the department whatever was necessary by way of seed, advances, and subventions to the peasants in any district which was without 'cultivating units'; these advances were to be repaid at harvest time. He was to collect peasants for any district which had none and set them to cultivate the land. In the event of a crop failure in any district his duty was similar to that of the *vazīr* in charge of crown lands.[2]

There was a special *mustoufī* who dealt, among other matters, with the accounts of these estates. He wrote drafts on and assigned the revenue from the crops and cleared the accounts of the peasants concerned and collected the *dīvān* and *vaqfī* dues. Similarly, conversion rates (*tas'īr*) were fixed in November by the *'āmils* and officials according to the customary rule (*dastūr*), the accounts of the peasants were closed and final receipts issued to them.[3] Partial or total crop failures being of frequent occurrence, and the revenue from the land being levied for the most part as a share of the actual crop, it was important to ascertain annually the amount of the harvest. In the capital, Iṣfahān, there was a special official in charge of this known as the *rayyā'*. His duty was to examine in the presence of the tax-collectors and other officials the crops of the Maḥāll of Iṣfahān in whatever year it was so decreed, whether because the quarter which was the government's share (? *chahār yaki nasaq*) was to be levied, or because the crops belonged to a category of land which had to be examined or was to be examined

[1] *T.M.*, ff. 82 a–b. Minorsky translates *tas'īr* by 'prices'. I would suggest rather 'conversion rate', the process denoted by *tas'īr* being the conversion of the share of the harvest due to the landowner or government from kind into cash.

[2] ibid. ff. 74 a–b.

[3] ibid. ff. 75 b–76 a.

[for some remission to be effected] because of blight, pest, or drought, etc. He was to take a sample of the crop in the presence of these officials, and the *ʿummāl* were then to make an estimate of the total harvest in accordance with this and adjust the assessment of the peasants and tax-payers on this basis; if it was then approved by the *vazīr* of the High Dīvān it became operative.[1]

Ouqāfi tafvīẓī[2] were under the supervision of the *ṣadri khāṣṣeh va ʿāmmeh*.[3] *Ouqāf* in the neighbourhood of Iṣfahān were administered by a special *vazīr* of the department, which was known as the *fayẓ āṣār* department, whose duty it was to see that estates and arable fields were being cultivated according to their capacity and to secure the prosperous condition of gardens, real estate (*musta-ghallāt*), and mills, and to see that *qanāts* were in good order. The estimated amount of the crops from the Maḥāll (i.e. the country-side of Iṣfahān and the districts which were *khāṣṣeh*) and real estate as well as other revenue accruing from the endowments of this department was collected from the peasants and tenants with the *vazīr's* knowledge and under his seal, and was employed by him for settled purposes. The *vazīr* was charged to exert himself to achieve the security of the property of the Maḥāll and to increase the prosperity of the Maḥāll and its agriculture.[4]

The administration of the *ouqāf* in the provinces was the duty of a special *mustoufī*. All *vazīrs*, *mustoufīs*, *mutaṣaddīs*, *mutavallīs*, and *mubāshirs* of the endowments both of the *khāṣṣeh* and the *dīvān* departments had to submit their accounts to the endow-ments office (*daftari mouqūfāt*) for audit.[5] A special *mustoufī* belonged to this department among whose duties it was to examine the accounts of the peasants and tenants and to issue to them receipts.[6] Charges for administration (*ḥaqq ut-toulīyeh*) and supervision (*ḥaqq un-naẓāreh*) were made on some *ouqāf* for the *ṣadri aʿẓam* (or chief minister).[7]

There was an important change in the Ṣafavid period in the position of the *qāẓīs* and the jurisdiction of *ʿurf* or customary law courts. Already under the Seljūqs the religious institution had been incorporated into the general structure of the state, but it was not till Ṣafavid times that the *sharīʿa* courts and the *qāẓīs* were made subordinate to the temporal powers as represented by the *ʿurf* courts and the semi-military hierarchy under the *dīvānbegī*.[8] Chardin states that the *qāẓī's* influence had been diminishing for several centuries. Minorsky suggests that the diminution in his

[1] ibid. ff. 83 a–b.

[2] i.e. those *ouqāf* of which the reigning monarch was the *mutavallī* (see above, p. 112).

[3] *T.M.*, f. 4 b

[4] ibid. ff. 71 a–b.

[5] ibid. ff. 71 b–72 a.

[6] ibid. ff. 81 b–82 a.

[7] ibid. ff. 85 a–b.

[8] See also ibid. pp. 110, 119.

powers had been achieved by creating the offices of the Ṣadr and Shaykh ul-Islām.[1] The *dīvānbegī*, moreover, controlled all *sharī'a* courts and acted as the executive power for the decision of the *sharī'a* courts.[2] Chardin maintains that there was no conflict of jurisdiction between the written (i.e. Qur'anic law) and customary law (i.e. *'urf*), because 'the latter being the stronger prevailed over the other without the least resistance'.[3] Criminal justice was according to Chardin entirely outside the jurisdiction of the *sharī'a* courts.[4]

Local administration was in the hands of *kadkhudās* who appear to have been responsible for the collection of taxes and dues and to have possessed certain authority over the inhabitants of villages. A *farmān*[5] dated 1006/1598, issued by Shāh 'Abbās I to a land-owner of Fārs, Shaykh Shahbāz b. Shaykh Ḥaydar, reads as follows:

> A royal command has been issued [as follows]: Since Shaykh Shahbāz, the son of Shaykh Ḥaydar, has pleaded that for a long time, generation after generation, [his family] have lived in the township of Iqlīd and engaged in agriculture and in making [the area] flourishing, and that the *kadkhudās* of the village of Bāzūncheh (?) where he has a small assessment (*bunīcheh*) demand that he should go there, we accordingly order that the *kadkhudās* of the above-mentioned village shall not force him to go there because he has lived generation after generation in that township and the decree of the royal prince, the august, sublime *khāqān*, has in this connexion been issued and he pays the taxes and dues to which he is subject there, and they shall not trouble him. The tax-collectors of the above-mentioned township shall not make drafts on him or his relatives on account of extraordinary taxes (*ikhrājāt*) or dues (*'avāriẓāt*) contrary to [this] order, whether by way of labour service (*bīgār*) or *shikār* or for any other purpose under any name whatsoever. Let the governor (*ḥākim*) of Fārs give effect to this. A new decree shall not be demanded every year. Dated Jumādī II A.H. 1006 (January–February 1598).

The extent to which land tax was levied and the rate at which it was levied is not entirely clear. The assigned lands were in some, but not all, cases exempt from the payment of land tax to the central treasury, whatever the grantees levied for their own benefit. From crown lands in the hands of individuals and *vaqf* land, except where specially exempted, something by way of land tax or, in the former case by way of rent, was no doubt levied. According to the *Lubb at-Tavārīkh* (composed in 1541) the tax-regime instituted by Uzun Ḥasan[6] continued to be operative long after his death.[7] In

[1] *T.M.*, p. 111. [2] ibid. p. 119.
[3] Chardin, vi. 75. [4] ibid. v. 98.
[5] In the possession of Ḥājjī Muḥammad Āqā Nakhjavānī.
[6] See above, p. 101.
[7] Hinz, *Z.D.M.G.* c. 1 (1950), p. 177. See also Minorsky, *B.S.O.A.S.* x (1940–2), p. 142, n. 3.

ʿIrāq, Fārs, and Āẕarbāyjān, Sharaf Bidlīsī, the author of the Kurdish history known as the *Sharaf Nāmeh*, states that this regime was still in operation when he wrote, i.e. in 1596.[1] Here, again, however, there were in all probability considerable differences from district to district and it is unlikely that Uzun Ḥasan's regime was operative in all provinces. From what has been said above it appears that in some cases the land tax was a quarter of the produce. According to Alessandri, Ṭahmāsp b. Ismāʿīl (930–84/1524–76) levied rather less. He writes:

> on the produce of the soil, such as wheat and other grain, the king gets one-seventh: from vineyards and pastures, on 1,000 *orchi* [? *sic*] of land he gets 60 shahi yearly which in our money make four gold sequins each and a little over. These *orchi* are measures of theirs, there may be upwards of 100 to a field (so that 1,000 would equal 9 fields; and thus they pay little less than half a ducat for a field): . . . on animals for every 40 sheep yearly they pay 15 bisti, which in our money make 3 lire, 15 soldi, while on male animals they pay 10 bisti annually, which in our money make 2 lire, 10 soldi.[2]

It would be unwise, however, to presume that a uniform system prevailed throughout the country.

Special exemptions from taxation were made from time to time on account of poverty due to natural calamity or other causes. Thus in 909/1503–4 Shāh Ṭahmāsp issued a *farmān* exempting the people of Ṭāliqān from *khumsi nassājī*, *mavāshī*, and *marāʿī*, on the grounds of their inability to pay. The governors (*ḥukkām*), holders of *tuyūl*, *dārūghehs*, *kalāntars*, and *kadkhudās* were forbidden to levy anything on anyone on this account, and the *mustoufīs* of the *dīvān* were to enter this exemption granted to the people of Ṭāliqān in their registers. The *farmān* itself was engraved on stone and set up in the area.[3]

In Iṣfahān water dues were also levied. According to Chardin lands and gardens in Iṣfahān and the neighbourhood paid 20 *sols* per *jarīb* a year to the *shāh* for river water. The rate for spring water was less.[4] The *mīrāb* was an important official and, again to quote Chardin, obtained 4,000 *tūmāns* from his charge apart from what his underlings collected for him.[5] His duties were to appoint the supervisors of the irrigation canals (*mādī sālār*), to clean the channels (*anhār va jadāvil*), to see the water of the Zāyandeh Rūd reached every part of the Maḥāll of Iṣfahān which was watered by

[1] Quoted by Hinz; *Scheref-Nameh*, ed. V. Véliaminof-Zernof (St. Petersburg, 1860–2), ii. 120. The regulations (*dastūr*) of Uzun Ḥasan are also quoted in the *Tadhkirat al-Mulūk*, according to which the fees of the *ṣāḥib jamʿ* of the *rikāb khāneh* were in some cases levied (f. 100 b).

[2] *Chronicle of the Carmelites in Persia*, i. 52.

[3] M.F.A., No. 730, pp. 354–5.

[4] Chardin, iv. 100–1.

[5] ibid. p. 100.

it, and to prevent the peasants trespassing upon each other's water rights or the strong oppressing the poor in this matter. He was to decide any dispute between individuals or districts concerning their water rights and carry out his decisions with the confirmation of the *vazīr*, *kalāntar*, and *mustoufī*.[1]

The holders of *tuyūl*, assigned annually or on a long-term basis, and of *soyūrghāl* were subject to the payment of certain dues. This is clear from the fact that the salaries of certain officials were recognized as consisting in part of 'dues' paid by the holders of *tuyūl*, annual grants (*hameh sāleh*), and *soyūrghāl*. Whether these dues were confined to a single payment on the issue of the document or levied annually is not clear. Some dues, such as those to the keeper of the august seal, may have been paid only once. Others, such as the payment to the *mustoufī ul-mamālik* and the *ṣāḥib toujīh*, may have been levied annually. The following dues paid by the holders of *tuyūl* amounting to 16·42 per cent of the income of the grant for one year as registered in the *dīvān* are mentioned in the *Tadhkirat al-Mulūk*:[2]

(In *dīnārs* per *tūmān*)

To the *vakīl* of the Supreme Dīvān	357
To the *vazīr* of the Supreme Dīvān	330
To the *nāẓir* of the *daftarkhāneh*	7
To the keeper of the August Seal	260
To the keeper of the *sharafi nafāẕ* seal	315
To the *davātdāri aḥkām*	25
To the *davātdāri arqām*	25
To the *dārūghehyi daftarkhāneh*	7½
To the *mustoufī ul-mamālik*	45
To the *majlis nivīs**	200
To the *ẓābiṭeh nivīs*	11¼
To the *ṣāḥib toujīh*	11¼
To the *avārijeh nivīs* of the province of 'Irāq, Āẕarbāyjān, Fārs, or Khurāsān	11¼

* Alternatively 25 *dīnārs* per *tūmān* to the *munshī ul-mamālik* (*T.M.*, p. 53, n. 5).

[1] *T.M.*, ff. 81 a–b. Minorsky translates 'to conduct the surplus water (*āb-i zā'ideh*) of the Zāyandeh-rūd river . . .'. I would suggest that *āb-i zā'ideh-rūd* is a scribe's error for *āb-i zāyandeh-rūd*, since the *mīrāb* is concerned with the allotment of water, not when the water is surplus, since no disputes are then likely to arise, but when the water is not sufficient to supply the various needs of the area, or only sufficient if carefully allotted. Further, he translates 'quarrels . . . between landowners (*arbāb*) and the peasants of a district . . .'. I would suggest here that the meaning is rather 'quarrels between the landowners and peasants of one district with those of another over the allotment of the water'. The water of the Zāyandeh Rūd was (and is) divided first among the various districts irrigated by it and then among the lands of each district. In so far as the landowners worked their lands on a crop-sharing basis, disputes between them and their peasants would not arise, whereas disputes between the different districts arose then as at the present day.

[2] ibid. pp. 85–93.

To the *lashkar nivīs*	25
To the *sar khaṭṭ nivīs*	8
To the *daftardār*	3¾

The holders of 'military' *tuyūl* paid instead of the above, or together with some, but probably not all, of the above, the following dues, which amount to 3·5 per cent of the income of the grant for one year as registered in the *dīvān*:

(In *dīnārs* per *tūmān*)

To the *vazīrs* of the *qūrchīs*, *ghulāms*, *tufangchīs*, and *tūpchīs*	200
To the *mustoufīs* of the *qūrchīs*, *ghulāms*, *tufangchīs*, and *tūpchīs*	100
To the *ṣāḥib toujīh*	50

Since many of the assignments to the military were hereditary, it seems likely that these dues, if not levied annually, were at least levied whenever a *tuyūl* was transmitted by inheritance.

A due of 11¼ *dīnārs* per *tūmān* is mentioned as forming part of the salary of the *avārijeh nivīsi maʿdan*. Again, whether this was paid by all *tuyūl* holders or merely those in which mineral deposits were found is not clear.

The following dues were levied on annual grants (*hameh sāleh*):

(In *dīnārs* per *tūmān*)

To the *vakīl* of the Supreme Dīvān	238
To the *vazīr* of the Supreme Dīvān	220
To the *nāẓir* of the *daftarkhāneh*	4⅔
To the keeper of the August Seal	133⅓
To the keeper of the *sharafi nafāẕ* Seal	157½
To the *davātdāri aḥkām*	16
To the *davātdāri arqām*	16
To the *dārūghehyi daftarkhāneh*	5
To the *mustoufī ul-mamālik*	30
To the *majlis nivīs**	200
To the *ẓābiṭeh nivīs*	7½
To the *ṣāḥib toujīh*	7½
To the *avārijeh nivīs* of the province of ʿIrāq, Āẕarbāyjān, Fārs, or Khurāsān	7½
To the *lashkar nivīs*	16⅔
To the *sar khaṭṭ nivīs*	5⅓
To the *daftardār*	2½

* Or alternatively 16⅔ *dīnārs* to the *munshī ul-mamālik*.

These total dues amounted to some 10·6 per cent of the income of the grant for one year as registered in the *dīvān*.

Similarly the holders of *soyūrghāl* paid the following dues:

(In *dīnārs* per *tūmān*)

To the *vakīl* of the Supreme Dīvān	714
To the *vazīr* of the Supreme Dīvān	714

To the *nāẓir* of the *daftarkhāneh*	14
To the keeper of the August Seal	520
To the *davātdāri aḥkām*	50
To the *davātdāri arqām*	50
To the *dārūghehyi daftarkhāneh*	15
To the *mustoufī ul-mamālik*	90
To the *munshī ul-mamālik*	50
To the *ẓābiṭeh nivīs*	22½
To the *ṣāḥib toujīh*	22½
To the *avārijeh nivīs* of the province of ʿIrāq, Āẕarbāyjān, Fārs, or Khurāsān	22½
To the *lashkar nivīs*	50
To the *sar khaṭṭ nivīs*	16
To the *daftardār*	7½

The total amount involved represents some 23·58 per cent of income of the grant for one year as registered in the *dīvān*. It may be that all dues were not paid by each holder, and that since the grant was a permanent one the sum paid represented a payment made once and for all, and was in effect a kind of capital investment. The *ṣadri aʿẓam* received 15 per cent on all *soyūrghāls*.[1] This was presumably an annual payment.

It must not be assumed, however, from the above either that practice was uniform throughout the empire or that all grants conformed to one or other type. As pointed out above it is not clear whether all dues were levied on all grants—indeed it seems likely that this was not the case—nor is it clear whether they were levied only on the issue of the original grant, on its periodic renewal, or annually. Here again a variety of practice probably prevailed. If the dues were levied on the issue of the grant or whenever it was renewed, this lends point to the phrase frequently met with in official documents to the effect that the grant was an 'eternal' grant, and that a new decree was not to be demanded every year by the tax-collectors and other officials. Lastly it must not be assumed that the only dues levied upon the holders of *tuyūls* and *soyūrghāls* were those set out above, or that the liabilities of the holders ended with the payment of these dues.

The most notable change in the composition of the landowning class in Ṣafavid times, apart from the usual changes consequent on the rise of a new dynasty (i.e. the adherents and officials of the new regime displacing those of the former regime) was the great increase in land held by members of the religious classes. Originally they probably held this land as *mutavallīs* of *ouqāf* or by way of hereditary grants or *soyūrghāls*. In due course much of this land became

[1] *T.M.*, ff. 85 a–b. The text is ambiguous. Other possible readings are '10 per cent or 5 per cent', and 'tithe [i.e. on land not granted by way of *soyūrghāls*] and 5 per cent of all *soyūrghāls*'.

private property. In certain parts of the country, notably Āẕarbāyjān, and Iṣfahān, the religious classes have continued to form an important element in the landowning class.

Of the condition of the peasants we have little detailed information. According to Chardin land round Iṣfahān paid 30 écus (6,600 *dīnārs* or 0·66 *tūmān*) per *jarīb*.[1] That is to say, instead of the usual crop-sharing agreement, which according to Chardin prevailed elsewhere, the peasant paid a cash rent. The difference was no doubt due to the fact that land round the town was used largely for growing vegetables, which found a ready market in the town. Where crop-sharing prevailed Chardin states that the owner provided all or half the manure and water according to the agreement. The peasant worked the land, sowed the seed, and harvested the crop. All the expenses of cultivation were the responsibility of the peasant. The produce was divided, the owner taking a quarter to a half according to the situation of the land. Generally he had one-third after the seed had been deducted. This arrangement prevailed both in land held by private persons and in crown lands. On fruit-trees the landowner took one-half to two-thirds and on ordinary trees two-thirds.[2] Kaempfer gives further details and states that in the neighbourhood of Iṣfahān if the *shāh* provided the seed and water and the peasant oxen, manure, labour, and additional servitudes, the peasant received one-third of the harvest. If the *shāh* provided oxen and agricultural implements and remitted the servitudes the peasant's share fell to one-quarter, and if the *shāh* provided the labour also the share of the peasant did not exceed one-eighth. This latter agreement was thus properly speaking not a crop-sharing agreement at all, the one-eighth representing wages paid to the peasant for his labour. On rice, millet, cotton, beans, fenugreek, melon, and pumpkins, the share of the peasant, even if he provided all the costs of cultivation, was two-fifths. On opium his share was eleven twenty-eighths. On *ṣayfī* crops the peasant paid the landlord's share in cash at current prices to which were added 15 per cent. The landlord's share of *ṣhatvī* crops was paid in kind with an additional 1½ *maḥmūdī* per 100 *mann*. In addition the *shāh* received 2 per cent in cash on the value of all crops.[3] In Chardin's opinion the landlord always had the worst of the bargain with the peasant in a crop-sharing agreement, and he describes the many ruses he alleged they used to obtain a larger share than was their due. He states that the peasants lived in tolerable comfort, and compares their condition favourably with that of peasants in the more fertile parts of Europe. He states

[1] Chardin, v. 384; *T.M.*, p. 21. [2] Chardin, v. 384.

[3] E. Kaempfer, *Amoenitatum Exoticarum politico-physico-medicarum fasciculi V* (Lemgo, 1712), p. 91 (quoted in *T.M.*).

that they everywhere wore silver ornaments and sometimes gold, and were well clothed and had good footwear. Their houses were well provided with utensils and furniture (? presumably carpets). On the other hand, they were exposed to rough treatment on the part of officials. Further, they were subject to heavy demands in the way of forced labour, particularly in crown lands and lands held by great nobles.[1]

[1] v. 386–92. Chardin states that in the reign of Shāh Sulaymān (1667–94) there was a great diminution in riches and bounty. This was accompanied by a depreciation in the silver coinage. The great everywhere, he goes on to say, extorted from the people (iii. 292).

CHAPTER VI

THE AFSHARID INTERLUDE: THE RISE OF THE QĀJĀRS

AFTER the reign of Shāh ʿAbbās II (1052–77/1642–67) the Ṣafavid empire declined. During the reign of Ḥusayn (1105–35/1694–1722) the Afghāns revolted and in 1135/1722 under Maḥmūd they took Iṣfahān, the Ṣafavid capital.

The period of Afghān domination is remarkable only for the ruin which it brought about, especially in Iṣfahān and the neighbourhood. It seems probable that during the siege of Iṣfahān many government records and papers were destroyed. It is not unreasonable therefore to conclude that in the Iṣfahān area, if not elsewhere, considerable disorder was introduced at this time into land administration and land ownership. In 1729 Iṣfahān was recovered for the Ṣafavids and Nādir Shāh put Ṭahmāsp on the throne and some months later defeated the Afghāns near Shīrāz. In 1732 Nādir deposed Ṭahmāsp in favour of his infant son ʿAbbās and in 1736 he formally assumed power himself.

The Afsharid period is not of great importance in the history of land tenure and land administration. It brought no lasting changes. The general tendency appears to have been towards a tighter control over the administration and a resumption of *tuyūls* and *soyūrghāls*. In a *farmān* dated Muḥarram 1146/June–July 1733 it was decreed that the taxes of Tabrīz should be collected by Mīrzā Muḥammad Shafīʿ, *munshī* of the *sarkār* of the *ayālat* of Tabrīz and expended as he saw fit. The document states

> we have decreed that the *dīvān* taxes of Tabrīz and its districts, whether *tuyūls* of the exalted *beglarbegs*, or all the old annual grants of the victorious soldiers (*sālajāti qadīmehyi ʿasākir*), *soyūrghāls*, and sums which were allotted to the *vazīrs* of Āẕarbāyjān, and the produce of the *khāliṣejāt* and the revenue of the *vaqf* properties situated in the abovementioned *dār us-salṭaneh* and its districts shall be collected by Mīrzā Muḥammad Shafīʿ,[1] with the help of Luṭf ʿAlī Beg, the *nā'ib* of the *dār us-salṭaneh* Tabrīz and governor with full powers of Āẕarbāyjān, and allotted to and expended on such purposes as the latter shall approve.

Greater care than ever was to be exercised over the matter of *dīvān* taxes, and the accounts of the transactions, whether pertaining to the *dīvān* or not (i.e. both civil and military?), of the governors and tax-collectors of each of the provinces of Āẕar-

[1] He subsequently became *mustoufī* of Tabrīz (see Lisān ul-Mulk, *Tārīkh va Jughrāfīā*, pp. 281–2).

bāyjān were to be passed by him and he was to enter the income and expenditure in his accounts and to allow no one to commit peculation or waste. His wages in return for his service were fixed as from the beginning of 1145/1732 at 50 *tabrīzī tūmāns*. In addition he was to receive the minor dues which were allotted as the salaries of the secretaries (*munshīs*) of Tabrīz. The document also makes provision for the payment of two secretaries or scribes, at the rate of 10 *tūmāns* each, who were to assist him. He was to collect all the *dīvān* taxes from the tax-payers and tenants in full. The governor, *vazīr*, and tax-collectors of Marāgheh, ʿAbd ur-Razzāq Khān the *ẓābiṭ* of Urumīyeh, and the governor and tax-collectors of the provinces of Āẕarbāyjān were to pass their accounts through him and to show to him the accounts of all the taxes put up to public contraction (*muʿāmalāt*), and the *mustoufīs* and scribes of the *sarkār* of the province (*ayālat*) and *vizārat* of Tabrīz were to hand over to him the old records of each district so that no draft or charge on the revenue or tax should be forgotten. They were not to write any drafts on the revenue without his authorization and were to obey him in all. The *vakīls*, *kadkhudās*, landowners, peasants, tax-payers (whether assessed separately or by a group assessment), tenants, the collectors of *dīvān* taxes and the produce of *ouqāf* were to act in accordance with this decree and the great *mustoufīs* were to enter this document in their registers.[1]

The army under Nādir Shāh was to some extent paid in cash; in another *farmān*, also dated Muḥarram 1146/June–July 1733, Luṭf ʿAlī Beg, the *nāʾib* of Tabrīz and governor of Āẕarbāyjān, was ordered to collect the arrears of Tabrīz in accordance with the registers and to provide the pay of the army of Āẕarbāyjān for six months. He was also to appoint honest receivers (*ẓābiṭ*) in Qarājeh Dāgh, Hashtrūd, Garmrūd, Gāvrūd, Marand, Khūy, Chūras, and Salmās, to collect the taxes of those places in full and to report whatever was expended on the army and their pay.[2]

It appears that Nādir Shāh in general discouraged his *amīrs* from acquiring property. A *farmān* from Nādir addressed to Mihrāb Beg, *vazīr* of Herāt, after referring to the report that Mihrāb Beg had made himself buildings in the *qalʿeh* of Herāt, states that he himself was always on the move (*khāneh bi dūsh*) and that Mihrāb Beg had no right to acquire land there. Accordingly he was ordered to take possession of the new buildings, bath (*ḥammām*), and estates which he had acquired in the *dār us-salṭaneh* of Herāt and its dependencies on behalf of the *dīvān* and to limit himself to the possession of a house for a dwelling. He was to devote the time he had spent in acquiring estates to the affairs of state.[3]

[1] Lisān ul-Mulk, *Tārīkh va Jughrāfīā*, pp. 278–80.
[2] ibid. p. 280.
[3] *Munshaʾāt* (folios not numbered).

Nādir's rule, however, was too short and perhaps too much taken up with foreign adventures permanently to reverse the trend in administration in so far as the practice of making land assignments was concerned. The main importance of the period from the point of view of the distribution of land and revenue administration lies in his policy with regard to *ouqāf* and his tribal policy. He adopted, more widely perhaps than preceding rulers, the policy of resettling tribal groups, in some cases in order to garrison newly conquered territory and in others to lessen the likelihood of the rebellion of contumacious elements. In 1730 he ordered 50,000 to 60,000 families of tribes-people to be transferred from Āẕarbāyjān, Persian ʿIrāq, and Fārs to Khurāsān.[1] In 1732 he moved 60,000 Abdālīs from the neighbourhood of Herāt to Mashhad, Nayshāpūr, and Dāmghān.[2] In the same year 3,000 families of the Haft Lang branch of Bakhtīārī were sent to Khurāsān.[3] A further group of Haft Lang together with some Chahār Lang, amounting to 10,000 families, were sent to Jām in Khurāsān, after a Bakhtīārī rebellion had been crushed in 1736.[4] When Nādir Shāh reached Tiflis in 1735 he banished 6,000 Georgian families of his opponents to Khurāsān.[5]

Nādir Shāh and his successors appear, like former rulers, to have largely governed the tribes through their own leaders. In 1159/1746–7 Nādir appointed ʿAlī Sāliḥ Khān head of the Haft Lang.[6]

When Nādir Shāh accepted the throne in 1736 he had made it a condition that the Sunnī sect should be substituted for the Shīʿī (which had been the faith of the Ṣafavids). In the last year of his reign he promulgated a decree for the resumption of *ouqāf*, the extent of which, it will be remembered, had greatly increased in Ṣafavid times. As a result of this decree a considerable number of *ouqāf* were taken over and entered with *khāliṣeh* estates in the land register subsequently known as the *raqabāti nādirī*.[7] Where the benefactors of a *vaqf* and the *mutavallī* were strong they did not in fact surrender the *vaqf*, although it became registered in the *raqabāti nādirī*. Other *mutavallīs*, fearing that the *ouqāf* under their charge would be confiscated, did not produce their *vaqf nāmehs*, and this gave an opportunity to others to register these properties in their own names. The *mustoufīs*, moreover, could not reject such demands for registration on the grounds that the land was *vaqf*,

[1] L. Lockhart, *Nadir Shah* (London, 1938), pp. 51–2.
[2] ibid. p. 54. [3] ibid. p. 65. [4] ibid. p. 110. [5] ibid. p. 91.
[6] Sardar Asʿad, *Tārīkhi Bakhtīārī* (? Tehrān, lithog.), pp. 148–9.
[7] Anṣārī, *Tārīkhi Iṣfahān* (Tehrān, 1322), p. 37. For example, various villages in the neighbourhood of Shīrāz and Marvdasht which were part of the *ouqāf* of the Ātashī Sayyids were made into *khāliṣeh* (Fasā'ī, ii. 46). Subsequently much of this land became *arbābī* (i.e. the estates of large landed proprietors). Similarly, various *ouqāf* in the neighbourhood of Nayshāpūr belonging to a group of Sayyids were made into *khāliṣeh* (ibid. p. 86).

since all *ouqāf* were supposed to have been confiscated. In addition to the concealment of the true ownership of *vaqf* properties induced by Nādir's attempt to resume all *vaqf* property there was a further difficulty in ascertaining the true ownership of many *ouqāf* in the Iṣfahān area owing to the fact that the registers of *ouqāf* property were burnt during the sack of Iṣfahān by the Afghāns.[1] Nādir died, however, before full effect could be given to his decree. His successor, ʿAlī Qulī ʿĀdilshāh, revoked the decree and gave back some of the confiscated estates.[2] However, Sir John Malcolm, writing at the beginning of the nineteenth century, states that these lands were never fully restored.[3] In any case there seems little doubt that in the troubled years between the end of the Ṣafavid dynasty and the establishment of Qājār dominion much *vaqf* property was resumed by the state or converted into private property. For example, according to the account of one authority the revenue of the shrine of the Imām Riẓā from its endowments, which at the end of the Ṣafavid period amounted to 15,000 *khurāsānī tūmāns* or 300,000 rs., had fallen by 1821–2 to some 2,000–2,500 *khurāsānī tūmāns*, or 40,000–50,000 rs.[4]

There is little reason to suppose Nādir's rule was anything but hard on the population. The constant campaigns were paid for by enormous taxes and heavy contributions. In Kirmān, for example, in 1736 the people were so denuded of supplies by the expedition which he had planned for the recapture of Qandahār that there was a famine for seven or eight years afterwards.[5] Further, in February 1738 men and women of the Kirmān district were compelled to act as porters to Qandahār owing to a shortage of draught animals.[6]

Otto, who travelled from Baghdād to Iṣfahān in 1737, described the state of the peasants and common people as by no means enviable and when he returned to Baghdād in 1739 he reported further deterioration.[7] On the other hand, Mashhad, which Nādir regarded as his capital, was about the year 1741 in a flourishing condition.[8]

In so far as security was concerned, it appears that under Nādir Shāh some improvement was brought about. Travel was made relatively safe as a result of his policy of making the head of each village responsible for any complaints of incidents within his boundaries.[9] On the other hand, frontier districts were liable, as in Ṣafavid times, to be devastated, especially where occupied by

[1] Anṣārī, pp. 77–80. [2] ibid. p. 39.
[3] *History of Persia* (London, 1829), ii. 313.
[4] J. B. Fraser; *Narrative of a Journey into Khorasān* (London, 1825), p. 455. About 1892 the annual revenue of the shrine of the Imām Riẓā was, according to Curzon, 60,000 *tūmāns* and 10,000 *kharvārs* of grain (*Persia and the Persian Question* (London, 1892), ii. 489).
[5] Lockhart, p. 112. [6] ibid. p. 116. [7] ibid. pp. 180–1.
[8] ibid. p. 197. [9] *Chronicle of the Carmelites*, i. 602.

minority groups. Writing of Nakhjavān Mgr. Dominic Salvani, O.P., in a letter dated 11 December 1746 states:

having killed all men of position, put out those eyes that saw well and sold their families to the soldiers, after having taken away from the community all their ploughing animals and removed all the grain for the army, he [Nādir Shāh] has turned to harass the people and fleece them with impossible taxes, which leave them as naked as worms, . . . and then dragging them off in troops and a promiscuous mass to Kalat on the farthest borders of Khurasan.[1]

After the decline of Afsharid rule Persia enjoyed a brief period of relative peace during the latter years of Karīm Khān Zand (1163–93/1750–79), the centre of whose power was Shīrāz. The main lines of the administration appear to have continued unchanged; as under Nādir the tendency was towards direct administration by the officials of the state rather than to a return to the practice of making assignments to the military leaders. In a *farmān* dated Ẕu'l Ḥijja 1177/June 1764 from Karīm Khān to Najaf Qulī Khān for the office of Beglarbeg of Tabrīz and its districts, the latter was entrusted with the collection of the revenue. He was also charged with the ordering of agricultural affairs, making the province prosperous, care for the subjects (*ra'īyat*), the punishment of the rebellious and contumacious, the prevention of robbery, the restraining of the hands of the unjust from the weak and the poor, the good treatment of the peasants (*ra'āyā*), and the collecting of them (i.e. preventing their dispersal). He was also specially ordered to treat with compassion the Shaqāqī tribes and other tribes in the province, and to settle them in their original dwelling places and to cause them to engage in agriculture and service to the government. In conclusion the nobles, subjects, cultivators, and all the inhabitants of Tabrīz and its dependent districts, the *khāns* and chiefs of the tribes, were to obey him.[2]

Abdāl Khān, who succeeded his father 'Alī Ṣāliḥ Beg as head of the Haft Lang, was appointed on somewhat similar terms over the province of Persian 'Irāq. The *farmān* appointing him was issued by Karīm Khān in the name of the Ṣafavid Shāh Ismā'īl (Mīrzā Abū Turāb). By it Abdāl Khān was entrusted with the collection of taxes, the ordering of agricultural affairs, the general administration of the province and the collecting of the peasants (i.e. he was to see they did not disperse), and was allotted an annual salary of 700 *tūmāns*.[3]

The death of Karīm Khān (1193/1779) was followed by another period of anarchy and the emergence of Āqā Muḥammad Qājār,

[1] ibid. p. 630.
[2] Lisān ul-Mulk, *Tārīkh va Jughrāfīā*, pp. 173–4.
[3] Sardār As'ad, pp. 152–4.

the founder of the Qājār dynasty, which ruled until A.D. 1925. A branch of the Qājārs, a Turkish tribe, had been settled at Astarābād by one of the Ṣafavid rulers. After the death of Karīm Khān, Āqā Muḥammad Khān united the Qājārs of Māzandarān under him, and on the death of ʿAlī Murād Khān, Karīm Khān's nephew, in 1785 marched on ʿIrāq. Gradually, as a result of increasing, though not uninterrupted success, he obtained the support of various contemporary leaders and extended his conquests, and eventually transferred the centre of his dominion from Māzandarān to Tehrān.

The position at the time of his rise to power was not promising. The leaders of the tribes were ambitious, had become accustomed to revolt and plunder, and were reluctant to submit to any kind of authority. The countryside had been ruined by repeated pillage. The people had been reduced to ruin and driven to exile. Security on the roads was virtually non-existent and commerce had greatly declined.[1] The first task of Āqā Muḥammad Khān was thus to restore order and to establish a measure of security.[2] In this he was to some extent successful, and increased security brought some alleviation in the condition of the peasants. The basis of his power was the army. He appears to have continued the policy of paying the army in cash and not to have reverted to the policy of making assignments of the revenue or land to them. His successors resorted to the policy of making assignments both to their civil and to their military officials. The revenue under Āqā Muḥammad Khān, however, was largely farmed.[3] He was a man of considerable vigour and energy. Fear of punishment to some extent restrained the exactions of provincial governors and others from the

[1] Malcolm, *History of Persia*, ii. 182–3.

[2] Under his successors security of the roads left much to be desired. It was placed under officials known as *rāhdār* who, according to Morier, 'in general, exercise their office with so much brutality and extortion, as to be execrated by all travellers. . . . They afford but little protection to the road, their stations being placed at too wide intervals to be able to communicate quickly; but they generally are perfectly acquainted with the state of the country, and are probably leagued with the thieves themselves, and can thus, if they choose, discover their haunts.' (*A Second Journey through Persia* (London, 1818), pp. 69–70). Tancoigne, on the other hand, speaks not unfavourably of the *rāhdārs* at the beginning of the nineteenth century. He states: 'highway robbers are very rare in Persia . . . the safety of the roads is maintained by a corps called the rahdars, who are at the same time collectors of the custom house duties and town dues. Detachments of these rahdars are met at regular distances, posted so as to be able to lend each other assistance in case of alarm; they scrupulously examine all travellers who appear suspicious, and are the more interested in performing their duty properly, as they are made personally responsible for the robberies committed in the districts confided to their care.' (*Narrative of a Journey into Persia and Residence at Teheran* (London, 1820), pp. 237–8.)

[3] Under the later Qājārs the government offices were largely farmed. ʿAbbās Mīrzā, when governor of Āẕarbāyjān, attempted to abolish the practice of selling governorships to the highest bidder (Morier, *Second Journey through Persia*, pp. 240–1).

people, and during his reign there was in some measure a revival of prosperity. His successor, Fatḥ 'Alī Shāh, however, had to deal with a number of rebellions before he was able firmly to establish his position.[1] This fact appears moreover to have affected the nature of the rule of Fatḥ 'Alī Shāh. Fraser writes:

He [Fatḥ 'Alī Shāh] views Persia, not as his country, which he should love, protect, and improve, but as a property of which he has a lease, uncertain in its duration, and of which it behoves him to make the most he can while in his power. The throne having come into the hands of his family by conquest, he treats the whole country (except, perhaps, the seat of his own tribe in Mazunderan) like a conquered nation; and his only concern is how to extort from them the greatest possible amount of money.[2]

The Qājār period sees in some respects a return to the Seljūq practice of government by the ruling *khān* and his family. Once more provincial governorships were given to members of the ruling family—a practice which had been largely abandoned by the Ṣafavids. Tabrīz in Āẕarbāyjān became the seat of the heir apparent. Fraser, writing in the early part of the nineteenth century, states that each of the Qājār princes appointed to provincial governorships had a *vazīr* appointed to assist him in his government, and if the prince was young, the *shāh* usually sent some person on whom he could depend to instruct the prince and to transact all business.[3] Elsewhere, writing of Iskandar Mīrzā b. Muḥammad Qulī Mīrzā b. Fatḥ 'Alī Shāh, whose father was governor of Māzandarān, Fraser states:

I understood that this boy had an establishment exclusively to himself, like the other princes of the blood; including a vizier, or minister, gholaums, or confidential guards, peishkidmuts, and other officers; and several of his younger brothers unprovided with separate governments, have the same; the prince [Muḥammad Qulī Mīrzā] has a family of about twenty-five children, and an extensive harem, which makes his annual expenditure exceedingly large, and renders him anxious to relieve himself, by establishing his sons in various subordinate governments. . . . This practice generally proves a severe aggravation to the burdens of the respective governments; for they have to supply the expence of keeping up a petty court and its rapacious officers, while they are relieved from little, if any, of the regular taxes due to the crown.[4]

The Qājārs inherited from the Ṣafavids the absolute nature of the monarchy and the attribution of sanctity to the person of the

[1] Malcolm, *History of Persia*, ii. 214.
[2] *Journey into Khorasān*, p. 199.
[3] ibid. p. 204. See p. 203 n. for a list of the provincial governorates held by the sons and grandsons of Fatḥ 'Alī Shāh. This policy recalls the practice of the Seljūqs in appointing *atābegs* to the princes of the royal house.
[4] *Travels and Adventures in the Persian Provinces* (London, 1826), p. 38.

monarch. Morier, writing in the early part of the nineteenth century, states: 'as the Persians allow to their monarch a great character of sanctity, calling him the Zil Allah[1] . . . they pay him almost divine honours.'[2] Fraser also comments on the absolute nature of the monarchy and expresses the view that the people took their tone from the monarch. He states that:

the character of government . . . despotic, insolent and treacherous naturally forms that of its servants. The nobles and superior officers of court, subjected absolutely to the caprice of a tyrant who can neither endure opposition nor disappointment, though they may continue cringing and abject to him, become in their turn, cruel, haughty and imperious to their inferiors; and these again are delighted, when they can exercise the same petty tyranny upon such as may be unhappily subjected to their power. The greatest noble in Persia is never for a moment secure either in his person or property.[3]

He points out the disastrous effect of this lack of security on the country at large. In his view

the nature of the government, and particularly the character of the last two sovereigns of Persia [i.e. Āqā Muḥammad Khān Qājār and Fatḥ ʿAlī Shāh], have had a lamentable effect upon the morals of the people. The increased insecurity of property, and consequent jealousy, has been fatal to candour and common honesty. While the business of each individual is to amass money by every possible expedient, and particularly by the obvious one of plundering all those unfortunately subjected to his power, no amelioration in these parts can take place.[4]

And again,

the principal direct check to improvement and prosperity in Persia is the insecurity of life, limb and property, arising from the nature of the government, as well as from the revolutions to which that government is constantly liable. This must always repress the efforts of industry; for no man will work to produce what he may be deprived of the next hour.[5]

The same writer comments unfavourably on the material condition of both the possessing classes and the people at large. He states: 'the nobles, and particularly the officers of government, are in truth, kept wretchedly poor, as well as the rest of the people; there is hardly one of them who is not deeply and ruinously in debt.'[6] As for the peasants, he writes:

there is no class of men whose situation presents a more melancholy picture of oppression and tyranny, than the farmers and cultivators of the ground in Persia. They live continually under a system of extortion

[1] i.e. the Shadow of God.
[2] *Second Journey through Persia*, p. 173.
[3] *Journey into Khorasān*, p. 171.
[4] ibid. p. 108.
[5] ibid. p. 190.
[6] ibid. p. 222.

and injustice, from which they have no means of escape; and which is the more distressing, because it is indefinite, both in form and extent, for no man can tell when, how, or to what amount demands upon him may, without warning, be made.

On the other hand, the writer qualifies this in a footnote in which he states the peasantry often appear to enjoy relative comfort, to have sufficient food, and to be adequately if coarsely clad. This he attributes partly to the fact that provisions were cheap and wages high.[1] Malcolm, on the other hand, writing in the third decade of the nineteenth century, gives a somewhat more favourable picture. He states that in spite of corruption and extortion the general condition of the people was not as impoverished as might have been expected. 'The ministers and chief nobles', he writes, 'appear to enjoy affluence; and all persons in the public service seem to have ample means of supporting themselves and their families. Some of the merchants and principal inhabitants of the towns possess considerable property; and among the other classes, though few are rich, hardly any are in actual want.'[2] He notes, however, a certain stagnation or a failure to improve conditions compared with several centuries earlier. This he attributes to the form and character of the government. He points out that effort at improvement is attended with danger and exposes those by whom it is promoted to the cupidity of power.[3]

The military forces of the Qājārs were composed of a standing army, or rather a royal body-guard, which was never disbanded and provincial, mainly tribal, contingents. Similarly, each prince holding a provincial government had his own body-guard.[4] For example, according to Morier, ʿAlī Mīrzā b. Fatḥ ʿAlī Shāh, governor of Shīrāz about the year 1808–9, had in his actual service and pay a force of 1,000 cavalry, of which 200, the quota furnished by the Bakhtīārī tribes, formed his body-guard. In an emergency he could send to war 20,000 horsemen. His troops provided their own arms and clothing, and they received annually in pay 40 piastres and a daily allowance of 1 *mann* ($7\frac{1}{4}$ lb.) of barley, 2 *mann* of straw, and $\frac{1}{4}$ *mann* of wheat, except in spring when their horses fed on new herbage. They had further, each in his own country, for the maintenance of their families, a certain allotment of land which they tilled and sowed, and of which they reaped the annual fruits. When a new levy was ordered the head of each tribe brought forward the number which the state required of him.[5]

[1] ibid. p. 173.
[2] Malcolm, *History of Persia*, ii. 353. [3] ibid. p. 378.
[4] Morier, *Journey through Persia* (London, 1812), p. 241.
[5] ibid. p. 110. It is not clear from this whether these troops held their grants of land directly from the ruler or from the tribal leaders, but since the tribal areas were not directly administered, it is probable that the grants were made by the

Fraser also notes that the irregular forces for the most part remained in their own villages employed in agriculture or trades, and were seldom called upon for duty.[1]

The somewhat haphazard method of military recruitment and training of early Qājār times did not provide a force able to resist the pressure of foreign invaders. If Persia was to retain her independence some change in the existing system was essential. A return to the earlier system of even greater decentralization was clearly out of the question. Modernization of the military forces was imperative if they were to resist Russian arms, and this required a greater degree of centralization. The problem of how to pay a regular army, however, was never squarely faced, and in the absence of a solution to that question such measures as were taken to reform the army inevitably proved wholly inadequate. A variety of military missions and instructors were employed.[2] Under ʿAbbās Mīrzā in Āẕarbāyjān decrees were issued in 1221/1806 for the levy of men from every part of the province. Their pay, provisions, clothing, and other necessities were to be issued from government funds.[3] In practice, however, the attempt to create a modern army trained and equipped by the government failed. The army continued to be composed of contingents furnished in times of emergency by tribal leaders and others to whom assignments of land were made, and the standing troops or *ghulāms* employed by the ruler and all provincial governors continued to live on the country. Fraser, writing about 1822, states:

> [The gholaums employed as standing troops and as messengers] are the terror of the country; they live at free quarters, levy contributions on various pretences in the name of their master; guides, horses, provisions, the house and its inmates must await their pleasure; and their only argument in case of remonstrance is the butt-end of their fire-arms, or the cudgel they carry. None dares to resist, far less to attack a gholaum; for dreadful would be his punishment if such an offender were carried before the prince.[4]

tribal leaders. Morier and Fraser reckon 1 *mann* at 7¼ lb. The *manni tabrīz* is actually 6.5464 lb. (see Appendix III).

[1] He states: 'the king [Fatḥ ʿAlī Shāh] commutes the monied revenues [of Māzandarān including Astarābād] for the service of 12,000 toffunchees and 4,000 horsemen, who should be in readiness for service at all times' (*Travels in the Persian Provinces*, p. 46).

Morier states that the Arabs and the Faylī tribes were exempt from the provision of contingents. In so far as other tribes were concerned, he states that the names of the men who formed such contingents, with the names of their fathers and other particulars of their family, 'are registered in the *Defter Khona* at the seat of government; and at the *Norooz*, they attend the king to inquire whether their services for that year are required; if required they wait the encampment of his Majesty; if not, they are permitted to return, but in either case they receive a stated pay' (*Journey through Persia*, p. 240).

[2] See Curzon, i. 576 ff.

[3] ʿAbd ur-Razzāq, *Dynasty of the Kajars*, tr. Sir H. J. Brydges (London, 1833), p. 310.

[4] *Travels in the Persian Provinces*, p. 256.

Moreover, the movement of troops through the countryside whether to meet some foreign incursion or put down some rebel was usually accompanied by the devastation of the countryside. For example, Fraser states that the country between Tehrān and Qazvīn was made a desert by the military movements just before and after the death of Fatḥ ʿAlī Shāh.[1]

After the reign of Āqā Muḥammad Khān the tendency under the Qājārs was for large areas of the country to be alienated in the form of *tuyūls* and for the indirectly administered area to grow in comparison with the directly administered area. The term *tuyūl*, as in the Ṣafavid period, covered a variety of grants. In some cases it was a grant on the revenue attached to certain offices. In others the *tuyūl* was a grant of *khāliṣeh* land in lieu of salary. In some instances, notably in tribal areas, the holder was under obligation to provide military contingents. In others the *tuyūl* was merely a grant of the right to collect the taxation of a given area, which might be crown land, the property of a third person, or the property of the person to whom the *tuyūl* was granted, in which case it represented merely an immunity from taxation.[2]

The second of the above-mentioned types was perhaps the dominant form of *tuyūl* in Qājār times. The general tendency, moreover, was for such *tuyūls* to become hereditary, and for this type and the first type to be assimilated to each other. Various offices, often sinecures, tended to become the hereditary right of certain families, and the property would continue to be held by them even when the office was no longer exercised. As the control of the government weakened so the tendency grew to convert *tuyūls* into *de facto* private property, inheritable and alienable by sale. The ranks of landowners proper thus came to be swelled by erstwhile or actual government officials and *tuyūldārs*. Originally these officials had collected taxes on behalf of the government from the peasants and others living on the land, while the *tuyūldārs* had been granted by the government the right to collect the taxes of a certain area in lieu of salary, or for some other reason, while the landowners had merely collected certain dues consisting mainly in a share of the crop. As the tendency to usurp the land granted as *tuyūl* spread and the land was converted into *de facto* private property, the taxes, which had formerly been collected on behalf

[1] *Travels in Koordistan, Mesopotamia*, &c. (London, 1840), ii. 296; see also *Journey into Khorasān*, p. 590, where Fraser mentions the destruction of gardens and the cutting down of fruit trees in the neighbourhood of Burūjird by troops.

[2] According to Fraser, lands held as *tuyūl* 'pay nothing to government; the assignee takes three-tenths, which includes the proprietors' rights, and all government dues, with what else he can get from the farmers, when the lands belong to the government; but when the assignment is given upon the estate of another, the grant then only extends to the government dues or two-tenths of the produce.' (*Journey into Khorasān*, p. 211).

of the government or by way of salary, continued to be collected by the government official or *tuyūldār* in his capacity as *de facto* landowner and came to be regarded, not as taxes due to the government, but as additional dues which the landowner levied on the peasants. In other words, government taxes tended to be assimilated to the landowner's share of the crop (*bahrehyi mālikāneh*) or to the rent he received from his tenants.

Possession of land conferred a not inconsiderable economic benefit upon the holder. It enabled him to keep a body of armed retainers. This in turn gave him considerable power. In effect, it meant that the government had often to defer to the larger landowner in the areas in which he held land. This again gave the landowner social prestige as well as political power. Throughout the Qājār period the landowning classes (which included the tribal *khāns*) were the most powerful element in the kingdom. The fact that land offered both a profitable field of investment and conferred social prestige meant also that the ranks of the landowning classes were increased, not only by government officials who made use of their official position to buy up property in the areas to which they were appointed, but also by merchants and others who had money to invest.

Large areas of the Qājār kingdom were tribal areas, notably Fārs, the Bakhtīārī, Khūzistān, Kurdistān, the frontier areas of Khurāsān, and parts of Āẕarbāyjān and Balūchistān. In the frontier areas of Khurāsān and Āẕarbāyjān there was an almost constant state of petty warfare, and the movement of rebellious elements backwards and forwards over the frontier into the Russian provinces, Afghānistān, or the Ottoman Empire made for instability. Foreign wars were frequent, and various frontier delimitations took place, for the most part resulting in loss of territory to Persia.

Under the Qājārs, as under earlier dynasties, there was a redistribution of tribes and a weakening of some groups and strengthening of others. For example, Fatḥ ʿAlī Shāh, with a view to weakening the family of Muṣṭafā Khān of Ṭālish, distributed the whole of Ṭālish among the principal families which remained there (after Muṣṭafā Khān, who had fought on the side of the Russians in 1812, had been driven out of Lankarān) confirming to each such portion of the country as it had become possessed of. He also made them *khāns* by way of increasing their importance.[1] In some cases hostages were taken from the tribes as a guarantee of their good behaviour. For example, Fatḥ ʿAlī Shāh kept families of Bakhtīārīs in separate villages about Tehrān as hostages for the good behaviour of the rest.[2] On the north-eastern frontier there were also

[1] Fraser, *Travels in the Persian Provinces*, p. 145.
[2] Morier, *Second Journey through Persia*, p. 126.

changes brought about in the tribal population. Āqā Muḥammad Khān, in return for the assistance the Turkomāns had afforded him and his father, allowed them to move from the banks of the Atrak into the plain of Gurgān and gave them as *tuyūl* the villages on the banks of the Qarā Sū.[1] The Turkomāns in particular were at this period responsible for a good deal of the prevailing insecurity. They repeatedly raided caravans on the Mashhad road and the neighbourhood,[2] and their slave-raids, together with those of the Uzbegs from over the border, depopulated northern Khurāsān. As a result of ʿAbbās Mīrzā's successful expedition to Sarakhs the raids temporarily stopped, but they recommenced again after his death.[3]

There are other instances of tribal movements at this period. The tendency for tribal groups to be moved or to move from one part of the country to another in times of anarchy is illustrated by the history of the Bīgirlū, who towards the end of the thirteenth century A.H. were alleged to own a third of the hamlets and a fifth of the gardens of Qumm. They had originally lived on the borders of Anatolia. After the eclipse of the Timurids they had come to Iṣfahān and held important offices under the Ṣafavids. After the Afghān troubles they left Iṣfahān for Kāshān. Subsequently, in the reign of Karīm Khān Zand, they had come from Kāshān to Qumm. The latter town was at that time still suffering from the effects of the Afghān invasion, and the Bīgirlū were able to obtain possession of most of the estates (*amlāk*) of Qumm.[4]

Other groups which were moved in Qājār times include the Saʿdvand, who were brought from Fārs to the neighbourhood east of Qumm in the reign of Muḥammad Shāh (1250–64/1834–48). Similarly, the Kā'īnī tribe were brought to the north of Qumm. They had originally been in charge of the camel transport of the *dīvān*, which office they resigned of their own volition and devoted themselves to agriculture and flocks. Their pastures along the Sāveh river were near those of the Shāhsivan and disputes between them were common. The ʿAbd ul-Malikī tribe from Fārs also came to Qumm in Qājār times. They acquired pastures to the south of Qumm. Most of them were camel drivers or government *farrāsh*.[5]

According to another account seven groups (*ṭā'ifeh*) came to Qumm from Fārs at this period. They did not at first possess flocks but in the course of time acquired camels, sheep, and goats,

[1] Rabino (di Borgomale), *Mázandarán and Astarábád* (London, Leyden, 1928), p. 80.

[2] See Fraser, *Journey into Khorasān*, pp. 330, 615, 622.

[3] Fraser, *A Winter's Journey (Tatar) from Constantinople to Tehran* (London, 1838), ii. 25–6, 33.

[4] History of Qumm in M.F.A., No. 725 (folios not numbered).

[5] ibid.

and obtained pastures in the neighbourhood of the town. They did not pay *dīvān* taxes. Each tribe was allotted to the train of one of the *ʿulamā*. Before long they began to create disturbances. Muḥammad Shāh accordingly ordered them to be fined 500 *tūmāns*. This sum was then exacted from them every year and added to until it reached 664 *tūmāns* and, after the assessment made by Mīrzā Ḥabībullāh Garakānī, it was fixed at 1,120 *tūmāns*.[1] The Shīnī and Karzeh tribes from Kirmānshāh also came to Qumm in Qājār times.[2] Some of the Mīsh Mast ʿArab tribes were settled in the neighbourhood of Tehrān about this time. Some of them, notably the Hudāvand, came from Khurramābād, whence they had been moved by Karīm Khān to Fārs. Āqā Muḥammad Khān Qājār moved them to Tehrān.[3]

For the most part the tribes, in so far as they were semi-nomadic, were left subject to their own leaders, who were responsible to the government for the collection and payment of taxes. The taxes were assessed on their flocks. Fraser, writing in 1821–2, states that the rate was 1 r. per mare or horse, four-fifths r. per ass or cow, one-third r. per sheep or goat, and one-sixth r. per hive of bees.[4] Jaubert, writing in 1805–6, states that the nomad leaders paid their taxes mainly in horses, animals, carpets, and other objects, but that for the last few years the *shāh* had required at least one-fifth to be paid in cash.[5]

In so far as land tenure was concerned, there were considerable local variations in the tribal areas. Rawlinson, writing in 1838, describes the somewhat complicated system of land tenure prevailing among the Mukrī Kurds of Souj Bulāgh. He states that

> the country, acquired in war, was originally held as direct property of the chief. From him it descended to his family, and thus, at the present day, the proprietorship of almost the whole of this extensive country is in the hands of a single family, the Bábá 'Amíreh.... This small family, which does not number above fifty or sixty people, cannot be supposed capable of cultivating all the lands, and a system has been thus introduced, by which the chief of the tribe can assign any portion of the country that he pleases to the care of other inferior leaders, called Aghás, with or without the consent of the proprietor. The produce is then divided according to the following proportions:—the Bábá 'Amíreh landlord receives a fifteenth in right of his hereditary proprietorship; the Aghá, or farmer, who is the responsible agent to government, a tenth; the Zeráʿet-chis, a class of people who are supposed to understand

1 List of Landed Properties and Districts of Qumm compiled in 1296/1878–9 in M.F.A., No. 725, f. 59.

2 History of Qumm in ibid. No. 725.

3 ibid. No. 726, Report on Lār, dated 1298/1880–1, f. 16.

4 *Journey into Khorasān*, p. 212, see also *Travels in Persian Provinces*, pp. 143–4.

5 *Voyage en Arménie et en Perse* (Paris, 1821), p. 270.

the science of agriculture, and who superintend the cultivation, a fifth; and the remainder is shared between the expense of tillage and the price of labour, according to the different arrangements for farming which exist between the ra'yyat and Aghá; the most common is what is called Niṣfehkárí. . . . The tenth claimed by the Aghá, independently of this arrangement, is ostensibly the government share . . . but, practically, it does not work so. The revenue to be realised is distributed by the chief among the different districts, at an average rate of two tómáns a family, and the Aghá, or Bábá 'Amíreh proprietor, if he farms his own land, is then at liberty to apportion the assessment among his ra'yyats, in reference to his own knowledge of their capability to contribute.[1]

Local administration was regulated largely according to *'urf* or customary law, which was administered by the *shāh*, his lieutenants, the rulers of provinces, governors of cities, and other local officials or village headmen. Their decrees were enforced by the strong hand of power. According to Malcolm they were prompt and arbitrary in their decisions, and as they seldom bestowed much time on the consideration of evidence, they were continually liable to commit injustice even if their intentions were pure. The principal check upon them was the dread of superiors, to whom the injured could always appeal. They regulated their actions by the varying disposition of the despot of the day, and were active and just, or corrupt and cruel, as he happened to be vigilant and virtuous, or avaricious and tyrannical. The heads of villages were allowed to inflict slight punishments or impose small fines; if the crime was serious, the delinquent was sent to the *ẓābiṭ* (the revenue collector of the district), and when the case, from the magnitude of the property concerned, the rank of the parties, or the heinousness of the crime, was above the latter's cognisance he would refer it to the governor. The jurisdiction of the *'urf* courts could not by the nature of the case be clearly defined, but the general tendency was for their jurisdiction to be extended since this added to the power and emoluments of the officials.[2] It was this tendency, moreover, which had already become more marked in Ṣafavid times, which was probably the most important factor in the gradual worsening in the position of the peasant that took place in the nineteenth century. There were other factors also which contributed to this, but the decision of land and other cases being placed within the competence of the *tuyūldār* and landowners the peasant was in fact deprived of the possibility of an appeal for redress to an impartial, or relatively impartial, tribunal.

Customary law among the tribes differed materially from that

[1] 'Notes on a Journey from Tabríz through Persian Kurdistán, to the Ruins of Takhti-Soleïmán', *J.R.G.S.*, 1841, x. 35–6.

[2] Malcolm, *History of Persia*, ii. 318–19; cf. also Tancoigne, *Narrative of a Journey into Persia* (London, 1820), pp. 233 ff.

of the rest of the population, according to Malcolm. Cases were decided by councils of elders. In the case of land disputes the council would consist of the principal land-holders.[1]

As stated above, the revenue was largely farmed. ʿAbbās Mīrzā, while governor of Āẕarbāyjān, to some extent abolished the practice of farming and made some progress in fixing the revenues of the province upon a systematic scale and in enforcing their collection. Although while he administered affairs in person there might have been less arbitrary exaction, every village was, in the view of Fraser, taxed to the utmost it could well bear.[2]

The mode of collecting revenue was, according to Malcolm, intimately connected with the general administration of justice. The same officer presided over both, and this mode of power was favourable or unfortunate for the inhabitants according to his personal character.[3] There was a continual struggle between the governor of a province and his myrmidons on the one side, and villagers, *ẕābiṭs*, and *kadkhudās* on the other. Few villages paid without requisition. Those sent to collect lived on the country. The giving and accepting of douceurs was common. The government was not blind to this but gave such jobs 'to persons whom it may be inconvenient to provide for otherwise; indeed it is a common mode of paying the wages of a servant or inferior officer'.[4]

Arrears were common. Fatḥ ʿAlī Shāh shortly before his death demanded the payment of arrears for Fārs from the Farmān Farmā who was governor of the province. Amīn ud-Douleh was ordered to proceed to Fārs with an army and levy contributions on all districts withholding their assessments. A war of extermination was to be waged against those who refused to comply. The country was to be ravaged by fire and the sword. Crops were to be destroyed, villages burned, and cattle plundered; and the survivors, whether villagers or tribesmen, were to be carried off captive to Tehrān. Fortunately for Fārs, however, before this plan was executed Fatḥ ʿAlī Shāh died.[5]

Government officials levied taxes for their own expenditure and that of their staffs in the area under their jurisdiction in addition to the ordinary tax. This levy was known as *tafāvuti ʿamal*. These dues, in the course of time tended to be added to the original tax, and yet further sums to be levied to defray the expenses of the local officials. In this way the peasants were often reduced to penury and unable to pay the demands which the *dīvān* made upon them.[6] An example of this is the following. The original tax of

[1] Malcolm, *History of Persia*, ii. 326–7.
[2] *Travels in Koordistan*, i. 8.
[3] *History of Persia*, ii. 335.
[4] Fraser, *Journey into Khorasān*, p. 221.
[5] Fraser, *Travels in Koordistan*, ii. 251.
[6] See also Mustoufī, *Sharḥi Zindagīyi Man*, (Tehrān, 1324) i. 139. Mention

Shamsābād near Qumm had been 600 *tūmāns*. This was increased by the addition of various taxes until the assessment finally reached 3,550 *tūmāns*. This ruined the peasants and the estates were eventually confiscated for arrears.[1] Similarly, the revenue assessment for the cultivated land of the five districts (*ayālāt*) of Qumm watered by the river and gardens, apart from Sarajeh, made by Mīrzā Āqā Bābā Muḥammad Āshtīānī in the reign of Fatḥ ʿAlī Shāh, amounted to 12,014 *tūmāns* and 3,000 *tūmāns* and 4,582 *kharvār* in kind. Subsequently, an additional assessment was made every year for the expenses of the administration. This in the course of time was included in the assessment until finally it rose from 12,000 *tūmāns* odd to 25,000 *tūmāns*.[2] In a similar way many of the villages in the neighbourhood became ruined and deserted.[3] According to Malcolm, the fixed revenue at the time when he wrote amounted to three million sterling and was chiefly derived from the produce of crown and government lands, from taxes and imposts on landed property, and on goods and merchandise.[4] The rate on the produce of the land, i.e. wheat, barley, silk, tobacco, indigo, etc., was one-fifth in kind, and on vegetables, fruits, and the lesser produce of the earth was, according to Morier, one-fifth in cash; this appears, however, to have been a theoretical abstraction because he goes on to state that the assessment was based upon 'the number of oxen kept by the landholder',[5] i.e. it was levied on the plough-land and not on the crop. In actual fact, then as now, conditions probably varied from area to area. This is borne out by Fraser who states 'there are various methods of ascertaining the amount of government dues; that most commonly adopted is, to measure the corn when ripe, upon the ground, before it is cut, and from that they form an estimate; but the officers of government sometimes take charge of it until cut, and separated from the straw, when they receive their due by measurement'.[6]

The rate before the reign of Fatḥ ʿAlī Shāh is alleged to have been one-tenth.[7] Unirrigated crops, however, appear to have con-

of the raising of assessments is common in the sources. The following is an instance. Qumisheh had declined because of the pillage of the Afghān invaders and the extortion of rulers. Under Fatḥ ʿAlī Shāh it was restored to some degree of prosperity by the Ṣadri Amīn, who fixed its assessment at 7,000 *tūmāns*. It was then assigned to the ruler's son-in-law Qāsim Khān, who raised the revenue in ten months to 23,000 *tūmāns* and drove the people to despair. (Fraser, *Journey into Khorasān*, p. 120.)

[1] List of Landed Properties, &c., in M.F.A., No. 725, f. 67.

[2] Mīrzā Sayyid Mihdī, History of Qumm, in ibid. f. 113.

[3] List of Landed Properties, &c., in ibid. f. 47.

[4] *History of Persia*, ii. 336.

[5] *Journey through Persia*, p. 236.

[6] *Journey into Khorasān*, p. 212.

[7] ibid. p. 211. Fraser states that formerly no claim was made on the peasant by the government but one-tenth of the crop. This would appear to be an overstatement, but his explanation of the reason for the doubling of the rate may well have some truth in it. He states that irregular taxes, or *saadurāut*, were levied in

tinued to pay one-fifth.[1] According to Fraser the government looked in all cases 'to the cultivator for its dues', although he goes on to state that the proprietor might make an agreement with the farmer so as to pay them himself or vice versa.[2] Gardens in or close to villages paid one-fifth of their produce in kind, but melon grounds, tobacco, cotton, and such like fields paid in money, the tax being assessed on a valuation of the produce.[3] Date palms in Dālakī were assessed as follows: each full-grown tree was calculated to yield a *hāshimī mann* (*c.* 116 lb. or 16 *manni tabrīz* of 7¼ lb. each) of fruit, which was worth to the proprietor 2–2½ rupees, and on this the duty was 1 *maḥmūdī* or 8 *pūli siāh*, one-eighth of which went to the village accountant and the rest to the governor of the district for the crown.[4]

According to Waring, who wrote about 1802, the holders of *arbābī* land were obliged to pay the same amount of taxation whether their land was cultivated or not.[5] *Arbābī* land was held in general by some person of consequence who cultivated it for himself. He furnished seed, cattle to plough and draw water, and, after deducting the quantity advanced for seed, assigned a fifth part of the produce to the cultivators and a tenth part was paid in tax to the government. On *nuqd* land[6] the government tax amounted to one-fifth. Land owned by peasant proprietors also paid tax to the government.[7]

The duty on estates, according to Malcolm's account, was generally farmed by the owners in order to avoid the vexatious

order to make good the deficiency in the revenue, each proprietor being called upon 'to furnish a share proportioned to his estate. The cattle were at first the chief objects of this impost; but as it was by no means adequate to the purpose, other duties were levied, till they increased so much, that at last they were compounded, for an additional one-tenth of the produce. This occurred not long ago, and the regular government dues are now one-fifth: but faith was ill kept on the part of the government, for the saaduräut, although not in their original form, continue to be levied in shapes so capricious and arbitrary, that they form one of the ryot's heaviest grievances' (ibid., and see below p. 149).

[1] *Journey into Khorasān*, p. 212.

[2] ibid. p. 212. Elsewhere he states that in Dālakī the rate per plough-land or *khīsh* worked by an ass was 8 rupees and by a mule or horse 16 rupees. The former yielded 60 *hāshimī mann* wheat or barley, worth respectively 2 rupees and 1 rupee per *mann* (ibid. p. 74). 'In Derrood [i.e. Dorūd] on the skirts of the range which separates the plain of Nishapore from Mushed and Koordistan, [i.e. Bujnūrd], the ploughs are taxed at twenty tomauns each, and the fruit trees at two reals for every hundred manns Tabreez of fruit' (ibid. 432–3).

[3] ibid. p. 212.

[4] ibid. p. 74. See above, p. 137, n. 5.

[5] *A Tour to Sheeraz* (London 1807), p. 88. The author enters a caveat concerning the reliability of information obtained by him on matters affecting land.

[6] *Nuqd* would suggest land on which the assessment is paid entirely in cash, but Waring goes on to state that he believed the taxes on *nuqd* land were always paid in kind (ibid. p. 86). He states that the produce of crown lands were 'subject to two divisions, the one called *Nuqd*, and the other *Jinsee*; or, in other words, the former yielding produce for manufacture, as cotton, silk, etc., and the latter crops of grain' (p. 85).

[7] ibid. p. 86.

interference of the subordinate officers of the revenue. In other words, the landowner compounded with the government for a fixed sum.[1]

Malcolm further states that according to the general and established rule the taxes ought to be paid in cash and kind in equal portions, but in practice the actual proportion varied. Some villages, where the inhabitants were poor, paid almost entirely in kind; but where the landowner was wealthy he preferred to pay in cash, thereby avoiding the interference of the minor revenue officials. These rates did not apply to rich and highly manured fields or gardens near towns, which were generally rented for money and often at a very high rate.[2]

Whereas *vaqf* land, as stated above, decreased in extent, *khāliṣeh* land formed an increasingly important category of land. It derived from various origins, partly from earlier periods, and partly from confiscations for arrears of taxation, rebellion, and other causes. Already at the beginning of Qājār times there were considerable *khāliṣeh* territories which were in time increased.[3] The vicissitudes through which *khāliṣeh* and other land in the neighbourhood of Iṣfahān went through is instructive of the changes which came about in land ownership. During the campaigns between the Qājārs and Zands, land in this neighbourhood had fallen into decay. Fatḥ ʿAlī Shāh's Prime Minister, Ṣadri Amīn, had been able to rent at a low rate considerable areas of *khāliṣeh*, *arbābī*, and *vaqf* land in the neighbourhood of Iṣfahān. His rival, Amīn ud-Douleh, who subsequently succeeded him, was able to secure the confiscation to the state of the Ṣadri Amīn's estates for arrears of taxation.[4] Amīn ud-Douleh then himself rented on easy terms a number of *khāliṣeh* villages and various other estates. He, too, was accused by his rival, Āṣaf ud-Douleh, of failing to pay in full his obligations to the state, and, finally, in settlement of the claims of the state against him, certain transfers of land to the state were made.[5] These estates became known as *khāliṣejāti ẓabṭī*.[6] Such estates, according to Morier, remained annexed to the crown until the family were again restored, when the estate might according to the pleasure of the sovereign be returned. The *shāh*, while he retained such property generally, allowed a portion of its produce to the relatives of the former owner, which allowance was known as *mustamarrī*.[7]

[1] cf. *muqāṭaʿeh* above, p. 33.

[2] *History of Persia*, ii. 338–9.

[3] For example, Āqā Muḥammad Khān (1779–97) bought considerable areas of land in Māzandarān which became *khāliṣeh*.

[4] Anṣārī, pp. 42–3. See also Morier, *Second Journey through Persia*, pp. 131–2, for the career of Amīn ud-Douleh.

[5] Anṣārī, p. 44.

[6] ibid. pp. 44–5.

[7] *Journey through Persia*, pp. 237–8.

During the reign of Muḥammad Shāh (1834–48) further increases in *khāliṣeh* land in the neighbourhood of Iṣfahān occurred. Many villages were ruined during the famine which broke out in the early years of his reign. With a view to restoring prosperity, the *mubāshirs* of the *dīvān* subsequently provided their inhabitants with seed, the names of these villages being thenceforward included in the list of state lands. Some years later, when prosperity returned, these lands were returned to their owners; they continued however, to be known as *khāliṣejāti bazrī*.[1]

According to Waring, one-eighth of the land of the province of Fārs and (Persian) ʿIrāq was probably in the hands of the *shāh*. Those who cultivated such land paid a rent of half the produce besides the deduction made on account of seed. Cattle for drawing water were, however, provided by the *shāh*, who also dug wells at his own expense. Rents were not always paid yearly and in some cases were not paid until troops were quartered on the district and the rents paid at the requisition of the *kalāntar*. In the event of a drought some allowance was made to the husbandman, but, states Waring, 'this depends chiefly on interest and favour'.[2]

According to Malcolm, crown lands were cultivated by the peasants on terms very favourable to the cultivator. When the crop had been measured by an officer appointed for the purpose, if the seed was supplied by the government it was returned. Ten per cent was then put aside for reapers and threshers; after which the remainder was equally divided between the cultivator and the king. Lands owned by individuals paid according to their situation in respect of water. If this came from a flowing stream they paid 20 per cent after the deductions mentioned above, if from *qanāts* 15 per cent, and if from wells and reservoirs 5 per cent.[3] Every encouragement was held out to cultivators to sow government *daym* lands. If the cultivator found the seed the king took 10 per cent. Such land belonging to private individuals was seldom cultivated. *Daym* crops were sometimes abundant but often failed altogether.[4] These rates applied to grain crops. Rice was regulated by the same rules. For other crops the cultivator provided the seed and one-third of the produce went to the government.[5]

Fraser states that the rights of the crown in the lands of which it was proprietor were precisely the same as those of a private proprietor, i.e. one-tenth part of the produce, with the price of water brought out by *qanāt*, the only difference being that the rentee besides his one-tenth of the grain was obliged to give also one-tenth of the straw.[6] Morier also describes the terms on which *khāliṣeh*

[1] Anṣārī, p. 45.
[2] *Tour of Sheeraz*, pp. 85–6.
[3] *History of Persia*, ii. 336–7.
[4] ibid. p. 337.
[5] ibid. pp. 337–8.
[6] *Journey into Khorasān*, p. 211.

land was cultivated round Iṣfahān. Amīn ud-Douleh rented this from the government and sub-let to the peasants. The latter provided the draught animals and Amīn ud-Douleh the seed. At harvest time three-quarters of the produce went to Amīn ud-Douleh.[1] The reason for the relatively high percentage going to him would appear to be the fact that he had made cuts from the Zāyandeh Rūd to irrigate the land. The manure used in these fields, Morier goes on to state, was generally the produce of flocks of sheep and goats, a small sum being paid to the shepherd, who kept them upon the appointed ground for whatever time may have been the agreement.[2]

Moreover, the government, according to Malcolm, was always ready to dispose of waste-land, particularly if it was to be built on or to be planted as a garden. A heritable lease would be given, subject to a small ground tax, which varied according to the age of the trees and the quality of the fruit.[3] This would appear to be a continuation of Ṣafavid practice and in opposition to Islamic practice.[4]

The responsibility of the landowner and cultivator did not, however, cease with the payment of these regular taxes. Public requisitions (or *ṣādirāt*) were frequent. Such extraordinary taxes were levied, for example, to provide for a variety of purposes, civil and military. To quote Malcolm:

> if an addition is made to the army—if the king desires to construct an aqueduct or build a palace—if troops are marching through the country, and require to be furnished with provisions—if a foreign mission arrives in Persia—if one of the royal family is married—in short, on any occurrence more than ordinary, an impost is laid, sometimes on the whole kingdom, at others only on particular provinces. This is regulated by the nature and extent of the occasion, and by a regard to its local or general extent.[5]

Morier, writing on the same subject, states that

> the *sader* is an arbitrary tax, and is the most grievous to the *Rayat*. It admits every species of extortion, and renders the situation of the peasant extremely precarious. This impost is levied on particular occasions, such as the passage of any great man through the country, the local expenses of a district, or on other opportunities which are continually recurring; so that the *Rayat* is never certain of a respite. It is assessed in the same manner [as ordinary taxes] upon the number of oxen which he may keep.[6]

[1] Amīn ud-Douleh undertook considerable irrigation works elsewhere. Morier also records the making of *qanāts* by him in the neighbourhood of Kāshān (*Second Journey through Persia*, pp. 162–3).

[2] ibid. p. 154.

[3] *History of Persia*, ii. 339.

[4] See above, pp. 118–19.

[5] *History of Persia*, ii. 342.

[6] *Journey through Persia*, p. 237; the tax was presumably levied on the plough-land.

Another burden laid on the peasants was that known as *sūrsāt*, or purveyance, claimed not only by the officials known as the *mihmāndārs* who were in charge of conducting foreign envoys through the country but also by all great men or messengers travelling on the part of the ruler. These provisions were extorted from the private stores of the villages. 'The villager', wrote Morier, 'groans under the oppression, but in vain shrinks from it; every argument of his poverty is answered, if by nothing else, at least by the bastinado'.[1]

The picture of the land revenue system and administration of the early Qājārs is one of decay, maladministration, oppression, and insecurity.[2]

[1] *Journey through Persia*, p. 37; see also Fraser, *Journey into Khorasān*, pp. 88, 113, 115.

[2] The relations between the peasants and the landowners were substantially the same under the early Qājārs as in the second half of the nineteenth century. Specific reference to this question has therefore been held over until Chapter VII.

CHAPTER VII

THE SECOND HALF OF THE NINETEENTH CENTURY: THE EVE OF REFORM

IN the latter part of the Qājār period certain new developments can be discerned. The old problems continued, such as the extravagances of the court, military weakness, and administrative inefficiency, but there were alongside of them a growing discontent and demand for reform. Those who demanded reform were influenced by the Young Turk movement and the pan-Islamic movement led by Sayyid Jamāl ud-Dīn Asadābādī (Afghānī). As the *shāh* in his search for money began to grant concessions to foreign companies, notably the Tobacco Concession of 1890, so the demand for change became increasingly vocal and culminated in the Constitutional Revolution of 1905–6.[1] In so far as the land system and the status of the landowner and peasant is concerned the Qājār period marks the final break-up of the old system of land-holding and the grant of the Constitution may be regarded as the outward sign of its dissolution. But the process of change was a gradual movement: there was no sudden transition from the medieval to the modern. Already before 1906 the breakdown in the administration which had occurred had led to considerable changes in practice, while, on the other hand, certain medieval survivals lingered on or have reappeared from time to time in the period after 1906.

The need for more money to pay for the extravagances of the court, to provide for the administration of the country and the upkeep of the army, became ever more pressing in the latter part of the Qājār period. Clearly the only sound way to provide extra funds was to reform the system of taxation and the administration. Some effort was made under Nāṣir ud-Dīn Shāh (1264–1313/1848–96) to bring about a measure of reorganization, but although there was a growing demand during the second half of the nineteenth century for reform, there is little evidence to show that the ruling class in general appreciated the need for reform or that those who were most vocal in voicing this demand realized its full implications.

The main source of wealth of the country at this period, as earlier, was the land and its produce, just as the possession of land

[1] For a discussion of the causes leading up to the Persian Revolution see E. G. Browne, *The Persian Revolution of 1905–9* (Cambridge, 1910).

was also the main source of power and influence. In spite of this, or perhaps because of it, the method of assessment and the effectiveness of the collection of revenue varied in different parts of the country. Some areas were over-assessed while some were under-assessed. To introduce some order and system into this state of affairs was a prerequisite to financial reform, upon which the success of any wide system of reform would in turn depend. The various types of land-holding which had existed at earlier times are found, though their relative extent varied. *Khāliṣeh* land at this period still occupied a considerable area of the country; it was for the most part in a state of decay and made little contribution to the revenue. In view of this, and because of the constant need of the ruler for money, the general tendency of the period was for *khāliṣeh* to be converted into private property by sale (and in some cases by usurpation also).

In a report dated 1296/1878–9 on Khwār and the *bulūks* of Tehrān it is stated that most of the villages of Khwār, whether *arbābī* or *khāliṣeh*, were in a state of decay,[1] and also that *arbābī* land was everywhere in better condition than *khāliṣeh*.[2] In view of the general decay prevailing in *khāliṣeh* land, Amīn us-Sulṭān, minister to Nāṣir ud-Dīn Shāh in the latter part of his reign, considered it would be in the interests of better cultivation to transfer the estates themselves to individuals instead of merely giving the latter drafts on their revenue. Accordingly decrees were in due course issued for their transfer. They were made subject to a relatively high rate of tax, which was estimated in kind and converted into cash at a fixed rate known as *tas'īr*. Reductions were granted for special purposes such as for the repair or making of *qanāts*. These *khāliṣeh* became known as *khāliṣejāti intiqālī*; the holder was able to transfer them to his heirs but could not sell the land to a third party. Moreover, since it was always possible that the state might reclaim the lands, their value was in general less than that of *arbābī* land. Further sales of *khāliṣeh* land subsequently took place towards the end of Nāṣir ud-Dīn Shāh's reign, when a decree was issued for the sale of all *khāliṣeh* land except that in the neighbourhood of Tehrān. In the space of ten years much was sold.[3]

The vicissitudes which *khāliṣeh* land in the neighbourhood of Iṣfahān underwent in the post-Ṣafavid period have been touched upon in the previous chapter. Further developments took place under Nāṣir ud-Dīn Shāh. At the beginning of his reign there were some 1,000 villages and hamlets (*mazra'eh*) in the neighbourhood of Iṣfahān, some of which were private property, some *ouqāf*, and some *khāliṣeh*, which had fallen out of cultivation. Fourteen

[1] M.F.A., No. 726, f. 163. [2] ibid. f. 158.
[3] Anṣārī, pp. 59–60.

thousand *tūmāns* in cash and 1,000 *kharvār* in kind were advanced to Mīrzā ʿAbd ul-Ḥusayn, the finance minister, in order that he should reclaim them. He spent the money instead on arms and rebelled. As a result of the ravages caused by the disorders occasioned by this rebellion further villages became ruined. When the rebellion was put down, the estates of those concerned were in part confiscated to the *dīvān* and although their owners recovered them some years later, the estates continued to be registered as *khāliṣejāti ẓabṭī*.[1] Shortly after these events Mīrzā ʿAbd ul-Vahāb made a new assessment of Iṣfahān and the lands were placed in two categories, *khāliṣehyi vaqfī* and *khāliṣehyi arbābī*.

Reductions in the assessments were in some cases given and extortion by government officials was prevented. As a result dead lands were brought into cultivation and irrigation works carried out. After the death of Mīrzā Taqī Khān in 1851 extortion once more recommenced and salaries were again assigned on certain *arbābī* villages.[2] The return of prosperity was thus cut short, and when in 1286–8/1869–72 there was a series of famine years much *khāliṣeh* and *arbābī* land again became dead land, and many landowners simply abandoned their lands, which were thereafter included in the *khāliṣeh*.[3] Certain villages had meanwhile been made over by their owners to members of the religious classes in order to avoid the payment of taxation. The result of these various events was that the registers of the *khāliṣeh*, *vaqfī*, and *arbābī* land in Iṣfahān were reduced to disorder.[4]

In the latter part of Nāṣir ud-Dīn's reign much of the *khāliṣeh* land in the neighbourhood of Iṣfahān was sold, and when Muẓaffar ud-Dīn Shāh came to the throne the only *khāliṣeh* lands which remained in Iṣfahān were the ruined villages of Barā'ān.[5] Land sales meanwhile were brisk. The court, as usual, was in need of money, and so Muẓaffar ud-Dīn's advisers suggested to him that a declaration should be made stating which land in the Iṣfahān neighbourhood was *khāliṣeh* land, with a view to its being sold. Accordingly the land register of Nādir Shāh, known as the *raqabāti nādirī*, was brought out. This, as pointed out in Chapter VI, had never corresponded to fact, and had been laid aside for a hundred years or so. Nevertheless, in accordance with the entries made in

[1] ibid. pp. 46–7. [2] ibid. p. 49.

[3] ibid. p. 54. The decrease in population (whether by actual death or migration) in central Persia as a result of the famine was considerable. A census made in Qumm in 1284/1867–8 showed the population to be 25,382 persons, while in a census made in 1291/1874–5 it amounted to 14,000 only (M.F.A., No. 725, History of Qumm by Mīrzā Sayyid Mihdī, f. 100). The Quhistān district of Qumm appears not to have recovered by that time from the famine years and its population, formerly some 8,000, was reported to be negligible (List of Landed Properties, &c., f. 69).

[4] Anṣārī, pp. 50–1. [5] ibid. p. 62.

it various lands were declared to be *khāliṣeh*. As a result of this measure further confusion was introduced into the situation. *Arbābī* land of old standing was declared *khāliṣeh*, and where the owners were unable to resist the demands of the government officials the land was confiscated.[1] The upshot of these and other measures was that *khāliṣeh* land was regrouped into the following categories: (1) *amlāki dīvānī* or true *khāliṣeh*, which was in the hands of bailiffs (*mubāshirs*) employed by the government and cultivated directly by the state or let to peasants or others; (2) *amlāki ẓabṭī*, estates temporarily confiscated by the state as punishment for rebellion, or estates whose owners were not known;[2] (3) *amlāki intiqālī*; (4) *amlāki ṣabtī*, estates which were never actually in the hands of the *dīvān* but were registered in the faulty *raqabāti nādirī* as belonging to the state; and (5) *amlāki bazrī*, estates which had been left uncultivated by their owners in bad years and for which the government had provided seed so that they could be reclaimed. After the harvest was reaped and the seed returned these estates, although they were handed back to their owners, remained wrongly registered in the name of the government.[3]

There were also cases of *arbābī* land being converted into *khāliṣeh* by arbitrary action by government officials. For example, under Ẓill us-Sulṭān, governor of Iṣfahān under Nāṣir ud-Dīn Shāh, a number of decrees are alleged to have been given in which *arbābī* land was declared to be *khāliṣeh*.[4] Stack, writing in 1882, also notes that there was a constant tendency for *dīvānī* (i.e. *khāliṣeh*) land to increase by resumption of religious grants, by confiscation, and by escheat.[5]

In addition to *khāliṣeh* proper certain areas were declared *quruq*, i.e. royal hunting grounds. Regions in the neighbourhood of Tehrān and Lār were set apart in this way.[6]

Curzon also mentions the reservation of pastures on the hillsides for the government mules and horses, and states that exemptions for the use of their own grounds would then be sold to the real proprietors. Similarly, in some cases a prohibition of shooting on the hills would be issued, and pasturage, on the ground of disturbance to game, would be prohibited; and then a grazing tax would be exacted as the price of redemption.[7]

The vicissitudes undergone by *vaqf* property in this period were

[1] Anṣārī, pp. 63–4.

[2] In the revenue assessments of the period references are frequently found to *amlāki ẓabṭī*, or *amlāki mutaṣarrifī*. (e.g. M.F.A., No. 727, ff. 81–2), which gives a revenue assessment of the *bulūks* of Fārs (ff. 82–108). The *amlāki ẓabṭī* were in some cases returned after a period to their owners.

[3] Anṣārī, pp. 76–7.

[4] ibid. pp. 81–2.

[5] *Six Months in Persia* (London, 1882), ii. 248.

[6] M.F.A., No. 726, Report entitled 'Shimīrān to Lār', f. 51.

[7] *Persia and the Persian Question*, ii. 473.

probably little less than those undergone by *khāliṣeh* land. The tendency under Nādir to convert *vaqf* into private property has been mentioned in the previous chapter. In the later Qājār period also misappropriation of *vaqf* funds and their conversion into private property was not unknown.[1]

A great deal of the country, as formerly, was alienated from the direct control of the central government in the form of *tuyūls*. These were in some cases allotted out of *khāliṣeh* lands and also on private property, which might or might not belong to the person to whom the *tuyūl* was granted. In some cases a certain area was the *tuyūl* allotted to the holder of a particular government office; in others they were personal grants.

It is difficult to estimate the relative extent of the land granted as *tuyūl* or of the different forms of land-holding. There were considerable variations in the different provinces. Thus, according to a list dated 1296/1878–9 referring to Zanjān and the districts under Zanjān, between 800 and 900 villages are listed. The most common type of village was the *arbābī* village; the most prevalent form of holding after this was the *khurdeh mālik* village. Unfortunately, it is not clear from the list whether the genuine peasant-proprietor village is meant by this term or merely a village owned by several owners owing to subdivision by inheritance or sale and run, in fact, as an ordinary *arbābī* village.[2] These two classes make up over a third of the villages. The next most prevalent type of village is the village allotted as *tuyūl*, and over half of the villages so allotted belonged to the holder of the *tuyūl*; the second most common type of *tuyūl* was the *tuyūl* allotted on a *khāliṣeh* village. The wages of various offices, as distinct from *tuyūls*, were allotted on certain villages and in a few cases the pension of an individual. Two villages were exempt from taxation. The number of *vaqf* villages was small. A certain number of villages belonged to tribal groups and to tribal *khāns*. Notable also is the number of villages which appear to have belonged to members of the religious classes. Many of the villages were held partially in different ways.[3]

In a report on Kharaqān dated 1298/1880–1[4] the following details emerge. The villages were mainly small. Of 34 villages whose

[1] Thus a certain *ribāṭ*, some 4 *farsakhs* from Ṭabas, had many *ouqāf* until the *ḥukkām* of Ṭabas gradually usurped these and converted them into their own private property. (M.F.A., No. 726, *Safar Nāmeh* of Mīrzā ʻAlī Khān Nā'īnī from Mashhad to Yazd and Nā'īn, f. 96.) Similarly, in a report on Ṭāliqān written in 1301/1883–4, it is stated on the authority of the *mutavallī* of the *imāmzādeh* of Tikīyeh in central Ṭāliqān that the *imāmzādeh* had many *ouqāf*, the proceeds of which were not devoted to their proper purposes (ibid. No. 730, f. 355). The same was alleged to be the case of the *ouqāf* set aside in Ṣafavid times for the shrine of Mahdī Ḥanafīyeh in Marjān (ibid. f. 357).

[2] See below, p. 267, for a discussion of this type of holding.

[3] M.F.A., No. 730, ff. 498–636.

[4] ibid. No. 728, ff. 343–72.

population is given 12 (3 of which were wholly or partially *khurdeh mālik*) were under 50 families, 12 (4 of which were wholly or partially *khurdeh mālik*) were over 50 and under 100, 9 (3 of which were wholly or partially *khurdeh mālik*) were over 100 and under 200, and 1 (which was *khurdeh mālik*) was over 200. Some half of the villages were partially *daym* and partially *ābī*. Three were entirely *ābī* and 4 predominantly *ābī*. One was entirely *daym*. The remainder were predominantly *daym*.

In so far as ownership was concerned some 46 villages were wholly *arbābī* and 13 partially *arbābī*. Of these some 17 villages were owned wholly and 5 in part by the Shāhsivan and 1 wholly and 1 in part by the Kurds. There were 4 *khurdeh mālik* villages and 10 villages partially *khurdeh mālik*. An interesting fact is that some 7 villages wholly or partially *khurdeh mālik* are recorded as becoming *arbābī*, of which 3 were purchased by the Ṣhāhsivan and 3 by Nāṣir ul-Mulk. Only a third of one village is recorded as being *khāliṣeh*, and half of one village, a third of another, and a sixth of another as being *vaqf*.

Another report, dated 1297/1879–80, on the villages of Malā'ir[1] shows that there were 59 villages with a population of under 50 families, 48 over 50 and under 100 families, 24 over 100 and under 200, 8 over 200 and under 300, and 15 over 300, making 154 in all. The population of a number of other villages was unspecified. Of a total of 236 villages 206 were wholly and 7 partially *arbābī*. Sixteen were wholly and 5 partially *khāliṣeh*, and 2 were *vaqf*. Eight of the *arbābī* villages belonged to Turkomān *khāns*. A great many of these villages were situated at the foot of mountains and many had both *ābī* and *daymī* cultivation. No mention is made of *khurdeh mālik* villages and it is possible that the term *arbābī* is used to cover all forms of private ownership.

A report on Nihāvand and Khazal dated 1298/1880–1[2] shows 7 villages with a population of under 50 peasants (not families), 14 with over 50 and under 100, 14 with over 100 and under 200, 20 with over 200 and under 300, 10 with over 300 and under 400, 7 with over 400 and under 500, 4 with over 500 and under 600, 2 with over 600. This report gives also the potential capacity of the village in *zouj*, or plough-lands.[3] Five had less than 5 *zouj*, 9 between 5 and 10, 20 between 10 and 15, 12 between 14 and 20, 17 between 20 and 30, 14 between 30 and 40, 7 between 40 and 50, 5 between 50 and 75, 1 between 100 and 150, and 1 between 150 and 200. The average number of peasants per *zouj* was 9·9, but this was unevenly distributed as follows: 37 villages with an average of less than 10 per *zouj*, 36 with 10 to 50 per *zouj*, and 4

[1] M.F.A., No. 729, ff. 1–151.

[2] ibid. ff. 124–94.

[3] See above, pp. 4 ff.

with over 20 per *zouj*. Thirteen villages were wholly *khāliṣeh*, 3 of which were in ruins, and 4 were partly *khāliṣeh*. The *khāliṣejāt* of Khazal (west of Nihāvand) were, according to the report, in a state of ruin, but seed had been advanced in the previous two years by ʿIzz ud-Douleh and they were improving in condition. The district of Khazal in general, moreover, was in a state of decay. No taxation was collected from it and most of the peasants had dispersed.

Another important class of land in Qājār times, as earlier, was tribal land, and there was probably little change in the latter half of the nineteenth century compared with the early years of the century either as regards the extent of this type of land or in the method of administration of the tribal areas. There was no clear delimitation between tribal land and non-tribal land: one merged into the other, and those of the tribes which were semi-nomadic passed through the land or along the borders of the land of the settled population, and in many cases their chiefs held land outside the tribal areas proper, where their position corresponded to that of ordinary landowners.

In certain areas, notably, in parts of Khūzistān, certain peculiar practices in regard to land tenure also prevailed. In Havīzeh and other districts the whole district would become the right of whoever became *vālī* or *shaykh* of the day, and even the landed property and houses of the late governor or *shaykh* would pass to the new governor, and the family of the late governor would be forced to migrate. This was the case in Fallāḥīyeh, Muḥammareh, and Rām Hurmuz. Najm ul-Mulk, who travelled to Khūzistān in the year 1299/1881–2, states that because of this no one dared develop the land.[1]

The majority of the various tribal groups in different parts of the country migrated annually from winter to summer pastures and back. They were no doubt often contumacious and lawless. In the areas through which they migrated extensive damage was frequently done to the crops and gardens of the settled population.

In Khūzistān, for example, no adequate measures were taken to protect the settled people from the nomads and the semi-settled element. In a report on Fallāḥīyeh written in 1286/1869–70 it is stated that the *bulūk* of Daymcheh, situated to the west of Shūshtar, which had formerly contained prosperous villages, was in a state of ruin because of the inroads of the Lurs and Bakhtīārīs. The crops of the peasants, moreover, were habitually damaged by the flocks of the Bakhtīārī and the Bū Isḥāq.[2] Najm ul-Mulk, travelling in Khūzistān some years later, ascribed the agricultural

[1] M.F.A., No. 725, *Safar Nāmehyi ʿArabistān*, ff. 278–9.
[2] ibid., No. 727, f. 309.

backwardness of the province to the prevailing insecurity caused by the semi-nomadic nature of the Arab tribes.[1]

A report on Khurramābād, written about the close of the thirteenth century A.H. (second half of the nineteenth century A.D.), also mentions the destruction caused to gardens and trees by the tribes in their passage through the area on their annual migration.[2] Similarly, a report on Zanjān mentions the damage done by the Shāhsivan Afshār and other tribes on their annual migration.[3]

Pastures were allotted to certain tribes in their summer and winter quarters as part payment for the military contingents which they were required to furnish. A tax was also levied upon families according to their wealth and the numbers of their flocks. It was collected by the chief or deputies appointed by him.[4] The rate varied. In the neighbourhood of Shīrāz it was levied at the rate of 300 *dīnārs* per milch cow, 200 *dīnārs* per ass, 1,000 *dīnārs* per mare in foal, 300 *dīnārs* per camel, and 700 *dīnārs* per sheep or goat.[5] In the Bakhtīārī the tribes were assessed on the number of their mares (*mādīān*), at the rate of 5 *qirāns* to 2 *tūmāns* per mare, the rate varying with different tribes. Four cows and twenty ewes or she-goats respectively were counted as one mare. No tax was paid by the Bakhtīārī on their agricultural holdings except for a nominal sum per *khīsh* (or plough-land) in the cultivated land in their winter quarters (*qishlāq*).[5]

Special levies were paid by the leaders of the tribes to the ruler at the new year. These were in due course collected by the tribal leaders from their followers and constituted a heavy imposition.[6] The rule of the tribal *khāns* often tended to be highly oppressive. ʿAbd ul-Ghaffār Najm ul-Mulk, on his way to ʿArabistān in 1299/1881–2, states that he travelled a few days in the neighbourhood of Kar Kunān and saw many ruined villages which had formerly constituted the *bulūk* of Chinārrūd. They numbered over 300, and the Bakhtīārī themselves told him that they had become ruined because of the oppression of the tribal *khāns*.[7]

To establish control over the tribal areas was indeed one of the hardest problems which faced the Qājārs. In general at this period they attempted, as had rulers before them, to rule the tribes

[1] M.F.A., No. 725, ff. 495–6.
[2] ibid. No. 729, f. 154.
[3] ibid. No. 730, ff. 508, 520, 522, 526, 529, 616, 624.
[4] Malcolm, *History of Persia*, ii. 339.
[5] Sardar Asʿad, pp. 197–8.
[6] ibid. (in section with pages unnumbered). See also Curzon, ii. 472–3.
[7] M.F.A., No. 725, f. 357. He also relates instances of the seizures by the Īl Khān of *vaqf* land in Bāb Ḥaydar, which had been constituted into a *vaqf* for the descendants of the Imām Mūsā and Sayyids of Bab Ḥaydar and had been exempt from taxation since the time of the Atābegs (f. 352).

through the tribal chiefs, but the control they established was seldom more than precarious.[1] Thus, an Īl Khān and Īlbeg were appointed over the larger tribes; they collected government taxes and were generally responsible for tribal affairs. These officers were usually, but not necessarily, tribal chiefs, and the tendency was for the office to be hereditary. In Fārs the two main groups were the Khamseh and the Qashqā'ī, the former of whom were in early Qājār times the more powerful. It was composed, as the name suggests, of five tribes, three Turkish (the Aynālū, Bahārlū, and Nafar) and two Arab (the Bāṣirī and the Īli 'Arab). The Aynālū, who ranged from winter quarters in Khafr, Dārāb, and Fasā to summer quarters in Rāmjird and Marvdasht, were a constant source of trouble in the latter part of the thirteenth century A.H. (mid-nineteenth century A.D.); they lived largely by plundering and highway robbery in Fārs, Kirmān, and Yazd. From 1293/1876–7 onwards they were brought under some sort of control by the efforts of Mu'tamid ud-Douleh Ḥājjī Farhād Mīrzā, and Mīrzā 'Alī Muḥammad Khān Qavām ul-Mulk Shīrāzī, and were settled in the neighbourhood of Qarā Bulāgh.[2] Similarly the Bahārlū, about the turn of the thirteenth and fourteenth centuries A.H., were becoming settled in the neighbourhood of Dārāb.[3] The Īli 'Arab were divided into the 'Arab Jabbāreh and the 'Arab Shaybānī, their leadership, since early times, having been in the hands of the 'Arab Shaybānī *khāns*. One group lived in the neighbourhood of Rām Hormuz, Jarrāḥī, and Dourāq, and spent the summer on the banks of the river; another group wintered in Haft Bulūk, Rūdān, and Aḥmadī and spent the summer in Bavānāt, Qūnqarī, and Sar Chāhān, the distance between their summer and winter quarters being nearly 100 *farsakhs* (some 350 miles).[4] The leadership of the Bāṣirī, whose winter quarters were in Sarvistān, Kurbāl, and Kuvār and summer quarters in Arsinjān and Kamīn, was in the hands of the Īli 'Arab, to whom it was entrusted in Ṣafavid times.[5]

The Qashqā'ī ranged from the *garmsīr* of Fārs in Chahār Bulūk Afzar, Jarreh, Khisht, Khunj, Dashtī, Dashtistān, Farrāshband, and Māhūr Mīlātī to their summer quarters in the districts of Dizgird, *sarḥaddi* Chahārdāngeh, *sarḥaddi* Shish Nāḥīyeh, Kām Fīrūz, and the area of Kākān and Kuhar in the Mamasanī. The office of Īlkhānī and Īlbegī belonged to the tribal *khāns*.[6]

There were several other tribal groups in Fārs of various origins, some settled, some semi-settled, and some entirely nomadic.[7]

[1] In 1896 in the reign of Muẓaffar ud-Dīn Shāh there was a proposal for the establishment of a special ministry or High Council to have charge of tribal affairs (G. Demorgny, *Essai sur l'administration de la Perse* (Paris, 1913), p. 8).
[2] Fasā'ī, ii. 309. [3] ibid. p. 310. [4] ibid. p. 311.
[5] ibid. p. 310. [6] ibid. p. 313. [7] ibid. pp. 330–2.

The Sharīfāt tribe, who lived near Bandar Hindīān, held the government (*ḥukūmat*) of the area.[1]

Control over the Turkomāns of the Gūklān and Yamūt, as in the earlier Qājār period, was of a somewhat precarious nature. Sayf ud-Douleh, who was made governor (*farmān farmā*) of Astarābād in 1320–1/1902–4, wrote an account of these two tribes for Muẓaffar ud-Dīn Shāh.[2] He states that on arriving in Astarābād he summoned all the *khāns* of the Gūklān and issued to them the necessary revenue rolls (*dastūr ul-ʿamal*) and lists of extraordinary taxes (*takālīf*), made a revenue survey and census, and defined the pastures and lands of each tribe.[3] Each tribe was composed of several *oubeh*, each of which had its leader, who held a private or hereditary *yurt*. There was no leader over the whole tribe; when necessary the elders of the *oubeh*, *shaykhs*, and old men assembled for consultation and decided upon action in accordance with the views of the prominent members, elders, and even of the ordinary members of the tribe.[4] The Yamūt lived primarily by raiding. Their lands were exceedingly fertile and each tribe wherever it took up its residence treated the surrounding plain as its personal and hereditary *yurt*. The muleteers of Simnān, Shāhrūd, and Astarābād used to entrust their beasts to the Turkomāns to graze and used to pay them in return 1 *tūmān* per head of cattle.[5] It was customary from ancient times for all the villages of Astarābād to pay tribute to the Yamūt. The peasants of Astarābād paid a certain share of their crops to the leader of the tribe in the neighbourhood. In return the latter and his tribe would refrain from stealing the peasants' goods and recover anything stolen from them by another tribe and return it to the villagers.[6]

Rabino gives a somewhat similar account. He states that

> [the Yamút and Gúklán] have no constituted authority although each section has an *áq-saqal* or 'grey beard'. His position, however, confers no authority and is simply attained by virtue of his age, experience, and personal influence. The inter-tribal feuds which prevail among the Turcomans are due to this want of a central authority and of some supreme chief to keep the various sections under control. The degree of influence or authority of the Persian government extends to the imposition of tribute, but leaves the movements of the people free, and does

[1] Fasā'ī, p. 331.

[2] MS. in the library of the National Assembly.

[3] ibid. ff. 52–5.

[4] ibid. f. 98. Fraser, writing in 1821–2, also notes that the Yamūts and Gūklāns had no chiefs but merely elders or 'reish suffeed' to whom considerable respect was paid and whose advice was taken in all matters affecting the interests of the community, and who adjusted petty disputes (*Journey into Khorasān*, p .262; cf. also G. C. Napier, *Collection of Journals and Reports from Capt. the Hon. G. C. Napier, on special duty in Persia*, 1874 (London, 1876), pp. 322 ff.).

[5] MS. in the library of the National Assembly, f. 110.

[6] ibid. f. 123.

not admit of the punishment of offences by the supreme power. This authority is submitted to or resisted at the caprice of the people or their leading men, and is increased or diminished as the action of the local governor is strong and resolute or weak and vacillating. The tribute is paid to certain agents, or *sarkardas* appointed by the Central Government, who are responsible for its collection as well as for the quota of horsemen which the various sections of the tribe are supposed to furnish when called upon to do so. The post of agent became practically hereditary in certain families, so that the holders of those posts soon abuse their position and entered into partnership with the Turcomans to plunder the unfortunate villages of Astarábád.[1]

The Yamūt were divided into two sections: cultivators known as *chumūr*, and nomads known as *chārwā*. The latter paid little if any tribute.[2]

The relations between the Yamúts and the Atak villagers are as a rule anything but friendly, and although the *chárwás* are supposed to be responsible for most of the raids, yet the Atábáy and even the Ja'farbáy *chumúr* often take part in these forays, and the villagers of Kurd-Maḥalla, whose only neighbours are Ja'farbáy, have to be constantly on the look-out to frustrate the attacks of their hereditary enemies. Not a day passes but what bloodshed occurs, or some plundering foray or retaliatory expedition is undertaken. . . . To guard against these raids many of the Atak villagers pay a Yamút chief an annual quantity of rice, in return for which he is bound to protect them and to make good any losses they may suffer at the hands of the Yamút. This arrangement is termed *sákhlú*.[3]

The Gūklān were not nomadic. They lived in constant dread of the Yamūts and were also on bad terms with the Kurds of Bujnūrd, the Ḥājjīlar of Kabūdjāmeh, and other inhabitants of the neighbouring district of Astarābād. Raids and counter-raids were of frequent occurrence.[4]

The Turkomāns, like other tribal groups, were an element making for insecurity, but as in the case of other tribal groups they, too, were often subject to oppression and provocation. In a letter from Iḥtishām ul-Vizāreh, a former Persian Commissioner at Gumbadi Qābūs, quoted by Rabino from a work by Nāṣir ul-Kuttāb on the Gurgān plain, the writer expresses his opinion that the Yamūt and Gūklān were loyal subjects of the *shāh* and that

If they have such a bad reputation, it is due to the fact that they have never had a representative at Court to remove misunderstandings. Governors and persons in authority, in the interest of their own pocket

[1] H. L. Rabino (di Borgomale), *Mázandarán and Astarábád*, pp. 94–5.
[2] ibid. p. 97.
[3] ibid. p. 99; cf. also Napier, who mentions the enmity between the settled villagers of Astarābād and the nomads (*Journals and Reports*, p. 266).
[4] Rabino, p. 100.

and to increase their reputation, have always represented some section or other of Turcomans as being in open rebellion, and the Persian Government has immediately sent instructions for the punishment of the rebels. I myself have often seen innocent tribes ruthlessly plundered. The chiefs and grey-beards more than once informed me that they dislike becoming Russian subjects, but that the governor of Astarábád forces them to rebel. . . .[1]

Rabino also mentions that many of the inhabitants of Astarābād admitted to him 'that the Turcomans received great provocation from the Atak villagers, who often stole their horses and cattle, whilst the governors of Astarábád made an excuse of their so-called punitive expeditions to impose heavy fines on the tribesmen and enrich themselves at their expense'.[2]

Similar tendencies were also to be found in other tribal areas. Sardar As'ad in his *Tārīkhi Bakhtīārī* quotes from a report written by 'Abdur-Rahīm Kāshānī in 1323/1905–6 in which the writer describes how the Bakhtīārī, because of the great tyranny and oppression they had suffered, fled when they saw a traveller, lest he should be an official of the *dīvān*, an envoy from the *khān*, or a tax-collector from the governor (*ẓābiṭi ḥukmrān*). Noting the absence of cultivation in the villages he passed through in the country between Puli 'Imārat and Malāmīr, the author of the report asked why the people did not grow vegetables, which they could eat themselves and sell any surplus to travellers. An old man replied to him as follows:

What you say is true provided we are left to ourselves. What benefit is there for me that I should spend my life and undertake labour, the fruits of which will be taken possession of entirely by the governor (*ḥākim*) and tax-collector (*ẓābiṭ*), who will prevent me from enjoying them. And, if I undertake this labour once, it will become a hereditary charge on my family. Every year the tax-collector (*ẓābiṭ*) and governors (*ḥukkām*) will demand it of me.[3]

A somewhat similar condition appears to have prevailed in Kurdistān; in a report written in 1296/1878–9 the writer comments upon the potential fertility of Kurdistān and regrets that this was wasted because of the prevailing poverty, disorder, frequent rebellions, and insecurity. He remarks on the wretched condition of the people and puts this down to the fact that the governors of the province were concerned only with the acquisition of personal wealth and were not concerned to prevent tyranny against the weak. He alleges that they neglected national interests, and were

[1] Rabino, p. 96. [2] ibid. pp. 99–100.

[3] p. 50. Cf. the tendency of the Egyptian *fellāh* to limit production (H. A. R. Gibb and Harold Bowen, *Islamic Society and the West* (London, 1950), vol. i, part i, p. 264).

concerned only with their own illegitimate interests. He points out that in such instances the people had no remedy but migration.[1]

In some of the frontier areas in the north-east various tribal groups appear to have held land free in return for the provision of military contingents or for the military services they performed in connexion with frontier defence. This was the case in Bujnūrd, Darigaz, and Ashraf. In 1874 Napier records that the *khān* of Darigaz maintained a body of 800 horsemen, mounted and armed, as a condition of his tenure, and goes on to state:

> Exposed as the whole northern border of the chiefship is to sudden attacks by overwhelming forces from the desert and the Akhal 'Atak', the burden of self-protection falls heavily on the people. In the 'Atak', where the Khan's cavalry can usually only arrive in time to pursue the assailants after all the mischief in their power has been done, the whole population may be said to be constantly on guard. Every village keeps watçh day and night on its walls, and every gang of sowers and reapers goes to work matchlock in hand, and stations watchmen on the high round towers that dot the field in all directions at very short intervals.
>
> The inner line of defence extends from the heights above the Rood Var, east of the valley, to Kalta Chenar, on the Koochan border, and every pass and pathway has its watch tower occupied constantly by parties of villagers.
>
> The Khan holds his lands free of any revenue, but subject to the payment of a yearly tribute in the shape of presents of money and horses, the amount of which regulates the treatment that he receives at the hands of the provincial and central Governments. A sum of 750 tomans is allotted yearly from the Mashad treasury to pay a portion of the horsemen entertained for the defence of the border. Formerly 1,500 tomans was the amount of the grant, but even that was quite insufficient; for the pay of 800 men would alone amount to at least 8,000 tomans. The arrangement is, however, nearly nominal, for no portion of the subsidy leaves the hands of the officials at Mashad.[2]

Similarly the Īlkhānīs of the Shādilū of Bujnūrd were exempt from the payment of revenue on condition of military service. Describing the situation Napier writes:

> they are bound to protect their own borders, and to guard the passes leading across it into the interior districts.
>
> No revenue is taken from the people, save such as the chief himself may choose to take. The whole of the permanent body of horse and foot for border defence being paid by assignments on the villages, and many villages being made over to the chief's relations and adherents, he is able to collect for his personal expenses only the small sum of 4,000 tomans = rupees 16,000 per annum. Of this 300 tomans is raised from the town dues on shops, sale of cattle, horses, etc., the balance is collected rateably from the free villages, *i.e.* those not assigned to dependents.

[1] M.F.A., No. 730, f. 454.

[2] *Journals and Reports*, pp. 303–4.

Four thousand tomans is the nominal sum assessed yearly, but I was given to understand that more than this is occasionally exacted; the excess usually falling on villages not inhabited by the chief's tribesmen. A tribute of horses, and usually of a sum of 1,000 tomans or more, in gold coins, is paid yearly to the Shah.[1]

The Ghilzay Afghans settled by Nādir Shāh in Qarā Tappeh in the Gurgān plain also held their lands free of revenue, and received a yearly sum of 400 *tūmāns* (not always paid), the pay of fifty horsemen they were bound to keep up armed and equipped for border defence.[2]

Although the Qājār period in some respects sees a reversion to Seljūq practice, the provincial contingents outside the tribal areas were levied on a somewhat different basis. This change was introduced by Mīrzā Taqī Khān, Nāṣir ud-Dīn's prime minister. It was made incumbent upon each area to provide, in addition to its tax assessment, so many soldiers or, in some cases, a sum equivalent to the wages of so many soldiers.[3] In theory, therefore, the loyalty of these soldiers was to the central government or to the provincial government, and not to the local landowner or *tuyūldār*. The latter had merely to expedite their dispatch to the capital or provincial capital. It was thus a service on the land. Formerly the duty of service was placed upon the *muqṭaʿ* or assignee and not upon the land as such. He was granted an *iqṭāʿ* or assignment of land to defray the cost of the contingent he was bound to provide as his service when called upon to do so; the contingent the *muqṭaʿ* provided was therefore loyal in the first instance to him and only secondly to the *sulṭān*.

In so far as local administration and the administration of justice was concerned there was little difference from the earlier Qājār period. In villages owned by large landed proprietors the landowner was the judge of all disputes affecting the population of the village, his authority being exercised through his bailiff (*mubāshir*) or through the *kadkhudā* or village headman. In villages held as *tuyūl* the *tuyūldār* exercised a similar authority. In *khurdeh mālik* villages the people would take their cases to whomever among the local men they considered to be impartial. If cases were not settled locally they were referred to the deputy-governor or governor, but this was not often necessary.[4]

The revenue administration was under the *mustoufī*. In the tax registers were entered the names of the provinces and the *bulūks* or districts and villages of each province together with their taxation. Any alterations made in the assessment were entered in the register. The *mustoufī* of each province prepared every year a revenue

[1] *Journals and Reports*, pp. 286–7. [2] ibid. p. 90.
[3] Mustoufī, i. 91. [4] ibid. p. 138.

assessment which was entered in a register known as the *daftari dastūr ul-ʿamal.* The total was the same as that entered in the *daftari juzvi jamʿ* under the province concerned. The revenue realized locally was used to defray regular local expenses. If any surplus remained over, it was allotted to such expenses as the authorities might decree in that particular year, and the payment of the grants of persons which had been made a charge on the province. Anything left after this was remitted to the treasury.[1]

The *dastūr ul-ʿamal* of each province was completed before the Nou Rūz, signed by the *mustoufī ul-mamālik* and the Prime Minister, and approved by the *shāh.* Taxes were then levied and expenses paid in accordance with the *dastūr ul-ʿamal.* Drafts endorsed by the *mustoufī* were sent to the local governors for the salaries of officials and others which were allotted on the provinces. These read: 'The sum of . . . for the wages of . . . on the *dastūr ul-ʿamal* of . . . has been allotted.' The recipients would give a receipt when they received the sums allotted to them.[2]

The villages were assessed in a lump sum, the division of this among the individual peasants being made by the local authorities and in the peasant proprietor areas by the village elders. This group assessment was known as *bunīcheh.* In it were included the number of soldiers or government servants (*noukari doulatī*) which each area had to provide. The collection of the various taxes and the levying of the soldiers and their expenses were often the cause of much oppression by the tax-collectors.[3]

In making these assessments water, land, the availability of labour, the state of cultivation, and the occupation of the people were in theory if not in practice taken into account. The reason for the assessment being made partly in cash and partly in kind was alleged to be in order that any loss or benefit resulting from a rise or fall in prices should affect the government and the tax-payer equally. In provinces such as Yazd and Kāshān, which were not self-supporting in grain, the tax was payable in cash and reckoned at the lowest rate of conversion. From time to time new assessments were made for different areas.[4]

[1] ibid. p. 565. [2] ibid. p. 566.

[3] See ibid. i. 139; see also Curzon, ii. 471.

[4] For example, land watered by various *qanāts* in Qumm was assessed during the vazirate of Mīrzā Taqī Khān Farāhānī and by Mīrzā Zayn ul-ʿĀbidīn Tabrīzī, the latter assessment being subsequently modified by Mīrzā Ḥabībullāh Garakānī (List of Landed Properties, etc., M.F.A., No. 725, ff. 47–8). Fārs was delimited about the middle of the thirteenth century A.H. by Muḥammad Ḥusayn Ra'īs Shayādānī (b. 1221/1806–7, see Fasā'ī, ii. 57). Under Muẓaffar ud-Dīn Shāh, Mīrzā Maḥmud Qarā increased the assessment of Khurāsān. Complaints were made from Qūchān and elsewhere of the heaviness of the assessment, the injustice of the governors (*ḥukkām*) and the way in which the increase was divided among the tax-payers. A commission of inquiry was eventually appointed and the taxes were readjusted (Mustoufī, ii. 651).

The unit on which the tax was assessed varied in different areas. Stack, writing in 1882, records that in the submontane and maritime villages of Fārs the assessment was made 'by the cow, that is to say by the plough'.[1] The rate varied from 4 *tūmāns* to 16 *tūmāns* according to the quality of the land.[2] He states that the landowner had to pay a money assessment to the local governor.

This assessment [he writes] has developed itself out of the custom of bygone centuries, with such reductions as a famine would necessitate, and such amplifications as the exigency of the State may have prompted. A village, for example, may be assessed at 500 tomans land-revenue and 50 tomans' worth of gratuitous labour (*khidmatana*); in the course of years these two demands coalesce into one demand of 550 tomans as land-revenue, with 10 per cent or 55 tomans extra as khidmatana. Some notion of the propriety of a periodical revision of assessment seems to hover in the minds of the people, but in a form entirely vague; nobody could tell me anything about the latest revision (*jamabandi*), save in Kavar, where an intelligent young arbab remembered hearing it spoken of as a thing done fifty years ago. The assessments of individual villages are valueless towards estimating the general incidence of the land-revenue; besides, it is next to impossible to ascertain what these assessments are, unless one had sight of the revenue-rolls in the Governor's office; for a village is always spoken of with its *bulukât* or dependent villages and hamlets, and the number and extent of these are uncertain. A few instances may be given, however, with the general remark that diwani villages seem to be more heavily assessed than arbabi; an arbab can make some kind of resistance, while a multitude of poor tenants can neither resist nor bribe effectually. Deh-i-Nau, in the Shiraz plain, pays 400 tomans a year; so does Fathabad in the Kavar plain; while Kavar itself, a much larger village than either of them, pays 120 tomans only, and forty kharwars of grain, the kharwar here being 100 Tabriz mans, worth about five tomans. Jawakan pays only 100 tomans, though considerably bigger than Deh-i-Nau; it lies higher, and the land is not so good.[3]

Stack comments that the assessment seemed heavy but, on the other hand, that land appeared to be a good investment since it was eagerly bought.[4] In the plains of Bīdshahr, ʿIwaẓ, and Lār, where wells were used to irrigate the land, the state levied a tax known as *sarcharkhī* on each well. These were private property even in *dīvānī* (i.e. *khāliṣeh*) villages.[5] In the Yazd plains and in Shīrkūh, however, the assessment of a village was based upon a calculation of its water-supply.[6] On *daym*, i.e. unirrigated crops in Marvdasht, in the Shīrāz and Kuvār plains, in Jawakān, Fīrūzābād, and Qīr, one-fifth was paid by way of tax, the amount being estimated on the threshing floor.[7] Stack mentions another type of

[1] ii. 249.
[2] ibid. p. 250.
[3] ibid. pp. 256–7.
[4] ibid. p. 257.
[5] ibid. p. 259.
[6] ibid. p. 273.
[7] ibid. p. 252.

assessment which he observed in the area between Furg and Sirjān; this recalls earlier practices connected with conversion rates.[1] He writes that the assessment and distribution of the land revenue was made by

> reference to a *bunicha* or imaginary assessment, which, being multiplied by a certain figure, gives the real assessment of the village. The bunicha (or *foundation*) is usually stated in tomans, and the land-revenue is got by taking so many qirans per qiran, or so many *pul* per *pul*, or *shahi* per *shahi*. Thus in Kaha the bunicha is five qirans but the revenue demand is 300 pul per pul, that is to say, 300 qirans per qiran of the bunicha, i.e. $5 \times 300 = 1{,}500$ qirans or 150 tomans. In Birakun and Dehistan the rate is the same; in the mountain villages north of the Sirjan plateau it seems to be less, varying from 120 to 150 qirans per qiran of the bunicha; in the villages on the foot-slopes of the range north of the Zarand plain, Sar Asiab, Khanuk, and Tughraja, the rate was said to be only 40 tomans per toman of the bunicha.[2]

In addition to the regular land tax the population were also subject to occasional taxes or reliefs. When Stack was travelling through Fārs he mentions that the people were paying a relief imposed on account of the Kurdish invasion of Āẕarbāyjān, which was collected as a poll tax.[3]

In the latter part of Nāṣir ud-Dīn Shāh's reign various steps were taken with a view to unifying the tax administration of the country, increasing the revenue, and ensuring that what was collected reached the central treasury. These efforts were not attended, however, by any conspicuous degree of success, and Curzon, who visited Persia in 1889–90, records that the assessments were in the main obsolete in date and character.[4] By the decree of 1303/1885–6 on the Shourāyi Tanẓīmāt, certain projects for reform in the collection of taxes were laid down. It was intended that these should be progressively extended to all the areas of Persia. In this decree there was an attempt to define the financial responsibility of the governor.

According to art. I the governors were to assemble in the first two months of the year, namely Ḥamal and Ṣaur, in the chief town of the area under their jurisdiction, all the *kadkhudās* and *rīsh sifīd* of the villages. The assessment of each village was to be fixed according to the registers of the *mustoufīs* and the advice of the local council for provincial reforms. A copy of this was to be given to the *kadkhudās* of the village concerned. The tax due was to be paid in regular monthly instalments by the *kadkhudā*, and as long as this was paid tax-collectors were forbidden to enter the village. Art. IV lays down that in order to protect the peasant from the

[1] See above, Ch. II.
[2] ibid. pp. 259–60.
[3] ibid. pp. 250–1.
[4] ii. 472.

exactions of the *kadkhudā* and tax-collectors the text of the decree should be publicly announced in the villages. Extraordinary levies were to be discontinued. The power to make levies to meet local expenses was removed from the competence of the tax-collectors; decisions concerning the making of such levies and their expenditure was to rest with the local inhabitants (art. V). A *mustoufī* and *sirishtehdār* was to be appointed to each province (*vilāyat*) to prepare the tax rolls. In villages in ruins, in poor villages, or villages newly created, special government agents were to be appointed to exercise financial control according to the instructions of the local administrative council (art. VIII). The owners of several villages could not be granted a reduction on the ground of one or more of their villages being in ruins provided their other villages could make good these alleged losses (art. X). Since government tax-collectors were by decree prevented from going into the villages, the central authorities had no longer the right to demand from the governors the payment of supplementary taxes such as *pīshkash*, *khalʿatbahā* (levied for royal favours), *ghulūq* (levied for tax-collectors), *nāzi shast* (levied for services performed), or levies made on feast days. The governors were not to be forced to pay personal levies except on the special orders of the central government (art. XII). Local officials and *kadkhudās* were to be paid regularly (art. XIV).

The next step was taken in 1307/1889–90 when instructions were issued for a new land survey to be carried out under the Ministry of Finance. By this survey land was divided into various categories and taxation was assessed on the basis of the produce per 10,000 square *ẓarʿ*: (1) crown lands (*amlāki salṭanatī*) consisting of buildings, gardens, factories, barracks, stores, forests (*jangalhā*), special state preserves (*quruqhāyi makhṣūṣīyi doulatī*), telegraph offices, guard houses (*qarāvul khānehhā*), embassies, consulates, and special hill stations (*yaylāqāt*) in the hands of the officials of foreign governments but belonging to the government, and similar property; (2) common property (*amlāki ʿumūmī*) such as mosques, *tikīyehs*, shrines (*zavāyā*), water-tanks, drinking places, places of worship of foreigners, public hospitals, public gardens, stations and railway centres, and cemeteries; (3) real estate consisting of baths, caravanserais, shops, similar state-owned rentable property, mills, and any land in the temporary possession of someone in return for a payment in money or kind; and (4) private property (*amlāki khāṣṣeh*) consisting of houses, gardens, orchards, and cultivable property.[1]

Provision was made for recording changes in the relative prosperity of estates.[2] One man per 180 male Muslims in each village was to be taken annually for military service, and 150 *tūmāns* for

[1] *Kurāsat ul-Maʿī*, ff. 1020–2. [2] ibid. f. 1037.

every 180 male non-Muslims.[1] Taxes were to be levied as follows: at harvest time an official was to go to the village and from every kind of grain, pulse, lucerne, and grass, 10 per cent was to be taken in kind and stored in government store-houses; from tobacco, cucumbers, melons, water-melons, marrow, opium, cotton, silk, sugar-canes and beet, 10 per cent in cash was to be collected in instalments.[2]

The camels, sheep, and goats of every village and tribe (*qabīleh*) were to be counted annually at the beginning of spring. Three *qirāns* (*si hazār*) per camel and 1 *qirān* per sheep or goat (*gūsfand*) was to be taken. On every hive of honey-bees 10 *shāhī* (½ *qirān*) was to be levied in the middle of autumn. Other animals in villages or belonging to the nomad tribes were exempt.[3]

Various other dues were to be levied. Thus marriage permits for virgins were to cost 2 *qirāns* (*do hazār dīnār*). The charge for the verification of documents concerning landed estates issued by religious authorities was to be 5 *shāhī* (¼ *qirān*) per 1 *tūmān* of the value of the property or of the annual rent; for permits to carry out repairs 10 *shāhī* (½ *qirān*); for permits to make new buildings 1 *ʿabbāsī* per sq. *ẕarʿ*; and for every transit permit 2 *qirāns* (*do hazār dīnār*).[4] If anyone from a province was sent to a government office (*idāreh*) and had no transit permit, that office was to send him back under guard to his own province.[5]

Certain services were also taken from the population by the law of 1307/1889–90 for the making of roads. All males from 16–50 years of age were bound to give a number of days' labour per annum on the roads, and those who could not give labour were bound to compound for a payment in cash so that labourers could be employed in their stead. The religious classes (of whatever religion), school-teachers, soldiers in service, and police were exempt.[6] Pack animals of every province (*vilāyat*) were to give 20–30 days in every five years for the transport of road-building materials.[7] Provisions were made for equalizing the service of labourers according to the distance they had to travel to the areas where the road was being constructed. Thus twenty-five men from a village close to the area were to serve five days per annum, whereas those from a village 4 *farsakhs* away (approximately 14 miles) would only serve four days.[8] Travel permits would be given only to those who had performed their road service.[9]

How far these various regulations were operative throughout the country is not certain. It is, however, clear that in so far as the

[1] ibid. f. 1059.
[2] ibid. ff. 1059–60.
[3] ibid. f. 1060.
[4] ibid. ff. 1060–1.
[5] ibid. ff. 1070–1.
[6] ibid. f. 1089.
[7] ibid. f. 1090.
[8] ibid. f. 1093.
[9] ibid. f. 1094.

central government was able to exercise control, certain services were exacted and the peasant was in some measure tied to the soil. Taxation was levied in a lump sum on each village, and in addition to taxes in cash and kind, each village had to produce a number of soldiers. Where the central government's authority did not extend, similar services were no doubt exacted by the landowners.

In so far as the assessment and collection of revenue was concerned, considerable variations appear to have persisted.[1] Moreover, a great deal of difficulty was experienced in the collection of taxes. On the whole, however, the general tendency was for such sums to be exacted by way of ordinary taxes, and above all in the form of extraordinary levies, as frequently to lead to the ruin of whole districts. Instances of decay due to oppression by government officials have already been quoted. Najm ul-Mulk bears witness to a similar state of affairs in Khūzistān, or ʿArabistān as it was then known, which province he visited in 1299/1881–2.[2] Describing the decay of various regions in ʿArabistān in spite of their potential fertility, he attributes this partly to the neglect of the central government and partly to the oppressive practices of local *shaykhs*, governors, and landowners.[3] ʿAqīlī, for instance, he states, had become ruined because of excessive oppression. It was customary to take up to 3 *tūmāns* per yoke of oxen, and taxation per *jarīb* had reached 20–30 *tūmāns*, and as a result the people had left their lands. In Dizfūl and Shūshtar he alleged that no one was able to live unless he farmed the taxes or rented *khāliṣeh* land, and if he farmed government taxes he would nevertheless be unable to pay the instalments at the proper time and would inevitably become in need of a loan. No rich people were to be found in Dizfūl or Shūshtar: all the families were ruined and the people poor and destitute.[4] Similarly, the population of Rām Hurmuz had declined to 200 families all of whom were poor.[5] The Arabs of

[1] According to Curzon, the assessment frequently amounted to 30 per cent of the total produce and 25 per cent could be taken as a fair average. He notes, however, the considerable local variations, and that the taxes were levied sometimes from the proprietor, and sometimes from the cultivator (ii. 471). He also states that 'religious endowments and lands held upon the basis of feudal service, were exempt from land tax (ii. 470).

[2] Another report, written in 1286/1869–70, states that the people of Gargar (belonging to Shūshtar) were unable to pay their taxes (M.F.A., No. 727, f. 309).

[3] An important factor militating against prosperity in Khūzistān was Arab-Persian hostility. Najm ul-Mulk mentions the aversion of the Arabs of Ahvāz to the building of a dam in Ahvāz and to the development of the town lest this should lead to the penetration of the Persians. He alleges that the Arabs brought up their children to fear the Persians, and goes on to state that there were reasons for this, namely, the oppression practised by the officials who came to Ahvāz with no thought other than that of filling their pockets (*Safar Nāmehyi ʿArabistān*, f. 263). He mentions a similar fear of Persian penetration among the Arabs of Shuʿaybīyeh should development schemes be undertaken (Report on Khūzistān, f. 185).

[4] *Safar Nāmehyi ʿArabistān*, f. 333.

[5] ibid. f. 337.

Khumays (?) practised *daym* cultivation; each *khīsh* paid 2 *tūmāns* or more. Irrigated land had no fixed tax, and as much as could be extorted was taken. The ordinary tax was 13,000 *tūmāns* and the extraordinary 1,500 *tūmāns*. This was beyond the taxable capacity of the land, and the peasants had dispersed. All kinds of dues were demanded from them such as *sar khānegī*, under which head 5–10 *tūmāns* was levied on every house according to its size. Formerly, Rām Hurmuz had fruit gardens, but when Najm ul-Mulk visited it in 1299/1881–2 only one garden of citrus fruits was in production. He attributes this decay to the oppression of tax-collectors and the dispersal of the peasants, and also to the fact that the available water was used for *ṣayfī* and *shatvī* crops.[1] In another report, written in 1300/1882–3, the same writer reiterates his view that the decay of Rām Hurmuz was due to the oppression of the tax-collectors and the frequent changes of governors.[2]

The relations between the peasants and the landowners varied considerably from district to district. In some cases, as in later and earlier times, the land was permanently apportioned, in others it was redistributed among the peasants annually or at intervals. In the submontane and maritime villages of Fārs, Stack asserts that the lands of the village were divided into various tracts known as (*ṣaḥrā*) according to position and local advantages. In winter, shortly before seed time, all the lands were divided among the number of ploughs which the village could muster. Each *ṣaḥrā* was parcelled out into longitudinal strips, and to every plough was assigned a strip or strips in each *ṣaḥrā*, so as to make the apportionment fair.[3] From Shīrāz to Lār and Furg to Lār he records that irrigated lands were annually distributed among the plough-owning cultivators. The lands were measured out in strips, and then these strips were assigned to the cultivator by lot, or by mutual agreement.[4] In Dashti Arjan the land was also annually apportioned among the ploughs of the village.[5] In some areas, however, the peasants had a more permanent tenure. In Jawakān the irrigated lands had been divided and were held permanently by the peasants, each in his several share; when a man died, the land went to his heirs; when a family became extinct, a stranger was brought into the vacant place. Such rights of cultivators were not saleable.[6]

According to Fraser, who wrote about 1820, in so far as Āẕarbāyjān was concerned the peasant had by customary law a certain security. He states:

> the original customary law regarding landed property, clearly provided with much consideration for the security of the ryot. The rights of the villager were guarded at least as carefully as those of his lord: his title to

[1] ibid. f. 338. [2] Report on Khūzistān, f. 216. [3] ii. 250.
[4] ibid. p. 253. [5] ibid. p. 255. [6] ibid. pp. 254–5.

cultivate his portion of land descends to him from the original commencement of the village to which he belongs, and can neither be disputed nor refused him; nor can he forfeit it, nor can the lord of the village eject any ryot, while he conducts himself well, and pays his portion of the rent. In fact, the proprietor has nothing to do with the individuals of the property; he has to treat with each village collectively, and none can forfeit his right to cultivate his share, save by general consent in an assembly of the whole, headed by the *Reish suffeed*, which is the only paramount authority in such a case. The ryot, however, if he dislikes the terms, his service, or desires it on other accounts, has a right to remove from any village, unless he be liable for a portion of the māleyāt or taxes; in which case he cannot move unless the rest of the villagers take on themselves the payment of his portion; but this right of removal is now often tyrannously refused, in despite of their anxiety to quit; and . . . the whole of the customary law is rendered nugatory by the encroachments and arbitrary character of the government and its officers.[1]

He goes on to state:

the ryot cannot increase the amount of his own particular cultivation at will, to the prejudice or exclusion of his fellow villagers. The land having been divided in portions among the community at the commencement, or fresh arrangements having been made as circumstances demanded, from time to time by common consent, no individual can contravene these; but if he can procure water, he may take in waste lands, or he may purchase from those who are willing to sell their right of cultivation, for such term as may be agreed upon. It is not unfrequent for a ryot to purchase a small field in the village ground, from the proprietor, and this property is disposeable like any other.[2]

This description by Fraser is of great interest and shows that in some areas in Āẕarbāyjān if not elsewhere the communal organiza- of the village was still strong at the beginning of the nineteenth century. Fraser himself, however, notes the encroachment of government and its officials in the field of customary law, and there seems little doubt that the old village organization, in so far as it remained, was broken down during the course of the nineteenth century. Moreover, such actual legislation as was passed in practice did not improve the status of the peasant. As pointed out above, by the survey of 1307/1889–90 the peasant was in some measure tied to the soil and made subject to labour service. No doubt this to some extent reflected the actual situation, but by giving to it legal recognition the disabilities which the peasant suffered were settled more firmly upon him.

In the area between Shīrāz and Lār the cultivator paid two-thirds of the crop to the landowner.

His status [Stack states] may be that of a tenant holding under an arbab, or of a tenant of the State, or he may be a kind of under-pro-

[1] *Journey into Khorasān*, pp. 208–9.

[2] ibid. p. 209.

prietor. In Marvdasht, the Shiraz and Kavar plains, and Firuzabad, the cultivators are mostly tenants of large non-resident arbabs. They pay two-thirds of the crop, or its equivalent in money, as happens to suit the arbab; and they receive some assistance from him in the matter of seed. Where irrigation depends upon a dam, as in Kavar, it is the arbab who finds the materials to repair the dam in case of need, but the villagers furnish the labour. The distribution of the water is regulated by a *mîrâb* or water-captain, who is a servant of the arbab, and receives payment in grain from the villages. The arbab's bailiff is similarly paid, whose business it is to supervise the distribution of the produce.[1]

In Jawakān, however, the peasants paid only one-half of the produce as the landlord's share.[2] Fraser states that in the neighbourhood of Nayshāpūr the landlord took two-thirds of the crops and was responsible for payment to the state of all dues.[3] In Āẕarbāyjān Fraser alleges that the rights of a proprietor in the land which he owned, or in *khāliṣeh* or *vaqf* land (which he held by virtue of some grant or by lease), amounted to one-tenth of the yearly produce in the case of *daym*, i.e. unirrigated land, while in the case of irrigated land he received something extra for the water if it had been artificially procured by him.[4] Where, however, the proprietor furnished seed and cattle he received two-thirds of the produce or more and satisfied the claims of the government.[5] The landowner's share was assessed in various ways, 'by valuing, and renting out the natural water by which it is irrigated; by measurement of the surface before sowing; or by that of the crop when standing when ripe etc., etc'.[6]

Fraser also mentions that

customary law is so far from encouraging a proprietor to cultivate his own land, that he is prohibited, in some cases, from residing on the estate, and a stranger is sent as governor to collect the rents; and this has been ordained expressly to prevent him from tyrannising over his ryots, a practice too common in many forms; for if extra payments be not exacted, severe demands of service are made, and assistance in various shapes indirectly required, by those proprietors who farm their own lands.[7]

It will be useful here, perhaps, to recapitulate the broad developments which have been sketched in the preceding chapters. With the rise of Islām and the incorporation of Persia into the Islamic

[1] ii. 253–4.
[2] ibid. p. 255.
[3] Commenting that these dues were neither accurately defined nor regularly collected he states that they appeared to consist of 10 *tūmāns* per yoke of oxen, which was calculated to produce 30 *kharvār* of grain; 'this', he states, 'valued at 7–8 mauns for the real would bring the duty pretty nearly to the usual standard of one-fifth of the produce'. The peasants paid a tax on whatever stock they kept, amounting to ½ rīāl for each sheep or goat (*Journey into Khorasān*, p. 390).
[4] ibid. p. 208.
[5] ibid. p. 209.
[6] ibid. p. 208.
[7] ibid.

empire, land ownership was of two main kinds: on the one hand was private property, and on the other was land which had no private owner, the ultimate ownership of which came to be vested in the Muslim community and in the *imām* as its representative. With the division of the *dār ul-islām* into a number of semi-independent and independent kingdoms, at times at war with each other, there was inevitably a modification in the theory that all land which had no private owner was held by the *imām* for the people, and the tendency was for the rights of the *imām* in this respect to pass to the temporal ruler. Under the Seljūqs there was a reintegration of the eastern part of the Abbasid Caliphate. Ultimate ownership of such land which had no private owner came to be vested in the Seljūq people and the *sulṭān* as their representative. The *imām*, meanwhile, played an uneasy part in the background. He no longer delegated his temporal power to the *sulṭān*, but was required merely to give legal and religious sanction to the activities of the 'ruling *khān*'. The conception of 'the people' was never very strong and tended to be overshadowed by the elements of absolutism which gained ground as the traditions of the steppe weakened. The Mongol position was broadly similar, but the element of consultation was weaker and the break-up on the fall of the Mongol Īlkhān dynasty greater because of the weakening and ultimate disappearance of the caliphate. With the disintegration of the Īlkhān kingdom and its break-up into constantly warring principalities, the emphasis came to be laid on the individual ruler. Under the Ṣafavids there was to some extent a reaffirmation of the idea of 'the people', not as a conquering horde who were the owners in common of their conquests, one group of whom or one of whose number was by common consent their leader, but as a national group ruled over by the *shāh*. Ultimate ownership and all rights vested in him, not as the representative of the people, but as a divinely appointed ruler, or, according to his more extreme followers, as an emanation of the Godhead. His rule, therefore, could not be other than absolute, and submission to his government could not involve any measure of consultation with the ruled, nor did it require their freely accorded consent. Under the Qājārs the religious element was considerably weakened, but the element of absolutism remained and was untempered by any element of responsibility. This increase in the element of absolutism ran right through society and affected the general attitude to land and also the position of the peasants on the land.

In so far as the landowning classes were concerned, the feudal landed aristocracy of Sasanian Persia disappeared after the Arab conquest. The *dihqāns*, on the other hand, continued to be responsible for local administration and the collection of tribute from the protected communities, and after conversion to Islām they largely retained their lands and furnished one of the main sources of supply for recruits to the bureaucracy. Meanwhile, a new class of landed proprietor grew up, drawn originally from the Arabs who acquired large landed estates partly by grant from the *imām*, partly by conquest, and partly by purchase. To them were added in the course of time converted non-Arabs. This class differed from the feudal landed aristocracy of Sasanian times in that its members did not hold their land in return for military service, and from the *dihqāns* in that they were not primarily either the representatives of the government *vis-à-vis* the peasants or tax-collectors, though such functions were often in the course of time taken over by them. With the rise of Turkish military government a new class was interposed between the state and the landowner, and the state and the peasant, i.e. the *muqṭaʿ*, to whom was assigned first the right to collect the revenue and eventually the right to the land itself. In the settled areas the old landowner was probably largely driven out by or, in so far as he accepted government service, assimilated to the *muqṭaʿ*. In the tribal areas and the more inaccessible districts such as the Caspian provinces, local leaders probably in large measure retained both their lands and their influence. Broadly speaking, the rise of new dynasties did not materially alter the structure of landowning classes, though it altered their personnel, and, to some extent, the relative importance of the different sections of the landowning class.

Throughout the pre-Mongol period a striking feature is the recuperative power of agriculture. This can in part probably be explained by the fact that the local village communities formed relatively stable and to some extent self-governing communities, under their own *kadkhudās*, who acted as middlemen between the village communities and the government, or the *muqṭaʿ*. Although large-scale resettlement sometimes took place there was on the whole little movement from one village to another. Neighbouring villages, indeed, often spoke different dialects. When one cultivator fell out his land was in all probability taken up by his fellow villagers. The main contact with the outside world was through the tax-collector. On the other hand, it is true that the villagers were, in many cases, virtually tied to the land and subject to heavy dues of one kind and another. It is true also that we know little of their actual conditions. It would seem, however, that as long as the various classes retained some sort of independence and corporate sense, as long as all power was not concentrated in the hands of one person or group of persons and some degree of local self-government was preserved, there was a possibility of obtaining redress, or in the last resort of taking refuge with neighbouring princes or landowners, while the need to maintain economic well-being broadly speaking set a limit to the exactions of the landowners and government officials upon the peasants, though many instances of places being ruined by over-taxation can be cited. With the rise of the Mongols the restraint afforded by Islām was temporarily at least removed, nor was there any longer a limit set to taxation by considerations of economic self-interest. Local communities were further subject to a greater degree of interference by the civil and military officials than heretofore, and this involved a corresponding weakening in local self-government. Further, certain practices, which had formerly been customary only, received the sanction of law through imperial decrees. The peasant, as a result, became more effectively tied to the land than was the case before. This dependence was further increased when military service under the Qājārs became a charge on the land and not on the individual.

As long as the peasant could appeal to a court presided over by the *qāẓī* which was independent of, or at least not entirely subordinate to, the landowner, *muqṭaʿ*, or *tuyūldār*, he had some possibility of redress. This was to some extent the case under the Seljūqs. The religious institution, it is true, had been virtually incorporated into the general structure of the state, but there was still some balance between the various organs of the administration.[1] Under the Mongols land disputes in some cases were still referred to courts presided over by *qāẓīs*.[2] Under the Ṣafavids a change occurred. On the one hand, the independence of the *qāẓīs* was reduced, while, on the other, in so far as they tended to become assimilated to the landowning class, they were less likely to support the claims of the peasants against their lords. Moreover, both the *tuyūldārs* and the holders of hereditary *soyūrghāls* were in many cases given full powers to decide all cases in the area granted to them, to the exclusion of the officials of the central or provincial government (see pp. 109–12, 117). This tendency to extend the jurisdiction of the local landowner and *tuyūldār* and to concentrate all power in their hands continued in Qājār times. The result was a further weakening in the element of local self-government and an increase in the dependence of the peasant.

Meanwhile, however, other influences began to be felt. Contact with foreign countries was increasing. Military reverses, especially at the hands of Russia in the early part of the nineteenth century, had already shown that some change was needed if Persia was not to be left behind by the technical superiority of certain European

[1] E. Tyan has pointed out that in the first half of the third century A.H. (mid-ninth century A.D.) *qāẓīs* began to be appointed over the *maẓālim* courts (*Histoire de l'organisation judiciaire en pays d'Islam* (Paris, 1938–43), ii. 234). Under the Seljūqs the prestige of the *qāẓīs* was high and this practice may well have continued.

[2] See above, pp. 87–8.

countries; in the latter part of the nineteenth century the Young Turk movement and the movement for reform headed by Jamāl ud-Dīn Asadābādī (Afghānī) had a profound influence. Further, the ever-growing financial stringency was exercising the minds of both the ruling classes and the intellectuals: but whereas the former were looking for ways to provide themselves with better military forces and more money to pay for the extravagances of the royal courts, the latter resented the tendency of their rulers to attempt to solve financial difficulties by the grant of commercial concessions to foreigners, on the grounds that such grants would reduce Persia to the economic and political tutelage of foreign powers. They sought rather a larger share in the government of the country, and looked to the acquisition of the technical knowledge of western European countries to provide them with greater material ease. These various and conflicting movements and tendencies came to a head in the Constitutional Revolution of 1905–6 and resulted in the grant of the Constitution by Muẓaffar ud-Dīn Shāh in 1906. With this began a new period in the history of Persia. In so far as land tenure is concerned, the break in legal theory was perhaps greater than the change in practice and in the general attitude to land, which in some ways remained essentially medieval. Power, moreover, still largely remained in the hands of the landowners and tribal *khāns*, and it was not till the reign of Riẓā Shāh that this was materially altered.

PART II

CHAPTER VIII

THE CONSTITUTION: THE RISE OF RIẒĀ SHĀH

THE grant of the Constitution in 1906 marks a new period in the history of the relationship of the various classes owning and occupying land. The Constitution recognizes the sanctity of private property. Art. 15 of the Supplementary Fundamental laws of 7 October 1907 states that no owner can be deprived of his land except by sanction of the *sharīʿa*, and even then only after the fixing and payment of a just price. Art. 16 further states that the sequestration of the estates and property of anyone as a penal measure is forbidden except by order of law. Gradually a body of law concerning land grew up and was formulated in the relevant sections of the Civil Code.[1]

One of the first actions of the newly convened National Assembly in 1907 was to appoint a committee[2] to examine the question of financial reform, which was closely bound up with the question of land tenure and the land revenue administration. As a result of the work of this committee four main measures of reform were adopted, all of which closely affected the land and the various charges made upon it:

1. After going carefully through the revenue accounts of the various provinces, the committee greatly reduced, and in some cases abolished, the pensions and grants which were paid to a large number of individuals, and in particular to persons of rank and princes of the royal house such as Shuʿā us-Salṭaneh, Ẓill us-Sulṭān, Kāmrān Mīrzā Nā'ib us-Salṭaneh, Sālār ud-Douleh, and ʿAẓud ud-Douleh.

2. The sums which local governors levied over and above the revenue assessment for their expenses and the expenses of their staffs[3] were added to the regular assessment and provision made for the expenses of provincial administration. Thus in Kirmān the assessment had been in the neighbourhood of 44,000 *tūmāns*, but the actual sum collected reached some 170,000 *tūmāns*, and in Balūchistān, where the assessment was 18,000 *tūmāns*, the actual sum collected was about 40,000 *tūmāns*.

3. The system of *tuyūl*[4] was abolished.

[1] See Ch. IX.

[2] This was known as the *anjumani mālīyeh*.

[3] i.e. the *tafāvuti ʿamal*.

[4] See above, p. 139.

4. The conversion rates[1] were abrogated. The rates had in many cases survived from former years, and whereas the value of grain crops had increased, the landowners or, in the case of crown lands, rentees, paid according to the old rate. The abolition of this practice considerably augmented the national revenue. In the case of *khāliṣeh* land certain other issues were raised.[2]

Of these four measures, the abolition of *tuyūls* attracted perhaps the most attention. Viewed in retrospect it may well be seen to mark the close of the medieval period. In practice the immediate effect of the measure probably varied considerably according to the remoteness or otherwise of the area concerned. One writer suggests that in fact this step was detrimental to the peasants. He argues that the holders of *tuyūls* had ceased by 1325/1907–8 to draw large benefits for their *tuyūls* and did not, therefore, suffer great loss when this form of land grant was abolished. The peasants, on the other hand, he maintains, became subject to all kinds of oppression and extortion practised by government officials, there being no longer any other force to counter the influence of the latter and to restrain their actions.[3] There is no doubt some truth in this, but it is unquestionable that the advent of government officials to the more remote areas after the abolition of *tuyūls*, while not wholly beneficial, nevertheless introduced a new factor into the local situation and in some measure reduced the dependence of the peasant on the landowner or *tuyūldār*. In many areas, however, the local officials were little but nominees of the landowners and they could not hope to exercise their functions without obtaining in some measure the good will of the latter, to whom they owed in large measure their appointment; this in turn was often only to be won by granting concessions. Power thus continued to be for the most part in the hands of the large landowners and the tribal *khāns*, who were still able to devote a considerable portion of the proceeds of their estates to the maintenance of irregular troops, and when necessary to defy the government.

The law of Rabīʿ II 1325 (May–June 1907) concerning the election of provincial councils was designed to bring about a measure of administrative decentralization,[4] but was never put into effect. It was followed by the law of 4th Ẕu'l Qaʿda 1325 (December 1907) which aimed at a reorganization of the provincial administration. In art. 51 an important distinction was made

[1] *tasʿīr*; see above, p. 152.

[2] See Ch. XII.

[3] Mustoufī, ii. 354.

[4] See G. Demorgny, *Essai sur l'administration de la Perse* (Paris, 1913), pp. 114–15. The question of the election of provincial councils was raised subsequently on several occasions, but no effective steps were taken to implement the law. New proposals for the establishment of provincial councils were under discussion in 1951, only to be dropped later.

between revenue for general and for local expenses. The effect of this law, which was in some measure a continuation of Nāṣir ud-Dīn Shāh's decree of 1303/1885–6, was to lessen the powers of the provincial governors and to increase the control of the central government. In practice, however, in spite of the provisions of arts. 52–60, which concerned the financial administration of the provinces, little change was brought about. In 1911 Shuster was appointed Treasurer-General of Persia with a view to reorganizing the archaic and chaotic state of the treasury. He describes the financial administration of Āẕarbāyjān as follows:

There was, during my service in Persia, a chief tax-collector, or *pishkar*, at Tabriz, the capital of the province, and second city of importance in the Empire. The province itself is divided into a number of sub-districts, each in charge of a sub-collector, and these sub-districts are in turn divided up into smaller districts, each in charge of a tax-agent. Within the third class of districts the taxes are collected by the local town or village headmen. The chief collector at Tabriz, for example, is called upon to collect and place to the credit of the Central Government at Teheran a given sum in money and a given sum in wheat, straw, and other agricultural products each year. Beyond a very indefinite idea in the heads of some of the chief *mustawfis*, or 'Government accountants', at Teheran as to what proportion of these amounts should come from the first class of districts within the province, the Central Government knows nothing as to the sources of the revenue which it is supposed to receive. Its sole connecting link with the tax-payers of the province of Azarbayjan is through the chief collector at Tabriz. The latter official, in turn, knows how much money and produce should be furnished by each of the sub-collectors under him within the province, but he has no official knowledge of the sources from which these sub-collectors derive the taxes which they deliver to him. The chief collector has in his possession what is termed the *kitabcha* (little book) of the province, and each of the sub-collectors has the *kitabcha* of his particular district. These little books are written in a peculiar Persian style, on very small pieces of paper, unbound, and are usually carried in the pocket, or at least kept in the personal possession, of the tax-collector. They are purposely so written as to make it most difficult, if not impossible, for any ordinary Persian to understand them. There is in Persia, and has been for many generations past, a particular class of men who are known as *mustawfis*. The profession or career of *mustawfi* is, in many cases, hereditary, passing from father to son. These men understand the style in which the *kitabcha* are written, and the complicated and intricate system by which the local taxes are computed and collected. Whether one of them is a chief collector of a province or the collector of a taxation district, he considers the corresponding *kitabcha* to be his personal property, and not as belonging to the Government. He resents most bitterly any attempt on the part of any one to go into details, or to seek to find out whence the taxes are derived or what proportion of them he himself retains. . . . One of the striking defects in the Persian taxation system is that even the *kitabcha* are out of date and do not afford a just basis for the levying of the duties. Most of them were prepared over a generation ago, and since that time many villages which were prosperous and populous have become practically deserted, the people having moved to other districts. Yet the *kitabcha* are never changed, and a few hundred inhabitants remaining in some village which has before harboured a thousand or more are called upon to pay the same taxes which were assessed on the entire community when it was three or more times as large. In like manner, a village which, when the *kitabcha* were prepared many years ago, had only a few inhabitants, is still called upon to pay, so far as the Central Government is concerned, only the amount originally fixed in the *kitabcha*, although the agent who collects the taxes in the name of the Government never fails to exact from each man in the community his full quota.[1]

Anglo-Russian rivalry in Persia complicated Shuster's task, and before he was able to take any effective measures to reorganize the finances of Persia, Russian diplomatic pressure forced him to leave the country. In the years leading to the First World War, Russian pressure upon Persia became stronger. Meanwhile, internally, Persia's finances were in a state of disorder and the administration generally failing to work effectively. Finally, during the war years the authority of the central government broke down completely. Local leaders, landowners, tribal *khāns*, and others were able to assert their virtual independence and to arrogate to themselves again the privileges and immunities which the *tuyūldār* had formerly held.

The Rise of Riẓā Shāh

After the war Riẓā Khān, who later became Riẓā Shāh Pahlavī, emerged as the most powerful figure in Persian politics.[2] Between the years 1921–5 some progress was made in internal reconstruction. Inspired 'by the ideal of effective national independence as against foreign powers and effective national sovereignty at home',[3] Riẓā Khān, having first devoted his attention to the formation of an efficient national army, undertook a series of campaigns against various recalcitrant tribal leaders in order to restore the writ of the central government throughout the country. These operations

[1] W. M. Shuster, *The Strangling of Persia* (London, 1912), pp. 245–6, 248–9.

[2] Riẓā Khān led the Cossack Brigade which marched from Qazvīn to Tehrān to make the *coup d'état* of February 1921. He was then appointed Commander-in-Chief of the Persian army and Minister of War. In October 1923 he became Prime Minister and in October 1925 the National Assembly deposed the Qājār dynasty, entrusting the conduct of affairs provisionally to Riẓā Khān. On 12 December the crown was conferred by the National Assembly on Riẓā Khān and his heirs.

[3] *Survey of International Affairs*, 1925, i. 535.

included the suppression of a revolt in Khurāsān and the defeat of the Jangalīs under Kūchik Khān in the Caspian provinces in 1921, operations against the Kurds under Simko (Sīmtqū) east of Lake Urumīyeh (Riẓā'īyeh) and the Shāhsivan in the neighbourhood of Ardabīl, and the crushing of a revolt in Luristān in 1922. Further operations against the Lurs were undertaken in 1924. Shaykh Khazʿal, a semi-autonomous ruler in Khūzistān, was also removed under the centralizing policy of Riẓā Shāh.

Meanwhile Riẓā Khān had realized that military reform could not be carried out without some measure of financial and administrative reform. In the summer of 1922 a group of American financial experts under Dr Millspaugh was engaged.

Already before the arrival of Millspaugh certain steps had been taken to reform the land revenue system. A bill had been introduced into the National Assembly providing for a survey of all landed property and fixing a uniform tax on land.[1] On 20th Dalv 1300 (1922) a law for the registration of property and documents was passed. Under this law a department for registration was set up in the Ministry of Justice (see also pp. 184 ff.).

On his arrival Millspaugh found the financial administration to be in a state of disorder. Some financial legislation had been enacted by the National Assembly, but it was for the most part not enforced. The internal taxation he describes as 'a chaotic mixture of customary survivals and legislative enactment'.[2] Land tax was levied at 10 per cent on the proprietor's net share of the produce or according to the amount fixed in the tax rolls in the hands of the *mustoufīs*. These rolls were out of date. Many changes had taken place since they had been compiled. New villages had been created which paid no tax, while others which had disappeared still appeared in the tax rolls. Other villages were under-taxed or over-taxed according to their growth or decline.[3]

Land disputes, moreover, were numerous. Many *khāliṣeh* villages, especially in Māzandarān, had fallen into private hands and the ownership of other villages which had been confiscated by the government was disputed by individuals. Various committees had been formed to decide cases of disputed ownership. Such cases were at the time of the advent of Millspaugh under the jurisdiction of a tribunal of the Ministry of Finance. The Council of Ministers had also set up a committee to examine and determine the validity of the documents concerning land grants possessed by individuals. It had, moreover, laid down that any village which had been in the continuous possession of one person for thirty years or more should

[1] A. C. Millspaugh, *The American Task in Persia* (London, 1925), p. 63.
[2] ibid. p. 61.
[3] ibid. pp. 62–3.

be considered as his private property.[1] In fact, however, the Council of Ministers had subsequently given decisions concerning disputed property at variance with this, and little progress, according to Millspaugh, had been made regarding the settlement of land disputes.[2]

On his arrival in Persia Millspaugh found not only the assessment obsolete but also the land tax in arrears.

> Exemptions and reductions had been given on no equitable or sound basis, and some of the largest tax-payers had failed for years to pay their taxes and owed amounts ranging from a few thousand tomans to several hundred thousand. . . . In the actual collections there were numerous irregularities. Collectors frequently gave personal receipts to taxpayers and the revenues received went into the pocket of the collectors. Occasionally receipts were given for large amounts where no money had been collected.[3]

There was also a miscellaneous collection of irregular taxes, tolls, and exactions of various sorts. Claims against the government had accumulated, and when a Persian claimant became unduly troublesome he would be given an order on a delinquent tax-payer for the amount due to him and was expected to collect this himself. Whether he collected or not the claim and tax would be entered in the accounts as paid.[4]

Gradually some sort of order was introduced into the finances of the country and as the writ of the central government was re-established in the outlying areas, financial agencies were established in them to arrange for the collection of taxes. Thus in the winter of 1923, after the military successes of the army, financial agencies were established in certain districts of Kirmān, Fārs, and Luristān,[5] and the financial administration of the whole province of Khūzistān was taken over. A cadastral survey was begun in 1926 under the law of 20th Day 1304. The whole of the country was not covered, however.[6]

The law of 20th Day 1304 (January 1926) established a uniform land tax throughout the country based on the gross produce, which was to be ascertained by the new survey. Irrigated and unirrigated land was to pay 3 per cent on the gross produce before the division of the crop between the landlord and the peasant and the deduction of any charges on the crop.[7] Pastures and forests were to pay 10 per cent of the owner's receipts, and mills 5 per cent. On water

[1] A similar period was laid down by Malikshāh and Ghāzān in attempts to settle questions of disputed titles (see above pp. 87 and 69).

[2] *The American Task in Persia*, pp. 65–6.

[3] ibid. p. 68. [4] ibid. p. 72. [5] ibid. pp. 216–17.

[6] Partial surveys were made subsequently in 1313/1934–5 and 1329/1950.

[7] The rate was subsequently raised to 5 per cent and in July 1930 to 8 per cent (A. T. Wilson, *Persia* (London, 1932), p. 300).

used for irrigation 5 per cent of the owner's revenue (i.e. of the rent or of the produce) was to be the tax-rate. By the same law a tax was imposed on animals at the rate of 10 *qirāns* per camel over three years old, 8 *qirāns* per three-year-old mare, 6 *qirāns* per three-year-old horse or three-year-old mule, 1 *qirān* per three-year-old donkey, and $\frac{3}{4}$ *qirān* per two-year-old sheep or goat. Each family was permitted to own 1 camel, 1 ox or buffalo, 1 mare, 1 horse, 1 mule, 1 donkey, and 5 goats or sheep tax free.[1] In the later years of the reign of Riẓā Shāh a major change was made in land revenue administration by the law of 24th Āẕar 1313 (December 1934), which abolished the law of 20th Day 1304. In place of these taxes, any products of the land or animals were to pay 3 per cent in kind on entry to a town or township (*qaṣabeh*) or on export from the country. The tax was payable on each item once only (art. 2). The taxable value of the various articles was to be fixed annually (art. 3). The effect of this law in practice was to increase the burden of taxation on the peasant.[2]

From about the year 1929 onwards the tendency was for the government to play a more active role in directing the economy of the country. In February 1931 by the law of 6th Isfand 1309 foreign trade was made into a government monopoly, and various other monopolies were subsequently established under the general authority given by this law. In many cases the state transferred its rights to companies specially formed to deal in the commodities concerned. Such were the monopoly companies for trading in sugar and tea, opium, silk, cotton, wheat, dried fruit, gum tragacanth, etc.[3] Under these monopolies the government in the case of wheat, and the monopoly company in other cases, bought the products in question at a fixed price. This in some measure was beneficial to the peasants since it assured them of a market for their crops at a known price. On the other hand, it meant the multiplication of the visits of government officials to the country districts, which, in so far as the officials tended to live on the countryside, increased the burden of the peasant.

Mention has already been made of the establishment of a Department of Registration (p. 182). Further legislation was subsequently

[1] F. Mochaver, *L'Évolution des finances iraniennes* (Paris, 1938), pp. 280–1.

[2] After 1941 various bills were submitted to the National Assembly on the subject of income-tax and land tax. In the majority of cases these were not passed, but in some cases the government acted on the bill on the grounds that since certain sums by way of land tax and income-tax had been voted for in the budget laws, authority was given to them to collect such taxes. It was on this basis that in 1948 a land tax was reimposed in some areas on the basis of the survey begun in 1304/1926.

[3] The cotton monopoly and the silk monopoly have been abolished. The monopoly company formed in 1935 for dealing with wheat was subsequently merged into the Ministry of Finance and became a department of the Ministry. It was abolished in 1949.

passed on 21st Bahman 1306 (1928), and a supplementary law for the registration of property on 11th Day 1307 (1929) fixed the charges to be made for registration. On 8th Khurdād 1308 (1929) an emendation was made to the period during which objection could be lodged against the registration of property. The law of Mihr 1308 (1929), which is concerned with the establishment of registration offices, made the registration of real estate compulsory (c. 2, s. 1, art. 16) within a period of two years after an office of the Department of Registration was set up in any given area. In the event of failure to register within that period the government was empowered to register the property in the name of the holder at that time. Thus art. 19 states that the property of those who took no steps to register it would be registered by the government, the owners would have no right of protest concerning the delimitation of the property, and ownership deeds would not be issued for five years. Property the owner or owners of which were unknown was to be registered under the supervision of the *muddaʿī ul-ʿumūm* or Public Prosecutor of the district, and if its owner did not come forward within twenty years it was to be registered in the name of the state and its proceeds devoted to charitable purposes. If the owner of a property was known but missing, the property was to be placed in charge of a receiver appointed by the court (art. 20). By art. 18 a period of four months was allowed for objections to be lodged to the registration of any property in a given area.

On 26th Isfand 1310 (1932) a further law concerning the establishment of registration departments was passed. In the regulations for this law (s. 3, art. 12, v) provision is made for the registration of any proprietary rights enjoyed in the property by others (*ḥuqūqi ʿaynī*) and of easements (or praedial servitudes), i.e. of subordinate titles. These are all to be mentioned in title-deeds (s. 4, art. 30, iv and s. 6, art. 51). Similarly, creation of any new proprietary rights is to be registered (s. 6, art. 52). Special provisions are made for the registration of *ouqāf* (s. 3, arts. 14–18), the responsibility for this resting with the *mutavalli*. Should he fail to apply for the registration of *vaqf* properties within the period stipulated by the law, the head of the local Department of Ouqāf is to apply for registration (and the *ouqāf* in question are presumably taken over by the Department of Ouqāf). In the case of private *ouqāf*, the responsibility for registration rests with the overseer (*mutaṣaddī*). S. 3, art. 20 states that 'applications by private persons for the registration of properties which have no private owner, such as roads, highways, dead lands and mountains, and common property will not be entertained'. A note to art. 20 states, 'applications by individuals for the registration of forests which are common property will not be entertained'. S. 7, art. 77 provides for the consultation of local experts where necessary.

In certain cases, notably in Fārs, there appears to have been some difficulty in deciding ownership owing to the fact that several people exercised rights over a property concurrently. It seems that in Fārs and various other regions there were estates in which the holders reaped the crops[1] and exercised certain rights of ownership, disposing of the property in various ways[2] while at the same time paying a fixed sum according to agreement or local custom to the real owners, who, while confirming the above-mentioned powers on the occupants, received their ownership dues. In an attempt to clear up this ambiguity a letter of 5th Day 1313 (1934), signed by the Director-General of the Department of Registration, was issued stating that occupancy of property (by virtue of subordinate title), though recognized by the owner, did not give legal title. In this letter it was further laid down that one property could not have two kinds of owners and that the occupants, therefore, in spite of the rights which were accorded to them, could not be recognized as owners. The true owners were those who received ownership dues from the holders according to arrangements agreed upon between them. The holders enjoyed only such rights as the owners allowed them. Accordingly, application for registration was to be accepted only from the true owners, but provisions were made for the confirmation of subordinate titles held by others.

In practice the registration of land, in the absence of an accurate and complete cadastral survey, is a matter of some difficulty. The usual practice is to register land with a statement of its limits rather than of its actual area. The attestation of the owners of the neighbouring land is accepted as proof of ownership. The preliminary step to registration is known as *plākkūbī*, i.e. the owner files in the local department of registration a claim to a certain piece of land. Subsequently the department examines this claim together with the relevant documents and witnesses, and any objections are heard.

Where a village is jointly owned, it can be registered as a joint holding known as *mushāʿ*, or the individual holdings may be defined, in which case it is known as *mafrūz*. Where a village is *mushāʿ* any agreement concerning the exploitation of the land or water has to be concluded with all the owners. For example, suppose an irrigation company wants to sink a well in the uncultivated land of a village jointly owned by several persons, the company has to conclude agreements with all the joint owners, each of whom holds a share in that land proportionate to their share in the

[1] *bahreh bardārī namūdeh.*
[2] *naql va intiqāl va ṣulḥ va hibeh va ijāreh va ghayreh dar ānhā mīnamāyand.*

cultivated land of the village. Clearly the completion of agreements in such a case is likely to be a lengthy business.

The 'borders' or *ḥarīm*[1] of a *khurdeh mālik* village, i.e. a village owned by several persons or a peasant-proprietor village, are normally registered jointly in the name of the owners of the village concerned (but these are not mentioned individually). The 'borders' can be registered on the production of a written statement (*istishhād nāmeh*) from the neighbouring village or villages that such and such a piece of land belongs to the claimant or claimants. If the *ḥarīm* is not registered, anyone who sinks a well in it and cultivates the land becomes the owner of that land and can register it in his own name.

Water rights can also be registered under the law of Mihr 1308 (1929). A circular (No. 143) issued on 10th Farvardīn 1309 (1930) by the Director-General of the Department of the Registration of Estates and Documents states that demands for the registration of water came under four heads: *qanāts* (underground irrigation channels),[2] springs, irrigation channels, and rivers. Where a *qanāt* was owned by more than one owner the precise shares of the individual owners in time and the period of rotation were to be stated. The registration of *qanāts* was to be separate from that of estates. Springs were to be registered in the same way. If the share of the various owners of the water of a spring was not known precisely it could only be registered as part of a property by way of *ḥaqq ābeh* (i.e. a right to a share of the water). Irrigation channels leading off from springs were subject to the same rules as springs; where they led off from rivers they were dealt with when the property on which they were was registered, the owner being required to declare how much water (measured in time) he had from the channel according to local custom under a formula such as 'one day and night's [water] of such and such an irrigation channel in accordance with local custom', or, if the division was not by time, that he had a *ḥaqq ābeh* in such and such a channel in accordance with local custom. Demands for the registration of the water of rivers were only to be accepted in the form of a right of irrigation (*ḥaqq ush-shurb*) belonging to a given property in the course of the registration of that property, because the method and manner of the distribution of water of the great rivers had not yet been regulated. An exception was made in the case of a river which had been divided among a specified number of owners; these could register the extent of their respective shares.

It is a striking fact that since the Middle Ages Persia has been backward in the matter of land registration. Various attempts in the past were made; all proved abortive. At the present day, also,

[1] See pp. 199–200. [2] See Ch. X.

although it is over twenty-five years since the law of registration was passed, considerable areas of the country have not been registered. Disputed ownership of land is of relatively common occurrence. In Āẕarbāyjān, with the exception of the Riẓā'īyeh area, the extent of village lands is not known with any accuracy. They are in most districts registered only with the limits (*ḥudūd*) defined, the actual area not being stated. The province of Balūchistān[1] is for the most part not yet registered. In Qā'ināt registration has only been carried out near the towns and in the case of the property of certain large landowners. In some districts the preparatory steps to registration (*plākkūbī*) have been taken. The major part of Fārs, on the other hand, has been registered. Certain areas in the mountains in the neighbourhood of Iṣṭahbānāt are an exception to this, and in various tribal districts a number of titles are still in dispute. In Khūzistān in the Khurramshahr-Shādagān area the land, which is mainly *khāliṣeh*, is largely unregistered. In other areas where the *khāliṣeh* land has been distributed, ownership documents are for the most part not in the possession of the occupiers.[2] In central Persia, in the Kāshān–Qumm–Iṣfahān–Yazd area, some areas still remain to be registered. In Sāveh approximately one-third of the land has been registered.

Rights of ownership have been further reinforced by legislation concerning dispossession and recovery. The law of Urdī Bihisht 1309 (1930) concerning the method of preventing dispossession permits the security officials, i.e. the police, or, failing them, the governors and district officers, or, failing them, the gendarmerie, to prevent dispossession of property. It is clear, however, that this law is intended to refer to actual and not to past acts of dispossession, i.e. cases which are observed by the security officials themselves, or where a complaint is preferred immediately after the occurrence of dispossession. In such circumstances it is incumbent upon the security officials, after the recovery of the land, to refer the plaintiff, if he wishes to assert a title to the property, to the relevant court. In the event of more than one month elapsing after dispossession has taken place the security forces have no right to interfere. Dispossession is divided into three categories: dispossession, prevention of right, and encroachment. Art. 749 of the *Ā'īni Dādrasīyi Madanī* (Regulations for Procedure in Civil Cases) states that possession acquired by force cannot become converted into an absolute title by virtue of 'lapse of time'. At the same time, however, there would appear to be a certain concession to the principle of force, because the article goes on to state that once force has ceased to be exerted 'lapse of time' begins from that

[1] Here and in the following pages the term Balūchistān refers to the Persian province of that name.
[2] See Ch. XII.

moment. In certain cases complaints of dispossession are rejected out of hand: thus if the allegations made conflict with the records of the property registers of the Department of Registration they are ruled out according to art. 331 of the Regulations for Procedure in Civil Cases. Art. 22 of the Law of Registration of Estates and Documents of 1310 (1932) states that the government recognizes as owner only that person in whose name the property is registered, or the person to whom the property has been transferred, the transfer having been registered in the property register, or the person to whom the property has been transmitted by inheritance from the official owner. There is, however, some safeguard in the penal law against dispossession, since it provides for the punishment of acts of dispossession. In spite of this, in the early days of registration these various regulations, designed no doubt with a view to the preservation of public order, probably led in some cases to the conversion of possession acquired by force into an absolute title. These laws concerning dispossession and recovery do not derive from Islamic law. It is probable that a French influence is to be found here.[1]

It is also alleged that influential persons in some cases have registered land in their own names in spite of the fact that the peasants claim to have had old titles to the land in question. While it is difficult to substantiate such cases without access to the relevant evidence, it is clear that the peasant has in practice less easy access to the courts and less ability to put his case than have the more influential classes, and it seems not unlikely that cases of this kind should have occurred.

Where cases of dispossession concern agricultural land the interests of a third party, namely, the crop-sharing peasant, are often also involved. Certain conditions are laid down to provide for such contingencies. If the harvest has ripened, the person in possession must reap this immediately, with the payment of a fair wage to the peasant. If the crop has not ripened, whether the seed has set or not, the successful party to the suit can choose between recovering possession of his property, paying the cost of cultivation in proportion to the provision of the seed and labour, or leaving the property in the hands of the person in possession until the harvest is reaped, taking from him a fair rent (art. 334).[2]

Gradually, under Riẓā Shāh, changes were brought about in local administration; in some cases the nature of this change was merely to give the force of law to what had been merely *ʿurf* or

[1] For a discussion of the various aspects of dispossession see Matīn Daftarī, *Āʾīni Dādrasīyi Madanī* (Tehrān, 1324), pp. 290 ff.

[2] This appears to bear the imprint of Islamic law. Ṭūsī deals with the question under the section on *muzāraʿeh* in his *Kitāb al-Mabsūṭ*. See below, Ch. IX, for *muzāraʿeh* contracts. See also Matīn Daftarī, pp. 317–18.

customary law before. On 20th Āẕar 1314 (December 1935) the law concerning *kadkhudās* (village headmen) was passed. According to this law, the *kadkhudā* was the representative of the landowner and was responsible for the execution of laws and regulations referred to him by the government (art. 1). In each village or group of villages a *kadkhudā* was to be appointed (art. 2). In *khāliṣeh* land he was to be recommended by the local Finance Office, in *vaqf* land by the *mutavallī* or his representative, in large landed properties by the landowner, and in villages owned by several persons by those who owned the greater part of the property, to the governor or deputy-governor of the district, who would issue his order of appointment (art. 3). The qualifications for a *kadkhudā* were Persian nationality, a clean record, a reputation for honest dealing, trustworthiness and capability, residence in one of the villages in the area over which he was to be appointed, and that he should carry out some cultivation in the area (art. 4). The *kadkhudā* was to oversee agricultural affairs in accordance with the orders of the landowner. He could decide minor cases in the villages up to 50 rs. (approx. 5*s.* 10*d.*). He was to prevent disputes breaking out among the people; if and when they broke out he was to settle them, as far as possible by conciliation (art. 7). He was, in accordance with art. 23 of the Law for Criminal Trials, to prevent the flight of accused persons and the destruction of evidence, and was to report his actions as quickly as possible to the nearest gendarmerie post or deputy-governor (art. 8). If there was a delay of over fifteen days on the part of the landowner or landowners in recommending a person to be *kadkhudā*, the governor would appoint someone (art. 10). If the *kadkhudā* showed negligence in agricultural affairs he could be dismissed on the demand of the landowner or landowners (art. 11).

The *kadkhudā* was thus looked upon as the servant of the landowner and the guardian of his interests. He was in no sense, therefore, the representative of the people, and there is no provision in the law, in the case of a landlord village, for consultation of the wishes of the local inhabitants other than the landowner or landowners in the matter of his appointment.

Further legislation concerning local administration was passed, notably the law of 16th Ābān 1316 (1937) affecting the division of the country and the duties of the governors (*farmāndārs*) and district officers (*bakhshdārs*). Art. 8 of this law states that a *dihdār* would be appointed by order of the governor (*farmāndār*) from among the inhabitants of the district (*bakhsh*) on the recommendation of the district officer (*bakhshdār*). According to a note, the Ministry of the Interior could choose the *dihdār* from among government officials on the recommendation of the *farmāndār*.

Art. 9 states that the *kadkhudā* would be appointed by order of the governor from among the permanent inhabitants of the village or villages on the recommendation of the owner and the proposal of the district officer. According to a note, if the *kadkhudā* showed negligence in agricultural affairs he could be dismissed on the demand of the owner or owners. Art. 21 lays down that in every district (*bakhsh*) a District Council was to be formed, consisting of the district officer and heads of government departments in the district. In addition, members from among the owners and cultivators would be chosen as necessity arose. Their representation was not to be less than three persons. The duties of the District Council were as follows: (*a*) to investigate the condition of each township and any causes for its decay, and to recommend the necessary means for better exploitation; (*b*) to supervise the provision of what was necessary for public health and other public needs of the townships in the district; (*c*) to endeavour to form agricultural companies; and (*d*) to give guidance in agricultural training to owners and peasants. A note to art. 22 states that the *dihdār* was the representative of the government and the *kadkhudā* the representative of the government and the owners. This law, therefore, also weights the scales against the peasant in favour of the owner; the local representation on the District Council would appear to be inadequate also. In fact the law has never been put into operation *in toto* throughout the country. District Councils are for the most part not in effective operation and the *dihdār* has never been appointed. Since, moreover, the *kadkhudā* was to be the representative of the government and the landowners, there would appear to be very little reason for the appointment of an extra official to represent government interests.[1]

[1] In Isfand 1323 (February 1945) a further bill concerning the formation of Agricultural Councils was tabled by the Prime Minister. It has yet to be put into effect. Art. 1 lays down that Agricultural Councils shall be formed in every sub-area (*shahristān*) and if necessary in every district (*bakhsh*) with a view to the promotion of agriculture. Art. 2 states that District Councils were to be composed of five to nine members, one of whom should be a representative of the Ministry of Agriculture and the other a representative of the Agricultural Bank (where a branch of this existed). The remainder were to be elected by those engaged in agriculture locally (arts. 3–5). The term of office was to be four years (art. 6). The Sub-area Agricultural Council was to be composed of two representatives from each district, as decided by the representatives of the Ministry of Agriculture and Agricultural Bank, and one to three agricultural experts appointed by the Ministry of Agriculture (art. 7). The period of office was to be four years (art. 9). Once a year a General Agricultural Council, composed of representatives of the Sub-area Councils, was to be convened in Tehrān (art. 10), to be presided over by the Minister of Agriculture or the Under-Secretary of State for Agriculture (art. 10). The Sub-area and District Councils were charged with the following duties: (*a*) to make recommendations regarding improvements to be effected for the promotion of agriculture and the study of methods to be employed for the accomplishment of these improvements; (*b*) to consider agricultural problems and bills connected with agriculture referred to

The increase of production and productivity has always been a matter which has interested the government of Persia, even if effective steps have seldom been taken to secure it. Increased production meant increased revenue. The reign of Riẓā Shāh was no exception to the general rule. On 25th Ābān 1316 (November 1937) the law for agricultural development (*qānūni ʿumrān*) was passed. This law contains certain far-reaching provisions. Art. 1 states that the owners of lands (*arāẓī*) were bound to bring them into cultivation. This duty in respect of *vaqf* property devolved on the *mutavallī* or his deputy. The meaning of the term *ʿumrān* is defined as the greatest possible agricultural development by means of the creation and repairing of *qanāts*, the reclaiming of waste-lands, the maintenance of irrigation channels, the improvement of housing with due regard to hygiene, the making of roads between villages, the establishment of public health posts, and the draining of marshes. A note to this article states that the improvement of the houses of the peasants is the responsibility of the owner of the *aʿyān*. Art. 2 states that the District Council would draw up a programme for agricultural development and stipulate the share of each landowner in it. It would be put into operation after the approval of the governor of the sub-area had been gained. Accord-

them by the Ministry of Agriculture; (*c*) to supply the necessary information to the Ministry of Agriculture concerning relevant affairs; (*d*) to consider suggestions made to the Agricultural Council by country people coming under this law; (*e*) to co-operate with the Ministry of Agriculture in the enforcement of all agricultural programmes and all measures to be taken for the promotion of agriculture, irrigation, war on plant and livestock diseases, medical facilities, and other measures to improve the lot of the country people; (*f*) to hold agricultural competitions and to encourage the giving of prizes; (*g*) to aid the Ministry of Agriculture with the preparation of statistics; (*h*) to make recommendations as to the prices to be set for agricultural products and to submit such proposals to the Ministry of Agriculture; (*i*) to draft an annual report on the activities of the Council and to submit such reports to the Ministry of Agriculture; (*j*) to prepare regular reports showing the agricultural situation in the Sub-area and to submit such reports to the Ministry of Agriculture; (*k*) to establish co-operative societies for the encouragement of the production of crops and of their disposal, such as societies for procuring agricultural and ploughing machinery, dairy-farming, dried-fruit processing, irrigation and the maintenance of *qanāts* and water channels, cattle breeding, insurance against the loss of livestock, wool, and hide, loan of capital to the country people and the provision of the necessary funds, artificial fertilizers, and transport; and (*l*) to fulfil the duties entrusted to the Council for the protection of country people as provided for in this law and the regulations concerned. Provisions were also made for the establishment of an organization for providing family bonuses and aid in the case of disability (arts. 12, 13), and for the building of primary schools (art. 14) and the setting up of clinics (art. 15). Funds to meet the expenses of the Agricultural Councils and the Organization for the Protection of Country People were to be provided by a levy of 3 per cent on all crops before division (i.e. to be levied on the total harvest), interest on capital in hand, donations from landowners and others, assistance afforded by the revenues of the General Irrigation Department, and various other sources (art. 19). The Ministry of Agriculture was to have the right to inspect and exercise permanent control over all affairs connected with the Organization or with Agricultural Councils (art. 21, note).

ing to art. 3, if the reason for the decay of any given property was lack of funds a loan could be granted. Art. 4 provides for the taking over of estates which were not properly managed through the failure of the owner to provide the necessary means of development even if he possessed the financial means to do so, or through negligence; and for the administration of the estate under lease by one of the agricultural companies (which were to be set up under the law of 20th Ābān 1316).

Although this law is on the statute book it has in fact never been put into operation. The regulations for it have never been drawn up. The reason for this is perhaps not far to seek. Art. 4 is clearly of a nature likely to arouse opposition among the landowning class. Further, in present circumstances the government is hardly in a position to implement the provisions of such a law.

The neglect into which this law, together with some of the other measures mentioned above, has fallen is typical of much of the modern law-making of Persia. The jurists of the early centuries of Islām, in their zeal to preserve what they conceived to have been the practice of the early Islamic community, became as time went on more and more divorced from reality. The legislative power of the present day is perhaps little less divorced from reality in that it tends to consider the putting on paper of a form of words to be an end in itself, while utterly disregarding the instruments by which the law is to be put into practice and the conditions under which it is to be implemented.

It would, however, be misleading to end this chapter on an entirely negative note. The period from 1906 onwards sees marked changes both in the structure of Persian administration and in Persian society. The effect of this on the question of land ownership will be discussed in Chapter XIII.

CHAPTER IX

THE CIVIL CODE

In addition to the various measures outlined in the last chapter a body of law concerning land was also promulgated in the Civil Code. This is largely a restatement of Islamic theory. In the following pages a comparison between various sections of the Civil Code and earlier Muslim practice will be made; in this way some of the apparent peculiarities of the Civil Code will be better understood. Certain features of Muslim law are naturally ignored by the Civil Code; the early Muslim jurists were concerned in part with the regularization of the situation which had arisen as a result of the Muslim conquest of the lands formerly belonging to the Byzantine and Persian empires, and certain points such as the distribution of the conquered lands,[1] which were of vital moment in the early period, have ceased to have any importance. Similarly, late Abbasid and post-Abbasid developments concerning the *iqṭāʿ* system and the later *tuyūl*,[2] since the practice of granting *tuyūls* was abolished after the grant of the Constitution,[3] are ignored. It is nevertheless indisputable that Muslim law is the largest single influence in the Civil Code. The Code largely consists of the broad general principles upon which the consensus of opinion among Shīʿī jurists of the Ithna ʿAsharī or Jaʿfarī rite agrees, which principles the compilers of the Civil Code have attempted to put in modern dress.[4]

The Shīʿī school of law, that from which the modern Civil Code draws its main inspiration, differs from the Sunnī in certain respects. The bases of Shīʿī law are the Qur'ān, 'the Traditions', *ʿaql* or Reason, and *ijmāʿ*, the Consensus of Opinion. The Sunnīs accept the first two, though the body of traditions accepted by them differs somewhat from those accepted by the Shīʿah. Neither the Qur'ān nor the Traditions contain a systematized body of law. Many questions arose which were not covered by clear and unambiguous commands, statements, and prohibitions in the Qur'ān and the Traditions. To overcome this difficulty the use of *qīās*, or analogy, was permitted by the Sunnīs, and became the third base of the law. The Shīʿah reject this and substitute for it the use of reason, or *ʿaql*, and confine its use to the outstanding men of the age, the *mujtahids*. Both schools accept *ijmāʿ*, which is in actual practice the foundation of the legal system, since it is *ijmāʿ*

[1] See above, pp. 18 ff. [2] See Chs. III–VII. [3] See above, p. 178.

[4] In the following pages, unless stated to the contrary, the term Shīʿī is to be taken as referring to the Ithna ʿAsharī or Jaʿfarī rite.

which guarantees the authenticity of the Qur'ān and of the Traditions. For the Sunnīs *ijmā'* in its original meaning meant the consensus of opinion of the companions of the Prophet and their immediate successors; later it came to mean the consensus of the orthodox *'ulamā*. The Shī'ah, on the other hand, take *ijmā'* to be the consensus of opinion of the *imāms*. As long as the *imāms* were in the community the position was clear. After the disappearance of the twelfth *imām* in 260/873–4 difficulties arose. Strictly speaking *ijmā'* ceased, but in practice a consensus of opinion grew up based upon the Qur'ān, the Traditions, the exercise of reason (*'aql*), and the *fatvās*, or decisions given throughout the ages by the *'ulamā*. This is embodied in a vast literature which includes the writings of the *'ulamā* of each age.[1]

Two points are for our purpose of special interest. First the Civil Code, like earlier Muslim law, is not concerned primarily with the abstract theory of ownership but rather with the practical consequences of ownership. Various distinctions between different kinds of property are made, but, for the most part, only in a secondary way; similarly, special types of land such as *vaqf* land and *khāliṣeh* are mentioned.[2] Secondly, the relations between landlord and tenant, which are the subject of detailed regulation in English law, receive but little attention in the Civil Code; nor has the Civil Code been supplemented in this respect by any considerable corpus of legislation in recent years. The section of the Civil Code on agricultural and harvesting contracts to some extent regulates the relation of the crop-sharing peasant and the landlord (see below), but for the most part custom plays a more important part than the written law in deciding what this relationship shall be.

The Civil Code is somewhat more precise in its division of property into two kinds, movable and immovable (art. 11) than is the exposition of the Shī'ī jurists. Under immovable property are included certain articles which are not properly speaking immovable property. Thus, as in Roman (and English) law, fruit and crops are deemed immovable provided that they have not been picked or reaped (art. 15). Similarly, trees and their branches,

[1] Muḥammad b. al-Ḥasan b. 'Alī Abū Ja'far at-Ṭūsī, who lived in the first half of the fifth/eleventh century, holds a central position in the development of Shī'ī law. In his numerous works, including the *Mabsūṭ*, the *Khilāf*, the *Nihāya*, the *Muḥīṭ*, and the *Risālayi Ja'farīya*, he sums up the previous law and becomes a leading authority. The *Sharāyi' al-Islām fī Masā'il al-Ḥalāl va'l Ḥarām* of the famous jurist Najm ud-Dīn Abu'l Qāsim Ja'far b. al-Ḥusayn b. Yaḥyā al-Muḥaqqiq al-Avval, who died in 676/1277, is largely a restatement of Ṭūsī. One of the best known commentaries on the *Sharāyi'* is the *Javāhir al-Kalām* of Shaykh Muḥammad Ḥasan an-Najafī. The expositions of these and other early jurists were reworked by their successors. European scholars, notably Baillie and Querry, have mainly based their work on the *Sharāyi'* of al-Muḥaqqiq.

[2] See Chs. XI and XII.

young plants, and cuttings, as long as they have not been cut down or dug up, are considered immovable (art. 16). Certain exceptions are also made with a view to safeguarding the position of the peasant. Thus,

> Animals and equipment which the owner thereof shall have provided specifically for cultivation, such as oxen, buffaloes, machines, implements and appurtenances of husbandry, seed, etc., and in general all movable goods which are necessary for the prosecution of farming operations, and have been devoted by the owner exclusively to this purpose shall, for purposes of the competence of courts and of attachment of property, be considered as forming part of the landed property and shall be treated as immovable property, as also shall pumps, oxen and other animals, appropriated for the irrigation of fields, houses and gardens (art. 17).

This corresponds to the *fundus constructus* in Roman law and also to certain provisions in the Turkish Mejelle concerning the *çiftlik*. Similarly

> The usufruct (*ḥaqqi intifā'*) of immovable objects such as a life interest (*ḥaqqi 'umrā*), the right of residence (*ḥaqqi suknā*), and similarly easements (*ḥaqqi irtifāq*) over the land of another, such as the rights of passage and of transit of water, and rights derived from immovable property such as demands for eviction and similar applications, shall follow the rules concerning immovable property (art. 18).

The transfer of the substance of the property by the owner to another party does not nullify the right of usufruct, but if the person to whom the property is transferred does not know that the right of usufruct has been granted to another party he has the option of dissolving the contract (art. 53).

Chapter 2 of the Civil Code describes the various rights which may be exercised over property or may accrue to persons from its possession. These are three—the right of ownership (whether of the substance of the thing or its benefit), the right of usufruct, and rights of easement in the property of another (art. 29). Concerning ownership (c. 2, s. 1) it is stated that every owner has unlimited rights of occupation and enjoyment of his property except in matters in which the law has made an exception (art. 30). No property can be capriciously expropriated (art. 31). This is merely a restatement of the Islamic principle that 'the people enjoy full power over their possessions' and recognizes wider powers of ownership than the practice of the post-Abbasid period. Art. 33 is also in accordance with the Islamic principle 'what is cultivated belongs to the cultivator'. It states that

> products and crops which have come out of the land are the property of the owner of the land, whether their growth is natural or the result of

the owner's operations, unless the product or crop has sprung from the roots or seeds of another party. If this is the case the trees or crops shall be the property of the owner of the roots or seed, even if they have been sown without the approval of the owner of the land.

Possession by way of ownership is taken as proof of ownership unless the contrary be proved (art. 35). In the case of waste-land, however, the fulfilment of certain other conditions is necessary in order to acquire ownership (see below). The object of art. 35 is probably mainly to prevent disorders likely to arise should the original owner of a property which has been usurped attempt subsequently to get it back. In keeping with this the courts which investigate cases of alleged dispossession are not competent to investigate at the same time the question of ownership.[1] The law, therefore, although intended primarily to protect private ownership, may in fact involve also the confirmation of an act of usurpation. That it should be so is in keeping with the tendency which began in early medieval times and has continued in political thought in Persia ever since, namely that the interests of law and order demand submission even to an illegal ruler.[2] A somewhat similar history concerning the confirmation of acts of usurpation will be known to students of the Roman Interdicts and of the English Possessory Assizes.

Concerning rights of usufruct the Civil Code is largely a restatement of the theory of al-Muḥaqqiq. Life rights, rights for a prescribed period, and rights of occupation, are recognized.[3] The right of usufruct can only be granted to or for the benefit of a person or persons alive at the time of the creation of the right, but it is possible for it to pass by inheritance to persons who were not alive at the time of the conclusion of the contract (art. 45). It is only possible for a right of usufruct to be granted if the property is such that it can be used without affecting its own existence (*res quae usu non consumata*, art. 46). The user must not misuse the property to which the right of usufruct applies and, being in custody of it, must not allow encroachment or waste (art. 48). The expenses necessary for the upkeep of the property which is subject to the right of usufruct is not an obligation on the user, unless a provision to the contrary has been agreed upon (art. 49). If the property which is subject to the right of usufruct becomes dissipated for any

[1] See also pp. 188–9.

[2] cf. G. E. von Grunebaum, *Medieval Islam* (Chicago, 1946), p. 168. See also, Ghazālī, *Kīmiā as-Sa'ādat*, p. 156 and *Iḥyā 'Ulūm ad-Dīn* (1346), ii. 125. It will be noticed that reference in the following pages is frequently made to Sunnī as well as Shī'ī authorities. Except where Shī'ī political doctrines are concerned there is often little difference in their theory, while some authorities, such as Ghazālī, who was a Sunnī but also a Persian, enjoy a wide reputation.

[3] See i. 593 (tr. Querry).

reason other than encroachment or waste by the user, the latter shall not be held responsible (art. 50). The right of usufruct lapses in the event of the time-limit expiring or the property which is the object of the right of usufruct being destroyed (art. 51). Art. 54, which states 'the rest of the circumstances concerning the right of usufruct in the property of another shall be as laid down by the owner or demanded by custom and usage', would appear to be a concession to customary law, and a tacit recognition that alongside the Civil Code customary law is still in force in many parts of the country. It is, moreover, reminiscent of the provision often contained in Ṣafavid and other documents concerning the observance of local custom in the regulation of relations between landlord and peasant.

Praedial and personal servitudes may be created by contract (art. 94). Wherever someone's channel for running water or rain-water passes through the land or house of another person, the owner of that house or land cannot prevent access unless he can prove it is not being used as a right (art. 95). If the owner of property has given permission to pass through it to someone who cannot do so by right, he may rescind his permission whenever he wishes; similarly with other rights of easement (arts. 98, 108). Whenever someone derives profit, such as the working of a mill or something similar, from water which is the property of someone else, in accordance with some right, the owner of the water cannot change the course of the channel in such a way as to prevent this right from being profitably exercised (art. 101), nor can the owner of a property on which another person has a right of easement use his property in such a way as to result in damage to, or suspension of, this right, except with permission of the owner of the right (art. 106). Similarly, a right of easement necessarily implies the means of exercising that right; thus, if a person has the right of taking water from the springs, tanks, or reservoirs of others, he has the right of passage to such springs, tanks, or reservoirs for drawing water (art. 104). Whenever an estate is transferred either in its entirety or in part to someone else, rights of easement over another estate or portion of it being included therein, such rights remain unchanged, unless there be a stipulation to the contrary (art. 102). Any expenses which may be necessary for the enjoyment of a right of easement are a charge upon the owner of that right, unless an agreement to the contrary has been arrived at between him and the owner of the property (art. 105). As in the case of the right of usufruct, reference is made to custom: thus art. 107 reads, 'the benefits attaching to a right of easement are varied to the extent agreed upon, or to the extent recognized by common usage, and demanded by what is essential to its enjoyment'. Certain rights and privileges also appertain to a property in relation to an adjacent property. Thus a wall situated between two properties is considered as common property of the owners of the two properties unless there is a supposition to the contrary (art. 109). A tree, a ditch, or anything similar between two properties is treated in the same way as a wall (art. 135). None of the partners in a ferry or watercourse can prevent the other partners from crossing it or taking water away (art. 134).

Ḥarīm (*'Borders'*)

According to Islamic law the ownership of a property also involves a right over its borders (*ḥarīm*) where necessary for its full enjoyment. There was a difference of opinion among the early Islamic jurists as to the extent of the 'border' of the various forms of property.[1] Subsection 3 of Section 3 of Chapter 2 of the Civil Code concerning the 'borders' (*ḥarīm*) of properties defines and delimits these as follows:

Art. 136. The 'borders' (*ḥarīm*) of a quantity of land are the boundaries of the property, the water channels, the streams and the like, which are necessary for the full enjoyment of the land.

Art. 137. The 'borders' of a well are 20 *gaz* [approx. 21 yds., 2 ft., 5 in.] for drinking water and 30 *gaz* [approx. 32 yds., 2 ft., 5 in.] for cultivation.

Art. 138. The 'borders' of a spring or a *qanāt* are 500 *gaz* [approx. 546 yds.] on all sides in soft soil and 250 *gaz* [approx. 273 yds.] in hard soil, but if the distances mentioned in this and the preceding article are not enough to avoid loss, distances to the extent required to prevent loss shall be added to them.

Art. 139. 'Borders' are governed by the provision applicable to the property of the owner of the 'borders', and any occupation of them or use of them which is contrary to the purpose of the 'borders' is invalid without the permission of the owner, and therefore nobody can dig a well or a *qanāt* within the 'borders' of another spring or channel. But activities which do not cause loss are permissible.

The Civil Code does not explicitly limit the right of *ḥarīm*, whereas among some of the Islamic jurists it is made subject to the qualification that it can only exist in land to which no one has any right, i.e. it cannot be exercised where it would interfere with the right of another person. Implicitly this follows, however, from other provisions of the Civil Code.

Ownership can be acquired in a variety of ways: by the cultivation of dead land and the annexation of unclaimed objects (see

[1] See Māwardī, pp. 313, 318–19, 321; al-Muḥaqqiq, ii. 297; Abū Yūsuf, tr. Fagnan, pp. 152–3.

below), by means of contracts and agreements, by acquisition in virtue of a right of pre-emption, by bequest, inheritance, or gift.

Gifts

The question of gifts is dealt with briefly in the Civil Code, in Book II, Part 2, s. 19.[1] Delivery of possession to the recipient or his representative is essential for the completion of a gift (art. 798). It is revocable even after delivery unless (*a*) the donor is the parent or child of the recipient; (*b*) some exchange was given for the gift; (*c*) the gift is no longer in the possession of the recipient, or a third person has acquired a right in it, either by inhibition, as in the case of the recipient having become bankrupt, or by mortgage; or (*d*) some change has occurred in the substance of the gift (art. 803).

One of the ways by which the excessive subdivision of estates consequent upon the laws of inheritance is to some extent limited is by the owner making gifts of his estates during his lifetime to one or more of his heirs. The form which this transaction takes, however, is not usually that of a gift, but rather of 'conciliation' or *ṣulḥ*. The Civil Code defines this transaction as follows: 'Conciliation is possible either in order to settle an existing dispute or to prevent a potential dispute concerning some transaction or other or which might arise over something else' (art. 752). For the 'conciliation' to be valid both parties must be competent to undertake the transaction and to take possession of the subject of the 'conciliation' (art. 753). A 'conciliation' without recompense is valid (art. 757). The right of pre-emption is not established in the case of 'conciliation' (art. 759). It is a binding agreement (art. 760), but 'conciliation' transacted under duress is not valid (art. 763). It is possible in a 'conciliation' agreement for one of the parties, in return for the subject of the 'conciliation', to undertake to pay as a pension an annual or monthly sum for a definite period to the other party or to a third person or persons (art. 768). Similarly, it is permissible to stipulate that such a pension shall be transmitted by inheritance to the heirs of the original beneficiary (art. 769). Such a pension, moreover, is not abrogated should the party who undertook to pay it become bankrupt or insolvent (art. 770). 'Conciliation' in the Civil Code is extended to cover a rather wider field than in the exposition of al-Muḥaqqiq who appears to regard it solely as means to terminate a dispute.[2] That this should be the case is indicative of the measure of importance which the practice of 'conciliation' has acquired in modern times as a means of preventing the subdivision of estates.

[1] al-Muḥaqqiq states that a father may favour one or more of his children by gift, but that it is better to abstain from such an action (i. 598).

[2] i. 487 ff.

Pre-emption

The right of pre-emption (*shufʿeh*) is discussed in Book II, Part 3 of the Civil Code. It is a question of some importance in view of the relatively common occurrence of jointly held property. The right of a co-proprietor of an undivided share in a property to recover from an outside purchaser the undivided share sold to him by another co-proprietor would appear to be of considerable antiquity. It is found in the various schools of Islamic law, and was, in all probability, taken over from pre-Islamic practice.[1]

The Civil Code limits the right of pre-emption to immovable property owned by two co-sharers, and makes no distinction between Muslims and non-Muslims. Art. 808 states that where immovable property capable of division is owned by two persons jointly, if one partner wishes to transfer his share by sale to a third person, the other partner has the right of pre-emption, and, by paying to the purchaser the price which he has paid to the original owner, can take possession of the share which has been sold. The right of pre-emption is capable of transmission by inheritance (art. 823) and thus although there must be only two owners when the action arises, there may be more when it is enforced. Art. 824 states that if one or several of the heirs of him who enjoyed the right of pre-emption forego their claim to pre-emption, the remaining heirs cannot exercise a right of pre-emption with reference to their share only: they must either relinquish it or exercise it with reference to the whole of the object purchased.

If buildings and trees without land are sold, the right of pre-emption is not established (art. 809). If a person sells a piece of land which is his exclusive property and with it his share in a jointly owned passage or watercourse, the right of pre-emption is established, but not if the property is sold without the share in the jointly owned passage or watercourse (art. 810). Where the property concerned is partly *vaqf*, neither the *mutavallī* nor the beneficiaries of the *vaqf* have the right of pre-emption (art. 811). The reason for this is that neither the *mutavallī* nor the beneficiaries can be regarded as the owners of the property, and ownership is a condition of the establishment of a right of pre-

[1] al-Muḥaqqiq accords the right of pre-emption in respect of dwellings, vacant spaces, and orchards. The person exercising the right of pre-emption is known as *shafīʿ*, and every owner of a share in a joint and undivided property, who is able to pay the price of the part sold, can exercise the right of pre-emption, but should the purchaser be a Muslim, the *shafīʿ* must also be a Muslim; a non-Muslim's right of pre-emption can only be established against another non-Muslim. al-Muḥaqqiq lays down conditions for the exercise of pre-emption (1) where the co-partners are two and (2) where they exceed two in number (ii. 271–94). He differs from the Ḥanafī school in that he does not accord the right of pre-emption to neighbours. (See also A. D. Russell and Abdullah al-Ma'mūn Suhrawardy, *Muslim Law* (London, 1925), p. 67.)

emption. The exercise of the right of pre-emption is not prevented by an option being stipulated in the contract for sale (art. 814). The right of pre-emption cannot be exercised with reference only to a portion of that which is sold. The owner of this right must exact his privilege in full or relinquish it entirely (art. 815). In the event of one of the partners exercising his right of pre-emption, the purchaser is responsible for handing over the property, unless it has not yet come into his possession (art. 817). The buyer is not responsible for any loss or damage which may take place in the period between the property coming into his hands and the right of pre-emption being exercised or after this right has been exercised unless he has shown negligence (art. 818).[1] Any natural growth which takes place on the land which has been sold prior to the establishment of the right of pre-emption belongs, if still connected (with the property), to the person who exercises the right of pre-emption, and if separated (from the property) to the purchaser. But the purchaser can pull down any building which he has erected or uproot any tree which he has planted (art. 819). The right of pre-emption must be exercised immediately (art. 821).[2]

Bequests

Islamic law limited to one-third the proportion of a testator's property which can be disposed of by bequest.[3] The Civil Code, which deals with bequests in Book II, Part 4, similarly stipulates that one-third only of a testator's property, reckoned on its value at the time of his decease, can be disposed of by bequest without the consent of all the heirs of the testator (arts. 843, 845). Various conditions attach to the validity of a bequest. The testator must be competent to make a transfer of the property (art. 841). Acceptance of the bequest made before the death of the testator is not effective because the testator can if he wishes revoke the bequest even if the legatee has taken possession of it (art. 829). The acceptance or rejection of the legatee is valid only after

[1] Negligence has been used to translate the terms *ta'addī* and *tafrīṭ*, which are defined in arts. 951 and 952 respectively as 'transgressing beyond the bounds of what is allowed or customary with regard to the property or right of another' and 'the abandoning of an action which by virtue of an agreement or custom is necessary for the preservation of the property of another'.

[2] This is presumably the meaning of the text which reads 'The right of pre-emption is immediate'. No limit is set to its preferment. al-Muḥaqqiq, on the other hand, sets a time limit of three days, which may in certain circumstances be prolonged (ii. 274).

[3] Shī'ī law differs from certain of the Sunnī schools in that it permits such a bequest in favour of either a legal heir or someone other than the testator's legal heirs (cf. al-Muḥaqqiq, i. 623), whereas according to all the Sunnī schools a bequest to an heir or heirs is only valid with the consent of the other heirs. Ismā'īlī law in this case follows the Sunnī practice.

the death of the testator. Thus, if the legatee has refused the bequest during the testator's life, he can after the latter's death nevertheless accept it. If he accepts it after the death of the testator and takes possession of it, he cannot then reject it. But if he should have accepted it before the testator's death, a second acceptance after the latter's death is not necessary (art. 830). A bequest which deprives one or several of the testator's heirs of their inheritance is not valid (art. 837). If the bequest is a general one, the definition of the individual shares is the responsibility of the heirs unless otherwise stipulated (art. 847). If the bequest is a common (or jointly held) share of the estate, such as a quarter or a third, the legatees share that proportion jointly with the heirs (art. 848). If the legatees are several and not possessed of full legal rights the bequest is divided equally among them unless otherwise stipulated (art. 853).

Inheritance

The Civil Code (Book II, pt. 4, c. 2) incorporates the main provisions of the Shīʿī law of inheritance; it is, in fact, substantially a restatement of the traditional forms. Heritable right is based on consanguinity (*nasab*) and upon special cause (*sabab*). Fixed shares are allotted to the various classes of heirs; the rules for the combination of these shares and the order of succession are minutely regulated. Where there are male and female heirs of the same degree and class of the same side each male has double the share of each female (art. 907). The wife inherits only on movable property, buildings, and trees (art. 946); and in the case of buildings and trees she does not inherit the substance but only their equivalent value reckoned on the assumption that they are left in or on the ground (art. 947). If, however, the other heirs refuse to pay her their value, she can have it paid by (the transfer of the) substance (art. 948). In the event of the deceased having no heirs his property goes to the temporal government (art. 866).[1] The law of inheritance is so framed as inevitably to lead to the subdivision of landed estates. The practice of 'conciliation', as stated above, in some measure offsets this tendency, but in general the weight of tradition is strong and the normal course of events is for landed estates to be broken up into relatively small holdings or into jointly held estates in the course of a few generations.

[1] The word used is *ḥākim*, i.e. governor. This is interpreted to mean 'the temporal government', which has become the successor of the *imām* or his deputy (see also p. 174). This is in some measure a departure from earlier Shīʿī practice, according to which there was no escheat to the public treasury. All escheats went to the *imām* or his representative, who distributed the proceeds among the poor of the intestate's native city (see Ameer Ali, *Lectures on Mahommedan Law* (Calcutta, 1885), pp. 11–12).

Dead Lands

According to Islamic theory legal government belongs to the *imām* or his deputy. It has been tacitly assumed that such privileges as belonged to the *imām* in matters of land have devolved, together with other privileges, upon the temporal government.[1] Further, since the temporal government as the successor of the *imām* is the representative of the people, what is owned by the community is also vested in the temporal government. The Civil Code does not, however, give a clear exposition of these points or an exhaustive list of what belongs to the temporal government as the successor of the *imām* or his deputy, or as representative of the people. It appears to be tacitly assumed that certain things, such as large rivers, cannot be privately owned; also that property having no private owner is vested in the temporal government.

In the case of pastures and uncultivated lands which are not owned by private individuals practice is not uniform. In some cases rights of passage and pasture appear to be enjoyed by tradition by certain groups in specified areas, in others these rights are free to the community in general (see also p. 357). Art. 27 of Section 3 of Chapter 1, Book I of the Civil Code concerning property which has no private owner reads:

the appropriation of property which is not private property and which private individuals, acting in accordance with the regulations contained in this law and the special laws dealing with each particular category, take into their possession and exploit, shall be termed permissible, and under this heading shall come dead lands (*arāẓiyi mavāt*), that is to say lands which have fallen into disuse and on which are neither habitations nor cultivation.

The question of dead lands occupies an important part in the exposition of the Islamic jurists, whether Sunnī or Shīʿī. According to the famous Sunnī jurist, Abū Ḥanīfa, reclamation of dead land conferred ownership only if undertaken with the permission of the *imām*.[2] Māwardī, on the other hand, states that whoever reclaimed a piece of dead land became the owner thereof with or without the permission of the *imām*.[3] al-Muḥaqqiq considers that dead lands acquired by force of arms belonged to the *imām* and that no one could cultivate them without his authorization if he was present. Whoever in the presence of the *imām* seized any piece of dead land had to pay rent for it. If, however, anyone reclaimed dead land in the absence of the *imām*, he acquired the ownership of it although by necessity he had not received authorization.[4] Dead lands, other than those acquired by force of arms, also

[1] See above pp. 18, n. 2 and 203, n. 1.
[2] Abū Yūsuf, tr. Fagnan, pp. 96–7.
[3] *Aḥkām as-Sulṭānīya*, pp. 379–82.
[4] i. 337.

belonged to the *imām*, and no one could take possession of them without his authority. Further, any occupation of such lands was only made valid by such authorization.[1]

Reclamation of dead land for agricultural purposes involved, according to Māwardī, three conditions: (1) the heaping up of the earth delimiting and isolating the land it was intended to reclaim, (2) the bringing of water to the land, or if it was water-logged, draining it, and (3) ploughing and levelling it. That person who marked out dead land was the best qualified to reclaim it, but if someone took it from him and reclaimed it, this person had the prior right.[2] In the view of Abū Yūsuf if the person who performed *taḥjīr*, i.e. the delimitation of the land he intended to reclaim, did not reclaim it within a period of three years he lost his right thereto.[3] According to some other authorities, however, it was improper for anyone to take land from the person who had performed *taḥjīr*, even if he did not cultivate the land for a period of three years.

At the present day the subject of dead lands is still of some importance. The Civil Code preserves the main features of Islamic tradition concerning their reclamation. In contradistinction, however, to the exposition of certain Islamic jurists, no stipulation is made that the permission of the government shall be necessary for the acquisition of ownership by virtue of the reclamation of dead lands. Art. 141 defines the actions directed towards the reclamation of land as those which make dead and unclaimed land exploitable by means of operations which are included by custom under the heading of cultivation, such as husbandry, tree-planting, building, etc. Art. 142 defines the preliminary steps, which are known as *taḥjīr*, as to begin to cultivate land, for example, by arranging stones round a plot or by digging a well, and states that this does not effect ownership, but it creates for him who has performed the *taḥjīr* a prior right to carry out the cultivation. A person who cultivates, with the intention of becoming the owner thereof, a part of a stretch of dead and unclaimed land, becomes the owner of that part (art. 143). The reclamation of the borders of a piece of land involves the ownership of the middle of it also (art. 164). The right of priority acquired by the person who performs the *taḥjīr* is not, according to the Civil Code, subject to any limitation in time and continues, therefore, to be exercised unless the owner thereof specifically renounces it.

[1] ii. 295; see also J. Schacht, *Origins of Muhammadan Jurisprudence* (Oxford, 1950), pp. 202–3.

[2] pp. 308–9.

[3] Tr. Fagnan, pp. 153–4. It seems probable that customs concerning the taking possession and cultivation of dead lands go back to pre-Islamic Arab practice in Syria; see V. Chauvin, *La Constitution du code théodosien sur les Agri deserti et le droit arabe, Mém. et publ. des sciences, des arts, et des lettres du Hainaut.*

Forests

The present situation with regard to forests is not entirely clear. It appears that the state, as representative of the community, nominally claims all forest land except where this has been registered in the names of individuals. In certain other cases forest land is in the effective possession of groups or persons. In such cases these persons would seem to exercise the traditional right open to all Muslims to benefit from forest trees. This would appear to be the case in certain parts of the Bakhtīārī country, Bāsht, and elsewhere. The Civil Code is silent on the question of forests, which is an indication, perhaps, that there is no general measure of agreement in the matter.[1]

Crop-sharing Agreements

Chapter 3, Section 5 of the Civil Code deals with contracts for agricultural and harvesting purposes.[2] Both are crop-sharing agreements. The former, known as *muzāraʿeh*, is defined in art. 518 as 'a contract in virtue of which one of the two parties [known as the *muzāriʿ*], gives to the other [who is known as the *ʿāmil*] a piece of land for a specified time so that he shall cultivate it and divide the proceeds'. This type of contract is of undoubted antiquity in Persia. It was recognized by the early Islamic jurists and would appear to have been in existence in Persia in Sasanian times.[3] Art. 519 of the Civil Code stipulates that the share of each party to the contract shall be specified by way of undivided shares, as, for instance, a quarter or a third or a half, etc. Art. 520 states that it is lawful to make a condition that one of the two parties shall give to the other party some other thing in addition to a share from the produce.[4] According to the Civil Code (art. 532) a *muzāraʿeh* contract is null and void if it is laid down that the whole of the harvest shall belong to one or other of the parties alone.[5] In case of deceit either party has the right of cancellation (art. 526).

[1] A note to art. 20 of the law of 26 Isfand 1310 (1932) concerning the establishment of registration offices, however, mentions 'forests which are common property (*jangalhāyi ʿumūmī*)' (see above, pp. 185–6). According to Abū Yūsuf trees which grow in marshes which have an owner cannot be used by anyone. If, however, the land has no owner or the owner is not known, the trees can be used by anyone. The same applies to wild fruit-trees in mountains, marshes, and valleys (tr. Fagnan, p. 157).

[2] See Appendix I for a translation of the text of this section of the Civil Code.

[3] Certain of the early jurists disputed the legality of this transaction. Abū Ḥanīfa disapproved of it, but his follower, Abū Yūsuf, considered such contracts to be in order and regarded them as analogous to the contract of *muẓārabeh*, a partnership of capital and labour, the proceeds of which were shared in a fixed proportion (p. 134).

[4] On this point al-Muḥaqqiq states that certain jurists disputed the legality of such a proceeding, but that it was better to admit it (tr. Querry, i. 516). See also N. B. E. Baillie, *The Land Tax of India* (London, 1873), pp. 52 ff.

[5] See Baillie, p. 56, who mentions various other conditions which invalidate

al-Muḥaqqiq lays down that the land subject to a *muzāraʿeh* must be handed over to the *ʿāmil* with the water needed for its exploitation.[1] The Civil Code is less definite on this point and merely states that

> the land which is the subject of a *muzāraʿeh* must be capable of being cultivated in the way desired, although it may need working or water, and if the cultivation of the lands demands operations of which the *ʿāmil* at the time of the contract was ignorant, such as the construction of a water-channel, or of a well, etc., he will have the right of cancellation of the transaction (art. 523).

al-Muḥaqqiq considers that in certain circumstances the contract becomes void. Similarly, the Civil Code states that 'If, owing to the loss of water or other causes of this nature, the land becomes unfit for cultivation, and it is impossible to remove the cause of this defect, the contract of *muzāraʿeh* is cancelled' (art. 527). al-Muḥaqqiq makes certain further stipulations to protect the interests of the *ʿāmil*. Thus, in the case of disputes over the amount of the respective shares, the declaration of the man who provided the seed was to be considered valid, and if both parties provided evidence in support of their claims, preference was to be given to the cultivator (though some jurists considered that a decision should be arrived at in such a case by the drawing of lots).[2] Art. 541 of the Civil Code states that the *ʿāmil* may take a wage-earner for the cultivation or take a partner, but the consent of the *muzāriʿ* is necessary for transferring the responsibility of the transaction or surrendering the land to another person. al-Muḥaqqiq, however, accords this right to the *ʿāmil* unless a special clause in the contract forbids it. Art. 542 states that 'the land tax (*kharāj*) is the responsibility of the proprietor unless the contrary is stipulated in the agreement; the rest of the expenses of the land depend upon the agreement of the two parties, or on custom'. This is in keeping with the traditional view of the early jurists who considered that the payment of *kharāj* was the responsibility of the owner of the land.[3]

Abū Yūsuf included under the term *muzāraʿeh* a contract which is also recognized by the Civil Code, namely, that whereby the owner of the soil provides all the means of cultivation, draft animals, seed and implements, and hands these over to a labourer who receives one-sixth or one-seventh of the produce. Abū Ḥanīfa did not recognize this form of contract and regarded any payment made in such a case to the cultivator as a wage.[4] Shīʿī

a *muzāraʿeh*; see also *The Mejelle*, tr. C. R. Tyser, D. G. Demetriades, and Ismail Haqq Effendi (Cyprus, 1901), Bk. X, Ch. VIII, s. 1.

[1] i. 517.
[2] i. 520.
[3] Abū Yūsuf, tr. Fagnan, p. 137.
[4] ibid. p. 138.

authorities regard such contracts as valid. al-Muḥaqqiq holds that the *muzāriʿ* can, with the consent of the *ʿāmil*, fix an approximate rent in place of a proportion of the crop, but the execution of this condition is subject to the ripening of the harvest. If the harvest is lost accidentally by hail or any other cause independent of the cultivator, the latter has no obligation towards the *muzāriʿ*.[1] This provision finds no echo in the Civil Code, but it would appear to survive in customary law; thus, in the case of abnormal conditions it is usual for the landowner to send his representative to estimate the extent of the damage suffered and to remit a proportion of the share due from the *ʿāmil*.

In general the provisions of the Civil Code dealing with *muzāraʿeh* would appear to be weighted in favour of the *muzāriʿ*. Thus, art. 528 states that

> if a third person, before the land which is the subject of a *muzāraʿeh* is delivered to the *ʿāmil*, seizes the land, the *ʿāmil* has an option of cancellation; but if the land is seized after delivery he has no right of cancellation.

Further, according to art. 534,

> if the *ʿāmil*, during the course of the work or at the beginning abandons it, and if there is no one to carry out the work in his place, the judge, at the demand of the *muzāriʿ*, can compel the *ʿāmil* to fulfil the work, or else may direct that the work be continued at the expense of the *ʿāmil*, and if this is impossible the *muzāriʿ* has the right of cancellation.

Similarly, art. 535 states that 'if the *ʿāmil* does not cultivate, and the period comes to an end, the *muzāriʿ* is entitled to a reasonable compensation'. Further, 'if the *ʿāmil* does not use proper care in cultivation, and the harvest becomes less owing to this fact, or any other loss results for the *muzāriʿ*, the *ʿāmil* will become liable for the difference' (art. 536).

A second type of contract, known as *musāqāt*, concerns a transaction which takes place between the owner of trees and similar things and another party, known as the *ʿāmil*, in return for a specified undivided share of the produce.[2] According to the Civil Code it is subject to the same provisions as the *muzāraʿeh*, except that if the contract becomes null and void or is cancelled, the whole of the produce is the property of the owner, the *ʿāmil* having the right to a reasonable compensation (art. 544). Further, the *ʿāmil* cannot, without the permission of the owner, hand over the transaction to someone else or enter into partnership with someone else (art. 545).

[1] Tr. Querry, i. 521.

[2] Some of the early jurists, including Abū Ḥanīfa, disapproved of this contract (Abū Yūsuf, tr. Fagnan, p. 134). al-Muḥaqqiq discusses it at some length (i. 521–8).

The question of crop-sharing agreements is one of considerable importance in Persia. From time to time there has been talk of fixing by law a minimum share for the *'āmil*, i.e. the crop-sharing peasant. In fact, however, no government has had the courage to tackle the question. Riẓā Shāh towards the end of his reign appears to have considered doing so. The law of 27th Ābān 1318 (1939) concerns the distribution of crops between the landowner and peasant. Art. 1 empowers the Ministry of Justice to fix the share of the produce of the landowner and peasant. Regulations taking into consideration the five factors—water, land, draft animals, labour, and seed—were to be drawn up and rates fixed, which, after confirmation by the Council of Ministers, were to be put into operation in all districts. Art. 3 empowers the Ministry of Justice to decide the terms on which peasants could have gardens and flocks in large landed properties. Draft regulations were drawn up on 25th Shāhrivar 1318 (1939) for the execution of this law, but Riẓā Shāh is alleged to have decided to shelve the matter in view of the international situation, considering it inexpedient to bring forward at that time a controversial measure such as this was likely to prove. A question was put in the National Assembly in July 1944 asking why the regulations had not been promulgated. No answer was given. A law was passed by the government headed by Aḥmad Qavām which came into office in September 1947, granting to the peasant a 15 per cent increase in his share. In fact this law has not been put into operation except in isolated cases.[1]

It will be seen that the influence of Islamic law on the Civil Code in so far as land questions are concerned has been strong. Indeed there would appear to have been very little attempt to supplement the old law, which has been largely re-enacted. It will further be clear that very little attention is paid by the Civil Code (or any other body of legislation) to the regulation of the relation of landlord and tenant. In general the scales are weighted in favour of the former, and little or no protection is afforded to the latter.

[1] In Bampūr in 1948 in the *khāliṣeh* properties 15 per cent was taken by the governor from the lessees and handed over to the peasants.

CHAPTER X

IRRIGATION

IN Chapters VIII and IX an outline of the constitutional and legal aspects of land has been given, but before going on to discuss the various types of land tenure and the relations of landlord and peasant, there is one subject inextricably bound up with legal considerations and with the general question of land tenure and land administration which must first be dealt with, namely, irrigation. Here also it will be necessary to refer in some detail to Islamic theory.

Water, as pointed out in the introduction, is one of the main limiting factors in Persian agriculture. It is not surprising, therefore, that there should be a body of law concerned with irrigation, based on the *sharīʿa* or Islamic law and on custom.[1] By law water cannot be bought and sold;[2] it is only the channel through which the water flows and the right to use it that can be sold. The origin of this would appear to be found in the tradition, related on the authority of Āʿīsheh, that 'the Prophet forbade the sale of water'. Abū Yūsuf, however, interprets this to mean water which has not been placed in receptacles or vessels.[3] The owner of a spring, a *kārīz* (i.e. a *qanāt*),[4] a well, or a canal cannot refuse the use of his water to travellers or flocks, but no one can use it for irrigation purposes without first obtaining his permission. This prohibition also goes back to a tradition of the prophet.[5] It is perhaps because of this prohibition on the sale of water that the question of water rights is dealt with by the Civil Code (in Bk. 2, s. 1, c. 2) under the annexation of unclaimed things.

According to Islamic theory water is divided into three categories: that coming from (1) rivers, (2) wells, and (3) springs. Rivers are further subdivided. First are great rivers, such as the Tigris, the Euphrates, and other large rivers, the water of which suffices for all the needs of cultivation and from which anyone can lead off a channel to irrigate his land. These are owned in common by all Muslims.[6] Secondly, there are lesser rivers, subdivided again

[1] See also Chauvin, 'Le Régime légal des eaux chez les Arabes', *Proc. 5th Int. Cong. Medical Hydrology* (Liége, 1899). Some of the practices in connexion with water go back to pre-Islamic times. See C. Bartholomae, *Zum sasanidischen Recht* (Heidelberg, 1918–23), iii. 40.

[2] cf. Blackstone, ii. 18, quoted by H. Potter. *The Modern Law of Real Property and Chattels Real* (founded upon the 5th ed. of Goodeve's *Real Property*): 'Water is a movable wandering thing, and must of necessity continue common by the law of nature, so that I can only have a temporary transient usufructuary property therein . . .' (p. 11 (t)).

[3] Abū Yūsuf, tr. Fagnan, pp. 144–5, 147.

[4] See below, p. 217.

[5] See Abū Yūsuf, tr. Fagnan, pp. 144–5, 147.

[6] ibid. p. 148.

into (1) those the water of which is sufficient to be led off without dams to irrigate the land situated along the river banks, and from which canals to irrigate other lands can only be led off if such action does not prejudice the position of the lands situated along the banks, and (2) those in which barrages have to be made, in which case lands situated higher up the river have a prior right to those situated lower down. The amount of water which can be taken off depends upon circumstances, local needs, and custom. Thirdly, there are canals dug to bring water to dead lands. These belong to those who dug them. The water of a canal is divided (1) by rotation by days or hours, (2) by a dam or sluice dividing the water into the requisite number of shares, and (3) by an opening or outlet hole through which the water flows from the main channel into each plot of land.[1]

The Civil Code does not clearly define the position as regards rivers and their ownership. It appears to be tacitly assumed, however, that large rivers, since they were included in what belonged to the community, now belong to the state.[2] The methods for dividing the water of a canal described by the Islamic jurists are those in common use to-day. The Civil Code states that land first cultivated has a prior claim to land cultivated later (art. 158); where priority cannot be proved land nearer the source has priority over landl ower down (art. 156). Land can be cultivated for the first time bordering a river only if there is a surplus of water and the owners of existing plots will not be hampered (art. 159). Many examples of the distribution of the water of a river on these principles are to be found.

Thus, Ṭuruq near Mashhad, which is watered by river water, can only take water after those villages situated higher up the river, namely Maghān, Khānrūd, and Ardameh, have taken all they want. There is no division into shares. Whichever village is higher takes all the water it requires; only then can the village lower down take its requirements from what is left over. In Kurdistān the *ḥaqq ābeh* of villages watered by rivers is of the same kind; those villages situated higher up the stream take the water first and each person can take as much of the water which flows through his property as he requires. Villages may not, however, build new dams or take off new irrigation channels without first obtaining the permission of landowners lower down the river. In some cases, however, villages and lands have a fixed share in the water of rivers on which they are situated; they receive this in one of the ways mentioned above. At Ābrūd (Ourū) near Turbati Ḥaydarī irrigation is partly by river water, which is divided into 21 *shabāneh rūz*. In the Riẓā'-īyeh area each village has a *ḥaqq ābeh*, the division being by the

[1] Māwardī, pp. 313–22.

[2] cf. above, p. 204.

hour. In some cases one village may have the sole right to the water of a river. Thus, Abīāneh, near Kāshān, has the sole right to the water of the river or stream upon which it is situated. Villages lower down the stream have no share in the water and are irrigated by *qanāt*. A similar situation prevails in So, which has the sole right to the water of the river on which it is situated. In Abīāneh the period of rotation is 24 days.

Most of the rivers of Persia are subject to a great diminution in volume at certain seasons of the year and consequently where the water is divided by rotation or by shares, this is subject to minute and careful regulation. The Zāyandeh Rūd affords an illustration of this.[1] The system of division of the Zāyandeh Rūd is traditionally attributed to the Ṣafavid period, and is based on a document supposed to originate in the time of Shāh Ṭahmāsp (930–84/1524–76). From Āẕar (November–December) to 15th Khurdād (5 June) the water was free, i.e. not subject to regulation. For the second half of Khurdād and the second half of Ābān (November) it was reserved for the two *bulūks* of Rūdashtayn and Barā'ān; for ten days in either period it was allotted entirely to Rūdashtayn and for five days it was shared by the two *bulūks*. From 1st Tīr (22 June) to 18th Mihr (10 October) it was shared by a system of rotation between five *bulūks*, Linjān, Alinjān, Mārbīn, Jay, and Barzirūd. From 19th Mihr (11 October) to 15th Ābān (6 November) it was shared by these five *bulūks* and by Karārij and Barā'ān. The system was designed to satisfy the various needs of the crops in the different districts, so that each would receive water when it was most needed. Within the *bulūks* the water was allotted to the various irrigation channels, and each piece of land watered by these channels had the right to the water for a certain period. It is stated in a report dated 1294/1877–8 that the division (*dastūr*) of Shāh Ṭahmāsp was no longer followed, though a copy of this existed in the record office (*daftar khāneh*) of Iṣfahān. This report states that the period when the water began to decrease in volume was one of great anxiety for those peasants who were poor or weak, because the rich and powerful, by bribes and the exercise of force, used to divert the water to their own lands. Whole villages and districts would usurp the water of their neighbours, and the overseers (*mubāshirs*) would connive at this.[2]

In 1308/1929 the earlier system was once more brought into operation, with certain modifications. In 1315/1936 the cultivation of rice in Linjān and Alinjān was forbidden. Trees and gardens

[1] See my article, 'The Regulation of the Waters of the Zāyande Rūd', *B.S.O.S.*, ix. 3, pp. 663–73.

[2] Ḥusayn b. Ibrāhīm Khān Iṣfahānī, *History of Iṣfahān*, f. 534, in M.F.A., no. 726.

were accordingly widely planted and sown instead, and further modifications became necessary in the regulation of the water which was designed specially for the needs of the wheat and rice crops of the area. At the present day rice cultivation has been restarted, but there is not enough water for rice as well as trees and gardens.[1]

The Jājī Rūd in the neighbourhood of Qishlāq, north of Varāmīn, is divided among the villages according to a traditional division. Certain villages have the right to so many *sang* of water.[2] Other villages which have no share have to buy water.

In view of the scarcity of water prevailing in many areas disputes over its use were and are common. The bringing of new land into cultivation, in spite of the provisions of Islamic law and of the modern Civil Code, often led to difficulties. The history of the Qumm river is one example of this. It is related that before the coming of the Arabs to Qumm (*c.* 99/717–18) the people of Taymareh and Anār used to stop the flow of water in the Qumm river one month after the Persian New Year, After the Arabs came to Qumm they asked the people of Taymareh and Anār to share the water with them equitably, or if they were not prepared to do this, to prevent the surplus water flowing into Qumm in winter, which often did much damage to Qumm and its estates. This request was refused. The Arabs accordingly broke down the dams of the people of Taymareh and Anār and let all the water flow into Qumm. As a result the fields of Taymareh and Anār dried up. Fighting over this went on until the people of Taymareh and Anār were reduced to extremities and forced to accept the Arabs' ultimatum. They protested, however, that the soil of their lands was sandy and did not hold water and so required more water, and when a test was carried out it was found that whereas the land in Qumm did not dry up for ten days, that of Taymareh dried up in five days. Accordingly, it was agreed that both parties should take their share of the water every month in two instalments. In the first fifteen days the people of Qumm were to have the water first for five days and the people of Taymareh and Anār were then to have it for ten days; the same arrangement was followed for the second fifteen days. According to another account the people of Qumm had the water in the second period for the last five days instead of the first. It was then agreed that the people of Qumm should send a horseman, who should start at sunrise and ride up the river bank from Qumm to Taymareh until sunset breaching every dam he reached to let the water flow down the Qumm river.

[1] The realization of the plan to draw off water from the Kārūn into the Zāyandeh Rūd by means of a tunnel into the Zardeh Kūh should relieve this shortage (see p. 215).

[2] See Appendix II, p. 408, for the meaning of this term.

This was done and tradition relates that the horseman rode so fast that by sunset he had reached the bridge of the township of Tabreh, one of the villages of Taymareh, twenty-nine *farsakhs* from Qumm. On reaching that place, within a few yards of the last dam, the time-limit being up, he threw his whip in front of him into the dam, while his horse, exhausted, collapsed beneath him. After this it became the custom for the people of Qumm to come out every month and breach the dams of the people of Taymareh and Anār to let water flow down the Qumm river.[1]

According to accounts dated 286/899–900 and 347/958–9 respectively, there were twenty channels taken off from the Qumm river to water the neighbouring area. This water was again divided into shares known as *mustaqeh*. Subsequently, after the Gīlānīs and Daylamites conquered the region, changes were made in the administration of the water,[2] which had up to that time been under a special *dīvāni āb*. A report dated 1296/1878–9 states that the division of the river water in Qumm prevalent at that time went back many centuries; the water was divided into seventy shares, and ten channels were led off from the river, nine of which were privately owned, the remaining one being *khāliṣeh*.[3]

Instances of division by dams or sluices can be seen in many parts of the country, whether the water derives from rivers, canals, or *qanāts*. In Khūzistān various dams exist and the ruins of others can be seen. These include a weir built by the Sasanian ruler Shāpūr by the labour of prisoners of war taken on the defeat of the Roman Emperor Valerian in A.D. 260. In a report written in 1300/1882 eleven dams in Khūzistān, ruined and otherwise, are enumerated.[4] At the present day, a number of companies are in charge of dams and the distribution of water from them. These are mainly financed and run by the government, as at Āhū Dasht where a dam has been made across the Shāʿūr, and at Ḥamīdīyeh. In other parts of Persia the ruins of various storage-dams are to be seen, among them a dam in the neighbourhood of Sāveh, the Bandi Amīr in Fārs, the Ghamsar and Quhrūd dams near Kāshān, and the Farīmān, Ṭuruq, and Gulistān dams in Khurāsān. The last three dams are still in use but furnish little water, being heavily silted up. During the reign of Riẓā Shāh a number of new dams and barrages were planned and constructed, both by the government and by private enterprise, notably at Simnān, Ravānsar, Shabānkāreh and at Āhū Dasht and Ḥamīdīyeh as mentioned above. Under the Seven-Year Plan it is proposed to construct a number of new dams; these include one, near Bampūr, where the

1 *T.Q.*, pp. 48–9. 2 ibid. pp. 50–3.
3 M.F.A., No. 725, List of Landed Properties, etc., f. 48.
4 Najm ul-Mulk, Report on Khūzistān, f. 195, in M.F.A., No. 725.

present distribution of water is unsatisfactory because it is divided into such small quantities that the flow is reduced below the level of efficiency. A scheme is also in progress for the construction of a tunnel to divert part of the water of the Kārūn into the Zāyandeh Rūd.[1]

Responsibility for the upkeep of the 'great rivers', which have never entered into division, is vested according to Islamic law in the *imām*. When these required to be dug or their banks to be repaired it was done by the *imām* with money from the public treasury, and if there were no funds in the public treasury, the Muslims were compelled to give their services for the purpose. If an individual Muslim wished to dig a channel from these rivers for the purpose of watering his own lands, he was permitted to do so, provided it was not injurious to the public. In the case of large rivers which had entered into division or distribution among villages, the cleaning and repairing of their channels was the duty of their owners. If they refused, they could be compelled, since a neglect of their duty resulted in injury to the community, and might diminish the supply of water to those who were entitled to it. From these rivers no one had a right to cut a channel to water his land, whether that would injure the owners of the stream or not.[2]

Although the Civil Code is silent upon the question of the upkeep of rivers and channels, the duty of the *imām* to repair the banks and channels, if necessary by labour furnished by corvées, and the right to compel the owners of lesser rivers to clean and repair watercourses, would appear to have been taken over by the state. It is this principle which presumably underlies the levy of *ḥashar* in Sīstān at the present day for the cleaning and repairing of the dykes and irrigation channels.[3]

The administration of rivers which belong to the state is under the Department of Irrigation, which is a department of the Ministry of Agriculture. Water dues are collected by government officials at various rates. Where, as in Khūzistān for example, the distribution is in charge of an irrigation company, water dues are collected by the latter. The basis on which these dues are levied varies. In Dūghābād near Turbati Ḥaydarī, which is watered by the Azqand river, the villagers pay so much per unit of land for the water. Four persons are in charge of the distribution and collect these dues from the peasants. In Mīāndoāb the rate paid to the government for river water in 1945 was 1 r. (approx. $1\frac{1}{2}$*d.*) per 100 sq. metres (approx. 119 sq. yds.) of land watered. In Sīstān water dues

[1] Shāh 'Abbās also had a project to bring the water of the Kārūn to Iṣfahān by cutting a trench through the ridge separating the springs of the Kārūn from those of the Zāyandeh Rūd. The work was abandoned after some 100 ft. had been cut.

[2] See Baillie, *Land Tax of India*, pp. 49–50.

[3] See Ch. XVIII.

paid to the Department of Irrigation amounted to 15 rs. (approx. 1*s.* 9*d.*) per share until 1948, when they were doubled, the extra money being earmarked to pay for a dam at Bandi Zahak.

Where irrigation companies (see below) have been formed water dues are often levied in the form of a share of the crops. In Shūsh the irrigation company takes one-quarter on irrigated grain crops, or in areas where the land is poorer or unfavourably situated, one-fifth. In Bihbahān the irrigation company takes one-eighth on winter crops, one-sixth on summer crops, and one-fifth on garden produce, levied in each case on the total harvest. Gardens are exempt for the first five years.

In the case of rivers which have entered into division, the cleaning and repair of channels is normally, as under Islamic law, the responsibility of the owners of these channels. This is the case in Dizfūl, for example. There, water is led off from the river for long distances in channels which require constant cleaning and repair. As the flow of water in the river bed, which at Dizfūl is of considerable width, becomes less during the summer, the channels have to be extended into the river bed; the following spring when flood water comes down, the mouths of these channels are washed away. They have, therefore, to be re-made annually. From spring to the month of Mihr (September-October) the flow of water decreases, and dams, made largely of brushwood, are made in the river bed to raise the water level; these, too, are subsequently carried away by the flood water. Crops receive water about 10th Isfand (1 March). Work on irrigation channels also begins some twenty days before the Persian New Year and continues till Mihr (September). Labourers in 1949 were paid 20 rs. (approx. 2*s.* 4*d.*) per diem (of some five hours' work) in Isfand (February–March). Later in the season when labour was in greater demand they got 40 rs. (approx. 4*s.* 8*d.*) per diem. The channels dug are some 6 ft. wide and the banks thrown up on either side are high. Some two to three hundred men are employed on each channel at the height of the work. The annual expenditure on these channels and dams is heavy. The total annual cost of the irrigation of the estates round Dizfūl was said to be in the neighbourhood of 4 million rs. (approx. £23,529). It is noteworthy that the work on these channels and dams is done by paid labour and not, as is often the case in similar works elsewhere, by *bīgārī* or corvée.

In Kurdistān, where irrigation channels leading off from rivers are required in land worked by the landowner and not on a crop-sharing basis, the work is done by the peasants as part of their labour service; but where they are required in land worked on a crop-sharing basis, the peasants combine together to make the necessary channels.

Qanāts or *kārīz*, underground water channels, are a special feature of Persia. They are found in most parts of the plateau, but especially in the neighbourhood of Tehrān, Qumm, Iṣfahān, Yazd, and Kirmān. These *qanāts* are underground conduits which, by using less slope than that of the soil surface, bring water to the surface. The *qanāt* starts in a water-bearing layer at a depth of from 50–80 ft. to as great as 300 ft. In the upper section the *qanāt* collects through one or more galleries; in the lower section, it conducts the water through dry layers to the spot where it reaches the surface. From this point it continues as an open channel. The cross section of a *qanāt* is some 4 ft. high and 2½–3 ft. wide. The excavated soil is lifted to the surface through vertical wells in buckets made of skin by rope on a wooden wheel. The wells also serve to provide fresh air for the *muqannī*, i.e. the man who digs the channel. Where the water-bearing layer is deep and the slope of the country slight, the *qanāts* are lengthy. Their discharge varies from a few quarts to some 21 gallons per second. The end well of a *qanāt*, i.e. that farthest away from where it comes to the surface, is known as the *mādar chāh*.

The making of a *qanāt* is a highly skilled operation, and the trade of the *muqannī*[1] is often hereditary. The most skilful *muqannīs* are said to come from Yazd. Practices connected with *qanāts* probably go back in part to customary law and pre-Islamic times. Gardīzī in the *Zayn ul-Akhbār*, written in the eleventh century A.D., relates that in the time of ʿAbdullāh b. Ṭāhir, who was governor of Khurāsān from 213–30/828–44, disputes about *kārīz* were continually taking place. In the books on *fiqh* (law) and in the Traditions of the Prophet there was nothing about *kārīz* and rules for the distribution of their water. Accordingly ʿAbdullāh assembled all the jurists (*fuqahā*) of Khurāsān and some from ʿIrāq to write a book on the laws of *kārīz*. This book, according to Gardīzī, was called the *Kitābi Qanī*. It was extant in his time.[2]

The Civil Code does not specifically mention *qanāts* or *kārīz*. The subject, however, is dealt with by the law of 6th Shahrīvar 1309 (28 August 1930). This law is clearly designed to encourage the making of *qanāts*. Art. 3 states that if anyone wishes to make a new *qanāt* or repair an old one and this necessitates the digging of a well in the cultivated land or garden of another the owners cannot prevent this, provided the land is not built upon and a fair price is paid in advance for the land where the well, pond (*istakhr*), or channel is to be made. In the case of land which cannot be alienated, such as *vaqf* land, a fair rent is to be paid. Moreover, according to art. 4, if a person wishing to make a water channel, to

[1] In Kirmān the *muqannī* is known as the *chāhkhū*.
[2] *Zayn ul-Akhbār*, p. 8.

drain a swamp belonging to himself, to make a dam or dyke or to lead off water from a river, or to cause a stream to pass over or under a *qanāt* or watercourse, needs to take possession of the property of another[1] and cannot come to an agreement with the owner for buying or leasing it, the courts will give an order in his favour.

In some cases the division of the water of the *qanāt* goes back hundreds of years. Thus Mīrzā 'Alī Khān Nā'īnī, travelling towards the end of the thirteenth century (mid-nineteenth century) through Ardistān, records that according to local tradition when Hūlāgū, the grandson of Chinghīz Khān, passed through Ardistān he ordered the water to be divided. This was accordingly done under the supervision of Naṣīr ud-Dīn Ṭūṣī. It was divided into 21 shares, or *firzeh*, and allotted to various villages and quarters. Mīrzā 'Alī Khān states that this division was still in force when he was writing.[2] The tradition that the division of the water goes back to Naṣīr ud-Dīn Ṭūsī is still current.

In Nayrīz tradition attributes the division of the waters of one of the local *qanāts* to Shaykh Bahā'ī (who is also popularly supposed to have regulated the waters of the Zāyandeh Rūd). This division begins on 16th Mihr (8 October), i.e. at the beginning of the agricultural year. From then until 30th Mihr (22 October) water is taken by those who have a share in it. There appears to be no fixed order of priority, it being alleged that whoever wants water comes and takes it during this first period. The round is then repeated in the same order until Bahman (January). Thus, whoever takes water on 16th Mihr has the right to take it on the 1st and 16th of every month until Bahman. Similarly, whoever takes it on 17th Mihr (9 October) has the right to take it on the 2nd and 17th of every month until Bahman. The number of shares with which the various *qanāts* are divided varies. The Huvar *qanāt* has 10,800 shares divided among some two to three hundred owners. Formerly the division was made by the stars and the sun. At the present day it is by the hour. The unit is a *fayn*, i.e. 20 minutes' water. (See also below.)

In Kāshmar *qanāt* water is divided into 12 *sahm* or shares each of 12 *dāng*, making 144 *dāng* in all. In Qā'ināt, which is mainly irrigated by *qanāt*, the rotation of the water[3] varies in the different villages. Twenty-four hours' water comprise 1 share, or *sahm*, which is divided into 120 *finjān*. The number and size of the *tīrkār*, i.e. the plots into which the village land is divided,[4] depends

[1] *Muḥtāj bi taṣarruf dar milki ghayr.*

[2] *Safar Nāmeh* of Mīrzā 'Alī Khān Nā'īnī from Mashhad to Yazd and Nā'īn, in M.F.A., No. 726, f. 131.

[3] The term used for the rotation of water in east Persia is *madāri āb* or *gardishi āb*. In central Persia the term *rashn* is used.

[4] See Ch. XVI.

largely on the rotation of the water. Thus in ʿAlīābād, east-south-east of Bīrjand, the water is divided into 14 shares and the land into 7 *tīrkār*, so that each *tīrkār* gets 2 shares. In Gīv the rotation of the water is in 16-day periods, in other words there are 16 shares, 2 again going to each *tīrkār*. Every year lots are drawn between the *tīrkār* for priority in the distribution of the water, and according to the results of the draw the rotation is fixed for the coming year. In Maʿṣūmābād west of Bīrjand 1 *finjān* of water irrigates 360 sq. metres (appox. 431 sq. yds.). In some areas in Āẕarbāyjān the village land is also divided on the basis of the rotation of the water.

In Gaz (Jaz), in the district of Burkhwār near Iṣfahān, irrigation is entirely by *qanāts*. Gaz has seven *qanāts*, each of which waters four groups of fields or *dasht*. The area watered by 1 *ṭāq* of water varies with the *qanāt*. Thus 1 *ṭāq* from the Gazābād *qanāt* waters 40 *jarīb*[1] (approximately 14 acres) *kulūkh* (i.e. land dug and prepared for cultivation) or 50–60 *jarīb* of land under crops (approximately 18 acres to 21 acres). Other *qanāts* water only 10–20 *jarīb* (approximately 3½ acres to 7 acres) per *ṭāq*. The rotation of the water of the various *qanāts* varies. For the Gazābād and Raḥmatābād *qanāts*, each of which are divided into 28 *ṭāq*, it is 14 days. For the Gilishābād *qanāt*, which is divided into 30 *ṭāq*, it is 15 days, and the Fīrūzābād, Ḥusaynābād, and Ḥaydarābād *qanāts* are each divided into 32 *ṭāq* and 16 days. The rotation of the Amīrābād *qanāt* is, however, 8 days; the fact that the period of rotation is shorter is due to the fact that the soil of the land watered by this *qanāt* is lighter and dries up quicker than in the immediate neighbourhood of Gaz, and therefore requires more frequent irrigation. In Tarq, between Mūrchehkhwart and Kāshān, the rotation varies between 9, 12, and 15 days according to the *qanāt*. In Bīdhand it is 12 days. In Mūrchehkhwart it is 14 days. In Iṣṭahbānāt in Fārs where there are five *qanāts* their water is divided into 250 shares or *rasad*.

In certain areas, if owing to drought the flow of the *qanāt* is materially decreased, the period of rotation is altered. Thus, in 1944 in the neighbourhood of Yazd, the flow of water in the *qanāts* in most areas except Ardistān was greatly reduced; for example, land in ʿAlīābād near Yazd, which normally received water every 8 days, was getting water only once in 16 days. In Yazd the rotation is for the most part 15 or 16 days. The unit of water is the *jurreh* or *sabū*, which varies from some 8½ minutes' water in Maybud to 11 in Yazd and 11½ in Ashkizār.

In the large landowner areas the ownership of the *qanāts* belongs to the owner of the land through which it flows. In some areas where the land is worked on a crop-sharing basis, the different

[1] *jarīb* in Gaz = 1,444 sq. *ẕarʿ* (approx. 1,731 sq. yds.).

pieces of land watered by a *qanāt* have a prescriptive right to a certain share of the water. Where this is the case, anyone who brings new land into cultivation has to buy water from someone who has water surplus to his own needs or is prepared for some reason or other to sell water. This is the case in many districts in Arāk. In certain areas the ownership of land and water is separated. Thus in Iṣṭahbānāt (but not in the neighbouring districts of Khīr and Īj) land and water are separately owned, though, in fact it often happens that the same person owns both the water and the land which it irrigates. In the Yazd area, except in Najafābād, Mihdīābād, Ṣadrābād, Jallālābād, and a few other areas, the ownership of land and water is separate, the latter belonging for the most part to an absentee owner and the former to the peasant who cultivates it. In Maymeh similarly land and water are separate. This is also the case in some districts of Ardistān.

It sometimes happens that a *qanāt* waters more than one village; where this is the case each village has a prescriptive right to the water for a certain period every so many days. For example, Khurramdasht some three *farsakhs* from Kāshān on the Natanz road, a peasant-proprietor village of some 20–30 families, shares a *qanāt* with the neighbouring village known as Jazbi Khurramdasht (i.e. the village adjoining Khurramdasht); the former has the water for 18 hours in 24 and the latter for 6.

The cost of the upkeep of a *qanāt* is greater or less according to the type of soil through which it flows, and the length of the *qanāt* from the source, or *mādar chāh*, to where it emerges above ground. The cost is almost always heavy. If a *qanāt* flows through soft soil, not only is constant cleaning required, but also hoops of baked clay have to be inserted in the tunnel to prevent subsidence.[1] In certain areas, notably Kirmān, the length of the *qanāt* is very considerable and the cost of upkeep therefore relatively heavy. Long *qanāts* are occasionally found in other areas also. Thus, the source of the Gazābād *qanāt* in Burkhẉār is some five *farsakhs* from where it emerges above ground.

The cleaning of *qanāts* (*lārūbī*) is normally done between the Persian New Year and the thirtieth day after the New Year (19 April) in Burkhẉār. Other repairs go on throughout the year. For the most part the cleaning of the *qanāt* is the responsibility of the owner, but the cleaning of the channels through which the water flows above ground is the responsibility of the peasants who cultivate that land. In the Yazd area the cleaning of the surface irrigation channels is the responsibility of the peasants, who, in those areas where there is a *mīrāb*, undertake this on the orders of

[1] These hoops are known as *kaval* (*kūl*) in Tehrān and the neighbourhood; in Fasā they are called *gum*. The term *nāy* is used for them in some areas.

the *mīrāb*. In view of the great labour and heavy cost often involved in the upkeep of *qanāts* it is not altogether surprising that there should be a vast number of ruined *qanāts* in different parts of Persia. Further, the capital outlay involved in making a new *qanāt* or reclaiming an old and disused one is usually heavy, and therefore for the most part this work is undertaken mainly by the large landowners, and then only if they are assured of reasonable conditions of security. In some areas, notably Gaz, some work has been done in recent years by local landowners in the repair and reclamation of old *qanāts*.[1]

The capital value of *qanāts* varies considerably in different parts of Persia. In Maʿṣūmābād, west of Bīrjand, the capital value of 1 *finjān* (i.e. water to irrigate approx. 431 sq. yds.) is some 2,500 rs. (approx. £14. 14*s*.). In Nayrīz the capital value of 1 *fayn* of water (i.e. 20 minutes' water) is 1,000 rs. (approx. £5. 17*s*.) and its annual rent 50–70 rs. (approx. 5*s*. 10*d*. to 8*s*. 3*d*.). These prices are said to show an increase relative to their value ten years ago. In Iṣṭahbānāt the capital value of 1 *rasad* (i.e. 1/250th part of the water of the five *qanāts* of the area) is 60,000 rs. (approx. £353). The total rentable value of the water is some 1 million rs. (approx. £5,882). In Ashkizār, near Yazd, water from what was alleged to be the best *qanāt* was selling in 1945 at some 1,000 rs. (approx. £5. 17*s*.) per *jurreh* (i.e. 11½ minutes' water) per annum; 1 *jurreh* bought occasionally cost 60 rs. (approx. 7*s*. 1*d*.). The price of water was said to vary from year to year. The capital value of 1 *jurreh* was 20,000 rs. (approx. £117. 13*s*.). Another *qanāt* in the same area was rented at 500 rs. (approx. £2. 18*s*. 10*d*.) per *jurreh* per annum. Rents are not necessarily in cash. For example, another *qanāt* in Ashkizār was rented on the terms that the owner of the *qanāt* provided the seed and took three-fifths of the crop. In Zāch near Yazd, the cost of water was 700 rs. (approx. £4. 2*s*. 4*d*.) per *jurreh* or *sabū* per annum. In Fīrūzābād the cost of 1 *jurreh* per annum in 1945 was 540 rs. (approx. £3. 3*s*. 6*d*.). The capital value per *jurreh* in this case was 15,000 rs. (approx. £88). In Dihshaykhī, also near Yazd, the capital value per *jurreh* was 14,000 rs. (approx. £82) in 1945. In 1949 water in the neighbourhood of Yazd was selling at 50–80 rs. (approx. 5*s*. 10*d*. to 9*s*. 5*d*.) per hour. Well-water worked by electric pump was selling at 50 rs. per hour (approx. 5*s*. 10*d*.). In Maḥvilāt, in the *garmsīr* of Turbati Ḥaydarī, water is exceedingly valuable. The rentable value of one hour's water per annum is in some cases as much as 50,000 rs. (approx. £294).[2]

[1] The flood of 1949 is said to have damaged many *qanāts* and to have destroyed others.

[2] Fraser, writing in 1833, mentions a *qanāt* in Jaʿfarābād near Ray in Tehrān the water of which was let for 1,000 *tūmāns* per annum and the capital value of which was 10,000 *tūmāns*, i.e. ten years' purchase (*A Winter's Journey*, ii. 64).

The local official in charge of irrigation is usually known as the *mīrāb*. In many areas, notably Marv, Iṣfahān, and Shīrāz, the office of *mīrāb* was an important one in the Middle Ages and tended to be hereditary. Iṣṭakhrī, describing the division of the Murghāb river in Marv, states 'there is a *mīrāb* over this river who enjoys greater respect than the governor (*vālī*)'.[1] In Shīrāz the office of *mīrāb* was held for many generations by the same family. Thus Ḥājjī Muḥammad ʿAlī Mīrāb, who had inherited the office from his father, became towards the end of the Ṣafavid period *mustoufī* also. His descendant, Āqā Khudādād Mīrāb, became *mīrāb* of Shīrāz in the time of Karīm Khān Zand (1163–93/1750–79). His son, Ḥājjī Taqī Mīrāb, also held the post of *mīrāb*, and after him his son, Āqā Hādī, who combined with it the office of *mubāshir*, or overseer, of the district (*ḥoumeh*) of Shīrāz. His son, Ḥājjī Mīrzā Muḥammad Mīrāb, held the office of *mīrāb*, and when he died in 1299/1881–2 was succeeded as *mīrāb* by his son, Mīrzā Faẓlullāh Mīrāb.[2]

According to the Ṣafavid *tūmār* for the regulation of the waters of the Zāyandeh Rūd quoted above, the *mīrāb* and his servants received 630 *tūmāns*, 2 *qirāns*, 12 *shāhīs*. In more recent times the annual salary of the *mīrāb* was in the neighbourhood of 60,000 rs. (approx. £353). This sum was apportioned among the *bulūks*, and, in the *bulūks*, among the villages. At the present day a *mīrāb* is not always appointed, nor is he appointed, as he was in Ṣafavid times, from among the *kadkhudās* of Jay. The water and the land irrigated thereby are divided into thirty-three shares, and from each share one representative is appointed to elect a *mīrāb*, whom they recommend to the Department of Agriculture. The Department, having assured themselves that he enjoys the confidence of the majority, issue an order for his appointment. His wages, which are paid by the people, are on a daily basis, the rates being fixed by the thirty-three representatives. If the thirty-three representatives cannot agree on a *mīrāb* and no one is appointed, each *bulūk* sends its representative to oversee the administration of the water when its turn to have the water comes round. Overseers of the irrigation channels (*mādī sālārs*) are appointed at the present day by the people and paid (in most cases) by the landowners.

In Ṭuruq (near Mashhad) there is a *sar mīrāb* who oversees the distribution of water throughout the area. He is under the *dārūgheh*, or village headman.[3] He is paid 1,500 rs. (approx. £8. 16*s*.) per month and 3 *kharvār* (approx. 17½ cwt.) of wheat per year and fodder for his horse, which amounts to 3 kg. barley (approx. 6 lb. 9 oz.), 6–9 kg. straw (approx. 13 lb. 2 oz. to 19 lb. 11 oz.), and 1½ kg. lucerne (approx. 3 lb. 4½ oz.) per month. Under

[1] pp. 261–2. [2] Fasā'ī, ii. 74–5. [3] See below, p. 338.

the *sar mīrāb* are four *mīrābs*. They each receive 330–50 rs. (approx. £1. 19*s*. to £2. 1*s*.) per month and some 4 *kharvār* wheat (approx. 23 cwt. 42 lb.) per year, and fodder for their horses as above. The payments in cash are made by the lessee (Ṭuruq being *vaqf* property); the payments in kind are deducted from the total harvest. In Khīābān, near Mashhad, there are two *mīrābs*. They each receive 400 rs. (approx. £2. 7*s*.) from the lessee and 6 *kharvār* (approx. 35 cwt.), two-thirds in wheat and one-third in barley, from the total grain harvest. In the Turbati Ḥaydarī area the *mīrāb* is usually paid by contract, and not by a share in the crops. In Ābrūd (Ourū) he gets 10 *mann* (approx. 65½ lb.) grain per share of water.

Whereas it is usual in districts such as Iṣfahān, where the distribution of water is a complicated matter, or in areas where water tends to become scarce at certain periods of the year, for some officer to be appointed to see to distribution, or for an appointment to be made during the period of scarcity, in many other areas the distribution of water is entirely in the hands of the peasants themselves. This is the case in Ardistān. In Khurāsān, where irrigation is by *qanāt*, it is not usual to appoint a *mīrāb*; this is also the case in Kurdistān, where even in the case of river water a *mīrāb* is seldom appointed. Where the duties of the *mīrāb* are not sufficient to occupy him full-time he is frequently appointed from among the peasants. For example, in Joushaqān, where a *mīrāb* is appointed only in those years when water is abnormally scarce, the peasants appoint someone from among themselves in whose integrity they have confidence. In 1948 a *mīrāb* and four assistants were appointed to oversee the distribution of water. All four were peasants. They were paid at the rate of 1 *manni shāh* (approx. 13 lb.) wheat and ½ *manni shāh* (approx. 6½ lb.) barley per 10 *kīleh* 478·4 sq. yds.). Their total wage amounting to 480 *manni tabrīz* (approx. 28 cwt.) wheat and 240 *manni tabrīz* (approx. 14 cwt.) barley was divided among them in equal proportions. In Abīāneh, on the other hand, a *mīrāb* is appointed annually by the larger landowners, who also fix his wages. He is paid in kind at harvest time.

In Nayrīz each *qanāt* has one or more persons known as *sar ṭāq* in charge of the distribution of water, and under each *sar ṭāq* are two *lāvāns* who supervise the distribution. All transactions concerning the division of the water and the purchase and sale of shares or part shares and their transmission by inheritance are entered by the *sar ṭāq* in a book kept by him for this purpose. In lieu of wages the water is allotted to him for five days a year, which are known as *khamseh*. They are taken as follows: 31st Farvardīn (20 April), 31st Urdī Bihisht (21 May), 31st Khurdād (21 June), 31st Tīr (22 July), and 31st Murdād (22 August). For the purposes of the division of water (as described above) the remaining seven months of the year are reckoned at thirty days each; thus, 1st Mihr falls on 31st Shahrīvar, and the succeeding months each begin one day earlier than the calendar month; an extra day is added to Isfand so that the 30th Isfand of the irrigation year corresponds to 29th Isfand (20 March), the last day of the calendar year. The *lāvāns* are paid by the owners in kind by a share of the produce of the gardens and fields, the irrigation of which they supervise; the payment amounts broadly to 20–30 rs. (approx. 2*s.* 4*d.* to 3*s.* 6*d.*) per day. The *sar ṭāq* and *lāvān* are appointed by the owner or owners of the *qanāt*. In Ashkizār (near Yazd) which has three *qanāts* there is one *mīrāb* with ten *pākārs* under him. The latter each received in 1945 50 rs. (approx. 5*s.* 10*d.*) per *jurreh* per annum. In the Mamasanī, where water is relatively plentiful, a *mīrāb* is appointed only for rice cultivation. In Kirmān a *mīrāb* is found usually only in the jointly owned villages. He receives a share from the total harvest.

In Sīstān the official in charge of irrigation is known as the *ābyār*. Until recently there were two types of *ābyārs*: one who brought the water to the village and the other who saw to the distribution of the water within the village. They were paid 1½ per cent of the crops. The latter type of *ābyār* has now been abolished and his functions transferred to the *kadkhudā*. The remaining *ābyārs* each receive 3 *mann* (approx. 19 lb. 10 oz.) of wheat per share[1] of land under their charge. In each *bulūk* there is a *sar ābyār* who is paid by the Department of Irrigation.

In some areas in Kirmān where the upkeep of *qanāts* forms a large proportion of the landlord's expenses and the *muqannī* (or *chāhkhū*, as he is called locally) are constantly at work, a special deduction is made from the harvest for the *muqannī*. For example, in Rafsinjān and Fayẓābād (near Rafsinjān) a proportion is taken from the total harvest for various officials including the *muqannī*.[2] The latter in Rafsinjān also takes an armful (*bāfeh*) of grain at harvest-time before threshing, amounting to 5–6 *manni tabrīz* (approx. 32 lb. 12 oz. to 39 lb. 4 oz.) of grain.

In 1943 legislation was passed which would appear to give the state a wider control over irrigation than was envisaged by Islamic law. Although the primary intention of this law was clearly to facilitate the undertaking of irrigation works, it contains provisions for widespread state control of irrigation, extending also to privately owned *qanāts*. As yet, however, these powers of supervision have not for the most part been exercised over already existing irrigation works. By the law of 29th Urdī Bihisht 1322 (1943) the estab-

[1] See Ch. XII for a description of the land system in Sīstān.
[2] See Ch. XIX.

lishment of an Irrigation Institute,[1] which was to be under the supervision of the Ministry of Agriculture, was authorized. Art. 2 provided for the provision of an annual grant of 45 million rials for ten years through the Agricultural and Industrial Bank. This Institute was to carry out irrigation works which had already been planned and to make plans for further development (art. 4). It was to provide, where required, technical assistance to landlords desirous of carrying out irrigation works at their own expense (art. 5). The charge for water supplied as a result of work carried out by the Irrigation Institute was to be in accordance with the rates usual in each locality (art. 6). Any revenue resulting from irrigation establishments was to be devoted to the expansion of irrigation (art. 7), with the exception of 10 per cent, which was to be devoted to the improvement of rural health conditions, rural education, and agricultural improvements (art. 8). The Irrigation Institute was to form companies for the purpose of carrying out irrigation works or drainage with capital provided by the Institute and the landlords. After termination of the work, if the landlords or other persons were prepared to buy all or part of the shares of the government, the Institute would be authorized by the Council of Ministers to dispose of its shares and to allot the proceeds thereof to irrigation purposes. Landlords using the water would have priority over others in purchasing the shares. Further, the Institute could buy the shares of other partners with their consent out of its funds (art. 9).

The Irrigation Institute was to exercise supervision over all matters connected with irrigation in the country, such as irrigation establishments, sluices for the division of river water, public channels, dams, reservoirs, and springs whose water was used for cultivation, paying due regard to the provisions of the Civil Code in respect of water rights, and to local custom (art. 10). For the purpose of ensuring the regular division and distribution of the water, and the maintenance of dams, cisterns, public channels, and jointly owned *qanāts*, the Institute was authorized to form boards, composed of landlords and persons receiving water supplies, and to create special funds for the purpose. All landlords were to pay a yearly sum to be decided by the Irrigation Institute and the boards a sum proportionate to the water they used or owned, so that when necessary these funds could be used under the control of the board for the repair of dams, water channels, water-dividing apparatus, and the repair of *qanāts*, etc. Expenditure on the repair of *qanāts*, however, was only to be carried out under the supervision of the landowners or of an elected committee of landlords

[1] The full title is The Independent Irrigation Institute, but it will be referred to as the Irrigation Institute in the following pages.

(art. 11). Provisions were made for the recovery of sums due from defaulting landlords (art. 12).

In respect of jointly owned *qanāts*, water channels, and lands suitable for the construction of *qanāts*, if it should become necessary to repair a disused *qanāt* or clean or increase the water of a *qanāt* already in operation, the Irrigation Institute, on the request of the owner or owners of one-twelfth of the *qanāt* water, was to make investigations, and after ascertaining that the operations were necessary, useful, and technically possible, and that these measures would not adversely affect other *qanāts* and thereby be contrary to the provisions of the Civil Code, was to inform the principal owners in writing and the lesser owners by notices in newspapers having a large circulation and by the posting of public notices in the locality. The landlords were obliged to take steps to repair their *qanāts* within the period fixed by experts, and in any case not later than two months from the date of notification. If one or more of them were not able or willing to take steps to start work on their *qanāts* within the said period, the Irrigation Institute was to entrust the work on the *qanāts* immediately to the joint-owner or owners who had applied to them, itself control the work, pay the share of the defaulters out of the funds of the Institute, and after completion of the work demand and collect from them the sum due from them, plus interest at 12 per cent and a fine of 10 per cent for the delay (art. 13).

Various irrigation companies were already in existence before this law was passed. One of these is the Irrigation Company of Bihbahān, which was established in 1939. Bihbahān is situated in the middle of a plain some 15 miles south of the Mārūn river. This river flows in an east to westerly direction and the plain slopes gently towards the south. In the Middle Ages the plain was irrigated by a complex system of *qanāts* and irrigation channels. The collapse of a weir, built in Sasanian times across the Mārūn river near the site of the city of Arrajān, resulted in the destruction of the system. The purpose of the Bihbahān Irrigation Company was first to irrigate a part of the plain, and secondly to supply the town with water. Water is led off the Mārūn river through a tunnel 4,400 m. (approx. 2 miles, 1,292 yds.) long. From the southern end of the tunnel a canal extends 3,322 m. (approx. 2 miles, 113 yds.) into the plain and from it three canals lead off, each feeding subsidiary canals. By June 1945 water was flowing through the canals with an irrigation potential of 5,000 acres. Lack of capital appears to have held up the company's operations for the next two years. In October 1947 work was resumed and in June 1948 the irrigation potential had been increased to 7,500 acres of land.[1]

[1] See also below, pp. 318–19.

Among those companies established after the setting up of the Irrigation Institute is that formed in Āẕarbāyjān in Bahman 1326 (January–February 1948), with some 30 million rs. capital (approx. £176,470), of which 10 million rs. (approx. £58,823) were provided by the Institute, 9 million rs. (approx. £52,941) by the Municipality of Tabrīz, and the remainder by private individuals.

Wells, according to Islamic law, are divided into those made (*a*) for public use; (*b*) for private use, such as wells in pastures to which flocks and their owners have a right of priority as long as they are in the area; and (*c*) for private use as personal property. Springs are divided into (*a*) natural springs, in which case he who first uses the spring to reclaim land has a right of priority; (*b*) springs which have been bored by individuals, and which belong with their *ḥarīm*[1] to them; and (*c*) springs bored in private property, which belong to the owners thereof.[2]

Wells in pastures are not for the most part subject to special levies. In the Turbati Ḥaydarī area, however, a due known as *ḥaqqi chāh* is taken by the owners of wells in pastures, amounting usually to one or more lambs and some clarified butter (*roughan*) from flocks making use of the pastures. In some cases the ownership of the well is not in the same hands as the ownership of the pastures. Where an individual has obtained permission from the landowner to sink a well, he then collects dues from the owners of the flocks which make use of this well.

Irrigation by well is found in widely dispersed areas: in Khūzistān, the Persian Gulf littoral, Fārs, Iṣfahān, some areas in east Persia and on the shores of Lake Riẓā'īyeh. In the neighbourhood of Shīrāz there is a considerable amount of cultivation of summer crops, especially melons and vegetables, by wells. In Qarā Bulāgh (Fārs) cultivation is mainly by wells, which are in constant operation except in those months when rain may be expected. The wells are worked by 1, 6, or 8 oxen. Each ox has two men working with it. The area round the town of Bihbahān is irrigated by well.[3] The land is divided into relatively small plots and devoted largely to *ṣayfī kārī* (i.e. summer crops and vegetables). The construction of the wells varies slightly in the different areas. The general principle, however, is, broadly speaking, the same, and in all cases primitive, laborious, and inefficient. A wooden wheel is set vertically in the jaws of the well. An ox or mule is harnessed to it and sets it in motion by walking up and down a run

[1] See above, p. 199.
[2] See Māwardī, pp. 320–2.
[3] This area is known as *chahābi aṭrāfi shahr*, i.e. the well [-watered land] around the town.

in front of the well, or a second horizontal wheel (as in the case of the *charkhi dūl* in the area round Shūshtar) is turned by an ox or mule which, walking round and round a circular run made about the well, sets the vertical wheel in motion. The water is raised on a belt in a skin bucket which, when it reaches the top of the belt, empties its contents into a channel communicating with the land it is desired to irrigate.

In recent years a number of wells have been sunk in various areas and are worked by machine. A number of deep wells have been sunk in the neighbourhood of Yazd, for example; some thirty were said to be in operation in 1949. As a result of the increase in the supply of water brought about in this way, the price of water was alleged to have fallen slightly. The owners of these wells are for the most part town-dwellers, but in some cases peasants and small landowners have shares in them. It was alleged that the owners could expect to get back their capital outlay (some 900,000 rs., approx. £5,294, per well) out of their profits in one to two years. If this is, in fact, the case the price charged for water would appear to be excessive. This development was not regarded with unqualified approval by the peasants. There was a fear that water would be sold relatively cheaply at first in order to encourage the peasants to make gardens, etc., and that once they had invested money and labour in their gardens, the cost of water would be raised, thus facing them with the alternative of paying an excessive price for water or allowing their gardens to go to rack and ruin for want of water. In Kāshmar three wells have recently been sunk by local people. The water from these wells is sold at the rate of some 100 rs. (approx. 11*s.* 8*d.*) per hour and compares favourably with the price of water from *qanāts*. Several wells operated by petrol-driven pumps have been installed in Jahrum and Qarā Bulāgh and are said to be cheaper and more efficient than the old-fashioned wells worked by oxen.

In Khūzistān a certain amount of irrigation is carried on by petrol-driven pumps raising water from the river. It would appear that the possibilities of irrigation by this means have not yet been fully exploited. In the division of the *khāliṣeh* land in Khūzistān[1] a condition of the allotment of land is that the holder should install a pump. According to one report, between Ahvāz and Khurramshahr there were in 1320/1941–2 over 100 pumps from 4 to 14 in. in operation. The 14-in. pumps were worked by 170 h.p. engines.[2] In 1326/1947–8, however, there were only sixty-seven pumps in operation on the Kārūn. The reasons for this decrease

[1] See Ch. XII.

[2] ʿAlī Razmārā, *Military Geography of Irān* (Tehrān, 1320), vol. on Khūzistān, p. 11.

were probably lack of spare parts and in some cases inheritance disputes. Most of the pumps are pre-war. In the Sūsangird–Havīzeh area the amount of land irrigated by pumps is very small. On the Karkheh there are five pumps from (but not including) Ḥamīdīyeh to (and including) Sūsangird. There are no pumps west of Sūsangird, and there is only one pump near Havīzeh.

CHAPTER XI

OUQĀF

TWO categories of land have been frequently referred to, *vaqf* (pl. *ouqāf*), i.e. lands immobilized for charitable or other purposes, and *khāliṣeh*, or crown lands. The Civil Code, as stated in Chapter IX, devotes a special section to *ouqāf* but barely mentions the question of *khāliṣeh*. No discussion of land tenure in Persia which neglected these types of land-holding would be complete. Accordingly this and the following chapter will be devoted to a discussion of *ouqāf* and *khāliṣeh* and their present distribution which, if less extensive than at certain times in the past, is by no means negligible. Both since early Islamic times have formed important categories of land. The institution of *vaqf* is essentially Islamic; in its modern form it differs little from the theory of the Islamic jurists, and it will be discussed here with reference to the earlier theories.

Professor Vesey-FitzGerald states that the essence of a *vaqf* is its perpetuity, but he goes on to point out that this was not always the case. There are traces, he writes, in Shīʿī law in which the word *ḥabs* is used for 'the purely secular grant of a usufruct, and Shīʿī authority may be found for the contention that in default of express trusts the property is not maintained for the benefit of the poor but reverts to the *waqif*' (i.e. the founder). The orthodox Shīʿī view, however, differs little from the Sunnī view, namely, that *vaqf* is a tying up or appropriation of an article in perpetuity.[1]

On different occasions in the past the government of the day has attempted to bring under control the administration of *ouqāf*. A similar tendency is found in the Constitutional Period. Shortly after the grant of the Constitution a Department of Ouqāf was set up under the Ministry of Education and Ouqāf and was placed in charge of *ouqāf* lands.

The legal position as regards *ouqāf* at the present day is set out in a Subsection of Section 2, Chapter 2, of the Civil Code. By the definition of the Civil Code a *vaqf* 'consists in the surrender of property and the devotion of its profits to some purpose'. Two kinds of *vaqf* are recognized: (1) those constituted in the general interest, i.e. charitable *ouqāf*, and (2) those constituted for private purposes, i.e. personal *ouqāf*, as, for example, property placed in trust for the settlor's descendants.[2] The Islamic jurists also recog-

[1] *Muhammadan Law* (London, 1931), p. 206.

[2] A charitable *vaqf* is known as a *vaqfi ʿāmm*, and a personal *vaqf* as a *vaqfi khāṣṣ*.

nize two types of *ouqāf*, charitable and personal.[1] In so far as the latter are concerned there is, however, a difference of opinion among them concerning the legitimacy of constituting a *vaqf* in favour of the settlor's descendants. According to all authorities, one generation at least must be born in order for this to be done. Some jurists consider that the *vaqf* reverts after the second generation to the poor. The Civil Code makes no limitation of this kind. According to its provisions an endowment takes place when the settlor makes an offer by any form of words which definitely carry this meaning, and when the first generation of beneficiaries or their legal representatives if they are not in possession of full civic rights, as in the case of children, accept it; or if the beneficiaries are in possession of full civic rights or the endowment be made for the benefit of the public, then the acceptance of a judge (*ḥākim*) is required (art. 56). It is permissible to endow only such property as can be exploited without detriment to its existence, whether it be movable or immovable, held as joint property in undivided shares (*mushāʿ*) or separately held (*mafrūz*) (art. 58). A *vaqf* is a binding contract and cannot be revoked or altered after completion of the contract and the taking possession of it by the beneficiaries (art. 61). Property of which the profits are temporarily granted to another party can be the object of an endowment, and similarly it is permissible to endow landed property to which a right of easement is attached, without prejudicing this right (art. 64). A person cannot make a *vaqf* wholly or partly in favour of himself (art. 72), but in the case of a *vaqf* for charitable objects, if the settlor falls within the category of persons for whose benefit the *vaqf* is constituted he can participate therein (art. 74).

According to Islamic law a *vaqf* must have an administrator. Except by Mālikī law, he may be the settlor. Failing the appointment of an administrator the judge, or *qāẓī*, appoints one. The conditions laid down in the Civil Code concerning the appointment and functions of the administrator, who is known as the *mutavallī*, do not differ materially from the theory of the Islamic jurists. According to art. 75 the settlor can designate himself during his lifetime or for a stipulated period as the *mutavallī*, or he can appoint another person as *mutavallī* to act as administrator jointly with himself, or appoint a person or persons to act as administrators severally or jointly. He can stipulate that he himself or the *mutavallī*, whom he has designated, shall appoint the (succeeding) *mutavallī* or make any other condition which he considers fit (art. 75). A person appointed as administrator may accept or refuse the office (art. 76). If the settlor designates two or more persons as administrators, on the death of one the other or others

[1] e.g. al-Muḥaqqiq, i. 575 ff.

may act alone, but if it was stipulated that the administration should be jointly exercised, in the event of the death of one of the administrators a judge (*ḥākim*) appoints someone to take his place (art. 77). The settlor can appoint a *nāẓir* (or overseer) over the *mutavallī* to approve and take cognizance of his actions (art. 78). Neither the settlor nor a judge (*ḥākim*) can dismiss someone designated as *mutavallī* unless such a right was a condition of appointment. If the *mutavallī* commits embezzlement (and is therefore removed from office), a judge acts as trustee of the *vaqf* (art. 79). If the settlor stipulates certain qualities in the administrator, if the latter does not possess these he is deemed dismissed (art. 80). Art. 81 states that in the case of charitable *ouqāf*, if the settlor has not appointed an administrator, the *vaqf* will be administered according to art. 6 of the law of 28th Shaʿbān 1328 (11 August 1910). The *mutavallī* cannot transfer the office of administrator to anyone else unless he has been given permission by the deed of settlement, but he can appoint a deputy unless (personal) stewardship was a condition of the deed of settlement (art. 83).

According to Islamic law the administrator receives 10 per cent of the produce. The Civil Code does not lay down any definite share as the right of the administrator. Art. 84 merely states that if no share has been laid down by the settlor he can take from the proceeds a share to recompense him for his work.

Once the proceeds of the *vaqf* and the share of each of the beneficiaries have been defined, the latter can take possession of their respective shares, even if the administrator has not given (them) permission, unless such permission was made a condition to their doing so by the settlor (art. 85). Unless the settlor otherwise stipulates, expenses for the repair of the endowed property and matters necessary for the exploitation of the *vaqf* have priority over the claims of the beneficiaries (art. 86). The settlor can lay down that the proceeds of the *vaqf* be divided among the beneficiaries in any way he sees fit (art. 87).

Among the Islamic jurists there was a difference of opinion concerning the legitimacy of the sale of a *vaqf* property.[1] The consensus of opinion was that it was only permissible if it was exchanged for a better property. While arts. 88–90 of the Civil Code permit sale only if the exploitation of the land is rendered impossible or likely to become so, the prevailing view among modern jurists is that exchange or sale is permissible if this results in the acquisition of a better property. Alienation of the property on a long-term lease is not expressly forbidden by the Civil Code. Consequently, where *vaqf* land is required for some public development project,

[1] See al-Muḥaqqiq, i. 590.

or in some cases merely for private purposes, it is sometimes let on a 99-years' lease.[1]

If the administrator, taking into consideration the interests of the *vaqf*, lets it, the contract does not become void by his death (art. 499).

Where a charitable *vaqf* was made for an object which is no longer known, or for a purpose which is no longer valid, its proceeds are devoted to charity (art. 91). This provision was of some importance during the reign of Riẓā Shāh (see p. 236).

The law of 3rd Day 1313 (1934) introduced certain changes into the administration of *ouqāf*. According to this law all *ouqāf* which had no administrator (i.e. by the terms of the deed of settlement of which no administrator had been designated, or if designated was unknown) were placed under the Ministry of Education and Ouqāf, though the Ministry was at liberty to leave the *vaqf* in the hands of whoever was its overseer at the time.[2] According to art. 2, in the case of charitable *ouqāf* with administrators, the Ministry of Education and Ouqāf exercised supervision. Note 2 to art. 2 excepted from this provision the *ouqāf* of which the reigning monarch was the administrator.[3] In the case of personal *ouqāf* the Ministry of Education and Ouqāf was not to intervene except in the case of sale, when its sanction was required.[4] In art. 9 there was a return to earlier Islamic practice. It was laid down that the Ministry of Education and Ouqāf was to receive a fee of 10 per cent of the net income of a *vaqf* for its administration unless special terms for administration were laid down in the deed of settlement. In the event of supervision alone being exercised, the remuneration of the Ministry of Education and Ouqāf was to be 5 per cent. An exception was made in the case of *ouqāf* constituted for the benefit of hospitals and schools, in which case the Ministry of Education and Ouqāf was to levy 3 per cent for administration and 2 per cent for supervision.

The purposes for which charitable *ouqāf* are constituted are many and various, ranging from the upkeep of shrines and religious schools, the support of *sayyids* (i.e. descendants of the prophet Muḥammad) and others of the religious classes, to the holding of *rouẓeh khwānīs*, i.e. the performance of religious plays, readings from the Qur'ān, and similar functions. They include, on the one hand, the valuable properties of the shrine of the Imām Riẓā, and, on the other, walnut trees in the mountains round Iṣṭahbānāt which have largely been constituted into *vaqf*, their produce to be given to children in the mosque, presumably in order to induce them to attend the mosque.

1 See also above, p. 115.

2 Art. 1.

3 See below, p. 234.

4 Art. 4.

The administration of *ouqāf* will be dealt with only very briefly here. In some cases *vaqf* land is worked directly, but more often it is leased. In such cases the administration of the land does not materially differ from that of a large landed property which is let. In either case a third party is interposed between the peasant and the owner of the land or the administrator of the *vaqf*. In many cases it is the *mutavallī* himself who rents the property: in other words he pays a fixed sum to the foundation and keeps the remainder of the profits from the land himself. In such cases no third person is interposed between the peasant and the administrator, who combines in his person the function of administrator and lessee. This is the case in the majority of *ouqāf* in Arāk. A similar practice is frequently followed in Fārs, where there are considerable *vaqf* properties. Where the *vaqf* property is leased to a third party, the latter may often be a neighbouring landowner. The general tendency is for *vaqf* property to be let on terms advantageous to the lessee; this is especially the case when the lessee is the *mutavallī* himself. There are many instances of lessees of *vaqf* property who have succeeded in making large profits. The sub-letting of *vaqf* property is not uncommon.

Where *vaqf* land is let on a short-term lease, as is for the most part *vaqf* land administered by the Department of Ouqāf, the lessee has no permanent interest in the land and no security of tenure. The result is that long-term improvements are not undertaken and the land tends to fall into decay. For example, I saw a village in the neighbourhood of Shāh ʿAbd ul-ʿAẕīm in 1945, the garden of which had been allowed to fall into complete disorder, though it had formerly been in production. The reason alleged for this was that the lease had come to an end: the Department of Ouqāf wanted to raise the rent, but the lessee was not prepared to accept the new figure and, being uncertain of his tenure, had allowed the garden to fall into decay.

As stated above, considerable areas of the country are *vaqf*. The most important group, both as regards extent and income, are the *ouqāf* belonging to the shrine of the Imām Riẓā in Mashhad. The office of administrator of these *ouqāf* is vested in the reigning monarch.[1] This is also the case with the *ouqāf* of the Sipahsālār and Shāh Chirāgh mosques in Tehrān. Ten per cent of the revenues of these *ouqāf* go to the *mutavallī*. The properties which constitute these *ouqāf* are exempt from taxation on the grounds that the income of the monarch is not taxable.[2] Other *ouqāf* pay taxes in the same way as other landed property.

[1] cf. above, p. 112.

[2] Before the grant of the Constitution *vaqf* land was subject to taxation unless granted immunity by a special decree or *farmān*.

The *ouqāf* of the shrine of the Imām Riẓā are situated in different parts of the country; but they are mainly concentrated in Khurāsān, where the shrine of the Imām Riẓā is one of the largest landowners of the province. The extensive properties which it owns in Darigaz and Sarakhs are directly administered by the shrine authorities. In other areas, such as Turbati Ḥaydarī, Kāshmar (Turshīz), Qūchān, Nayshāpūr, Sabzavār, Gunābād, and elsewhere, it lets its properties. The negotiations are normally in the hands of the deputy administrator (the *nā'ib ut-toulīyeh*). Formerly, under Riẓā Shāh and in the early years of Muḥammad Riẓā Shāh's reign, the shrine properties in Khurāsān were let to a company, known as the Shirkati Filāḥatī. This arrangement is alleged to have proved unsatisfactory. The rent is said to have been comparatively low and not to have been paid in full. The company was dissolved in 1948 and the various properties were leased to different groups and individuals. In some cases, notably Kāshmar and Turbati Ḥaydarī, the shrine properties were rented by local landowners. A small company, known as the Shirkati Kishāvarzīyi Riẓā, was formed from the remnants of the former Shirkati Filāḥatī; this rents some twenty of the shrine properties in the neighbourhood of Mashhad, including Ṭuruq, Shādkan, Mihrānkhān, and Khīābān. The rent paid for Ṭuruq by the Shirkati Kishāvarzīyi Riẓā in 1949 was 1,200,000 rs. (approx. £7,059) per annum and 100 *kharvār* grain (approx. 29 tons, 4 cwt., 56 lb.), paid two-thirds in wheat and one-third in barley. The lease was for a period of five years. In Khīābān the rent was 11 *kharvār* grain (approx. 64 cwt., 33 lb.) paid two-thirds in wheat and one-third in barley and 20,000 rs. (approx. £117. 13*s*.) per *juft* (or plough-land), there being some hundred such units in the village.

In addition to the *ouqāf* of the Imām Riẓā, there are various other *vaqf* properties in Khurāsān. For example, in Kāshmar the shrine of the brother of the Imām Riẓā, known as the Bāghi Niẓār, also owns property, mainly in the form of shares in the *qanāt* which flows through the garden of the shrine. This *qanāt* is divided into twelve shares, of which four are *vaqf*. The annual rent per share in 1949 was 200,000 rs. (approx. £1,176).

In Kurdistān there is a good deal of *vaqf* property, mainly consisting of relatively small units. In Arāk there are large endowments belonging to various Shī'ī shrines. In 1944 the capital value of these endowments was estimated at some 30–50 million rs. (approx. £176,470–£294,100). There are also considerable *vaqf* properties in Fārs, some of them valuable. Elsewhere, scattered throughout the provinces, there is a good deal of *vaqf* property, but mainly in relatively small units. In Kirmān there are numerous *ouqāf* consisting of villages, or shares in villages, and *qanāts*, or shares in these. Iṣfahān was formerly, especially in Ṣafavid times,[1] an important centre of *vaqf* property. Although the majority of this has disappeared or been usurped, a considerable amount nevertheless remains.[2] In the neighbourhood of Shāh ʿAbd ul-ʿAẕīm, near Tehrān, there is also a good deal of *vaqf* land. Approximately half of the Khalafābād area in Khūzistān is *vaqf*, having been constituted by the late Niẕām us-Salṭaneh into *ouqāf* for the *sayyids* and *ʿulamā*.

Certain charitable *ouqāf* which were constituted for purposes such as the holding of *rouẕeh khwānīs* became under Riẕā Shāh *mutaʿazzir ul-maṣraf*, i.e. their proceeds could no longer be devoted to the purposes for which they were founded, since *rouẕeh khwānīs* were prohibited under Riẕā Shāh. In some cases these *ouqāf* were taken over by the Ministry of Education, in others usurped by individuals. Since the abdication of Riẕā Shāh the proceeds of some of these *ouqāf* have again been devoted to the purposes for which they were founded.

Various other instances of usurpation are alleged; it is claimed, for example, that much *vaqf* land was registered in the name of private individuals on the pretext that if supervised by the government the revenue of the property would not be devoted to the purpose intended by the founder. Cases of this sort are alleged to have occurred in Āẕarbāyjān and elsewhere. Similarly, some of the *ouqāf* of the Chahār Bāgh *madraseh*, or college, in Iṣfahān were usurped by private persons; these properties, however, were recovered by the *madraseh* after litigation.

In addition to charitable *ouqāf* there are also, as has been stated, personal *ouqāf*. The area occupied by these is probably not large. The main reason for the constitution of this type of *vaqf* was to protect the land from usurpation. The founder would normally vest the office of *mutavallī* in himself and his descendants after him, and in this way his family would preserve their estates and live on the revenue therefrom. The office of administrator of personal *ouqāf*, unless otherwise stipulated, is vested in 'the eldest and and most learned' survivor.

Although in theory the state exercises supervision over 'personal' *ouqāf* as well as over charitable *ouqāf*, in practice the supervision exercised over the former is of the most perfunctory kind; and the administration of this type of *vaqf* differs little, if at all, from that of an ordinary landed estate.

[1] See Ch. V.

[2] It is perhaps not out of place to mention here that the historic buildings, mosques, and shrines, etc., to which some of the *ouqāf* belong, were in many cases in a state of ruin until restoration was begun some years ago under the auspices of the Tehrān Museum and the Ministry of Education.

To recapitulate, it will be seen from the foregoing that the institution of *ouqāf* survives largely in its medieval form, although it has been brought under some measure of state control. But whereas in the past it was not uncommon for persons to constitute part of their estates into charitable *ouqāf*, this is seldom the case at the present day.

CHAPTER XII

KHĀLIṢEH

THE Civil Code does not concern itself with *khāliṣeh* or crown lands. The origins of this form of land-holding, as shown in Chapter I, go back to pre-Islamic times. At the time of the Islamic conquests the early Muslims were forced to evolve a theory to include this type of land within the general framework. Subsequently, when the rights of the *imām* were transferred to or vested in the temporal ruler, the latter took over the rights exercised by the *imām* over *khāliṣeh*. It has also been pointed out that the extent of these lands varied considerably with the rise and fall of dynasties. The period since 1906 is no exception to this. New political exigencies led to the disappearance of some groups of *khāliṣeh* and to the creation of new *khāliṣeh* and legislation to deal with it. These laws are concerned mainly with the sale, acquisition, and administration of *khāliṣeh*, and do not formulate any general legal principle underlying the existence of such lands. The Civil Code is also silent on this point.

At the time of the grant of the Constitution the *khāliṣeh* then in existence could be divided into three main groups according to their origin: lands entered in (1) the Nādirī Land Register, which comprised lands confiscated by the state in the time of Nādir Shāh (1736–47); (2) the Muḥammad Shāhī Land Register;[1] and (3) in the Nāṣir ud-Dīn Shāhī Land Register or the Nāṣirī Land Register.[2] In the last two groups were included lands which had been confiscated for arrears of taxation and other reasons, and some lands which had been acquired by the state by purchase. These various lands were not for the most part directly administered by the state. Some of them had been handed over to individuals for life or a shorter period, with the right of transfer. Such lands were known as *khāliṣejāti intiqālī* (or *vā guzārī*).

One of the early measures taken after the grant of the Constitution was the abolition in 1325/1907–8 of conversion rates (*tasʿīr*)[3] for the *khāliṣejāti vā guzārī*. The result of this measure was to increase the revenue considerably both in cash and in kind.[4] In addition to the fixing of the conversion rate reductions (*takhfīfāt*) for special purposes had, in some cases, been stipulated in the deed of transfer, while in others they had been fixed by decree subsequently to the transfer. An attempt was made to abolish these

1 Called after Muḥammad Shāh, reg. A.D. 1834–48.
2 Called after Nāṣir ud-Dīn Shāh, reg. A.D. 1848–96.
3 See above, p. 179.
4 Mustoufī, ii. 353.

reductions also, but when claims were made by the state against the holders for the exact amount in cash and kind as shown in the assessment, the holders protested that they had invested their capital in the land on the understanding that they would be granted certain reductions and would pay their taxes according to the conversion rate fixed. The dispute dragged on for some years. Shuster, who became Treasurer-General of Persia in A.D. 1911, held that the full tax as shown in the assessment (*juzvi jam'*) should be paid or the property be returned to the government. Eventually a compromise was reached, some adjustment being made in the assessment and a proportion of the reductions which had been granted formerly being confirmed.[1]

A second type of *khāliṣeh*, the *khāliṣejāti tuyūlī*, were *khāliṣeh* the possession of which carried with it the obligation to furnish military contingents. This type of *khāliṣeh* was found chiefly, if not entirely, in the tribal areas. Lastly there were *khāliṣejāti dīvānī*, which remained in the full possession of the government in contradistinction to the *khāliṣejāti intiqālī*. Some of these properties were sold to private owners in the early years of the Constitutional Period. This was the case in the province of Kirmān where there were formerly large areas of *khāliṣeh*. The area occupied by crown lands, however, does not appear to have been materially reduced. In 1926 the Persian government is recorded by Millspaugh as owning

> extensive and numerous villages, agricultural and pastoral lands, scattered over all parts of the country, the annual produce of which exceeds, under present conditions, krs. 12,000,000. Virtually the whole of the vast grain-producing district of Sistan, 3,000 square miles in area, for example, belongs to the Government as part of the public domains.[2]

The tendency was for *khāliṣeh*, in the period after 1906, no less than in preceding periods, to be in a state of decay and to make little or no contribution to public finance. For this reason it became official policy to decrease the amount of *khāliṣeh* by sale. On 14th Mihr 1310 (September–October 1931) a law was passed permitting individuals to purchase *khāliṣejāti intiqālī*. By the terms of this law the holder was able by the payment of ten years' rent to buy the land outright. A further law, the law of 17th Day 1312 (January 1934) concerning the sale of *khāliṣejāt* and agricultural and industrial loans, empowered the government for a period of ten years to sell the *khāliṣejāt*, with the exception both of cultivated lands in the neighbourhood of Tehrān and in Mīāndoāb, and of estates which the state held jointly with individuals; the *khāliṣejāt*

[1] ibid. pp. 490–1.

[2] *The Financial and Economic Situation of Persia* (Imperial Persian Government, Washington, 1926), p. 36.

of Sīstān, Balūchistān, Pushti Kūh, Luristān, Banī Ṭurūf, and Hindījān (part of which might be transferred to the cultivators against payment in instalments or free); and *khāliṣeh* situated in the Gulf Ports or on the coast, except in areas specified by government decree and any estates which the government might require for model farms. The estates were to be sold to the highest bidder, the minimum price being fixed in each area by a commission composed of three heads of government departments in the area chosen by the Ministry of Finance after the advice of two local experts had been obtained. Land bought for less than 10,000 rs. (approx. £59) was to be paid for in cash; that of which the price was over 10,000 rs. could be paid for in instalments over a period of five years provided a quarter of the price or at least 10,000 rs. (approx. £59) was paid down. In the budget for the year 1315 (1936–7) 2 million rs. (approx. £11,764) is shown as the estimated profit from the sale of the *khāliṣejāti intiqālī*.

The law of 20th Ābān 1316 (November 1937) permitted the sale of *khāliṣeh* round Tehrān (which had been excluded by the law of 17th Day 1312) to the highest bidder. This law was to remain valid for ten years. The minimum price was to be ten times the average annual value of the crops for the three years immediately preceding sale. Properties worth less than 50,000 rs. (approx. £294) were to be sold for cash and others were to be paid for in instalments over five years provided a first payment of a quarter the value or at least 50,000 rs. (approx. £294) was made. When this law was passed there were some 200 *khāliṣeh* villages in the neighbourhood of Tehrān. The number, at the time of writing, has fallen to about fifty. Art. 5 of the same law permitted the Ministry of Finance also to transfer by instalments or without exchange the *khāliṣejāt* of Khūzistān, Dashtistān, and parts of the southern ports (i.e. the Gulf Ports) in such allotments as might be necessary for the settling of cultivators in accordance with regulations drawn up by the Council of Ministers. As a result of these various laws much of the *khāliṣeh* in Āẕarbāyjān, where it was formerly extensive, in Arāk, Khurāsān, and Kurdistān was sold to private owners.

In addition to the policy of selling *khāliṣeh* to private individuals, which was dictated mainly by a desire to improve the state of cultivation of the country and thereby to increase the revenue, *khāliṣeh* lands were used in part to implement Riẓā Shāh's policy of settling the tribes. For example, by the law of 14th Tīr 1311 (5 July 1931) for the sale of *khāliṣeh* situated in the neighbourhood of Puli Ẕahāb the Minister of Finance was empowered to sell the *khāliṣeh* in that area as a whole or in allotments on condition that the buyers 'should prepare, in the period stipulated at the time of the transaction with the government, all the buildings and villages [needed] for the settling of the tribes in those areas and make available to them whatever was needed for agricultural purposes'. If from among these tribes any individuals were prepared to buy allotments from the estates mentioned which would suffice to furnish the means of livelihood for them and their families, land could be transferred to them, but such allotments were not to exceed two plough-lands.

Similarly, by the law of 28th Mihr 1311 (October 1931) for the transfer of *khāliṣeh* in Luristān to the Lurs, the Ministry of Finance 'is permitted to transfer free a share of the *khālisejāt* situated in Luristān to any individual among the Lurs who abandons nomadic life and becomes settled, such as will suffice to provide means of livelihood for him and his family'. Again, by the law of 7th Day 1311 (December 1932), the Ministry of Finance was empowered to transfer without exchange from the pastures and crown lands in the province of Āẕarbāyjān, in the area where the Shāhsivan reside, whatever amount it considered necessary as private property to the *khāns* and individuals of those tribes. The conditions of transfer were to be laid down by the Ministry of Finance.

Connected with Riẓā Shāh's tribal policy and his policy of reducing the power of the large landowners by breaking up their estates was another series of laws permitting the transfer of *khāliṣeh* to persons who were exiled from their original homes in part exchange for their original estates. An example of these is the law of 17th Khurdād 1311 (June 1932) permitting the exchange of Ibrāhīm Qavām's estates in Shīrāz for *khāliṣeh* in other parts of the country, namely, Ashraf, Simnān, Dāmghān, Nayshāpūr, Kāshān, and Tūrqūzābād in Ghār, the exchange to be on a basis of equivalent incomes; if these estates were not sufficient for this purpose certain others in Ghār were to be added to them. In a similar way the valuable properties of Ev Oghlī (near Khūy) were exchanged, their erstwhile owners being given properties in Māzandarān. After Shahrīvar 1320 (August–September 1941), when these estates in Māzandarān were returned to their original owners, Ev Oghlī again became *khāliṣeh*. Saʿīdābād, another valuable *khāliṣeh* property in Āẕarbāyjān, which had been given to Ibrāhīm Qavām in exchange for estates elsewhere, was sold after Shahrīvar 1320 to the reigning monarch, who transferred it to the Shīri Khurshīdi Surkh (the Persian Red Cross). In the Jīruft area some twenty *khāliṣeh* villages were during the reign of Riẓā Shāh exchanged for properties elsewhere. These also after Shahrīvar 1320 reverted to the government as *khāliṣeh*, since the properties for which they had been exchanged were taken back by their original owners.

In addition to this tendency to sell *khāliṣeh* there was also a movement in the opposite direction. During the early years of Riẓā Shāh's reign considerable areas of land were confiscated by the state from rebels and others. Among these estates were large areas in Khūzistān taken from Shaykh Khazʿal and considerable areas in Kurdistān and Mākū. In some cases those whose land was expropriated were, as mentioned above, given estates in exchange or part exchange in other parts of Persia. The form these confiscations usually took was *touqīf*, i.e. confiscation for alleged arrears of taxation, so that the transaction should not have the appearance of arbitrary confiscation (*muṣādireh*).

In certain cases, especially *qanāts* in the neighbourhood of towns, *khāliṣeh* properties have been transferred to the local municipalities. For instance, the hamlet (*mazraʿeh*) of Birinjzār was transferred by the Ministry of Finance as private property to the municipality of Nayrīz by the law of 5th Bahman 1310 (January 1932), so that the municipality could bring water from Birinjzār to Nayrīz for the use of the inhabitants of the town.

After the abdication of Riẓā Shāh certain further developments regarding *khāliṣeh* took place. By Regulation No. 313/2 dated 19th Farvardīn 1323 (April 1944) issued by the Administrator-General of the Finances, a special institute was charged with the exploitation of *khāliṣeh*, with which had been amalgamated the Ceded Properties, i.e. the personal estates of Riẓā Shāh (see *amlāk*, pp. 256–7 below). Among the duties of this office were the following:

1. The provision and keeping in order of the tax rolls for all the estates, *khāliṣeh* and Ceded Estates.
2. The provision of special books for the registration of rent documents.
3. The collection of the products of the estates which are directly administered and the collection of the rent of estates which are leased.
4. The digging of canals, the building of dams, and the supervision of the development of the irrigation of *khāliṣeh* and Ceded Estates.
5. The supervision and the provision of help to the cultivators of the estates.
6. The preparation of measures concerning the development and exploitation of these estates.
7. The collection of land and water rates and any other dues which the government may impose on the lands and the water.
8. The preservation and exploitation of the pastures belonging to the Ceded Estates, *khāliṣeh*, and forests which are not privately owned.

9. The allocation of the *khāliṣeh* which, according to the relevant regulations and instructions, were to be transferred to the peasants.
10. The performance of the formalities in connexion with the sale of *khāliṣeh* and the purchase of lands and estates for the government.
11. Looking after the government and royal gardens which are under the supervision of this department.
12. The maintenance of agricultural machines and their use.
13. The maintenance of peasant buildings.
14. Looking after the well-being of the peasants and raising their standard of living.

The Administrator of the Ceded Estates was meanwhile given the task of preparing the ground for the registration of the government estates and the obtaining of ownership documents from the registration department.

Subsequently steps were taken for the selling and distribution of *khāliṣeh* by a decree dated 15th Tīr 1325 (6 July 1946), which was subsequently emended by the decrees of 22nd Tīr 1325 (13 July 1946) and 12th Ābān 1325 (3 November 1946) respectively. The purpose of the decree of 15th Tīr was to extend peasant proprietorship. Art. 1 reads

To encourage peasant proprietors and to provide facilities for those who are engaged in agriculture as a profession to obtain freehold possession of land the following capital is placed at the disposal of the Ministry of Agriculture from this date:

(*a*) All *khāliṣeh* irrespective of whether it is cultivated or uncultivated land, and whether original *khāliṣeh* or *khāliṣeh* which derives from the estates ceded [by the ex-Shāh], with the exception of pasture lands and woods belonging to the state, as well as state-owned rentable property in towns and property with respect to the ownership of which the government or private individuals may have total or partial claims, or which may be subject to disputes or differences as regards registration or other matters, so long as such disputes are not definitely settled and the ownership of the Government is not clearly and indisputably established. . . .

The apportioning of these domains was to be carried out by the Agricultural Bank. By art. 6, as emended by the decree of 22nd Tīr 1325, the Agricultural Bank was authorized to apportion into plots the *khāliṣeh* which was to be divided among the cultivators in accordance with the decree, taking into consideration local conditions and methods of farming regarding the practice of fallow, irrigation, and the quality of the land, and to give such plots of land into the possession of local cultivators, sending a statement concerning the apportionment to the Ministry of Finance through the Ministry of Agriculture, in order that a definite and final transfer of the land to the cultivators should be made, and asking for the issue of title deeds. Land needed by the Ministry of Agriculture for creating model farms was excepted from the distribution. According to an amendment to note 1 of art. 6 the apportionment of the land was to be so arranged that each holder should receive without partiality or favouritism an equal quantity of good and bad land. In passing, it might be mentioned that this provision, though possibly in the circumstances desirable in order to achieve equality in the holdings, makes strip cultivation inevitable. Note 2 of art. 6 gives preference to local peasants. Immediate exploitation of the land is made a condition of apportionment in note 3, art. 7. Art. 8, as emended by the decree of 12th Ābān, limits the size of the holdings as follows:

> Any person becoming possessed of land and water by virtue of this decree shall not receive more than ten hectares [24·71090 acres] of land and must not own more than two hectares [4·94218 acres] of arable land in any other part of the country.
>
> The basis of application shall be three hectares [7·41327 acres] for each tillage turn, that is to say, in localities where the land is tilled every alternate year every tiller shall receive six hectares [14·82654 acres] and where the land is cultivated every third year each cultivator shall receive nine hectares [22·23981 acres]. In all cases, however, an extra hectare [2·47109 acres] is allowed for a garden, orchard, stables, etc.

In actual fact these various attempts made to encourage and extend peasant proprietorship have not been marked by conspicuous success. In general there has been a failure to implement the decrees, however excellent the intention may have been behind them. Where land has in fact been distributed, it has either never got into the hands of the peasant proprietors or, where it has, they have been subjected to pressure of various kinds and in due course have been expropriated in many cases. An example of this, as will be shown in the following section, has occurred in Sīstān. This episode in the history of *khāliṣeh* will be described in some detail because it illustrates some of the difficulties which any far-reaching measures of land reform are likely to encounter.

Sīstān[1]

The *khāliṣeh* of Sīstān goes back to the early years of the reign of Nāṣir ud-Dīn Shāh Qājār, the province being occupied in 1866–7. The authority of the Persian government was subsequently disputed by various local chiefs and the province was finally occupied

[1] In the following pages 'Sīstān' has been used to denote the Persian province of Sīstān, unless otherwise stated.

by Mīr ʿAlam Khān, the Amīr of Qā'in, who was given Sīstān as his *tuyūl* in 1874, and on his death it passed to his son. Mīr ʿAlam Khān is alleged, during his term of office, to have urged various of the local *mullās* to propose to the government that they should rent certain lands, which they accordingly did; further, he forced the *sardārs* (the local landowners and tribal leaders) to make certain payments in kind by way of taxation, and to provide a number of government servants as part of the service on their lands. In due course these payments and services came to be looked upon as rent for the land, and Sīstān came to be regarded as *khāliṣeh*. The subsequent history of Sīstān is largely one of intrigues between the various factions among the *sardārs*, in particular ʿAlī Khān Sarābandī and the family of the Amīr of Qā'in.

The physical conditions of Sīstān offer peculiar problems. In the north and west it is bounded by the inland lake known as the Hāmūn. The Hīrmand river enters Sīstān and then divides into two branches. The first, known as the Pariān, flows in a northerly direction and divides into a number of streams, the most important of which are the Niātak and Mulkī. The former waters part of the north-west of Sīstān and the latter the district of Miān Kangī, i.e. the north and north-eastern part of Sīstān. The Pariān continues in a northerly direction and forms the Perso–Afghān frontier until it finally turns north-east into Afghānistān. The second branch, known as the Sīstān river, flows through southern and south-westerly Sīstān. Near the frontier the Kahak dam has been constructed across this river and diverts the water into the Pariān. Lower down another dam, known as Bandi Zahāk, has been made, from which a number of streams, including the Hasankī, are led off. By these various canals and streams the lands of Sīstān are watered; the surplus water is conducted into the Hāmūn, whence it flows out through a watercourse known as the Shīlā. The land is entirely dependent upon irrigation. In the event of flood, owing to the flatness of the country there is danger of widespread inundation. In order to ensure the irrigation of the land on the one hand, and to prevent flooding on the other, dykes known as *kūreh*, made of mud and tamarisk brushwood, have to be constructed along the banks of the river. Every year the channels have to be cleaned. The maintenance of the dykes throughout the area is a matter of common interest. A breach may lead to widespread inundation. If the proper regulation and control of water breaks down the area may be damaged by flood or by drought, as happened when a series of dry years culminated in floods in 1949. During these years of drought large areas of reed-beds and pasture, in which cattle normally graze, dried up and contributed materially to the prevailing poverty.

The control of the water is a matter which is beyond the individual efforts or resources of the peasants, and necessitates some kind of central control. The making and repairing of irrigation channels is done by corvée, known locally as *ḥashar*,[1] under the supervision of the local department of the Irrigation Office of the Ministry of Agriculture, which is in general charge of irrigation affairs.

Up to the year 1311 (1932–3) the *khāliṣeh* of Sīstān was rented to the *sardārs* and local notables. In that year a decision was taken to distribute the *khāliṣeh* of Sīstān to peasants, on the ground that the *sardārs* and others who held the land had taken no steps to increase the productivity of the area, had practised extortion against the peasants, and often refrained from paying the rent due to the government. Accordingly the land was divided into shares of 36,000 sq. *ẕarʿ*, or *gaz* (approx. 8 acres, 4,336 sq. yds.). Areas nominally consisting of 1–120 shares were transferred to the peasants, *sardārs*, and others, on the basis of their ability to cultivate the land. An annual tax (*mināl*) of 50 rs. (approx. 5*s.* 10*d.*) per share was levied. This transfer did not, however, involve a change in ownership. Subsequently, in 1316/1937, by a decree of the Council of Ministers (No. 3124 of 27th Khurdād 1316/June 1937), it was laid down that (1) the *khāliṣeh* of Sīstān should be sold and divided into shares of 36,000 sq. *ẕarʿ*, or *gaz* (approx. 8 acres, 4,336 sq. yds.);[2] (2) the price of each share was to be 500 rs. (approx. £2. 18*s.* 10*d.*) in a lump sum in cash or 800 rs. (approx. £4. 14*s.* 1*d.*) to be paid in ten annual instalments of 80 rs. (approx. 9*s.* 5*d.*); (3) the land was to be sold in blocks; the subsequent division of these blocks among the peasants and arrangements concerning the crop rotation to be practised in them was the responsibility of the Department of Agriculture; (4) priority was to be given to those at present exploiting the land; (5) land could only be re-sold to those resident in Sīstān or to persons who would reside in Sīstān after purchasing the land; (6) more than ten shares might only be sold to those who were at present working more than ten shares; (7) land in the neighbourhood of the peasants' houses suitable for gardens could be transferred to them gratis.

No survey work was carried out with a view to the implementation of this decree. The division was in the hands of the officials of the Department of Agriculture in Sīstān. Complaints of irregularities were received almost immediately. The Ministry of

[1] See above, p. 215.

[2] i.e. an amount of land in which 600 kg. (11 cwt., 91 lb.) wheat could be sown annually on the basis of *do āyish*, i.e. half the share being left fallow every year.

Finance, anxious to avoid entanglement in what was obviously going to be a complicated business, did not at first press its claims to have a say in the division, or for the division to be put in the hands of a local commission. By 1318/1939–40, however, the volume of complaints, and the fact that the Ministry of Finance was not receiving taxes and government dues in respect of Sīstān (the collection of which since 1316/1937–8 had been the responsibility of the Department General of Agriculture) forced the Ministry of Finance to intervene. In that year responsibility for all matters, except irrigation, relating to the division of the *khāliṣeh* in Sīstān was transferred from the Department General of Agriculture to the Ministry of Finance. This had no effect on the number of complaints received.

Matters were brought to a head towards the end of 1318/1940 or the beginning of 1319/1941 by two cases. The first was the case of Muḥammad Amīn Nārū'ī, who complained that land which had been in his possession for several years and which he was cultivating was taken away from him and sold to Arbāb Mihdī, a merchant dwelling in Tehrān. Investigations made into the case by a commission sent by the General Staff showed that 196½ shares of land in Zābul had been let to Muḥammad Amīn Nārū'ī and were cultivated by him and local peasants. Meanwhile this land was sold to Arbāb Mihdī, contrary to the decree of the Council of Ministers (mentioned above) which clearly stated that priority was to be given to those at present exploiting the land. Further, the investigations of this commission showed that land had been sold to thirty-three persons who were not, and never had been, landowners in the Zābul area. Most of them were government officials.

The second was the case of Ghulām Ḥusayn Bārānī, who complained of the extortionate action of the officials of the Department of Agriculture in selling the lands of the Bārānīs to Muḥammad ʿAlī Kayānī. On investigation it appeared that 252 shares of land had been taken from the Bārānīs and been handed over to Muḥammad ʿAlī Kayānī on a lease and these were subsequently sold to his relatives and dependants, so that the 252 shares appeared in the names of twenty-two persons, although in reality all these shares in fact belonged to Kayānī and were in his effective possession.

As a result of the gravity of the complaints, Riẓā Shāh ordered the whole question of the division to be reviewed by means of a commission, which was in due course set up, composed of the local representatives of the Ministries of Finance, the Interior, Justice, and War. It reported on 19th Farvardīn 1319 (April 1940). The conclusion arrived at in the report, which would appear to be somewhat timorous and (probably intentionally) vague, was that the area and population of the *khāliṣeh* lands were such as to permit roughly one share per family. It was proposed that the land should be surveyed and the shares transferred accordingly. The price and conditions of payment were to be unchanged. Various proposals were made for the practical application of the above proposal to each village: (1) Where the number of families equalled the number of shares no action was to be taken. (2) If the number of families was less than the number of shares, surplus shares could be taken up to a maximum of five by local inhabitants who had previously held more than one share. (3) If the number of families was greater than the number of shares the surplus families were to be removed to the nearest village with surplus shares. (4) Where the number of shares was surplus to the number of families even after the steps proposed under (2) above had been taken, the surplus could be taken up by (*a*) local inhabitants, and (*b*) non-Sīstānīs provided they settled in the area, up to a maximum of five shares each in either case. If surplus shares still remained landowners were to be allowed to retain large holdings or a proportion of them.

The report also proposed that waste-land and brackish land, the reclamation of which required some capital expenditure, should be transferred free to the holder of the neighbouring land if he was prepared to reclaim it, and if he was not prepared to undertake this, to anyone else who was so prepared.

The local commission in reply to questions raised by the Ministry of Finance stated that it had not meant that where shares in excess of one had been allocated to individuals these should be reallocated, and alleged that the holding of these shares had not been the subject of complaint. This reply would appear, in fact, to make nonsense of the original report. The report was passed to the *shāh*, who ordered that the Council of Ministers should arrange for a commission to review the matter (12th Day 1319/January 1941). The Council of Ministers accordingly decreed (29th Day 1319) that representatives of the Ministries concerned should meet and agree on the instructions to be given to this commission. The report duly submitted by the representatives of the Ministries concerned, after enumerating the complaints arising from the misapplication of the decree of 27th Khurdād 1316 (June 1937), suggested that a commission should be sent to Zābul charged with the application of the following programme: (1) the division of *khāliṣeh* land into shares each of 5 ha. (approx. 12 acres, 88 sq. yds.); (2) the sale of these shares to local inhabitants at the rate of 250 rs. (approx. £1. 9*s*. 5*d*.) per ha. (approx. 2 acres, 2,280 sq. yds.) payable in instalments over ten years, or 160 rs. (approx. 19*s*.) in a lump sum cash down; (3) the sale of the land in blocks to be held jointly; (4) the prohibition of holdings of more than 10 shares each; and (5) the formation of a company for the development of Sīstān, half the capital of which would consist of the immovable property of the peasant proprietors and half of funds to be subscribed by capitalists, who should preferably be Sīstānīs.[1]

Meanwhile, towards the end of 1319/1941 conditions in Sīstān deteriorated, and as a result of the extortion practised against the peasants, a flight from the area began. In due course, a commission composed of the representatives from the Ministries of Finance, Justice, and the Interior, and the Department General of Agriculture was formed and reached Zābul on 8th Urdī Bihisht 1320 (April 1941), but its terms of reference were not as recommended. It reported on 1st Tīr 1320 (June 1941). It divided the plaintiffs into the following categories: those who complained that (1) they had not received any land, (2) the share allocated to them was less than the regulation, (3) their shares had been allocated to someone else, (4) others had usurped their shares, (5) the limits of the shares allotted to them were not defined, and (6) the land allotted to them was not capable of cultivation. The report went on to condemn the principle of small holdings mainly on the following grounds: (1) It claimed that the population was insufficient. The number of potential peasant proprietors was estimated at 30,000, while the total number of shares, put officially at 36,000, was estimated at not less than 40,000. (2) It was alleged that ignorance, lack of capital and equipment, and lack of mutual co-operation of the peasant proprietors made the plan unworkable. (3) It examined and rejected as unpractical the proposal that the government should make loans to peasant proprietors through the Agricultural Bank, although it was in favour of loans being made to large landowners to enable them to plant gardens, orchards, and to buy tractors, etc. The commission recommended that (1) the *khāliṣeh* lands should be sold by villages or large blocks of land at the rate of 250 rs. (approx. £1. 9*s*. 5*d*.) per ha. (approx. 2 acres, 2,280 sq. yds.) payable in instalments, or with a reduction of the total price if paid in a lump sum cash down. Residence should not be an essential qualification but present holders of land should have preference over newcomers; (2) the order to the Zābul Finance Office dated 15th Urdī Bihisht 1320 (May 1941) forbidding the sale of any more land until a survey had been carried out and a decision reached by the Council of Ministers, should be confirmed. This report was submitted to the Council of Ministers on 13th Murdād 1320 (August 1941). No action was taken. The Ministry of Finance, however, confirmed its order to the Zābul

[1] The functions of this company and its relations to those to whom lots had been or were to be transferred are not described.

Finance Office. Further applicants for land were, as a temporary measure, to be given shares in proportion to their ability to cultivate it, and on them they were to pay annually the government share (*bahrehyi mālikānehyi doulat*). The Finance Ministry also agreed that minor complaints should be dealt with by a local commission composed of the governor (*farmāndār*) and heads of the Offices of Justice and Agriculture.

Early in 1321/1942, on the Prime Minister's orders, a local commission, composed of the Governor-General, the officer commanding the S.E. Division, the head of the Agriculture Office of the 8th Ustān, and the heads of the Offices of Finance and Agriculture of Zābul, was formed to report on the situation. In its report the commission attributed the existing state of affairs to (1) the ignorance, laziness, and selfishness of the peasants; (2) the absence of any controlling authority in the villages; (3) the actions of government officials, either as shareholders or as agents provocateurs; and (4) the conflicting interests and claims of the various local government departments. The commission cited the following figures as being indicative of the current state of affairs: whereas in 1319/1940–1 21,500 *kharvār* (approx. 6,283 tons, 7 cwt., 91 lb.) of wheat and barley were sown, in 1320/1941–2 only 16,500 *kharvār* (approx. 4,822 tons, 4 cwt., 32 lb.) were sown. The average surplus (*māzād*) of wheat and barley before the division of the *khāliṣeh* was 40,000 *kharvār* (11,690 tons); after the division it fell to 7,000–10,000 *kharvār* (2,045 tons, 15 cwt. to 2,922 tons, 10 cwt.). The commission proposed that (1) the existing system should be abolished, and the lands rented or sold by auction so that the land should be in the hands of large landowners or lessees from whom the government should demand the maximum possible surplus; (2) if the government decided to continue with the existing system temporarily, those shares at present held by government officials should be taken from them and reallocated to the peasants or landowners. No action, however, appears to have been taken on this report.

In Tīr 1323 (June–July 1944) another report was made; this time by representatives of the Ministries of Finance and Agriculture. In this report it was stated that from 1317/1938–9 to the date of the report, 179 shares had, according to the records, been sold at 500 rs. (approx. £2. 19*s*.), and 25,083 on the instalment system. The total money collected was 8,548,708 rs. (approx. £50,287). In addition 441 shares had been transferred for exploitation against annual payment of the government's share (*bahrehyi mālikānehyi doulat*). The report described the method—or more properly speaking the absence of method—of recording transfers of these lands, and the chaos which prevailed in the registration records. It gave a list of the various types of complaints. In some cases cultivators, although they had paid some of the instalments due on the lands allocated to them, when these lands had been flooded, had abandoned them. Subsequently others had usurped possession of these lands and brought them into cultivation. The original holders had then reclaimed them. In other cases the lands of persons who had gone on a journey or gone to perform their military service had been allocated to others in their absence. In some cases persons had usurped lands the holders of which had been dispersed or died, and neither paid the government's share nor the instalments due. In other cases, since the limits of the allotments were not defined, holders frequently transgressed their limits and took in land properly belonging to their neighbours. In 1318/1939–40 the shares of a large group were flooded and the holders of some 1,860 shares claimed that they had received no compensation. Further, since there had been no survey a number had usurped land over and above the amount due to them. The commission attributed responsibility for these difficulties and disputes to the malpractices of officials of the Agriculture Office up to 1318/1939–40 and of the officials of the Finance Office from 1319/1940–1 onwards. A list of the shares held by government officials —in their own names only and excluding therefore shares acquired in the names of their dependants—was given and amounted to 1,223½ shares; in addition, 352 $\frac{1}{20}$ shares had been transferred to government officials for exploitation (*bahreh bardārī*) by them. The report pressed for a survey of the land as a prerequisite of any reform. It pointed out that a partial survey was made in 1314/1935–6, and showed the difference between the number of shares as surveyed and the number actually transferred. It alleged that it was not unintentional that no use was made of the maps prepared in 1314/1935–6. It recommended that (1) no more transfers of land should take place until a survey was made, (2) a local commission composed of the governor and heads of the local Offices of Agriculture and Justice should meet weekly to deal with minor complaints; and (3) an attempt should be made to estimate the area held in excess of shares officially allocated and the government's share levied on this. Implicitly it was implied that shares held by government officials should be confiscated. It appears that the Ministry of Finance took some action on the lines of (2) and (3) above; this led merely to an increase in the number and shrillness of complaints. Moreover, it was alleged that the local Finance Office made further transfers of land to government officials.

Another report about the same date, namely, 20th Tīr 1323 (July 1944), gave a detailed description of the alleged misconduct of government officials, and listed the shares held by government officials in their own names with the date of transfer or sale from 1311/1932–3 to 1323/1944–5. This list agreed substantially with the list mentioned above. Late in 1324/1946 a commission was formed at the instance of the Ministry of the Interior. It included representatives from the Ministries of Finance, Agriculture, and Health, the gendarmerie, and the Land Registration Office. The report of this commission, submitted to the Prime Minister, recommended that a commission should be sent to Sīstān, with full powers, and that a survey party be attached to it. This proposal was reiterated in several other ministerial reports dated from late 1324/1946 to mid-1325/1946. There is no record of any action having been taken.

Although over twelve years had elapsed since the original distribution no ownership documents had been issued by mid-summer 1949. The allocations of land appear to have been based on no legal contract. The only documents in the hands of the holders are the receipts for the instalments they have paid. In spite of the absence of ownership documents, however, the shares are in fact bought and sold and documents for their sale officially issued. The fact that no proper survey or measurement has been carried out materially contributes to the prevailing confusion. By the exertion of pressure and use of bribery the peasants have largely been expropriated. In many cases by interference with the distribution of water, and by withholding water, the land of the peasants has been made valueless. The holder has thus been forced to sell out at a low price or has merely abandoned the land, which has then been usurped. Further, in 1948 when famine conditions prevailed shares were sold for nominal sums. As a result of these various developments a great deal of Sīstān is once more in the hands of large landowners.

Not only the agriculturalists have been subject to extortion. The cattle-breeders and fishermen have also suffered. The former graze their cattle in the reed-beds of the Hāmūn. Grazing dues (*ḥaqq ul-marta'*) are paid to the government at the rate of 2 rs. (approx. 2¾*d.*) per head of cattle per annum. In recent years (1946 onwards), however, the pastures and reed-beds are alleged to have been usurped by the *sardārs* and others. The land has, in some cases, been rented from the Finance Office on the pretext of turning it into arable land, for which, in fact, it is unsuitable. The rent to be paid to the Finance Office for the exploitation of the land was to be one-third of the produce. Since, however, no crops were raised no rent was paid. What in many cases happened was that those who had leased the lands on the pretext of turning them into arable lands in fact did not take steps to do this, but instead let the land at a higher rate to the cattle-breeders, from whom the 2 rs. per head of cattle was still collected by the government. Similarly, tracts of alluvial land along the shores of the Hāmūn are said to have been acquired by dubious means and under dubious pretexts by the *sardārs* and others from the Finance Office. Formerly the fishermen numbered some 800 families. At the present day they probably do not exceed 400.

It would appear from the above that the attempt by the government to encourage peasant proprietorship, and to decrease the influence of the *sardārs* and local notables, and thereby to increase the productivity and prosperity of Sīstān, has failed dismally. The present standard of living in Sīstān is probably as low as anywhere else in Persia or lower; the cattle-breeders and fishermen are among the most primitive communities in the country. The land, in spite of its potential fertility, is not fully exploited or well cultivated. Disease, especially trachoma and syphilis, is rife. The use of opium in the form of *shīreh*[1] is widespread. A general air of dereliction prevails. The population of the area would appear to be decreasing. In 1948 local difficulties were added to by the fact that the normal flow of water from Afghānistān to Sīstān was interfered with; drought and famine was the result. The fundamental reason for the decay of Sīstān, its poverty and its depopulation must, however, be sought in the oppression of the *sardārs*, the malpractices of government officials, inadequate control of irrigation, absence of health services, and the fact that the peasant, having no security of tenure or title to the land, is not prepared to undertake any improvement of it.

Khūzistān

After Sīstān the most important concentration of *khāliṣeh* is to be found in Khūzistān. The properties here fall into two classes: the pre-Riẓā Shāh *khāliṣeh* and the Riẓā Shāh *khāliṣeh*, the latter deriving mainly from the confiscation of Shaykh Khazʿal's properties. According to Najm ul-Mulk in Qājār times the land and water of Havīzeh, Ahvāz, Fallāḥīyeh, Muḥammareh (Khurramshahr), and Rām Hurmuz, and of virtually the whole of Khūzistān were *khāliṣeh*.[2] Part of these properties was sold up in late Qājār times. At the present day there are still considerable areas of *khāliṣeh* between Shuʿayb and Ahvāz, in Dashti Mīshān, in the Khurramshahr–Abādān area, two areas in the Dizfūl district, namely, Chughāmīsh and Ijayrūb (Gayrūb), two villages south of Shūshtar, some areas in the Kūhgīlūyeh (which have been usurped by the Boir Aḥmadī) and some properties in the plain south of the

[1] A preparation made from the residue of opium.
[2] M.F.A., No. 725, *Safar Nāmehyi ʿArabistān*, f. 279.

Kūhgīlūyeh, including Tilahū, Mangalū, and Hindījān. In the last-named place the government work the land directly; elsewhere *khāliṣeh* properties are leased. In some areas the rents are fixed annually by a *mumaiyiz*.

The conditions and terms of the leases for *khāliṣeh* in the Ahvāz area are said to vary considerably. The salient points in a lease for a farm in the neighbourhood of Kūt ʿAbdullāh, dated November 1945, were as follows: In the first four-year period the government would make no charges; in the second four-year period it would take 8 per cent on all crops, *ṣayfī* or *shatvī*, and on trees; in the third period 10 per cent, in the fourth 12 per cent, and in the fifth 15 per cent. The lessee undertook to change the crop to money at the government rate, to erect a pump capable of irrigating the area, and to complete these installations during the first four-year period. The government could renew the lease after twenty years. If it did not the trees, gardens, and machinery belonged to the lessee and he undertook to continue to pay 15 per cent. He could, however, sell his rights to these. All else, buildings, canals, etc., belonged to the state.

Much of the *khāliṣeh daym* land is in the *de facto*, but not *de jure*, possession of the Arabs. Many of the remaining areas have been handed over to new owners as a result of the laws of Farvardīn 1306 (March–April 1927) and 16th Farvardīn 1314 (April 1935). Further regulations for the transfer of *khāliṣeh* in Khūzistān were issued by the Council of Ministers on 16th Ābān 1326 (November 1947).

The main intention of the regulations of 1306/1927 was apparently to increase cultivation and to encourage peasant proprietorship. Preference was to be given, other things being equal, to local peasants. Full rights of ownership, however, were not granted. If the holder did not cultivate the land within one year the grant lapsed; further, the land could be resumed by the state if the public interest so demanded and the transfer of the right to cultivate the land was forbidden if to a foreigner and required the Department of Finance's approval if to a Persian subject. One-fifth or one-tenth of the produce, according to the situation of the land, was to be paid by way of land tax. The regulations of the law of 1314/1935 provided for the transfer of land to individuals or companies who were prepared to irrigate the land by means of pumps. The size of the holdings was limited to 2½ times the area which could be irrigated by the pump the holder undertook to install. The holdings were to become the private property of the holders, but the transfer of the land during the first three years required the sanction of the Ministry of Finance. The regulations of 1326/1947 are also concerned with the transfer of land to persons prepared to irrigate the land by the instalment of pumps. Preference was to be given to local cultivators but only providing that they filed their applications within a period of six months of the date of issue of the decree. The extent of each lot was to be 3 ha. (approx. 7 acres, 200 sq. yds.). No limit was set to the number of lots which could be held by one person. Rights of ownership are left somewhat in the air by these regulations; but the right of transfer is withheld until the holders have fulfilled their undertakings concerning the cultivation of these lands. Whereas the regulations of the law of 1306/1927 state that the holders were as far as possible to sow cotton in their lands (art. 6), the regulations of 1326/1947 state that applicants were for every 100 ha. (approx. 247 acres, 528 sq. yds.) of land transferred to them within the space of five years to plant 1 ha. (approx. 2 acres, 2,280 sq. yds.) with citrus fruits and dates (art. 11). Art. 9 of the regulations for the law of 1306/1927 forbade the holders of permits to turn out the peasants from their homes or to treat them badly, whereas art. 20 of the regulations of 1326/1947 seems concerned rather to preserve the *status quo*, and states that 'the landowners are to deal with the peasants dwelling in the transferred lands on the crop-sharing basis prevailing in the area'.

The decree of 1326/1947 had not been put into operation at the time of writing. Demands for *khāliṣeh* are alleged to have been filed, mainly by landowners, merchants, and others of the wealthy classes.

In Sūsangird and Havīzeh the land is *khāliṣeh*. In 1317/1938–9 in the Sūsangird area the land was divided among the local peasants and *shaykhs*; the former were given 1 ha. (2 acres, 2,280 sq. yds.) with a title-deed, and the latter 20 ha. (49 acres, 2,042 sq. yds.) each. In some cases, however, the land given to the peasants was above flood level and therefore valueless. In this way a labour force for the *shaykhs*' allotments was obtained. In Havīzeh a similar division was made.

Other areas

Apart from Sīstān and Khūzistān, the main areas in which *khāliṣeh* are still found are Balūchistān and certain frontier districts in Āẕarbāyjān. The latter are retained in government possession for reasons of policy. They include some forty villages in Qarājeh Dāgh, and some property which formerly belonged to Shaykh Tahā in Targivar Margivar between Riẓā'īyeh and Shāpūr (Salmās). There are also some six villages in Mīāndoāb and pastures in the neighbourhood of Mount Sahand and Mughān.

In Balūchistān, as in Sīstān, the *khāliṣeh* goes back mainly to the reign of Nāṣir ud-Dīn Shāh (A.D. 1848–96). After the death of Nādir Shāh in 1747, what is now Persian Balūchistān had for a time been under the Durrānī rulers of Afghānistān. From 1795 onwards it was split up under local chieftains. Towards the middle of the nineteenth century it was brought under Persian control again. The land largely became *khāliṣeh*, its former owners having disappeared and records of their ownership not being available. At the present day the *khāliṣeh* of Balūchistān includes some property and *qanāts* in the towns of Khāsh and Zāhidān and some twenty-odd villages in the neighbourhood of Bampūr and Īrānshahr. This land is leased mainly, if not entirely, to non-local people. In the leases it is stipulated that the relations of the lessees with the peasants shall be in accordance with the prevailing custom (cf. p. 255 above).

There is little *khāliṣeh* remaining in Khurāsān; it includes the pastures of Shaṣt Darreh in the neighbourhood of Turbati Ḥaydarī, and seven shares of the water of the Azqand river. In Kurdistān, where there were formerly considerable areas of *khāliṣeh*, some of this has been sold and some usurped by neighbouring landowners. A few areas only remain. Elsewhere there are *khāliṣeh* properties, scattered throughout the various provinces, but they do not for the most part occupy large areas.

Apart from such special areas as Sīstān and Khūzistān, where there has been or is in process an attempt to distribute the *khāliṣeh* among peasant proprietors, *khāliṣeh* is administered in two main ways. Either the proceeds of the land are leased for a period of three to five years, the land (or village) being put up to tender, or the right to harvest the crop is sold each year after valuation. Where there are large areas of *khāliṣeh* the second method tends to be followed. The practice or putting up villages to tender for a short-term lease leads on the whole to bad farming and an attempt by the lessee to extract the maximum from the land without regard to its future productivity. In so far as administration is concerned and the relations between the lessee and peasants, there is little difference between *khāliṣeh* land and the estates of the large landed proprietors.[1]

Amlāk

During the later years of the reign of Riẓā Shāh there emerged another form of *khāliṣeh*, namely, the personal estates (*amlāk*) of the ruler himself. These were acquired nominally by purchase, and the title-deeds were handed over under a formal transaction, but in many cases this was merely a cloak for virtual confiscation. In some cases the holder was forced to exchange his property for property elsewhere, not always of an equivalent value. These estates were kept separate from *khāliṣeh* and administered by the

[1] See Ch. XIII.

personal bureau of the ruler. Most of Māzandarān in this way became part of the personal estates of Riẓā Shāh. Since the abdication there have been certain changes in the extent and status of these estates.

By a royal decree dated 20th Shahrīvar 1320 (September 1941) they were transferred to the state. On 12th Khurdād 1321 (2 June 1942) a law was passed for the return of these estates to their original owners. Special courts were set up to deal with cases arising under this law.

These estates, which became known as the Ceded Properties (*amlāki vā guẕārī*), were divided into four categories: (1) land bought from its former owners for a price of over 10,000 rs. (approx. £59); (2) land exchanged for estates elsewhere; (3) land taken by usurpation; and (4) land bought from its former owners for a price less than 10,000 rs. (approx. £59).

Land in classes (3) and (4) is now mainly in the possession of its former owners with or without the issue of a formal decree to that effect. Where a decree has not been issued, the case has to be referred to the courts. Once a decree has been issued in favour of the former landowner the land is removed from the register of *amlāk*. If the decision is in favour of the crown, the land is taken back together with the income for the past year or years when it was in the possession of the claimant. Such cases are relatively few in number. Land in classes (1) and (2) has to be referred to the courts. If a decision is given in favour of the crown the land becomes *khāliṣeh*. Possibly some 90 per cent of the land which fell into these two classes has been settled. Notable exceptions are the estates of the Khalʿatbarī family and the Vālī of Pushti Kūh. Some 170 cases, involving areas of different sizes, have been settled in favour of the crown. In order to make a claim for the return of land in class (2) the claimant has to be in possession of the land which he received in exchange for his original estate. This land when returned to the crown, if the case is decided in favour of the claimant, becomes *khāliṣeh*.

The latest development with regard to the Ceded Properties is contained in the law of 20th Tīr 1328 (11 July 1949), under which those estates which had not yet been recognized as private property and were not *sub judice* reverted to the reigning *shāh*, and were to be constituted into a *vaqf* for the Pahlavī family and the income therefrom devoted to charitable objects. Moreover, those estates which had been recognized as the undisputed property of the state, and any estates concerning which the relevant courts might give a decision in favour of the state subsequently, were similarly to revert to the reigning *shāh*.[1]

[1] On 27 January 1951 it was reported in the British press that the *shāh* had

Quruq

Lastly, there is a category of land known as *quruq*, i.e. royal hunting preserves. This class of land is not extensive. There is some in the neighbourhood of Tehrān which dates back to the reign of Nāṣir ud-Dīn Shāh (1848–96).[1] The grazing rights of the villagers in this area are limited to a certain number of flocks. Outsiders are not allowed to graze their flocks in the *quruq*.

ordered all the crown lands he had inherited from his father to be distributed among peasants. It was asserted that the lands would be sold on favourable long-term conditions and that the money received would be spent in productive purposes and on the formation of agricultural companies to benefit the peasants. The annual revenue from these lands, which included some 800 villages, was alleged to exceed £500,000. It is interesting to observe that such a procedure would appear to be contrary to the provisions of the Civil Code, since the land had meanwhile been made into *vaqf*, though perhaps authority for such action can be found in the earlier Shīʿī authorities (see above, p. 230).

[1] See also p. 154

CHAPTER XIII

THE LARGE LANDED PROPRIETORS

The relations between landlord and tenant in the forms of land-holding discussed in the previous two chapters, *vaqf* and *khāliṣeh*, do not differ materially from those prevailing in the large landed estates. Before, however, discussing the relations between landlord and tenant, it is necessary to describe the position of the landed proprietors. These can be broadly divided into large landed proprietors and peasant proprietors with various intermediary holdings, the small landowner merging into the more prosperous class of peasant proprietor. It will have been seen from Part I that whereas the power and privileges of the landowning class have been relatively constant over a long period, its composition has undergone many changes. From time to time it has incorporated new elements into its ranks and lost others.

Never, however, has a stable landed aristocracy, transmitting its estates in their entirety from generation to generation, emerged. The principal reasons for this are twofold. First, the nature of society and the Islamic law of inheritance[1] militates against it. Subdivision inevitably occurs within a few generations. Of necessity, therefore, with some exceptions, notably in the tribal areas where leadership derives from the tribe in the first instance and only secondly, if at all, from land, the modern landowning class is of relatively recent growth. The same has been true of the landowning class of any given period in the last thousand years or so. It is misleading, therefore, to compare the landed aristocracy of Persia to the former landed aristocracy of Britain or any other Western European country. Secondly, conditions of recurrent anarchy and repeated dynastic changes have also prevented the emergence of a stable landed aristocracy. The rise of the Pahlavī dynasty has been no exception to the general rule that a new dynasty is accompanied by a change in the composition of the landowning class. The old landed proprietors and the tribal *khāns*, in so far as they were also landowners, tended under Riẓā Shāh to lose their land, on the one hand by confiscation to the state and on the other to the rising class of merchants and contractors, to the new bureaucracy, and to the military classes, all of whom began to acquire land both for its economic value and perhaps even more for the political power and social prestige which its ownership conferred, considerations to which these classes were especially susceptible.

[1] See above, p. 203.

The change in modern times, however, has not been limited simply to a change in the composition of the landowning class: there has been some change also in the nature of land ownership, in the position of the landowner and in the size of his estates. The general trend of events since the grant of the Constitution in 1906, beginning with the abolition of *tuyūl* and continuing with changes in the administration,[1] has been in fact to alter the status of the large landed proprietor from that of a petty territorial prince to that of an ordinary landowner. The change has not been, as pointed out in Chapter VIII, an abrupt one: it began in the early Constitutional Period, and culminated in the reign of Riẓā Shāh.[2]

In addition to the reduction in the power of the large landed proprietors, there has also been a tendency towards a reduction in the size of their estates. This was brought about partly by confiscation, as described in Chapter VIII. On the other hand, it is doubtful whether it can be said that the total area owned by the large landed proprietors has sensibly decreased. In so far as the confiscated lands became *khāliṣeh* while other areas became the personal estates or *amlāk* of Riẓā Shāh, there was a decrease, but this was offset to some extent by the distribution of certain areas of existing *khāliṣeh* to those who had been deprived of their property elsewhere. Moreover, in the case of both *khāliṣeh* and *amlāk*, with the exception of the areas subject to the experiment of division among peasant proprietors in Sīstān, Khūzistān, and Luristān,[3] the regime to which they were subject differed little in its essentials from the regime of the estates of the large landed proprietors, the latter being replaced in the case of *khāliṣeh* by the state, and in the case of *amlāk* by Riẓā Shāh. Further, in many areas there has been a tendency—not perhaps a very marked one—for the land of peasant proprietors to be bought up by large landed proprietors or by new recruits to the landowning class. What change there has been thus probably consists rather in a general diminution in the size of the areas held by the individual landed proprietors than in a diminution in the total area held by them.

Riẓā Shāh's policy of land confiscation had, moreover, not only direct but also indirect effects upon land ownership. It weakened the position and power of the tribal *khāns* and reduced their economic status to such an extent that they were often forced to sell property. For example, the Bakhtīārī properties in certain parts of Khūzistān were in part sold when the Bakhtīārī fortunes declined under Riẓā Shāh. The Bakhtīārī leaders were formerly large landowners in the Dizfūl area. At the present day the estates

[1] See Ch. VIII.

[2] Since the abdication there has been, in certain areas, a movement in the opposite direction.

[3] See Ch. XII.

held by them in that area have decreased in number and the size of the landed estates in the area has considerably declined, the landowners for the most part owning lots in several villages rather than one village outright. Similarly, in the Rām Hurmuz area the former Bakhtīārī owners have been largely bought out, though they still own a quarter of the land in the neighbourhood. Some thirty villages in Maḥallāt, Gulpāyagān, and Khumayn, which formerly belonged to Bakhtīārī owners, have also largely been sold. In the Bihbahān area there have been similar changes in land ownership in relatively recent times. The newcomers are mainly persons who have made their money in trade. Similarly, in the province of Kirmān the amount of land held by the landlord of relatively long standing is decreasing in comparison with that held by merchants and *nouveaux riches*.

Further changes in land ownership tend to come about whenever there is a series of bad years. Speculators and those susceptible to the social and political advantages offered by the possession of land frequently take the opportunity offered by such occasions to buy up the property of peasants or small landowners who have insufficient reserves to tide them over the bad years.

The landowning class at the present day can roughly be divided into the following groups. First, there are those whose landholdings go back several generations. In many cases it will be found that their family fortunes were laid by government service, which enabled a preceding generation in the course of its duties to acquire local influence and land, the family subsequently being transformed into a landowning family. Secondly, there are the tribal *khāns* who have acquired by purchase, government grant, or hereditary transmission estates in or on the outskirts of their tribal territory. Thirdly, there are the religious classes, who became an important element in the landowning class in Ṣafavid times.[1] In certain areas of the country, notably Āẕarbāyjān and the neighbourhood of Iṣfahān, they still own considerable areas of land. Many members of the religious classes also hold land in the province of Kirmān. In some cases the fortunes of these members of the religious classes have been laid by their holding the office of *mutavallī* of some *vaqf* property. Fourthly, there are the relatively new recruits to the landowning classes, who may be broadly divided into three main groups. First are the bailiffs (*mubāshirs* and *kadkhudās*) of the large landed proprietors who have used or misused the influence of their position to acquire estates for themselves. There are many such instances. Secondly, there are government officials, civil and military, who have acquired property in the areas where they have held office. This applies to all ranks from

[1] See above, p. 115.

the sergeant or private in the former *amnīyeh* or gendarmerie to governors-general. Thirdly, there are the merchants and contractors who have invested their money in land for economic reasons or in order to acquire political or social prestige.

The attitude to the land among landowners in some measure varies according to the class from which they spring. In general land is looked upon as a source of gain, whether in the form of social prestige, political power, or economic advantage. The extent to which this attitude is tempered by any measure of responsibility for the well-being of the land and its inhabitants would, broadly, appear to be proportionate to the length of landowning tradition in the family, though it would be a misrepresentation to suggest that this is always the case. There are oppressive landowners among those whose period of tenure has been longest, as well as enlightened landowners among newcomers. Among all types of landowner the tendency to prefer extent to quality is widespread. Thus it would probably not be unfair to say that the average landowner would rather own several villages in bad condition than one or a few in good condition. This arises partly from the fact that political power and social prestige were in the past and are still, though to a lesser extent, derived from the possession of land as such rather than primarily from the income derived therefrom. Among landowners of long standing the sale of land is, on the whole, regarded as a discreditable operation, and is avoided as long as possible. The following is an illustration of the attitude to land of the older type of landowner who tends to regard the possession of land as a matter of social prestige. Financial pressure made it necessary for the owners of the village of Raḥmatābād near Rafsinjān to sell part of their property. The village, like most villages, consisted of 6 *dāng*. These were arbitrarily increased to $7\frac{1}{2}$ *dāng* and $1\frac{1}{2}$ *dāng* were sold. In this way the original owners still retained 6 *dāng*, the normal equivalent of a whole village.

Since the interest of the landowner of long standing in his land is relatively permanent, self-interest dictates that a limit should be set to his demands upon the peasants and cultivators. If he reduces them to absolute penury, at best his own income will suffer on a long-term view, and at worst the peasants will emigrate—and in most areas there is a deficiency rather than a surplus of peasants. Moreover, in a bad year—and bad years in Persia are of frequent occurrence—the landowner who has a relatively permanent stake in the land, although he may squeeze his peasants to the limit in a good year, will, out of self-interest if no more, tide them over bad times by the provision of seed and advances, or draught animals if necessary. It is in bad years that the difference between the landowner with a permanent stake in the land and the newcomer is most clearly seen. The latter, particularly if he is drawn from the merchant or contractor class, is all too prone to seek a short-term advantage and to exploit the land and its inhabitants without regard to its future productivity or their well-being.

Broadly speaking, however, between the landowner as a class, no matter what his origin, and the peasant there is a wide gulf. In no sense is there a spirit of co-operation or a feeling of being engaged in a mutual enterprise. The attitude is on the whole, though not without exceptions, one of mutual suspicion. The landowner regards the peasant virtually as a drudge, whose sole function is to provide him with his profits and who will, if treated with anything but severity, cheat him of his due. It is widely believed in land-owning circles that anything above the barest consideration of the well-being of the peasant would be taken by the latter as a sign of weakness and as a result he would not pay the dues of the land-owner. Education, better hygiene, and improved housing for the peasant are similarly regarded as unnecessary, except by a minority of the more enlightened landowners. On the other hand, the peasant himself is highly conservative and resists tenaciously any efforts to change his age-long habits, whether as regards his living conditions or traditional agricultural methods. In order to see the relation of the landowner to the peasant in its true perspective, it must be viewed against the background of Persian society in general. When so seen it will not perhaps compare unfavourably with that of the employer to the employee in industry or with the relation of the landowner to the peasant in pre-Constitution days. The landowner almost as much as the peasant is a victim of the social and political system under which he lives and the all-pervading insecurity which goes with it. However, it would be mere casuistry to attempt to defend the relations which exist between the landowner and the peasant merely on the grounds that the position of the peasant is at least no worse, and perhaps better, than that of certain other sections of the community.

In recent years a major change in the economic field has taken place which materially affects the position of land and landowners in the general framework of society. Whereas in the past land offered, in addition to its social and political value, a field for economic investment which, on the whole, gave as high a return as other fields, or even a higher one, this is no longer the case. The return on large landed properties in most areas is probably not more than 10 per cent, or, when grain prices are high, perhaps 15 per cent, excluding certain districts situated near the frontiers where advantage can be taken, from time to time, of higher prices prevailing in the neighbouring countries and grain can be smuggled over the frontier. It is alleged in some quarters that profits on land in Āẕarbāyjān for the last eight years or so have been 15–20 per cent. It is not easy to estimate the truth of this but it would seem that certain landowners in Āẕarbāyjān have made relatively high profits in spite of the political troubles in the area. In Kurdistān, on the other hand, the capital value of villages is estimated at ten times the annual income from all sources. This is probably typical of other provinces also. In 1945 the Agricultural Bank in general based its transactions on an estimated dividend of 10 per cent on capital expenditure.[1] The return to be obtained from large-scale commerce in recent years has been higher.

Among the landowning class in Persia there are still many rich men, but their fortunes do not, as a whole, unless they are supplemented from other sources, compare favourably with the fortunes made by contractors and big merchants in recent years. Further, in spite of the apparent prosperity of many of the landowners, it is alleged that there is widespread indebtedness among them. This may well be true and arises in part, in the case of the landowner of relatively long standing, from the somewhat patriarchal fashion in which he lives. This type of landowner has a host of dependants of one kind or another whom he virtually keeps. Further, because it is the tradition of his class to do so, he lives on a grand scale. Extravagance is a virtue, economy unbecoming to his status. Moreover, in addition to the expenses of the upkeep of his dependants, he is forced by his position to undertake other, but no less heavy, expenses. For example, the entertainment of the gendarmerie and other government officials is a very considerable item in his budget. Further, it is essential for the landowner to maintain constant touch with the capital himself or through a representative, or at least with the provincial capital, if he lives in one of the remoter provinces. The expenditure involved thus is virtually unavoidable because failure to watch over his own interests in this way may result in all kinds of burdens being imposed on him or on his peasants. It is true that the more powerful landowners in attempting to secure their own interests often go to lengths which can hardly be regarded as legitimate, and seek to obtain the appointment of their own nominees to local positions of influence, and in some cases to reduce them to the position of mere puppets. Such proceedings cannot be defended, but, in the absence of an efficient civil service with traditions of integrity and public service, it is not entirely surprising that they should arise. The country is still largely administered on a personal basis. The rise

[1] As stated in Ch. XII (p. 240) the minimum purchase price of the *khāliṣeh* round Tehrān which was to be sold under the law of 20th Ābān 1316 (November 1937) was to be ten times the average annual value of the crops for the three years immediately preceding the sale.

of one group is liable to result in a change of officials right through the administration, often followed by a working off of old scores and personal vendettas. Since the struggle between the various conflicting groups and interests is the keynote of Persian society, and since power and money are ends in themselves, it is natural that the landowner should use all the means at his disposal to defend what he conceives to be his interests.

The position is further aggravated by the rivalry between factions, which has been a characteristic feature of Persian life throughout history, and has contributed in no small measure to the country's misfortunes. While perhaps more marked in rivalry between towns and more still between different quarters in the same town, factions are not by any means absent from rural life. They range from major factions between landowners who may control large tracts of country, to minor factions which tend to split even the smallest villages. It is probably in the more remote areas that this rivalry between factions is to be seen at its height. At best the factions are forced to defend themselves in order to prevent their rivals gaining the upper hand, and at worst they adopt the offensive and despoil their rivals. Where the landowners are sufficiently strong to influence the appointment of government officials, the securing of office by the nominee of one group is frequently followed by the despoliation of the villages of the other group. As long as such a situation is likely to arise it is clear that the landowner cannot remain indifferent to the appointment of local officials.

The Sanandaj area of Kurdistān, for example, is rent by two major factions. In other areas of Kurdistān factional strife is not absent but partakes rather of the nature of tribal warfare.[1] The situation in Sīstān and Qā'ināt is not dissimilar to that in Kurdistān. Here again there are two main factions, one centred in Bīrjand and the other in Zābul. The situation differs, however, from the situation in Kurdistān in that both factions belong to the same family and outwardly their relations are cordial. The difference in tactics employed by the two factions is significant. During the reign of Nāṣir ud-Dīn Shāh (1848–96), Mīr ʿAlam Khān was entrusted with the campaign to subdue Rafīʿ Khān, who had rebelled in 1264–5/1848–9, and with the restoration of order in Qā'ināt. He was successful in this and meanwhile established his own position as Amīr of Qā'ināt. Since then the most influential family in Qā'ināt has been the ʿAlam family. In due course Bīrjand and the neighbourhood became the seat of the late Shoukat ul-Mulk, while his brothers, Ḥisām ud-Douleh and Ṣamṣām ud-Douleh, succeeded to property in the Zābul area.

[1] See Ch. XV.

Shoukat ul-Mulk, who was the leading member of the family during his lifetime, exercised his influence in what is now known as the Persian province of Balūchistān by the careful selection of officials—mainly Bīrjandīs—loyal to himself, whereas the other branch of the family sought to acquire and maintain influence largely through land. In the first instance the use of political power was broadly in the interests of the land, whereas in the latter case it conforms to the normal pattern, land being treated as an instrument to attain and to hold political power, which is regarded as an end in itself.

Arāk also is split into two mutually hostile factions led by the Muḥsinīs and Bayāts respectively. The rivalry between these two factions also goes back several years.

In Khūzistān factional strife is found throughout most of the area. In some cases, as in Bihbahān, it takes the ancient form of strife between the quarters, between Qanavātīs and Bihbahānīs. In so far as the local townspeople are the main landowners of the district, this factional strife extends also to the rural districts. In some parts of the province the opposition is between Arab and Persian, and is a legacy from the oppression which the Arabs have suffered in the past at the hands of Persian officials.

In Fārs the standing opposition is between Turk[1] and Tājīk (i.e. non-Turk), and between settled and semi-settled.

Even in the peasant-proprietor villages factional strife is by no means unknown and militates against the prosperity of the area and the solidarity of its inhabitants in the face of pressure from outside, whether economic, political, or of any other kind. In some of the villages on the southern borders of the Kūhi Kargis, for example, the population is split internally into bitterly hostile factions and part of their energies is wasted in factional strife.

The almost complete absence of statistics makes it impossible to estimate with accuracy the total area of land held by the large landed proprietors in comparison with other forms of land-holding, or even to guess at the average size of the large landed estates. For the most part properties where registered are registered only with a statement of their boundaries, the actual area which they occupy not being measured. Further, although all land held by the class of large landed proprietors is broadly subject to the same regime as regards internal administration and the relations between the landowner and the peasantry, there are certain differences in the nature of the holdings. In the first place there are the large landed proprietors, known as *ʿumdeh mālikīn*; their estates range from single villages to several villages, the number of which, in certain exceptional cases, is alleged to run into three figures. These

[1] i.e. the Turkī-speaking element of the population.

villages tend to be consolidated in one area, but in some cases the landowner may hold land in widely separated areas. A similar scattered distribution of property is to be found in some cases among those landowners who have been given estates out of *khāliṣeh* land, in whole or part compensation for their own estates which were taken over by the government or the ruler for one reason or another. Secondly, there are the landowners who own shares in several villages. Technically they are known as *khurdeh mālikīn*, but the total aggregate of their shares is such as to put them in the class of large landowners.[1] Thirdly, there are jointly owned estates. For example, when a large landed estate is transmitted by inheritance, it frequently happens that villages become the joint property of the original owner's heirs. This form of holding is known as *mushāʿ*. The individual shares are not delimited, each of the joint owners having a right to a specific share of the total proceeds. In such cases it usually happens that one of the joint owners is appointed by the rest to administer the property.[2] This form of holding is technically known as *khurdeh mālik*, but it nevertheless conforms to the general pattern of the large landed estate, with this difference, that since any major changes in the administration of the estate require the sanction of all the joint owners, measures involving change are more difficult to bring about than in an estate owned by one person.[3] Where a village is jointly owned in Kirmān, a proportion of the harvest is taken from each of the joint owners and placed in a common store to defray expenses in connexion with the cleaning and repair of *qanāts*. In some cases, however, this measure is dispensed with and the joint owners merely draw bills on one another when necessary.

Broadly speaking, large landed estates are found less commonly in the areas immediately round the large towns and in the hill districts. In Arāk it is estimated that 75 per cent of the land is owned by large landed proprietors. The majority of these own some five to six villages each; a few own as many as twenty to thirty. In some cases, however, the landowner does not own the whole of a village but merely the major part of it, the remainder

[1] The term *khurdeh mālik* is somewhat misleading in that it is also used to designate the genuine peasant proprietor.

[2] Such a practice is also frequently adopted when the shares of the various heirs are delimited (*mafrūz*).

[3] When a *mushāʿ* village is delimited for the first time this is done in the following way in Kirmān: the village is divided into 6 *dāng* which are shared out by lot among the various owners, the shares differing in size in so far as the land varies in quality. Suppose a village has thirty owners, these will be divided into five groups according to the number of *ḥabbeh* which they own so that the *ḥabbeh* owned by each group totals sixteen, and the land is then divided among them.

being either owned by peasant proprietors or *vaqf* land. Nevertheless, the fact that the major part of a village is owned by one man gives it the character of an *arbābī* village and usually enables that individual virtually to control the affairs of the village. There are several families of large landed proprietors, of whom the Bayāts and the Muḥsinīs own the largest properties. The rise of the Muḥsinī family as landowners goes back some two generations to the time of Ḥājjī Āqā Muḥsin, a local *mujtahid*, who during the course of his career succeeded in acquiring very considerable properties, amounting to some 5,000 *kharvār* of land.[1] Most of this property was constituted into a 'personal' *vaqf* and the income divided among some twenty-five descendants of the first generation. In 1945 three of these survived and one of them held some thirty villages.[2] Burūjird, which borders on Arāk, is almost entirely owned by large landed proprietors.

In Āẕarbāyjān land ownership is mainly in the hands of large landed proprietors. In some cases the number of villages held by one proprietor is very considerable. Riẓā'īyeh is an exception to the general rule: in this area peasant proprietors are found as well as large landed proprietors. In the Qarājeh Dāgh area the land is mainly owned by large landed proprietors either as *'umdeh mālikīn* or as *khurdeh mālikīn*.

Land ownership in Balūchistān is also mainly in the hands of large landed proprietors, who are for the most part Balūch *sardārs*.[3]

Qā'ināt is chiefly in the hands of large landed proprietors. A good many of the villages are owned *in toto* by one person, and others are held jointly by two or more large landed proprietors.

The relatively prosperous *bulūk* of Burkhvār to the north and west of Iṣfahān is technically mainly *khurdeh mālik*, but the character of the area is rather that of a large landed proprietor area. It contains some thirty to forty large villages, including Doulatābād, Dastgird (Dastjird), Gaz (Jaz), Sīn, and Gurgāb. Each of these villages has attached to it a number of hamlets (*mazāri'*), which are owned by the principal landowner or landowners of the village. Sīn and Gurgāb are also owned by large landed proprietors, and Doulatābād is mainly so owned. Gaz and Dastgird, on the other hand, are split up among a large number of owners.

In other districts round Iṣfahān land ownership is predominantly in the hands of large landed proprietors. Najafābād, although technically *khurdeh mālik*, is mainly in the hands of persons who

[1] Approx. 54,553 bushels (of 60 lb.). Assuming some 5 bushels are sown per acre, this would amount to some 10,910 acres.

[2] As stated in Ch. XI, in so far as administration goes, land constituted into a personal *vāqf* differs little from an ordinary large landed estate.

[3] See Ch. XV.

belong to the class of large landed proprietors. The size of the landed estates round Iṣfahān is alleged to have decreased in recent years.

In Fārs land is owned predominantly by large landed proprietors. In most areas the landowners are absentees; Iṣṭahbānāt is a notable exception to this. It is not perhaps fortuitous that it appeared (in 1949) to be exceptionally well cared for and flourishing.

Khurāsān is said to be mainly *khurdeh mālik*, but although there are a good many areas owned in relatively small lots, genuine peasant proprietors are not numerous. The predominant land tenure of the province is that of the large landed proprietor. The fact that much of the land, as stated in Chapter XI, is *vaqf* for the shrine of the Imām Riẓā in Mashhad does not alter the character of the province, since in so far as administration goes these properties conform to the general pattern of the large landed estate. Sabzavār and Nayshāpūr are alleged to be largely *khurdeh mālik*, and some genuine peasant proprietorship is found in the area.

Kurdistān is almost entirely in the hands of large landed proprietors. In the neighbourhood of Sanandaj there are two main landowning families, various members of which hold considerable numbers of villages or parts of villages. In northern Kurdistān round Mahābād the Kurdish tribal *khāns* are the main landowners.

Khūzistān is predominantly in the hands of large landed proprietors. Kirmān is almost entirely owned by large landed proprietors, whether as *ʿumdeh mālikīn* or as *khurdeh mālikīn*. In the Kirmānshāh area, although there may be some small landowners and peasant proprietors round the towns and in the more remote districts, land is, nevertheless, mainly owned by large landed proprietors. A few of the properties are extremely large and some include over fifty villages.

Sāveh, which is the centre of a relatively important agricultural area, is seven-tenths *khurdeh mālik*, but not mainly of the peasant-proprietorship type.

In the neighbourhood of Tehrān, where some large and valuable estates are to be found, the predominant form of ownership is that of the large landed proprietor.

The Pushti Kūh area of Yazd is entirely owned by large landed proprietors, though the relative size of the estates is probably less than that of the large landed properties in areas in the west and north-west of Persia.

In an unpublished report prepared by engineer Khwājeh Nūrī for the Seven-Year Plan on the ownership of villages and the connexion between this and the production of wealth, the distribution of large landed properties in various regions is analysed on the basis of figures for agricultural production furnished to the Department of Statistics for 1326/1947–8. He divides the country into twelve areas throughout each of which, he alleges, relatively similar agricultural conditions prevail:

1. Āẕarbāyjān, including Mākū, Khūy, Marāgheh, Riẓā'īyeh, Mahābād, Ardabīl, and Khalkhāl.
2. Kurdistān and Luristān, including Sunqur, Sanandaj, Bījār, Shahābād, Īlām, Hamadān, Malā'ir, Kirmānshāh, Qaṣri Shīrīn,[1] Burūjird, Khurramābād, and Zanjān.
3. Khūzistān, including Ahvāz, Khurramshahr, Ābādān, Bihbahān, Sūsangird, Shūshtar, and Dizfūl.
4. Fārs, including Ābādeh, Shīrāz, Kāzirūn, Bushire, Fasā, and Jahrum.[2]
5. The Gulf Ports, including Lār, Bandar 'Abbās, and Chāh Bahār.
6. Kirmān, including Bam, Jīruft, Sīrjān, Rafsinjān, and the district (*bakhsh*) of Shahri Bābak of Yazd.
7. The *kavīr*, including Zāhidān, Sarāvān, Īrānshahr, and Yazd (excluding Shahri Bābak).
8. Southern Khurāsān, including Zābul, Bīrjand, Gunābād, and Firdous (Tūn).
9. Northern Khurāsān, including Mashhad, Turbati Ḥaydarī, Kāshmar, Sabzavār, Qūchān, Bujnūrd, and Nayshāpūr.
10. The southern littoral of the Caspian Sea, including Gurgān, Sārī, Shāhī, Bābul, Āmul, Noushahr, Shahsavār, Lāhījān, Rasht, Pahlavī, Fūmināt, and Ṭavālish.
11. Central areas other than the *kavīr*, including Tehrān, Qazvīn, Sāveh, Arāk, Qumm, Kāshān, Gulpāyagān, Maḥallāt, Iṣfahān, Dārāb, Shahri Kurd, Shahriẓā, and the districts of Damāvand and Ayvāni Kay (in the sub-area or *shahristān* of Damāvand).[3]
12. Cities north of the *kavīr*, including Shāhrūd, Dāmghān, Simnān, and the districts of Fīrūzkūh and Garmsar in the sub-area of Damāvand.

From the statistics given by Khwājeh Nūrī a significant point emerges. The left-hand column in the table below gives the twelve areas in the order of their percentage of large landed properties, beginning with the highest; the right-hand column shows the average annual rainfall.

[1] Qaṣri Shīrīn seems in fact to have little in common with Hamadān.

[2] Here again the *sardsīr* and the *garmsīr* are classed together, Ābādeh, for example, having little in common with Kāzirūn or Bushire.

[3] Parts of Qumm and Kāshān seem to have closer affinity with (7) or (6) than with places such as Shahri Kurd.

Area	*Annual rainfall (mm.)*	*Average rainfall (mm.)*
1	350	
9	250	500
10	900	
2	250	
3	350	265
4	250	
12	210	
11	270	270
8	160	160
5	180	165
6	150	
7	150	150

It is obvious that the land with a higher average rainfall will have a higher and more stable yield.

The common characteristic of the large landed proprietors as a class is that they are for the most part absentees. Seldom does the large landed proprietor live on his estate. In cases where he owns several villages situated in widely separated areas he is inevitably an absentee. In many cases he lives in the capital or provincial capital, and perhaps never sets foot in the more remote of his properties. The nearer ones he may visit at harvest time to collect his dues, after which he returns once more to the town whence he came. Or he may merely send his agent to perform this task for him. There are, however, landowners who spend the major part or a considerable part of their time on their properties. Where this is the case, greater prosperity and better relations between the landowner and the peasantry are frequently found to prevail.

Where the landowner is an absentee his affairs are entrusted to a bailiff who often practises extortion on the peasants. The reasons for this are many. On the one hand, the bailiff is tempted to feather his own nest. That he is often able to do so is shown by the frequency with which bailiffs become themselves petty landowners. Further, where the landowner is an absentee the peasant has little chance of obtaining redress against the extortion of a bailiff. On the other hand, where the bailiff watches closely over the interests of his master, there is a tendency to consider him, perhaps unfairly, a hard task-master. Clearly, moreover, since in such a case his main concern is to raise the income of his master and thereby render his services the more valuable, he is reluctant to make concessions which the owner of the land himself might make. Nor has he the same permanent interest in the land as the owner. In addition to these tendencies the bailiff is on the whole less likely than his master to be able to stand up to undue pressure from local officials. In Kurdistān the large landed properties are mainly administered by bailiffs. It is alleged that these often appropriate to themselves a considerable portion of the revenue of the land, sometimes becoming themselves landowners in due course. In spite of this it is said that they are seldom turned out by their masters. The practice of leasing property (see below) appears to be less common in Kurdistān than in many other areas. Some of the smaller landowners, however, let their villages.

In many cases not only is the landowner an absentee, but a third party in the shape of a rentee is interposed between him and the peasant. The landowner may well prefer to free himself of the trouble of administering his property and collecting his dues, and so he lets his property. The fact that the landowner is often forced to have recourse to somewhat doubtful practices[1] is an added inducement to the less vigorous among the landowners to lease their property. In some cases the lessee may be the local *kadkhudā*, or the landowner's own bailiff, or some other local person, living in the neighbourhood and perhaps owning a small property himself. More often, however, the lessee is not a local person, but some merchant or contractor who rents the property mainly for the economic advantage to be obtained therefrom. Such a person has no permanent interest in the property and tends to squeeze out of it what he can and then to abandon it. In other cases the lessee may make such profit out of the transaction as eventually to buy out the original owner and himself become a landowner. It sometimes happens that not only is the landowner an absentee, but the lessee also. This practice is clearly indefensible and contrary to the interests of the peasants and the land.[2]

Considerable variety of practice exists concerning the actual terms on which land is leased, depending upon the nature of the crop and the type of irrigation. A cash rent prevails in many areas such as certain parts of the Caspian Provinces, Khurāsān, Fārs, Kirmānshāh, northern Khūzistān, and the Gulf Ports. The rent for land growing winter crops in certain areas, such as Ardakān, Sabzavār, parts of Iṣfahān, Mashhad, and the Gulf Ports, and certain areas round Tehrān, and for land growing summer crops in the Tehrān area, Qazvīn and Khamseh is in many cases reckoned in kind at the rate of half the produce which would accrue to the landlord under the crop-sharing agreements prevailing locally.

The usual period for a lease is three to five years, on the assumption that during such a period an average yield, allowing for good,

[1] See above, p. 264.

[2] There is another type of renting, namely, a contract concluded between the landowner and the peasant, which does not involve the interposition of a third person. This type of rent will be discussed in Ch. XVII.

bad, and normal years, may be expected. In Arāk the normal period of a lease is three to six years, which corresponds to two periods of crop rotation.

Rents during the latter part of Riẓā Shāh's reign were chiefly in cash. Subsequently there was a reversion to payment partly, if not wholly, in kind owing to the uncertainty of the price of grain. In Āẕarbāyjān few of the large landowners work the land themselves: the common practice is to lease it for a varying number of years.

In Kullīyā'ī a good deal of the land is leased; the rent is paid in cash and kind. The term of the lease is normally three years. Leases for a longer term are rare.

In the Burkhw̱ār district some of the hamlets (*mazāriʿ*) such as Khw̱urzuk are leased. In Khurāsān, where it appears also to be a common practice to lease land, the period of lease tends to be five years. Malikābād, a small village of twelve plough-lands near Turbati Ḥaydarī, is owned by two persons. One of these also owns a large garden in the village. This together with six plough-lands was let in 1949 for five years at the rate of 75,000 rs. (approx. £441) and 75 *kharvār* (approx. 818 bushels) wheat per annum. In that year the lessee was said to have had a deficit of 30 *kharvār* (approx. 327 bushels) owing to a partial crop failure.

It is usual for a stipulation to be included in a lease to the effect that the relations of the lessee with the peasant, in so far as crop-sharing and the collection of dues are concerned, shall be in accordance with local practice. Similar conditions were laid down in Ṣafavid and Qājār times, as shown in many of the documents which have come down to us. The original intention behind this proviso may have been to safeguard the peasants in some measure from detrimental innovations, but whatever its original intention, it is difficult to regard it at the present day in any light other than as bearing witness to the conservative nature of society. Any change in established practice is viewed by landowner and peasant alike with suspicion, and should any landowner introduce in his own property measures designed to improve the lot of his own peasants and to lessen the demands made upon them, he is likely to meet with the bitter opposition of his fellow landowners.

In addition to the large landed estates which are leased, much *khāliṣeh* and *vaqf* property is in the hands of lessees.[1]

The relations between the landowners and the peasants are for the most part based on a crop-sharing agreement. In some cases, however, the land is rented by the peasant. These questions will be discussed in subsequent chapters. Occasionally it happens that the landowner or lessee works the land himself with hired labour, but this is the exception rather than the rule; in some villages,

[1] See Chs. XI and XII.

especially where the landowner is not habitually an absentee, a portion of the village land is exempted from the distribution among the crop-sharing peasants and worked by the landowner with hired labour. The payment of this labour may be—indeed usually is—partly in kind; where the labour is relatively permanent it is usually paid by a percentage of the crop. In other cases the labour is taken on only when the work is at its heaviest, for example, at harvest time.

To sum up, it would seem that although there have been changes in the economic position of the land relative to other fields of investment, and in the status of the landowner, the large landed proprietor still holds an immensely important position in society and is able to exert great influence in the political field. By far the greatest part of the country, including the most fertile areas, is in the hands of the large landed proprietors. Lastly, the traditional cleavage between landowner and peasant persists, and a strong element of conservatism running through society enables the large landowner to maintain his privileged position *vis-à-vis* the peasant.

CHAPTER XIV

PEASANT PROPRIETORS AND OTHER SMALL OWNERS

PEASANT proprietorship is found in different parts of Persia but is nowhere widely spread. It occurs alone and mixed with other types of tenure. In some areas, notably in Kirmān, it is virtually non-existent. The main reason for this is perhaps the fact that irrigation in the Kirmān province is abnormally costly: the *qanāts* for the most part are lengthy, the soil through which they flow is often soft, and the capital cost and annual repairs therefore heavy, requiring on the one hand an outlay which is beyond the pocket of the average peasant and on the other a degree of co-operation which is seldom found among them. The main concentration of peasant proprietors is probably to be found along the south-western and southern borders of the central desert, from Qumm (where the prevalent tenure is that of large landed proprietors) through Kāshān (where the prevalent tenure in the immediate neighbourhood is also that of large landed proprietors), and Ardistān, excluding Nā'īn which is mainly owned by large landed proprietors, to Yazd, stretching in the south-west through the mountain district of the Kūhi Kargis to Maymeh and Mūrchehkhwart. In the Ardistān area, with some 330 villages, the dominant tenure is that of small local landlords and peasant proprietors. This is also true of the Kūhi Kargis area, Mūrchehkhwart, and Maymeh. There is a certain amount of peasant proprietorship also in the neighbourhood of Yazd, where practice differs in that the ownership of land and water is separate.[1] Many of the villages are technically *khurdeh mālik* but owned chiefly by absentee landlords in Yazd; some, such as Mazvīrābād, Khwurmīz, Mihrīz, Dihābād (near Ardakān), and Maybud, are partly owned by peasant proprietors. In Burkhwār there is a little peasant proprietorship: thus in Gaz (Jaz), the largest village of the district, roughly half of the 12,000 inhabitants are said to be peasant proprietors. Sedih in the Linjān district of Iṣfahān, with a population of some 40,000, is predominantly owned by peasant proprietors. One-fifteenth of Qahdrījān, a village of some 10,500 persons also in Linjān, is owned by peasant proprietors, the remainder being owned by a large landed proprietor. In Firaydan there are a few Armenian peasant proprietors.

In Arāk there is little peasant proprietorship: what there is

[1] See also above, p. 220.

consists mainly of small enclaves in various villages. In Āẕarbāyjān, except in the Riẓā'īyeh area, there are few peasant proprietors. Among those villages where this type of tenure is found are Kilaybar and some villages in the immediate vicinity of Ahar in Qarājeh Dāgh. In Kurdistān also there is little peasant ownership except in the more remote areas; there are, however, occasional instances of villages held in part by peasant proprietors. In Fārs, villages owned by peasant proprietors are the exception. There are said to be some in Khafr, one village in Bayẓā, one near Dārāb, and a few in the *sarḥadd* of the Īli ʿArab. Similarly, in Balūchistān there is little land ownership of this type. There are a few such villages round Īrānshahr; Dāman is mainly owned by peasant proprietors. A few peasant proprietors are found in Qā'ināt. Kalāteh Ḥājjī near Bīrjand is wholly and Isfīdrūd partly so owned. In Khurāsān peasant proprietors are probably more widespread than in many other districts. There are some in the Sabzavār and Nayshāpūr areas, as stated above; Quzhd and Fidāfin near Kāshmar are owned by peasant proprietors; in both cases certain gardens in these two villages are owned by townspeople of Kāshmar. Similarly, part of the land in the immediate vicinity of Turbati Ḥaydarī is owned by peasant proprietors, as are certain villages in the neighbourhood, including Būrīābād, Manẓar, Dih Pā'īn and part of Ḥouẓ Surkh, and Dūghābād in Maḥvilāt. Certain other villages, including Noughān, Ṣoumʿeh, and Sabūkh, are owned in part by peasant proprietors and in part by the large landed proprietors of Turbati Ḥaydarī. There is also probably some peasant proprietorship in the more remote mountain districts of Khurāsān.

This type of tenure is not common in Khūzistān. Vays, near Ahvāz, belongs in part to peasant proprietors. Sabīli Khākī, to the north of Dizfūl on the east side of the river, is entirely owned by peasant proprietors. Under Riẓā Shāh and subsequently it was intended to encourage peasant proprietorship by the distribution of *khāliṣeh* in Khūzistān among local peasants. Such steps as have so far been taken, however, have not materially altered the general character of the province as regards land tenure. This and a similar experiment in Sīstān have been discussed in Chapter XII.

In the neighbourhood of Tehrān there are a few peasant-proprietor villages, mainly in the poorer areas, scattered among the large landed estates. For the rest, except in remote mountain areas, there is little peasant proprietorship.

In the absence of reliable and complete statistics it is impossible to estimate with any accuracy whether there has been an increase or decrease in the amount of land held by peasant proprietors. It would seem to be generally borne out by the evidence available that the peasant proprietor (as distinct from other types of smallholders) has been on the whole confined to the less fertile and more remote parts of the country. As has been pointed out, where the rainfall is relatively high the prevailing type of tenure is that of large landed proprietors,[1] which bears out the view that the most productive land tends to be held by large landed proprietors. How far this is a recent trend it is impossible to guess. The tendency for the peasant proprietor to lose land to merchants, speculators, and others after a bad year or series of bad years would seem to be relatively widespread. Merchants and others from the towns or their agents are often to be met with in the country after a bad year looking for possible bargains in land. Further, money-lending at exorbitant rates of interest by merchants and others to the peasant proprietors to tide them over bad times frequently ends in a loss of the latter's land to the money-lender. Similarly, the landowners often buy up land owned by neighbouring peasant proprietors in such circumstances. Thus Ṣārī Chaman in Qarājeh Dāgh was bought by the present owner's father from its peasant proprietors after a bad year.

There is little information concerning the actual size of the holdings of peasant proprietors. For the most part these are worked as a family concern. In the poorer areas the holdings are often too small to afford an adequate living to the family unless supplemented by income from some outside source such as casual labour on the roads, weaving (chiefly by the female members of the family), or the keeping of flocks. In Joushaqān, a peasant-proprietor village south of Kāshān, where the pressure on available irrigated land is high, the size of holding owned by most peasants varies from 2–3 *jarīb* (approx. 956–1,434 sq. yds.),[2] although one man and his family can cultivate some 30 *jarīb* (approx. 2 acres, 4,666 sq. yds.). Where a peasant owns a holding of 6–7 *jarīb* (approx. 2,868–3,346 sq. yds.) he will normally own two oxen, two donkeys, and fifty to sixty goats, the droppings of which are used chiefly to manure the ground. Peasants holding 2–3 *jarīb* normally own two donkeys, but for ploughing borrow or hire an ox or oxen from a more prosperous neighbour. Five *mann* (approx. 32 lb., 12 oz.) wheat is sown per *jarīb*; the yield is on an average 35 *mann* (approx. 3 bushels, 49 lb.) per *jarīb*. There is no system of fallow, since land is in short supply. The average income of a peasant from his land in 1945 was between 10,000 rs. (approx. £59) and 50,000 rs. (approx. £294). In the absence of any supplementary source of income this was clearly not sufficient to cover his and his family's annual expenses. In the neighbouring areas of

[1] See above, pp. 270–1.

[2] 1 *jarīb* = 400 sq. m., or approx. 478 sq. yds.

Maymeh and Mūrchehkhwart the peasants were slightly better off, largely owing to the fact that they were able to grow cotton, which fetched a relatively high and stable price. In the latter place the average holding is 2–10 *jarīb* (approx. 1,435 sq. yds.–1 acre, 2,335 sq. yds.).[1] In Maymeh the available land is divided into 2,016 *ḥabbeh*, and the average holding is 2–5 *ḥabbeh*.[2] The holdings of the individual peasant proprietors are not necessarily consolidated but may be found in different parts of the village land. In Abīāneh, for example, there is considerable fragmentation of holdings. The land is divided into small plots which are subdivided among different owners, the boundary being marked by a stone[3] placed in the border of the plot.

Where the peasant owns a garden or gardens in addition to arable land his economic condition is usually more favourable. Thus the cultivated lands of Farīzand, Kumjān (with its gardens in Karvand), Tarreh, Barz, and Abīāneh, all in the Kūhi Kargis area, consist largely of gardens and orchards, and these villages in 1948 appeared relatively prosperous compared with neighbouring villages which were engaged mainly in the raising of grain crops. Similarly Maymeh, which also appeared to be fairly prosperous, has a considerable revenue from vineyards. In areas which grow a large proportion of *ṣayfī* crops, such as Burkhwār, the peasant proprietors are also, in some cases, relatively men of substance.

If a holding is broken up by inheritance into units too small to afford a livelihood to a family, the usual practice is for the holding to be sold, or for the joint heirs to lease their shares to one of their number and themselves to emigrate elsewhere in search of permanent or casual employment.

The supposition that the average small-holding in many areas does not provide an adequate livelihood in present circumstances is corroborated by the fact that there has been in recent years a marked tendency to leave certain areas for the towns. In Joushaqān between 1946–8 some 312 persons left the village mainly for Tehrān, leaving a population of some 1,679 persons in 1948. Similarly, large numbers have left So, Tarq, Bīdhand, Mūrchehkhwart, and Abīāneh in the same neighbourhood in recent years. From the latter place it was alleged that 200 families had gone, leaving some 500 in the village. As stated above, in many cases these émigrés often keep some stake in the village; they may even leave their families behind and may return themselves from time to time. In such cases where a number of persons from any

[1] In Mūrchehkhwart 1 *jarīb* = 600 sq. *gaz* (approx. 717½ sq. yds.).

[2] The available water of the village is divided into 2,016 *ḥabbeh*, and 1 *ḥabbeh* of land represents the amount of land watered by 1 *ḥabbeh* of water.

[3] This stone is known locally as *dāvar*.

one district have gone to some town in search of work, there is often some system devised by which one of their number collects money periodically to take back to their families left in the village. Similarly, in Jougand (near Ardistān), which in a good year produces enough wheat, barley, and maize—the chief local crops—to enable the peasant to make ends meet, there was an exodus of almost all the men of the area to Tehrān and elsewhere in search of work owing to two bad years in 1943 and 1944. In Maymeh, on the other hand, which has a fairly constant water-supply from deep-water *qanāts*, good arable land, and vineyards, there would appear to have been no flight from the land in recent years.

The pasture and waste-land round a *khurdeh mālik* village, as distinct from the cultivated lands, belong in common to the villagers, each person having a share commensurate with his share of the cultivated land. In some cases, however, it may happen that one or more of the more prosperous members of the community have registered the adjacent pasture or waste-land as private property. Where this is not the case the villagers have the right to graze their flocks on this land. Further, any proceeds from the renting of the right to graze in this land or to tap the gum tragacanth plant (which is found in certain areas, especially in central Persia) are divided among the villagers in proportion to their shares in the cultivated land of the village, or spent on public works such as the repair of the local *ḥammām*, or bath, where there is one, or mosque.

It is often alleged that the peasant proprietor is no better off than his crop-sharing fellow, and that the tendency is for their incomes to be roughly the same because the peasant proprietor, being satisfied with a minimum, makes no effort to increase the land under production and to provide himself with anything beyond his minimum needs. In proof of this it is alleged that when, during the short period of Democrat rule in Āẕarbāyjān in 1946–7, certain large landed estates were handed over to the peasants, the latter relying on the fact that they would henceforth enjoy a larger share of the produce, immediately reduced the area under cultivation. If—as seems to have been the case—there was in fact a reduction in the area cultivated at this time, I would suggest that this was due in the main to the prevailing insecurity rather than to any lack of initiative on the part of the peasants. Further, in view of the fact that peasant proprietors are found mainly in the less productive parts of the country it is misleading to compare their incomes with those of crop-sharing peasants living on more productive land. Where peasant-proprietor villages are found in the same area as landlord villages with crop-sharing peasants, although both are often poor, the position of the peasant proprietor compares favourably with that of the crop-sharing peasant, and villages owned by the former, in most cases, have the appearance of being better cared for and better cultivated. In relatively fertile areas which are not specially subject to natural calamity the peasant proprietor, in so far as he is found, is usually considerably better off than his crop-sharing fellow, as for example in Gaz. On the other hand, in the poorer areas where the crop failures are more frequent it is probably true that the peasant proprietor may suffer more in a bad year than the crop-sharing peasant. The difference is that whereas the crop-sharing peasant in such circumstances is able to obtain an advance from the landowner, to whom he often becomes permanently indebted with the result that he is virtually tied to the land,[1] the peasant proprietor has to seek a loan from a money-lender. The latter in due course will probably foreclose on him, in which case he loses his land.

Where grain land is concerned it is probably true that the maximum productivity is not achieved when the land is split up into small holdings. In the report quoted in Chapter XIII the writer, on the basis of the figures quoted by him and according to the division of the country into twelve geographical areas, shows that the production of wealth per person in wheat is greater wherever large landed proprietors are more numerous. Although he admits that this fact can be partly explained by a higher average rainfall in the areas in which the large landed proprietors predominate, he nevertheless maintains that even were rainfall constant throughout the whole area the production of wealth would be higher in proportion as the large landowners were more numerous (though he sets an upper ceiling to the extent of their properties beyond which he believes productivity declines). How far these conclusions are valid is uncertain. Where the main income is derived from crops other than grain, i.e. *ṣayfī* crops or fruit, it is doubtful whether productivity rises with the number of large landed estates. On the other hand, it is true that in areas where heavy capital expenditure on irrigation is required the peasant proprietor is wholly at a disadvantage. Further, he has devised no co-operative organization to aid him in the marketing of his produce and the purchase of implements and seed, or to tide him over a bad year.[2]

From the foregoing it seems clear that peasant proprietorship is not, in so far as its extent is concerned, an important form of land-holding in Persia. The natural conditions under which agriculture are carried out would seem on the whole to favour large landed proprietorship, but it is clear that this advantage is more than offset by the disabilities resulting from the social conditions attendant upon the régime of the large landed proprietors in its

[1] See Ch. XXI. [2] See also Ch. XXII.

present form. The greater security of tenure enjoyed by the peasant proprietor and the larger measure of independence of character which accompanies it undoubtedly make for better cultivation and better social conditions. On the other hand, it is clear that the economic problems involved are of greater complexity than may be solved merely by an increase or decrease in one form of holding relative to the other.

Between the peasant proprietor who lives on and works his own holding and the large landed proprietor are certain intermediate groups. On the one hand is the landowner who owns a small share in a village but is an absentee living in the neighbouring town, and on the other hand the man who lives on, but does not work the land himself, and enjoys a social standing above that of the ordinary peasant proprietor. There is a general tendency for small merchants in the towns to invest their profits in land in the neighbourhood because, in spite of what has been said in Chapter XIII concerning the greater profits offered by trade and certain other fields for large-scale investment, land still offers to the small man greater security for the investment of his earnings. The small absentee landowner is thus found mainly in the neighbourhood of the towns. In many cases much of the land in the immediate vicinity of a town is owned by landowners of this type. For example, an area extending some 14 miles round Saqqiz is owned mainly in this way. In such cases land is seldom the main or only source of income.[1] In some cases the main motive of this kind of ownership of land is not an economic one, but the desire to obtain a refuge to which to retire from the town in the summer.

For instance, many of the villages in the foothills of the Elburz Mountains to the north of Tehrān are owned in part in this way by absentee town proprietors. This type of small-holding is seldom the only type of holding in any given area but tends to be mixed with other forms of holding, especially with ownership by peasant proprietors. This is the case, for example, in Ghamsar and various other villages in the neighbourhood of Kāshān, and in Maʿṣūmābād and Tuqāb near Bīrjand, which are partly owned by town-dwellers of Kāshān and Bīrjand respectively and partly by peasant proprietors.

There is, however, another type of small absentee land ownership which derives from hereditary right; this type of ownership is found in different parts of Persia and not only in the neighbourhood of the towns. It occurs where economic pressure has driven the owner or his forebears out, or ambition has induced them to

[1] There are instances of landowners of this type buying up or leasing neighbouring estates, and eventually becoming large landed proprietors themselves, but this is the exception rather than the rule.

migrate to seek economic advancement in the neighbouring town or elsewhere. In such cases the villager will not always cut himself off completely from his roots, but often retains some land in his original home. This type of absentee proprietor is perhaps especially common along the southern and south-western borders of the central desert. Many of them return in summer to their villages to collect their dues from the harvest.

The small-holder who is not mainly an absentee, but lives in the village, differs from the peasant proprietor in that he does not work on the land himself. In most cases he also derives his property from hereditary right, subdivision by inheritance having reduced his own status or that of his forebears to the position of a small-holder. In other cases he may be a comparative newcomer, or a peasant proprietor who, by greater industry or greater fortune, has succeeded in increasing his own holding. Where small-holders of this type are found in peasant-proprietor villages, it frequently happens that they own small areas of land in neighbouring villages also. Thus in Abīāneh, near Kāshān, which is mainly owned by peasant proprietors, some of the more prosperous people own land in the neighbouring villages; in a similar way part of the land of Abīāneh is owned by the people of the neighbouring village of Hanjan, which is also mainly owned by peasant proprietors. In most peasant-proprietor villages there are in any case usually one or two families who own rather more land than their fellows, which they work either on a crop-sharing basis or by employing paid labour. This type of landowner, in so far as he does not work the land himself but employs labour usually on a crop-sharing basis, resembles the large landed proprietor, but his social, political, and economic position is vastly different from that of the large landed proprietor: he enjoys none of the power and influence wielded by the latter. For this reason he has here been classed with the peasant proprietor rather than with the large landed proprietor.

CHAPTER XV

TRIBAL AREAS

In so far as the tribal leaders or *khāns* merge into the class of large landed proprietors, so their lands also fall into the category of large landed estates discussed in Chapter XIII. There are, however, certain differences between the position of the tribal *khāns* and that of the large landed proprietors. The power of the *khāns* derives from two sources: on the one hand, from the tribe of which they are the leaders, and, on the other, from the land which they own. In their capacity as landowners they collect their share of the produce of the land or their rents and dues as other landowners, while in their capacity as tribal leaders they collect certain levies from their followers. The extent to which they exercise a dual role varies. In many areas they have become settled and barely distinguishable from the large landed proprietors.

The main tribal areas are in Fārs, the Bakhtīārī, Gurgān, Balūchistān, Āẕarbāyjān, Kurdistān, Khurāsān, and Khūzistān; each area exhibits certain peculiarities in social structure and ethnological composition. The tribes are for the most part semi-nomadic only; in some cases they are settled but nevertheless retain to some extent their tribal organization. The tribal migrations vary considerably in length and in the extent to which the group as a whole takes part. In most cases a few members of the tribe remain behind in the *qishlāq*, or winter quarters, when the migration to the *yaylāq*, or summer quarters, takes place in order to look after the crops which have been sown in the *qishlāq*. In some cases there is also a small permanent or semi-permanent element in the *yaylāq*. Often the tribal leaders own arable land in the *qishlāq* and, in some cases, in the *yaylāq* also. In so far as the intervening country is concerned this may or may not belong to the tribal leaders. Where the migration route is a long one it usually passes through non-tribal lands.

By custom the tribes follow a certain well-defined migration route. Each sub-group (or *tīreh*) has by tradition the right to pass through certain areas.[1] These rights are seldom more than customary; in some cases it is alleged that old grants or leases are in existence. Where the route passes through open country little difficulty arises, but where it skirts the borders of or actually passes through cultivated land considerable losses may be inflicted on the

[1] The area through which a tribe moves by customary right from winter to summer quarters and back is known in Fārs as the *ravāl* of the tribe.

crops of the settled population unless a strict control is exercised by the tribal leaders. As against this the settled areas situated along or in the neighbourhood of the migration routes gain in so far as a plentiful supply of clarified butter or *roughan* and meat at relatively advantageous prices becomes available to them.

When the Īli ʿArab section of the Khamseh tribes of Fārs migrate from their winter to their summer pastures or vice versa, they follow a special route, decided upon beforehand by their leaders, in consultation with the local government authorities. Along that route each group and sub-group has its special camping places and pastures, to which it has by tradition a right. These rights, as stated above, are customary and often of long standing, and if one group encroaches on the pastures of another trouble is likely to ensue.

On the borders of the territory of two hostile tribal groups, such as the Qashqā'ī and the Khamseh, disputes sometimes arise over the pastures and are usually decided by *force majeure*. In the neighbourhood of Jahrum, for example, the pastures lie on the borders of Khamseh and Qashqā'ī territory. They are not divided and anyone can use them provided the land is not sown. They are a frequent bone of contention between the Qashqā'ī and the Khamseh.

The main body of the Shāhsivan range from the Mughān steppe, with its fertile wheat land, to Sablān Kūh, where they possess numerous gardens. The distances which they migrate are relatively small and hence they are able to carry on agriculture without much difficulty. This differentiates them from the Qashqā'ī, who are almost continually on the move. The Shāhsivan follow traditional routes from the *qishlāq* to their *yaylāq* and move on fixed dates. Some thirty-two groups (or *ṭā'ifeh*) go to the Mughān steppe in the winter months.

Tribal pastures belong in some cases to the tribal leader in whose name they have been registered; this is largely the case in Fārs. In others they are *khāliṣeh*, as in parts of Āẕarbāyjān, such as Mt. Sahand and the Mughān steppe, which are the *yaylāq* and *qishlāq* respectively of the Shāhsivan, and in parts of Khurāsān; in these the government levies a pasture due or lets the pasture. In other cases the pastures belong to the settled population, who similarly either lease them to the tribes for a lump sum or levy pasture dues.

In the Qashqā'ī different sections and individuals of the tribe appear to have traditional rights in the pasture lands owned by the tribal leaders or *khāns*. These rights are not registered or absolute, although they are sometimes based on documents going back 200 years or so. The practice is for the *khān* to allot these pastures to his followers every year. In fact the same person is usually given the same pasture, but the formality of allotment is carried out every year in order to prevent the tribesmen acquiring an undisputed title and so that the holder can be turned out if he commits some act of insubordination. Formerly it was customary to exact some payment when the pastures were re-allotted. This practice is said to have been abandoned by the Qashqā'ī. In Qarājeh Dāgh, in the Chilibīānlū and Muḥammad Khānlū country, the pastures belong mainly to the *khāns*, who also own arable land, especially in the *qishlāq*.

Riẓā Shāh, as was stated in Chapter VIII, greatly reduced the power of the tribal leaders and attempted to settle the tribes. The fact that successive governments had failed to integrate the tribal element into the social and political structure of the country, and that the settled population regarded the tribes as a potential threat to their security, constituted a problem of no small magnitude which called for a solution. Moreover it would seem that Riẓā Shāh in his attempt to modernize Persia regarded the tribal element as an anachronism. He sought to solve the problem in a radical fashion by destroying the tribal organization, preventing migration, and attempting to convert the tribesmen into agriculturists. In this policy there is little doubt that he had the general support of the non-tribal element of the population of the country. It is also clear that the policy was put into operation without adequate preparation. No detailed survey of the possibilities of settlement or the effect the destruction of the tribal element would have upon the economy of the country was made. Many of the tribal leaders were exiled and the annual migration of the tribes from winter to summer pastures was largely prevented. Suitable areas in which to settle the tribes were not always chosen, adequate provisions for health and education were not made, and sufficient facilities by way of agricultural training and the provision of agricultural implements were not given to the tribesmen to enable them to change over from a pastural to an agricultural life. Further, there is little doubt that many welcomed the decline in the fortunes of the tribes and took the opportunity to retaliate for tribal depredations in the past; while on the part of the government little attempt was made to conciliate the tribes. Sometimes whole groups were forced to move to different parts of the country, areas where they would no longer be able to carry on their traditional mode of existence. For example, the Galbaghī were moved from Kurdistān to Hamadān, Iṣfahān, and as far afield as Yazd. Such was the pressure brought to bear upon them in the course of this move that they took to the hills and fought as rebels for many months. When they were eventually overcome and moved, their numbers were very greatly reduced. Since the abdication they have returned to their former homes while most of the Turkī-speaking population who had been settled in the Galbaghī villages have left Kurdistān.

The tribal policy of Riẓā Shāh, ill conceived and badly executed, resulted in heavy losses in livestock, the impoverishment of the tribes, and a diminution of their numbers. The adverse effect of these factors on the economy of the country was such that he was forced in the latter years of his reign to modify this policy. Limited migrations were once more permitted. After his abdication in 1941 the tribal problem, which he had by no means solved, re-emerged. Many of the exiled tribal leaders returned to their tribal areas. Some of the tribal elements which had been settled in villages abandoned these and once more took up a semi-nomadic life. That this should have been the case is in part no doubt due to the natural inclinations of the tribesman to follow a nomadic life and his reluctance to submit to the authority of the central government, but it is also unquestionable that this reluctance was heightened by the extortion to which the tribes were subjected during the period of settlement.

The general tendency since 1941 has been for the tribal leaders to increase their power. In some areas the government has been forced to reverse the policy of Riẓā Shāh and to entrust public order and security to the tribal leaders. The extent to which this has been done and the success with which it has met varies considerably.

It is in Fārs that the increase in the power of the tribes has been most marked. In the Qashqā'ī country the gendarmerie, which was formerly responsible for security, ceased to act. A token military force was in Fīrūzābād, the Qashqā'ī capital, in 1949. Responsibility for law and order, however, was the concern of the Qashqā'ī leaders. In the Khamseh country, on the other hand, the security forces of the government were operating in 1949, but responsibility for law and order in so far as the tribes were concerned was the charge of the leader, or *sar parast*, of the tribe. The latter was appointed by the government and was responsible to the Commander of the Fārs Division. He was, in 1949, one of the tribal leaders.[1] The latter were provided by the government with a limited supply of arms and ammunition to enable them to keep order. In the case of the Khamseh the tribal leaders recommended to the government persons for the position of *kalāntar* or chief of the various sub-groups. *Kalāntars* could not be appointed without government confirmation, but in the case of the appointment of *kadkhudās*, i.e. the leaders of smaller groups, confirmation by the government was not required. In the Mamasanī area, on the other

[1] He was subsequently replaced by an army officer.

hand, gendarmerie posts in 1949 were in existence. In the Kūhgīlūyeh area the military were engaged in collecting the arms of the Boir Aḥmadī in 1949.

Security in the various tribal areas in Fārs in 1949 was on the whole good; it was only in the border land between two tribal areas, for which there was no clearly defined responsibility, that conditions were not satisfactory. In the Qashqā'ī security was admitted by the settled population to be better than ever before. This was probably due to the relative prosperity of the tribesmen in general at the time. This in turn was probably largely due to the success of the tribal leaders in limiting the activities of the government in their area. The *kalāntars* and *kadkhudās* of the tribes have in many cases amassed considerable wealth, largely, so it is asserted, by the sale of sugar in the days during the war and the years immediately after when this was issued against coupons. In so far as the Khamseh territory is concerned security was also good, due probably mainly to the relatively satisfactory administration of their *sar parast*, rather than to any increase in the general prosperity of the tribe, which was not as marked as it was in the case of the Qashqā'ī.

The gendarmerie were also virtually excluded from 'Aqīlī and Bāsht in Khūzistān. Here, too, by 1949 security had in effect become largely the responsibility of the tribal *khāns*, who maintained riflemen (*tufangchīs*) and received a limited supply of arms and ammunition from the government. Security in Khūzistān, except for some petty raiding in the Arab areas, was on the whole good.

The practice of making the tribal *khāns* responsible for security within their areas appears, in the circumstances, to work tolerably well in Fārs and Khūzistān provided the better elements among the tribes are chosen. It would seem preferable to the practice of Riẓā Shāh, who exiled the *khāns* and reduced the tribes to poverty. On the other hand, a similar system followed in the country of the Chilibīānlū, its subsections the Qarā Khānlū and Ḥājjī 'Alīlū, and the Muḥammad Khānlū in Qarājeh Dāgh has not worked well. It would seem that the leaders of these tribes have used their arms to overawe their settled neighbours and to levy illegal dues. Encroachments of the tribes on the settled people and their crops were not infrequent in 1949. In a bad year, such as 1949, the temptation to allow one's flocks to graze in one's neighbours' crops is no doubt strong, and applies not only to the tribes but also to the settled element; the former, however, being armed, had the upper hand. Petty robbery was also relatively frequent.

It is clear that a policy of delegating authority to the tribal leaders, dictated by weakness and unaccompanied by adequate control, whatever its temporary advantages, can hardly be a satisfactory long-term policy. The personal element is unduly emphasized and considerable power is placed in the hands of individuals who may well be tempted to misuse it. The administration of tribal affairs by the tribal *khāns* in the old-fashioned way requires a large budget; this is not provided by the government and therefore involves the making of levies directly or indirectly upon the tribes by the *khāns*, a practice which is clearly open to abuse. In 1327/1948–9 the Governor-General of Fārs, for example, agreed that a levy of 1 per cent on sheep and goats which had had young should be made by the *sar parast* of the Īli ʿArab on the tribe to defray his expenses as *sar parast*. It is, moreover, doubtful whether future generations of *khāns* will be prepared to live the kind of life which the system demands: even with jeeps it is a relatively hard life and lacks the amenities of modern city life which most Persians find attractive.

On the whole, in many of the tribal areas the government would appear to be conscious of a certain weakness and to seek to maintain its position by a policy of 'divide and rule'. It tends, whenever possible, to put into power those of the *khāns* who will be subservient to it and who will share the proceeds of office, stirs up intersectional strife in the tribe, and foments intrigue. This has been the case to some extent in Khamseh territory, where the rivalry between the Bāṣirī and ʿArab has at times been fanned, while in the Bakhtīārī local governors have frequently been selected from among those of the Bakhtīārī *khāns* who are prepared to practise and connive at extortion and to reduce the tribespeople to poverty. Further, the Bakhtīārī tribesmen have been disarmed by the army but are given no protection from the depredations of other groups situated along their migration routes who have not yet been disarmed. In so far as this represents government policy it would seem short-sighted in the extreme. It is true that there is a long history of antagonism between the settled element and the semi-settled. On the one hand, the tribal element has undoubtedly been responsible for much of the insecurity in the past; and the settled element, subject as it has been for years to recurrent raids, not unnaturally fears a return of insecurity if the tribes are not held in check. On the other hand, there is no question that the officials of the settled government have in the past oppressed the tribes whenever they have been strong enough to do so.[1]

The influence and power of the tribal *khāns* depends largely on the personal element. Where the tribe is semi-nomadic and the tribal organization is relatively strong the *khāns* enjoy very con-

[1] The conduct of the officials of Sanjar's government (see pp. 58–9) is typical not only of the sixth century A.H.

siderable powers. Tribal affairs are directly administered, and since the personal position of the *khāns* depends largely on the support they receive from their followers the extortion they practise is limited by the need to retain the loyalty of their followers. Where, however, the tribes are settled or partially settled, the tribesmen have little possibility of attaching themselves to a rival leader if they are dissatisfied with their own leader: once settled their freedom of movement and action is limited. The *khāns*, therefore, are not forced to the same extent to retain the consent of their followers; they take on more the character of large landed proprietors, while retaining the powers of the tribal *khān*, upon the autocratic use of which the exigencies of tribal life no longer impose a limitation. It is broadly in those areas where the *khāns* have abandoned or largely abandoned tribal life that the heaviest dues and impositions are imposed upon the peasant population. If, moreover, as is sometimes the case, the local *khāns* make common cause with government officials to bleed the countryside the condition of the peasants is further worsened.

Land ownership in the tribal areas of Fārs is partly in the hands of landowners belonging to the settled population, who are mainly absentees, and partly in the hands of the tribal *khāns*. Disputed tenures are not uncommon. The fortunes of the tribes and their different subsections have been subject to considerable vicissitudes which have affected also the ownership of the land. The basis of land ownership in the tribal areas is force, although it is given a legal veneer by registration. Thus, when registration was first introduced, whoever was strong enough or rich enough to do so registered land in his own name irrespective of his title thereto. At the present day the title to much of the Mamasanī is disputed between the tribal element represented by the Rustamī *khāns* and settled (and absentee) claimants in the persons of the Muʿīn ut-Tujjār Bushihrī family. There are also cases of disputed ownership between the Darashūrī and the Qashqā'ī. Since the abdication of Riẓā Shāh the Qashqā'ī have in several cases retaken possession of their erstwhile properties without giving up those which they had received in exchange under Riẓā Shāh. They are alleged also to have forced some of the settled and absentee landowners in the Fīrūzābād area to lease their property to them at relatively low rentals.

In the Qashqā'ī area the *khāns* formerly levied 3 per cent per annum on the flocks of their followers. Nāṣir Khān, the present leader of the Qashqā'ī, abolished this as a regular annual due after his return to Fārs on the abdication of Riẓā Shāh, but is said to have levied it on two occasions since 1941. It is probably still levied on occasion by the minor *khāns*, *kalāntars*, and *kadkhudās*.

Pasture dues are not taken where the pastures are owned by the *khāns*, but if there are two or more good years consecutively there is what is known as a *galleh bigīr*, i.e. the tribesmen out of gratitude for the blessings of these good years and in order that this bounty may not, as it were, turn against them, give one or two head of sheep and goats per hundred to the *khān*, this due being brought, so it is alleged, by the tribesmen of their own free will. To what extent compulsion would be exercised were these gifts not brought is open to conjecture. This also applies to the New Year offerings brought by the tribesmen throughout the tribal areas to the *khāns*, *kalāntars*, and *kadkhudās*. These also are nominally gifts; one *kalāntar*, however, when asked what he would do if the tribesmen did not bring these offerings at the New Year said such a thing could not happen, but that if it did he would take them by force. In Nūrābād the *khān* expects New Year gifts of clarified butter (*roughan*) and lambs, etc., from his followers. Formerly, in addition, a levy per annum of one lamb in fifty was made.

In general in the tribal areas, whether in Fārs or elsewhere, the *khāns*, the *kalāntars*, and *kadkhudās* and their servants make levies on the tribes of clarified butter and meat for their own expenses. The Kurdish chiefs and the Shāhsivan leaders similarly, in addition to the dues which they receive as landowners, receive certain dues, usually in the form of animals, by virtue of their position as tribal leaders.

The *kalāntars* and *kadkhudās* in some of the tribal areas are responsible for the collection of the government dues, in which case they retain part of what is collected by way of commission.

In the Pīshkūh and Pushti Kūh of Luristān a levy known as *shākh shumārī* (the counting of horns) is still made in some cases. If the *khān* is in need of money he levies a due based on the number of sheep, goats, and cattle owned by his followers. Goats and sheep are counted as two *shākh*, cows and oxen as four, asses three, and horses and mares four, so much being levied per *shākh*.

Another levy formerly made but now rare is *tash shumārī*, i.e. a hearth tax by which every household which has an oven in which a fire is lit, even if the household owns no cattle, pays so much to the *khān*.

Dues for the entertainment of guests are also levied by some of the *khāns* on their followers and on the peasants in the area. Under Riẓā Shāh these various dues had begun to die out; since the abdication and the revival of the influence of the tribal leaders the tendency has been for some of them to be reimposed.

Although the Kurds are not mainly even semi-nomadic except in a few cases on the ʿIrāqī border, society in Kurdistān (though to a lesser extent in the Sanandaj area than in the Mahābād area) is essentially tribal except round the towns. Kurdistān has always been a problem area for the Persian government. From the time of Nāṣir ud-Dīn Shāh onwards and especially under Riẓā Shāh interference by government officials has added to rather than diminished the general insecurity. There is a long tradition of hostility towards government officials, who have done little to overcome this in recent years by way of refraining from corruption and extortion. Formerly intertribal strife was common and at the present day factions rend the countryside. During the period of the movement for an autonomous Kurdistān in 1946 guerrillas (*chateh*) ravaged the countryside. Insecurity prevailed. A return to such conditions is felt by the local population to be an ever-present threat. The peasants, moreover, have little or no security from their own *khāns*, who tend to look upon them as chattels. Where the *khān* or landowner is relatively benign conditions are tolerable; this depends, however, entirely on the personal factor. In practice, the peasant has no security of life or livelihood.

In the outlying areas of various provinces, notably in Khurāsān, the power and influence of the large landed proprietors, which is often considerable, has in part a semi-tribal basis, and the regime prevailing in the districts which they dominate to some extent resembles the semi-tribal regime of Qājār days.[1] A similar situation exists in parts of Kirmān, especially in the neighbourhood of Bam. This is also the case on the borders of Kurdistān in Kulliā'ī. The leaders of the rival groups go about accompanied by armed retainers. Clashes between them and robberies of each others' flocks are common.

The tribal areas of Khūzistān are mainly inhabited by Persian tribes in the north and Arab tribes in the lowlands. Under Riẓā Shāh an attempt was made to bring the whole of Khūzistān under the effective control of the central government. In furtherance of this policy many of the local *khāns* and *shaykhs* were exiled. Some measure of security from raiding and the depredations committed by migratory bodies as they passed through the land of the settled people was achieved. As against this the peasants and tribesmen were left entirely at the mercy of government officials, whose nature had not greatly changed since earlier times. The result was that the peasants in Khūzistān were reduced to an even more abject state of poverty than formerly. Since the abdication of Riẓā Shāh in 1941 a number of the *khāns* and *shaykhs* have returned and there has been some decrease in the pressure of government officials upon the peasants.

The Persian tribal element consists mainly of Lurs, Bakhtiārīs,

[1] See Chs. VI and VII.

and Kūhgīlūyeh; these groups are settled and semi-settled. The Lurs are found mainly in the neighbourhood of Dizfūl, Ahvāz, and Ābādān, and the Bakhtīārīs in Dizfūl, Rām Hurmuz, and Masjidi Sulaymān. The semi-settled element begin to move down with their flocks from the uplands to the foothills at the beginning of autumn and thence to the plains about the Persian New Year (21 March). They start their upward migration again about a month or six weeks after the Persian New Year.

At the present day the distribution of the Arab tribes is broadly as follows: In the neighbourhood of the Kārūn and the Nahri Hāshim are the Mālik and Banī Tamīm, in Dashti Mīshān the Sharafeh, Havīzeh, Savārī, Banī Ṭuruf, and Banī Ṣāliḥ; in the neighbourhood of the Karkheh, the Chanāneh, Humayh, Rubūt, and Banī Lām, in the neighbourhood of the Shaṭṭ ul-ʿArab and Khurramshahr the Muḥassin and Durais Nisar; in Shādagān, the Banī Kaʿb, in the neighbourhood of Jarrāḥī and the Gulf Ports the Jarrāḥī Arabs, and in the neighbourhood of Rām Hurmuz the Āli Khamsīn.[1] In the Arab areas the tribes are not nomadic but their organization is in some respects tribal. Interposed between the peasant and the state is a *shaykh* who may or may not be the owner of the land on which the peasant works. This system goes back many years. In a description of Havīzeh written in 1299/1881–2, it is stated that certain dues were levied on the crops by the *shaykhs*. The government tax on rice was half the crop, and one-quarter of the government's share went to the *shaykh* unless he was a *sayyid*, in which case he got one-half. On irrigated grain the government tax was one-third, on which the *shaykh's* share was also one-third; on unirrigated grain the government tax was one-fifth or one-fourth according to the remoteness or otherwise of the district, and on this the *shaykh's* share was one-fifth and one-fourth respectively. The *shaykhs* had no right to any dues on other crops such as various pulses.[2] This limitation of their dues, however, appears to have been largely theoretical. The writer goes on to say that the tax on Havīzeh which Moulā Muṭallib paid was about half of what he collected in cash and kind from the peasants, and that he used to leave grain with the peasants for two to three years until prices rose.[3] He also states that according to investigations made secretly in 1299/1881–2, the peasants in certain Arab areas suffered from the injustice of the Arab *shaykhs*, who were said to levy taxes five to six times a year.[4] In Fallāḥīyeh, as a result of the extortions of the Arab *shaykhs*, the number of date palms had

[1] Razmārā, *Military Geography of Persia* (volume on Khūzistān, p. 11).
[2] Najm ul-Mulk, *Safar Nāmehyi ʿArabistān*, f. 281.
[3] ibid. f. 287.
[4] Report on ʿArabistān in M.F.A. No. 725, f. 499.

declined;[1] the *shaykhs* also levied 3 *tūmāns* per *khīsh* in this district.[2]

The Arab *shaykhs* are still used in parts of Khūzistān as collecting agents. In the *khāliṣeh* areas under Riẓā Shāh they took 12 per cent commission, a practice instituted during the period of the first Millspaugh mission.[3] At the present time they receive as commission one-fifth of the crop. In those areas where they do not cultivate the land, a third party may be interposed between the *shaykh* and the peasant between whom and the *de facto* land-holder there is a crop-sharing relationship. In ʿArab ʿAbbās (near Kūt ʿAbdullāh), which is in the effective possession of Shaykh Jābir, the government demand on the village amounted in 1949 to some 40 *manni ahvāz* (approx. 39 cwt., 41 lb.). It is collected from the *shaykh*, who in turn levies it from the peasants. There are some fifteen to twenty plough-lands in the village, the land of which is entirely *daym*. Seven *manni tabrīz* (approx. 46 lb.) per *khīsh*, some clarified butter (*roughan*), and one lamb if available are taken by the *shaykh*, and one day's labour per man per year. In addition, some 5 *manni ahvāz* (approx. 4 cwt., 103 lb.) per *khīsh* are sown and reaped for the *shaykh* on his own land; the *shaykh* provides the seed for this. In the Bāvī country comprising some sixty villages the tax is also collected by the *shaykh* or by his bailiff (or *mubāshir*) who collects it from the *kadkhudās* and they from the villagers at so much per plough-land. In the Baḥreh area (south of Kūt ʿAbdullāh) the tax per plough-land is 66 rs. (approx. 7*s*. 9*d*.) and 2 *manni ahvāz* (approx. 1 cwt., 108 lb.) wheat and 1 *manni ahvāz* (approximately 110 lb.) barley. The cash payment is levied whatever the harvest, but the payment in kind may be reduced if the harvest is bad. The *shaykh* acts as the government collector and keeps 6 rs. (approx. 8¼*d*.) of the 66 rs. In the neighbouring area of Suwayeh the tax is 63 rs. (approx. 7*s*. 5*d*.) and 3 *manni ahvāz* (approx. 2 cwt., 106 lb.) grain per *khīsh*. In Shādagān the *shaykh* in the Arab areas takes one-third to one-half. All costs of cultivation are borne by the peasant.

In the case of complaints of over-taxation, as occurred, for example, in the Banī Ṭuruf in 1326/1947–8, a valuer (*mumaiyiz*) may be sent to investigate the case.

Balūchistān also contains tribal areas which have certain peculiar features. The Balūch are settled and semi-settled; but their social organization is broadly speaking tribal. In so far as groups of them migrate from summer to winter pastures, their migration is for the most part a relatively short one. The Balūch leaders, known as *sardārs*, wield very considerable local influence. They own large areas of land and exercise a kind of tribal jurisdiction over even

[1] ibid. f. 504.
[2] ibid. ff. 504–5.
[3] See Ch. VIII.

larger areas. Owing to lack of communications government officials have remained for the most part in a few isolated centres. In the time of Riẓā Shāh they had little direct contact with the people. The *sardārs*, moreover, prevented their followers from getting in touch with government officials lest their own influence should thereby be weakened. They made themselves as far as possible the only channel of communication between the government and the tribesmen. More recently some of the *sardārs* have established relatively close relations with government officials, thereby providing themselves with an additional *point d'appui* and strengthening their position *vis-à-vis* their followers.

The *sardārs* claim 10 per cent of all produce by virtue of their position as *sardārs*. This levy was forbidden recently by the authorities, except where the *sardārs* have been recognized by the government as *kadkhudās*, or tribal leaders. In fact it continues to be levied except in the less remote areas such as Zāhidān, where the people, having come to realize that power is not a monopoly of the *sardārs*, are no longer prepared to pay. Where the patriarchal basis of tribal life has remained strong this 10 per cent is regarded by the tribesmen to some extent as a return for the services the *sardārs* render them in the defence of their (the tribesmen's) interests against the interference of government officials and the depredations of rival groups. In the remoter areas it is often levied several times a year according to the degree of extortion or otherwise practised by the local *sardār*. It is alleged that various officials, civil and military, get a 'rake-off' from this due levied by the *sardārs*. The latter are, as a class, astute; this, coupled with the absence of communications and the lack of any attempt by the government to improve local conditions and extend agriculture, has enabled the *sardārs* to preserve their power and prevented the spread of government influence.

While the above is in no way a complete description of the tribal areas and their organization, the complexity of the tribal problem, the importance of the tribal areas, and the influence of tribal customs on land tenure and on the relations of the landowner and the peasant have been indicated. It has also been shown that the tribal problem still awaits a settlement. Conflicting interests, social, political, and economic, remain to be reconciled, and it is by no means clear along what lines the problems will ultimately be solved.

CHAPTER XVI

THE CROP-SHARING PEASANT: SECURITY OF TENURE

THE position of the peasant proprietor and the small landowner has been briefly discussed in the previous chapters. The vast majority of the peasant population of Persia is, however, composed not of peasant proprietors, who are a small minority, but of crop-sharing peasants or tenants and 'landless' labourers. It is with the former that this chapter is concerned. They, too, strictly speaking are landless, but by virtue of a contract, written, or more often merely verbal, a certain area of land is handed over to them on a crop-sharing basis for a specified or unspecified period of time, the peasant providing the seed, draught animals, and agricultural implements, or only one or two of these in addition to the labour, whereas the landless labourer, although he may be also paid by a share of the crop, is differentiated from the crop-sharing peasant by the fact that he provides only labour and can be dismissed at will.[1]

Security of tenure is a matter of vital concern to the peasant. Some slight security is given him by the law with regard to any crops which he may have sown (see p. 189), but in practice in the majority of areas he has no real security of tenure. The landlord (or lessee) can, in fact, turn him out at will, except in a few areas. Custom, however, gives the peasant a measure of protection in some areas, and lays down certain rules.[2] In Kirmān, for example, the peasants' share of the crop is divided into three parts, known as *ābdār*, *kishtdār*, and *bārdār* (i.e. the return due for the preparation of the land for cultivation, for the sowing and tending of the crop, and for the reaping and harvesting of the crop). Thus, if the peasant is turned out at the Persian New Year he is entitled to one-third of his full share. This, in turn, is recovered by the landowner from the peasant who takes over. It is alleged that the peasant in Kirmān can only be turned out at the New Year (i.e. March) or in Mihr (September to October).

The peasant enjoys certain customary rights of occupation in

[1] As will be seen in the following chapter, the peasant may undertake to pay a fixed rent in cash or kind or both in place of a share of the crop. What is said in this chapter is, however, equally applicable to him and to the crop-sharing peasant proper.

[2] For example, in many areas if a landowner gives a peasant permission to cultivate lucerne, it is tacitly recognized that the peasant has a right to the land as long as the roots of the crops remain in the ground, which with some types of lucerne may be seven years.

some areas. This is the case in parts of Āẕarbāyjān. Such rights are known locally as *jivar* (*juvar*), and represent a kind of right of priority, which is acquired by a peasant who brings land into cultivation on a landlord estate and works on it for some years. For the most part these rights are acquired by virtue of the labour which the peasant has put into the land and refer to fruit-trees, vines, and trees which have been planted by the peasant, but not to the land itself. If the landowner wishes to evict a peasant who has *jivar* rights he has to pay him compensation, the amount of which is decided locally by agreement. Further, if the landlord sells his land the new owner cannot deprive the peasant of his rights. These rights, moreover, can be transferred by the peasant to a third person. They can also be registered, in which case they are no longer merely customary, but legally recognized. *Jivar* rights are found mainly in Bāsminj, in some areas in Marāgheh, and in Qarājeh Dāgh. For the most part the landlords refuse to allow the peasants to acquire these rights, preferring to keep full ownership and unlimited power to evict the peasants. In a few areas round Tehrān similar occupancy rights, known as *qarāpishk*,[1] are found.

A somewhat peculiar situation exists in Riẓā'īyeh. The land is divided into *ṭannāb*, i.e. shares of 4,000 sq. metres (4,784 sq. yds.) and for the most part registered in the names of the individual holders; the rights of these persons, however, appear to be occupancy rights and not full rights of ownership, which remain in the hands of absentee owners. The relationship between these two groups, both enjoying rights over the land, is not altogether clear. It appears that formerly the occupiers (*ṭannābdār*) paid 13 *qirāns* per annum to the landowners. When registration was introduced, the occupiers registered the land in their own names, and it often came about that the former landowner was either left with the village and no land, or the land was registered in the name of both the original landowner and the occupier. When, during the first Millspaugh mission, a land survey was made and land tax levied on the basis of this, difficulties arose. The *ṭannābdār* said: 'we pay 13 *qirāns* per annum to the landowner: if the government is now to demand land tax from us, why should we continue to pay 13 *qirāns* per *ṭannāb* to the landowner also?' No solution was found to this problem because, it is alleged, the government did not wish to disturb the existing system of land ownership by deciding against the landowner. At the present day if the landlord wishes to evict a *ṭannābdār*, he has to buy any trees and gardens which the latter may have planted. This situation may have developed out of some sort of *jivar* right.

[1] See glossary for other meanings of this term.

The peasants are said to transmit their holdings by inheritance and by sale in certain areas round Iṣfahān, but such transfers are not registered. Similarly, in Sāveh the peasant transmits his land by inheritance. His title to it is, however, merely customary (*ʿurfī*).

The peasants for the most part have no title to the land in Fārs; Kāzirūn is an exception to this. There the peasants, although they have no legal title to the land, are able in fact to transmit their occupancy rights (known as *sar quflī*) by sale and inheritance.

In Khūzistān in general the peasant has no security of tenure. ʿAqīlī is an exception to this; there the peasant has by custom, though not by law, some degree of security of tenure. Some fifty years ago the land of the village was divided. Each plough-land was made to comprise three to four strips known as *kurteh*, containing good, medium, and bad land, and distributed among the peasants. The latter are able to transmit this land by inheritance but not by sale.

If a peasant is evicted by the landowner in the Yazd area it is customary for the latter to pay him some compensation (*dastranj*) for the labour he has put into the land during the period of his occupation. A similar practice prevails in Nūqāt and Nūq near Rafsinjān. It may well be that the practice has spread to this region from Yazd, since most of the landowners are Yazdīs. Elsewhere in the province of Kirmān the landowner appears to be able to evict the peasants at will, subject only to the payment of compensation for ploughing and other current operations as mentioned above.

In certain villages in Khurāsān if a peasant, after having brought land into cultivation in the *muḥavvaṭeh*,[1] i.e. land near the village or *qalʿeh* which is manured annually, leaves the village, the landowner (or lessee) pays him for the labour he has expended on the land; if, however, he merely takes over from another peasant, the land having already been brought into cultivation, he receives nothing when he gives up the land.

In Māzandarān any clearings made in the forest belong by custom to the person who performs this work. The right so acquired is known as *ḥaqqi tabar tarāshī* (i.e. the right derived from the felling of trees). This would seem to be an extension of the practices in connexion with dead land[2] according to which whoever reclaims dead land establishes ownership thereby.

For the most part, however, the peasant's tenure is not guaranteed, even for a period, much less permanently. He may spend his whole lifetime in one village, but the land which he cultivates will

[1] In Turbati Ḥaydarī the term *muḥavvaṭeh* is applied to land near a village; the different parts of the *muḥavvaṭeh* are enclosed by walls and belong to individual peasants.

[2] See above, pp. 204–5.

vary, an annual or periodic redistribution being made by lot. This practice prevails notably in Khurāsān, Kirmān, parts of Fārs, and parts of Āẕarbāyjān. The basis of the division of the land varies: in some areas it is based on the rotation of the water-supply or the number of shares into which the water is divided, in others it is divided into plough-shares. Thus in Kirmān the unit of division is a *dāng*, i.e. one-sixth of the water-supply together with the land watered thereby. The number of *juft*, or yoke of oxen, to each *dāng* varies with the amount of water. Individual *juft* may help each other out in time of need but they work as separate units and there is no formal co-operation between them. In ʿAbdullāhābād near Rafsinjān there are four men, one yoke of oxen, and four to six asses per *dāng*; in Raḥmatābād in the same area there are some six persons to each *dāng*, consisting of a head peasant (known as the *sar zaʿīm*), three peasants (each known as *mard*), and two children. The landowner transmits his instructions through the *sar zaʿīm*.

In some areas the village land is divided into groups of fields worked by a varying number of yoke of oxen. For example, land in the landlord villages in Qā'ināt is divided into a number of *tīrkār*, each of which has a number of peasants, oxen, and asses attached to it under a *sālār*. The number and size of the *tīrkār* in the different villages depends in part on the rotation of the water-supply, which comes mainly from *qanāts*. Twenty-four hours' water comprise one share, or *sahm*, and each share is subdivided into 120 *finjān*. In ʿAlīābād, east-south-east of Bīrjand, the water is divided into fourteen shares, two shares going to each *tīrkār*. Each *tīrkār* has eight men attached to it. In Gīv the water is divided into sixteen shares, two shares similarly going to each *tīrkār*, each of which has one *sālār*, who is the head peasant of the unit, and five *dihqāns* attached to it. In Kākh, in the neighbourhood of Gīv, there are one *sālār*, two *dihqāns*, two oxen, and two asses to each *tīrkār*. Every year lots are drawn between the *tīrkārs* for the distribution of water, and the rotation for the coming year is fixed according to the result.

In Sīstān in the landlord areas (or where relatively large holdings have been acquired, see Ch. XII) the peasants are grouped together in units composed of six shares which are known as *pāgāv*. At the head of the unit is a *sālār*, and under him six peasants and one ox. The *sālārs* tend to be permanent, but the area they cultivate changes from year to year.

The villages in the landlord areas in Khurāsān are divided into a number of *ṣaḥrās*, or areas of land worked by a varying number of pairs of oxen. This type of division is a marked feature of rural organization in Khurāsān and east Persia generally, and differentiates it from other parts of the country.[1] The number of *ṣaḥrās* into which a village is divided varies, as does also their size. In Turbati Ḥaydarī the *ṣaḥrās* are worked by a maximum of six and a minimum of two yoke of oxen; in Kāshmar, however, the number of yoke to a *ṣaḥrā* varies from one to sixty. In Ṭuruq near Mashhad there are fourteen *ṣaḥrās*, each with six yoke of oxen. Shādkan and Mihrānkhān in the same area both have three *ṣaḥrās*, each with four yoke. In Khīābān the number of yoke to a *ṣaḥrā* varies from four to six. Each *ṣaḥrā* is under a *sar sālār*, who is in charge of the distribution of water and the weeding and manuring of the crops. Under him are a number of *sālārs*. Ploughing and sowing is the responsibility of the *dihqāns*, who are similarly under a *sar dihqān*. The *sar sālār* and *sar dihqān* are chosen by the village headman or *kadkhudā*.[2] Reaping is a joint undertaking, threshing is the responsibility of the *dihqāns*, and winnowing the charge of the *sālārs*. In Shādkan there are four *sālārs* and four *dihqāns* to each *ṣaḥrā*, under a *sar sālār* and *sar dihqān* respectively. The *sar sālār* and the *sar dihqān* each receive one day's free labour per annum from other members of the group, known as *sar sālārī* and *sar dihqānī* respectively. In Khīābān there are six *sālārs* and six *dihqāns* to each *ṣaḥrā*, one of whom is the *sar sālār* and one the *sar dihqān* respectively. In Ṭuruq there are twelve peasants to each *ṣaḥrā*.

In Kāshmar and Turbati Ḥaydarī the nomenclature is somewhat different, the man in charge of a *ṣaḥrā* being known as the *sālār*, while the term *sar sālār* is used in Turbati Ḥaydarī to designate the man who is the head of all the *sālārs* of the various *ṣaḥrās*. In Kāshmar the number of men to a *ṣaḥrā* varies from two to ten; in some cases the *ṣaḥrā* is worked on a family basis.

It would appear in the majority of cases that the land of the village is redistributed among the *ṣaḥrās* annually. In Khīābān the annual redistribution of the land is the responsibility of the *sar sālārs* and is done by the drawing of lots. A similar practice is followed in Shādkan. In Turbati Ḥaydarī the *sar sālār*, i.e. the head of the *sālārs* of the various *ṣaḥrās*, draws lots at the beginning of the agricultural year for the rotation of the water between the various *ṣaḥrās*. The peasants working in a *ṣaḥrā* are known as *ṣaḥrādārs*. They have no tenancy rights and there is no question, therefore, of their transmitting by sale or inheritance the right to cultivate a given piece of land.

There is in Khurāsān another type of peasant known as a *ballak*, in contradistinction to the peasant who belongs to one of the *ṣaḥrās* and is known as a *ṣaḥrādār*. The *ballaks* are of two kinds. (1) They

[1] Stack, writing in the late nineteenth century, mentions a similar type of division in the maritime villages of Fārs (see above p. 171).

[2] He is called in Khīābān the *dārūgheh* (see Chapter XIX).

sow unirrigated (i.e. *daym*) land with grain, receiving permission from the landowner or lessee to do so. In Ṭuruq the *ballaks* are given permission by the lessee, i.e. the Shirkati Kishāvarzīyi Riẓā, to sow a specified quantity of grain in a defined area every year.[1] The *ballak*, by sowing a particular piece of land, establishes some right of priority to the cultivation of that particular piece of land. (2) They borrow land from the *ṣaḥrādārs* for the cultivation of melons, etc. It is in the interests of the *ṣaḥrādārs* to let them have a certain amount of land for this purpose, since they manure it for the cultivation of summer crops and vegetables. The *ṣaḥrādārs* have priority over the *ballaks* in the matter of the water-supply.

Two to four *juft* are grouped together in Jahrum in a unit known as *harāṣeh*, in charge of which is a peasant known as the *rīsh safīd*.[2] In the irrigated land of the villages in this area there is, for the most part, a threefold rotation, and the land is divided into three portions. Two months before the Persian New Year, when the ploughing season begins, lots are cast for one of the three portions each year, each portion being held for a period of three years.

In Kurdistān in a few areas a number of *juft*, usually some three to five, are grouped together and work as a unit, known locally as *jūq*. In Ḥasanābād near Sanandaj the village is divided into *jūq*, each having four *juft*. At the head of each *jūq* is a peasant known as the *sar jūq*. He has no special privilege, and is merely the oldest and most experienced or respected of the group. He decides who shall perform labour service (*bīgārī*) and at what time this shall be performed.[3]

In certain areas of the country a limited amount of the land only is distributed by lot, the remainder being permanently distributed. Thus in the Asadābād area near Hamadān when a certain piece of land, apart from that already divided into plough-lands, is to be sown in a given year with a special crop, for example cotton, this land is divided into a number of shares corresponding to the number of plough-lands in the village, and lots are drawn by the holders of the plough-lands for shares in this land. This drawing of lots is known as *pishk*. Similarly, when new land is brought into cultivation, lots are drawn in the same way but the division is permanent; this drawing of lots is known as *qarāpishk*.[4]

Similarly part of the land in the Bakhtīārī is redistributed by lot every seven to ten years; this process is also known locally as *qarāpishk*.

Redistribution by lot is not usual in Iṣfahān. In the majority

[1] A piece of *daym* land sown by a *ballak* with grain is known as *namūneh*.

[2] Lit. the white-bearded, i.e. an elder. [3] See Ch. XVIII.

[4] See *qarāpishk* above, p. 296, in a different meaning.

of cases the peasant remains in occupation of the same piece of land. If a new piece of land is brought into cultivation after lying fallow for some years the *kadkhudā* and peasants of the village, or the village elders (the *rīsh safīd*), customarily assemble and divide it among themselves. In Sāveh also there is no periodic redistribution of land. The same is true of the *khāliṣeh* villages near Īrānshahr in Balūchistān.

In Āẕarbāyjān if the peasant has no occupancy rights or *jivar* (*juvar*) rights the land is redistributed between the *juft* of the village every so many years, this distribution being known as *hampā'ī*. The period varies usually from six to ten years. In Qarājeh Dāgh the village land is redistributed every ten years or so. In Burūjird a redistribution of village land by the *kadkhudā* is usual.

A similar practice is followed in many parts of Fārs. This places an undue measure of power in the hands of the *kadkhudā*. The consequence of any measure of independence on the part of the peasant, or, indeed lack of subservience to the *kadkhudā*'s wishes, is likely to be a failure to obtain an adequate share of the good land of the village at the next year's redistribution of the land. In Nayrīz and Dārāb an annual redistribution of the village lands is made by the drawing of lots.

In the Bihbahān area the land is annually redistributed in Mihr (September–October) or Ābān (October–November) by the *kadkhudā* or *mubāshir*. In Dizfūl an annual drawing of lots for land is usual.

Whether the peasant holds a piece of land for one year or a number of years depends in Kirmān entirely on the will of the landowner. It is alleged that the land in Shahdād is usually left in the hands of the same peasant, and only re-allotted if the total land under cultivation is increased.

In Kurdistān the land of a village is redistributed whenever the landowner sees fit; the period usually varies from some five to fifteen years. The land of Ḥasanābād near Sanandaj was redistributed in 1948 after some fifteen years. In Dīvān Darreh the land is redistributed every ten to fifteen years. Where the landowner retains a portion of the village land which he works directly, i.e. not on a share-cropping basis,[1] this land is excluded from the annual or periodic redistribution. Unirrigated or *daym* land both in Khurāsān and Kurdistān is normally also excluded from redistribution, probably mainly for the reason that there is no shortage of *daym* land or great difference in quality between one area and another, whereas in irrigated land the relative distance from the head of the water-supply may make a material difference to the productivity or otherwise of the land.

[1] This land is known locally as *khāliṣeh*.

The peasant in the cases described in the preceding paragraphs either owns the draught animals with which his holding is cultivated or belongs to a group one of the members of which owns the draught animals, or is provided by the landowner with draught animals. In some areas, however, notably the neighbourhood of Tehrān, a third person known as the *gāvband* is interposed between the peasant and the landowner or the peasant and the lessee. The *gāvband* usually manages some four to six units known as *buneh*, sowing some 8 to 10 *kharvār* (approx. 87 bushels, 18 lb. to 109 bushels) of grain. Each unit or *buneh* comprises one ox and four men, with whom the *gāvband* makes a contract. Each ox has attached to it one *sar ābyār* and one *dumbi ābyārī*, who are engaged mainly in irrigating and weeding the land, and two labourers (*barzigar*), who attend mainly to the ploughing. The initial division of the crop is between the *gāvband* and the landowner or lessee; the share of the *gāvband* is then divided between the *gāvband* and the peasants after the deduction of any dues for local officials.[1]

In some areas a certain security is given the peasants by the fact that they own their houses and gardens, known collectively as *aʿyān*. Where this is the case the landlord, should he wish to evict them, has to buy the *aʿyān*, i.e. the trees, fruit-trees, vines, etc., and any buildings the peasant may have put up; in some areas the landlord has to compensate the peasant also for the labour which he has put into the land. Ownership of the *aʿyān* can be registered.

The general tendency is for the landowners not to encourage the peasants to make gardens. The reason for this is that the landowners know that the possession of gardens is likely to make the peasants more prosperous, and fear lest easier circumstances may make them independent. There is a minority of landowners who adopt a more liberal policy, and take the view that if the peasant has some permanent stake in the land, he is more likely to be contented and, therefore, to work better. In such cases they encourage the peasants to make gardens and give them land in which to do so.

In some parts of Khurāsān a somewhat different practice prevails. Anyone wishing to make a garden in a landlord area enters into a contract with the landlord for a period of ten to twenty years. During this period one-half or one-third of the produce goes to the landlord, and after the expiry of the period the land, together with the garden made on it, reverts to the landlord. In some cases a stipulation is made that when the contract expires one-tenth or so of the value of the garden is paid by the landowner to the man who made the garden.

In so far as housing is concerned the landlords probably prefer

[1] See Ch. XXI.

the peasants to own their own houses because they (the landlords) are not then liable for the expense of repairs. In certain villages in the Asabādād area near Hamadān the peasants own their houses, and most of the peasants in the Tabrīz area own their own houses. In Qarājeh Dāgh, on the other hand, the *aʿyān* mainly belong to the landowners; Varzaqān in the Uzum Dil region is an exception to this. In the Bīrjand area the *aʿyān* have in some cases been transferred by the landowners to the peasants. This, for example, is the case in Gīv, which was rebuilt after destruction by an earthquake in 1948. The peasant does not own his house in the majority of villages in Burkhwār; Sīn is an exception to this. In Qahdrījān near Iṣfahān the *aʿyān* belong to the peasants. For the most part this is also the case in the villages in the immediate neighbourhood of Iṣfahān. In Sāveh the *aʿyān* belong mainly to the landowners.

In various areas in Fārs the peasants own their houses. This is so in Qarā Bulāgh and Iṣṭahbānāt, except where the peasants live in a *qalʿeh*, or walled enclosure, belonging to the owner. In the Nayrīz area, on the other hand, the housing in most villages belongs to the landowner.

Most of the houses in Dizfūl formerly belonged to the landowners. In many cases these have been transferred to the peasants. In villages where there is a *qalʿeh* this usually belongs to the landowner, and the peasants working for him normally live inside the *qalʿeh*; in some cases they build rooms inside it for themselves. This, for example, is the case in Dayijī, near Dizfūl. In Vays, Bandi Qīr, ʿAqīlī, Rām Hurmuz, Khalafābād, and, for the most part, in the Bihbahān area the houses belong to the peasants. In Sayyid Khalaf, near Ahvāz, on the other hand, the housing belongs to the landowner.

In Sahneh the *aʿyān* belong to the principal landowner. In 1945 he was alleged to take one-sixth of the tenant's revenue as rent, a levy which was regarded locally as being somewhat heavy. In the Sanandaj area the housing for the most part belongs to the landowner. In Ḥasanābād near Sanandaj it is related that the landowner told the peasants they could register the houses and gardens in their own names subject to the condition that they did not sell them to outsiders. It is alleged that few of them took advantage of this; they argued that, as things were, when their houses needed repair, the landowner's bailiff saw to the matter, whereas if they were to register the houses in their own names this would no longer be the case. Further, they are alleged to have declared that the houses were for them *ḥalāl*, i.e. not lawful property. It is possible that something of the sort did in fact occur. In any case by 1949 only about half the villagers had in fact registered their houses and gardens in their own names. There is no doubt that in some areas there is a feeling that certain things are the lawful due of the landowner and therefore not proper to the peasant. This feeling, in so far as it exists, has its roots in tradition, and has been fostered by centuries of subservience by the peasant to the landowning class, and by a distrust on the part of the peasant of his own capabilities. It has been largely broken down by recent events but probably still lingers on in the remoter areas.

In some areas those peasants who cultivate the arable land of a village on a crop-sharing basis, or against the payment of a rent, enjoy certain advantages over those inhabitants of the village who are not crop-sharing peasants or tenants and who are known as *khwushnishīn*.[1] The former, on the whole, where they hold gardens, tend to hold them on more favourable terms. For example, in Lakkān, in Arāk, while the crop-sharing peasants paid in 1945 a due of 6 rs. (approx. 8½*d.*) per 100 vines, the *khwushnishīn* paid 50 rs. (approx. 5*s.* 10*d.*).[2]

Further, although the peasant has no right to transmit his holding by inheritance (except in a few areas) if the holder of a plough-land or a share of the water dies, it usually happens that the landlord makes an agreement with one of his sons, who continues to cultivate the land which his father cultivated before him. Where, moreover, the peasant is able to transmit his holding by inheritance, since the holding is a unit which in theory can support and be cultivated by a family, the usual practice is for one member of the family to succeed to the holding, and to work it on behalf of and with the help of the others. Subdivision beyond a certain limit is avoided in the same way as it is avoided in the peasant-proprietor areas. Eviction, although the peasant has for the most part no legal security of tenure, is not usual. The reasons for this are probably twofold. In the first place tradition is strong, and it is not the custom for the landowner to turn his peasants out, although they may be driven by poverty to leave of their own accord; in the second place the pressure on the available land is not great except in certain areas. In some places there is a shortage rather than a superfluity of peasants. In the west of Persia, in the neighbourhood of Kirmānshāh on the borders of Kurdistān, it seems that there is a shortage of peasants and that the land is not cultivated to its full capacity. In Arāk also in many cases all the plough-lands of the villages are not in cultivation.[3] The villages

[1] In Khurāsān they are known as *āftābnishīn*.

[2] cf. the division of the peasants in Hashtrūd into *zāri'* and *gharībeh*. The latter pay higher pasture dues (see below, p. 334).

[3] The total potential of a village in plough-lands is known in this area as *nasaq*.

range from a potential capacity of 24 to 120 plough-lands; few, if any, have 120 in cultivation, the average being 36 to 48.

In some areas it may happen that a village has more land than its inhabitants can cultivate, or more water than it can use. In the latter case, which is rare, the water will be leased to a neighbouring village. In the former case peasants sometimes come from a neighbouring village and cultivate the land, paying the landowner's dues in the village in the usual way, although actually living in another village.

On the other hand, the pressure on the land is considerable in certain areas, especially in the neighbourhood of the large towns. In the neighbourhood of Tehrān, for example, it is extremely difficult for a peasant to acquire a holding on a crop-sharing basis in a landlord estate, the available holdings being for the most part taken up. In the neighbourhood of Kirmān there is a superfluity of peasants, and it is customary when a new peasant takes over from an outgoing peasant to pay a premium (known as *taʿāruf*) to the landowner for the right to cultivate the land. This practice was formerly more widespread than it is at the present day; it still prevails in some areas of the province of Kirmān. A similar practice exists in the *garmsīr* of Turbati Ḥaydarī.

In some areas, on the other hand, there has been a flight from the land. This has already been mentioned in so far as it concerns the peasant-proprietor areas on the edge of the central desert. It is also noticeable in east Persia, in Qā'ināt, and Sīstān. The exodus from these areas is due mainly to the poverty of the peasants. In southern Persia also on the borders of the oil-producing area there is a flight from the land, the peasants seeking more profitable employment in the oil-fields; this movement is to some extent a seasonal one, the peasants coming down in winter and returning to their villages at harvest time. There is also a movement into the towns where work is offered by industrial concerns, such as the textile factories in Iṣfahān. There has been in recent years an influx into Tehrān of people from relatively remote areas also in search of work; it is significant that the few rials they are able or hope to earn in a town offer them a more attractive prospect than life in a village at a bare subsistence level.

CHAPTER XVII

THE DIVISION OF THE CROP: RENTS

THE relations between the peasant and the landowner are, for the most part, based on a crop-sharing agreement. Another type of relationship is based on a fixed rent.[1] In either case the payment to the landowner is usually made partly in kind and partly in cash. The crop-sharing agreement, which is by far the most common, will be discussed first. The basis of this relationship is primarily and mainly local custom, which, although it displays a certain homogeneity throughout the country, differs considerably in detail from district to district. An attempt was made in early times by the Islamic jurists and in modern times by those who framed the Civil Code to bring this type of relationship within the legal system.[2] It nevertheless remains largely regulated by custom. Traditionally, five elements are taken into account in dividing the crop: land, water, draught animals, seed, labour; theoretically one share is allotted to each element and goes to whoever provides that element. In fact, however, this is little more than a theoretical abstraction, and the actual division, although it is materially affected by the ownership and provision of these different elements, is seldom made on the basis of the allotment of five equal shares for each element. Some jurists hold that if the peasant provides only his labour, the agreement is not a crop-sharing agreement, or *muzāraʿeh*. In certain areas, however, land is in fact handed over to a peasant who cultivates it with draught animals, seed, and implements provided by the owner in return for a specified share of the crop. The position of such peasants differs from that of labourers who work for the landowner on land which he has exempted from the general distribution among the peasants on a crop-sharing basis, and will, therefore, be included here. Such peasants are subject to dues and servitudes as are the crop-sharing peasants proper, and their land to periodic redistribution in those areas where periodic redistribution is made.

A great variety of practice concerning the division of the crops prevails: the major differences concern irrigated and unirrigated crops, and *shatvī*, or winter crops, and *ṣayfī*, or summer crops and vegetables. The type of irrigation, whether by river, *qanāt*, or well also affects the division of the crop. In some cases straw is included in the division, in others it goes to one or other of the two parties concerned. In the majority of cases the actual division of the grain

[1] cf. *muqāsameh, masāḥat,* and *muqāṭaʿeh* agreements (Ch. II).
[2] See Ch. IX.

crop is made on the threshing-floor, the grain and straw being divided up into the requisite number of heaps. Thus, supposing the landlord's share is two shares to the peasant's one, the grain and straw are each divided into three heaps. In some areas, notably Kurdistān, it is the right of the landlord or his agent to choose which heap he will have. The grain and straw are measured into the heaps, usually with a relatively small hand measure, a process which is in itself laborious. Normally the peasant has not permission to move his share of the harvest from the threshing-floor until the landlord takes his in person or through an agent acting on his behalf. When the harvest is collected into heaps some sort of mark is placed on them[1] which becomes displaced if anyone touches the grain. Watchmen are stationed in the fields at night to guard the grain against theft. The cost of the transport of the grain and straw to the granary varies: in many areas it is the responsibility of the peasant to transport both his share and that of the landlord to the granary.[2]

The landowner's share of *ṣayfī* crops (summer crops and vegetables), in contradistinction to grain crops, is usually decided by valuation. In some areas, however, the landowner's share not only of *ṣayfī* crops but also of *shatvī* crops is decided by valuation. This is the normal practice in the Mamasanī area. A valuer (*mumaiyiz*) comes round in the person of the *kadkhudā* or some other individual, looks at the crop, often, it is alleged, in the most cursory fashion, and estimates it at so much, on which estimate the peasant is required to pay the landlord's share. This process causes much discontent, and it is alleged that over-estimation is common. In the neighbouring district of Nūrābād, where the proportion taken by the landowner as his share of the crop is the same, but where the harvest is divided on the threshing-floor, the peasant appears to be rather better off. In Fīrūzābād the share due from the peasant is fixed annually by a valuer (*mumaiyiz*). The latter represents both the landowner and the village elders (*rīsh safīd*), but is paid for his services by the landowner. In some properties in the neighbourhood (but not in those owned by the Qashqā'ī leaders) the peasant's contribution is fixed by taking the average share due over a period of three years. In Qarā Bulāgh the landowner's share of unirrigated crops is estimated by valuation, but irrigated crops are divided on the threshing-floor.

For the most part the landowner's share on grain crops is paid in kind. In a few areas it is converted wholly or in part into cash. This, however, is not the usual practice. On *ṣayfī* crops the landowner's share is more often paid in cash. In some parts of the

[1] This is known as *muhr kardan*, i.e. 'to seal' the grain.
[2] See p. 330.

Bakhtīārī the landowner's share of *ṣayfī* crops is converted into and paid in grain.

In addition to the share of the crop which goes to the landlord (or lessee) there are also a number of dues deducted from the crop. Great variety of practice prevails in the form and method of deduction of these.[1] Only after all the various dues have been taken into account can an accurate estimate be made of the share of the crop remaining to the peasant. In general, it would appear that in those areas where the peasant receives a larger share of the crop under the crop-sharing agreement he has to pay heavier dues under other heads, while in those areas where his share is smaller the extra levies made on him are fewer.

The extent to which the peasant provides draught animals, seed, and labour varies in different parts of the country. As a rule, where he provides all three his economic position tends to be more favourable. In many areas of the country seed is provided by the landowner. Where this is the case, and the harvest is divided into five shares, one share is set aside for the seed; in other cases an equivalent amount is deducted for the landowner (or lessee) from the total harvest, i.e. before it is divided between the peasant and the landowner according to their allotted shares.

Irrigated wheat and barley

In Arāk the usual practice is *seh kūt*, i.e. one share goes to the landowner and two to the peasant who provides the oxen, seed, and labour. In Farāhān, however, the division is mainly *niṣfī*, i.e. half goes to the landowner and half to the peasant. In a few areas where the landowner provides the seed two-thirds of the harvest goes to him. This division is known as *seh kūti maʿkūs*.

In the Iṣfahān area, including Linjān, the division is for the most part two shares to the landlord and one to the peasant. The former provides the land, water, and seed, and the latter the draught animals and labour. Where the peasant provides the draught animals, agricultural implements, and seed, he gets two shares to the landlord's one. This, in contradistinction to the practice in Arāk, is also known as *seh kūti maʿkūs*.

In certain parts of Burkhwār, such as Ḥaydarābād and Amīrābād, three shares go to the landowner and two to the peasant. The division in some areas in Burūjird is half to the landlord and half to the peasant, who provides the draught animals, implements, and seed; for the most part, however, three-fifths go to the landowner, who provides the seed, which in some cases is deducted from the total harvest before the division between the two parties is made. In certain villages in the Varāmīn area where the peasant provides

[1] See Ch. XVIII.

the seed, draught animals, and labour the division is also *niṣfī*, i.e. half going to either party.

In Maʿmūnīyeh, the principal village of Zarand (near Sāveh), in some large landed properties the landlord provides the seed and takes two-thirds of the crop. In other parts of Zarand the landowner takes three-fifths. In Bayāt, another district of Sāveh, four-fifths go to the landowner, who provides the seed. This was formerly the division in Kharaqān also. During famine years, some twenty-six years ago, the chief landowner made an adjustment to lighten the burden on the peasant: by this the landowner's share was reduced to one-third, the peasant providing the seed, and straw was exempted from the division, all of it going to the peasant.

Considerable variations are found in Khurāsān. In Ṭuruq, Khīābān, Shādkan, and Ābkūh the lessee, and in Vakīlābād the owner, takes one-half. The lessee or the owner provides the seed, which is deducted from the total harvest. In some of the neighbouring landlord areas the peasant receives seven-tenths. In Turbati Ḥaydarī the division in the *garmsīr* differs from the division in the *sardsīr*. In the latter the landlord provides the seed and takes three-fifths of the grain and half of the straw. In Andishghūn, however, the landlord takes two-thirds, and in Zāveh three-fifths, the seed being provided by the landlord and deducted from the total harvest. In the *garmsīr* the landlord also provides the seed and takes two-thirds of the crop. In Kāshmar the prevailing division is two-thirds to the landowner, who provides the seed, which is deducted from the total harvest. In some landlord areas which were formerly *khāliṣeh* three-fourths of the crop goes to the landowner.

In certain villages in Hamadān the landowner takes one-third of the grain and the straw. In the Asadābād area draught animals and seed are both provided by the peasant, whose share is three-quarters of the crop. Before the division is made one *qafīz* (or *āb mīān*) is deducted from the total harvest for the landowner.[1] The predominant division in the Kirmānshāh area is two-thirds to the peasant. A great variety of practice is found in the province of Āẕarbāyjān. In Hashtrūd the landowner's share is one-third, one-fourth, or one-fifth; this is also the case in Qarājeh Dāgh, Ūjān, ʿAbbās, and Mihrānarūd; for the most part the highest of these rates is taken in the case of land watered by *qanāts*. In Sarcham (between Zanjān and Tabrīz) and Khurramdasht three-quarters of the crop goes to the peasant. In Marāgheh, Khūy, and parts of Riẓā'īyeh one-third is the prevailing rate at which the landlord's

[1] This is somewhat similar to the custom found in certain areas of southern Persia where the holder of a plough-land is required to cultivate a certain amount of grain for the landlord (see p. 332).

share is taken: the peasant supplies the seed and provides the draught animals and implements. In Mīāndoāb the peasant also gets two-thirds of the crop. In some areas of Āẕarbāyjān, including parts of Qarājeh Dāgh, two-ninths are the landlord's share, together with one-fortieth (known as *kharman chillak*) on crops which grow on the land after the grain harvest has been reaped. In Varzaqān in Uzum Dil straw is exempted from this division, but the peasant has to give the landowner instead 20 *sabad* (37 cwt.) of straw per *pānzdah*,[1] each *sabad* holding approximately 10 *manni ahar* (approx. 1 cwt., 95 lb.). The rough heads[2] left on the threshing-floor after the grain and straw have been separated by threshing and winnowing are also divided on the basis of two-ninths to the landowner. Lucerne is divided in a different way: on the first crop the land-owner takes half, and on the second one-fifth.[3] In Kilaybar in Qarājeh Dāgh the landlord takes two-fifteenths of the crop in certain properties.

In Kurdistān, broadly speaking, the crop division is less favourable to the peasant in the immediate neighbourhood of the towns than in the more remote districts. In the neighbourhood of Sanandaj in the area extending for some 7 miles from the town the landowner takes one-half on wheat and barley. Straw, the rough heads of which remain on the threshing-floor after threshing and winnowing,[4] and grass go entirely to the peasant. In other districts of Kurdistān the prevailing division is one-fifth to the landowner. In Zhāvirūd, where the soil is unduly stony, the landowner's share is less, namely, two-fifteenths.

The usual division in Bakhtīārī is three-quarters to the peasant, or two-thirds. Where the landowner provides the seed, however, he gets two-thirds. In Firaydan if the peasant provides the seed and oxen he takes two-thirds.

In Fārs, in view of the widely different climatic conditions prevailing, it is not surprising that many variations are found. In the Mamasanī in Kūpān the peasant provides the draught animals, labour, and seed and takes three-quarters of the crop; in Nūrābād a similar division prevails. In Bālādeh and for the most part in Noujayn the landowner takes one-third; in Farrāshband the land-owner's share, which was formerly one-quarter, has been reduced to one-sixth. In Fīrūzābād the owner provides the seed and in some cases the oxen also, and takes half or two-thirds. In Fasā the landowner normally provides the seed and draught animals and takes four-fifths of the crop. In Jahrum the division is *niṣfī*, i.e. half

[1] The village land is divided into 93 *pānzdah*.
[2] Known locally as *kuzar*.
[3] The second crop is known as *pishi dirou* (*pisha dura*), and the third crop as *āva dura*.
[4] Known locally as *kutal*.

going to either party, including straw; the landowner provides the seed. This is also the case in Dobarān. In Dārāb and its five *bulūks* (Khusū, Fasārūd, Shāhījān, Rūdbār, and Kashīvar) the landowner provides the draught animals, implements, and seed; the latter is deducted from the total harvest, after which the peasant gets one-quarter of what remains. If, however, the peasant owns the oxen and provides the seed he takes two-thirds. In Qarā Bulāgh and Nayrīz, in land watered by well the peasant undertakes all the expenses of cultivation, provides the seed and draught animals, and takes nine-tenths of the crop. On the other hand, in land watered by *qanāt* in Qarā Bulāgh the landowner is responsible for all the expenses of cultivation, provides the seed and draught animals, and takes three-quarters of the crop. This is also the case in Iṣṭahbānāt. In Khīr and Īj in the same neighbourhood the landlord takes two-thirds. In Nayrīz (except in land watered by well) the peasant usually provides the draught animals, but other expenses, including seed, are the responsibility of the landowner, who takes three-quarters of the harvest. In the *sarḥadd*, i.e. the *yaylāq* of the Īli ʿArab the owner provides the draught animals and seed and takes three-quarters of the harvest.

The division in the province of Kirmān is for the most part either seven-tenths or two-thirds to the landowner. In Gāvkhāneh, Akbarābād, and Muḥammadābād, near the town of Kirmān, the owner's share is seven-tenths. Oxen belong to the peasant, who also provides the seed. In Sīrjān the landowner's share in the villages in the plain (*julgeh*) is 82 per cent, in Quhistān 75 per cent, and in the hill districts 67 per cent. In Bam, Narmāshīr, Jīruft, Rūdbār, and Sar Dū'īyeh the landlord takes 70 per cent. In Bāft he takes in some cases 75 per cent and in others 70 per cent; the expenses of cultivation are the responsibility of the peasant. In certain villages in Zarand the landowner's share is two-thirds of the crop. He provides the seed. In others the landowner takes 70 per cent of the crop, the expenses of cultivation, such as manure, the digging of the land, and the provision of seed, being the responsibility of the peasant. In Shahdād, similarly, the landowner's share is 70 per cent. In this area wheat straw goes to the landowner and barley straw to the peasant; if, however, the amount of one is in excess of the other, the surplus is equally divided between the two parties. In Tikābād the landowner provides the seed; in Andūjird this is also the case, but an equivalent amount is subsequently deducted for the landlord from the total harvest. In Bardsīr the landowner's share is 70 per cent or, in some cases, two-thirds of the crop. In Rafsinjān, in the villages of Nūq, where the soil is brackish or where the land has recently come into cultivation, the landlord takes half the produce, the draught animals and seed being provided by the peasant; where the landlord provides these he takes 75 per cent of the crop. In other areas where the landlord provides the seed and the peasant the draught animals, the former takes 70 per cent of the crop. Formerly in the neighbourhood (*ḥoumeh*) of Rafsinjān the division was 75 per cent to the landowner, except for straw, which was *niṣfī*, i.e. half going to either party. About the year 1946, when agitation by the Tūdeh party was active, the landowner's share in many villages was reduced to 70 per cent. The provision of draught animals and asses is the responsibility of the peasant, and expenses in connexion with *qanāts* the responsibility of the landowner. Other expenses, such as digging the land and the provision of seed, are shared between the two parties in the same proportion as the crop is shared, i.e. 30 per cent is paid by the peasant and 70 per cent by the landowner; the provision and purchase of manure, however, is the responsibility of the landowner and its transport that of the peasant. In Raḥmatābād, near Rafsinjān, the division is 70 per cent to the landlord on the grain and half on the straw. In the more productive villages of Rafsinjān the division is still 75 per cent to the owner. In most areas of the province of Kirmān the rough heads of wheat and barley[1] remaining on the threshing-floor after winnowing and threshing goes to the peasant. It would thus appear that the share of the peasant relative to that of the landowner in the province of Kirmān, taking into consideration the fact that he provides the draught animals and in many cases the seed also, is considerably less favourable than in most other areas. One of the reasons for the larger share of the landowner is that the expenses in connexion with the upkeep of *qanāts* in Kirmān are heavy owing to the great length of many of the *qanāts* and the nature of the soil through which they flow.

In Bīrjand and Qā'ināt the peasant for the most part provides the oxen and asses and the landowner the seed. When, however, the peasant loses his ox it is frequently replaced by the landlord. The landlord's share of the crop in most cases is three-quarters or two-thirds of the crop. In Kākh the landowner takes three-quarters on the grain and half on straw. In Ḥasanābād, a village near Kākh, on the other hand, the landowner's share is two-thirds. In Isfīdrūd, south of Shoukatābād, the landowner takes three-quarters on wheat, five-sixths on barley, and half on straw.

The peasant provides the draught animals in the *khāliṣeh* land of Bampūr in Balūchistān and takes three-fifths of the crop. One hundred *manni tabrīz* (approx. 5 cwt., 95 lb.) of seed per *juft* is provided by the government or, if the property is leased, by the lessee, and recovered at harvest time after the government's (or

[1] Known locally as *kurūsheh*.

the lessee's) share has been deducted from the total harvest. In the neighbourhood of Khāsh three-fifths go to the owner, who provides the seed. The draught animals are let to the peasant by the landowner for ploughing, at a rate of some 50 rs. (approx. 5*s.* 10*d.*) per day; in some cases, however, the peasant merely pays for their keep while using them.

In Sīstān the landowner usually provides the seed and the peasant the draught animals. Where this is the case the landowner takes two-thirds or three-fifths of the harvest; in some areas, where the seed is provided in equal parts by the peasant and the landowner, the crop is divided in equal shares between the two parties.

There are certain differences between the various areas of Khūzistān, especially between the Arab tribal areas and the Persian settled areas. Usually the landowner's share is the first charge on the harvest before any dues are deducted. In Bandi Qīr, Sayyid Khalaf, and Ismāʿīlīyeh the landowner takes one-third, the peasant providing the seed and draught animals. In Bandi Qīr, if the landowner supplies the seed (which is not customary), he takes half the crop. In the Bāvī areas the landowner provides the seed and takes half the crop. In the Bihbahān neighbourhood the landowner takes one-fifth on the grain and 300 kg. straw per *juft*. The peasant provides the seed and draught animals. In Dizfūl the landowner takes one-tenth to one-fifth. The peasant here, too, provides the seed and draught animals. In Rām Hurmuz the landowner takes one-quarter in grain and straw, or, in some cases, one-third, the peasant providing the seed and draught animals; this is also the case in Shūsht (near Bāsht). In most of the Arab areas which were *khāliṣeh* one-quarter of the grain crops was paid to the government; in some of the properties which had formerly belonged to Shaykh Khazʿal, as for example Qalʿeh Saḥar, one-third was levied as the landowner's share, and this continued to be the rate when the properties became *khāliṣeh*. In 1316/1937–8 the government dues (*mināl*) on *khāliṣeh* were remitted by virtue of a royal proclamation. This, however, was never ratified by the National Assembly. Although the Minister of Finance expressed the view after the abdication of Riẓā Shāh in 1941 that the proclamation was no longer valid, the *mināl* were not in fact reimposed until 1326/1947–8, and then at a slightly different rate, namely, one-fifth to one-fourth. In the *khāliṣeh* of Havīzeh and Sūsangird when the government dues were reimposed in 1326/1947–8 the cash equivalent of 3 *manni havīzeh* (approx. 2 cwt., 71 lb.) per share of 1 ha. (2·47109 acres) was taken.

In some of the villages round Qumm and Kāshān the landlord provides seed and draught animals and takes four-fifths of the crop. In the Pushti Kūh district of Yazd crop-sharing is found only in the newer villages: the older foundations are rented. The reason for this difference in practice appears to be that no one is prepared to pay a fixed rent down for the right to cultivate the land of a village until the area has been under cultivation for some years, because in the beginning the yield is problematical. Where crop-sharing prevails the crop is usually divided equally between the landowner and the peasant, seed being deducted from the total harvest and repaid to whoever provided it.

Crop-sharing is also found in a small way in those areas in central Persia where the prevalent tenure is peasant proprietorship. Thus in Mūrchehkhw̱art and Abīāneh where land is worked on a crop-sharing basis, the landowner provides seed and draught animals and takes three-quarters of the crop; straw goes entirely to him and is used as fodder for his animals. This is also the case in Khusrouābād and Vandādeh (near Maymeh in the district of Joushaqān); if, however, the peasant provides the draught animals the division is *niṣfī*, i.e. half goes to either party. In Tar (near Tarq) the landowner takes two-thirds and provides the seed and draught animals.

Unirrigated wheat and barley

Daym, i.e. unirrigated or dry, crops are only found in certain parts of Persia. Usually the seed and draught animals are provided by the peasant. This is the case in the areas mentioned below unless otherwise stated. In Arāk one-fifth goes to the landowner. In the Sāveh district the division in Kharaqān is as for irrigated crops; but in Bayāt one-fifth only is the owner's share. There are considerable areas of dry farming in Khurāsān. In Ṭuruq the lessee takes one-tenth of the crop, which is divided on the threshing-floor. In a year when water is plentiful some water is given to *daym* crops, in which case the division of the crop is modified; if water is given twice the lessee takes three-tenths, and if once one-fifth. In Khīābān, in the same area, the division is also one-tenth to the lessee. Here too, when water is plentiful, it is used to irrigate the *daym* crops also, in which case the lessee takes one-fifth if the crop is watered once and half if it is watered twice. In Shādkan and Vakīlābād the lessee and landowner respectively take one-tenth. In Ābkūh the division is as for irrigated crops, namely, *niṣfī*; the landowner (or lessee) provides the seed, which is deducted from the total harvest. In Turbati Ḥaydarī the landowner's share is one-tenth.

In Hashtrūd in Āẕarbāyjān one-quarter, occasionally one-third, and in some areas one-fifth, is the landowner's share. He also gets one-fortieth of the total harvest. These shares together with various other dues amount roughly to two-ninths of the total.

A similar division is made in Ūjān, ʿAbbās, Mihrānarūd, and Qarājeh Dāgh. In the Tabrīz area, the landowner's share is one-quarter. In the neighbourhood of Sanandaj and in most parts of Kurdistān the landowner takes one-fifth. In the Bakhtīārī and Firaydan the landowner's share is for the most part one-quarter, but if the landowner provides the seed he takes half the crop.

In Fārs in the Mamasanī, Nūrābād, and Kāzirūn the landowner takes one-fifth; in Fasā, Fidiskān, Dobarān, and Dārāb one-tenth; in Jahrum the proportion varies from one-fifth to one-tenth according to the proximity or otherwise of the land to the town. In Fīrūzābād one-sixth is taken by the landowner. In the Bīrjand area in general nothing is taken on unirrigated crops. It is said that until some fifteen years ago the government used to take *ʿushr* (tithe), i.e. one-tenth, on *daym* crops. This was apparently levied by way of a tax and was not a share levied for the benefit of the landowner. One-eighth is taken by the landowner in Khūzistān in Bandi Qīr and Sayyid Khalaf; and one-fifth in Bāsht, Shūsht, and in Khalafābād in areas near the river.

In the Bāvī areas, if the draught animals are provided by the peasant, who is in that case known as a *nīmkār*, and the seed by the landowner, the produce in *daym* land is equally divided. In some cases, however, the landowner provides the draught animals also, in which case the peasant gets only one-quarter of the crop; the landowner gives him also food, an *ʿabā*, or cloak, in summer, a *namad*, or felt, in winter, and two pairs of *gīveh*, or cotton shoes, per annum. Such a peasant is known as a *sumkār*. In the Arab areas which are *khāliṣeh* 33 to 100 rs. (approx. 3*s.* 11*d.* to 11*s.* 9*d.*) per plough-land was levied under Riẓā Shāh, except in some properties formerly belonging to Shaykh Khazʿal, which continued to pay 70 rs. (approx. 8*s.* 3*d.*) as they had paid under Shaykh Khazʿal. These dues were remitted, as were the dues on irrigated wheat, by royal proclamation in 1316/1937–8 (see p. 313), and when reimposed in 1326/1947–8 the rate was increased to 140 rs. (approx. 16*s.* 6*d.*) per plough-land, or ½ *manni ahvāz* (approx. 55 lb.) wheat and ½ *manni ahvāz* barley. These dues are paid to the local Department of Finance.

Ṣayfī crops, i.e. summer crops and vegetables

In some areas the division is the same as for irrigated grain or *shatvī* crops, but usually the peasant's share is higher than in the case of *shatvī* crops. The provision of seed is of less importance than in the case of wheat and barley; manure, however, is more frequently used. Weeding has to be carried out with some crops. In the neighbourhood of Tehrān cotton is mainly *niṣfī*, i.e. equal shares going to either party if the landowner provides the manure;

if the peasant furnishes this, he takes two-thirds of the crop. In Shahrīār and Souj Bulāgh *ṣayfī* crops are divided at the rate of two-thirds or three-fifths to the peasants and one-third or two-fifths to the landlord, except where the peasant pays a fixed rent per *jarīb*.

The division for *ṣayfī* crops in Arāk is as for *shatvī*. In the Sāveh area the peasant's share is two-thirds. The usual division in Iṣfahān is *niṣfī*. In Burkhw̱ār, where the main wealth of the area comes from *ṣayfī* crops, especially melons, which have largely replaced cotton, formerly widely grown, the peasant provides the seed and spades for cultivation and takes half the produce. Normally the peasant converts the landowner's share into cash and pays him in money and not in kind. Various oil-seeds and pulses such as castor-oil, sunflowers, rape, *shāhdāneh*, and *sīāh tukhm* are grown round the edges of the melon fields and known as *sar marzī*. They are divided on the basis of two-sevenths to the landowner and five-sevenths to the peasant.

The division of *ṣayfī* crops, such as cotton, beet, etc., in Ṭuruq, Khīāban, Ābkūh, Shādkan, and Vakīlābād in Khurāsān is *niṣfī*, the shares being estimated by a valuer (*mumaiyiz*); on crops known as *bāgh tarreh*, i.e. melons, water-melons, cucumbers, etc., the lessee takes one-third or two-fifths according to the method of cultivation.[1] In Shādkan if the lessee provides the manure he takes half. In Turbati Ḥaydarī the landowner takes half in most villages in the *sardsīr*; in Malikābād and Andishghūn he takes two-thirds; in Zāveh he takes three-fifths and in the *garmsīr* two-thirds. In Kāshmar the landowner takes three-quarters of the crop, or, in land which was formerly *khāliṣeh*, four-fifths. In Quzhd, which is mainly owned by peasant proprietors, where the land is cultivated on a crop-sharing basis the landowner's share is three-quarters.

In the Hamadān area in some places such as Dastjird and Sulaymānābād the landowner takes one-third; in Asadābād the landowner's share is one-quarter. The division in Āẕarbāyjān in most areas is as for irrigated *shatvī* crops. The landowner's share on tobacco in Marāgheh is taken in kind. In Kurdistān the landowner's share in the neighbourhood of Sanandaj is one-third; elsewhere it is as for irrigated *shatvī* crops. In the Bakhtīārī the rate is also as for irrigated *shatvī* crops.

In Fārs in the Mamasanī, Fidiskān, Jahrum, and Fīrūzābād the division is *niṣfī*; in the last-named place in the Qashqā'ī property

[1] In the former case the plants are sown on a flat surface and each covered with earth. This type of cultivation is known as *takhti pal*. It involves considerable labour, but it is alleged to give better results than the more usual method of planting in trenches.

the landlords levy no share on beans. In Kāzirūn the landowner takes one-third on rape and peas and one-fifth on beans. In Dārāb and in the *sarḥadd* of the Īli ʿArab the division is as for irrigated *shatvī* crops. In Khīr, Īj, and Iṣṭahbānāt the landowners mainly take two-thirds. In Nayrīz the landowner takes three-quarters. In land watered by well in Qarā Bulāgh and Nayrīz the landowner's share is one-tenth, the peasant undertaking all the expenses of cultivation.

The division in the Kirmān neighbourhood, including Zarand and Shahdād, is mainly as for irrigated *shatvī* crops. Millet is *niṣfī*; four-fifths of the henna crop in Bam, Narmāshīr, Jīruft, Rūdbār, Sar Dū'īyeh, and Shahdād goes to the landowner; in Bāft 67 per cent is the landowner's share of *ṣayfī* crops. In Rafsinjān the landowner's share on indigenous cotton is four-fifths if he is responsible for all the expenses of cultivation, or 73 per cent if he provides the seed and the peasant is responsible for the other expenses of cultivation. On other *ṣayfī* crops (melons, marrows, cucumbers, etc., lucerne, rape, castor-oil, millet, maize, madder, turnips, beet, etc.) he takes three-quarters and pays all the expenses of cultivation, except in Raḥmatābād near the town of Rafsinjān, where the landowner takes three-fifths on melons, marrows, cucumbers, etc., beet and millet, and three-quarters on other crops.

In Bīrjand the landowner takes for the most part three-quarters or two-thirds of the crop. In Kākh three-quarters is taken on cotton and two-thirds on millet. In Ḥasanābād near Kākh half the crop is taken on cotton, millet, beet, and turnips; in Isfīdrūd, south of Shoukatābād, three-quarters of the crop is the landowner's share. In Balūchistān in the neighbourhood of Khāsh the landowner takes half. The division in Khūzistān is in some areas as for irrigated *shatvī* crops. In Bihbahān the landowner takes one-quarter, in Dizfūl half, except on millet and a pulse known as *māsh*, on which he takes one-third, and in Rām Hurmuz one-third. In Mūrchehkhwart, Abīāneh, and the neighbourhood the division is as for irrigated *shatvī* crops. In the Pushti Kūh district of Yazd in those villages where crop-sharing prevails the division is *niṣfī*.

Opium

In the Iṣfahān area the division is *niṣfī*, i.e. half goes to either party; the peasant in this case provides the manure. In the neighbourhood of Mashhad the division is also *niṣfī*, but the expenses of cultivation are halved between the peasant and the landowner (or lessee) in most areas. In Khīābān, however, weeding is the responsibility of the peasant. In Turbati Ḥaydarī the landowner's share is two-thirds; the expenses of cultivation, apart from those in connexion with weeding, which are the responsibility of the peasant, are deducted from the total crop. In Kāshmar three-fifths go to the landowner, the expenses of cultivation being divided between the landowner and the peasant. In certain cases the peasant only ploughs the land for the opium crop, in which case he gets one-tenth.

The landowner pays all the expenses of cultivation in Fasā and takes eight-ninths of the crop. In Dārāb and its five *bulūks* the division is *niṣfī*. In Fīrūzābād the landowner takes two-fifths.

In certain villages in the neighbourhood of the town of Kirmān, and in Zarand, Rafsinjān, and the Pushti Kūh district of Yazd the division is also *niṣfī*, all expenses in connexion with the cultivation of the crop being the responsibility of the peasant. In Bardsīr it is also *niṣfī*, the landowner providing the seed and the peasant being responsible for all the other expenses of cultivation.

Rice

In Kurdistān the landowner takes half. In the Qaṣri Shīrīn area the peasant takes two shares to the landowner's one, and is responsible for all the expenses of cultivation.

In Kāzirūn, if the expenses of cultivation are deducted from the total harvest, the division is *niṣfī*, but if these are shouldered entirely by the peasant the landowner takes one-third. In the rice-growing areas in the Qashqā'ī the division is *niṣfī*, the costs of cultivation being the responsibility of the landowner.

In Rām Hurmuz the landowner takes one-third. In Havīzeh the peasant working on land belonging to the *shaykhs* provides the seed and takes three-quarters of the crop. In the Arab areas, which were *khāliṣeh*, one-third of the crop was taken by the government in the reign of Riẓā Shāh. As in the case of grain crops the government dues were remitted in 1316/1937–8 (see p. 313) and reimposed in 1326/1947–8, the rate being altered from one-third to one-fourth. In the *khāliṣeh* in the Sūsangird and Havīzeh areas when the government dues were reimposed in 1326/1947–8 the rate was fixed at the cash equivalent of 3 *manni havīzeh* (approx. 2 cwt., 71 lb.) per ha. (2·47109 acres) which amounted in 1326/1947–8 to 300 rs. (approx. £1. 15*s*. 3*d*.) and in 1327/1948–9 to 370 rs. (approx. £2. 3*s*. 6*d*.).

In Ṭālish the owner provides the seed and the division is *niṣfī*. In Māzandarān, which is the main rice-growing area of the country, the peasant pays for the most part a fixed rent based on the area held (see below, pp. 321–2).

Where irrigation companies have been formed another element is introduced into the crop-sharing system. In Bihbahān, for example, the irrigation company takes one-eighth on *shatvī* crops, one-sixth on *ṣayfī*, and one-fifth on garden produce,[1] all of which dues are levied on the total harvest before division between the various parties concerned. Similarly, in Shūsh the irrigation company takes one-quarter on irrigated crops, or where the land is less favourably situated or poorer one-fifth. In the case of the *khāliṣeh* in the Arab areas of Khūzistān, where irrigation is in charge of an irrigation company, the government dues are paid to the irrigation company.

The second type of relationship, where the peasant pays a fixed rent in cash or kind or in both, according to the area of land (or the amount of water) which he holds is not found in many areas. The contract is often merely a verbal one. When a written contract is entered into some stipulation is usually made safeguarding the peasant in the event of natural calamity such as drought or pest. On the whole there would appear to be a marked preference on the part of the landowners for crop-sharing agreements rather than for leasing at a fixed rent. On the other hand, the incentive to the peasant to increase the output of the land is greater in the case of a fixed rent, since the whole increase belongs to him and is not divided with the landowner or lessee, as is the case when the relationship is on a crop-sharing basis.

One of the main areas where this type of rent is found is in the neighbourhood of Yazd. Here again practice is not uniform: the rent may be for a period of years or may be adjusted annually. In the Pushti Kūh area the contracts are usually for a period of three to five years. The rent in Jīnābād, for example, in 1949 was some 75 *manni tabrīz* (approx. 4 cwt., 43 lb.) wheat and 35 *mann* (approx. 2 cwt., 5 lb.) barley and straw per *ṭāq* (or 12 hours' water). The rent is usually paid in two instalments, the first being paid when the barley is harvested and the second when the wheat is harvested. In certain villages near Yazd the rent represents a payment for the water rather than a rent for the land and is fixed annually by a valuer[2] who visits the area concerned on behalf of the owner of the *qanāt*, estimates with the peasant the amount which the land will yield during the current year, and fixes the rent accordingly. The valuer, who is usually a man of local reputation, does not normally take money for his services. In ʿAlīābād, Ḥusaynābād, and Ḥasanābād, near Yazd, the average rent in 1945 was 7–10 *manni tabrīz* (approx. 46–65 lb.) of wheat or barley per *sabū* (10 minutes' water). This was usually converted into and paid in cash. In an exceptionally good year it was said the yield of a piece of land watered by one *sabū* might be some 20 *manni tabrīz* (approx. 2 bushels, 11 lb.), but in a bad year the yield might perhaps

[1] Gardens are exempt from this due for the first five years.
[2] Known locally as a *muṣaddiq*.

not be more than 5 *manni tabrīz* (approx. 32½ lb.). In Khẉurmīz the rent was some 10 *manni tabrīz* (approx. 65 lb.) grain per *qafīz* (approx. 1,196 sq. yds.); and in Mihrīz 6½ *manni tabrīz* (approx. 39 lb.) grain and 300 rs. (approx. £1. 15*s.* 3*d.*) for *ṣayfī* crops. In Yakhdān (near Aqdā) the rent was 50 *manni tabrīz* (approx. 2 cwt., 101 lb.) of barley (of which 10 *manni tabrīz*—approx. 65 lb.—might be in wheat) per *qafīz* (approx. 1,196 sq. yds.) and 300 rs. for *ṣayfī* crops; in Ṣadrābād (near Ardakān) the rent was 7 *manni tabrīz* (approx. 46 lb.) wheat and 50 rs. (approx. 5*s.* 10*d.*) per *jurreh* (approx. 11 minutes' water).[1] In Dihābād it was 20 rs. (approx. 2*s.* 4*d.*) for *shatvī* and 20 rs. for *ṣayfī* crops per *jurreh*. In Maybud the rent is also reckoned according to the water; the actual amount of the rent varies with the different *qanāts*; thus, one of them paid in 1945 1 *manni tabrīz* (approx. 6½ lb.) of wheat and 1 *manni tabrīz* of cotton per *jurreh* of 8½ minutes' water. Certain villages in the neighbourhood of Nā'īn paid 120 *manni tabrīz* (approx. 6 cwt., 103 lb.) wheat or cotton per *ṭāq*. In bad years the landlords give reductions. In Bāqf the rents are for the most part paid in grain and cotton. In Jougand (near Ardistān), the centre of some twenty-four hamlets and villages, 7½ *manni tabrīz* (approx. 49 lb.) of wheat, barley, or maize was paid per *kīleh* (approx. 191 sq. yds.) in 1945.

In Natanz rents averaged in 1945 some 20 *manni tabrīz* (approx. 1 cwt., 19 lb.) wheat per *jarīb* (approx. 957 sq. yds.). In Barzuk they were higher: 10 to 20 *manni tabrīz* (approx. 65 lb. to 1 cwt., 19 lb.) of wheat per *jarīb* (approx. 478 sq. yds.).

In Gaz in Burkhẉār crop-sharing and rents are both found: rents are usually in cash and tend to prevail over crop-sharing in a good year. The procedure is for a valuer (*muṣaddiq*) to value the crop and fix the rent per *jarīb* which the peasant has to pay the landowner. In a good year the right to collect the melon crops of Ḥaydarābād, for example, is sold for some 170,000 rs. (approx. £1,000). In Gilishābād, which is mainly *khurdeh mālik*, the rent per *jarīb* (approx. 1,731 sq. yds.)[2] in 1948 was some 2,000 rs. (approx. £11. 15*s.*). In the neighbourhood of Iṣfahān also, in some cases, the peasants pay a rent to the landlord; rates are some 1,000–1,500 rs. (approx. £5. 17*s.* 6*d.*–£8. 16*s.* 4*d.*) per *jarīb* (approx. 1,495 sq. yds.).[3]

In Sarāb and Garmrūd (in Āẕarbāyjān) rents are usually fixed in kind.

Most of the land in the Dizfūl area of Khūzistān was formerly held by the peasants in return for the payment of a fixed rent, but

[1] The length of the *jurreh* varies. In Ṣadrābād 130 *jurreh* = 24 hours' water.

[2] 1 *jarīb* in Gaz = 1,444 sq. *ẕar'*, or approx. 1,727 sq. yds.; the rate is the equivalent of approx. £37. 17*s.* per acre.

[3] 1 *jarīb* = 1,250 sq. metres.

this has largely been replaced by crop-sharing. Where a fixed rent prevails it is usually as follows: 225 kg. (approx. 4 cwt., 48 lb.) wheat, 150 kg. (approx. 2 cwt., 107 lb.) barley, and 1 *kharvār* (approx. 5 cwt., 95 lb.) straw per plough-land of irrigated land, and 75 kg. (approx. 1 cwt., 53 lb.) and upwards of wheat and barley each per plough-land of unirrigated land. Seed and draught animals are provided by the peasant. Major irrigation works are the charge of the landowner and the cleaning and up-keep of the sub-channels only are the responsibility of the peasant. This fixed payment is said to have come down from earlier times; in so far as it has changed it has been increased. In ʿAqīlī the relation between the landowner and the peasant is based on a fixed rent. The peasant pays a fixed sum per annum for the land. The payment on land growing wheat and barley is taken in kind, and on cotton in cash. In 1945 the payment was 457 kg. (8 cwt., 111 lb.) wheat, 301 kg. (approx. 5 cwt., 103 lb.) barley, and 50 rs. (approx. 5*s.* 10*d.*) per plough-land on irrigated land, and 225 kg. (approx. 4 cwt., 48 lb.) wheat, 150 kg. (approx. 2 cwt., 107 lb.) barley, and 50 rs. on unirrigated land. On cotton the payment was 1,000 rs. (approx. £5. 17*s.* 6*d.*) and on other *ṣayfī* crops one-third of the produce. In many of the dry-farming areas of Khūzistān also there is a fixed payment per plough-land. This is the case in the Bāvī area and Qalʿeh Saḥar where 140 rs. (approx. 16*s.* 5*d.*) per plough-land or ½ *manni ahvāz* (approx. 55 lb.) barley and ½ *manni ahvāz* (approx. 55 lb.) wheat is paid to the Finance Office (the land being *khāliṣeh*). In ʿArab ʿAbbās, which is also *khāliṣeh*, 40 *manni ahvāz* (39 cwt., 41 lb.) grain per plough-land is taken. In Bihbahān 150 kg. (2 cwt., 107 lb.) grain per plough-land is taken on *daym* land. In Gundūzlū 5 *manni gundūzlū* (approx. 1 cwt., 53 lb.) wheat and 5 *manni gundūzlū* barley per plough-land is taken. In Khalafābād in the remoter areas 30 kg. (66 lb.) barley and 50 kg. (110 lb.) wheat is taken.

In Ṭālish certain areas are let to the peasants, usually for a period of one to five years, though in the case of a peasant of some standing, a lease is sometimes concluded for as long as ten years.

In Langarūd (in Māzandarān) there is for the most part a fixed payment based upon 100 *darz* of 24 sq. *qabẓeh* of land.[1] This in most areas amounts to 150 kg. (2 cwt., 107 lb.) of rice, though in some areas it is 225 kg. (4 cwt., 48 lb.), i.e. rather more than half the crop. All the expenses of cultivation are the responsibility of the peasant. In some villages this rent of 150 kg. rice is converted

[1] 1 *qabẓeh* = the average breadth of the closed fist of the hand. A hundred *darz* of 24 sq. *qabẓeh* are reckoned as 2 *jarīb* or 2,000 sq. metres. (= 2,392 sq. yds.) in most of the villages of Langarūd.

into cash, with a reduction of one-thirtieth. In other parts of Māzandarān the payment is also based on the area held.

The following tables show the rents paid in various areas per plough-land (the size of which varies), per unit of water (the amount and volume of which varies), and per acre.

Rent per Plough-land

Area	*Rent in kind*	*Rent in cash*	
		£ s. d.	
'Aqīlī	8 cwt., 111 lb. wheat 5 cwt., 103 lb. barley	5 10	Irrigated
	On cotton*	5 17 6	
	4 cwt., 48 lb. wheat 2 cwt., 107 lb. barley	5 10	Unirrigated
'Arab 'Abbās	39 cwt., 41 lb. grain	..	..
Bihbahān	2 cwt., 107 lb. grain	..	Unirrigated
Dizfūl	4 cwt., 48 lb. wheat 2 cwt., 107 lb. barley 5 cwt., 95 lb. straw	..	Irrigated
	1 cwt., 53 lb. grain	..	Unirrigated
Gundūzlū	1 cwt., 53 lb. wheat 1 cwt., 53 lb. barley	..	..
Khalafābād	66 lb. barley 110 lb. wheat	..	..
Qal'eh Saḥar	55 lb. wheat 55 lb. barley } or	16 5	..

* One-third of the produce is paid on *ṣayfī* crops other than cotton.

Rent per Unit of Water

Area	*Rent in kind*	*Rent in cash*	*Unit of water*
		£ s. d.	
Maybud	6½ lb. wheat 6½ lb. cotton	..	8½ mins.
Nā'īn	6 cwt., 103 lb. wheat or cotton	..	12 hours
Pushti Kūh: Jīnābād	4 cwt., 43 lb. wheat 2 cwt., 5 lb. barley 2 cwt., 5 lb. straw	..	12 hours
Yazd: 'Alīābād	46–65 lb. grain	..	10 mins.
Dihābād	For *shatvī* crops	2 4	11 mins.
	For *ṣayfī* crops	2 4	
Ḥasanābād Ḥusaynābād	46–65 lb. grain	..	10 mins.
Ṣadrābād	46 lb. grain	5 10	11 mins.

*Rent per Acre**

Area	*Rent in kind*	*Rent in cash*					
		£	*s.*	*d.*	£	*s.*	*d.*
Barzuk . . .	5 cwt., 98 lb. 11 cwt., 84 lb. } grain		..			..	
Havīzeh†. . .	1 cwt., 7 lb. grain		..			..	
Iṣfahān . . .	..	19	0	0 –	28	0	0
Jougand . . .	11 cwt., 10 lb. grain		..			..	
Khwurmīz . .	2 cwt., 39 lb. grain		..			..	
Māzandarān . .	5 cwt., 110 lb. grain 8 cwt., 109 lb. rice		.. ..			.. ..	
Mihrīz . . .	1 cwt., 46 lb. grain	7	2	8		..	
Natanz . . .	4 cwt., 78 lb. grain		..			..	

* The figures have been worked out per acre, but the reader should remember that the holdings may in some cases be less than 1 acre.

† This land is *khāliṣeh*. Land growing rice also pays 1 cwt., 71 lb. rice per acre.

In some cases the leasing of small-holdings to peasants merges into the leasing of villages or parts of villages to persons of local influence. For example, 1 *dāng* of the village of Ḥabashī in Kulliā'ī in 1945 was let to the *kadkhudā* for three years for 50 *kharvār* (approx. 292 cwt., 28 lb.) of wheat and 500 rs. (approx. £2. 18*s*. 10*d*.) in cash. Such a case forms an intermediate category between the plough-lands leased to peasants and villages leased to individuals.

Gardens

As in the case of arable land, gardens and orchards are (1) handed over by the landowner to the peasants (*a*) on a crop-sharing basis, or (*b*) in return for the payment of rent; (2) worked by the landowner himself with paid labour; or (3) leased to a third person who cultivates them with paid labour or on a crop-sharing basis.

In Arāk in many of the villages the peasants have gardens, for which they pay an annual rent to the landowner for the land and water of some 50–60 rs. (approx. 5*s*. 10*d*. to 7*s*. 1*d*.) per annum. The vines and fruit-trees in the gardens and their produce belong to the peasants. In the case of trees other than fruit-trees, such as walnut, while the walnuts belong to the peasant, once the tree is cut down the wood is divided between the landowner and the peasant, two-thirds going to the latter. In Sarāb 'Amārat the peasants paid 7 rs. (approx. 10*d*.) per *jarīb* (approx. 741 sq. yds.)[1] for their gardens in 1945. No due is levied on gardens until they are actually in production. The period of exemption depends on local agreement and varies from two to six years.

[1] Sixteen *jarīb* irrigated land are reckoned as 1 ha. (approx. $2\frac{1}{2}$ acres) in Sarāb 'Amārat.

Gardens are not common in the west in the neighbourhood of Kirmānshāh. Where they exist they usually belong to the landlord. This is the case, for example, in Harsīn, where most of the gardens and orchards belong to the landowners and are in charge of a gardener known as the *bustānchī*. The value of the produce is estimated annually by an expert (*khibreh*) and sold on the tree. The *bustānchī* is usually given the first option to buy the produce. In the Pushti Kūh area of Kangāvar also the gardens and orchards belong to the landowners and are usually leased. Trees, however, other than fruit-trees, are mainly divided on the basis of two shares to the peasant and one to the landowner. In Kurdistān there are on the whole few gardens. Where they exist they also belong for the most part to the landowner. In Ḥasanābād (near Sanandaj) the gardens belong in some cases to the landowner and in others to the peasants. In the former case some are let to the peasants, the rent being paid in three instalments. In Dālān the produce of a garden belonging to the landowner, growing vegetables and melons in 1949, was divided on the basis of two-thirds to the landowner and one-third to the three gardeners who looked after it. In the Saqqiz area the peasant pays a rent for his garden if he has one. In Kulliā'ī gardens are not common. Where they are held by peasants a rent is paid to the landowner, based on the area of the garden. In Mīāndoāb trees and fruit-trees belong mainly to the peasants, who paid 1 r. (approx. $1\frac{1}{2}$*d.*) per 100 sq. metres (119·6 sq. yds.) to the landowner in 1945, or, in the case of *khāliṣeh*, to the government. Water dues are also paid to the government.

A rent, known as *jarībāneh*, is normally paid in the Tehrān district by the peasants to the landowner for their gardens and the water used therein. In 1945 some 30 to 100 rs. (approx. 3*s.* 6*d.* to 11*s.* 9*d.*) per *jarīb* (1,196 sq. yds.) was paid. In Yāftābād one landowner received 30 rs. (approx. 3*s.* 6*d.*) per 1,700 sq. metres (2,033 sq. yds.). In Shahrīār the rate in the same year was 10 to 15 rs. (approx. 1*s.* 2*d.* to 1*s.* 9*d.*) per *jarīb* (1,196 sq. yds.). Disputes have been going on for some years concerning the rate of *jarībāneh*, which, it is alleged, was fixed many years ago and bears little relation to present-day prices. In the Tehrān neighbourhood in some areas the rate has been raised in recent years to 200–500 rs. (£1. 3*s.* 6*d.*–£2. 18*s.* 10*d.*). There have been similar disputes in other parts of Persia. In Sa'īdābād, near Tabrīz, which was given during the reign of Riẓā Shāh to Qavām ul-Mulk Shīrāzī (Ibrāhīm Qavām) in part exchange for his estates in Fārs, an attempt was made to raise the rate of *jarībāneh*. The peasants objected and recourse was had to the gendarmerie. After the abdication of Riẓā Shāh it was not possible to continue to collect the increased rates, and eventually the estate was sold. In Rām Hurmuz, also, similar disputes took place in 1949, because of an attempt by the local landowners to raise the prevailing rate of 20 rs. (approx. 2*s*. 4*d*.) per *jarīb* (1,196 sq. yds.) for garden land (growing mainly citrus fruits).

In Khurāsān the division of fruit-trees and trees is in many areas *niṣfī*, i.e. half to the landowner or lessee and half to the peasant.

Gardens do not play an important part in Qā'ināt. In some villages the landowner takes three-quarters of the produce of fruit-trees, except on mulberries, on which he takes half.

Considerable planting of fruit-trees and timber has been going on since 1314/1935–6 in Kharaqān (near Sāveh). The division is *niṣfī*, i.e. half to the peasant and half to the landowner.

In central Persia on the borders of the central desert stretching from Qumm through Kāshān to Yazd there is no uniform practice concerning the ownership of gardens. In some cases the gardens belong to the peasants, in others the produce only belongs to the peasant, and in others the gardens and their produce belong to the landowner; in the areas near the larger towns where this is the case the gardens are often leased for considerable sums to a third party. In Dihābād, near Ardakān, the gardens belong to the peasants. In Ṣadrābād near Yazd this is also so in the majority of cases. In Ardistān a due or rent is paid by the peasants to the landowner for their gardens.

Gardens are not important in Fārs. Where they exist they belong for the most part to the landowners. One of the main reasons for the lack of gardens in Fārs is insecurity. The movement of tribes in the various areas of the province creates conditions in which the preservation of gardens may often present difficulties. In the neighbourhood of Shāpūr where certain groups of the Qashqā'ī were settled by Riẓā Shāh a number of gardens were planted. After the abdication these were largely abandoned and destroyed by the passage of flocks from their winter to their summer pastures. In Kāzirūn the gardens are usually leased by the landowner to a third party. In Nayrīz the gardens belong mainly to the landowner, and the gardener gets one-fifth or one-sixth of the produce. In Jahrum the rate paid to gardeners who look after landlord gardens is usually one-tenth of the produce. In some cases, however, the gardens have been made by the peasants on the land of the landowner; in such cases the division is *niṣfī*. When the garden crops ripen their value is estimated and the amount of the landowner's share fixed. In the Jahrum neighbourhood there is a shortage of peasants, and they are encouraged to plant gardens so that they may become attached to the soil. This does not appear to be the practice, however, in other parts of Fārs.

In the Iṣṭahbānāt area the main revenue of the population comes from wild fruit-trees, almonds, walnuts, figs, and vines. These grow in the neighbouring mountains and are grafted. They are not irrigated. The trees, which grow in profusion to a distance of several miles round the town, have every appearance of being well cared for. They are largely owned by peasants and small landowners. In spite of the impossibility of guarding these trees—they grow wild on the mountain-side and are not enclosed by garden walls—it is alleged that cases of theft are rare. The example of Iṣṭahbānāt is being followed on a small scale in a few isolated areas elsewhere in Fārs.

In Kirmān also the gardens mainly belong to the landowners. The relationship between the gardener and the landlord is usually based on a contract, the gardener undertaking to look after the garden in return for a fixed sum or, in some cases, on a crop-sharing basis. In Bam, Narmāshīr, Jīruft, Rūdbār, and Sar Dū'īyeh four-fifths of the produce of gardens go to the landlord, who is responsible for the provision of manure. In Bāft he takes 70 per cent, the expense of cultivation being the responsibility of the peasant. In the Zarand area the landowner takes three-quarters of the fruit crop, all the expenses of cultivation, such as the provision of manure and the digging of the land, being the responsibility of the peasant. In Shahdād the landowner takes 90 per cent on citrus fruits.

The nuts from pistachio trees are an important crop in Rafsinjān and the neighbourhood. The gardens in which they are grown belong to the landowners. They are generally worked on a contract basis. In some cases the landowner collects the pistachios himself, but more often he lets the right to do this. Where this is done the value of the crop is first estimated by a valuer (*mumaiyiz*). The man who rents the right is usually a local man and the rent is paid in kind.

In Khūzistān the gardens mainly belong to the landowners. In Dizfūl the chief produce of gardens is citrus fruits. Usually these gardens are let. Thus, in Dayijī, a small landlord village near Dizfūl, the right to collect the produce of a garden growing citrus fruits of some 3 ha. (7·4 acres) which had been brought into cultivation recently was let in 1949 for 90,000 rs. (approx. £529)[1] per annum. Older gardens with trees of greater maturity and more closely planted are let at higher rates. In the event of blight or disease a reduction is made in the rent by mutual agreement. Fruit-sellers come out from the towns, buy the fruit on the spot, and transport it to the towns for sale. In 'Aqīlī where gardens have been made by the peasants the latter pay a rent to the landowner.

[1] This is the equivalent of £71 per acre.

In some areas in the neighbourhood of Bihbahān, where gardens have been made by the peasants, one-quarter or one-third of the produce goes to the landowner; in other cases the peasants pay *jarībāneh*, i.e. a rent based on the area held.

Some 40–50 rs. (approx. 4*s.* 8*d.*–5*s.* 10*d.*) per tree of citrus fruits is taken in Māzandarān in the estates of the large landed proprietors. This sum is approximately half the income of the tree; in the former *amlāk*[1] 20 rs. (approx. 2*s.* 4*d.*) per tree is the rate. The relative lowness of the rate in the former *amlāk* is alleged to have given rise to protests on the part of the landowners; it is also alleged that the landowners have in some cases bought up the trees of the peasants in the *amlāk* and have re-let these at the rate of 50 rs. (approx. 5*s.* 10*d.*) per tree.

The following table shows the approximate rent per acre of gardens in various areas:

Area	*Rent per acre* £	*s.*	*d.*	£	*s.*	*d.*
Miāndoāb		3	4			
Rām Hurmuz		1	0			
Sarāb ʿAmārat		3	10			
Shahrīār		4	8–		7	3
Tehrān		14	1–	2	7	6
	4	15	2–	11	18	0*
Yāftābād		8	3			

* See p. 324.

Date plantations are important in certain areas. For the most part so much per tree is paid to the landowner or, in the case of *khāliṣeh* land, to the government. In Khurramshahr the holdings may be from 100 to 6,000 or 7,000 trees. The latter figure, however, is exceptional; 2,000–3,000 trees is considered a good holding. All expenses relating to the clearing of the main irrigation channels are borne by the holder of the land; the fertilizing of the palms, cutting, and basketing is entrusted to a peasant who receives one-quarter of the crop.[2] He may also grow what subsidiary crops he likes, whether winter crops or summer crops. He keeps the whole produce of these unless the landowner has advanced the seed, in

[1] i.e. estates taken over by Riẓā Shāh (see Ch. XII).

[2] There is a marked difference between the ʿIrāqī and Persian standards of date cultivation. In ʿIrāq palms are felled when they grow old and replaced by young shoots; the ground is relatively well weeded and irrigation channels are cleaned regularly. In Khūzistān, on the other hand, the palm is left to grow until it falls down. Plantations are generally speaking weed-choked and ditches not cleaned.

Casual labour moves from the north just before the date-picking season starts. This labour is paid no fixed wage, but feeds on the dates while picking and each family is given about 4–6 *istayleh* (i.e. baskets holding ½ *manni baṣreh*, approx. 82 lb., 11 oz.) to take away. The date-picking season lasts some three months.

which case the produce is shared equally between them. The main date-growing areas in the district are mostly *khāliṣeh*. The government dues or *mināl* were not levied during the period 1316–26/1937–48. In 1326/1947–8 and 1327/1948–9 they were reimposed in the form of a cash sum per tree, varying from ½ to 1½ rs. (approx. ¾*d*.– 2*d*.). Payment was to be reckoned against the arrears which would have been due from 1323/1944–5 had the *mināl* been levied in those years, and the holders were given to understand that their title to the holdings would depend upon the payment of these arrears. In November 1949 Ministry of Finance notices were put up in Khurramshahr of which the following is an extract:

> In the course of letter No. 22125 dated 3rd Shahrīvar [13]28 in pursuance of the decree of the Council of Ministers, orders were given that the land (*'arṣeh*) of the palm groves, which are *khāliṣeh*,[1] shall be transferred to the owners of the trees and buildings therein provided that they pay the claims outstanding against them from the year [13]23 [1944–5] to the end of [13]27 [1948–9] at the rate of 1½ rs. [approx. 2*d*.] per ordinary palm (*nakhli 'ādī*)[2] and 2 rs. [approx. 2¾*d*.] per special palm (*nakhli mumtāz*)[3] by the 20th Mihr.

It is alleged that this notice produced no results.

In the Bihbahān area in certain properties the date groves are largely planted by the peasants. One rīāl (approx. 1½*d*.) per tree per annum is levied by the landowner once the tree is in production. Formerly the rate was 3 rs. (approx. 4¼*d*.) per tree, a reduction being made in 1300/1921–2 because the properties were in a bad condition. In Manṣūrīyeh, near Bihbahān, one-quarter or one-third of the produce of the tree is taken by the landowner.

Date groves in Fārs are in some cases rented.[4] In Farrāshband, where there are some 30,000 date palms, 1½ rs. (approx. 2*d*.) per annum per palm is taken by the landowner. In Dihrām and Kārzīn, on the other hand, one-sixth and a half of the produce respectively is taken. In Jahrum there are some 80,000 date palms, all belonging to the large landowners. The man who looks after the date palms and gathers the harvest receives one-twentieth of the harvest. One man looks after some 200 palms. In Dārāb, on the other hand, nothing is levied on the peasant's date palms by the landowner. Date palms do not form an important part of the local economy, and the object of exempting them from dues is to encourage peasants, of whom there is a shortage, to settle in the area.

In the province of Kirmān, in Jīruft and Rūdbār the landlord

[1] i.e. which belong outright to the government.

[2] i.e. those palms known locally as *zanā'ib*.

[3] i.e. those palms known locally as *ṣudār*.

[4] Date palms do not bear fruit for some ten to fifteen years according to their situation and do not reach full maturity until they are some thirty years old.

takes 70 per cent of the date crop, in Bam 75 per cent, and in Shahdād 75 per cent or 90 per cent. In Balūchistān the produce of date palms in *khāliṣeh* land is divided at the rate of three-fifths to the government or lessee and two-fifths to the peasant. On other land the man who tends the date palms obtains one-fourth or one-fifth of the produce. The extent to which a government tax is levied on date palms in this area varies. In some cases it appears that a tax of 1 r. (approx. 1½*d.*) per palm is levied.

CHAPTER XVIII

PERSONAL SERVITUDES AND DUES

As pointed out in the previous chapter, the peasant, in addition to the share of the crop or the rent which he pays to the landowner or lessee, is, in many areas, liable to various dues, which may be regarded, in part at least, as personal servitudes. The number of these and the rate at which they are levied varies from place to place. One of the most common is the liability of the peasant to transport the landowner or lessee's share of the harvest from the threshing-floor to the granary. Thus in Āẕarbāyjān the transport both of the landlord's share from the fields to his granaries and of the grain which the landlord delivers to the state granaries by way of taxation is commonly a charge upon the peasant. This is also the case in Kurdistān, Kirmān, and in the vicinity of Kāshmar. In Souj Bulāgh and Shahrīār in the neighbourhood of Tehrān the landlord takes delivery of his share of the harvest at the granaries in the villages, and the cost of transport from the fields to the granaries falls upon the peasant; in the nearby area of Khw̱ār and Varāmīn, however, the peasant is not responsible for the delivery of the landlord's share to the granaries.

The most onerous of the personal servitudes is probably labour service, or *bīgārī*. The performance of such service or the provision of so many men for labour service was a normal obligation upon those who held land in Ṣafavid and Qājār times and probably in earlier times also. One of the most common immunities granted to those in receipt of royal favour was immunity from such service. Clearly, therefore, it was regarded as a service to be rendered to the ruler by those who held land grants or who owned land. It was presumably performed by those who actually tilled the soil, but in so far as rights over the land, whether of ownership or merely of jurisdiction, were granted to a third person, the obligation to provide men for the performance of labour service, unless special immunity had been granted, was a charge upon the grantee or the owner. But, in so far as the grantee was in effect often the local governor, he would in many cases have levied labour service on the population in the area under his jurisdiction in his capacity as the local representative of the government. In the course of time many of the dues levied on behalf of the government by those holding grants of land came to be regarded by the grantees, as they were transformed into ordinary landowners, as services due to them. When the status and nature of the landowning class began to change at the beginning of the twentieth century,[1] and the custom of paying officials by grants of land or its revenue was abolished, and public services such as road-making were taken over by the central government and were no longer a charge upon the local landholder in the person of the *tuyūldār* or grantee, labour service died out in some areas; in others the landlord continued to levy it on his own behalf.

At the present day, although labour service is no longer demanded in all parts of the country, and its incidence, where it is levied, is less than was the case formerly, it still survives in many areas, notably Kurdistān, Āẕarbāyjān, Khūzistān, parts of Fārs, Kirmān, and in east Persia.

It is levied in a variety of ways: on each household, plough-land, or share of water, or, occasionally, upon the male peasant population, and consists of so many days of free labour by a peasant or the provision of an ass for free labour on so many days of the year.[2] In the latter case the asses are used, for example, for the transport of the landowner's produce from the village to the town, or for the transport of building materials, etc. The labour service of the peasants usually takes the form of labour on the construction of buildings, irrigation works and road-building, or agricultural labour in the fields which the landowner cultivates himself, i.e. those fields not worked on a crop-sharing basis or leased, or in his gardens.

So many days' labour service of men and asses per *juft* per annum is exacted in the landlord areas of Kurdistān. In Ḥasanābād (near Sanandaj) the levy is made per *juft* and amounts to seven days' free labour of a peasant and four days' free labour of an ass per annum.[3] In addition the peasants have to dig the landowner's garden in spring, providing two free days' labour per household. In Dabbāgh seven free days' labour per *juft* are taken; in Dālān four free days' labour of a peasant and two free days' labour of an ass. Similar levies are made in the neighbouring villages. In the Saqqiz area also each *juft* has to provide several free days' labour in men and asses. In addition to this, agricultural labour has to be performed for the landowner whenever required. Thus, if the landowner wants his land ploughed, or the harvest reaped, or any other agricultural work performed, it is done by corvée. Food is provided for those taking part but no other payment is made. This levy, which is taken in certain other parts of Kurdistān also, is

[1] See Ch. VIII.

[2] In some areas this is known as *khari siāh*.

[3] In other words it is stipulated in the contract (which is usually a verbal one between the landowner and the peasant) that the latter shall give in addition to a share of the crop seven days' free labour, known as *haft nafar*, and four days' free labour of an ass, known as *chahār ulāgh*.

known as *gal*, and is in addition to the peasant's liability to perform free labour on a fixed number of days per annum. It differs from *bīgārī*, in that the latter, in Kurdistān, is levied not mainly for agricultural work but for building and road-making, etc. In certain areas it would appear that *gal* also takes the form of mutual self-help and is performed not only for the landowner, but also for peasants or small landowners when necessary to help them get in their crops.

In Āẕarbāyjān also *bīgārī* is commonly levied by the landowners. For example, in Varzaqān in Uzum Dil, four days' free labour in men and asses is levied per *pānzdah*.[1]

Similarly in Khūzistān *bīgārī* is levied in some areas, but the rate is rather less heavy, being usually one day's labour a year per plough-land. In certain areas it is the practice for the holder of a plough-land to be required also to plant, reap, and thresh a certain amount of grain free in the land which the landowner reserves for himself, i.e. land excepted from that distributed among the crop-sharing peasants or tenants. For this the landowner provides the seed.[2]

In Fārs, in the Mamasanī, *bīgārī* is levied. In Shāpūr also every peasant is bound to give one day's labour in the rice fields per annum. In Nūrābād, however, free agricultural labour is not usually levied, but the holder of each plough-land is required to sow and reap for the landowner without payment a small quantity of rice.

Bīgārī, known locally as *qalūn*, is common in most areas in the province of Kirmān, though it is alleged to be less heavy than was formerly the case. It usually takes the form of corvées levied for the performance of some project or other which the landowner wishes to undertake. It is said to be the heaviest in those areas where the rule of the old-fashioned *khāns* survives. In Shahdād it is less common than round Kirmān; in Rafsinjān it is no longer demanded.

In Khurāsān in the more remote areas *bīgārī* is still common. In Turbati Ḥaydarī it is taken from all crop-sharing peasants and landless peasants but not from the *sālār*, i.e. the peasant in charge of an agricultural unit (see p. 299). In Zāveh this form of labour service has taken on a somewhat different guise: attached to each *ṣaḥrā* (see p. 298) there is an individual known as the *bīgāreh*; he is paid by the peasants who work the *ṣaḥrā* but is in effect the servant of the landlord.

Until relatively recent times labour service in men and asses was taken in Qā'ināt. The late Shoukat ul-Mulk abolished it.

[1] See p. 310, n. 1.
[2] This is known as *gārā* in Dizfūl, and *shikarteh* in the Arab areas.

A special form of labour service known as *ḥashar* is levied in Sīstān for the making, cleaning, and repairing of irrigation channels. Since most of the land in Sīstān is *khāliṣeh*,[1] this labour service is levied by the government. Originally *ḥashar* may conceivably have been performed in part at least as a kind of public service and to have been a form of 'self-help'. Whatever may have been the position in the past, however, no such conception attaches to it at the present day. It has become a source of oppression, an occasion for bribery and corruption, an important factor in the prevailing decay in the area, and a cause of great discontent. It is levied by government officials not only for irrigation works but also for the performance of all kinds of work including road-building, both in Sīstān and Balūchistān.[2] Men have to be provided for this labour service by those who have the right to a share of the water, in proportion to the number of their shares, whenever called upon to do so by the officials of the government (see also below).

Another form of labour service is the duty to provide a certain number of loads of firewood, or camel-thorn. This levy, which only survives in a few areas including parts of Āẕarbāyjān, is made upon the holder of a plough-land.

In certain areas, notably west Persia and Āẕarbāyjān, it is the common practice of landowners to levy per plough-land or per share of water (where the village land is divided in this way) a due payable in clarified butter (*roughan*) or in cash or in both. This due is known as *sar juftī*. The sum varies somewhat from village to village. Collection is made on behalf of the landowner by the *kadkhudā* or by a collector (*ẓābiṭ*). On a given day a crier is sent out to announce that the holders of plough-lands should bring their clarified butter on such and such a day. In Dastjird and Sulaymānābād, near Hamadān, *sar juftī* consists of a cash payment and two loads of lucerne, one dry and one fresh, per annum. In Asadābād, near Hamadān, it was levied in 1945 at the rate of 50–100 rs. (approx. 5*s.* 10*d.*–11*s.* 9*d.*), and 5–6 *manni tabrīz* (approx. 32 lb., 12 oz.–39 lb.) of clarified butter per annum. In the Pushti Kūh area of Kangāvar *sar juftī* was levied in the same year at the rate of some 1 *manni tabrīz* (approx. 6 lb., 9 oz.) clarified butter, three hens, and 200 rs. (approx. £1. 3*s.* 6*d.*) per annum. In Kulliā'ī the rate was some 50 rs. in some properties; in others owned by the old-fashioned type of *khān* higher rates were taken. For example, in 1945 it was alleged that there were cases of *sar juftī* being levied at the rate of 1,000 rs. (approx. £5. 17*s.* 6*d.*). In

[1] See Ch. XII.

[2] The argument put forward in support of, or rather to excuse the levy of, *ḥashar* by the government for public works, that the capital expenditure on such works is prohibitive, and that only in this way can they be carried out, can hardly be regarded as relevant.

Kurdistān also a number of dues are levied in various areas, such as ½ *mann* (approx. 3 lb., 4½ oz.) clarified butter per plough-land, a number of hens and eggs, and a quantity of *dūgh* (a kind of whey) and butter, etc. In Ḥasanābād (near Sanandaj) three to four hens, ½ *manni tabrīz* (approx. 3 lb., 4½ oz.) clarified butter, and 100 rs. are levied per plough-land. In Dabbāgh, near Dīvān Darreh, the levy is five hens, 100 rs. and 1 *manni kurdistān* (approx. 5 lb.) clarified butter. In Dālān in the same area it is 35 rs. (approx. 4*s*. 1*d*.) and four hens. Similar dues are paid in the neighbouring villages. In Saqqiz some 50 rs., 1 *manni tabrīz* clarified butter, and one sheep are taken per plough-land. In the Kirmānshāh area *sar juftī* usually amounts to some five to ten hens, 1 *manni tabrīz* clarified butter, and some fuel. In Āẕarbāyjān a number of dues were, and to a lesser extent still are, levied per plough-land or per share of water, as in parts of Qarājeh Dāgh. These include cheese, clarified butter, hens, eggs, lambs, kids, and money. In Hashtrūd a sum in cash is levied upon the peasant according to the area of land he occupies, or so much per head of livestock. The peasants in this area are of two kinds, *zāriʿ* and *gharībeh*. The latter, who are landless peasants, pay more per head of livestock than the former, who are crop-sharing peasants or tenants.

In the Kirmān area it is usual to provide one or two loads of firewood or camel-thorn a year and occasionally a number of hens per *juft*.

A poll tax[1] was formerly levied in most areas. It has now largely died out, but is still found in Āẕarbāyjān.[2]

The entertainment of government officials and travellers in former times was a charge upon the inhabitants of the country through which they passed. In some areas a due is still levied by the landowner for this purpose. This is known in Āẕarbāyjān as *qunāghliq*. A similar due is also levied in parts of Kurdistān and parts of Fārs. Elsewhere it survives only in isolated instances. For example, in Āb Shīrīn, a small place on the Qumm–Kāshān road, the proceeds of two *āb mīān*[3] were still set aside in 1945 to meet the expenses of government servants, visiting officials, and the *kadkhudā*.

Various other dues are still found in isolated areas. For example, in Kilaybar in Qarājeh Dāgh in one village the peasants provide the landowner with an annual due in partridges, which are caught in winter in the snow. In some parts of Kurdistān a due

[1] Known as *sarāneh*.

[2] The Democrats during the regime of Pīshehvarī (1945–6) forbade the levying of this and other dues. In fact, however, many of them have been re-imposed and continue to be levied.

[3] i.e. a share of the water and the land irrigated by it set aside for a special purpose.

known as *sūrāneh* is still levied. This is a payment which the peasant makes to the landowner for permission to marry. This due illustrates the essentially personal nature of the link between the landlord and the peasant.

Formerly at the Persian New Year a due known as *nourūzī* was levied. This has been abolished in many areas, but in the more remote places and especially in the tribal areas, 'presents' of sheep, hens, eggs, clarified butter, etc., are given to the landowner by the peasant according to their means. Occasionally a return of equal or greater value is given. In some of the more remote districts similar presents are expected on other occasions, such, for example, as the birth of an heir to the landowner.

In certain areas where the affairs of the landowner are looked after by a bailiff, usually known as the *mubāshir*, as distinct from the *kadkhudā*, he is often paid in part by the peasants. For example, in Hashtrūd a levy known as *takhteh* was formerly made for the *mubāshir*. It is now seldom made. Similarly when the landowner sends a collector (*ẓābiṭ*) at harvest time to a village to collect his share of the harvest, the collector usually lives on the country. This, in Ṣārī Chaman in Qarājeh Dāgh, the landowner's *mubāshir* visits the village at harvest time. His entertainment is a charge on the villagers, who also pay him a certain quantity of *roughan* and a number of hens. These, however, were stated to be the only extra dues levied on the villagers in that village. From the landowner the *mubāshir* received 1 *kharvār* (approx. 5 cwt., 95 lb.) grain. In Havīzeh 4 *manni havīzeh* (approx. 3 cwt., 85 lb.) is deducted from the total harvest on irrigated crops and 2 *manni havīzeh* (approx. 1 cwt., 84 lb.) on unirrigated crops for the *mubāshir*, where there is one.

Until recently in Sīstān there were *mubāshirs* representing the Ministry of Finance. Although they had no function after the distribution of *khāliṣeh*, they nevertheless lingered on for a period, receiving 6 per cent of the total harvest. In the *khāliṣeh* of Bampūr the *mubāshir* receives a small payment in cash from the government or the lessee; his main income derives from the plough-lands which he works himself and on which he does not pay the landlord's share.

In many areas the *mubāshir* and *ẓābiṭ* are paid entirely by the landowner. In Kirmān the *mubāshir* usually receives 10 per cent of the owner's share. In certain properties in Qā'ināt the *mubāshir* also gets 10 per cent of the landowner's share, or in the more prosperous properties, 5 per cent. In Gīv the *mubāshir* shares the 5 per cent with an official known as the *taḥvīldār*, who is virtually his assistant. At harvest time, further, a *ẓābiṭ* comes on behalf of the landowner to collect the crop in many areas in Qā'ināt. In

Kāshmar in certain districts a *ẓābiṭ* is employed by the landowner for three to four months to collect the harvest. His wage is deducted from the total harvest.

The various dues mentioned in this chapter will give the reader an idea of the variety of practice which prevails. In many cases the actual amount of these dues is not heavy, but they reflect the continuance of a certain attitude of mind and of the survival of a certain type of social organization. Indeed, it is perhaps in the field of personal servitudes that the survival of medieval customs and even more of a medieval attitude of mind is most striking. Other aspects of land tenure, such, for example, as the crop-sharing system, may perhaps be partly justified on the grounds that the economic and social conditions which engendered them still persist. For personal servitudes there can be no such defence. The system of labour service was originally designed to meet political and social needs which no longer prevail and cannot be regarded as anything but an anomaly, while the special form which labour service takes in Sīstān is an enormity which may well make life intolerable for those upon whom it is imposed.

CHAPTER XIX

THE PAYMENT OF LOCAL OFFICIALS

IT was suggested in Part I that the recuperative power of agriculture and rural life was due to the fact that the village communities were largely self-supporting and self-contained units. From this it follows that they had developed a technique of local administration and some degree of self-help. This feature of early medieval life, as has been pointed out, was modified with the growth of absolutism. With the spread of administrative centralization it was largely swept away. Certain features of the early organization nevertheless persist. Among these is the custom of making deductions from the harvest in lieu of payment for certain services. The manner in which these deductions are made varies: they may be a charge on the landowner or the peasant or a joint charge, i.e. they are deducted from the total harvest of the plough-land before this is divided between the landlord and the crop-sharing peasant according to the terms of the crop-sharing agreement. These deductions are clearly not confined to the landlord areas. Many of them are found also in the peasant-proprietor areas and are paid by the peasant proprietors. The actual deductions made in any given area vary. Broadly speaking they can be classed under three heads: for local administration, for the performance of certain services, and for the benefit of the religious classes. Various of these deductions such, for example, as the due levied for the payment of the *kadkhudā* in so far as he has become a government official are, like the servitudes considered in the proceeding chapter, anomalies; many of them, on the other hand, are a reflection of social and economic conditions.

The custom of making deductions[1] for the payment of local officials goes back to the days when the inhabitants of any given area were virtually autonomous in internal affairs, and used to appoint for their own protection and convenience one or more of their number to represent them *vis-à-vis* outsiders and to be responsible for certain local affairs. At the present day there is far more direct intervention by the government in local affairs than was formerly the case, and the office of the *kadkhudā*, who is the most important of the local officials, has been brought within the general hierarchy of the government.[2] Certain changes have been made

[1] The deductions made from the harvest for local officials are collectively known as *mouẓūʿāt* or *rusūmāt*. Those made in favour of the irrigation officials have already been discussed in Ch. X.

[2] See Ch. VIII. The term *kadkhudā* has a long history during which it has undergone various changes. At the present day it has two main usages: one in

in the status of the *kadkhudā*, the general effect of which has probably been to weaken local self-determination. In landlord areas he is in effect the servant or the bailiff of the landlord. The general tendency is for him to receive a cash payment from the landlord and dues in kind, with or without labour service from the crop-sharing peasants or tenants in the area under him. The dues are calculated in a variety of ways, the most common being for them to be reckoned at so much per plough-land, per share of water, or per household. In addition to his regular wage, the *kadkhudā* has a number of perquisites, and his position gives him a number of opportunities of levying irregular dues upon the villagers. He is responsible for the general order of the village, and reports thefts, disputes, and disorders to the security officials. He can call upon the villagers for the performance of public works such as the cleaning of irrigation channels. He settles minor disputes and can inflict minor degrees of punishment by imprisonment, flogging, or fines.

In Khurāsān there is a variety of usage in the different areas. Terminology also varies. In Ṭuruq, one of the properties of the shrine of the Imām Riẓā leased by the Shirkati Kishāvarzīyi Riẓā, the *kadkhudā* (known locally as the *dihdār*) survives in his original form, i.e. he is the villagers' representative and is chosen by them. They recommend their nominee to the lessees who put his name forward to the government; if the latter are satisfied that he is in fact the choice of the villagers, a warrant is issued for his appointment. He receives 2,000 rs. (approx. £11. 15*s.*) per annum from the lessees, two days' free labour per annum from all peasants who own an ox (one day's sowing and one day's reaping), and one day's labour from those who do not own an ox. The official who is the lessees' representative, and who would in most districts be called the *kadkhudā*, is known as the *dārūgheh*; he oversees on their behalf Ṭuruq and the neighbourhood. He is appointed by them and receives 4,000 rs. (approx. £23. 10*s.*) per month from them and 3 *kharvār* (approx. 17 cwt., 60 lb.) wheat together with fodder for his horse, deducted in each case from the total harvest. In Ābkūh the due of the *kadkhudā* is levied on the total harvest. In Khīābān and Shādkan the official who carries out the duties performed elsewhere by the *kadkhudā* is also known as the *dārūgheh*. He receives one-tenth of the lessees' share of the harvest as delivered at their granaries and storehouses in Khīābān, a monthly wage and a payment in kind deducted from the total harvest in Shādkan.

the settled areas to denote the village headman and the other in the tribal areas of Fārs, the Bakhtīārī, and elsewhere to designate the head of a tribal sub-group or clan.

In Turbati Ḥaydarī in the landlord areas the functions of the *kadkhudā* are performed by the landowner's bailiff, known as the *ṣāḥib kār* or *mubāshir*. He is paid 1,000–2,000 rs. per annum (£5. 17*s.* 6*d.*–£11. 15*s.*) by the landowners and 4 *kharvār* (approx. 23 cwt., 42 lb.) wheat, 2 *kharvār* (approx. 11 cwt., 77 lb.) barley, 10 *kharvār* (approx. 58 cwt., 50 lb.) straw, and 2 *kharvār* (approx. 11 cwt., 77 lb.) lucerne in kind. From each of the peasants he gets one day's free labour (known as *yāvarī*) a year; he also levies other forms of labour service (*bīgārī*) such as the provision of so many loads of firewood or camel-thorn. In some cases he receives, instead of the above payments in cash and kind from the landowner, 5 per cent or 10 per cent of the landlord's share of the produce as delivered to the latter's granaries and store-houses.[1] In the *khurdeh mālik* villages of the same area the *kadkhudā* is paid by a due levied per household,[2] or a free share of the water is allotted to him.[3] Thus, supposing that the water of a *qanāt* is divided into twelve shares, the size of the shares is decreased and their number increased to thirteen, the extra share going to the *kadkhudā*.

In Āẕarbāyjān the dues levied for the *kadkhudā* are deducted for the most part from the peasant's share. In Varzaqān in Uzum Dil the *kadkhudā* receives 15 *manni tabrīz* (approx. 98 lb.) in equal quantities of wheat and barley and 15 rs. (approx. 1*s.* 9*d.*) per *pānzdah*[4] from the peasants. These payments in theory are supposed to recompense him for his expenses in the entertainment of travellers and officials passing through the village. In fact, however, it has been alleged that separate levies for entertainment (*mihmānī*) are made upon the peasants.

The *kadkhudā* in certain districts holds one plough-land or *juft* or part of a plough-land free, on which he does not pay the landowner's share of the crop or dues (*bahrehyi mālikāneh*). This is the case in many of the villages of Kurdistān. Further, in Kurdistān a share of the dues in clarified butter or *roughan* levied by the landowners on the peasants goes to him to defray his expenses in entertaining travellers and officials, since in this part of Persia, except in those villages which are situated on a main road, where it is no longer customary to give hospitality, the *kadkhudā* entertains all travellers and officials passing through. In some cases the income from a mill or a proportion of this is allotted to the *kadkhudā* for *mihmānī*, i.e. for entertainment. Thus, in Ḥasanābād (near Sanandaj) the *kadkhudā* has half the income of one of the seven mills; in Dālān (near Dīvān Darreh) the *kadkhudā* holds a quarter of two plough-lands free, i.e. he does not pay the landowner's share or any dues on these.

[1] See also p. 335.
[2] This due is known locally as *khānehshumārī*.
[3] Known as *far'khīz*.
[4] See p. 310, n. 1.

In various areas in Fārs one-tenth of the total harvest is deducted for the *kadkhudā*. In the Mamasanī this one-tenth is paid by the peasant although it is reckoned on the total harvest. In Jahrum the *kadkhudā's* due on *ābī* crops is also one-tenth of the total; it is similarly paid by the peasant. In Farrāshband the *kadkhudā* gets 4 per cent of the landowner's share, which was formerly one-quarter of the crop but has been reduced recently to one-sixth. In Dārāb the *kadkhudā* gets 5 per cent of the total harvest; this is also the case on *ābī* crops in Qarā Bulāgh; on well-watered land the equivalent of 10 per cent of the total crop is taken from the peasant's share and divided between the *kadkhudā* and the *kalāntar*.[1] In Khīr and Īj the *kadkhudā* gets 1 per cent of the total produce of the village. In Nayrīz, on the other hand, the *kadkhudā* is paid by the landowner.

This is also usually the case in Arāk. In Lakkān the *kadkhudā* receives 6 *kharvār* (approx. 35 cwt., 81 lb.), half in wheat and half in barley, per annum. In the Asadābād area the *kadkhudās* in most properties receive a monthly payment of some 1,000 rs. (£5. 17*s.* 6*d.*) and hold one plough-land on which they do not pay the landowner's share or due. In the neighbourhood of the village of Asadābād the *kadkhudā* also levies some 5–6 *manni tabrīz* (approx. 32 lb., 12 oz.–39 lb.) grain from the holder of each plough-land. The *kadkhudā* in Firaydan gets a payment in money from the landowner and also something in kind from the landowner and the peasants. Thus in Ghargūn he receives 2 *manni tabrīz* per *kharvār* from the peasants and 1 *manni tabrīz* per *kharvār* from the landowner, i.e. 2 per cent and 1 per cent respectively of the total harvest. In Burūjird the *kadkhudā* receives some 2 *manni tabrīz* (approx. 13 lb., 2 oz.) grain per plough-land from the peasants and a cash payment from the landowner. In Qahdrījān, near Iṣfahān, the *kadkhudā* is paid 20,000 rs. (approx. £117. 13*s.*) per annum and he levies in addition a certain amount in cash or kind from each peasant.[2] In Sāveh the *kadkhudā* is paid by the landowner at the rate of 2–3 *kharvār* (approx. 11 cwt., 77 lb.–17 cwt., 60 lb.). One to two *manni tabrīz* (approx. 6½–13 lb.) are deducted from the total harvest in the Tehrān area for the *kadkhudā*; he also receives a cash payment of some 3,000 rs. (approx. £17. 12*s.* 11*d.*) per annum. In Bābā Salmān the *kadkhudā* receives 2–8 *manni tabrīz* (13 lb., 2 oz.–52 lb., 6 oz.) per *kharman*. In Khūzistān the due of the *kadkhudā*, who is in effect in the settled areas the landowner's representative, is levied in some areas on the landowner's share

[1] The *kalāntar* is the head of a tribal group. Qarā Bulāgh is inhabited largely by the 'Aynālū tribe, who belong to the Khamseh; although they are settled, they retain, in part, their tribal structure.

[2] This is known as *toujīh sari kharman*.

and in others on the peasant's. In Havīzeh the *kadkhudā*, where there is one, receives 2½ *manni havīzeh* (approx. 2 cwt., 21 lb.) on *ābī* crops levied on the total harvest, and 1 *manni havīzeh* (approx. 98 lb.) on *daym* crops.

In Kirmān the *kadkhudā* sometimes receives a due which is levied at the rate of some 5 per cent, 7 per cent, or 10 per cent of the total harvest. In most cases, however, he is paid by the landowner. In *khurdeh mālik* villages he receives so much per share of water. Thus in Māhān he receives 10 *sīr* (approx. 1 lb., 10 oz.) grain per share of water.[1] In ʿAbdullāhbād near Rafsinjān he receives some 1 *manni tabrīz* (approx. 6 lb., 9 oz.) wheat and 1 *manni tabrīz* cotton per *ḥabbeh* water. In Fayẓābād, also near Rafsinjān, he is paid by the landowner at the rate of 1 *manni tabrīz* per *ḥabbeh*.

The *kadkhudā* in Qā'ināt is paid by the villagers at the rate of some 1–2 *manni tabrīz* (approx. 6 lb., 9 oz.–13 lb., 2 oz.) per family. It appears, however, that the payment is not made regularly: some families pay, but others do not. In Kākh the *kadkhudā* gets 1 *manni tabrīz* cotton and 1 *manni tabrīz* wheat from each peasant. In Sīstān the *kadkhudā* receives 5 *manni zābul* per share from the peasant. In Bampūr in Balūchistān the *kadkhudā* receives some payment from the landowner or lessee. His main income comes from the plough-lands which he works himself and on which he does not pay the landlord's share.

In the peasant-proprietor areas the *kadkhudā* is either paid so much per household or per unit of water or land. Thus, in Joushaqān he received in 1948 10 rs. (approx. 1*s.* 2*d.*) per household and certain services when required. In Mūrchehkhw̦art the *kadkhudā* has no regular wage.

The number of village officials varies from district to district. Moreover, the use of the technical terms is not in all cases the same. In different areas the same official may be known by a different name; in others the same term is used to cover different functions. The *pākār* is found in some districts and is normally a subordinate of the *kadkhudā*, carrying out the latter's decisions and orders. In Āẕarbāyjān, Balūchistān, Linjān, and Khūzistān the dues for the *pākār* are taken from the peasant's share. In ʿAqīlī the *pākār* receives 3 *manni tabrīz* (19 lb., 11 oz.) grain per plough-land, 6 lb., 9 oz. being paid when the crops begin to shoot and 13 lb., 2 oz. at harvest time. In the *khāliṣeh* of Bampūr 5 *manni tabrīz* (approx. 32 lb., 12 oz.) per plough-land is deducted from the peasant's share and divided between the *qāẓī*[2] and the *pākār*.

[1] This has been the case for the past three years, the rate having been fixed by the *bakhshdār*.

[2] The Balūch are predominantly Sunnī: hence the existence of the *qāẓī* in Balūchistān. He is a member of the religious hierarchy and decides disputes affecting personal status and religious matters.

In the neighbourhood of Īrānshahr the *pākār* gets 2 *manni tabrīz* (approx. 13 lb., 2 oz.) grain per plough-land. In the district surrounding Asadābād the *pākār* receives 5–6 *manni tabrīz* (approx. 32 lb., 12 oz.–39 lb.) from the owner of each plough-land. In the Mamasanī in Fārs the *pākār* is allowed to cultivate one plough-land free, i.e. he does not pay the landowner's share or dues on this. In Kurdistān the main duty of the *pākār* would appear to be the levying of labour service (*bīgārī*). He is paid in some cases by the landowners, and in others special levies in grain, bread, etc., are made on the peasants on his behalf.

In certain areas the *pākār*, while executing the orders of the *kadkhudā*, also watches over the interests of the peasants and corresponds rather to the *dashtbān* (see below). This is the case in Arāk. His share of the harvest in some villages in Arāk is deducted from the total harvest and in others from the share of the peasant. Thus in Sarāb ʿAmārat and Lakkān respectively there are two *pākārs*. In the latter the *pākār's* due is deducted from the total harvest and amounts to 5 *manni tabrīz* (approx. 32 lb., 12 oz.) per plough-land, paid in equal portions of wheat and barley. When it is necessary to clean irrigation channels, mend roads or bridges, or carry out some other public work, the *kadkhudā* informs the *pākār*, who then transmits his orders to the peasants and makes a levy on them of so many men per plough-land. In Joushaqān there are two *pākārs* who are appointed by the villagers from among their number. Their duties are to see that the fields of the villagers are secure from depredations from whatever source. They receive ½ *manni tabrīz* (approx. 3 lb., 4½ oz.) grain per *jarīb ābī* (approx. 478·4 sq. yds.). In Lāstān, a district composed of gardens adjacent to Joushaqān, there are also two *pākārs*, who are similarly appointed and paid in kind in grapes, walnuts, etc. In the Yazd area the *pākār* is in some cases a subordinate official of the *mīrāb*. Thus in Ashkizār, which has three *qanāts*, the *mīrāb* has ten *pākārs* under him, each of whom is paid 50 rs. (approx. 5*s*. 10*d*.) per *jurreh*, i.e. 11½ minutes' water, per annum, by the peasant.

The *dashtbān* bears witness to a tendency towards self-help among the peasant community by whom he is appointed. He is himself usually a peasant. His duties are to watch over the peasant's fields and crops and in some cases to oversee or help in the distribution of water. He is usually paid in kind, a deduction being made in most cases from the peasant's share of the harvest. The fact that the appointment of such an official should be necessary is evidence of the somewhat rudimentary nature of public security and the absence of adequate protection for the peasant's interests. The number of *dashtbāns* in a village depends on the extent of the cultivated fields.

In Qā'ināt practice varies somewhat. In some cases the due of the *dashtbān* is taken from the total harvest, in others from the peasant's share. In 'Alīābād, east-south-east of Bīrjand, he receives 300 *manni bīrjand* (approx. 9 cwt., 108 lb.) of grain, two-thirds in wheat and one-third in barley, 10 *manni bīrjand* (approx. 37 lb.) of cotton, 1,000 *manni bīrjand* (approx. 33 cwt., 3 lb.) each of beet and carrots. In the Mājān area his share is deducted from the total harvest, and amounts to 10 *manni bīrjand* (approx. 37 lb.) of every crop from each *tīrkār*.[1] In Gīv there are three *dashtbāns* who get 300 *manni bīrjand* millet, wheat, and barley respectively, which they share.

In Fārs also practice varies. Thus, in Jahrum the *dashtbān* gets 100 *manni jahrum* (approx. 6 cwt., 62 lb.) each of wheat, barley, and millet per *kharman* on *ābī* crops and 500 rs. (approx. £2. 18*s*. 10*d*.) per plough-land. In Dārāb he is paid a fixed sum, the amount varying from place to place and year to year. In Qarā Bulāgh in *ābī* villages the landowner pays him 30–45 *manni shīrāz* (approx. 1 cwt., 108 lb.–2 cwt., 106 lb.) grain per month. In Nayrīz he is paid by a deduction made from the total harvest.

Similarly, in some villages in the Iṣfahān area, as in Qahdrījān, the due of the *dashtbān*, who is known in some areas as the *nāẓūr*, is deducted from the total harvest.

In Khurāsān the *dashtbān* is paid in a variety of ways. In Ṭuruq, near Mashhad, he is paid 1,500 rs. (approx. £8. 16*s*. 5*d*.) per month, 3 *kharvār* (approx. 17 cwt., 60 lb.) wheat per annum, and fodder for his horse, which amounts to 3 kg. (approx. 6 lb., 10 oz.) barley, 6–9 kg. (approx. 13 lb., 4 oz.–19 lb., 13 oz.) straw, and 1½ kg. (approx. 3 lb., 5 oz.) lucerne per month. The payment in cash is made by the lessees and the payments in kind are deducted from the total harvest. In Khīābān, where there are six *dashtbāns*, each receives 400 rs. (approx. £2. 7*s*.) per month from the lessees and 6 *kharvār* (approx. 35 cwt., 8 lb.) grain, two-thirds in wheat and one-third in barley, taken from the total harvest. In Shādkan and Ābkūh the *dashtbān's* wages are deducted from the total harvest. In Turbati Ḥaydarī he is usually paid by contract, his wage amounting to some 2–4 *kharvār* (approx. 11 cwt., 77 lb.–23 cwt. 42 lb.) grain which he receives from the owner, 1 plot or *kart* of opium (which gives some 8 *miṣqāl*—approx. 1 oz., 8 dr.) from each *ṣaḥrā*,[2] some 20–50 *manni tabrīz* (approx. 1 cwt., 19 lb.–2 cwt., 101 lb.) melons, some lucerne, and a levy on other crops, and one load (i.e. 25–30 *manni tabrīz*—approx. 1 cwt., 42 lb.–1 cwt., 84 lb.) of beet and carrots from each *ṣaḥrā*. In winter the *dashtbān* has no work in the fields and acts as an assistant to the

[1] See p. 298 for the meaning of this term.
[2] See pp. 298 ff. for the meaning of this term.

ṣāḥib kār or *mubāshir* (see above). In Kāshmar he is paid from the total harvest, the amount being usually in the neighbourhood of 100 *manni tabrīz* (approx. 5 cwt., 95 lb.) per *ṣaḥrā*. The number of *dashtbāns* attached to each *ṣaḥrā* depends upon the size of the *ṣaḥrā*.

The *dashtbān* in the province of Kirmān is selected by the peasants who hold plough-lands, with the concurrence of the landowner. In this area the due of the *dashtbān* is in some cases included in a deduction of 7 per cent made from the total harvest, which is shared with other officials such as the blacksmith, carpenter, and bath-keeper (see below). Elsewhere he is paid a fixed wage amounting to some 300–360 *manni tabrīz* (approx. 17 cwt., 60 lb.–1 ton, 1 cwt., 4 lb.) per village in wheat, barley, and millet, which is taken from the total harvest. In certain properties near Zarand he receives so much per *dāng*, i.e. per unit of water; in others, including Jannat which has three *dashtbāns*, he is paid so many *mann* per *kharman*; in this area the *dashtbāns* cultivate the land along the edges of the irrigation channels for themselves and keep the produce.[1] Similarly in Akbarābād and Muḥammadābād, near Kirmān, the *dashtbān* is paid per *dāng*, i.e. per share of water, the levy being made from the total harvest. In Shahdād he gets 18 *manni tabrīz* (approx. 1 cwt., 6 lb.)[2] from the total harvest and 5 *manni tabrīz* (approx. 32 lb., 12 oz.) per plough-land paid by the landowner. In Andūjird, as in Zarand, the *dashtbān* sows the land along the edges of the irrigation channels and keeps the produce thereof; if there should occur any thefts from the land under his charge, these are made good from the produce of the grain he sows along the edges of the irrigation channels. In ʿAbdullāhābād near Rafsinjān the *dashtbān* gets something in the neighbourhood of 150 *manni tabrīz* (approx. 8 cwt., 86 lb.) millet and cotton respectively and 350 *manni tabrīz* (approx. 1 ton, 51 lb.) wheat and barley per six *dāng*, i.e. from all the village lands. In Fayẓābād in the same area 360 *manni tabrīz* (approx. 21 cwt., 4 lb.) partly in winter crops and partly in summer crops is deducted from the total produce of the village lands for the *dashtbān*,[3] blacksmith, carpenter, and *muqannī*.[4] The *dashtbān* gets three shares to the *muqannī's* one. In addition, in the Rafsinjān area the *dashtbān* takes an armful of wheat or barley[5] containing some 5–6 *manni tabrīz* (approx. 32 lb., 12 oz.–39 lb.) grain from each *kharman* before the threshing takes place.

The *dashtbān*, or *qukhil* as he is known in Kurdistān, is paid in

[1] This is known locally as *jūbī*.
[2] Or 12 *musht* (1 *musht* = $1\frac{1}{2}$ *manni tabrīz*).
[3] Known locally as *nāẓūr*.
[4] Known locally as the *chākhū* or *kahkīn*.
[5] Known locally as *shūmī*.

that province by the peasant in the crop-sharing areas, and by the landowner in the land retained and cultivated by him not on a crop-sharing basis. In Sīstān the *dashtbān*[1] gets in the landlord areas 20 *manni tabrīz* (approx. 1 cwt., 19 lb.) per *pāgāv* (i.e. per six shares worked by six peasants and one ox) levied on the total harvest, usually in equal shares of wheat and barley. In the Tehrān area the *dashtbān* gets 1–2 *manni tabrīz* (approx. 6 lb., 9 oz.–13 lb., 2 oz.) per plough-land. In the Pushti Kūh area of Yazd he receives from the peasants something in the neighbourhood of 1 *manni tabrīz* wheat and 1 *manni tabrīz* barley per *ṭāq* (or unit of water), and some fruit where this is grown. In Mūrchehkhwart there are two *dashtbāns* who receive 2–3 *manni tabrīz* (approx. 13 lb., 2 oz.–19 lb., 11 oz.) grain per *kharman*. In the district of Asadābād the *dashtbān* receives 5–6 *manni tabrīz* from the owner of each plough-land. In Khūzistān he is also paid by the peasant. In ʿAqīlī he is paid approximately 3 *manni tabrīz* (19 lb., 11 oz.) grain per plough-land, 6 lb., 9 oz. being paid when the crop begins to shoot and 13 lb., 2 oz. at harvest time, and a cash payment for *ṣayfī* crops. In Rām Hurmuz the *dashtbān* receives approximately 13 lb. wheat and 13 lb. barley per plough-land.

The second type of deductions are those made for the payment of certain village craftsmen and servants. These deductions are not made in all areas: in some cases the craftsmen and servants concerned do not exist, in others they are paid as and when they carry out a piece of work or perform a certain service. In many cases, especially in eastern and southern Persia, however, the village blacksmith and carpenter receive a payment in kind at harvest and carry out in return running repairs for the peasant throughout the year. These dues are known as *āhangarī* or *ḥaddādī*[2] and *najjārī*[3] respectively. In the *khāliṣeh* of Bampūr 20 *manni tabrīz* (approx. 1 cwt., 19 lb.) grain per plough-land is taken from the peasant's share for the blacksmith and carpenter together. In return they provide for the peasant anything he needs which appertains to their two trades respectively. In Īrānshahr *āhangarī* and *najjārī* are levied at a similar rate. In Qā'ināt these dues are deducted either from the total harvest, from the peasant's share, or from the owner's share. In ʿAlīābād, east-south-east of Bīrjand, they are levied at the rate of 80 *manni bīrjand* (approx. 1 cwt., 71 lb.) in equal parts of wheat and barley each per *tīrkār*. In Mājān and Kākh the rate is 15 *manni bīrjand* (approx. 55½ lb.) on all crops per *tīrkār*. In Gīv, on the other hand, *najjārī* and *āhangarī* are paid by the owner.

In Jahrum on *ābī* crops *āhangarī* and *najjārī* are collected under

[1] Known locally as *mushrif*.
[2] From *āhangar* and *ḥaddād* respectively, 'a blacksmith'.
[3] From *najjār*, 'a carpenter'.

two heads, i.e. as wages in cash or kind and a payment in kind which consists in that amount of grain and straw (before threshing) which can be carried off under one arm.[1] Recently this has been commuted to 5 *manni tabrīz* (approx. 32 lb., 12 oz.) wheat and 5 *manni tabrīz* barley per plough-land taken on the total harvest, and the wages of the blacksmith and carpenter have been fixed at 8 *manni tabrīz* (approx. 52 lb.) barley and 8 *manni tabrīz* wheat and, on summer crops, 8 *manni tabrīz* millet if it is grown; if not, a further 8 *manni tabrīz* barley per plough-land. These amounts are taken from the peasant's share. In Dārāb *āhangarī* and *najjārī* are fixed by contract and usually amount to some 2 per cent of the total harvest, from which they are deducted. The amount taken in Fasā is rather less. In Qarā Bulāgh in *ābī* villages the landowner pays 10 *manni shīrāz* (approx. 73 lb.) each of wheat, barley, and millet per month by way of *āhangarī* and a similar amount for *najjārī*. In Nayrīz, on the other hand, *āhangarī* and *najjārī* are levied on the total harvest.

In Khurāsān practice varies. In Ṭuruq *āhangarī* and *najjārī* amount to 40 *kharvār* (approx. 11 tons, 13 cwt., 89 lb.) each for the whole village; this levy is divided among and collected from the various plough-lands. In Khīābān these dues amount to 9 *kharvār* (approx. 52 cwt., 68 lb., two-thirds in wheat and one-third in barley) each, and are paid by the *ṣaḥrādārs*.[2] In Shādkan they are deducted from the total harvest at the rate of 30 *mann* (approx. 1 cwt., 84 lb., two-thirds in wheat and one-third in barley) per *ṣaḥrā*. In Turbati Ḥaydarī and Kāshmar they are deducted from the total harvest of the village, amounting in some villages in the former area to about 4 *kharvār* each (approx. 23 cwt., 42 lb.).

In some villages in the province of Kirmān, as stated above, some 7 per cent of the total harvest is said to be deducted for *āhangarī*, *najjārī*, and *ḥammāmī*, i.e. the due of the bath-keeper and the due of the *dashtbān* together. What happens in fact appears to be that each of them takes an armful of grain after it is cut, but before it is threshed, and a further quantity of grain after it is threshed. Similarly, their dues on summer crops are taken in kind.

In some villages, as in Gāvkhāneh, *āhangarī* and *najjārī* are levied on the peasants at so much per *dāng* of water. In Shahdād these dues, together with *ḥammāmī* and *salmānī*, amount to some 10 *manni tabrīz* (approx. 65 lb., 8 oz.) grain per plough-share and are paid by the peasant. In Bardsīr the dues for *āhangarī* and *najjārī* are at the rate of 5–10 *mann* (approx. 32 lb., 12 oz.–65 lb., 8 oz.) per *kharman* and are deducted from the total harvest. In ʿAbdullāhābād near Rafsinjān *āhangarī* and *najjārī* are levied at

[1] Known locally as *muzd* and *baghalī* respectively.

[2] See above, p. 299.

the rate of some $1\frac{3}{4}$ *mann* (approx. 11 lb.) wheat and barley and something on summer crops per *ḥabbeh* or unit of water. Broadly speaking, in the neighbourhood of Rafsinjān where the crop division is three-quarters to the landowner these dues are taken from the landowner's share, but where the landowner takes 70 per cent of the harvest they are levied on the total harvest.

In Khūzistān *āhangarī* and *najjārī* are usually paid by the peasant. In Kurdistān (near Bihbahān) 110 lb. grain per plough-land is the rate for *najjārī*, and in Shūsht 15–23 lb. grain are paid to the man who makes ox-yokes. In Sāveh also *āhangarī* is the responsibility of the peasant.

In Sīstān *āhangarī* and *najjārī* are not everywhere levied, since the craftsmen concerned are not found in all villages. Where these dues are levied they are deducted from the total harvest and amount to 20 *manni zābul* per share.[1] In the landlord areas of Sīstān they are less, being some 5 *manni zābul* per *juft* or share.

Āhangarī and *najjārī* are for the most part not found in Kurdistān or central Persia, the blacksmith and carpenter being paid in these areas for work as it is done.

In those villages where there is a bath, or *ḥammām*, the bath-keeper is in some cases also paid by a share of the harvest in return for which the peasant and his family use the bath throughout the year. This due is known as *ḥammāmī* and is levied per household or sometimes per head. Thus, in Lakkān in Arāk the levy is 5 *manni tabrīz* (approx. 32 lb., 12 oz.) per working man or woman and 1 *manni tabrīz* (approx. 6 lb., 9 oz.) per child below working age. In Joushaqān *ḥammāmī* is paid at the rate of 3–4 *manni tabrīz* (approx. 19 lb., 11 oz.–26 lb., 3 oz.) grain per family per annum. In the Pushti Kūh area of Yazd the bath-keeper gets 1 *manni tabrīz* wheat and 1 *manni tabrīz* barley per household.

In some areas a similar due for the barber, known as *salmānī*,[2] is levied. This also is usually paid per head or per family and not per plough-land. The barber circumcises the children and, on the occasion of weddings, the performance of passion plays (*taʿzīehs*), etc., acts as a kind of head servant (*pīshkhidmat*). In the Mamasanī *salmānī* is levied on the peasant at the rate of 10 *manni tabrīz* (approx. 65 lb., 8 oz.) per *kharman*. In the Qashqā'ī the amount taken from the peasant for *salmānī* and *ḥammāmī* varies; it is taken from the total harvest and amounts usually to 1 *ruhn*, i.e. the amount of grain that will go into a receptacle known by

[1] See Ch. XII for the division of the land into shares.

[2] Barbers are commonly known in Persia as *salmānī* (as also the due levied for their services), after one of the companions of the Prophet Muḥammad whose name was Salmān. He was a Persian and plays an important part in Muslim legend and in the development of various Ṣūfī orders and guilds. According to a tradition, he was the Prophet's barber. (See under 'Salmān al-Fārisī' in *E.I.*)

that name. Wheat, barley, and straw are taken.[1] In Jahrum *salmānī* and *ḥammāmī* are taken from the peasants, the former at the rate of 3 *manni tabrīz* (approx. 19 lb., 11 oz.) grain per person. In Qarā Bulāgh in *ābī* villages 10 *manni shīrāz* (approx. 73 lb.) grain per plough-land is taken from the total harvest for *salmānī* and *ḥammāmī* respectively, and in well-watered areas 2½ *manni shīrāz* (approx. 17 lb., 7 oz.) per plough-land from the peasant's share.

In Khurāsān *salmānī* and *ḥammāmī*, where they exist, are for the most part paid by the peasant. In Turbati Ḥaydarī the due is some ½–1 *manni tabrīz* (approx. 3 lb., 4½ oz.–6 lb., 9 oz.) grain per annum per head. The *salmānī* usually serves several villages. In Khūzistān *salmānī* is usually paid by the peasant. In Dizfūl a levy for this purpose is made at the rate of 2–4 *manni dizfūl* (154 lb.–308 lb.) per plough-land and one load of rice. In Khalafābād it is ¼ *manni jarrāḥīyeh* (68 lb.) barley and ½ *manni jarrāḥīyeh* (136 lb.) wheat per plough-land, and in Kurdistān (near Bihbihān) it is 35 kg. (77 lb.) wheat and 35 kg. barley. In some villages in Qā'ināt *ḥammāmī* and *salmānī* are paid by the owner. This is the case in ʿAlīābād, east-south-east of Bīrjand, and in Gīv. In certain areas in Sīstān the due for *salmānī* is 2 *manni zābul* per share and is paid by the peasant.

Finally, there are certain dues deducted from the harvest for the religious classes. The origin of these dues goes back to early Islamic times, when it was an established practice to give alms at harvest time.[2] At the present day the collection of dues on the harvest for the religious classes has died out in most areas, but such dues are still found as regular charges on the harvest in east Persia and Kurdistān. In addition, there are itinerant members of the religious classes who tend to follow the harvest, collecting what they can as they go.[3] In certain villages in Qā'ināt these payments to the religious classes are made by the landowner. Thus, in ʿAlīābād, east-south-east of Bīrjand, the dues for the prayer-leader (*pīsh namāz*) and servant of the mosque (*khādimi masjid*) are paid by the landowner. In Balūchistān, as stated above, in the *khāliṣeh* villages of Bampūr 5 *manni tabrīz* (approx. 32 lb., 12 oz.) per *juft* is divided between the *qāẓī* and the *pākār*.[4] In Qarā Bulāgh a small deduction from the total harvest is made for the *sayyids* and *ākhunds* or *mullās*. In Khurāsān these deductions for the religious classes, known as *māl ullāhī*, are made either from the total harvest or from the peasant's share. In Ṭuruq and Shād-

[1] The taking of this levy is known as *taleh*.

[2] See Yaḥyā b. Ādam, *Kitāb al-Kharāj*, ed. Juynboll (Leyden, 1896), p. 89.

[3] These persons are known in some quarters as *muftkhwār*, and in many cases are nothing more than beggars who, adopting the garb of a religious mendicant, trade on the good nature of the peasants.

[4] See p. 341, n. 2.

kan a deduction of 5 *manni tabrīz* (approx. 32 lb., 12 oz.) per *kharman* is made for this purpose. In Kurdistān in most villages of any size there is a *mullā*. He is usually paid some 1–5 *kharvār* (approx. 5 cwt., 95 lb.–29 cwt., 25 lb.) by the landowner and given at the festivals known as *'īdi fiṭr* and *'īdi qurbān*[1] a suit of clothes.[2] The peasants also pay him some 5–20 *manni tabrīz* (approx. 32 lb., 12 oz.–1 cwt., 19 lb.) per household.[3] Fuel for the mosque, where there is one, is usually provided by the landowner; in some cases the revenue from a mill is set aside to defray the expenses of the mosque. Thus, in Ḥasanābād near Sanandaj $1\frac{1}{2}$ mills are set aside in this way. In Sīstān the *mullā* gets 2 *manni zābul* per share.

To sum up, various survivals of former customs are to be found in the field of local administration and in the dues which are levied for various purposes in many villages, particularly in the outlying areas. Although these dues survive from the days when the economy of the village was entirely a grain economy, and the village was a self-contained unit to a greater extent than is the case at the present day, they nevertheless to some extent still reflect prevailing social and economic conditions. In the second class of dues, namely those made for the payment of local officials, a trend can be distinguished similar to that mentioned in Chapter VIII; in so far as the force of law has been given to what was formerly custom, the scales are weighted in favour of the landowner. Significant of this is the fact that the *kadkhudā*, who has been incorporated into the hierarchy of government officials, is or has become the representative of the landowners, while the *dashtbān*, who is the representative of the peasants, has no official status.

[1] The *'īdi fiṭr* is the festival celebrated on 1st Shavvāl on the breaking of the fast at the end of the month of Ramaẓān. The *'īdi qurbān* is celebrated on the 10th Ẓu'l Ḥijjeh, the day when the pilgrims offer their sacrifices in the valley of Minā on the way to Mecca. (See art. 'Ḥajj' in *E.I.*)

[2] This is locally known as *khil'at*, which term was formerly used to designate a robe of honour which the ruler gave to ministers, envoys, and others as a mark of favour.

[3] This payment is referred to as *zakāt*, the original meaning of which is alms tax. See above, p. 31.

CHAPTER XX

FLOCKS AND PASTURES

APART from the flocks belonging to the semi-settled element of the population, two main types of flocks owned by the settled population can be distinguished: the large flocks owned by the landlords and the small flocks owned by the peasants. In the former case the ownership of flocks is independent of the ownership of the land, and although the flocks may and often do constitute an important source of income for the landowner, this revenue is seldom of vital importance to him and is a sideline rather than an activity which is closely bound up with his ownership of the land. For the most part this is not so where the peasant is concerned. As stated in Chapter XIV, the peasant supplements the income which he obtains from agriculture, and which in many cases is insufficient to support him and his family, by the keeping of flocks. This applies not only to the peasant proprietor but also to the crop-sharing peasant.

The relative importance of flocks in the local economy varies and is largely determined by the climate of the different areas. On the borders of the central desert, as, for example, in the Yazd area and in Qā'ināt, flocks do not play an important part in the local economy. In west Persia, on the other hand, the livelihood of the peasants is based perhaps as much on flocks as upon agriculture. Three main purposes are served by the keeping of flocks. First, the animals to some extent provide manure for the land; secondly, their produce, in curds, clarified butter (*roughan*), and cheese, etc., is an important article in the diet of the peasant and his family, and the sale of their produce where surplus to his needs supplements his income. Thirdly, the hair of goats is used in some areas to weave cloth for tents and to make ropes, and the wool of sheep for making carpets.

In Sīstān there is a section of the population which is engaged solely in cattle-breeding. They are known as *gāvdārān*. The cattle graze in the reed-beds (*nayzār*) in the lagoon. They cross over the water daily in the morning into the reed-beds and return in the evening. The Trayfī (?Turayfī) Arabs in the Dizfūl-Shūstar-'Aqīlī-Shu'ayb area also make their living from tending cattle, but in this case they do not actually own the herds. They take buffaloes on a *tarāz* contract. In other words, the buffaloes are taken over for a fixed period and so many *mann* per head of buffalo per year, usually 4–6 *manni tabrīz* (approx. 26 lb.–39 lb.) being paid to the owner, and after the expiry of the period the animals are returned to their owner; any progeny they have had in the meanwhile is divided equally between the owner and the man who farmed them out, or their value is estimated and a payment made to the former amounting to half of the value of the increase. In a good year the profit in clarified butter to the man who looks after the buffaloes is 5–6 *manni tabrīz* (approx. 32 lb., 12 oz.–39 lb.) per head. If any of the buffaloes entrusted to him die a natural death he has no responsibility, but if any losses occur through his negligence he has to compensate the owner for half the value of the animal lost. A pasture due of 50 rs. (approx. 5*s.* 10*d.* per annum) per buffalo is paid by the man who looks after the buffaloes to the owner of the pastures in which they graze.

In so far as the flocks of the landlords are concerned, they are in most cases farmed out to a shepherd on a contract, which in some respects resembles the crop-sharing contract made between the landlord and the peasant for the cultivation of land. The produce of the flock is shared in varying proportions between the two parties. There are two main types of contract; one is known as *dandānī* and the other is the *tarāz* contract, mentioned above. The main feature of the *dandānī* contract is that when it expires an equal number of animals of the same age as the animals at the time of the commencement of the contract are returned to the owner; any surplus over this is retained by the shepherd.

Landowners in the neighbourhood of Tehrān are in the habit of letting out their flocks on one or other of these types of contract. For example in 1949 in the Jājī Rūd valley ½ *manni tabrīz* (approx. 3 lb., 4½ oz.) *roughan*, or clarified butter, was paid to the owner by the shepherd for every animal in milk. In some areas of central Persia a similar amount was paid per head (i.e. whether male or female, in milk or barren).

In the Turbati Ḥaydarī area various arrangements are made with shepherds.[1] One practice is to farm out the sheep and goats after lambing for a specified period in return for a certain amount of clarified butter (*roughan*) or a kind of dried curd known as *kashk*. The maximum rate is ½ *manni tabrīz* clarified butter per head for a period of seventy days, and 5 *sīr* (approx. 13 oz.) *kashk*.

Tarāz and *dandānī* contracts are widely found in the Jahrum neighbourhood. It is common to entrust sheep and goats to a peasant shortly before they lamb or kid. Under a *tarāz* contract the peasant undertakes to milk the animals and give so much of the produce to the owner, and to return the animals at the end of the

[1] A flock of 600 head is looked after by two shepherds, one ass, and two sheep dogs. The sheep dogs receive a ration of 10 *sīr* (approximately 1 lb., 10 oz.) barley flour per day from the owner of the flock in winter until the lambing season.

period to their owner. The amount which the peasant undertakes to give is usually 1 *manni tabrīz* (approx. 6 lb., 9 oz.) per cow and ¼ *mann* (approx. 1 lb., 10 oz.) of sheep or goats. The *dandānī* contract is used only for sheep and goats. A number of animals, say sixty goats of two years old, are handed over to the peasant and a receipt taken from him to the effect that on a certain date he will give back to the owner sixty two-year-old goats and 1 *manni tabrīz* (approx. 6 lb., 9 oz.) clarified butter per three goats per annum, i.e. 20 *manni tabrīz* (approx. 1 cwt., 19 lb.) for the period of the contract. The progeny of the goats meanwhile and their wool belong to the peasant. Any losses are his responsibility. In the Mamasanī area sheep, goats, and buffaloes are let out on *tarāz*. The sum taken is usually in the neighbourhood of 1 *manni tabrīz* per annum per buffalo (*gāvmīsh*) and ½–1 *vaqeh* (approx. 11½–23 lb.) per sheep or goat.

In Arāk the period of a *dandānī* contract is normally four to seven years. The peasant undertakes to give the owner of the animals ½ *manni tabrīz* clarified butter per ewe and 1 *mann* (approx. 6 lb., 9 oz.) per goat per annum.

Both the types of contract mentioned above are found where the number of animals concerned is considerable. They are not, however, confined to such cases. It frequently happens that a peasant takes a small number of animals under one or other forms of contract, either from the landlord or from more prosperous peasants who have more animals than they are able to look after themselves.

In the same way as the landlord in some cases exempts some land from the general distribution of the village land among the crop-sharing peasants, so he does not always let all his livestock out on a *tarāz* or *dandānī* contract, but employs a shepherd to whom he pays a wage in cash or kind or both. In the Turbati Ḥaydarī area shepherds are paid in a variety of ways: (1) by a wage in cash and kind, such as 1,000 rs. (approx. £5. 17*s*. 6*d*. per annum), 2 *kharvār* (approx. 11 cwt., 77 lb.) wheat, one *namad*, or felt coat, and one pair of shoes; or (2) an agreement is made by which they receive a proportion of the progeny of the flock, for example, 10 per cent of the lambs or kids handed over to the owner after lambing and weaning, i.e. not counting any losses incurred. Shepherds who graze unweaned lambs and kids are paid at the rate of 5–10 *manni tabrīz* (approx. 32 lb., 12 oz.–65 lb., 8 oz.) grain per month, and receive the proceeds of one day's milking per week. These shepherds are known as *khalāmehcharān*.

In Khūzistān shepherds are remunerated in a number of ways. In some cases they are paid so much per head on the animals entrusted to their care. Thus, in ʿArab ʿAbbās in the neighbourhood of Ahvāz they were paid 2 rs. (approx. $2\frac{3}{4}d.$) per head of sheep and goats per month in 1949.

In one of the peasant-proprietor villages in the Kūhi Kargis area the shepherds of the leading man in the village were each given in 1948 a monthly allowance for tea, sugar, tobacco, and clothing, and a wage of 1,000–3,000 rs. (approx. £5. 17*s.* 6*d.*–£17. 12*s.* 11*d.*) per annum.

The extent to which the peasants own flocks varies considerably. In Qahdrījān, for example, the villagers own some 15,000 goats and sheep between them. In Burkhw̤ār a few of the more prosperous peasants own 1,000–2,000 head. In Mūrchehkhw̤art where agriculture does not provide a living in itself, the population mostly own small flocks.[1] Climatic conditions in the villages along the borders of the central desert stretching from Qumm through Kāshān and extending southwards through the Kūhi Kargis area to Yazd are not favourable to the keeping of large numbers of flocks. For the most part the peasants usually own a few goats apiece. Some of the more prosperous have up to 200. In Joushaqān the peasants have some fifty to sixty apiece which they keep mainly for manure. In Ardistān the number owned by the peasant is on an average rather smaller. In the Yazd area, owing to the absence of grazing, the peasants seldom have more than three to four apiece. In the Pushti Kūh district of Yazd they have rather more, since grazing conditions are better. There are few flocks in Qā'ināt owing to the absence of pastures. Most of the villagers do not own more than a few head of sheep and goats which graze in the neighbourhood of the villages. In the Saqqiz area, although the landlords own large flocks, the peasants mostly own some ten to twenty head of sheep and goats each. In the Asadābād area, which also has large landlord flocks, the villagers mainly own four to six head each. In the Turbati Ḥaydarī area they have five to ten head each. In the Jājī Rūd neighbourhood of Tehrān the main income of the peasants comes from flocks. Part of the land in the neighbourhood is *quruq*,[2] and the number of flocks which the villagers have the right to graze in this area is therefore limited. Further down the river towards Varāmīn in Touchāl the population also lives mainly on its flocks. The size of these is relatively small: the largest are probably not more than 400–500 head. The people of this area are semi-settled and move to the Lār valley in summer.

Where the number of animals belonging to the peasants is small some co-operative arrangement is often made for taking them to

[1] Formerly the people of Mūrchehkhw̤art supplemented their livelihood by the keeping of camels which they let out for transport. With the increase in motor transport this practice has fallen into desuetude.

[2] See above, p. 258.

pasture, and the shepherd placed in charge is paid so much per animal entrusted to him. For example, in Bagī Jān there were eight flocks of sheep and two herds of cows belonging to the villagers in 1949. Each flock or herd had its own shepherds who were paid according to the number of animals in their charge. In Asadābād in 1945 shepherds were paid 5–10 rs. (*7d.–1s. 2d.*) per head.

In some villages in Qā'ināt there are communal shepherds from whom a deduction is made from the produce of the *tīrkār*.[1] Thus, in Ḥasanābād, Mājān, and Kākh there is one shepherd to each *tīrkār* who gets 42 *manni bīrjand* (approx. 1 cwt., 42 lb.) of all crops from the *tīrkār*.

Whereas the large flocks owned by the landlords are usually sent to summer pastures, the extent to which the village flocks are sent outside the area varies. In the hotter parts of Persia they are usually sent in summer to pastures in the cooler regions. In the more temperate parts the villagers also tend to move their flocks in summer, if only to the outskirts of the village; in such cases, a number of their womenfolk accompany the flocks, pitch their tents outside the village, and spend the summer or part of it in tents. When the flocks are sent farther afield they are usually accompanied only by the shepherds. The distance travelled by the village flocks depends largely upon climatic conditions. In a year when pasture is bad they go farther afield than in a good year. In winter in the upland country, when prevented by snow from pasturing in the open, they are fed on hay or lucerne and kept in stables. In the area to the north of Iṣfahān round Maymeh underground caverns are dug, known as *būmkan* (or *būmkand*), in which the sheep and goats are kept during the severest part of the winter. Their droppings are subsequently collected and used as manure. In the Iṣfahān area if the combined flocks of the villagers are large they are usually sent to summer pastures. In Qahdrījān the village flock is sent in summer to Firaydan or Chahār Maḥāll. In Burkhwār the flocks belonging to the peasants also usually go in summer to some upland district such as Firaydan. In Mūrchehkhwart also the larger flocks are taken to Firaydan or Muta'. Throughout the area stretching from Qumm through Kāshān to the Kūhi Kargis, and extending southwards to Yazd, the village flocks as well as the landlord flocks go in summer to the upland districts to graze. In the event of drought they may be forced to travel considerable distances to find pasture. For example, in 1948 there were flocks from Nā'īn at Gilahrūd near Joushaqān.

In Kurdistān the village flocks are in most cases sent to pasture, but in Ḥasanābād near Sanandaj, since there are a considerable

[1] See above, p. 298, for the meaning of this term.

number of gardens in the village, the villagers usually graze their own sheep and goats, feeding them, for example, on the leaves of the trees, stubble, and weeds growing in the gardens. In Kirmān also the small communal flocks composed of the animals belonging to the peasants, each of whom own a few head, graze in the neighbourhood of the villages on stubble in the fields after the crops have been reaped, on weeds in the village gardens, branches pruned from trees, and lucerne, etc.

Another practice is found in the Yazd area in connexion with livestock. The Qashqā'ī and other tribesmen are in the habit of bringing sheep to the district before the Persian New Year and selling them to the local people on credit. The latter then fatten the sheep, sell them some forty to sixty days later, pay off their debt, and keep any profit. Landowners sometimes sell sheep to the peasants on similar terms; it frequently happens that a peasant in this way has two or three sheep to fatten for sale.

The legal position of village pastures has been briefly covered in Chapter VIII, while reference has also been made to them in Chapter XV in so far as the tribal areas are concerned. In the peasant-proprietor areas the pastures round a village are usually held in common, and are grazed by the flocks of the villagers. In the landlord areas the peasants usually have the right to graze their animals in the pastures surrounding the village in which they live, although these belong to the landowner. In the tribal areas where the pastures are owned by the sedentary landowners these are often let to the tribes; the pastures immediately round the villages, however, are not included in such leases, and the right of the settled villagers to use these is not affected. Where, as happens in some areas, outsiders use the village pastures, a pasture tax is usually levied.

The pastures in Āẕarbāyjān are owned mainly by the large landowners or are *khāliṣeh*. In some areas, as in the property of the Afshār *khāns*, one day's milk of the village flocks per annum goes to the landowner by way of a pasture due.

In the Iṣfahān area the pastures round the villages are also usually the property of the landowner.

In Kurdistān the pastures belong mainly to the large landowners. In the Sanandaj area no pasture dues are taken from the villagers. In the Saqqiz area, however, a pasture due is levied amounting to some 150–200 rs. (approx. 17*s.* 7*d.*–£1. 3*s.* 6*d.*) per household per annum.

Similarly, in the Asadābād area the pastures are owned by the landowners and are let out to tribal groups and others. The villagers, however, have the right to use the grazing round the villages.

The pastures round the landlord villages in Arāk belong to the landowners. The peasants are in most cases allowed to graze their flocks in these. Flocks coming from outside districts paid 700–1,500 rs. (approx. £4. 2*s.* 4*d.*–£8. 16*s.* 5*d.*) per 100 head of sheep or goats in 1945.

The pastures in certain other areas in the neighbourhood of Tehrān, notably the Lār valley, are *khāliṣeh*. These are in some cases leased and sub-leased. A due of some 12 rs. (approx. 1*s.* 5*d.*) per head is levied on the flocks which use the pastures.

In Ṭālish the pastures are for the most part owned by the large landowners.

The villagers in the Sāveh area have the free use of the village pastures. From outsiders, on the other hand, a pasture due is taken.

A pasture due (*ḥaqq ul-marta*ʿ) is taken in many areas in Khurāsān by the owner of the pasture. In some cases the villagers are required to pay this even for the pastures immediately round the village in which they live. In Ṭuruq near Mashhad, for example, a pasture due of 10 rs. (approx. 1*s.* 2*d.*) per head of sheep and goats per annum is taken from the villagers and 15 rs. (approx. 1*s.* 9*d.*) from outsiders for the use of the village pastures. In Khīābān the village pastures are in some cases sub-let by the lessees and pasture dues collected by the sub-tenant. The holder of each plough-land has the right to graze ten head of sheep or goats free. A pasture due is not paid on oxen and asses. The right to graze on stubble is let at the rate of 35 rs. (approx. 4*s.* 1*d.*) per head of sheep or goats. In Shādkan one cow and up to five sheep or goats per peasant are exempt from pasture dues. Eight rs. (approx. 11½*d.*) is paid on anything above this number in pastures near the town of Mashhad and rather less farther out. In Turbati Ḥaydarī the flocks of the peasants grazing in landlord areas pay a due known as *ḥaqq us-sahm*, i.e. the produce of two milkings during the sixty-odd days when the flock is in milk must be given to the landowner, or one to the landowner and one to the *kadkhudā*. This is in addition to a pasture due, or *ḥaqq ul-marta*ʿ, which is payable on flocks numbering more than 400 head of sheep or goats. The villagers, who usually own five to ten head each, have a right to graze a communal flock of 400 head free. A pasture due is usually levied in a lump sum for a given period. Flocks of outsiders passing through pay a transit due. In Shaṣt Darreh, which is *khāliṣeh*, a due of ½ r. (approx. ¾*d.*) per head is taken or the right to use the pasture is let for a lump sum. The pastures in Kūhi Surkh were formerly also *khāliṣeh*. Pasture tax at the rate of 1 r. per head used to be levied for their use. In the late Qājār period these pastures were usurped by landowners, who are said to levy a higher rate at the present day. When flocks graze on stubble fields usually some charge is made for this by the landowner.

Pasture dues, or *ḥaqq ul-marta'*, are not normally levied in the provinces of Kirmān. In some cases if the flocks of an outsider graze in the village pastures a pasture due is taken; this is the case in Shahdād. On the whole, however, the landowner welcomes the presence of flocks on his land because of the manure which they afford.

In Fārs much of the pasture land is owned by the tribes or they have a traditional right to certain areas,[1] but as stated above, this does not affect the pastures immediately round the villages which belong to the owner or owners of the village in question. In Qarā Bulāgh the pastures are registered in the name of the landowner but are enjoyed in common by the villagers. In Iṣṭahbānāt and Nayrīz no pasture dues are taken.

In Khūzistān the pastures round the villages are used by the peasants. The practice over pasture dues varies. In Rām Hurmuz, where the pastures are owned by the landowners, a pasture due, *ḥaqq ul-marta'*, at the rate of three sheep or goats per 100 is levied; only those animals whose wool has been clipped are counted. The custom of levying a pasture due in this area is said to survive from the days when it was owned by the Bakhtīārī *khāns*. In the Khalafābād area no pasture dues are taken; formerly five head per 100 head of sheep and goats were taken. In the *daymī* villages (i.e. where dry farming is practised) in 'Aqīlī the people for the most part move with their flocks to summer quarters, leaving only a few persons behind in the villages.

To sum up, there are few districts in Persia where the peasant does not keep flocks, and in some areas their produce forms an important part of his livelihood. This is reflected in the fact that in many areas, especially in west Persia and Āẕarbāyjān, among the dues levied by the landlord on the peasant is usually a certain amount of clarified butter or *roughan*.[2] Whether this represents a former pasture due or an old servitude, it clearly presupposes the possession of flocks by the peasant, and assumes that his mode of life is both pastoral and agricultural. In ancient times the emphasis was on the first and even in modern times the peasant, although his forbears long since adopted a settled life, is still in some areas partly a keeper of flocks. As in the case of other aspects of land tenure there are considerable local variations concerning the ownership of pastures and grazing rights. These, like crop-sharing arrangements, are largely based on custom. A greater or less degree of liberality is shown by the landlords with regard to the use of pastures by the peasants in the different areas; it does not,

[1] See Ch. XV. [2] See Ch. XVIII.

however, always follow that in an area where the demands made upon the peasant by the landlord in other fields are relatively heavy, pasture dues are also heavy. For example, in Kirmān, where the relations between landlord and peasant are not unduly favourable to the latter, no pasture dues are levied. In the Saqqiz area, on the other hand, pasture dues are levied, and it is a noteworthy fact that in spite of relatively favourable climatic conditions in that area the peasants do not usually own more than a few animals apiece. Broadly speaking, it would seem that the levying of pasture dues is a deterrent to the keeping of flocks by the peasants, and that though the keeping of flocks is an important element in the peasant economy it is the exception rather than the rule for the individual peasant to own more than a few head apiece. One other point worthy of note is that a certain degree of co-operation is to be observed among the peasants in the arrangements made for the pasturing of their animals. This, like other measures of self-help which are still found in the village communities, would seem to be a survival of the days when the village community was a self-contained, self-governed, and relatively stable unit.

CHAPTER XXI

THE PROBLEMS OF THE PEASANT: AGRICULTURAL METHODS

THE problems which affect the crop-sharing peasant and the peasant proprietor alike arise from natural conditions and technical deficiencies. Poverty of the soil, soil erosion, pests, occasional floods and deficient rainfall can, to some extent, be mitigated by improved techniques. But large-scale measures to counteract soil erosion, control pests, and improve irrigation require a capital expenditure well beyond the means of the peasant. His technical problems concern agricultural methods, financial questions such as the provision of credit, commercial questions such as marketing methods, communications, the fixing of rents, and security of tenure. All these questions, apart from the last two, are of vital concern both to the peasant proprietor and to the crop-sharing peasant.

Terracing in mountain valleys is carried out with considerable skill and care in many places. This is noticeable particularly in many of the peasant-proprietor villages in the Kūhi Kargis area. Apart from this, however, little attention is given to the problem of soil erosion, which is widespread in many areas on the Persian plateau. It is at the foot of the mountains rather than in the mountain valleys that the problem is the more urgent. The soil tends to break away: in the hot summer it bakes hard and cracks and is then eroded by the wind; moreover the relatively steep slopes and in many areas the rapid rate of water-flow when rain comes tend to form gullies. Contour ploughing is seldom carried out efficiently, partly owing to the relatively small size of holdings. There are few places in Persia where erosion is not abundantly evident: it is particularly striking in the area round Zanjān. On the borders of the central desert, especially in the south-east and east, in the neighbourhood of Yazd, Kirmān, Qā'ināt, and Sīstān the encroachment of the desert on the sown can be clearly seen; in these areas blown sand is a nuisance to cultivation.

Agricultural methods are primitive in the extreme. Ploughing in most areas is carried out by a wooden nail plough, drawn by an ox; the plough-share merely scratches the soil and does not invert the furrow slice.[1] In the dry-farming belt round Ahvāz and Bandi Qīr in Khūzistān the Arabs use a donkey, mule, horse, or mare for ploughing. In Bandi Qīr donkeys are most commonly used. The

[1] For a brief discussion of the merits or otherwise of this method of shallow ploughing see Keen, *Agricultural Development of the Middle East*, p. 51.

speed at which a mare or mule ploughs is considerably greater than that of an ox or donkey. In certain parts of Fārs mules are used as draught animals, but mainly on unirrigated land. Buffaloes are also used in various areas including the northern littoral of the Persian Gulf, Mīāndoāb in Āẕarbāyjān, and Mahābād in Kurdistān. In 1945 the average price of a buffalo in Mahābād was 5,000–10,000 rs. (approx. £29. 8*s*. 3*d*.–£58. 15*s*.). In some areas in Balūchistān the camel is used as a draught animal. In certain areas, especially in the *garmsīr* of Fārs, the process of ploughing is considerably complicated by the growth, often in profusion, of the *kunār* bush, the roots of which have to be removed.

In the Mārbīn district of Iṣfahān and Yazd and in some villages in the neighbourhood of the Kūhi Kargis, such as Maymeh, Tarq, and Bīdhand, a plough is not used, the land being dug by spade. The depth dug and the turnover of the soil is considerably greater than when a plough is used but the labour involved is heavy. It is customary for several men to dig together. A long-handled spade is used; above the blade is a wooden cross-piece upon which the man who wields it places his foot, and drives the spade into the earth with a jump or lunge forward, three or more men usually working together in unison side by side. The reason for the use of the spade rather than the plough is probably threefold. In the first place the land is better dug. Secondly, in some of the areas mentioned above fodder for draught animals is not easily obtainable. Thirdly, the size of the holdings has something to do with the practice, the size of the holdings in Mārbīn, for example, being smaller than those in some of the neighbouring districts of Iṣfahān. This is not, however, a complete explanation, because in many areas where the holdings are as small or smaller than in Mārbīn the spade is not used. In Burkhw̤ār near Iṣfahān the land is first dug by spade and then ploughed by a plough drawn, usually, by two oxen.

Seed is sown broadcast, the amount sown relative to the area of land being greater in the case of irrigated land than of unirrigated land. In many areas the land is measured by the amount of seed it will take, e.g. its area is reckoned as capable of taking so many *manni tabrīz* of seed.

A few landowners have tractors, but they are the exception rather than the rule. In Khīābān, near Mashhad, five tractors are in use in the property which is rented from the shrine of the Imām Riẕā by the Shirkati Kishāvarzīyi Riẕā. The expenses of running these are said to be high, amounting to some 400 rs. (approx. £2. 7*s*.) for the sowing of 1 ha. (2.47 acres). The results, however, are said to be better than when the land is ploughed by an ox-drawn plough. These tractors belong to the company and are hired out to the peasants, who pay the costs of cultivation.

Few ancillary implements in addition to the plough are used. A primitive kind of harrow (known as *māleh*) is employed in some districts. Hoes are unknown in most districts. Weeding, if done at all, is done by hand. Where it is necessary to divide the land into deep ridges and furrows, as for example in melon cultivation, after the land has been ploughed or dug an implement known as a *katar* is pulled backwards alternately by two men facing each other so that the earth is heaped up into a ridge.

Reaping, threshing, and winnowing are done by hand. For the first-named operation a scythe, or in some cases a sickle, is used. The grain is then collected in heaps[1] and threshed by a wooden threshing machine (known as *chūn*), to the under-carriage of which circular knives are attached. Drawn by an ox, donkey, or mule the *chūn* is driven round and round the heap, the unthreshed grain being strewn in the path of the threshing machine which gradually cuts it up into small pieces. In certain areas, however, even more primitive methods are adopted. In Qarājeh Dāgh, for example, the threshing machine[2] has pieces of stone attached to the bottom instead of knives. In other areas, notably in certain parts of Kurdistān and Sīstān, the harvested grain is trodden out by some five or more oxen tied together. Winnowing is done by tossing the grain in the wind with a wooden-pronged fork (usually known as *chahār shākh*), after which the heaps of grain having been thus separated from the straw are passed through a coarse sieve, by which means the heads from which the grain has been removed are separated from the grain. The whole process employs a considerable number of hands and takes considerable time.[3]

Rice cultivation is carried on in two ways. In a few areas, as in parts of Khūzistān, it is sown broadcast, but in the important rice-growing area of Māzandarān and also in Linjān and Alinjān, near Iṣfahān, the rice is first sown out and later transplanted. The yields obtained by this method of cultivation are considerably higher than when the rice is sown broadcast. The process of transplantation is a laborious one as also is the preparation of the ground for planting; it is carried on of necessity in waterlogged ground. In Māzandarān labour in the rice-fields is largely performed by women. This is not, however, the case in the rice-growing areas of Kurdistān. In the seasons when the rice is transplanted and

[1] The size of the heaps varies. Usually the peasant collects his grain harvest into one heap, unless he holds strips in different areas of the village land, in which case he will construct a heap in each area. The word *kharman*, which means harvest in general, is also applied in particular to a heap comprising the grain harvest for a particular piece of land.

[2] Known locally as *val*.

[3] In some areas landless labourers follow the harvest round on the chance of casual employment.

reaped the labourers can be seen at work in the fields from morning till evening up to their ankles or knees in mud and water, and, in the case of women, often accompanied by their children.

Manure is not widely used.[1] In some areas, such as Qarājeh Dāgh, no manure at all is used. Animal dung is for the most part burnt as fuel. Sheep and goats, however, are often allowed to graze on stubble partly with a view to fertilizing the land by their droppings. Household sewage is mixed with earth and used as manure; in the areas round the towns the land is better manured than in the outlying districts, since household sewage is more easily obtainable. Where the land is manured the tendency is to raise crops on it every year; in the outlying districts land is left fallow to renew its fertility. In the Iṣfahān district pigeon manure, collected in pigeon towers situated in the neighbourhood of the town, is used in the cultivation of melons and pear trees. In Kirmān some landowners have recently started to use a preparation made of the waste product of fish from the canning factory in Bandar ʿAbbās to manure land growing pistachio trees. Near many of the towns and the villages of Persia there are ruined buildings and old walls—relics of earlier phases of the development of the town—and the earth of these old ruins is used in lieu of manure.[2]

Practices in connexion with fallow and crop rotation vary widely, except for land in the immediate neighbourhood of a town or village, which is cultivated annually. In Farāhān (in Arāk) crop rotation is either threefold or twofold (*seh bikār* or *do bikār*). In the first case one-third of the land is sown with grain, one-third with clover (*shabdar*) or spring wheat, and one-third is ploughed in preparation for sowing. In the second case half the land is sown with grain and half with *ṣayfī* crops or clover. This last type of rotation tends to be found in those districts which have a less plentiful water-supply and a poorer peasantry. Thus in the district of Kazzāz, in the relatively prosperous villages of Hafteh and Ḥiṣār, a threefold rotation is practised, whereas in Aṃbarteh, which has a less plentiful water supply and the peasants of which are relatively poor, a twofold rotation is practised. Land in Farāhān is left fallow every fourth, fifth, or sixth year.

In Asadābād, near Hamadān, the land is left fallow in alternative years. Most of the land in Qarājeh Dāgh is, similarly, cultivated in alternate years.

In Gaz in Burkhẉār there is a four-yearly crop rotation; the land watered by each *qanāt* is allotted to four areas known locally

[1] In some of the dry-farming areas this may be partly because there is not sufficient rain to rot the manure.

[2] Fraser, writing in 1833, noted the breaking down and spreading of the earth of old walls on cultivated land (*Winter's Journey*, ii. 65).

as *dasht*, one of which lies fallow each year. The crop rotation is as follows: in the first year wheat or barley is sown in the autumn; in the second year twenty to eighty days after the Persian New Year[1] *ṣayfī* crops are sown; in the third year the land lies fallow, and in the fourth year it is prepared by digging and ploughing for sowing in the following year. Gilishābād, one of the hamlets of Gaz, is, however, an exception to the general rule, having only three *dasht*. In the districts in the neighbourhood of Iṣfahān much of the land is left fallow in alternate years.

Much of the land in the mountain valleys on the borders of the Kūhi Kargis is cultivated every year. Thus in Tarq (on the Mūrchehkhwart–Kāshān road) autumn barley is sown after the wheat harvest has been gathered. When the barley is harvested, clover is sown and after the clover is cut, melons are planted. In Abīāneh in the same area, clover is sown after the wheat or barley have been harvested and when this is cut wheat is sown again in the autumn.

In Fārs practices concerning rotation vary with local conditions, depending upon the amount of land and water available. The *garmsīr* of the Qashqā'ī is mainly sown every year. In Fīrūzābād in the *sardsīr* irrigated land is sown in alternate years. In Jahrum in most villages the irrigated land lies fallow once in three years, the irrigated land of each village being divided into three *dasht*. Unirrigated land in the neighbourhood of Jahrum is sown every year, but a crop is raised on an average of one year in every three only owing to lack of rainfall. In Nayrīz the land is, for the most part, cultivated in alternate years.

Similar variations are also found in Khūzistān. *Daym* land is more often left fallow than irrigated land. In the neighbourhood of Dizfūl, in irrigated land a threefold rotation is mainly practised, the land being divided into three lots. One-third is sown with rice, which is reaped in the month of Ābān (October–November). The land, being waterlogged, cannot then be immediately re-sown. The other two portions are sown with wheat, barley, or beans. When the wheat or barley has been reaped, one-third of the total land is again sown with rice. In Bandi Qīr, near Ahvāz, irrigated land is cultivated every year, and unirrigated land every other year. This is also the case in ʿArab ʿAbbās (near Kūt ʿAbdullāh). In ʿAqīlī rice land is separate from the grain-growing land. The latter, where irrigated, is divided into two portions and sown every year, alternately with wheat or barley and cotton.

The most common method of irrigation is by inundation. In vineyards, melon land, and market gardens, the water is let into the land by irrigation trenches.

[1] 20, 21, or 22 March.

The yield on wheat is reckoned not at so much per acre or per area sown, but at so many *tukhm*, i.e. at a return of so many times the amount of grain sown. The yield in different areas varies considerably, but with few exceptions it is low. Better methods of cultivation and improved seed might be expected to give higher yields, but it is alleged by some who have tried imported seed that although the yield in the first year or two is increased it falls thereafter to the rate of indigenous seed. Exact information on the yield in the various areas is not available. In its absence the figures in the table below are given as a rough estimate, based on local information. Special circumstances may give rise to heavier crops while pests and deficient rainfall frequently result in partial or total crop failures. It will be noticed that in most areas the yield on *daym* land is higher than on *ābī*; this is possibly due partly to the fact that *daym* land is left fallow more often than *ābī* land. It must be remembered, however, that the percentage of total or partial failure of *daym* crops is considerably higher than of *ābī* crops.

Area	*Yield*	
	Ābī	*Daym*
Arāk		
Farāhān	10–15	..
Kazzāz	6–7	..
Sari Band	6–7	..
Asadābād	4–5	10
Āẕarbāyjān	10–15 (?)	5–10
Qarājeh Dāgh	..	5–15
Balūchistān	..	..
Bampūr	5–17*	..
Khāsh	5	..
Bīrjand	5–15	..
Central Persia	5–15	..
Burkhwār	..	..
Amīrābād	20	..
Ardistān	10–15	..
Jougand	5	..
Kūhi Kargis	..	..
Abīāneh	15–20	..
Joushaqān	6–20	..
So	10	..
Tarq	10	..
Sāveh	..	..
Kharaqān	5–7	..
Maʻmūnīyeh	10	..
Tehrān	6–10†	..
Yazd	..	..
Pushti Kūh	5–25	

* According to one informant, considerably higher yields are obtained in a good year.

† In a good year in districts such as Varāmīn it may be 20.

Area	Yield	
	Ābī	*Daym*
Fārs	..	..
Dārāb	10–15	..
Dobarān	up to 50	..
Fasā	up to 50	up to 25
Fidiskān	up to 50	..
Fīrūzābād	10–25	..
Iṣṭahbānāt	25–30	10–12
Jahrum	12	5–8‡
Kāzirūn	25–30§	..
Nayrīz	12‖	..
Shīrāz	10	..
Hamadān	10	3–10
Khurāsān	..	..
Kāshmar	5–15	..
Khīābān	15	up to 25¶
Shādkan	5–18**	..
Turbati Ḥaydarī	5–20	..
Ṭuruq	7–8	..
Khūzistān	..	..
Ahvāz	..	up to 20
Bandi Qīr	6–8	10
Bāsht	..	10–20
Bihbahān	5–10	5–10
Dizfūl	5–6	12
Khalafābād	..	12–15
Qalʿeh Saḥar	..	up to 25
Shuʿaybīyeh	..	10–20
Kirmān	4–10	..
Jīruft	up to 50††	..
Kurdistān	..	..
Darband	20‡‡	..
Dīvān Darreh	4–6	4–6
Sanandaj	5–6	8

‡ Up to 15 in an exceptionally good year. Crops are successfully raised on *daym* land approximately one year in three only.

§ The actual amount by the time the harvest is transported to the village is considerably less owing to losses to sparrows. Further, since reaping is a long and laborious process, a proportion of the grain falls out of the heads if the grain gets over-ripe, as may happen if there is any delay in harvesting.

‖ 14–15 in a good year, 6 in a bad year, but 12 in an average year.

¶ In a good year.

** Usually about 8.

†† Usually about 7.

‡‡ In an exceptionally good year.

The transport of the crop from the field to the barn is in almost all areas by donkey or some other pack animal. The straw is placed in nets and the grain in sacks and loaded on to pack animals. The transport of agricultural produce from the villages to the towns is also mainly by pack animal. This method is slow and wasteful. The amount of produce which can be transported by pack animal is relatively small. Moreover, if the peasant himself is to transport it—and in the absence of co-operative arrangements for marketing he is usually obliged so to do—he has to absent himself from his village, often for relatively long periods of time. Again, his costs are so greatly increased by the high cost of transport if he lives in a remote area that he is unable to compete with growers who live closer to the markets.

A small two-wheeled bullock cart is used in certain parts of western Āẕarbāyjān in the neighbourhood of Riẓā'īyeh and in some of the Armenian villages of Firaydan.

Camel transport and lorry transport are also used. But these means are seldom used by the peasant for the transport of his surplus to the markets; their use is rather confined to the large landed proprietor or the merchant, who is concerned with the transport and sale of relatively large quantities of agricultural produce.

The life of the peasant is largely governed by the agricultural cycle. The seasons follow each other with regularity and the periods during which the different crops are sown are clearly defined, though of course subject to dislocation by the failure or undue lateness of rain. Adequate rainfall between November and January and from the second half of February to April is essential to a good crop. Failure of the rains may mean starvation. The writer remembers travelling through a remote part of Fārs in the spring of 1949 and how the first question the peasants and tribesmen put as they met anyone coming up from the *garmsīr* was 'Have the rains come?' and the joy which the local population showed when the rains began.

On the whole the Persian peasant makes good use of the opportunities he has. With courage and perseverance he turns to account the smallest store of water in the most remote and inhospitable districts. In the sowing season and at harvest time he works long hours. Winter, on the other hand, is a slack time when he often has little to occupy himself with. In south Persia wheat and barley are sown between the first week in November and the first week in January. Barley is reaped about 15 to 20 April and wheat about the end of April to the beginning of May. In the uplands of the province of Fārs the harvest begins roughly one month later, and on the plateau generally some two and a half months later.

The following is the agricultural cycle in a typical area in the uplands of central Persia. Wheat is sown between 29 October and 22 November. Five *manni tabrīz*, i.e. some 32 lb. 12 oz., are sown to every 400 sq. metres (478 sq. yds.).[1] It is irrigated four times. Spring wheat is sown from 20 February to 29 April. Spring barley is sown from 20 February onwards, barley of the kind known as *jou-i*

[1] Approx. 5½ bushels per acre.

tursh is sown from 29 July to 11 August, and autumn barley from 29 October to 22 November. Barley is irrigated three times. Peas are sown from 20 February to 29 April, and water melons, cucumbers, and melons from 24 to 29 May. These crops receive water as it becomes available. Barley is harvested at the end of June, wheat in the beginning of September, and potatoes from the end of September onwards. Over a normal cycle of five years one harvest is bad if not a complete failure, three indifferent, and one good. It is not infrequent, however, for two bad years or two good years to occur successively.

In Khurāsān wheat and barley are sown in the autumn and reaped in Khurdād (May–June). Grain land receives water once before sowing, and three to five times in spring. Cotton is sown in Urdī Bīhisht (April–May) and reaped in autumn. Cotton land receives water once before sowing and seven times during the period of vegetation. Opium is sown in the autumn and reaped in Khurdād (May–June), and receives water once or twice. Lucerne is irrigated ten to twelve times. Rape receives water twice: once at the end of spring and once at the beginning of summer. Vines are irrigated three times in winter and three times in summer.

The amount of land which a peasant can cultivate is limited by the primitive nature of the agricultural methods employed. Other factors such as the nature of the soil, the irrigation system, the relative plenty of the water-supply, and the nature of the draught animal used also affect the amount of land held by peasants. As stated in the introduction, the village land is divided into lots, the basis of which is either a share of the village water or the plough-land, i.e. a lot which can be cultivated by one yoke of oxen. The size of the lots into which a village is divided varies considerably in different parts of the country. In Khūzistān, for example, such a lot represents an amount of land which takes 8 *mann* (7 cwt., 97 lb.)[1] of wheat and 6 *mann* (5 cwt., 100 lb.) of barley if a donkey is used, 12 *mann* (11 cwt., 90 lb.) of wheat and 8 *mann* of barley if a mule is used, and some 15 *mann* (14 cwt., 85 lb.) of wheat and barley each if a mare is used. In the Iṣfahān area where cultivation is mainly by spade, as in Mārbīn, the average size of holding is some 3 *jarīb* (approx. 4,485 sq. yds.); in the other districts where cultivation is by ox, the holdings range up to 30 *jarīb* (approx. 9 acres 1,290 sq. yds.).

The lot is usually run as a family concern by the peasant and his sons or other members of his family. One man alone cannot run one plough-land, and extra labour is essential. When it is provided by outsiders, the extra hands are usually paid in kind by a share of the crop. Such labourers often form part of the household

[1] One *manni ahvāz* = 50 kg. (approx. 110 lbs.)

of the holder of the plough-land and are clothed and fed by the latter. At harvest time also if the peasant's family cannot provide the extra hands, additional labour is employed and paid in cash or kind on a daily basis.

The amount sown by one yoke of oxen ranges from 1–6 *kharvār* (approx. 5 cwt., 95 lb.–35 cwt., 8 lb.). The yield on this varies greatly from district to district.[1] Seldom, however, is the grain harvested by one yoke of oxen sufficient, after the deduction of the landowner's share and the other dues which are levied on it, to provide for the needs of the peasant and his family. In the majority of cases, unless the peasant is able to supplement his income by garden produce, the produce of flocks, or some cottage industry such as cloth-weaving or carpet-weaving, he is barely able to subsist.

In Arāk a plough-land is usually run as a family concern; the amount of grain (wheat and barley) harvested averages 10 *kharvār* (approx. 58 cwt. 50 lb.), of which the peasant keeps on irrigated land two-thirds, less various small deductions. This, unless supplemented in various other ways, as for example by garden produce, the produce of flocks or weaving, is not enough to support the holder and his family. The capital required by the holder of a plough-land in 1945 was some 30,000 rs. (approx. £176. 9*s*.). Among the items making up this total were the following:

A pair of oxen (5,000–20,000 rs., approx. £29. 8*s*. 3*d*.–£117. 13*s*.).
A minimum of 1 donkey (3,000–10,000 rs., approx. £17. 12*s*. 11*d*.–£58. 15*s*.).
2–3 spades.
1 threshing machine.
2 ploughs.
1 ox-shaft.
1 ox-yoke.
1 harrow.

The amount sown by one yoke of oxen in certain of the grain-growing areas is considerably more than in Arāk, and the amount harvested per plough-land is thus greater than the figure given above for Arāk. In Asadābād, for example, one yoke of oxen sows, according to land and circumstances, some 2½–6½ *kharvār* (approx. 14 cwt., 69 lb.–37 cwt., 111 lb.) of grain. One plough-land requires at least two peasants. In Dastjird and Sulaymānābād near Hamadān up to 3½ *kharvār* (approx. 20 cwt., 51 lb.) are sown per plough-land.

The amount sown in Kirmānshāh per plough-land is of a similar order, averaging 3–5 *kharvār* (approx. 17 cwt., 60 lb.–29 cwt., 25 lb.) of grain. There are, however, yokes of greater power than the

[1] See above, pp. 364–5.

average, which sow as much as 10 *kharvār*.[1] In the Pushti Kūh district of Kangāvar the harvest of a plough-land is normally some 28 *kharvār* (approx. 163 cwt., 74 lb.).

In Ma'mūnīyeh in Zarand in the district of Sāveh one yoke of oxen sows on an average 4–5 *kharvār* (23 cwt., 42 lb.–29 cwt., 25 lb.).

The area of a plough-land varies considerably in Āẕarbāyjān. The holder of the plough-land is known as a *hampā*: two other men are normally attached to it, one known as the *kishāvar* and the other as the *nirseh*. In Varzaqān and the neighbourhood each plough-land has four men attached to it and some 1–5 *kharvār* (5 cwt., 95 lb.–29 cwt., 25 lb.), of which two-thirds is normally wheat and one-third barley, are sown in it. In Āẕarshahr about 1 *kharvār* (5 cwt., 95 lb.) only is sown per plough-land.

In Burkhwār, where cultivation is largely by spade, a peasant and his family do not normally cultivate more than 3,000 sq. metres (3,588 sq. yds.), or 15 *manni bazr afkan*.[2] At Qahdrījān near Iṣfahān one yoke of oxen sows 1–2 *kharvār* (approx. 5 cwt., 95 lb.–11 cwt., 77 lb.) or 15 *jarīb* (approx. 4 acres, 3,056 sq. yds.).[3]

In Burūjird 5–6 *kharvār* (approx. 29 cwt., 25 lb.–35 cwt., 8 lb.) are sown per plough-land, to each of which two men are attached.

There are considerable variations in the size of the plough-land and the amount sown by one yoke of oxen in Fārs. In Fīrūzābād one yoke sows some 600–700 *manni fīrūzābādī* (approx. 41 cwt., 38 lb.–48 cwt., 25 lb.) and ploughs 300 *mann* of land[4] twice over for fallow. In Fidiskān 1 yoke sows 1½ *kharvār* (approx. 8 cwt., 86 lb.), in Dārāb 1½–2 *kharvār* (approx. 8 cwt., 86 lb.–11 cwt., 77 lb.), in Qarā Bulāgh 75 *mann* with *shatvī* crops and 30–35 *mann*[5] with *ṣayfī* crops if the land is irrigated by well (*chahāb*) and 25 *mann* sown with *shatvī* crops and 10–12[6] *mann* sown with *ṣayfī* crops if the land is irrigated by *qanāt*, in Nayrīz 150 *manni nayrīz*[7] and in Iṣṭahbānāt 250 *manni shīrāz*[8] of wheat and barley. The number of men attached to a plough-land varies. In Jahrum, Dārāb, and Qarā Bulāgh there are usually two men per plough-land, extra help being obtained at harvest time. In the Mamasanī there are two men attached to a plough-land, the owner of the oxen (the

[1] These are known locally as *jufti nādirī*.
[2] i.e. land taking 98 lb. of seed (Anṣārī, p. 154).
[3] 1 *jarībi iṣfahān* = 1,250 sq. metres (1,495 sq. yds.).
[4] i.e. land taking approx. 20 cwt., 75 lb. of seed. These figures, given by a local informant, are probably somewhat exaggerated.
[5] Land taking approx. 4 cwt., 43 lb. and 1 cwt., 84 lb.–2 cwt., 5 lb. of seed respectively.
[6] Land taking approx. 1 cwt., 42 lb. and 65–78½ lb. of seed respectively.
[7] i.e. land taking approx. 10 cwt., 9 lb. (1 *manni nayrīz* = 736 *miṣqāl* = approx. 7½ lb.).
[8] i.e. land taking approx. 16 cwt., 49 lb. (1 *manni shīrāz* = 720 *miṣqāl* = approx. 7 lb. 6 oz.).

gāvband) and a peasant known as the *bāzyār*. In some areas the latter receives one-quarter of what remains after the landowner's share of one-fifth on *daym* crops, one-fourth on *ābī*, and one-half on *ṣayfī* has been deducted.

In Jahrum the division between the men attached to the plough-land is as follows: if they are two and each owns one of the oxen the share is equally divided between them. If, on the other hand, one man owns both oxen and is helped by two men, the share of the owner of the oxen, which is known as *gāv bahreh*, is half, and the remaining half is divided between the other two men. In *daym* land the owner of the oxen generally pays the peasant he employs in one of two ways:

1. if it does not rain and the crop fails, he provides half the seed and the keep of the ox, or
2. if the crop ripens and is reaped the peasant employed by him reaps the crop and keeps one-fifth of it.

This system is known as *yak kār*.

In Qarā Bulāgh in land watered by well the peasant pays the reaper and the thresher, who get 5 per cent and 2 per cent respectively of the crop. The man who transports the harvest to the village[1] gets 1½ per cent. On *ṣayfī* crops a similar proportion is paid to each of the labourers[2] employed in harvesting the millet and cotton crop respectively.

In Khīr there are five men per plough-land or *band gāv*, which takes two yoke of oxen; one of these men, the *gāvband*, usually owns the oxen. He receives half what is left of the harvest after the landlord's share and certain dues have been deducted; the remainder is divided among the four peasants, who thus get roughly one twenty-fourth of the total crop each on *ṣayfī* crops and one thirty-secondth each on *shatvī* crops. In addition they receive a payment or due known as *tahi qubbeh*, which amounts to 25 *mann* per 1,000 *mann*, i.e. 2½ per cent of the harvest. This is divided among the four peasants, the *gāvband* receiving no share of this. This sum, i.e. the *tahi qubbeh*, is taken from the total harvest before it is divided between the landowner and the *gāvband*. A small amount is also taken from the total harvest and given to the four peasants, but not to the *gāvband*, under the three headings of *malikīyi gāvband* (i.e. for shoes),[3] *diroukunī* (i.e. for reaping), and *kharmankūbī* (i.e. for threshing).

In Turbati Ḥaydarī some 450 kg. (8 cwt., 96 lb.) of grain are sown per plough-land. It is run by two men who work with the

[1] Known locally as the *kashak*.
[2] i.e. the *zurratshikan* and the *paṃbehchīn*.
[3] *malikī* is the name of a type of *gīveh*, worn especially in Fārs.

oxen; they are assisted by one labourer and require two asses. In Ṭuruq near Mashhad one yoke of oxen sows 20 *mann* (approx. 1 cwt., 19 lb.) per day or some 3 *kharvār* (approx. 17 cwt., 60 lb.) during the sowing season, two-thirds in wheat and one-third in barley, if water is available. The actual amount sown is in fact usually less because of insufficient water. In Khīābān in the same area one yoke of oxen sows 1–1½ *kharvār* (approx. 5 cwt., 95 lb.–8 cwt., 86 lb.) wheat and 75 *manni tabrīz* (approx. 4 cwt., 43 lb.) barley, 1 ha. (2·47 acres) beet, 1 *manni tabrīz* (approx. 6 lb., 9 oz.) opium, and 2 ha. (4·94 acres) pulses, lucerne, etc. In Ābkūh, also near Mashhad, some 10 *kharvār* (approx. 58 cwt., 50 lb.) is sown by a plough-team of three yoke of oxen.

The plough-land in Khūzistān is known as a *khīsh* and usually has attached to it an ox and plough worked by two men. Extra help for reaping and threshing is required. If this cannot be provided by the peasant's own family casual labour is employed. In ʿAqīlī there are, however, four men, known as *sumkār*, attached to each *khīsh*, four oxen, and two labourers.[1] In Khalafābād a *khīsh* corresponds to the ordinary plough-land and has two oxen and one to three men attached to it. In Bāsht there are normally two labourers[2] attached to each plough-land in addition to the holder. The land in this area is full of thorn and fewer hands are unable to do the work. Further, wild pig are troublesome and one man has to remain on guard over the crops at night when they begin to ripen. The size of the plough-land in Khūzistān varies: in Dizfūl it is the amount of land which takes 3–3½ *kharvār* (approx. 17 cwt., 60 lb.–20 cwt., 51 lb.) seed of *ābī* land and 2,000 kg. (approx. 39 cwt., 4 lb.) of *daym* land. In the latter case mules are used and not oxen, which explains the greater extent of land which is sown. In Shūshtar 2–3 *kharvār* (approx. 11 cwt., 77 lb.–17 cwt., 60 lb.) are sown per plough-land. In the Ahvāz area it would appear that rather less is sown. In Rām Hurmuz one yoke of oxen sows 9 *manni ahvāz* (approx. 8 cwt., 96 lb.) in *daym* land and 10–12 *manni ahvāz* (approx. 9 cwt., 94 lb.–11 cwt., 90 lb.) in *ābī* land; in Khalafābād 3 *manni jarrāḥīyeh* (approx. 7 cwt., 42 lb.) wheat and 1½ *manni jarrāḥīyeh* (approx. 3 cwt., 77 lb.) barley; in Bihbahān some 300–700 kg. (5 cwt., 101 lb.–13 cwt., 87 lb.); and in Shūsht near Bāsht some 60 *manni shūsht* (approx. 8 cwt., 30 lb.). The amount of rice sown depends largely on the amount of water available. In Dizfūl it is 75–225 kg. (approx. 1 cwt., 53 lb.–4 cwt., 47 lb.) per plough-land.

The estimated initial cost of cultivating one plough-land in Bandi Qīr near Ahvāz in 1947 is given overleaf.

1 Known locally as *barzigar*.
2 Known locally as *bāzyār*.

	Rs.	£ s. d.	Rs.	£ s. d.
Two donkeys	..	..	6,000	(35 3 0)
Sowing:				
8 *manni ahvāz** wheat at 500 rs.	4,000	(23 10 7)		
6 *manni ahvāz*† barley at 200 rs.	1,200	(7 1 0)		
Plough	300	(1 15 3)		
			5,500	(32 6 10)
Harvesting:				
4 sickles	120	(14 1)		
Nets and rope	200	(1 3 6)		
Water skin	120	(14 1)		
Hire of 2 extra donkeys (30 days each at 10 rs. per day) .	600	(3 10 7)		
Hire of 2 extra labourers (each 12 *manni ahvāz*‡ wheat at 300 rs. and 8 *manni ahvāz*§ barley at 150 rs. . . .	9,600	(56 9 4)		
Two pairs *gīvehs* for the 2 extra labourers	100	(11 9)		
			10,740	(63 3 4)
Threshing and bagging:				
Hire of additional donkeys .	200	(1 3 6)		
Threshing fork	100	(11 9)		
Two mule panniers . . .	600	(3 10 7)		
Rope	50	(5 10)		
Ten bags	200	(1 3 6)		
			1,150	(6 15 2)
TOTAL			Rs. 23,390	(£137 8 4)

* Approx. 7 cwt., 98 lb.
† Approx. 5 cwt., 101 lb.
‡ Approx. 11 cwt., 90 lb.
§ Approx. 7 cwt., 98 lb.

In the *khāliṣeh* of Bampūr in Balūchistān three men are normally attached to a plough-land. The following is an estimate of their income. The peasant provides the seed and draught animals. The crown or the lessee provides 100 *manni tabrīz* (approx. 5 cwt., 95 lb.) of seed per plough-land, which is recovered at harvest time. Taking the average yield as fivefold the produce of one plough-land is 500 *manni tabrīz* (approx. 29 cwt., 25 lb.). The crown or the lessee's share of this is 200 *manni tabrīz* (approx. 11 cwt., 77 lb.) and is deducted from the total harvest. One hundred *manni tabrīz* is then deducted for seed, 20 *manni tabrīz* (approx. 1 cwt., 19 lb.) for the village blacksmith and carpenter, and 5 *manni tabrīz* (approx. 33 lb.) for the *qāẓī* and *pākār*, leaving 175 *manni tabrīz* (approx. 10 cwt., 26 lb.). Of this, one-fifth, i.e. some 35 *manni tabrīz* (approx. 2 cwt., 5 lb.), is set aside as *ḥaqqi gāv*, i.e. the 'share of the ox', which goes to the owner of the ox, and 40 *manni tabrīz* (approx. 2 cwt., 38 lb.) for the man who looks after the ox. This leaves some 100 *manni tabrīz* which is divided between the owner of the ox[1] and the two peasants[2] working with him. It is clear from this that the share of the peasants is extremely small; even supposing the average yield was in the neighbourhood of twenty and not five, the

[1] i.e. the *sar zaʿīm*.
[2] i.e. the *zaʿīm* and the *dihqān*.

amount to be divided between the *sar za'īm* and the two peasants working with him would only be some 10 *kharvār* (approx. 58 cwt., 50 lb.). The duties of the *sar za'īm* are to provide the necessary implements for tilling the land and reaping, i.e. spades, a plough, a mattock and pick, and two sickles. Further, if the two peasants require an advance he provides this. When wheat and millet are sown he gives them 12–15 *manni tabrīz* (approx. 78½ lb.–98 lb.) of wheat and millet and at the time when dams are constructed he provides whatever the labourers engaged thereon require by way of food.

In the Kirmān area one plough-land[1] has usually three persons attached to it, the owner of the oxen, a peasant whose duties include sowing,[2] and a labourer, and two asses. If, on the other hand, the owner of the oxen does not himself work, three labourers are usually employed on a contract basis. In Shahdād one plough-land is worked by two oxen, two asses, one *sar za'īm*, two labourers, and one ploughman or *gāvrān*. The first-named provides the plough, spades, and other implements. Four plough-lands are run as a unit. The combined area sown amounts to 1,000 *qaṣab āb*[3] (approx. 6 acres). One yoke sows 1–2 *kharvār* (approx. 5 cwt., 95 lb.–11 cwt., 77 lb.) wheat and 50 *mann* to 1 *kharvār* (approx. 2 cwt., 101 lb.–5 cwt., 95 lb.) barley, according to the amount of water available. In Bardsīr one plough-land has two men attached to it, one of whom is the ploughman and the other the *tukhmrīz*. In Zarand (near Kirmān) one yoke sows some 400 *manni tabrīz* (approx. 23 cwt., 42 lb.) wheat and barley. On an average, in the neighbourhood of Kirmān one yoke sows 12 *manni tabrīz* (approx. 78½ lb.) of wheat per day or 75 *qaṣab* (2,242·5 sq. yds.) land. In Kirmān the division of the peasant's share between the various individuals attached to the plough-land varies. In Fayẓābād near Rafsinjān a peasant who owns one ox and one ass takes one-quarter on *ṣayfī* and *shatvī* crops, whereas a peasant without an ox gets only one-eighth of *ṣayfī* and *shatvī* crops and 240 *manni tabrīz* (approx. 14 cwt. 3 lb.) wheat and barley.[4] In Raḥmatābād in the same district the share of the peasant, which is 30 per cent of the total less various deductions, is divided into five and shared between the persons concerned, namely, the *za'īm* or owner of the ox, two peasants, and two children; the latter do not receive a full share, part of their share being retained by the *za'īm*. The share on *shatvī* crops of such a group in a good year amounts to some 1,500–2,000 *manni tabrīz* (approx. 87 cwt., 75 lb.–116 cwt., 100 lb.) in all.

1 Usually known locally as *band gāv*.
2 Known locally as *tukhmrīz*.
3 1 *qaṣab* = 25 sq. metres or 29·9 sq. yds., 400 *qaṣab* = 1 ha. or 2·47 acres.
4 The former type of peasant is known as *mard* and the latter as *nīm mard*.

The number of men per plough-land varies in Kurdistān as does also the size of the plough-land. In perhaps the majority of cases there are two men per plough-land, and the amount sown is 2½–3 *kharvāri tabrīz* (approx. 14 cwt., 69 lb.–17 cwt., 60 lb.).[1] In the Saqqiz area there are two to four men per plough-land. Extra help is required at harvest time, and is paid at the rate of 15–20 rs. (approx. 1*s.* 9*d.*–2*s.* 4*d.*) per day with food.

In Shahriār, near Tehrān, a plough-team of four oxen and four peasants sows 8 *kharvār* (approx. 46 cwt., 84 lb.) of seed (5 wheat and 3 barley). In those areas where the landlord takes three-fifths of the crop, the peasants' share amounts to some 29 *kharvār* (approx. 170 cwt., 45 lb.). At government prices prevailing in 1945 this was worth some 18,000 rs. (approx. £105. 17*s.* 8*d.*) or 4,500 rs. (approx. £26. 9*s.* 5*d.*) per peasant and per ox together. In fact, however, the actual share of the peasant in most areas in the neighbourhood was much less and did not amount to more than some 2 *kharvār* (approx. 11 cwt., 77 lb.) wheat and 1 *kharvār* (approx. 5 cwt., 94 lb.) barley and some 5,000 rs. worth (approx. £29. 7*s.*) of pulses.

As stated in Chapter XVI, there is often interposed between the landowner and the peasant in the Tehrān area a third party in the person of the *gāvband*.[2] In Khwār and Varāmīn the land which he manages consists of four plough-lands known as *buneh*, each worked by four peasants and one ox; the grain harvest of such a unit comes to some 100 *kharvār* (approx. 584 cwt., 52 lb.) on an average. From this 2 *kharvār* (approx. 11 cwt., 77 lb.) or 50 *manni tabrīz* (approx. 2 cwt., 101 lb.) per *buneh* are deducted from the total harvest for the religious classes.[3] The payment of the *dashtbān*, amounting to 3 *kharvār* (approx. 17 cwt., 60 lb.) per *gāvband* or 25–30 *manni tabrīz* (approx. 1 cwt., 42 lb.–1 cwt., 84 lb.) per *buneh* is also deducted from the total harvest. Some 95 *kharvār* (approx. 555 cwt., 31 lb.) remain. This is divided between the landowner and the *gāvband*. The latter then deducts from his share of 47½ *kharvār* (approx. 277 cwt., 71 lb.) the seed, leaving some 37½–40 *kharvār* (approx. 219 cwt., 21 lb.–233 cwt., 90 lb.). He then deducts the due for the blacksmith, carpenter, and bathkeeper,[4] amounting to some 3 *kharvār* (approx. 17 cwt., 60 lb.). The remainder is then divided in equal shares between him, on the one hand, and the four peasants, on the other. In Souj Bulāgh, however, the *gāvband* usually gets three-fifths instead of half the crop; the reason for his

[1] It is alleged that some landowners restrict the amount which each peasant is allowed to sow to 1 *kharvār* (approx. 5 cwt., 95 lb.).

[2] The term is also used in the same way as *juft*, to mean both the yoke of oxen and the men who work it and also the land cultivated by them.

[3] Known as *kūchīn va māli khudā*. See Ch. XIX.

[4] See Ch. XIX.

receiving a higher share is that the land in this area has to be ploughed three times. The division of the three-fifths between the *gāvband* and the peasants is made on the basis of four-fifths to the former and one-fifth to the latter. The share of the *gāvband* and the division of his share between him and the peasants in the eastern parts of Ghār and Fashāpūyeh are as in Varāmīn, and in the western parts as in Souj Bulāgh. The share of the peasant in grain on the above calculation is clearly insufficient to support him and his family unless supplemented from other sources.

The inadequacy of the peasant's income is particularly apparent where a third party in the person of the *gāvband* is interposed between the peasant and the landowner. But even where this is not the case the share of the peasant is meagre. Moreover the liabilities of the peasant do not end with the payment of the landlord's share and the various dues described in Chapters XVIII and XIX. In many cases payment for extra labour required at harvest time or for special operations connected with such crops as opium is the responsibility of the peasant, or is a charge on the total harvest.[1] Casual labour at harvest time is mainly paid in kind. The amount paid is not large, but the share of the peasant is often so meagre that even the relatively small deductions made for casual labour materially reduce his income.

In some areas a fixed share is allotted to various operations. In Jahrum the reaper (*dirougar*) gets in a good year 100–120 *manni tabrīz* (approx. 5 cwt., 95 lb.–7 cwt.) per 100 *mann* of seed-land, but in a bad year some 80 *manni tabrīz* (approx. 4 cwt., 76 lb.) only. The man who threshes gets 6–8 per cent of the grain threshed. He threshes and delivers the grain to the peasant or the landowner as the case may be. In Turbati Ḥaydarī those employed in reaping carry off at the end of the day what they can carry under one arm. This, in some cases, is commuted to 1 *manni tabrīz* (approx. 6 lb., 9 oz.). In Kāshmar reapers take one-twentieth of what they reap.

In the Kirmān area male labour at harvest time gets a maximum of 1 *manni tabrīz* (approx. 6 lb., 9 oz.) per day and female labour ½ *manni tabrīz* (approx. 3 lb., 4½ lb.). In Shahdād they receive 1 *bāfeh* per day, i.e. the amount which will go in a small receptacle known by that name. A special share is sometimes allotted to the man who winnows and the man who weighs the grain respectively. In Shahdād *kayyālī*, i.e. the due for weighing the grain, is taken at the rate of 7½ *manni tabrīz* (approx. 49 lb.) per *kharman*[2] from the total harvest; in Rafsinjān the rate is ½ per cent or less according to the dirtiness or otherwise of the grain. The man who winnows the grain[3] also gets ½ per cent. Those who collect the grain from

[1] See Ch. XVII.

[2] See p. 361, n. 1 for a definition of *kharman*.

[3] i.e. the *boujār* or *būjār*.

the threshing-floor and what falls off the stalks in the fields and is left behind when the stooks are moved[1] get 1 *bāfeh* per day.

The thresher in Sīstān is paid at the rate of 3 per cent of the grain threshed and the reaper at the rate of 4 stooks per 100 stooks of barley and 3 stooks per 100 stooks of wheat. In Sīstān oxen are let out by the cattle breeders for ploughing, a payment being made at harvest time at the rate of 1 *mann* per 3 *manni zābul* of seed sown, one pair of oxen sowing 4–7 *manni zābul* per day.

In the opium fields a good deal of casual labour is employed and mainly paid by day. In Turbati Ḥaydarī it was paid in 1949 at the rate of some 10 rs. (approx. 1*s.* 2*d.*) per day for some 3½ hours in the case of men and 5 rs. (approx. 7*d.*) per day in the case of women. The cutting of the poppy was for the most part done by men and the collecting of the opium from the poppy by women. This operation is performed twice on each crop, or if the crop is above the average, three times at an interval of several days. The poppy is cut or perforated in the evening and the opium which oozes out of the cut is scraped off the poppy-head the following morning.

In Ābkūh, near Mashhad, casual labour was paid 13 rs. (approx. 1*s.* 6¼*d.*) per day in 1949 at all seasons of the year; at Mihrānkhān, on the other hand, labour was paid only 6–8 rs. (approx. 8½*d.*–11*d.*) per day. In Maymeh agricultural labour was paid in 1948 at the rate of 10 rs. (approx. 1*s.* 2*d.*) a day.

In so far as the rice-growing areas of the Caspian provinces are concerned, the economic position of the peasant is no better than that of the peasant in the grain-growing areas of the plateau: indeed, for the most part it compares unfavourably. The following estimate of the annual outlay on, and produce of an average peasant holding in Langarūd, illustrates the poverty of the peasantry in this area. The average-size holding is 2,000 sq. metres.[2]

The produce of a holding of 2,000 sq. metres (2,392 sq. yds.), i.e. 100 *darz* of 24 sq. *qabẓeh*), provided the land does not suffer pest and is properly cultivated and looked after, is some 450 kilos (approx. 8 cwt., 96 lb.). In most areas the landowner's share of this amounts to 150 kg. (approx. 2 cwt., 107 lb.), although in some villages 225 kilos (approx. 4 cwt., 48 lb.) are taken. Three

[1] The person who performs the operation is known locally as *tahi bāfeh jamʿ kun*.

[2] Land is measured by *darz*, which consist usually of 24 sq. *qabẓeh* but may also be 12 as in Mālājān, 20 as in Sālkūyeh, or 48 sq. *qabẓeh* as in Sāristāq. One *qabẓeh* equals the length of the fist; 100 *darz* of 24 sq. *qabẓeh* are reckoned as 2 *jarīb* (of 2,000 sq. metres or 2,392 sq. yds.) in most of the villages of Langarūd. Land is measured as follows: the surveyor takes the fists of several persons with different sized hands and puts these together so that he obtains 12, 20, 24, or 48 *qabẓeh*. He then cuts a stick of that length and using this as his measuring stick, marks a rope into lengths with it and then proceeds to measure the ground.

	Rs.	£. s. d.	Rs.	£. s. d.
1. Preparing the land for seed:				
Hire of ox	250	(1 9 4)		
Upkeep of ox during the ploughing season	50	(5 10)		
Hire of labourer for sowing at the rate of 45 rs. per day for three days (the labourer providing his own food)	135	(15 10)		
			435	(2 11 0)
2. Further preparation for sowing which is carried out by the labourer for two days, at the rate of 45 rs. per day (the labourer providing his own food)*	..	..	90	(10 7)
3. Levelling the land by the breaking up of clods of earth, done as above and at the same rate†	..	..	90	(10 7)
4. Stamping the weeds into the mud and preparing the land for planting (*nishā'*), which is done by one labourer in one day at the rate of 45 rs. per day with food‡ .	..	..	45	(5 3)
5. Planting:§				
16 kilos *shālī* (rice) in the form of *soum* are required.	90	(10 7)		
Three women for one day to plant this at the rate of 20 rs. per day (the women providing their own food) .	60	(7 0)		
			150	(17 7)
6. Weeding‖ which is done on two separate occasions, by three women at the rate of 20 rs. per day	..	..	120	(14 1)
7. Irrigation, i.e. the letting of water into the cultivated area according to certain regulations for which a *mīrāb* is appointed, the average payment per 100 *darz* being	..	..	25	(2 11)
8. Reaping, i.e. cutting off the heads of the rice after they ripen, for which two labourers are employed at the rate of 50 rs. per day for one day, with food	..	..	100	(11 9)
9. The transport of the rice from the field to the store, paid at the rate of 4 per cent of the total moved .	..	..	100	(11 9)
10. Threshing ¶ the heaps of rice** for which two labourers are required for one day and paid at the rate of 30 rs.	..	..	60	(7 0)
11. Cleaning†† the rice in the husk (*shālī*).	..	..	180	(1 1 2)
TOTAL			1,395	(8 3 8)

* This operation is known as *vākār*.
† This operation is known as *lāt zadan*.
‡ This operation is known as *dāmārdeh zadan*.
§ This operation is known as *nishā' kardan*.
‖ This operation is known as *vijīn kardan*.
¶ This operation is known as *kharak zadan*.
** Known as *kurpeh*.
†† This operation is known as *ābdang*.

hundred kg. (approx. 5 cwt., 101 lb.) thus remain to the peasant; half of this is required to defray the expenses of cultivation as set out above, leaving him with 150 kg. on which to live. Even suppose the labour in the fields is provided by his family and therefore unpaid, the margin is still insufficient to provide for him and his family; in order to maintain himself and his family at a minimum standard he is forced to supplement his agricultural earnings by labour on the roads, porterage, and other unskilled manual labour.

CHAPTER XXII

THE PROBLEMS OF THE PEASANT: DEBT; STANDARD OF LIVING

SINCE primitive methods of agriculture and unfavourable natural resources result in poor yields, of which a relatively large proportion goes to the landlord or to pay the various dues deducted from the harvest, the share remaining to the peasant is of the most meagre kind. When it is remembered that this share is subdivided among a minimum of two, and perhaps among as many as four or five persons who are attached to the *juft* or plough-land, it will be realized that the living afforded by agriculture to the crop-sharing peasants is in most cases totally inadequate to maintain him and his family in security or comfort. Even in the peasant-proprietor areas the inadequacy of technical resources is such that in many cases only the barest subsistence is obtained from the land.

The methods of the peasant, whether he is a crop-sharing peasant or a peasant-proprietor, resemble those of subsistence farming, but Persian farming to a greater or lesser extent is undertaken for marketing, although the amount of the crop which is sold varies. In certain areas, notably in central Persia, which are not self-supporting in grain, grain crops are not normally sold. Elsewhere any surplus grain over and above the annual requirements of the peasant (which in view of the methods employed is inevitably small) is disposed of. Similarly, various pulses are sold where the produce is surplus to the peasants' need. Cotton, tobacco, and opium in certain areas, and beet, which under Riẓā Shāh were made into government monopolies, and other commercial crops are grown for the market. Fruit, vegetables, and melons, etc., are grown almost entirely for the market.

The peasant performs all the operations concerned with the production and disposal of his crops himself.[1] He is closely concerned, therefore, with questions of price and credit. His prosperity or otherwise depends upon the margin between costs and price. This fact makes him particularly sensitive to seasonal and other variations in price. He has no co-operative marketing arrangements. This, together with the fact that he seldom has any reserve and is often ignorant of conditions outside his immediate neighbourhood, puts him in a weak position to drive a bargain.

[1] Fruit in the neighbourhood of the towns must in some cases be excepted from this. It often happens that merchants buy the fruit on the trees, in which case they arrange for the picking of the fruit and its transport to the city.

His need almost always forces him to take the price offered however disadvantageous it may be.

Inadequate communications and costly means of transport greatly add to his costs of production and make it more difficult for him to do anything but sell his goods at the nearest market at whatever price is offered. The almost permanent state of need and the series of temporary crises which are the normal concomitant of peasant life force him to dispose of his produce immediately after harvest, if it is not already pledged before. This means that he has no alternative but to sell or barter his surplus crops at the period when prices are lowest. Barter is more usual than sale. If, moreover, his reserves are exhausted before the winter is over, as is often the case, he then has to buy when prices are at their peak. If the peasant's crop is a relatively small one, grain, fruit, or pulses are exchanged for some commodity such as tea, sugar, or cloth. In some cases he also barters the produce of his flocks. Such transactions are usually carried on with brokers or merchants who come out from the neighbouring towns, or with the village shopkeeper. The transaction is seldom to the advantage of the peasant, the other party being able to manipulate prices to his disadvantage.

It is thus not surprising that debt should be one of the curses of Persian rural life. The peasant is constantly in need of money for capital requirements, to replace livestock and agricultural implements, for seed, and for other current expenses. To provide these he has to borrow. Often, in many areas his reserves are almost always exhausted before the winter is over and he has to borrow merely in order to feed himself and his family. When this is so the current harvest in some cases suffices only to pay off his debts, and in others is not sufficient even for this, and so the peasant remains permanently in debt.

In such circumstances the peasant may have recourse to a money-lender for a loan or to the landowner for an advance.[1] The former appears in a variety of guises: he may be a merchant in a neighbouring town, or a pedlar working for himself or for a third party, or the village shopkeeper, or a fellow peasant who for some reason or other is in more prosperous circumstances. But, whoever the money-lender may be, the rates of interest are almost always exorbitant. In certain areas in Arāk where peasants gave

[1] The Agricultural and Industrial Bank, founded in 1933 mainly with the object of granting credits for agricultural and irrigation projects, in practice does most of its business with the large landowners. For the early history of the establishment of this bank, see Chams-ed-Dine Djazaeri, *La Crise économique mondiale et ses répercussions en Iran* (Paris, 1938), pp. 243 ff. The agricultural and industrial functions of the bank were subsequently separated, a new bank known as the Industrial Bank being set up, and the old bank being thenceforward known as the Agricultural Bank.

advances to their less prosperous neighbours they were alleged in 1945 to take some 25 per cent by way of interest. A story is related of a merchant in Kāshān who made a practice in recent years of giving loans to needy peasants; it is alleged that in one case the sum due after some ten years on a loan of 130 rs. (approx. 15*s.* 3*d.*) with the payment of interest and compound interest came to 70,000 rs. (approx. £411. 15*s.* 3*d.*). Although this is, no doubt, an extreme case, it illustrates the difficulties of the peasant in freeing himself from debt once he is forced to have recourse to a money-lender.

Loans are normally raised on the security of the next harvest. The terms are usually highly unfavourable to the peasant, since, apart from anything else, he is forced to negotiate when prices are high and to repay his loan when prices are low. In many rural areas, and in particular in Kurdistān, wandering merchants or pedlars are in the habit of selling cloth, tea, sugar, and similar goods on account against the coming harvest. The peasants and their families in many cases are ignorant of the true value of their purchases and the prices paid are usually exorbitant.

Where the landowner gives an advance to the peasant, the terms on which he gives this vary. A limit is set to the rates of interest he charges by expediency: it does not pay him to reduce the peasantry below a certain level of poverty, since in that case the usefulness of the peasant will be impaired. Here again the landowner who is a relative newcomer tends to drive a harder bargain with the peasants to whom he gives advances than the landowner who has been longer established. Where tribal *khāns* own land in the settled areas they also are alleged to take high rates of interest on advances.[1]

In certain parts of Fārs two types of advances are found, which are known respectively as *musāʿideh* and *taqavī*. The former represents an advance given to the peasant to tide him over bad times. The normal practice is for an advance to be given in kind in winter, that is, when prices are high, and for repayment to be demanded in summer in cash or in the equivalent amount of grain at current prices, i.e. when prices are at the lowest and the amount of grain required to pay off the debt is therefore considerably greater than the amount originally given as an advance. In effect, the peasant pays a high rate of interest, and once forced by poverty to take an advance, he is likely to be kept in a permanent state of poverty. It is obvious, therefore, that unless the present system is considerably modified, there is a need for the provision of advances to the peasants on more favourable terms.

[1] Where the tribal leaders own villages in their own tribal territory, and in which members of their own tribal groups cultivate the land, they are less likely to take unduly high rates of interest.

The second form of advance, known as *taqavī*, which is found notably in Jahrum, is of a different nature. When a peasant first starts to cultivate a piece of land, he can take up to 1,000 rs. (approx. £5. 17*s.* 6*d.*) per ox without interest from the landowner and need not return this until he is able to do so. He cannot, however, leave the land until he pays off this sum. In the first year the peasant requires this money to enable him to buy the necessary implements to start work. In the second year he is encouraged to buy livestock or asses instead of repaying the loan immediately, or to take cows or other animals on a *nīmeh* basis, i.e. he buys a part share in a cow, feeds and tends it, giving half the produce and progeny to the other partner. Only after his affairs have been put on a relatively firm foundation is he expected to pay back the loan.

In Kirmān the poverty of the peasants is very marked. The fact that it is the normal practice for peasants to receive advances every year bears witness to this. In Zarand, for example, the peasants are seldom able to get through the winter without an advance. In due course this is repaid at harvest time, only to be required again before the following winter is over. In certain areas, as in Narmāshīr, a practice similar to that prevailing in Jahrum is found, the peasant receiving an advance, also known as *taqavī*, from the landlord when he first takes up a holding in a landlord estate. It is not customary for him to repay this as long as he stays on that estate. In actual fact he is generally unable to repay this money since the general level of poverty is greater in Narmāshīr than in Jahrum; consequently in practice he is unable to leave the estate. Thus an advance which in Jahrum is used to set the peasant on his feet and to help him to improve his economic status is in Narmāshīr a means of virtually tying him to the soil.

In Kurdistān when necessary seed is given to the peasants in a bad year and taken back at harvest time without interest. The type of advance given to a peasant when he first comes to a village in Jahrum and Narmāshīr, though not unknown in Kurdistān, where it goes by the name of *nān sufreh*, is not usual. If, however, a new village is made by a landowner he sometimes gives the peasant money to build his house. In a recent case of a new village being founded the landowner divided the land into thirty-two plough-lands and gave to the holder of each 7,000 rs. (approx. £41. 3*s.* 6*d.*), 2 *kharvār* (approx. 11 cwt., 77 lb.) of wheat, and wooden beams for his house. Formerly, it was the custom in Kurdistān to give 350 rs. (approx. £2. 1*s.*) and 2 *kharvār* of wheat to the peasants settled in a new village.

In certain parts of Varāmīn it is customary for the peasants to receive so much per month by way of an advance, which is repayable at harvest time.[1] This again illustrates the inadequacy of the living afforded by agriculture to the crop-sharing peasant.

The practice of giving advances is not common in Khūzistān. This fact is not to be ascribed to any greater prosperity among the peasants—indeed in many areas their poverty is striking—but rather to lack of interest on the part of the landowner in developing the land; this in turn is partly, no doubt, the result of insecurity of tenure and uncertainty as to the future. Advances are usual only when the crops have been destroyed or damaged by pest or some such natural calamity. In 1949 many of the peasants in Khūzistān had been reduced to a state of abject poverty by a succession of dry years. Few of them had sufficient seed for sowing, and adequate advances were not being made to them either by the landowners or in *khāliṣeh* land by the government to enable them to obtain seed. In the neighbourhood of Rām Hurmuz the practice of giving advances would appear to be more common than elsewhere in Khūzistān and it was alleged in 1949 that repayment was made in kind, *mann* for *mann*, at harvest time.

Insecurity is the dominant note in Āẕarbāyjān and, as a result of this, the landowners, as a whole, are unwilling to give advances to their peasants, even when these are repayable from the following year's harvest. The effect of this policy already in 1949 was to produce an agricultural decline, which, in turn, is likely to result in unemployment and unrest and, therefore, increase still further insecurity in the province. In Qarājeh Dāgh and other areas of Āẕarbāyjān in 1949 the peasants, who had no reserves to tide them over bad times, were being forced by poverty to sell up their belongings, including their draught animals. These were in most cases being sold for slaughter. The dangers of allowing such a state of affairs to continue are obvious. Already it would appear that poverty has forced many to abandon their villages.

In certain areas of the country the peasants are often forced to sell their crops in advance. The period just before the harvest, as stated above, is the time when the peasant is most subject to economic pressure: his accumulated reserves, such as they are, are often exhausted and he may well be tempted, if not forced, to sell in advance to tide him over the period till the crop is harvested. In many areas near the towns, notably round Tehrān, brokers are in the habit of visiting the country districts and tempting the peasants to sell their crops in advance at relatively low prices. This applies both to grain and *ṣayfī* crops and to garden produce.

Another practice is found in a few areas, which also works to the detriment of the peasant. The landlord, on the threat of withholding water, draught animals, or seed can (and sometimes does) force

[1] In one village this was 100 rs. (approx. 11*s.* 9*d.*) in 1949.

the peasant to sell him his (the peasant's) share of the crop on the threshing-floor at prices which he (the landlord) fixes.

Special methods are adopted in some cases to finance market gardening which, as pointed out in Chapter XVII, is carried on on a large scale only in areas in the immediate neighbourhood of the town. For example, in Khīābān, near Mashhad, the usual crop-sharing arrangement prevails between the lessee and the peasants (see p. 316), the latter being responsible for all the expenses of cultivation. In all some 1,200 daily labourers are employed in the area and were paid in 1949 at the rate of 20 rs. (approx. 2*s*. 4*d*.) per day. To finance the undertaking three methods are adopted. Either the Shirkati Kishāvarzīyi Riẓā (which leases the property from the shrine of the Imām Riẓā) advances the money for the payment of this labour to the peasants and takes it back at harvest time, or a greengrocer (*baqqāl*) in the town of Mashhad advances the money to the peasant and recovers it in kind when the crops ripen. The third but less common way of financing this type of cultivation is for the value of the crop to be estimated by a valuer. A third person then buys the crop, undertaking to pay one-third of the estimated value to the lessee. The lessee, however, is not forced to sell his share of the crop in this way and can, if he wishes, retain his right to one-third of the crop and collect it in kind at harvest time.

In Rafsinjān in some cases when the right to collect the pistachio nut crop is rented, the prospective rentee negotiates first with a merchant for the eventual disposal of the crop, and only when he has done so and has obtained a written pledge from the merchant is the garden entrusted to him.

There is another matter which is of vital concern to the peasant whether he is a crop-sharing peasant or peasant-proprietor, and which closely affects his material well-being, that is, his relations with the government. He comes into contact with government officials in a variety of ways. This increased contact has perhaps been one of the marked features of the twentieth century in Persia.[1] The activity which most concerns him is the preservation of order. Clearly without security he cannot carry on his daily occupations, and unless he can rely on adequate protection from disorder, there is little inducement to him to increase the extent or productivity of his holding, and thereby to improve his economic status. Fear that he will not be able to defend his goods from the depredations of others, deters him from undertaking labour the fruits of which he has little hope of enjoying. In the pre-Riẓā Shāh period, periodic inroads by lawless elements who would suddenly fall upon a village, drive off its cattle, and seize the possessions of its inhabi-

[1] See Ch. VIII.

tants were an important factor in the decay of some areas. Various marauding groups, such as bands of Turkomāns, would range far and wide;[1] others would confine their activities rather to the country bordering their own tribal territories. In these areas the fear of raids was seldom absent. At the present day security, in so far as the suppression of raiding goes, has been established virtually throughout the country. From time to time some crisis arises and security in the remoter areas, perhaps, breaks down temporarily, but generally speaking the peasant has no longer to be prepared at short notice to defend his land and possessions against armed marauders.

The insecurity which threatens the peasant and also the landowner at the present day is of another kind; it, too, affects his economic status adversely. What he has to fear to-day is the exaction of officials and false charges trumped up by unfriendly persons or by dishonest officials. Clearly this problem is not only one of rural organization but concerns the establishment of political and judicial security, the integrity of the civil service, and the creation of an effective administration to which the individual owes allegiance. Here it is treated only in so far as it adds to the problems of the peasant. Many officials both civil and military are, of course, honest and carry out their duties with integrity, but unfortunately they are probably in a minority. One of the results of the reign of Riẓā Shāh and his policy of centralization was for the countryside to be invaded by a horde of government officials, most of whom are inadequately paid. At best they live on the country and at worst look upon office as an opportunity to grow wealthy. In so far as promotion is obtained in return for the payment of a commission by the lower grades to the higher—and there is very little doubt that there have been instances of this kind among the security officials—it is clear that the local population is likely to suffer. A favourite method of extorting money, for example, is to stir up disputes in order to collect money from the parties concerned for their eventual settlement. Moreover, the tendency to extortion is one of the factors, though not perhaps the most important one, making for absenteeism. Local officials are inclined to make heavy demands upon the hospitality of the landowners if nothing more. Tradition demands that hospitality should be offered to all comers on as lavish a scale as possible: anything else would not be consistent with the dignity and status of the landowner. Consequently many feel that the only way of avoiding such impositions is to remain away.

Requisitions of provisions, of labour, and of animals by the security forces in the more remote areas are complained of. These,

[1] cf. Sir John Malcolm, *Sketches of Persia* (London, 1815), ii. 7 ff.

when they are made, contribute to the impoverishment of the peasant both directly and indirectly, since not only do they interfere with his work but by increasing his sense of insecurity they deter him from undertaking measures to increase or improve cultivation.

Compulsory military service is imposed on the male population. It is perhaps through this that the rural dweller comes into closest contact with the government. Recruits are called up annually. The men who are to serve are usually designated by the Military Service Department in consultation with the local *kadkhudā*. The fact that all men of any given age-group are not necessarily called up opens the way to corruption and bribery. The conscripts, who can often ill be spared from the land, once rounded up, are taken off to the nearest garrison town. Here they come in contact for the first time, perhaps, with town life and not only with its amenities but also with its vices and temptations. Not infrequently they contract disease and return to their villages less fitted than before they left to carry on their former calling.

The creation of a number of state monopolies such as the cotton and opium monopolies also brought about increased contact between the peasants and the government officials. This development, in so far as it meant that the peasants could rely upon a fixed price in cash for their crops, was beneficial to the peasants, but the fact that the officials concerned frequently lived on the country and were given to extortion considerably detracted from this advantage.

On the other hand, the advent of government officials in the country districts, as was pointed out in Chapter VIII, meant that the peasant had the possibility of appeal to a third party against oppression by the landowners. But in practice this was vitiated by various factors. Moreover, no adequate means of redress have been devised against the extortion of either landlords or government officials. Resort to the law is a lengthy process and even when made there is little guarantee that the decision reached will be impartial or impartially carried out. In any case it is virtually out of the question for the peasant. He has little chance of successful appeal against the landlord, who is usually able to influence the giving of a decision and its execution in his own favour, and still less against the official.

The establishment of political security primarily concerns the landowner[1] rather than the peasant, but in so far as its absence makes for uncertainty, and therefore militates against prosperity, he is also affected.

Some mention has already been made of housing in Chapter XVI.

[1] See Ch. XIII.

For the most part, whether the housing belongs to the peasant or to the landowner, overcrowding is the rule. The houses are mainly buildings of one story made of mud-brick. The quality of the brick varies from district to district according to the nature of the soil. In most areas it requires constant repair after the winter snow or rain. In districts where wooden rafters are available the roofs are usually flat and serve for sleeping quarters in summer. Elsewhere domed brick roofs are made. In the lowlands of Māzandarān and Gīlān sloping roofs of wood are constructed in order better to resist the heavy rain.

The rooms of the houses are usually dark, small, and ill ventilated. Windows are for the most part lacking, partly, no doubt, to make for warmth in winter and coolness in summer. The extent to which the interior of the room is furnished depends upon the relative prosperity of the peasant. In the case of the poorer it is empty except perhaps for a rough mat, carpet, or felt on the floor, and some bedding. In the better-to-do houses the floors are carpeted and curtains of some cotton-weave are hung over the door. Bedding consists of quilts, mattresses, and bolsters or pillows; it is rolled up in the day-time and put round the walls of the room to serve as supports against which to sit. Any surplus clothes or goods which the peasant has are usually stored in chests or boxes. For the rest there is perhaps a small mirror on a recess in the wall and perhaps a Qur'ān.

On the plateau warmth is provided in winter by a *kursī*; this consists of a charcoal brazier, placed on the floor, in some cases in a hole or declivity specially made in the floor, over which is placed a low wooden table covered by a large table-cloth or quilt. The family sit round this with the lower part of their bodies under the quilt; the brazier is refilled once or twice a day with charcoal which is specially prepared to prevent it giving off fumes. In cold weather the family also sleep round the *kursī*.

Cooking is done mainly in copper vessels on a charcoal fire, or on a fire made of camel thorn, wood, or animal dung. Copper bowls are largely used for eating; crockery is rare. In summer the cooking is done in a corner of the courtyard and in winter in an outhouse. In many cases, however, one room serves the peasant and his family for all purposes: sleeping, living, and cooking. Tea is usually made in a brass samovar, or in the case of the less prosperous peasants in a tin samovar, and is drunk out of small glasses.

Lighting is provided by kerosene lamps or storm lanterns. The poorer peasants and those in outlying districts largely dispense with lamps. Kerosene is obtained from the village shop, if such exists, or is brought by the peasant himself from the neighbouring town.

The more prosperous peasants often have some sort of veranda in front of their houses or a courtyard. In the courtyard there is sometimes a pool or even running water which serves the family for washing household utensils, etc. The houses in some areas may have trees and small gardens in the courtyard, but this is the exception rather than the rule. The family animals are often kept next to the living quarters. Partly for this reason, and because of the general lack of sanitation, there are swarms of flies in summer. In some villages each house has its own latrine; in others there is a common latrine which serves the village or the quarter. The use of neighbouring water-courses is also not uncommon.

In some landlord villages and hamlets a *qalʿeh* or walled enclosure in which the peasants have their quarters is found.[1] Here, again, overcrowding is common, and one family per room usual; in some cases the animals are kept in one part of the *qalʿeh* separate from the living quarters.

The water-supply varies according to natural conditions. It is usual for drinking water to be fetched in earthenware pitchers or skins from the village spring or well. Houses seldom have their own supply.

In some of the *garmsīr* areas permanent housing has not been built, the peasants living in huts made of reeds and branches of trees, or in houses the walls of which are made of mud-brick and the roofs of reed matting, and branches of trees. In Balūchistān, for example, many of the peasants live in reed-matting huts or in tents. In Sīstān also in certain areas huts made of reeds are used. Such conditions, especially in certain parts of Fārs and Khūzistān, are in part due to the fact that many of the people in these areas have recently changed from a semi-settled to a settled life. Nevertheless, such housing conditions are also witness to the poverty of the people.

Some of the more enlightened landowners are building new and improved housing in their villages. This is the case in some of the properties belonging to the shrine of the Imām Riẓā in Khurāsān and in some villages in the Bīrjand area, to mention two instances. Gīv, which was rebuilt after destruction by an earthquake in 1948, offers a striking example of the improvement in living conditions which can be brought about by better housing.

Throughout the country the main diet of the peasant is bread except in the rice-growing area of Māzandarān where it is rice, and in the date-growing areas where it is dates.

The grain in the grain-growing areas is mainly locally milled. In those villages which have no mill the peasant, unless he relies on a

[1] See above, p. 8.

hand-mill, which is extremely laborious, often has to take his grain considerable distances for milling. Payment is usually taken in kind for this service. In Mājān in Qā'ināt the miller takes some 5 per cent in kind on what is ground and also 1½ *sīr* (approx. 3 oz.) *zinjī*, i.e. the heads remaining on the threshing-floor when the grain is separated from the stalk, per peasant at the beginning of the harvest time and a further 1½ *sīr* at the end of the harvest. In Khūzistān the majority of the larger villages have mills. In Rām Hurmuz 30 rs. (approx. 3*s.* 6*d.*) per *manni ahvāz* (approx. 110 lb.)[1] was taken in 1949; in Khalafābād 35 rs. (approx. 4*s.* 1*d.*) per *manni jarrāḥīyeh* (approx. 2 cwt., 51½ lb.); in Shādagān the rate was 4½ rs. (approx. 6¼*d.*) per *vaqeh* (approx. 23 lb.) of wheat or barley at 5 rs. (approx. 7*d.*); in the village of Kurdistān near Bihbahān one-sixteenth of the wheat and one-twelfth of the barley ground is taken by way of payment.

Outside the rice-growing areas the peasant seldom eats rice except on festive occasions such as New Year's Eve. The main feature of his diet apart from bread is *ābgūsht*, or soup, made chiefly by boiling a little meat with split peas and occasionally with some other pulses. In summer he supplements his diet in the fruit-growing areas with fruit and vegetables such as cucumber. If he owns flocks he also eats a small quantity of cheese and curds. His only luxuries, if they may be termed such, are tea and sugar. These, in the outlying areas, are often in short supply. In Havīzeh the rice diet of the peasant is supplemented by fish, and along the shores of the Persian Gulf also fish forms an important article of diet.

The clothing of the peasant and that of his wife and children is often of the scantiest and most ragged kind. It is not unusual for the peasant's wardrobe to consist only of those clothes which he wears, with perhaps a spare shirt in addition. In some areas a rough cotton cloth is woven partly for use as clothing and partly for sale. A variety of this cloth, known as *karbās*, is used for the most part for the peasant's trousers and shirt. In winter he supplements this by a piece of felt cut in the rough shape of a coat. On his head he also wears a round felt hat, somewhat in the shape of a skull-cap, with, in the colder areas, ear-flaps which can be pulled down. His wife commonly wears a pleated skirt also of *karbās*. For the rest she mainly wears garments made of brightly coloured printed calico and cloth obtained from the village shop or pedlars. The long trousers which she commonly wears under her skirt are usually made of black calico. On her head she wears a large kerchief. In the tribal areas the women wear a heavily pleated skirt.

[1] In the town of Ahvāz 280 rs. (approx. £1. 13*s.* 1*d.*) per ton was taken on barley and 240 rs. (approx. £1. 8*s.* 2*d.*) on wheat in 1949.

This is an expensive item, since it requires many yards of material. Footwear on the plateau usually consists of a locally made shoe known as a *gīveh*. This has a woven cotton upper and a sole usually made of pulped rags, or in some cases of rope or coarse thread. In winter on the plateau a kind of clog is also worn, and in Balūchistān a sandal made of the fibre of the date palm.

Public health and education services do not cover all rural districts. For the most part they are found only in the less remote districts. The low standard of living of the peasants makes it impossible for health and education services to be to any extent self-supporting, while the absence of such services helps to perpetuate the prevailing standards. Further, the absence of amenities in rural districts makes the average doctor reluctant to practise in the villages, a reluctance which is reinforced by the fear (often not without foundation) that once out of the way in a rural district he will be forgotten and will fall behind his fellows in matters of promotion. The result is that doctors are few and far between in the rural districts, and there are hardly any nurses. Medicines are insufficient and often costly. In the bigger and less remote villages there are occasionally doctors, possibly serving several villages. But in the remoter areas if the peasant or one of his family falls ill, he has to make a long journey to the nearest town. If it is mid-winter the road may well be under snow and the journey difficult, while if it is harvest time or the sowing season he can ill spare the time to make such a journey. In such circumstances it is not surprising that disease takes a heavy toll—how heavy it is impossible to estimate. Malaria is endemic in many parts of the country and results in a loss of efficiency and, with secondary diseases, probably in great loss of life also. Trachoma is widespread. Infant mortality by all accounts is unduly high. In addition, sporadic outbreaks of minor infectious diseases such as measles often take a heavy toll in the villages, owing to the absence of doctors, nurses, and medicines.

A law providing for compulsory education was passed in 1943. It yet remains to be implemented throughout the country. In few villages except in those near the towns are there schools.[1] The main difficulties are the shortage of teachers and of buildings. Like doctors, and for the same reasons, teachers are reluctant to accept rural posts. In present social conditions, moreover, it is difficult if not impossible for women teachers to go out into the villages. The poverty of the village population is another obstacle to the spread of education. The children are from the earliest age

[1] Bīrjand is a notable exception. Literacy among the rural population in this area is relatively high. Some 80 per cent of military conscripts are said to be literate.

needed to help in the fields or to supplement the family income by tending sheep or carpet-weaving, and even if they are not put to work at an early age economic pressure prevents most of them from attending school regularly or over any considerable period of years. In some of the landlord villages the landowner provides accommodation for a school and the Ministry of Education an instructor. In many cases the buildings are dark and cramped; the curriculum and textbooks, moreover, are not suited to the needs of the country child.

The daily life of the peasant and his family is largely determined by the agricultural seasons.[1] The struggle for daily bread is such that he has little time or energy for other occupations. In any case there are no facilities for recreation or amenities in the average village. By far the most important festival of the year is the New Year, which falls at the spring equinox. It is a time for general rejoicing[2] and the celebrations last several days. The villagers for once forget their anxieties. Decked in their best they occupy themselves in visiting each other, disporting themselves in the neighbourhood of the village and, in some cases, in playing traditional games. For the rest the daily round is broken only by the Muhammadan feasts and days of mourning, or by births, weddings, and deaths. In the month of Muḥarram, in commemoration of the death of Ḥasan at Karbalā, passion plays are held in many villages. The local cemetery is a favourite place of assembly for the village women, especially on Thursday evenings; the object of their visits is to mourn the dead but at the same time these visits are in some measure a social event also, an opportunity to meet and to exchange gossip. In those areas where there is a local shrine in the neighbourhood, a visit to this is probably undertaken at least once, while it is the ambition of all (and an ambition not infrequently realized) to visit the shrines of the Imām Riẓā in Mashhad and of his sister Fātimeh in Qumm.

Two facts will have emerged from what has gone before. The first is that the dominant feature of the life of the peasant is insecurity, insecurity because of the frequent threat of crop failures due to natural causes,[3] insecurity because of market fluctuations, and insecurity from the exactions of his fellow men. Secondly, it will be clear that his almost constant problem is poverty. This is

[1] See Ch. XXI.

[2] Unless it coincides, as is sometimes the case, with the month of Muḥarram, which the Shīʿīs keep as a month of mourning.

[3] See above, p. 367. Partial or total crop failures occur on an average probably one year in five. Widespread famine is not any longer common, but local famines occur from time to time. For example, in 1948–9 there were crop failures in east Persia and deaths from starvation. In 1948 there were heavy losses in cattle in Khūzistān owing to drought.

true not only of the crop-sharing peasant but also to a lesser extent of the peasant proprietor, and even more of the agricultural labourer. In such circumstances it is not altogether surprising that he should have developed a certain technique of fatalism to enable him to exist in an environment whose capricious nature must frequently impress itself upon him.

CHAPTER XXIII

THE FUTURE

AN attempt has been made in the foregoing chapters to describe the salient features of land tenure and rural organization in Persia and their historical background. There has been a striking continuity of tradition over a period of some 1,200 years, and some features can be traced even farther, to pre-Islamic times. It is true that in law the traditional forms were from time to time virtually suspended, but they have repeatedly reasserted themselves, modified, it may be, by the incorporation of new customs and theories, the latest instance being the land law as set forth in the modern Civil Code.[1]

Certain major problems have reappeared throughout Persian history. The two most notable are the problem of the relations between the settled and the semi-settled elements of the population, and the problem of financing the administration of the state. The first has still to be solved. The second, which greatly affected the question of land revenue administration in the past, has, with the increasing diversity of economic activity in recent years, ceased to turn entirely, or even mainly, on land questions.

The background against which these various developments have unfolded is insecurity: the insecurity of the landowner against the caprice of the government, insecurity in the face of attack by hostile elements, whether internal factions or foreign invasion, and the insecurity of the cultivator *vis-à-vis* the landowner and others. The law was not backed by a predominant and impartial force; effective power therefore rested with whoever wielded the greatest force and, in the absence of control by the law, the exercise of this force depended almost entirely on personal caprice. Insecurity, political and economic, is no less the keynote at the present day than in the past, although there have been changes in emphasis.

Over-taxation and the tendency of government officials towards extortion, together with insecurity, were the main causes of the agricultural decay which became apparent on the disintegration of the Abbasid empire and has continued, with certain breaks, down to the present day. In the past the main burden of taxation fell upon the peasant. In modern times, although there has been a change of emphasis this is still true. The peasant contributes through indirect taxation a considerable proportion of the revenue of the country and continues to pay to the landowner many of the

[1] See Ch. IX.

dues the latter had formerly collected in his capacity as local governor or in return for the provision of military contingents. In the past the only remedy of the peasant was flight. At the present day, when driven to extremity, he still has no remedy but to leave the land to seek a perhaps even more precarious living in the town. The result of these tendencies was to fix a gulf between the government and the people; this in turn was reflected in the political quietism which became a marked feature of the Middle Ages and has continued to a greater or less degree down to modern times.

A widespread conservatism is another obstacle to change: there has always been an endeavour on the part of the government and the landowners to preserve the *status quo*; a tendency in which, it must be admitted, the peasants largely acquiesce. There is on the whole a reluctance on the part of the state to interfere in the relations between the landlord and his peasants and a refusal to regulate the position of the peasants. The main feature of medieval rural organization, the making of land assignments, was, it is true, abolished after the grant of the Constitution, but the conception of rural society is still essentially medieval, and it is this underlying conception which has decided the way in which new institutions have worked.

The economic status of the peasant has probably changed little in recent years, although some observers compare it unfavourably with that of thirty years ago. On the other hand, his social status, although he is still regarded as a hewer of wood and drawer of water, has probably been somewhat improved. His position in the landlord areas, it is true, still depends very largely on the personal qualities of the landowner, but nevertheless he enjoys a greater freedom of action than was formerly the case. This is due mainly to the increased power of the central government and the ensuing changes in provincial administration and to improved communications. Whereas formerly the landowner or tribal chief often combined in his person the functions of governor and landowner, a new element has been introduced into rural society in the person of government officials, to whom the peasant can refer. On the other hand, as pointed out in the preceding chapter, this increased contact with government officials is more often than not a burden rather than a relief to the peasant.

Whatever the changes, few people would honestly assert that the present situation is satisfactory. The peasant lives, for the most part, in conditions of grinding poverty, the landowner, although he enjoys comparative affluence, is in constant fear of being despoiled of his wealth by intrigue or of being cheated of it by a discontented peasantry, and the government official, often inadequately paid, finds it difficult to support himself and his family unless he has some source of income other than his pay. Distrust, insecurity, and intrigue prevail on all sides.

The means by which intrigue is carried out are provided by the relatively large sums of money which are at the disposal of the privileged classes. As long as this continues to be the case, and there is neither a tradition of public service nor a civil service with a high standard of integrity, this money is likely to be used both to maintain the privileges and monopolies of whatever class controls it and to exploit other classes. Any attempt to escape from the burdensome and unhappy conditions of the present day must be concerned primarily with the prevention of exploitation of man by man, which springs from the relation between the community and the individual. Merely to exchange one form of exploitation for another or to shift wealth, power, and privilege from one set of men to another, is no solution to the problem. But, in view of the prevailing political uncertainty and social insecurity, which threaten to dissolve the bonds of society, there is no doubt that any movement the proclaimed aim of which is to help the mass of the people (and to tear down the present political and social fabric) is likely to appeal to many sections of the public irrespective of its programme. The question at issue is not the need for reform, which is abundantly clear, but the means by which it is to be carried out. Any measures which fail to relieve the peasant of his poverty, to dissipate the prevailing distrust, or which neglect the importance of the provision of security for all are unlikely to succeed. Moreover, it is futile to suppose a movement of reform can be brought about by an act of the legislature alone. Its successful accomplishment presupposes changes so great as to amount to a social revolution. This, too, assumes an element of leadership, but it is by no means clear whence this is to come. The landowners are hardly likely to come forward as the standard-bearers of a movement the immediate effect of which is likely to be a reduction in their privileges. The experience of the past and the present situation hold little hope that they will even seek to maintain the substance of their privileged position by a compromise.

Neither past experience nor the present trend of events give reason to suppose that the government will, in practice, lead such a reform. There has often been talk of reform and social justice, but effective steps to secure it have been lacking. As long ago as 1881 Jamāl ud-Dīn Asadābādī (Afghānī), writing to Sayyid Ḥājjī Mastān Dāghistānī, said, 'Persian statesmen have great skill in politics and the art of talk, but their science is without practical application. If they expended on action one-hundredth part of the energy they expend in talking, Persia would take her place as regards progress, wealth, greatness, and power in the ranks of the Great

Powers. . . .'[1] These words might have been written at the present day.

Direct intervention by the government in the past, moreover, has not led uniformly to an improvement in the position of the peasant. There is, for example, the sorry story of the distribution of crown lands in Sīstān.[2] Nor is the position of the peasant in lands directly administered or supervised by the state on the whole any better than elsewhere. Were the government to start rural co-operative societies or to supervise the redistribution of land, there is little reason to suppose that such steps would in practice benefit the peasant.

As for the peasants themselves, they, no less than the landowners and other classes in Persia, are unpractised in the art of co-operation; there is no evidence which suggests that they would be able in the immediate future to run any co-operative undertaking successfully. In most areas the peasant is so fully occupied with the problems of day to day existence that he has little energy left for political or other activities. Moreover, centuries of oppression and struggle with a capricious environment and an unfavourable social system have caused him in many parts of the country to look upon his situation with resignation as part of the natural order of events. Even in Āẕarbāyjān, where physical conditions are more favourable and the proximity of the U.S.S.R. is likely to have awakened his political interests, the peasant shows little tendency to co-operate. During the Democrat rising in 1945–6, no leader emerged from the peasant community, the movement being led by townsmen and foreign-trained agitators. It would be foolish, however, to suppose that news of changed conditions elsewhere will not in due course reach the Persian peasant, arouse his interest, and spur him on to demand an amelioration of his own position. Leaving aside the fundamental problem of the relation of the individual to society, there are several technical problems to be tackled in order to achieve increased production.

1. Improved communications and the provision of cheap transport are vital. This has been touched upon in Chapter XXI. The problem is no easy one. The area to be covered is large and climatic conditions in some parts of it unfavourable. The towns are situated at long distances from one another. The cost of the upkeep of roads in such circumstances is bound to be heavy. Many areas are ill served by communications; a few have no roads at all. Fundamental, therefore, to increased production in the remoter

[1] Quoted from *al-Muqṭaṭab* (published in Cairo, Shavvāl 1343) by *Ṣadāyi Vaṭan*, 5th Shahrīvar 1328 (27 August 1949), in an article entitled 'Wherever tyranny exists and tranquillity is non-existent there will be no trace of a government'.

[2] See Ch. XII.

areas are improved communications and cheap transport. Without these the peasant cannot get his produce to market. The opening up of communications, moreover, has also an educational and social importance.

2. Improved marketing methods, better credit facilities, and some degree of co-operation are required if the economic position of the peasant is to be improved. Settled markets are also a prerequisite to increased production. In so far as the internal demand is concerned, no very great difficulty is involved, but where produce is grown for export—and increased production presupposes increased export—it is of vital importance that the grower, or those who handle his produce, should have some understanding of the requirements and trends of world markets.

3. Better agricultural methods, the introduction of new crops, a better management of crop rotation and fallow, pest controls, greater use of manure and fertilizers, and improved tools and machinery would increase production. Improved grain seed would probably materially affect the yield of crops. A certain quantity of special grain seed is made available at the present day by the Ministry of Agriculture, but further research and greater co-operation between the Ministry of Agriculture, the landowners, and peasants is desirable in this connexion. How far mechanization is desirable or practical is a matter for careful inquiry. It would mean a certain displacement of labour, and unless the area under cultivation is extended to absorb the displaced labour or alternative employment created, the immediate effect of widespread mechanization would not necessarily contribute to a solution of rural poverty. Further, it would be essential, if mechanization were advocated, to ensure that repairs to machinery were rapidly carried out and spare parts made available.

4. Improved irrigation and methods of water conservation are essential in many areas. Although water is the limiting factor in most agricultural development in Persia, considerable quantities of water run to waste every year. Total or partial crop failures occur on an average of one year in five, or in some areas as often as one year in three. The problem of irrigation has two main aspects: (*a*) large-scale measures, chiefly in the form of dams, which require considerable capital expenditure,[1] and (*b*) the better use of available water. In some areas a considerable portion is probably lost by evaporation and absorption as it flows through the water channels, while the relatively thick growth of weeds usually found in the cultivated fields and gardens also absorbs an unduly large proportion.

5. Afforestation and steps to prevent soil erosion are also

[1] See also Ch. X.

measures which will contribute ultimately to increased production. The result of neglecting these matters is likely to be disastrous.

6. The improvement of animal stock is highly desirable. The British Middle East Office reported very unfavourably on the quality of cattle and sheep in Persia. The question of animal population is, however, bound up with increased production. The present animal population is probably greater than the country can bear in its present state, and unless a higher proportion of cattle feed is grown it is probably not practicable to improve or increase present stock.

In the field of land tenure a variety of problems are involved. Certain measures could be taken which would undoubtedly improve the social and economic lot of the peasant and result in greater all-round prosperity.

1. The most important measure is to give the peasant security of tenure. It is no accident that where the peasant enjoys some security of tenure the land tends to be better cultivated and the peasant less poverty-stricken. The system of annual or periodic distribution by lot of the village lands among the peasants does not make for good cultivation. It is not, however, only the possibility of eviction which makes for insecurity in the position of the peasant, but also the almost unlimited power which the landowner or his representative in the person of the *kadkhudā* exercises *vis-à-vis* the peasant, and the constant fear of unfair discrimination and extortion.

2. The substitution of fixed rents for crop-sharing and the fixing of minimum periods for leases is desirable.[1] The traditional relationship in most areas is a crop-sharing relationship, but this does not encourage the exercise of initiative on the part of the peasant, who knows that only a fraction of the benefit of any extra labour which he may put into the land will accrue to him, the remainder going to the landowner. Here, again, it is no accident that in those areas where the peasant pays a fixed rent the standard of cultivation and prosperity is higher than in the neighbouring crop-sharing areas.

It is clear that the large share taken by the landlord in some areas, coupled with various dues demanded from the peasant, is an important factor contributing to the poverty of the peasant, but it is also true to say that in some areas even if the peasant's share were materially increased he would still in many cases not receive adequate subsistence. Suggestions for increasing the peasant's share of the crop are sometimes made. The great diversity of

[1] Where there are great fluctuations in price level crop-sharing has advantages. If, however, some measure of price control is maintained, there is a strong case for fixed rents.

practice in connexion with crop-sharing has been shown in Chapter XVII. It would be difficult to devise measures which would fit all localities. More fundamental measures are required to solve the problem of rural poverty than merely an adjustment of the crop-sharing system. But, clearly, some scheme for the control of crop-sharing (where this continues to exist) and rents should be devised to ensure an improvement in the condition of the peasants.

3. Labour service should be abolished. The element of personal subjection implicit in the performance of labour service is an anachronism and an important factor in depressing the status of the peasant. Where services are required these should be paid for. The abolition of labour service would improve both the economic and the social status of the peasant.

4. The peasants should be encouraged to plant gardens and be given land in which to make them. Where possible the ownership of their houses should be transferred to them.

5. The high proportion of absentee landlords and abnormally large landed estates makes neither for agricultural prosperity nor for social contentment. Some limitation upon the size of the large estates is desirable. Experience also suggests that the joint ownership of property by various small landowners, as distinct from peasant proprietors, is unsatisfactory. The absence of co-operation between the various partners does not make for the full development of the land.

Although it has been suggested in Chapter XIV that the villages held by peasant proprietors tend to be more carefully cultivated and the standard of living of the peasant proprietors to be higher than that of share-cropping peasants, it would nevertheless be unwise to assume that an abrupt change from large landed proprietorship to peasant proprietorship is practical. As already pointed out, in areas requiring heavy capital and current expenditure on irrigation the peasant proprietor is not in a position to undertake this (and co-operative societies with or without government participation have yet to show that they can function satisfactorily). Further, in areas where the peasant has for years been living in abject poverty and virtual submission to the landowner he has probably not the initiative or experience successfully to accomplish an abrupt change in status. At the same time, some scheme for the gradual distribution among peasant proprietors of a proportion of the large landed estates would appear to be desirable. Land for such a distribution might perhaps be acquired by the imposition of death duties. A further distribution of *khāliṣeh* under adequate supervision among peasant proprietors is another way of increasing peasant proprietorship. The failure of the experiments in Sīstān and Khūzistān to accomplish this object make it clear, however, that the success of any such scheme depends upon the integrity with which it is carried out.

6. Steps to bring about the development of undeveloped areas should be encouraged. This would involve the provision and control of capital. The form which this development should take will vary in the different areas. In some districts there are possibilities of increased arable farming. In other districts conditions are suitable for fruit-growing. In this connexion an interesting experiment has been carried out in the Jabal Bāriz and in Bāft in the province of Kirmān. Woodland in those areas belonging to the state has been rented by one of the local landowners, who has started to graft almond and pistachio on to the wild *bāneh* tree.[1] As long as the return on capital offered by non-agricultural investment gives a larger and quicker return than land, the wealthy are unlikely to invest considerable sums in land development. Coupled with this is the problem of those areas which as a result of natural circumstances do not offer an adequate livelihood to the peasant. Some scheme for the resettlement of the population of these areas in more fertile regions might be devised, but unless it offers a certain degree of security (which no government in the present state of affairs can really offer), it is unlikely that any but a few would wish to move.

Lastly there is the question of social services. Failure to improve them, if not fatal, will at least reduce the possibilities of the success of any reforms. The country urgently needs (1) health services, and in particular public hygiene and preventive medicine; and (2) an extension of education services, improved methods of research, and the dissemination of information.[2] As long as there are no social services or amenities in the rural districts the tendency to abandon country life for town life is likely to increase rather than decrease.

To sum up, the central problem is a political or a social problem. If the present situation as regards land tenure and rural organiza-

[1] The lease of these woodlands is for a term of forty years. The lessee undertakes to graft the trees and to pay one-quarter of the produce to the state. He has been engaged in this work for ten to fourteen years. Several permanent keepers are employed and a number of grafters in the grafting season. The nut harvest is gathered mainly by casual labour. Considerable expenditure is involved in bringing these woodlands into production, and for their full development security is essential. For example, for a period after Shahrīvar 1320/August–September 1941 work was stopped because of the prevailing insecurity.

The example of Iṣṭahbānāt (see above, p. 326) might well be followed in other areas where natural conditions are similar. A prerequisite to the spread of such a development, however, is the establishment of security greater than that which prevails at the present day. However, Iṣṭahbānāt is a glowing example of what can be done by local enterprise.

[2] For a discussion of some of the problems of rural education see H. B. Allen, *Rural Education and Welfare in the Middle East* (London, H.M.S.O., 1946).

tion results from the social system, nothing short of a fundamental change in the conception of society and the relation of the individual to society is likely to bring about a reform of conditions. Rural Persia is not in a vacuum, and reform in rural matters can only take place as part of a general reorganization of the country. Similarly, events in Persia as a whole are to some extent conditioned by her position in the world and interrelated with international events. Consequently it would be unreal to expect any substantial measure of rural reform in Persia in isolation, and apart from a settlement of the general social, political, and financial problems of the country.

APPENDIX I

THE CIVIL CODE, CHAPTER 3, SECTION 5

On Contracts for Agricultural and Harvesting Purposes

SUBSECTION 1

On Contracts for Crop-Sharing (muzāra'eh)

Art. 518. A *muzāra'eh* is a contract in virtue of which one of the two parties gives to the other a piece of land for a specified time so that he shall cultivate it and divide the proceeds.

Art. 519. In a contract of *muzāra'eh* the share of both the *muzāri'* and *'āmil* must be specified by way of undivided shares, as, for instance, a quarter, or a third, or a half, etc., and if the share is specified in any other way the rules for a *muzāra'eh* shall not apply.

Art. 520. In a *muzāra'eh* it is lawful to make a condition that one of the two parties should give to the other party some other thing in addition to a share from the produce.

Art. 521. In a contract of *muzāra'eh* it is possible for both the seed and the means of cultivation to belong either to the *muzāri'* or the *'āmil.* In this case also the share of each party will be as set out in the contract or as laid down by the customary law of the district.

Art. 522. In a contract of *muzāra'eh* it is not necessary that the possessor of the land should be the proprietor, but it is necessary that he should be the proprietor of the profits of the land; or that in some other manner, such as by way of guardianship (*vilāyat*), etc., he has the right of possession of the land.

Art. 523. The land which is the subject of a *muzāra'eh* must be capable of being cultivated in the way desired, although it may need working or water, and if the cultivation of the land demands operations of which at the time of the contract the *'āmil* was ignorant, such as the construction of a water-channel, or of a well, etc., he will have the right of cancellation of the transaction.

Art. 524. The kind of cultivation must be specified in the contract of *muzāra'eh*, unless it is known from local custom, or unless the contract was for cultivation in a general sense; in the latter case the *'āmil* will be entitled to choose the kind of cultivation which he prefers.

Art. 525. The contract of *muzāra'eh* is a binding contract.

Art. 526. Either the *'āmil* or the *muzāri'* may, in case of deceit, cancel the contract.

Art. 527. If, owing to the loss of water or other causes of this nature, the land becomes unfitted for cultivation and it is impossible to remove the cause of this defect, the contract of *muzāra'eh* is cancelled.

Art. 528. If a third person, before the land which is the subject of a *muzāra'eh* is delivered to the *'āmil*, seizes the land, the *'āmil* has an option of cancellation: but if he seizes the land after delivery the *'āmil* has no right of cancellation.

Art. 529. A contract of *muzāra'eh* will not be void owing to the death of the parties or of one of them, unless a condition has been made that the *'āmil* should supervise the work himself; in that case the contract is cancelled when he dies.

Art. 530. If a person has a life interest in the profits of a property and has given that property for development under a *muzāra'eh*, the contract of *muzāra'eh* will be cancelled by his death.

Art. 531. After the appearance of the harvest resulting from the cultivation, the *'āmil* becomes the owner of his share of the harvest.

Art. 532. If, in the contract of *muzāra'eh*, it is laid down that the whole of the harvest shall belong to the *muzāri'* alone or to the *'āmil*, the contract is void.

Art. 533. If a contract of *muzāra'eh* for some reason becomes void, the whole of the harvest becomes the property of the owner of the seed, and the other party, who was the owner of the land or of the water or [who provided] the labour, is entitled to a reasonable compensation in proportion to that which he owned.

If the seed was furnished partly by the *muzāri'* and partly by the *'āmil*, the harvest and the compensation will also be divided among them in the same proportions as the seed was owned.

Art. 534. If the *'āmil*, during the course of the work or at the beginning, abandons it, and if there is no one to carry out the work in his place, the judge at the demand of the *muzāri'* will compel the *'āmil* to carry out the work, or will continue the work at the expense of the *'āmil*, and if this is impossible the *muzāri'* has the right of cancellation.

Art. 535. If the *'āmil* does not cultivate the land, and the period comes to an end, the *muzāri'* is entitled to a reasonable compensation.

Art. 536. If the *'āmil* does not use proper care in cultivation, and the harvest becomes less owing to this fact, or any other loss results for the *muzāri'*, the *'āmil* will become liable for the difference.

Art. 537. If in the contract of a *muzāra'eh* it is laid down that a particular thing shall be cultivated, and the *'āmil* cultivates something else, the *muzāra'eh* is void and the provisions of Art. 533 will be applied.

Art. 538. If the *muzāra'eh* is cancelled during the period previous to the appearance of the harvest, the harvest belongs to the owner of the seed, and the other party will be entitled to a reasonable compensation.

Art. 539. If the *muzāra'eh* is cancelled after the appearance of the harvest, both the *muzāri'* and the *'āmil* share the harvest in proportion to the arrangement between them, but, from the date of the cancellation, up to the gathering of the harvest, each will be entitled to a reasonable compensation for the land, the work, and the implements belonging to him, payable from the proportional share of the other party.

Art. 540. If the period of the *muzāra'eh* comes to an end and it happens that the harvest is not ripe, the *muzāri'* has the right to destroy the crops, or to let them be in return for a reasonable compensation.

Art. 541. The *'āmil* may take a wage-earner for the cultivation, or take a partner, but the consent of the *muzāri'* is necessary for transferring the responsibility of the transaction or for the surrender of the land to another person.

Art. 542. The land tax (*kharāj*) is the responsibility of the proprietor, unless the contrary is stipulated in the agreement; the rest of the expenses of the land depends upon the agreement of the two parties, or on custom.

SUBSECTION 2

On Contracts for Sharing the Produce of Trees, etc. (*musāqāt*)

Art. 543. By a contract for irrigational purposes (*musāqāt*) is meant a transaction which takes place between an owner of trees and similar things and an *ʿāmil*, in return for a specified undivided share of the produce, the word 'produce' including fruit, leaves, flowers, etc.

Art. 544. In a case where the contract of *musāqāt* is void or is cancelled, the whole of the produce is the property of the owner, and the *ʿāmil* will have the right to a reasonable compensation.

Art. 545. The dispositions relating to a *muzāraʿeh* mentioned in the previous subsection will also apply to contracts of *musāqāt*, except that the *ʿāmil* cannot, without the permission of the owner, hand over the transaction to someone else or enter into partnership with someone else.

APPENDIX II

WEIGHTS AND MEASURES; CURRENCY

THE geographers give a bewildering picture of the variety of weights and measures used in the Persian provinces in early and medieval Islamic times. The nomenclature to some extent coincides with that of the present day; then, as now, there was a close connexion between weights and surface measures. Not only did the value of the various weights and measures vary from place to place, but they also varied with the article to be weighed and the type of land to be measured.

The *jarīb* was a surface measure in Fārs where, according to Iṣṭakhrī and Ibn Ḥauqal, there was a large *jarīb* and a small *jarīb*; the former was three and two-third times the latter, which was 60 sq. *z̤ar'* of 9 *qaṣab*.[1] Muqaddasī, however, states that the large *jarīb* was 70 sq. *z̤ar'* of 9 *qaṣab*.[2] In addition to these two main types of *jarīb*, there were a great many local variations also. In Shīrāz, according to Iṣṭakhrī and Ibn Ḥauqal, the *jarīb* was composed of 10 *qafīz* of 16 *riṭl* each, with slight variations according to the nature of the crop to be measured. The *jarīb* and *qafīz* of Iṣṭakhr were half those of Shīrāz:[3] those of Bayẓā were three-twentieths larger than those of Iṣṭakhr,[4] or according to Ibn Ḥauqal, one-quarter larger;[5] those of Kām Fīrūz were two-fifths those of Bayẓā, of Arrajān one-quarter larger than those of Shīrāz, of Shāpūr and Kāzirūn three-fifths larger, of Fasā one-tenth smaller.[6] In the Jibāl the *jarīb* comprised 10 *qafīz* and 6 *kaff*; in Ardistān it comprised 17 *mann*[7] and in Jahūdīyeh 13 *mann* of the Ardistān measure.[8] Māwardī states that the *jarīb* was 3,600 sq *z̤ar'*. He mentions seven varieties of *z̤ar'*.[9] The *Tārīkhi Qumm* describes the *jarīb* as 10 *qafīz* of 10 *'ashīr* of 36 *gaz*.[10]

The large *mann* in Shīrāz weighed 1,040 *dirhams* and the small *mann* 260 *dirhams*. The former corresponded to the *riṭl* of Ardabīl and the latter to the *mann* of 'Irāq.[11]

According to Muqaddasī the *qafīz* in Fasā comprised 6 *mann* of 300 *dirhams* for wheat: whereas the *qafīz* for almonds and barley was 6 ordinary *mann*, for rice, chickpeas, and lentils 8 *mann*. In Nayrīz the *qafīz* was 3 Baghdād *riṭl* for barley, raisins, and millet, while for wheat it was larger. The *mann* of Arrajān was 3 *riṭl*, except for sugar (which was reckoned at about 2 *riṭl*).[12] In 'Irāq the *qafīz*,

[1] Iṣṭakhrī, p. 157; Ibn Ḥauqal, ii, 301. Ḥamdullāh Mustoufī states that the *jarīb* of 'Irāqi 'Arab was 60 sq. *gaz* (*Geographical Part of the Nuzhat-al-Qulūb*, p. 28).

[2] p. 451.

[3] Iṣṭakhrī, p. 156; Ibn Ḥauqal, ii. 301.

[4] Iṣṭakhrī, p. 156.

[5] ii. 301.

[6] Iṣṭakhrī, p. 156; Ibn Ḥauqal, ii. 301.

[7] The practice of the Arab geographers in the writing of the word *mann* has been followed; the correct form of the word is *man*.

[8] Muqaddasī, p. 398.

[9] *Aḥkām as-Sulṭānīya*, p. 265.

[10] See above, pp. 38–9.

[11] Iṣṭakhrī, p. 156; Ibn Ḥauqal, ii. 301.

[12] p. 452.

according to Muqaddasī, comprised 30 *mann* or 6 *makkūk*,[1] but in Marāgheh it equalled 10 *mann*.[2]

Muqaddasī states that the measures of weight in Khūzistān were the *makkūk*, *kurr*, *makhtūm*, *kaff*, and *qafīz*. The *makkūk* of Jundī Shāpūr was 3½ *mann*, the *kurr* 480 *mann* of Jundī Shapūr, which corresponded to 1,250 *mann* of Ahvāz. The *makhtūm* of Ahvāz was 2 *ṣāʿ* and was divided into 3 *kaff*; the *qafīz* for wheat was 7 *mann*, the *kurr* for wheat 1,250 *mann*, and for barley 1,000 *mann*.[3] Abū Yūsuf gives slightly different figures for the *qafīz*, *riṭl*, *ṣāʿ*, and *makhtūm*.[4]

At the turn of the thirteenth and fourteenth centuries A.D., Ghāzān Khān, the Īlkhān ruler, attempted to unify weights and measures throughout his empire.[5] 'In each province there was a [different] *kīleh*, *qafīz*, *jarīb*, and *tughār* for wheat and barley. There were many different terms, which differed in value.'[6] According to a decree issued by Ghāzān, the weights used in Tabrīz were to be taken as the standard weight. One *kīleh* was to equal 10 *manni tabrīz*, 1 *manni tabrīz* being 260 *dirhams*, and 10 *kīleh* were to equal 1 *tughār*.[7] Although it is unlikely that Ghāzān was successful in imposing a unified system throughout his empire, it is perhaps due to the measures he took that the *tabrīz mann* came to be widely used in later times.

At the present day a great variety of usage is found. In 1926, by the law passed on 31 May, an attempt was made to equate Persian measures with the metric system,[8] and finally, in March 1935, the metric system was officially introduced.[9]

The correspondences between the Persian weights and measures and the metric system were fixed by the law of 1926 as follows:

Measures of weight

10 *nukhud* (or 2 *dirhams*) = 2 grammes
1 *miṣqāl* (or 10 *dirhams*) = 10 grammes
1 *sīr* (or 75 *dirhams*) = 75 grammes
1 *chārak* (or 750 *dirhams*) = 750 grammes
1 *sang* (or 1,000 *dirhams*) = 1 kg.
1 *mann* (or 30,000 *dirhams*) = 3 kg.
1 *kharvār* (or 3,000,000 *dirhams*) = 300 kg.

Measures of length

1 *girih* = 1 decimetre
1 *gaz* = 1 m.

Measures of area

1 *qafīz* = 1 sq. decametre
1 *jarīb* = 1 ha.

[1] p. 129. [2] p. 381. [3] pp. 417–18. [4] p. 81.
[5] *T.G.*, p. 288. [6] ibid. p. 289. [7] ibid. p. 290.
[8] E. R. Lingeman, *Report on the Finances and Commerce of Persia*, 1925–7 (Dept. of Overseas Trade, 1928), p. 5.
[9] *Persian Review of Commercial Conditions, April, 1945* (Dept. of Overseas Trade, 1945), p. 5.

In fact the weights which were in common use when this law was passed and are still in use (apart from local variations) vary somewhat from the table given above, and are as follows:

Persian weight	*Metric system*	*English weight*
1 *miṣqāl*	4·64 grammes	71·6 grains
1 *sīr* (= 16 *miṣqāl*)	74·24 gr.	2 oz. 185 gr.
1 *manni tabrīz* (= 40 *sīr*)	2·970 kg.	6·5464 lb.
1 *manni shāh* (= 2 *manni tabrīz*)	5·9400 kg.	13·0928 lb.
1 *manni ray* (= 2 *manni shāh*)	11·880 kg.	26·1856 lb.
1 *kharvār* (= 100 *manni tabrīz*)[1]	297·00 kg.	654·64 lb.
3 *kharvār*	1 short ton (approx.)	1963·92 lb.
3½ *kharvār*	1 ton (approx.)	2291·24 lb.

1 *zar'* (= 16 *girih*) = 39–42 inches according to local custom.

Many districts, however, still use local weights and measures. The *jarīb*, for example, represents an area varying from some 400 sq. metres (478·4 sq. yds.) to some 1,450 sq. metres (1744·2 sq. yds.). Its size, moreover, varies in some areas according to the nature of the farming practice, a *jarīb* of unirrigated land being larger in some areas than a *jarīb* of irrigated land. This is due probably in part to the fact that the *jarīb* is not purely a surface conception but is bound up with measures of weight: since the amount of seed sown per acre of irrigated land is greater than the amount sown per acre of unirrigated land, the size of the *jarīb* varies in proportion. In some areas, in fact, land is still measured, not by area, but the amount of seed it takes, i.e. a holding is reckoned at so many *manni bazr afkan* (or an area which takes so many bushels of seed).

In Tehrān the *jarīb* is usually reckoned at 1,000 sq. metres (1,196 sq. yds.). In Iṣfahān and certain areas in the neighbourhood and in Yazd the *jarīb* equals 1,250 sq. metres (1,495 sq. yds.) and some 15 *manni tabrīz* (approx. 98 lb., or 1 bushel, 38 lb.) are sown on an average per *jarīb* in Iṣfahān.[2]

The *jarībi shāh* comprises 1,200 sq. metres (1,435 sq. yds.), and the *jarībi rasm* 760 sq. metres (908·96 sq. yds.). In various villages to the north of Iṣfahān the *jarīb* varies from locality to locality. For example, the *jarīb* of Gaz comprises 1,444 sq. *zar'* (approx. 1,732 sq. yds.), of Mūrchehkhwart 600 sq. *gaz* (approx. 717·6 sq. yds.), of Joushaqān 400 sq. metres (478·4 sq. yds.), of Kāmū 500 sq. metres (598 sq. yds.), of Natanz 800 sq. metres (957 sq. yds.), and in Ardistān 1 *jarīb* is 1,600 sq. metres (1,914 sq. yds.). In Sarāb 'Amārat (in Arāk) 16 *jarīb* irrigated land equal 1 ha., i.e. 1 *jarīb* equals 741 sq. yds. (See also below.)

A *qafīz* in the neighbourhood of Yazd is reckoned at 1,000 sq. m. (1,196 sq. yds.) and takes 6–10 *mann* (approx. 39 lb., 6 oz.–65 lb., 10 oz.) seed according to the area.[3] In Joushaqān, on the other hand, 1 *qafīz*

[1] The number of *miṣqāl* to 1 *kharvār* varies. The variations in the *kharvār*, however, are less widespread than in the *mann* and the *jarīb*, the *kharvār* of 100 *tabrīz mann* being employed in most areas. In some villages in the Qumm-Kāshān area a weight known as a *khar*, which equals 20 *manni tabrīz* (approx. 1 cwt., 19 lb.), is used.

[2] i.e. approx. 5 bushels per acre.

[3] i.e. approx. 3½–4½ bushels per acre.

comprises only 40 sq. m. (47·84 sq. yds.) and is synonymous with 1 *kīleh*.

Measures of water also vary considerably in the different areas. They are based on time, but they are also in many cases equated with the amount of land which is watered during the period. The official measurement is by *sang*, which equals so many litres of water per second. In Tehrān 1 *sang* is reckoned as that amount of water which flows through an aperture of 0·20 sq. m. (2·1528 sq. ft.) at the rate of 1 m. (1·0936 yds.) in 3 seconds.

In Kirmān 1 *sang* of water equals 24 hours' water sufficient to irrigate 2 ha. (4·94128 acres) of land. The usual term, however, for measuring water in Kirmān is *qaṣab* or *jarīb*, and is (in some areas) that amount of water needed to irrigate 25 sq. m. (29·9 sq. yds.) in 24 hours. In Iṣfahān 1 *sang* of water is reckoned as the amount of water which will irrigate 1 *jarīb* (1,495 sq. yds.) of land in 1 hour. In Shirāz the unit of water known as the *sangi dīvānī* is reckoned as the amount of water which flows through an aperture 20 cm. (7·874 in.) ×80 cm. (31·496 in.) at the rate of 1 m. (1·0936 yds.) per second. It is divided into 8 *charkh*. Five *sangi dīvānī* are reckoned as 1 *sangi āsīā gardān*. In Arāk 1 *sangi dīvānī* is that amount of water which flows through four bricks placed to form an aperture 0·20×0·20 m. (7·8632 in.×7·8632 in.). In Hamadān a similar amount of water is reckoned as 1 *sang*. In addition to the *sang*, water is measured by *ṭāq*, *dāng*, *sabū*, *sarijeh*, *jurreh*, etc., the value of which varies from place to place. In Kirmānshāh the unit of water is known as *ṭāq* or *bīl* and is the amount of water which flows through an aperture 0·25×0·25 m. (9·7212 in.×9·7212 in.). In Kāshān 1 *ṭāq* represents 12 hours' water and is subdivided into 75 *sarijeh*, and each *sarijeh* into 6 *dāng*. In Joushaqān 1 *ṭāq* comprises 80 *sarijeh*, each *sarijeh* being 8 minutes' water; in Lāstān, however, where the gardens of the village are situated, 1 *ṭaq* = 90 *sarijeh*, each *sarijeh* being 9 minutes' water. In the former case 1 *ṭāq* = 200 *jarīb* (of 478·4 sq. yds.) of land, and in the latter 35 *jarīb* of land, while in Kāmū, a neighbouring village, 1 *ṭāq* = 100 *jarīb* (of 598 sq. yds.). In the Yazd area the terms *jurreh* and *sabū* are used in many cases to denote so many minutes of water of a given *qanāt*. The amount in time varies from district to district and in volume of water from *qanāt* to *qanāt*. In Tabrīz the unit of water is known as *lūleh*, 50 *lūleh* being equal to 1 *sangi tehrān*. In Khurāsān the unit of water is in some areas known as *zouj*; approximately 5 *zouj* are equal to 1 *sang* of water as reckoned in the neighbourhood of Tehrān. In many areas the water of a *qanāt* is divided into *dāng* or *sahm*, which in turn are subdivided into *finjān*. The size of these units varies with the volume of water of the *qanāt*, a *finjān* representing usually the amount of the water which flows through a given channel during the time which a vessel with a hole in the bottom takes to sink when in a bowl of water: clearly the time varies with the size of the vessel and the hole made in it.[1]

The most commonly employed weight is the *mann*. The *manni tabrīz* and the *manni shāh* are widely employed throughout the country, but in addition there are numerous local *mann*.

[1] See also Ch. X.

In Mashhad the *tabrīz mann* of 40 *sīr* of 16 *miṣqāl* is used, but in Bīrjand a *mann* of 40 *sīr* of 9 *miṣqāl* (1·67042 kg. = 3·69095 lb.) is used and in Ṭabas a *mann* of 40 *sīr* of 8 *miṣqāl* (1·485 kg. = 3·2732 lb.).

In Khūzistān there are several *mann* in use:

1 *manni ahvāz* = 50 kg. = 110·2315 lb.
„ „ *jarrāḥīyeh* (in use in Khalafābād) = 125 kg. = 275·57875 lb.
„ „ *bihbahān* = 67 kg. = 147·71021 lb.
„ „ *ḥoumehyi bihbahān* (i.e. the *mann* used in the area surrounding Bihbahān as distinct from the town itself) = 70 kg. = 154.3241 lb.)
„ „ *zaytūn* (also in use in the neighbourhood of Bihbahān) = 80 kg. = 176·3704 lb.)
„ „ *dizfūl* = 35 kg. = 77·16205 lb.
„ „ *rām hurmuz* = 25 kg. = 55·11575 lb.
„ „ *shūsht* (in use in Shūsht, near Bāsht) = 7 kg. = 15·43241 lb.
„ „ *shādagān* = *c.* 128 kg. = *c.* 282·19264 lb.
„ „ *khurramshahr* = *c.* 75 kg. = *c.* 165·34725 lb.*
„ „ *havīzeh* = 15 *manni tabrīz* = 44·55 kg. = 98·196 lb.
„ „ *gundūzlū* = 15 kg. = 33·06945 lb.

* This is approximately equal to the *manni baṣreh.*

Similarly in Fārs there are considerable local variations:

1 *manni farrāshband* = 4 kg. = 8·81852 lb.
„ „ *fīrūzābād* = 3½ kg. = 7·71616 lb.
„ „ *nayrīz* = 736 *miṣqāl* = 7·52886 lb.
„ „ *shīrāz* = 720 *miṣqāl* = 7·36470 lb.
„ „ *kāzirūn* = 4·8 kg. = 10·58222 lb.
3 „ *jahrum* = 10 kg. = 22·04630 lb.
1 „ *shāpūr* varies from village to village.
1 *sangi hāshim* (used in Dashtistān) = 16 *manni kāzirūn* = 76·8 kg. = 169·31552 lb.

There is a variety of other local *mann*, including the *manni ahar*, which is the equivalent of 9·4 kg. (20·72352 lb.) and the *manni sāveh*, which equals some 12 kg. (approx. 26·45556 lb.), in use in Ahar and Sāveh respectively, the *manni kurdistān* which is 5·23704 lb. and the *manni zābul* used in Sīstān.

CURRENCY

The official unit of currency is the *rīāl* composed of 1,000 *dīnārs*. The term *tūmān*, while not in official use, is commonly employed to designate 10 rs. Similarly, *qirān*[1] is sometimes used synonymously with

[1] In the 30th year of his reign Fatḥ ʿAlī Shāh (A.D. 1797–1834) adopted the title Ṣāḥib Qirān. This title was added to coins struck thereafter in his name, and the coin which was formerly known as *yak hazār*, which was equal to one-tenth of a *tūmān*, came to be known as *qirān*. Subsequently, in the reign of Riẓā Shāh, the term *rīāl*, which had formerly, in the time of Muḥammad Shāh (A.D. 1907–9), been a silver coin equal to 1,250 *dīnārs*, came to be used in place of *qirān* and the earlier *yak hazār* (Mustoufī, *Sharḥi Zindagīyi Man*, i. 53).

rīāl. The official rate of exchange at the time of writing is 89·40 rs. to the pound sterling. During recent years the rate on the free market has varied from 120 to 240. In order to avoid confusion 170 has been taken as an average rate for the conversion of *rīāls* to the pound sterling in Part II of this work.

For a discussion of the currency of the rulers of Persia from 1500 to 1941 the reader is referred to the monograph by Mr. H. L. Rabino di Borgomale entitled *Coins, Medals, and Seals of the Shāhs of Irān, 1500–1941*.

BIBLIOGRAPHY

I. PERSIAN MANUSCRIPT SOURCES

ʿAbd ar-Razzāq b. Jalāl ad-Dīn Isḥāq Samarqandī, *see* Kamāl ud-Dīn.

Abu'l Qāsim Īvāghlī, *see* Īvāghlī Ḥaydar.

Afẓal ul-Mulk, *Safar Nāmehyi Afẓal ul-Mulk bi Qumm.* Dated 1324/1906, Library of the National Consultative Assembly, Tehrān.

Ḥāfiẓ Abrū, *Jughrāfīā.* B.M. Or. 9316.

—— *Jughrāfīā.* In possession of Ḥājjī Ḥusayn Malik. (Unless otherwise stated the references in the text are to this manuscript.)

—— *Khulāṣat ul-Buldān.* B.M. Or. 8375.

Ḥusayn b. Ibrāhīm Khān Iṣfahānī, *Tārīkhi Iṣfahān.* In M.F.A., No. 726.

Ḥusayn b. Muḥammad b. Abī Riẓā al-Ḥusaynī, *Majmūʿehyi Rasā'il dar Tārīkhi Iṣfahān.* B.M. Or. 10,980. (This is a Persian rescension of Māfarūkhī's *Maḥāsin Iṣfahān.*)

Īvāghlī Ḥaydar: Abu'l Qāsim Īvāghlī Ḥaydar Beg. *Majmaʿ al-Inshā,* or *Nuskhehyi Jāmiʿehyi Murāsilāti ūlu 'l-Albāb.* B.M. Add. 7688.

Kamāl ud-Dīn: ʿAbd ar-Razzāq b. Jalāl ad-Dīn Isḥāq Samarqandī (Kamāl ud-Dīn), *Maṭlaʿ as-Saʿdayn.* B.M. Add. 17928.

Kurāsat ul-Maʿī. Library of the National Consultative Assembly, Tehrān.

Māfarūkhī, *see* Ḥusayn b. Muḥammad b. Abī Riẓā al-Ḥusaynī.

Mīrzā ʿAbd ar-Raḥmān b. Muḥammad Ibrāhīm al-Qāsānī, *Mir'āt al-Qāsān.* B.M. Or. 3603.

Mīrzā ʿAlī Khān Nā'īnī, *Safar Nāmeh.* In M.F.A., No. 726.

Mīrzā Sayyid Mihdī, *Tārīkhi Qumm.* Dated 1295/1878, in M.F.A., No. 725.

Munsha'āti ʿAhdi Saljūqī va Khwārazmshāhīān va Avā'ili ʿAhdi Mughul. Photostat copy of manuscript which is in the Asiatic Museum in the Academy of Sciences, Leningrad. *See* Victor Rosen, *Les Manuscrits persans de l'Institut des Langues Orientales,* St. Petersburg, 1886, No. 26, pp. 146–59.

Muntakhab ud-Dīn Badīʿ al-Kātib al-Juvaynī, *ʿAtabat al-Katabat.* Photostat copy of manuscript which is in the Dār ul-Kutub ul-Miṣrīya, Cairo.

Najm ul-Mulk: ʿAbd ul-Ghaffār Najm ul-Mulk, *Report on Khūzistān.* In M.F.A., No. 725.

—— *Safar Nāmehyi ʿArabistān.* In M.F.A., No. 725.

Niẓām ul-Mulk, *Naṣā'iḥ Nāmeh* (also called *Vaṣāyā Nāmeh*). In my possession.

Sulūk va Sijillāti Taymūrī. In the Library of the Shrine of the Imām Riẓā in Mashhad.

II. PERSIAN AND ARABIC PRINTED AND LITHOGRAPHIC SOURCES

ʿAbd ul-Fattāḥ Fūminī, *see below,* Dorn, B. (3).

ʿAbd ur-Razzāq b. Najaf Qulī, *The Dynasty of the Kajars, translated from the . . . MS. presented . . . to Sir H. J. Brydges* [by Sir H. H. Brydges and David Shea] . . . *to which is prefixed a succinct account of the history of Persia, previous to that period.* London, 1833.

Abū Naṣr Aḥmad b. Muḥammad b. Naṣr al-Qubāvī, *see* Narshakhī.

Abū Nu'aym, *Ẕikr Akhbār Iṣbahān* (*Geschichte Iṣbahāns*), ed. Sven Dederin. Leyden, 1931–4. 2 vols.

Abū Yūsuf (Ya'qūb b. Ibrāhīm), *Kitab El Kharadj* (*Le Livre de l'impôt foncier*), tr. E. Fagnan. Paris, 1921.

Abu'l Ḥasan b. Muḥammad Amīn Gulistāneh, *Mujmal ut-Tavārīkh pas az Nādir*, ed. Mudarris Riẕavī. Tehrān, 1320/1941–2.

Ādamīyat, *Amīr Kabīr va Irān*. Tehrān, 1323/1944–5. 2 vols.

Afẕal ud-Dīn Abū Ḥamīd Aḥmad b. Ḥamīd Kirmānī, *'Iqd ul-'Ūlā*, ed. 'Alī Muḥammad 'Āmirī Nā'īnī. Tehrān, 1311/1932–3.

Aḥmad b. Abi 'l-Khayr Zarkūb, *Shīrāz Nāmeh*, ed. Bahman Karīmī. Tehrān, 1310/1931–2.

Aḥmad b. Ḥusayn b. 'Alī al-Kātib, *Tārīkhi Jadīdi Yazd*. Yazd, 1317/1938–9.

'Alī b. Abī Ṭālib, *Nahj al-Balāgha*. Beyrut, 1307/1889. 2 vols.

'Alī b. Shams ad-Dīn, *see below*, Dorn, B. (2).

'Alī b. Zayd al-Bayhaqī (Ẓahīr ud-Dīn), *Tārīkhi Bayhaq*, ed. Aḥmad Bahmanyār. Tehrān, 1317/1938–9.

Anṣārī: Ḥājjī Mīrzā Ḥasan Khān Shaykh Jābiri Anṣārī, *Tārīkhi Iṣfahān*. Tehrān, 1322/1944.

Bahā ud-Dīn 'Āmilī: Muḥammad b. Ḥusayn Bahā ud-Dīn 'Āmilī, *Jāmi'i 'Abbāsī*. Bombay, lith., 1884.

Bahā ud-Dīn Muḥammad b. Mu'ayyad Baghdādī, *at-Tavassul ila 't-Tarassul*, ed. Aḥmad Bahmanyār. Tehrān, 1315/1936–7.

al-Balāẕurī, *Kitāb Futūḥ al-Buldān* (*Liber expugnationis regionum, &c.*), ed. M. J. de Goeje. Brill, Leyden, 1866.

Bāvar: Maḥmūd Bāvar, *Kūhgīlūyeh va Tlāti Ān*. Tehrān (?), 1324/1945.

Bayhaqī: Abu'l Faẕl Muḥammad b. al-Ḥusayn Bayhaqī, *Tārīkhi Bayhaqī*, ed. Ghanī and Fayyāẕ. Tehrān, 1324/1945–6.

al-Bayhaqī, *see* 'Alī b. Zayd.

Bidlīsī: Sharaf Khān b. Shams ad-Dīn Bidlīsī, *Scheref-Nameh*, ed. V. Veliaminof-Zernof. St. Petersburg, 1860–2. 2 vols.

al-Bukhārī, *see* Peltier, F.

Bundārī: Muḥammad al-Iṣfahānī Bundārī, *Zubdat an-Nuṣrat wa Nukhbat al-'Uṣrat* (in *Recueil de textes relatifs à l'histoire des Seldjoucides*), ed. M. T. Houtsma. Leyden, 1889.

Dorn, B., *Muhammedanische Quellen zur Geschichte des südlichen Küstenländer des Kaspischen Meeres*. St. Petersburg, 4 pts.

—— (1) *Sehir Eddin's Geschichte von Tabaristan, Rujan und Masanderan*. Pers. text, 1850.

—— (2) *'Aly ben Schems-Eddin's chanisches Geschichtswerk oder Geschichte von Gilan in den Jahren 880 (–1475) bis 920 (–1514)*. Pers. text, 1857.

—— (3) *'Abdu'l-Fattāh Fumeny, Geschichte von Gilan, 1517–1678*. Pers. text, 1858.

—— (4) *Auszüge aus muhammed. Schriftstellern betreffend die Gesch. und Geogr. d. südl. Küstenländer des Kasp. Meeres*, 1858.

Fasā'ī: Ḥājjī Mīrzā Ḥasan Fasā'ī, *Fārs Nāmehyi Nāṣirī*. Tehrān, lith., 1894–6. 2 vols.

Gardīzī, *Zayn ul-Akhbār*, ed. Muḥammad Nāẓim, ed. *Iranschähr*. Berlin, 1928.

Ghazālī, *Iḥyā 'Ulūm ad-Dīn*. Cairo, 1346/1929. 4 vols.

—— *Kīmīā as-Sa'ādat*. Bombay, lith.

—— *Naṣīḥat ul-Mulūk*, ed. Jalāl Humā'ī. Tehrān, 1315–17/1936–9.

Ḥamdullāh Mustoufī, *The Geographical Part of the Nuzhat-al-Qulūb*, ed. G. Le Strange. G.M.S. London, Leyden, 1919.

Ḥamdullāh Mustoufī, *Ta'rīkh-i-Guzīda*, ed. E. G. Browne. G.M.S. London, Leyden, 1910–13. 2 vols.

Ḥasan b. 'Alī b. 'Abd al-Malik Qummī, *see* Ḥasan b. Muḥammad b. Ḥasan al-Qummī.

Ḥasan b. Muḥammad b. Ḥasan al-Qummī, *Tārīkhi Qumm*, translated into Persian by Ḥasan b. 'Alī b. Ḥasan b. 'Abd al-Malik, ed. Sayyid Jalāl ud-Dīn Tehrānī. Tehrān, 1313/1934.

Hilāl as-Sābī: Hilāl b. al-Muḥassin as-Sābī, *The Historical Remains of Hilāl al-Sābī*, ed. H. F. Amedroz. Leyden, 1904. *See also* Amedroz.

Ḥusayn b. Abdāl Zāhidī, *Silsilat an-Nasabi Ṣafavīyeh*, ed. *Iranschähr*. Berlin, 1924–5.

Ḥusayn b. Muḥammad b. Abi'l-Riẓā Āvī, *Tarjumehyi Maḥāsini Iṣfahān*, ed. 'Abbās Iqbāl. Tehrān, 1328/1949–50.

Ibn ul-Athīr, *Histoire des Atabecs de Mosul*, 1876, in *Recueil des historiens des Croisades*, ii. 2.

—— *al-Kāmil fi't-Ta'rīkh*, ed. C. J. Tornberg. Brill, Lugduni Batavorum, 1851–76. 14 vols.

Ibn Bābūyeh: Muḥammad b. 'Alī (Ibn Bābūyeh), *Kitāb Man lā Yaḥẓuruh al-Faqīh*. Tehrān, lith., 1324/1906–7.

Ibn Balkhī, *Fārs-nāma*, ed. G. Le Strange and R. A. Nicholson. G.M.S. London, Leyden, 1921.

Ibn Bībī, *Mukhtaṣari Saljūqnāmeh* (*Histoire des Seldjoucides d'Asie Mineure*), ed. M. T. Houtsma. Leyden, 1902.

Ibn ul-Faqīh al-Hamadānī, *Kitāb al-Buldān*, ed. de Goeje. *Bibl. Geog. Arab.* Brill, Leyden, 1885.

Ibn Ḥauqal, *Kitāb Ṣūrat al-Arẓ* (*Liber imaginis terrae*), ed. J. H. Kramers. *Bibl. Geog. Arab.* Leyden, 1938–9. 2 vols.

Ibn Isfandīār: Muḥammad b. al-Ḥasan b. Isfandīār, *Tārīkhi Ṭabaristān*, ed. 'Abbās Iqbāl. Tehrān, 1320. Vol. 1, 2 pts.

Ibn Jamā'a, 'Tahrīr al-Aḥkām fī Tadbīri Ahli Islām', *Islamica*, vi. 4, 353–414.

Ibn Jouzī, *al-Muntaẓam fi't-Ta'rīkhi 'l-Mulūk wa'l-Umam*. Vols. 5–10. Haydarabad, 1357–9/1938–41.

Ibn Khallikān, *Biographical Dictionary*, tr. from the Arabic by Baron M. G. de Slane. Paris, 1842–71. 4 vols.

Ibn Khurdādbeh, *Kitāb al-Masālik wa'l-Mamālik*, ed. de Goeje. *Bibl. Geog. Arab.* Brill, Leyden, 1889.

Ibn Miskawaih, *The Eclipse of the 'Abbasid Caliphate*, ed. H. F. Amedroz and D. S. Margoliouth. Oxford, 1921. 7 vols.

—— *Tajārib al-Umam*, ed. L. Caetani. Vols. 1, 5, and 6. G.M.S. London, Leyden, 1909–17.

Ibn an-Niẓām al-Ḥusaynī: Muḥammad b. Muḥammad, called Ibn an-Niẓām al-Ḥusaynī, *al-'Urāẓa fi'l-Ḥikāyat as-Saljūqīya*, ed. Süssheim. Leyden, 1909.

Ibn Rustah, *Kitāb al-A'laq an-Nafīsa*, ed. de Goeje. *Bibl. Geog. Arab.* Brill, Leyden, 1892.

Ibn Wāẓiḥ: Aḥmad b. Abī Ya'qūb b. Wāẓiḥ, *Kitāb al-Buldān*, ed. Gaston Wiet. Cairo, 1937.

—— *Ta'rīkh* (*Ibn Wādhih qui dicitur al-Ja'qūbī historiae*), ed. M. T. Houtsma. Brill, 1883. 2 vols.

Iskandar Beg (Iskandar Munshī), *Tārīkhi 'Ālam-ārāyi 'Abbāsī*. Tehrān, lith., 1314/1896–7.

Iṣṭakhrī, *Kitāb Masālik al-Mamālik* (*Viae regnorum*), ed. de Goeje. *Bibl. Geog. Arab.* Brill, Leyden, 1927.

I'timād as-Salṭaneh, *see* Muḥammad Ḥasan Khān Marāgheh'ī.

AL-JAHSHYĀRĪ: Muḥammad b. 'Abdūs al-Jahshyārī, *Kitāb al-Wuzarā wa'l-Kuttāb*, ed. Muṣṭafa as-Saqqā, Ibrāhīm al-Ābyārī, and Abd al-Ḥāfiẓ Shalabī. Cairo, 1938.

JALĀL UD-DĪN DAVVĀNĪ, *Practical Philosophy of the Muhammadan People, being a translation of the Akhlāk-i-Jalāly*, by W. F. Thompson, London, 1839.

JUVAYNĪ: 'Alā ud-Dīn 'Atā Malik b. Bahā ad-Dīn, *The Ta'rīkh-i-Jahān-Gushā*, ed. Mīrzā Muḥammad Qazvīnī. G.M.S. London, Leyden, 1912–37. 3 vols.

KASRAVĪ: Sayyid Aḥmad Kasravī, *Tārīkhi Pānṣadsālehyi Khūzistān*. Tehrān, 1313/1934–5.

KĀ'ŪS B. ISKANDAR B. QĀBŪS SHAMS AL-MA'ĀLĪ, *Qābūs Nāmeh*. Tehrān, lith.

KHWĀNDAMĪR, *Habīb us-Sīār*. Bombay, 1847. 3 vols.

AL-KHWĀRAZMĪ: Muḥammad b. Aḥmad al-Khwārazmī, *Mafātīḥ al-'Ulūm* (*Liber Mafâtîh al-Olûm*), ed G. van Vloten. Leyden, 1895.

LISĀN UL-MULK SIPIHR, *Tārīkh va Jughrāfīāyi Dār as-Salṭanehyi Tabrīz*. Tehrān, lith., 1223/1808–9.

—— *Tārīkhi Qājārīyeh, being the final part of the universal history entitled the 'Nāsikh ut-Tavārīkh'*. Tabrīz, lith., 1319/1901–2. 3 vols. in 1.

MĀFARŪKHĪ, *Maḥāsin Iṣfahān*, ed. Sayyid Jalāl ud-Dīn Tehrānī. Tehrān, 1933(?).

MAR'ASHĪ, *see* Ẓahīr ud-Dīn al-Mar'ashī.

MAS'ŪDĪ, *Kitāb at-Tanbīh wa'l-Ischrāf*, ed. M. J. de Goeje. *Bibl. Geog. Arab*. Brill, Leyden, 1894.

—— *Murūj az-Ẕahab* (*Les Prairies d'or*), text and tr. by C. Barbier de Meynard and Pavet de Courteille. Paris, 1861–77, 9 vols.

MATĪN DAFTARĪ, *Ā'īni Dādrasīyi Madanī*. Vol. 1. Tehrān, 1324/1945–6.

MĀWARDĪ: Abu'l-Ḥasan 'Alī b. Muḥammad Māwardī, *al-Aḥkām as-Sulṭānīya* (*Maverdii constitutiones politicae*), ed. R. Enger. Bonn, 1853.

MĪRZĀ MUḤAMMAD KALĀNTARI FĀRS, *Rūznāmeh*, ed. 'Abbās Iqbāl. Tehrān, 1325/1946.

MUḤ. ḤASAN KHĀN MARĀGHEH'Ī, SANĪ' UD-DOULEH (I'timad as-Salṭaneh), *Kitāb al-Ma'āṣar wa'l-Āṣār*. Tehrān, lith, 1306/1888–9.

—— *Maṭla' ash-Shams*. Tehrān, lith., 1301–3/1884–5. 3 vols.

—— *Mir'āt ul-Buldān*. Tehrān, 1294–7/1877–80. 4 vols.

—— *Tārīkhi Muntaẓami Nāṣirī*. Tehrān, lith., 1881–3.

MUḤ. IBRĀHĪM, *Tārīkhi Saljūqīāni Kirmān* (*Histoire des Seldjoucides du Kirmân*), ed. M. T. Houtsma. Leyden, 1886.

MUḤ. JA'FAR KHWURMUJĪ, *Āṣāri Ja'farī*. Tehrān, 1860.

MUḤ. NĀṢIR (Furṣat) and MĪRZĀ ĀQĀ ḤUSAYNĪ, *Āṣāri 'Ajam*. Bombay, lith., 1314/1896.

MUḤ. QAZVĪNĪ, *see* Qazvīnī.

MUḤ. B. 'ABDŪS AL-JAHSHYĀRĪ, *see* al-Jahshyārī.

MUḤ. B. AḤMAD AL-KHWĀRAZMĪ, *see* al-Khwārazmī.

MUḤ. B. 'ALĪ (Ibn Bābūyeh), *see* Ibn Bābūyeh.

MUḤ. B. AL-ḤASAN B. 'ALĪ ABŪ JA'FAR ṬŪSĪ, *see* Ṭūsī.

MUḤ. B. ḤUSAYN BAHĀ AD-DĪN 'ĀMILĪ, *see* Bahā ud-Dīn 'Āmilī.

MUḤ. B. MAḤMŪD ĀMULĪ, *Nafā'is ul-Funūn fī 'Arā'is il-'Uyūn*. Tehrān, lith., 2 vols. in one.

MUḤ. B. MUḤAMMAD, called Ibn an-Niẓām al-Ḥusaynī, *see* Ibn an-Niẓām.

MUḤ. B. MUḤAMMAD NAṢĪR UD-DĪN ṬŪSĪ, *Akhlāqi Nāṣirī*. Lahore, lith., 1865.

MUḤ. B. ẒUFAR B. 'UMAR, *see* Narshakhī.

AL-MUḤAQQIQ: Najm ud-Dīn Abu'l-Qāsim Ja'far b. 'Alī Yaḥyā al-Muḥaqqiq al-Avval, *Sharāyi' al-Islām fī Masā'il al-Ḥilāl wa'l-Ḥarām* (*Droit musulman*), tr. by A. Querry. Paris, 1871–2. 2 vols.

Mujmal at-Tawārīkh wa'l-Qiṣaṣ, ed. Malik ush-Shu'arā Bahār. Tehrān, 1318/1939–40.

Munsha'āt, being a Collection of Nādir Shāh's Farmāns. Lith., 1294/1877.

MUQADDASĪ, *Kitāb Aḥsan at-Taqāsīm fī Ma'rifat al-Aqālīm* (*Descriptio imperii moslemici*), ed. de Goeje. *Bibl. Geog. Arab.* Leyden, 1906.

MUSTOUFĪ: 'Abdullāh Mustoufī, *Sharḥi Zindagīyi Man: Tārīkhi Ijtimā'ī va Idārīyi Dourehyi Qājārīyeh.* Tehrān, 1324–5/1945–6. 3 vols.

NĀDIR SHĀH, *see* above, *Munsha'āt.*

NAJM UD-DĪN ABU'L-QĀSIM JA'FAR B. 'ALĪ YAḤYĀ AL-MUḤAQQIQ, *see* al-Muḥaqqiq.

NAJM UD-DĪN RĀZĪ, *Mirṣād al-'Ibād min al-Mabda' ila'l-Mi'ād*, ed. Ḥusām al-Ḥusaynī an-Ni'matullāhī. Tehrān, 1312/1933–4.

Nāmehyi Tansar, ed. Mujtabā Mīnovī. Tehrān, 1314/1935–6.

NĀMĪ: Mīrzā Muḥammad Ṣādiq Mūsavī Iṣfahānī Nāmī, *Tārīkhi Gītī Gushāy*, with *Ẕayl* by Mīrzā 'Abd ul-Karīm b. 'Alī Riẓā ash-Sharīf, and *Ẕayl* by Āqā Muḥammad Riẓāyi Shīrāzī, ed. Sa'īd Nafīsī. Tehrān, 1317/1938–9.

NARSHAKHĪ: Abū Bakr Muḥammad b. Ja'far Narshakhī, *Tārīkhi Bukhārā*, tr. into Persian by Abū Naṣr Aḥmad b. Muḥammad b. Naṣr al-Qubāvī, adapted by Muḥammad b. Ẓufar b. 'Umar, and ed. by Mudarris Riẓavī. Tehrān, 1317/1938–9.

NAṢĪR UD-DĪN ṬŪSĪ, *see* Muḥammad b. Muḥammad Naṣīr ud-Dīn Ṭūsī.

NIẒĀM UL-MULK, *Sīāsat Nāmeh*, ed. Ch. Schefer. Paris, 1891–3.

OULĪĀ ULLĀH ĀMULĪ, *Tārīkhi Rūyān*, ed. 'Abbās Khalīlī. Tehrān, 1313/1934–5.

QAZVĪNĪ: Mīrzā Muḥammad Qazvīnī. 'Farmāni Sulṭān Aḥmadi Jalā'ir', *Yādgār*, Āẕar 1323/Nov.–Dec. 1944.

QUDĀMA B. JA'FAR, *Kitāb al-Kharāj.* Text and French tr. in de Goeje, *Bibl. Geog. Arab.* Brill, Leyden, 1889.

RASHĪD UD-DĪN FAẒLULLĀH, *Histoire des Mongols de la Perse*, ed. M. Quatremère. Vol. 1. Paris, 1836.

—— *Makātībi Rashīdī*, ed. Shafī'. Lahore, 1945.

—— *Tārīkhi Mubāraki Ghāzānī* (*Geschichte Ġāzān-Ḫāns aus dem Ta'riḫ-i-Mubāraki-Ġāzānī*), ed. K. Jahn. G.M.S. London, Leyden, 1940.

AR-RĀVANDĪ: Muḥammad b. 'Alī b. Sulaymān ar-Rāvandī, *The Rāḥat-uṣ-Ṣudūr wa Āyat us-Surūr*, ed. Muḥammad Iqbāl. G.M.S. London, Leyden, 1921.

RAZMĀRĀ, 'ALĪ, *Jughrāfīāyi Niẓāmīyi Īrān* (Military Geography of Īrān). Tehrān, 1320/1941–2. 20 vols.

AS-SĀBĪ, *see* Hilāl as-Sābī.

ṢADR UD-DĪN ABU'L-ḤASAN 'ALĪ B. NĀṢIR B. 'ALĪ AL-ḤUSAYNĪ, *Akhbār 'ud-Dawlat 'is-Saljūqiyya*, ed. Muḥammad Iqbāl. Lahore, 1933.

SARDAR AS'AD (Ḥājjī 'Alī Qulī Khān), *Tārīkhi Bakhtīārī.* Tehrān (?), lith., 1333/1914–15.

SHARAF KHAN B. SHAMS AD-DĪN BIDLĪSĪ, *see* Bidlīsī.

SULṬĀN AḤMADĪ JALĀ'IR, *see above under* Qazvīnī.

ṬABARĪ, *Ta'rīkh ar-Rusūl wa'l-Mulūk* (*Annales quos scripsit Abu Djafar Mohammed ibn Djarir at-Tabari*), ed M. J. de Goeje and others. Leyden, 1879–1901. Series I, i–iv; Series II, i–iii; Series III, i–iv.

Tadhkirat al-Mulūk, Persian text in facsimile translated and explained by V. Minorsky. G.M.S. London, Leyden, 1943.

Tansar Nāmeh, see *Nāmehyi Tansar*.
Tārīkhi Sīstān, ed. Malik ush-Shuʿarā Bahār. Tehrān, 1314/1935–6.
THAʿĀLIBĪ, *Histoire des rois des Perses, par Aboû Mansoûr Abd Al-Malik ibn Mohammad b. Ismaʿil Al-Thaʿâlibî*, ed. and tr. by H. Zotenberg. Paris, 1900.
ṬŪSĪ: Muḥammad b. al-Ḥasan b. ʿAlī Abū Jaʿfar Ṭūsī, *Kitāb at-Tahẕīb min al-Kutub al-Arbaʿah*. Tehrān, lith., 1317/1899.
ʿUNṢUR UL-MAʿĀLĪ KĀʾŪS B. ISKANDAR, *see* Kāʾūs b. Iskandar b. Qābūs Shams al-Maʿālī.
VAṢṢĀF: Shihāb ud-Dīn ʿAbdullāh Sharaf Shīrāzī Vaṣṣāf, *Tārīkhi Vaṣṣāf*. Lith., 1269.
YAḤYĀ B. ĀDAM, *Kitāb al-Kharāj* (*Le Livre de l'impôt foncier*), ed. Th. W. Juynboll. Leyden, 1896.
YAʿQŪBĪ, *see* Ibn Wāẓiḥ.
YĀQŪT, *Irshādu 'l-Arīb ilā Maʿrifati 'l-Adīb*, ed. D. S. Margoliouth. G.M.S. London, Leyden, 1907–13. 7 vols.
—— *Muʿjam al-Buldān* (*Jacut's Geographisches Wörterbuch*), ed. F. Wüstenfeld. Leipzig, 1866–73. 6 vols.
ẒAHĪR UD-DĪN AL-MARʿASHĪ, *Tārīkhi Ṭabaristān va Rūyān va Māzandarān*. *See above*, Dorn, B. (1).
Ẕayli Tārīkhi ʿĀlam-ārāyi ʿAbbāsī, ed. Suhayl Khwānsārī. Tehrān, 1317/1939.

III. EUROPEAN SOURCES AND SECONDARY SOURCES

ABBOT, K. E., 'Extracts from a Memorandum on the Country of Azerbaijan', *Proc. R.G.S.*, 1863–4, viii. 275–9.
ADONTZ, N., 'L'Aspect iranien du servage', *Le Servage* (*Communications présentées à la Société Jean Bodin*, Réunions des 16, 17, et 18 Octobre 1936).
AGHNIDES, N. P., *Mohammedan Theories of Finance: with an introduction to Mohammedan Law and a bibliography*. New York, London, 1916.
ALESSANDRI, *see* Barbaro, Josafa, and Ambrogio Contarini.
ALLEN, H. B., *Rural Education and Welfare in the Middle East*. London, H.M.S.O., 1946.
AMEDROZ, H. F., 'Three Years of Buwaihid Rule in Baghdad, A.H. 389–93, being a Fragment of the History of Hilāl as-Sābī', *J.R.A.S.*, 1901, 501–36, 749–86.
AMEER ALI, *Lectures on Mahommedan Law*. Calcutta, 1885.
BAILLIE, N. B. E., *The Land Tax of India, according to the Moohummudan Law, translated from the Futawa Alumgeeree*. London, 1873.
BARBARO, JOSAFA, AND CONTARINI, AMBROGIO, *A Narrative of Italian Travels in Persia in the 15th and 16th Centuries*. Hakluyt Society, 1st ser., vol. 49.
BARTHOLD, W., 'İlhanılar Devrinde Malî Vaziyet', *Türk hukuk ve iktisat tarihi mecmuası*, 1931, i. 136–59.
——*Turkestan down to the Mongol Invasion*, 2nd ed., tr. and rev. by the author with H. A. R. Gibb. London, Leyden, G.M.S., 1928.
—— *Zwölf Vorlesungen über die Geschichte der Türken Mittelasiens*, tr. by Theodor Menzel. Berlin, 1935.
BARTHOLOMAE, C., *Zum sasanidischen Recht*. Heidelberg, 1918–23. i–v.
BECKER, C. H., 'Historische Studien über das Londoner Aphroditowerk', *Der Islam*, ii. 359–71.

Becker, C. H., *Islamstudien*. Leipzig, 1924–32. 2 vols.
—— 'Neue arabische Papyri des Aphroditofindes', *Der Islam*, ii. 245–68.
Bellew, H. W., *From the Indus to the Tigris*, London, 1874.
Bent, J. T., 'Village Life in Persia', *New Review*, October 1891.
Berchem, Max van, *La Propriété territoriale et l'impôt foncier*. Geneva, 1886.
Bouvat, L., 'L'Administration de la Perse', *R.M.M.*, xxiv. 219–45.
Browne, E. G., 'Account of a Rare MS. History of Isfahan', *J.R.A.S.*, 1901. 411–96, 661–704.
—— *The Persian Revolution of 1905–9*. Cambridge, 1910.
Bulsara, Sohrab Jamshedjee, *The Laws of the Ancient Persians as found in the 'Mâtîkân ê Hazâr Dâtastân'*. Bombay, 1937.
Cambridge Ancient History, ix and xi.
Chardin, J., *Voyages du Chevalier Chardin, en Perse, et autres lieux de l'Orient* . . ., ed. L. Langlès. Paris, 1811. 10 vols.
Chauvin, V., 'La Constitution du code théodosien sur les agri deserti et le droit arabe', *Mémoires et Publications des Sciences, des arts, et des lettres du Hainaut*, Mons, 1900.
—— 'Le Régime légal des eaux chez les Arabes', *Proc. 5th Int. Cong. Medical Hydrology, Climatology, and Geology, Liége, 1898*. Liége, 1899.
Christensen, A., *L'Iran sous les Sassanides*. Copenhagen, 1936.
—— 'Introduction bibliographique à l'histoire du droit de l'Iran ancien', *Arch. d'hist. du droit orient.*, ii. 243–57.
Chronicle of the Carmelites in Persia and the Papal Mission of the Seventeenth and Eighteenth Centuries. London, Eyre and Spottiswoode, 1939. 2 vols.
Curzon, G. N., *Persia and the Persian Question*. London, 1892. 2 vols.
Czaplika, M. A., *The Turks of Central Asia in History and at the Present Day*. Oxford, 1918.
De Morgan, J., 'Feudalism in Persia: its Origin, Development, and Present Condition', *Smithsonian Institute Report*, 1913, 579–606.
Demorgny, G., *Essai sur l'administration de la Perse*. Paris, 1913.
—— *Les Institutions financières de la Perse*. Paris, 1915.
Dennett, D. C., *Conversion and the Poll Tax in Early Islam*. Harvard University Press and Oxford University Press, 1950. (Harvard Historical Monographs, XXII.)
Djazaeri, Chams-ed-Dine, *La Crise économique mondiale et ses répercussions en Iran*. Paris, 1938.
Don Juan of Persia, a Shi'ah Catholic, 1560–1604, tr. and ed. by G. Le Strange. London, 1926.
Drouville, G., *Voyage en Perse fait en 1812 et 1813*. Paris, 1825. 2 vols.
Du Mans, R., *Estat de la Perse en 1660, par le P. Raphael Du Mans, Supérieur de la Mission des Capucins d'Isfahan*, ed. Ch. Schefer. Paris, 1890.
Encyclopaedia Britannica. 11th ed.
Encyclopaedia of Islam. Leyden, 1913– .
Fevret, E., 'Le Groupement des centres habités en Perse d'après la nature du sol', *R.M.M.*, 1907, ii. 181–98.
Fischel, W. J., *The Jews in the Economic and Political Life of Mediaeval Islam*. London, 1937. (R.A.S. Monograph.)
—— 'The Origin of Banking in Medieval Islam: a Contribution to the Economic History of the Jews in Baghdad in the Tenth Century', *J.R.A.S.*, 1933, 569–603.
FitzGerald, S. G. Vesey-, *see* Vesey-FitzGerald.

FOURNAUX, DE G., 'L'Industrie, le commerce et l'agriculture en Perse', *Bul. Soc. Geogr. Commerce. de Bordeaux*, 1887, 1–33.

FRASER, J. B., *Narrative of a Journey into Khorasān in the Years 1821 and 1822*. London, 1825.

—— *Travels and Adventures in the Persian Provinces on the Southern Banks of the Caspian Sea*. London, 1826.

—— *Travels in Koordistan, Mesopotamia, &c*. London, 1840. 2 vols.

—— *A Winter's Journey (Tâtar) from Constantinople to Tehran*. London, 1838. 2 vols.

FRYER, JOHN, *A New Account of East India and Persia, being nine years travels, in Eight Letters, Begun 1672 and Finished 1681*. London, 1698.

GEIGER, W., *Civilization of the Eastern Iranians in Ancient Times*, tr. by Darab Dastur Peshotan Sanjana. London, 1885. Vol. 1.

GIBB, H. A. R., and H. BOWEN, *Islamic Society and the West*. London, 1950. Vol. 1, pt. 1.

GOLDSMID, F. J., ed., *Eastern Persia, an Account of the Journeys of the Persian Boundary Commission, 1870–1–2*. London, 1876. 2 vols.

GONZALEZ DE CLAVIJOS, RUY, *Embassy to Tamerlane, 1403–6*, tr. from the Spanish by G. Le Strange. London, 1928.

GREAT BRITAIN, Department of Overseas Trade, *Persian Review of Economic Conditions, April 1945*.

—— *Report on the Finances and Commerce of Persia, 1925–7*, by E. R. Lingeman, 1928.

GRUNEBAUM, G. E. VON, *Medieval Islam, a Study in Cultural Orientation*. Chicago, 1946.

GURLAND, A., *Grundzüge der Muhammedanischen Agrarverfassung und Agrarpolitik*. Dorpat, 1907.

HANWAY, JONAS, *An Historical Account of the British Trade over the Caspian Sea*. London, 1753. 4 vols.

HARLEY WALKER, 'Jāhiz on the Exploits of the Turks', *J.R.A.S.*, 1915, 631–97.

HINZ, W., 'Das Steuerwesen Ostanatoliens im 15. und 16. Jahrhundert', *Z.D.M.G.*, c. 1. (New Series, xxv. 1950), 177–201.

—— 'Steuerinschriften aus dem Mittelalterlichen Vordern Orient', *Türk Tarih Kurumu Belleten*, October 1949, xiii. 745–69.

HOUTUM-SCHINDLER, A., *Eastern Persian Irak*. (Special publication of the *R.G.S.*, 1898.)

—— 'Notes on the Karun River', *Proc. R.G.S.*, 1891, xii.

—— 'Notes on the Kur River in Fars, its Sources and Dams, and the Districts it Irrigates', ibid. 1891, xiii. 287–91.

—— 'On the Length of the Persian Farsakh', ibid. 1888, x. 584–88.

IVANOV, V., 'Notes on the Ethnology of Khurasan', *Geog. Journal*, 1926, 143–58.

JAMĀLZĀDEH, 'Some Aspects of Labour Conditions in Persian Agriculture', *Asiatic Review*, April 1935, cvi. 334–47.

JAUBERT, P. A., *Voyage en Arménie et en Perse, fait dans les années 1805 et 1806*. Paris, 1821.

JENKINSON, A., *Early Voyages and Travels to Russia and Persia by Antony Jenkinson and other Englishmen*. Hak. Soc., Nos. 72 and 73, 1885–6. 2 vols.

KAEMPFER, E., *Amoenitatum exoticarum politico-physico-medicarum fasciculi V, quibus continentur variae relationes, observationes et descriptiones rerum Persicarum et Ulterioris Asiae*. Lemgo, 1712.

KEEN, B. A., *The Agricultural Development of the Middle East*. London, H.M.S.O., 1946.

KINNEIR, J. MACDONALD, *A Geographical Memoir of the Persian Empire*. London, 1813.
KREMER, A. VON, *Culturgeschichte des Orients unter den Chalifen*. Vienna, 1875–7. 2 vols.
—— *Über das Budget der Einnahmen unter der Regierung des Hârûn al-Rašîd*. Vienna, 1887.
—— *Über das Einnahmebudget des Abbasiden-reiches vom Jahre 306 H (918–919)*. Vienna, 1887.
LAMBTON, A. K. S., 'An Account of the Tārīkhi Qumm', *B.S.O.A.S.*, 1948, xii. 3 and 4, 586–96.
—— 'The Regulation of the Waters of the Zāyande Rūd', *B.S.O.S.*, 1937–9, ix. 3, 663–73.
LAMMENS, H., *Le Berceau de l'Islam*. Rome, 1914. Vol. 1.
LAYARD, A. H., 'A Description of the Province of Khūzistān', *J.R.G.S.*, 1846, xvi. 1–105.
LE STRANGE, G., 'The Cities of Kirman in the Time of Hamd-Allāh Mustawfī and Marco Polo', *J.R.A.S.*, 1901.
—— *The Lands of the Eastern Caliphate*. Cambridge, 1905.
LEWY, H., 'Système féodale et exploitation du domaine royal d'après les textes de Nuzi', *Arch. d'hist. du droit orient.*, iii. 161–5.
LINGEMAN, E. R., *see* Great Britain, Department of Overseas Trade.
LOCKHART, L., *Nadir Shah: a Critical Study Based Mainly on Contemporary Sources*. London, 1938.
LØKKEGAARD, F., *Islamic Taxation in the Classic Period*. Copenhagen, 1950.
LORINI, E., *La Persia economica contemporanea e la sua questione monetaria*. Rome, 1900.
MACGREGOR, C. METCALFE, *Narrative of a Journey through the Province of Khorassan and on the N.W. Frontier of Afghanistan in 1875*. London, 1879. 2 vols.
MALCOLM, SIR J., *The History of Persia from the Most Early Period to the Present Time*. London, 1829. 2 vols.
—— *Sketches of Persia*. London, 1815. 2 vols.
The Mejelle, tr. by C. R. Tyser, D. G. Demetriades, and Ismail Haqq Effendi. Cyprus, 1901.
MEYER, E., *Geschichte des Altertums*. Stuttgart, 1884.
MEZ, A., *Die Renaissance des Islams*. Heidelberg, 1922.
MILLSPAUGH, A. C., *Americans in Persia*. Washington, 1946.
—— *The American Task in Persia*. New York and London, 1925.
—— *The Financial and Economic Situation of Persia*. Washington, 1926.
MINORSKY, V., 'A Soyūrghāl of Qāsim b. Jahāngīr Āq-Qoyunlū', *B.S.O.A.S.* (1937–9), ix. 927–60.
MĪNOVĪ, M., and V. MINORSKY, 'Naṣīr al-Dīn Ṭūsī on Finance', *B.S.O.A.S.*, 1940–2, x. 755–89.
MOCHAVER, F., *L'Évolution des finances iraniennes*. Paris, 1938.
MOLON, C. DE, *De la Perse: Études sur la géographie, le commerce, la politique, l'industrie, l'administration, &c.* Versailles, 1875.
MORELAND, W. H., *The Agrarian System of Muslim India*. Cambridge, 1929.
MORIER, J., *A Journey through Persia, Armenia, and Asia Minor, to Constantinople in the Years 1808 and 1809*. London, 1812.
—— *A Second Journey through Persia, Armenia, and Asia Minor, to Constantinople, between the Years 1810 and 1816*. London, 1818.
NAFIÇY, HASAN (Musharraf ud-Douleh), *L'Impôt et la vie économique et sociale en Perse*. Paris, 1924.

NAPIER, G. C., *Collection of Journals and Reports received from Capt. the Hon. G. C. Napier, on Special Duty in Persia, 1874.* London, 1876.

—— 'Extracts from a Diary of a Tour in Khorassan, and Notes on the Eastern Alburz Tract', *Trans. R.G.S.*, 1876, xlvi. 62–171.

NÖLDEKE, T., *Geschichte der Perser und Araber zur Zeit der Sasaniden.* Leyden, 1879.

D'OHSSON, A. C. MOURADJA, *Histoire des Mongols.* The Hague, Amsterdam, 1834–5. 4 vols.

OLEARIUS, A., *Voyages très curieux et très renommez faits en Moscovie, Tartarie et Perse.* Amsterdam, 1719. 2 vols. in one.

OTTER, J., *Voyage en Turquie et en Perse.* Paris, 1748. 2 vols.

PELTIER, F., *Œuvres diverses* (*El-Boukhari, livres de l'ensemencement et de la mousaqat*). Algiers, 1949.

POLIAK, A. N., *Feudalism in Egypt, Syria, Palestine and the Lebanon, 1250–1900.* R.A.S. Monograph, London, 1939.

—— 'La Féodalité islamique', *R.E.I.*, 1936, x. 247–65.

—— 'The Influence of Chinghiz-Khān's Yāsa upon the General Organization of the Mamlūk State', *B.S.O.A.S.*, 1940–42, x. 862–76.

POOLE, R. S., *Catalogue of Coins of the Sháhs of Persia . . . in the British Museum.* London, 1887.

PURVES, P. M., 'Commentary on Nuzi Real Property', *J.N.E.*, April 1945, iv. 2, 68–86.

RABINO [DI BORGOMALE], H. L., *Coins, Medals, and Seals of the Shāhs of Irān, 1500–1941.* London, 1945.

—— 'L'Histoire du Mâzandarân', *J.A.*, 1943–5, ccxxxiv. 211–44.

—— *Mázandarán and Astarábád.* London, Leyden, G.M.S., 1928.

RAWLINSON, H. C., 'Notes on a Journey from Tabríz through Persian Kurdistán to the Ruins of Takhti-Soleïmán, &c.', *J.R.G.S.*, 1841, x. 1–64.

—— 'Notes on a March from Zohab, at the foot of the Zagros, along the Mountains of Khuzistan (Susiana) and from thence through the Province of Luristan to Kirmanshah, in the Year 1836', *J.R.G.S.*, 1839, ix. 26–116.

RIEU, C., *Catalogue of Persian MSS. in the British Museum.* London, 1879–83. 3 vols. (Supplement, 1895).

ROSS, E. D., ed., *Sir Antony Sherley and his Persian Adventure.* London, 1933.

RUBRUCK, WILLIAM OF, *The Journey of William of Rubruck to the Eastern Parts of the World, 1253–55.* Hak. Soc., 2nd ser., iv.

RUSSELL, A. D., and ABDULLAH AL-MA'MŪN SUHRAWARDY, *Muslim Law: an Historical Introduction to the Law of Inheritance.* London, 1925. Vol. 1.

SANDJĀBĪ, K., *Essai sur l'économie rurale et le régime agraire de la Perse.* Paris, 1934.

SCHACHT, J., *The Origins of Muhammadan Jurisprudence.* Oxford, 1950.

SCHWARZ, P., *Iran im Mittelalter, nach den arabischen Geographen.* Leipzig, 1929–36. 9 vols.

LE SERVAGE, *Communications présentées à la Société Jean Bodin*, Réunions des 16, 17, et 18 Octobre 1936.

SHERLEY, A., *see* ROSS, E. D.

SHUSTER, W. M., *The Strangling of Persia.* London, New York, 1912.

SPIEGEL, F., *Eranische Altertumskunde.* Leipzig, 1871–8. 3 vols.

STACK, E., *Six Months in Persia.* London, 1882. 2 vols.

STEELE, F. R., *Nuzi Real Estate Transactions.* Philadelphia, 1943.

SYKES, P. M., *Report on the Agriculture of Khorasan*. Government of India, 1910.

TANCOIGNE, J. M., *Lettres sur la Perse et la Turquie d'Asie*. Paris, 1819. 2 vols.

—— *Narrative of a Journey into Persia, and Residence at Teheran*. London, 1820.

TAVERNIER, J. B., *Voyages de M. J. B. Tavernier en Turquie, en Perse et aux Indes*. Paris, 1713. 6 vols.

TISCHENDORF, P. A. VON, *Das Lehnswesen in den moslemischen Staaten*. Leipzig, 1872.

TORNAUW, N. VON, 'Das Eigentumsrecht nach moslemischen Rechte', *Z.D.M.G.*, xxxvi. 285–338.

TOYNBEE, A. J., *A Study of History*. London, 1934– . 6 vols. (in progress).

TYAN, E., *Histoire de l'organisation judiciaire en pays d'Islam*. Paris, 1938–43. 2 vols.

VALLE, PIETRO DELLA, *Fameux voyages de Pietro della Valle*. Paris, 1664. 4 vols.

VESEY-FITZGERALD, S. G., *Muhammadan Law: an Abridgement according to its Various Schools*. London, 1931.

WARING, E. S., *A Tour to Sheeraz by the Route of Kazroon and Feerozabad*. London, 1807.

WARRINER, D., *Land and Poverty in the Middle East*. London, 1948.

WELLHAUSEN, J., *Das arabische Reich und sein Sturz*. Berlin, 1927.

WILSON, A. T., *Persia*. London, 1932.

YULE, H., ed., *The Book of Ser Marco Polo*, tr. and ed. by Sir H. Yule, rev. by Henri Cordier. London, 1921. 2 vols.

GLOSSARY

THE terms included in the list below consist mainly of expressions used in connexion with (1) land tenure and revenue administration, and (2) irrigation and agricultural implements. The general as distinct from the technical meaning of the terms has not usually been included.

Some of the terms have become obsolete either because the institution they were used to denote has disappeared or because they have been replaced by other terms; others have changed their meaning in the course of time. Both processes will be familiar to the student of Islamic technical terms. If the term is obsolete this has been indicated in parenthesis; similarly, if its use in the past has been restricted to a limited time range this also has been indicated, though it must not be assumed from this that a term which was characteristic of, for example, the Seljūq period will never be found in an earlier or later period.

A number of dialect expressions in use at the present day have been included in the list. The area in which the term has actually been met with is given in brackets; in many cases it may well be that the geographical range of the term is wider than stated. The list is not a complete one. Usage varies from district to district and often from village to village. A broad transcription[1] has been used which does not represent exactly the dialect pronunciation. The latter often varies from that of standard Persian, especially as regards the length and quality of the vowels. Dialect words or words used in a special sense in a given area have been marked with an asterisk unless the common usage of the word has been given, in which case the latter is given first and the dialect usage afterwards, with an indication of the area in which it is used.

āb, water; *gardishi āb* and *madāri āb*, rotation period of water used for irrigation.

āb miān, extra share of the water inserted in the normal rotation period, the proceeds of which are allotted to some special purpose.

**ābbān*, man whose duty it is to see that water reaches the crops according to the proper allotment (Kirmān).

**ābdang*, cleaning rice in the husk (Māzandarān).

**ābdār*, that part of the peasant's share under a crop-sharing agreement which is due to him for sowing and tending the crop (Kirmān).

ābī, irrigated (farming).

**ābyār*, official in charge of irrigation (Sīstān); *sar ābyār*, peasant attached to a plough-land who is engaged chiefly in looking after the irrigation of the land and weeding it (Tehrān area).

ābyārī, irrigation; *duṃbi ābyārī*, peasant who assists the *sar ābyār* (Tehrān area).

**āftābnishīn*, those inhabitants of a village who do not own land or hold land on a crop-sharing basis (Khurāsān and east Persia).

āhangarī, due paid to the village blacksmith in return for his services.

ʿ*ajam* (obs.), non-Arab, i.e. Persian.

ājnād, pl. of *jund*.

ʿ*ajz*, tax-deficit (*T.Q.*, pp. 31, 190); contribution levied on a tax-community to make good the sum owed by defaulters (*T.Q.*, p. 144).

akareh (pl. of *akkār*), cultivators (*T.Q.*).

ākhund, member of the religious classes, *mullā*.

akireh, the peasant's share of the harvest (*T.M.*, f. 73 a); compensation due to anyone who has rented land for the labour which he has put into it in the event of the lease being terminated by the proprietor.

[1] See pp. xi–xiii for a note on transcription.

akkāreh, peasants living in a village in which they have no share of the cultivated land and who go to the surrounding villages to work.

ʿalafeh, levies for the food of officials (Timurid and Ṣafavid periods).

aʿmāl (obs.), reports of tax-districts and their revenue accounts.

**amāreh*, stubble (Joushaqān).

ambār, storehouse.

ʿāmil, tax-collector (obs.); in early times the *ʿāmil* was the chief revenue official of a province in contradistinction to the *amīr*, who was the chief military officer. In a crop-sharing agreement (*muzāraʿeh*) the *ʿāmil* is the term used to designate the person who is given a piece of land for a specified period to cultivate on a crop-sharing basis.

amīr (obs.), the chief military officer of a province (see above under *ʿāmil*). In Seljūq times the term *amīr* was used as a general term to denote those members of the Turkish military classes who had become freedmen; subsequently the term *amīr* was applied to leading members of the military classes in general.

amlāk (pl. of *milk*), privately owned landed estates; under Rizā Shāh the term was also used in a special sense for those estates which he had acquired in various ways and which after his abdication became known as *amlāki vā guzārī*.

amlāki mutaṣarrifī, *amlāki zabṭī*, estates temporarily confiscated by the state as punishment for rebellion (Qājār period).

amnīyeh, gendarmerie.

andākhtan, to deduct (*T.Q.*).

angusht, one-quarter of a *qabzeh* (*T.Q.*, p. 109).

anhār, pl. of *nahr*.

āq saqal, grey-beard, elder (Turkī).

āqcheh, a coin (Īlkhān period); (Andūjird and Shahdād), unit of water varying in quantity, normally approximately 12 hrs.

arāzī (pl. of *arz*), lands, especially cultivated lands.

arbāb (pl. of *rabb*, lord), master, landowner, 'squire'.

**arbābī*, belonging to a large landed proprietor.

**arzī*, arrangement between the owner of flocks and a shepherd by which the latter is entrusted with the flock for a fixed period in return for a wage (Iṣfahān).

**arzyāb*, valuer, assessor (Khurāsān).

asbāb, apparently used to mean some right or property in land (obs.); (Seljūq period) *arbābi asbāb*, (?) persons given the right to collect direct from a given area the sums which were due to them or which had been allotted to them.

ʿashīr, one-tenth of a *qafīz* or 36 sq. *zarʿ* (*T.Q.*, p. 109; cf. Khwārazmī, p. 67).

ashl, 60 *zirāʿ*, or 60 *hāshimīyeh gaz* or 10 *bāb* (*T.Q.*, p. 109; Khwārazmī, pp. 66–7).

ashrafī, see *dīnār*.

aṣl (obs.), original tax assessment (without the addition of extraordinary taxes, arrears, etc.); estimated yield (of a tax); fully grown (of trees, vines, etc., *T.Q.*).

**aujin*, wooden hoop attached to an ox-yoke and put round the ox's neck (Abīāneh).

**āva dura*, third cutting of a lucerne crop (Varzaqān).

ʿavāmili panjgāneh, the five factors, i.e. land, water, seed, draught animals, and labour, taken into consideration in a crop-sharing agreement.

avārij, *avārijeh* (obs.): *daftari avārij*, register in which the various items of revenue and expenditure were separately entered and in which were shown the various charges met from the revenue from different taxes and funds; register in which the liability of the individual taxpayer was entered and the instalments which he had paid in discharge of his liabilities.

avārijeh nivīs, the official in charge of the *daftari avārij*.

ʿavāriz, *ʿavārizāt*, dues, tolls. In documents of the fifteenth and sixteenth centuries A.D. the phrase *ʿavārizāti ḥukmī va ghayri ḥukmī* is met with and appears to mean 'dues demanded by virtue of a decree or otherwise'.

ayālat (pl. *ayālāt*), governorate-general; district, province. In modern usage *ayālat* has been replaced by *ustān*.

aʿyān, tangible property; land and chattels corporeal; in popular usage the house, outhouses, and trees of a holding as distinct from the land itself.

aʿyānī, what pertains to the *aʿyān*.

āyish, leaving fallow; crop rotation; *do āyish*, cultivated in alternate years (land); *seh āyish*, cultivated once in three years (land); having a three-

fold crop rotation (i.e. the land of a village is divided into three lots, one of which lies fallow every year).
ʿaynī, ḥuqūqi, subordinate titles.
**azhdār*, beam of a plough (Kirmān).

bāb, 6 *gaz* (*T.Q.*, p. 109).
**bāfeh*, armful of grain taken at harvest time by the village carpenter and others as part of their dues (Kirmān, Joushaqān, and elsewhere).
**baghalī* (Jahrum), the amount of grain which can be carried under one arm and is taken by the village carpenter and blacksmith as part of their dues. This was commuted in 1949 to 5 *manni tabrīz* (approx. 32 lb., 12 oz.) wheat and 5 *mann* barley per *kharman* per annum.
**bāgh tarreh*, melons, water-melons, and cucumbers, etc. (Khurāsān).
bahreh, share, portion; *bahrehyi mālikāneh*, the landlord's share of the harvest under a crop-sharing agreement.
**bahreh*, wooden spade (Vafsī).
bahreh bardārī, collecting a share of the harvest, drawing revenue (from the land).
bahrijeh (obs.), share, portion, especially of the harvest, etc.
**baj*, unirrigated farming (Mamasanī).
**bajī*, unirrigated (Mamasanī).
**bakhs*, unirrigated; unirrigated farming (Fārs).
bakhsh, sub-area, small administrative district.
bakhshdār, official in charge of a *bakhsh*.
**bāl*, spade (Abīāneh).
**bāleh*, spade (Simnān).
**ballak*, peasant who works alone (and not as one of a team), usually cultivating *daym* crops or *ṣayfī* crops (Khurāsān).
band, dam; yoke of oxen; plough-land.
**band gah*, dam (Kurdistān).
band gāv, yoke of oxen (especially Kirmān).
baqāyā (obs.), arrears of taxation.
baqqāl, chandler (who sells groceries such as tea, sugar, pulses, etc.).
**bār*, manure (Khurāsān).
barāt (= *bara'āt*), quittance, bill, draft (obs.; cf. Khwārazmī, pp. 55–6).
**bārdār*, landed proprietor (Bīrjand); the share of the peasant under a crop-sharing agreement due for reaping and harvesting the crop (Kirmān).
bar dāshtan, to reap, gather in (the harvest).
**bardū*, threshing-machine (it is equipped with knives on the under-carriage and is drawn by oxen or asses, a man sitting on it; Bīrjand).
**barjīn*, threshing-machine (Nayrīz).
**barm*, place where the banks of an irrigation channel are opened to let water through into the neighbouring fields (Nayrīz); clod of earth used to block an opening made in the side of an irrigation channel (Joushaqān).
**barq*, measure of water (Shahdād); opening made in the side of an irrigation channel to let the water through into the neighbouring fields; *barq bastan*, to close or stop such an opening; *yak barq āb*, the amount of water which one man can stop by placing his spade across the opening of an irrigation channel (Turbati Ḥaydarī); *barqi qanāt*, the place where a *qanāt* first emerges on the surface of the ground (Joushaqān).
**bārrīz*, manured (of land; Khurāsān).
**bart*, spade (Gaz).
barzigar, cultivator, agricultural labourer (not a crop-sharing peasant).
bāsqāq, local revenue official (Īlkhān period).
**bayl*, spade (Nayrīz).
bayt ul-māl (obs.), the state treasury.
bāz jūshīdan, to dry up (a *qanāt*, etc.; *T.Q.*, p. 157).
**bāzeh*, ridge dividing one plot of land (*kart*) from another (Kirmān).
**bāzūleh*, threshing-machine (Simnān).
**bāzyār*, agricultural labourer, not a crop-sharing peasant (Khalāfābād and certain other parts of Khūzistān and Fārs).
beglarbeg, beglarbegī, title held by provincial governors or governors-general (Ṣafavid period); kind of chief police officer or military governor (Qājār period).
bīgār, see *bīgārī*.
**bīgāreh*, man attached to a *ṣaḥrā* who is paid by the peasants but is in effect the servant of the landlord (Zāveh).
bīgārī, labour service. According to Poliak the term *bīgār* was used by the Mamlūks for the military service of the Turkish-speaking troops ('The influence of Chinghiz Khān's Yāsa . . . upon the Mamlūk State', in *B.S.O.A.S.*, x. 869).
**bījeh*, area taking some 100 *manni tabrīz* (approx. 5 cwt., 95 lb.) seed (Kāshmar); pistachio sapling which has been transplanted (Kirmān).

bīl, spade; (Balūchistān) 12 hours' water.

**biray*, irrigation channel flowing through a village (Gaz).

**birīneh*, kind of harrow (Simnān).

bītikchī, revenue official (Īlkhān period).

**boujār*, winnower (Linjān).

**būjār*, winnower (Kirmān).

bukāvul, official in charge of the commissariat arrangements of the army. (Īlkhān period). According to Barthold, the term means overseer of food and drink (*Turkestān*, p. 382). In the Timurid period the *bukāvul* was not only a military official but was also sometimes found in charge of the arrangements for feeding the inmates of *madrasehs* and *khānqāhs*.

bulūk, district (this is no longer an official term; the modern *dihistān* corresponds broadly to the earlier *bulūk* but the boundaries of the individual districts have largely been redrawn).

**buṃbakhsh*, having the shares delimited (of jointly owned land; Kirmān).

**būmkan*, *būmkand*, dug-out into which flocks are put in winter for shelter (Maymeh).

**bundār*, landed proprietor (Khurāsān). According to Løkkegaard a *bundār* was a wholesale buyer of *kharāj* in kind (*Islamic Taxation*, p. 244, n. 110).

buneh, household furniture, goods; especially the draught animals and plough, etc., of a peasant; (Tehrān) plough-land.

bunīcheh (obs.), group assessment of a village, etc. (i.e. the village was assessed in a lump sum, the amount due from the individual tax-payers being apportioned among them locally); *ṣāḥib bunīcheh*, person who was liable to taxation under the group assessment.

**bunjehbakhsh*, see *buṃbakhsh*.

buqʿeh, piece of ground in which a shrine is situated.

**bur*, flock of sheep of 400–600 head (Turbati Ḥaydarī).

**bureh*, threshing-machine (Sīvandī).

bustān, garden; orchard; any enclosure of trees planted sufficiently apart to allow cultivation of the intervening space (see Aghnides, *Muhammadan Theories of Finance*, p. 379, n. 3).

bustānchī, gardener who looks after a garden under a crop-sharing agreement or who farms the right to reap the crop.

chāh, well; *ḥaqqi chāh*, due levied by the owner of a well situated in pasture land (Turbati Ḥaydarī); *mādar chāh*, the end well of a *qanāt*, i.e. that well which is nearest to the source of the *qanāt*.

**chahāb*, well worked by oxen, etc. (Fārs and Khūzistān).

chahār shākh, wooden fork used in winnowing.

**chāhkhū*, man who constructs and cleans *qanāts* (Kirmān).

chak: *chak kardan*, to prune (a tree).

**chak*, wooden fork used in winnowing (Bīrjand and Turbati Ḥaydarī).

**chap*: *chap kardan*, to plough land for sowing, in contradistinction to ploughing land for fallow (Khūzistān).

charkhi dūl, contraption for raising water consisting of a wooden wheel set vertically in the jaws of a well which is set in motion by a second horizontal wheel to which an ox is harnessed (Shūshtar).

charwā, the nomadic branch of the Yamūt tribe.

**chateh*, guerrillas, irregular troops (Kurdistān and Āẕarbāyjān).

**chikineh*, jointly owned land (Bīrjand); flock composed of animals belonging to a number of different persons, who each own 3–4 head (Kirmān); shepherd who takes a flock composed of 20–30 of the villagers' sheep and goats to graze (Gaz).

chirīk, irregular soldier.

chumur, the settled branch of the Yamūt tribe.

chūn (? = *chān*), *chūn parreh*, threshing machine (which is equipped with knives on the under-carriage and is drawn by a donkey or mule, a man sitting on it).

**dā*, corn (which has been separated from the straw and cleaned; Kirmān).

dādbeg, official in charge of the administration of justice by secular courts (Qājār period).

daftar, (pl. *dafātir*) register.

**dāgh guẕāshtan*, to sink (the water-level; Mūrchehkhwart); to let water into a *mādī* (Iṣfahān).

dah o nīm, some due levied possibly for the expenses of the tax-collectors (Īlkhān period).

dah yak, some kind of tax or levy on land (Ṣafavid period).

dahaneh jazval (*jadval*), place where a *qanāt* comes to the surface.

dālīeh (obs.), water-wheel.

**dāmārdeh zadan*, to stamp weeds into the mud in preparation for the planting of rice (Māzandarān).

**dānāneh*, levy made on the peasants at harvest time for the landowner's horses (Kurdistān).

dandāneh, dandānī, contract by which sheep and goats are entrusted by their owner to someone for a stipulated period, during which a certain quantity of clarified butter, etc., is paid per annum to the owner of the animals by the person who takes charge of them and who, when the contract expires, returns to the owner the same number of animals as he originally took over and of the same age as when he took them over.

dāng, one-sixth part of any piece of real estate; (Kirmān) unit of water comprising 16 *ḥabbeh* or 24 hours' water; (Kāshmar) one hundred and forty-fourth part of the water of a *qanāt*; (Kurdistān) unit of property comprising 16 *sha'īr*.

dāniq (obs.), 4 *ṭasūj* or one-sixth of a *miṣqāl* (Khwārazmī, pp. 62–3).

dār ul-ḥarb (obs.), territory outside the lands held by the Muslims and with the people of which they were at war.

dār ul-islām (obs.), territory held by the Muslims.

dār us-salṭaneh, capital city (of a country); in the Ṣafavid period Tabrīz, Iṣfahān, and Qazvīn were known by this title.

**dāra*, sickle (Simnān).

**dārmālāneh* (obs.), house tax (Kurdistān).

**darū*, scythe (Ḥasano).

dārūgeh, kind of police official in charge of a town or ward, resembling in some respects the earlier *muḥtasib* (Ṣafavid and Qājār periods); the overseer of a village or group of villages (Khurāsān).

**darvāzeh*, threshing-machine (which has no knives and is drawn by an ox or ass, a man sitting on it; Bīrjand).

**darz*, approx. 23·7 sq. yds. (Langarūd).

**dāseh*, the rough heads of wheat or barley remaining on the threshing floor after the grain and straw have been separated (Tehrān); spikelet (of barley; Bīrjand).

dasht, plain; the cultivated fields, or a part of these, surrounding a village.

dashtbān, village official whose duty it is to protect the villagers' fields from damage and theft; in some areas he also oversees irrigation.

**dastak*, flock of 400 head (Turbati Ḥaydarī).

dastandāz, (?) perquisites, tips (Qarā Qoyunlū and Ṣafavid periods).

dastranj, compensation paid to a peasant for the labour he has put into the land if he is evicted (Yazd).

dastūr (obs.), revenue assessment; *dastūri aṣl*, original or basic settlement; *dastūr ul-'amal*, revenue assessment; *daftari dastūr ul-'amal*, the revenue roll (of a district, etc.).

**dāvar*, boundary stone marking the division between the various plots in a field (Abīāneh).

daym, unirrigated (dry) farming.

daymī, unirrigated (dry).

**dazh*, stick with a seal on the end used to mark heaps of harvested grain (Ḥasano).

**dīānāneh*, levy made for the landowner on his first visit to a village (Kurdistān).

dihāqīn, pl. of *dihqān*.

dihdār, village headman (Khurāsān).

dihqān, head of a village who held certain lands by hereditary right and acted as the government tax-collector; landed proprietor (obs.); peasant; (Balūchistān) peasant attached to a plough-land (but not the owner of the draught animals); (Khurāsān) peasant attached to a plough-land responsible for ploughing and sowing; *sar dihqān*, peasant in charge of the *dihqāns* of a plough-land.

dīnār, unit of gold currency which was replaced in the Qājār period by the *tūmān*, sometimes called the *ashrafī* (obs.); one-thousandth part of a *tūmān*.

dīnāri rāyij (obs.), currency *dīnār*.

diram, dirham, unit of silver coinage (obs.).

dirougar, reaper.

**diroukunī*, due levied for reaping at the rate of $2\frac{1}{2}$ per cent on the total harvest for the peasants attached to a plough-land (Iṣṭahbānāt).

dīvān (obs.), public register of receipts and expenditure; offices of the treasury; ministry; state (i.e. belonging to the state).

dīvānī (obs.), belonging to the state (land).

dīvāni inshā', the office from which official documents were issued on behalf of the ruler (pre-Mongol period).

**do bikār*, land cultivated in alternate years (Arāk).
**do galleh*, wooden two-pronged fork (Joushaqān).
**dous*, threshing-machine (Fasā and Nayrīz).
do ʿushr, some kind of tax or levy on the land (Ṣafavid period).
**do yak kardan*, to thin out and prune cucumbers by removing their surplus leaves and to cover them in part with earth (Joushaqān).
dūgh, kind of buttermilk.
dūlāb, water-wheel.
dūn, immature (of walnut trees, etc.; *T.Q.*).
**dunt*, wooden shaft to which the coulter of a plough is attached (Ḥasano).

**fālīz*, summer crops and vegetables (Sīstān).
faqīh, man learned in *fiqh* or Islamic jurisprudence.
farāyish, see *firash*.
farʿkhīz, free share of water allotted to the *kadkhudā* (Turbati Ḥaydarī).
farmāndār, governor.
**faryāb*, irrigated farming (Khūzistān).
**fatā*, sharp-pointed stone used for dividing water into different channels (Simnān).
fatvā, judicial or religious decision given by a *muftī*.
fay', in its primitive sense means all goods taken from the enemy (cf. Qudāma, *Kitāb al-Kharāj*, vii. 1), but in general *fay'* means all things which may be taken from unbelievers 'without fighting', i.e. only those things taken by peaceful means and placed apart from the booty (*ghanīma*). It included land the inhabitants of which had surrendered by virtue of a treaty of capitulation. Such land 'belongs to God and to his prophet' (Bukhārī, *al-Jāmiʿ as-Ṣaḥīḥ*, ed. Krehl and Juynboll, Leyden, 1862–1908, ii. 294). According to the *Taʿrīfāt* of ʿAlī b. Muḥammad al-Jurjānī, '*fay'* is what God most high returns to the people of his religion from goods belonging to someone who has opposed them in religion, without fighting but by reason of flight or by a treaty of capitulation in return (for an undertaking to pay) *jizya* or something else' (ed. Flügel, p. 177). According to most jurists one-fifth of the *fay'* was set aside and devoted in five equal parts to the five categories of beneficiaries, as was the fifth deducted from *ghanīma*. The basis for this is the Qur'ān, Sūra lix. 5–7. There was a difference of opinion among the jurists over the division of the other four-fifths. According to some it was to be expended by the *imām* on the army, while others held that it was to be expended on the public interest including the stipends of the army (Māwardī, *Aḥkām*, p. 219). The beneficiaries from *fay'* differed from those who had a right to the proceeds of *ṣadaqa* (see ibid. pp. 219–20, and also Wāqidī, *Kitāb al-Maghāzī*, B.M. Or. 1617, f. 100*b*). *Fay'* land was of two kinds, land the inhabitants of which had renounced their rights of ownership under the terms of capitulation, and land the inhabitants of which had been accorded under the terms of the treaty of capitulation rights of ownership. In the former case the inhabitants enjoyed only the usufruct of the land. The earliest example in Islamic times of usufruct is the case of Khaybar, when Muḥammad allowed the Jews to cultivate the land in return for half the produce of the land and its date-palms (Ibn Hishām, *Sīrat an-Nabī*, ed. Flügel, p. 764; al-Balāẓurī, *Futūḥ al-Buldān*, p. 27). Ibn Isḥāq states that Khaybar became *fay'* among the Muslims. The Jews in Fadak, on the other hand, by the terms of the treaty of capitulation renounced their rights of ownership to one-half of the land, which became the private property (*khāliṣa*) of the Prophet (Ibn Hishām, p. 764; see also al-Balāẓurī, p. 29). By implication the Jews retained rights of ownership over the other half because when ʿUmar subsequently expelled them from Fadak he paid them the just value of one half of the soil (al-Balāẓurī, p. 29). The properties of the Banī Naẓīr are also said to have become the private property (*khāṣṣa*) of the Prophet, who divided them among the early *muhājirīn* (Ibn Hishām, p. 653); al-Balāẓurī states that he assigned part of these properties to Abū Bakr and others (p. 18).
**faymān*, 3,025 sq. m. (approx. 3,618 sq. yds.; Nayrīz).
**fayn*, 20 minutes' water (Nayrīz).
fiddan (obs.), a surface measure.
fiqh, Islamic jurisprudence.

**firash, firaysh*, sown early (of crops; Khurāsān).

**firzeh*, a measure of water (Ardistān).

fuqahā, pl. of *faqīh*.

**gal*, corvée for agricultural work (Kurdistān).

**galleh bi-gīr*, levy on cattle and sheep formerly made annually by the *khāns* but now said to be levied only when there are two or more successive good years (Qashqā'ī area).

gamāneh, trial shaft sunk for a *qanāt*.

**gārā*, grain sown, reaped, and threshed free for the landowner by the peasant (Dizfūl).

**gardanehyi gāv*, 50 *manni tabrīz* (2 cwt., 103 lb.) wheat and 50 *manni tabrīz* barley which is deducted from the peasant's share of the crop in a crop-sharing agreement and set aside for the owner of the ox (Shahdād).

**garjīn*, threshing-machine (Kirmān).

garmsīr, relatively low-lying lands with a hot climate, as opposed to *sardsīr*, relatively high lands with a temperate climate.

**gārt*, plot of land in which citrus fruits are planted in the shade of date palms (Kīrmān).

gāv bahreh, the share of the crop belonging to the owner of the ox in a crop-sharing agreement (Jahrum).

gāvband, person interposed between the landlord and the peasant who manages several plough-lands run together as a unit (Tehrān); yoke of oxen (Shahdād and elsewhere); the owner of the oxen in a crop-sharing agreement (Khīr, Shahdād, and elsewhere).

gāvdārān (pl. of *gāvdār*), cattle-breeders.

gāvrān, ploughman.

ghalleh ṭarḥ, the dumping of grain from *khāliṣeh* lands on peasants and forcing them to buy this at a price above the current market price (Qājār period; the term also occurs in Āq Qoyunlū times, but its meaning in that period is uncertain).

ghanīma, booty consisting of captives, women and children, lands and movable property taken in war by force. One-fifth of this, according to Islamic usage, belonged to Allāh, and was divided into five equal portions between Muḥammad, those who were near to him (i.e. his family), orphans, the poor, and wayfarers, the authority for this being found in sūra viii. 41, which was revealed after the battle of Badr (see *khums*). The rules for the division of this and the remaining four-fifths of the booty as expounded by the various rites differ in matters of detail. The extensive conquests made by the Muslims made inevitable some modification in the application of the theory of booty, particularly in so far as land was concerned. The early practice of dividing the booty, apart from the one-fifth, among the conquerors was modified, though the jurists were at pains so to describe actual practice as to make it fit the legal theory and thereby to justify the actions of the leaders of the community. In fact it seems that the general practice came to be to treat all conquered land (whether it was taken by force or not) as if it were *fay'* land (see also above, pp. 17 ff.).

**gharībeh*, landless peasant not enjoying equal rights with the crop-sharing peasant (Hashtrūd).

ghaṣb, usurpation, dispossession.

ghulām (obs.), slave, especially a Turkish military slave.

ghulūq, due levied for the entertainment of officials.

**gīn* (Ḥasano), see *kharman*.

**gīv*, ox-yoke (Ḥasano).

gīveh, shoe the uppers of which are made of a cotton weave and the soles of a preparation made of pulped rags or from coarse thread.

**gouhak*, the upright shaft of a plough, fixed at an angle to the beam (Sīstān).

**gul*, the ox on the inside of a string of some ten oxen used to tread out the grain harvest (Sīstān).

**gulāl*, sheaf of wheat (Simnān).

**gum*, covered water channel (Abīāneh).

**guṃbeh*, mud-brick hut in which the *ābbān* takes shelter in winter (Kirmān).

**gunj*, short pipe used to drain land (Kurdistān).

**gūreh*, dyke (Sīstān).

gusfand, gūsfand, sheep and goats; (Turbati Ḥaydarī) *gusfand bi mīhan dādan*, to entrust sheep and goats to someone for a specified period in return for a fixed amount of clarified butter (*roughan*) or dried curds (*kashk*).

gūshīeh, place where water used for irrigation is divided into shares (*T.Q.*, p. 33).

ḥabbeh, one-sixth of a *dāniq* (obs.); measure of land (which varies in extent in different areas).
ḥabs, secular grant of usufruct; servitude.
ḥadd, limit; boundary.
ḥaddādī, due paid to the village blacksmith.
ḥaddi mīāneh, some kind of tax (Ṣafavid period).
ḥākim, judge, governor; in Qājār times all crimes, breaches of the peace, etc., were brought before the *ḥākim* or his deputies. The term is sometimes used in modern times to mean 'the temporal government'.
ḥammām, bath.
ḥammāmī, bath-keeper; due paid to the bath-keeper.
**hampā*, peasant who owns an ox and sufficient agricultural implements to enable him to work a plough-land on a crop-sharing basis (Āẕarbāyjān; cf. Bartholomae, *Zum Sasanidischen Recht*, i. 39, *hamba*, associate).
**hampā'ī*, distributing the plough-lands of a village among the crop-sharing peasants (Āẕarbāyjān).
ḥaqq ābeh, right to a share in the water of a *qanāt*, etc.
ḥaqq ul-marta', grazing dues.
ḥaqq un-naẓāreh, due of the supervisor of a *vaqf*.
**ḥaqq us-sahm*, grazing due paid by the peasants in landlord areas (Turbati Ḥaydarī).
ḥaqq us-sa'ī, perquisite (of an official; Ṣafavid period).
ḥaqq ush-shurb, right to a share of the water of a river.
ḥaqq ut-toulīyeh, due of the *mutavallī* of a shrine.
**haqqā*, the annual division by lot of the cultivable land among the peasants (Bīhbahān).
ḥaqqi khazāneh, some kind of due (Īlkhān period).
**harāṣeh*, *hirāṣeh*, two to four *juft* working together as a unit; two to four plough-lands grouped together as a unit (Jahrum); part of the village land in possession of a *za'īm* (Kirmān).
**harāteh* (see *harāṣeh*), plough-land (Nayrīz).
ḥarīm, the 'borders' of a property (see above, p. 199).
hars: *hars kardan*, to prune vines; (Jahrum) to estimate the value of a crop (cf. *kharṣ kardan*).
ḥashar, irregular troops (obs.); (Sīstān and Balūchistān) labour service (cf. *Tārīkhi Sīstān*, p. 31, and Narshakhī, *Tārīkhi Bukhārā*, p. 41).
hastāt, gardens (*T.Q.*, p. 60).
ḥazr (obs.), estimating the value of a crop, especially of corn. According to Hinz, *ḥazr* is the due for the man who collects or assesses the government due on the harvest ('Steuerinschriften', *Belleten*, xiii. 52, p. 747).
ḥīāzāt, special pastures set aside for the caliph's flocks in the Nihāvand and Karaj areas (*T.Q.*, p. 185).
**hīchāneh*, levy paid by the *khwushnishīn* of a village to the landowner for permission to reside there (Kurdistān).
ḥimā (obs.), the collective reserve of a tribe; common pasture land lying around a town in which the cattle and sheep of the inhabitants grazed; special reserves in which army remounts were grazed.
**hirākish*, sown early (of crops; Simnān).
ḥiṣār, walled enclosure.
**hish*, plough (Abīāneh).
ḥiṣṣeh, share, portion.
ḥoumeh, environs of a town.
**ḥubbeh*, measure of land (Maymeh; see also *ḥabbeh*).
ḥudūd, pl. of *ḥadd*.

'ibreh (obs.), the valuation of a crop arrived at by taking the average yield over a period of years (cf. Khwārazmī, p. 61).
ibtīā'ī, (?) purchase tax (Āq Qoyunlū period).
īdājī, an official attached to the commissariat of the army (Ilkhān period).
īghār (obs.), grant of land, carrying with it complete or partial immunity from taxation.
iḥdāṣ, (?) some kind of tax innovation (Āq Qoyunlū period).
iḥrāz, occupying something which is common property.
iḥtisāb (obs.), official credit (for a sum of money).
iḥyā, reclaiming (land), bringing (dead land) into cultivation.
ijmā' (obs.), consensus of opinion.
ikhrājāt (obs.), extraordinary taxes; *ikhrājāti dīvānī*, taxes levied for the expenses of the *dīvān*; *ikhrājāti mamlakatī*, extraordinary provincial taxes; *ikhrājāti qilā' va ṭavāyil va jouqehgāh*, taxes levied for the upkeep of fortresses and garrison posts, etc.
īl (pl. *īlāt*), tribe.
īlbeg, leader of a tribe (mainly Fārs and Bakhtīārī).

īlchī, official travelling on government business (Īlkhān, Ṣafavid, and Qājār periods).
īlīātī, tribesman; tribal.
īlkhān, leader of a tribe (mainly Fārs and Bakhtīārī).
iltijā' (obs.), placing oneself under the protection of another by ceding one's land to him (see Khwārazmī, p. 62).
iltizām (obs.), revenue farm.
imām, prayer-leader (see also *shī'ah*).
īnjū, crown land (Īlkhān period).
**insabā*, the peasant's share of the harvest under a crop-sharing agreement (Kirmān).
intifā' (pl. *intifā'āt*), usufruct.
iqṭā' (pl. *iqṭā'āt*; obs.), land assignment (the term *iqṭā'* was gradually replaced in the Īlkhān period by *tuyūl* and is seldom met with in post-Īlkhān times); *iqṭā' al-istighlāl*, the assignment of the revenue of a piece of land; *iqṭā' at-tamlīk*, the assignment of the land itself.
irtifā' (pl. *irtifā'āt*), usufruct; the harvest; gathering in the harvest.
irtifāq, easement; servitude.
**isahal*, coulter (Bihbahān).
**ishkaft*, place where a *qanāt* wells out of a rock (Joushaqān); cave (Fārs).
**ishkanak*, breach in an irrigation channel through which water runs to waste (Dizfūl).
**ishtin*, wooden many-pronged fork (Sīstān).
**iskam*, fall in the level of a water channel (Bīrjand). The level of a water channel in sloping ground is lowered by a series of steps, the intervening sections being roughly level, so that the water is prevented from running too fast and thus washing the channel away.
istakhr, water-tank or pond.
istīfā (obs.), function of a *mustoufī*; tax-settlement.
iṭlāq: *ḥaqq ul-iṭlāq* (obs.), due paid to the writer of a deed of quittance.
iṭlāqāti dīvān (obs.), requisitions by the *dīvān*.

jadval, irrigation channel.
jahbaẕ (obs.), broker, middle-man through whom taxes were remitted by the tax-payers to the government (see above, p. 42).
**jākār*, land cultivated every year (Joushaqān).
jālīz, melon bed or trench in which cucumbers and similar vegetables are cultivated.
jālīzkārī, melon cultivation, etc.
**janjar*, threshing-machine (Kurdistān and parts of Āẕarbāyjān).
**jār*, stubble-field (Kurdistān).
jarībāneh, tax or due assessed by measurement of the land.
**jī*, ox-yoke (Sīvandī, Bihbahān, and Sīstān).
**jīb*, ox-yoke (Nayrīz).
jihāt, *māl o jihāt*, taxes (Ṣafavid period; cf. *māl ul-jihāt*, tax the proceeds of which were used to provision the annual caravan to Mecca (R. Dozy, *Supplément aux dictionnaires arabes* (Leyden, 1927), ii. 787). Hinz states that *jihāt* means taxes on industry, *vujūhāt*, taxes and dues in money, and the phrase *māl u jihāt u vujūhāt* all possible forms of tax (*Belleten*, xiii. 52, p. 765).
**jivar*, occupation rights (Āẕarbāyjān; see above, p. 296).
jizya (obs.), poll tax.
**joug*, ox-yoke (Kirmān).
**jougah*, irrigation channel (Kurdistān).
**jouq*, ox-yoke (Bīrjand).
jūb (for *jūy*), irrigation channel, stream.
**jūbī*, right of the *dashtbān* to cultivate crops along the banks of irrigation channels (Kirmān).
juft, yoke of oxen; plough-land.
julgeh, plain; relatively flat land.
jund (obs.), local troops; army.
jundī (obs.), soldier (especially one levied for local duties).
**jūq*, three to five plough-lands grouped together (Kurdistān).
**jūqbandī*, dividing the land into *jūq* (Kurdistān).
**jur'eh*, *jurreh*, small child employed in agricultural work (Kirmān and Muta').
**juvar*, see *jivar*.
jūy, irrigation channel, stream.
**jūyeh*, ox-yoke (Simnān).
juzvi jam' (obs.), revenue assessment; *daftari juzvi jam'*, the register in which the assessment of a given area was entered.

kadkhudā, village headman; head of a clan or tribal sub-group; head of a craft-guild; (obs.) head of a *maḥalleh* or ward of a town.
kad shumārī, (?) family tax or poll tax (Āq Qoyunlū period).
**kadval*, implement used to remove earth which is drawn by an ox or pulled by a man (Kirmān).
**kaft*, wooden spade used to collect grain when it is being threshed and winnowed, etc. (Kirmān).

**kahkīn*, man who makes and repairs *qanāts* (Sīrjān).
kahrīz (obs.), see *kārīz*.
**kal*, plot of land (Sīstān); cultivated land (Sīstān); *kal kardan*, to cut a small amount of grain before it is ripe to be used as food in time of shortage (Joushaqān).
**kalā*, land left fallow without being ploughed (Joushaqān and Simnān).
**kalake darvāzeh*, pole or shaft joining the *darvāzeh* or threshing-machine to the yoke (Bīrjand).
kalāntar, overseer of the wards of a city (obs.); overseer of the trade guilds (especially in Iṣfahān; Ṣafavid to Qājār periods); head of a tribal sub-group (larger than that under a *kadkhudā*).
**kalār*, crops sown early (Dārāb).
**kalāteh*, village (Balūchistān); *zamīni kalāteh*, unproductive, barren land (Joushaqān).
**kalkī*, stook of wheat (Sīstān).
**kandeh*, dugout into which sheep and goats are put in winter for shelter (Joushaqān).
karbās, coarse hand-woven cotton cloth.
kard, plot of land.
kardbandī, dividing the land into plots.
**kardū*, plot or field (Joushaqān; cf. *T.Q.*, p. 108).
kārīz, underground water channel (especially Kirmān, Yazd, and east Persia).
karm, vineyard; closely planted trees (opp. of *bustān*; see Aghnides: *Muhammadan Theories of Finance*, p. 379, n. 3).
**kashak*, man who transports the harvest from the threshing-floor to the village (Qarā Bulāgh).
kashk, kind of dried curd.
katar, contraption used to heap earth up into ridges, and which is pulled to and fro by two men standing opposite each other.
kaval, hoop of baked clay placed in the tunnel of a *qanāt* to prevent it falling in (Tehrān).
kavīr, salt desert.
**kay*, water which comes to the surface in relatively flat land as distinct from *jūshi zamīn*, i.e. the water of springs (*chashmeh*) which is drawn from hilly land (Iṣfahān).
kayl, a measure of capacity.
kayyālī, due paid to the man who weighs the harvest.
**khalāmehcharān*, shepherd who takes flocks of unweaned lambs and kids with their dams to graze (Turbati Ḥaydarī).
khāliseh (pl. *khāliṣejāt*) crown land; (Kurdistān) land excepted from the village land distributed among the crop-sharing peasants and worked by the landlord himself.
khān, a complimentary title (obs.); tribal leader.
khānehshumār, *khānehshumārī*, house tax; poll tax.
khānqāh, Ṣufī hospice.
kharāj (obs.), tax; tribute; land tax; *kharāj valad al-ab*, a system of collecting *kharāj* from the Arabs in Qumm by which certain persons were made surety for the tax-payers (*T.Q.*, pp. 155–6).
**kharak zadan*, to thresh rice (Māzandarān).
**khardal*, one-eighth of a *sha'īr* (Kurdistān).
khārijīāt, some kind of tax (Āq Qoyunlū period).
**khari sīāh*, an ass taken for labour service, i.e. the ass provided by the peasant to work free for the landlord on so many days per annum (Kurdistān and Āẕarbāyjān).
kharman, harvest; the grain which has been cut and brought to the threshing-floor. The number of *kharman* per plough-land varies with the configuration of the plough-land.
kharman chillak, crops sown on land immediately the grain harvest has been reaped (Āẕarbāyjān).
kharmangāh, threshing-floor.
kharmankūb, threshing-machine.
kharmankūbī, due paid to a peasant in some areas for threshing.
kharmanpā, man who guards the harvest.
kharṣ (obs.), valuation; *kharṣ kardan*, to estimate the value of a crop (especially date palms and vineyards).
khāṣṣ, *khāṣṣeh* (obs.), crown land.
khīār, full grown (of walnut trees, etc.; *T.Q.*).
**khīd*, plot of land (Bīrjand).
**khil'at* (obs.), robe of honour.
khil'atbahā, due levied in return for the grant of a royal favour (Qājār period).
khīsh, ploughshare, plough; (Khūzistān) plough, plough-land.
**khou kardan*, to weed (Khurāsān).
khums, one-fifth. Originally a deduction of one-fifth from booty (*ghanīma*) and (according to most jurists) from *fay'* also was made. This fifth was itself divided into fifths in

favour of Muḥammad, those who were near to him (i.e. his family), orphans, the poor, and wayfarers. After the death of the Prophet differences of opinion arose as to the disposal of the fifth which had gone to him. Some jurists considered that it went to his heirs; others considered that it belonged to the *imām* who had replaced him in the administration of affairs; Abū Ḥanīfa held that it lapsed after his death; and ash-Shāfiʿī maintained that it was expended on the interests of the Muslims, such as stipends of the army, fodder for their horses, and weapons, the building of fortresses and bridges, and the stipends of *qāẕīs* and *imāms*. The right of the family of Muḥammad to the second fifth of *khums* according to Abū Ḥanīfa lapsed; ash-Shāfiʿī held that it remained but was confined to the Banī Hāshim and the Banī ʿAbdi'l-Muṭṭalib, others of the Quraysh having no right to it (see Māwardī, *Aḥkām*, pp. 218–19). In the later Ithna ʿAsharī theory the meaning of *khums* was modified and appears to have been loosely used to cover *zakāt* also. Bahā ud-Dīn ʿĀmilī states that *khums* was obligatory on (1) *ghanīma* (booty), (2) mineral deposits, (3) anything got out of the sea by divers, (4) property, (5) land bought from a *ẕimmī* (i.e. one-fifth of the land and its price or one-fifth of its revenue annually), (6) gold deposits, and (7) net profits on trade, agriculture, or any craft. Half the revenue derived from *khums* belonged to the *ṣāḥibi zamān* (i.e. the hidden *imām*) and the other half to the *sayyids* descended through the male line from Hāshim (even if they were not descended from Fāṭima provided they were Ithna ʿAsharīs), to orphans, to the poor, and to wayfarers. The latter half the payer could himself distribute to those to whom it was due but the half which belonged to the *ṣāḥibi zamān* was to be paid, during the occultation of the *imām*, to a *mujtahid* who would also distribute it among Hāshimī *sayyids* provided they were Ithna ʿAsharīs, orphans, the poor, and wayfarers (*Jāmiʿi ʿAbbāsī*, B.M. Add. 23578, f. 54 *b*). The term *khums* also denotes some tax or due in the post-Seljūq period but its precise meaning is not clear.

khurdeh mālik (pl. *khurdeh mālikīn*), joint owner of an estate; peasant proprietor; owned by several owners in divided or undivided shares (land); owned by peasant proprietors (land).

khureh, rotation period of water used for irrigation.

khurehbandī, fixing the rotation period of water used for irrigation.

khwānsālār (obs.), official in charge of the commissariat arrangements for the court.

khwushnishīn, the inhabitants of a village who are neither landowners nor crop-sharing peasants.

**kibar*, shelter made of branches and brushwood (Kirmān).

kifāyat, some kind of additional tax or levy possibly connected with the conversion rate (*T.Q.*, pp. 147 ff.).

**kihin*, land which has lain fallow for one year and is then prepared for sowing (ʿAqīlī).

**kimū*, fine sieve used for winnowing (Kirmān; cf. the Joushaqānī word *kameh*, sieve).

**kirār*, see *katar* (Dārāb and the neighbourhood).

kirbās, a kind of cotton homespun.

**kirou* (Sīvandī), see *katar*.

**kirs*, manure which accumulates in a *kandeh* (Joushaqān); the ridge dividing one plot of land or *kard* from another (Kirmān).

**kishān*, cultivated land (Māzandarān); *bī kishān*, land lying fallow (Māzandarān).

**kishāvar*: two peasants, in addition to the owner of the oxen, are attached to a plough-land, one of whom is known as the *kishāvar* and the other as the *nirseh* (parts of Āẕarbāyjān).

**kishmān*, the area immediately around a village which is cultivated every year and regularly manured (Bīrjand; see also *kishtmān*); crop rotation (Kirmān).

kisht, cultivation.

**kishtdār*, share of the crop to which the crop-sharing peasant has a right by virtue of having sown and tended the crop (Kirmān).

**kishtkhān*, land cultivated every year (Iṣfahān).

**kishtmān*, the area immediately around a village which is cultivated every year and regularly manured (Bīrjand; see also *kishmān*).

kitābcheh (obs.), the revenue roll or register in which the revenue of the district was entered by the *mustoufī* of a district.

**koujil*, rough heads which remain on the threshing-floor after the grain has been threshed and winnowed (Simnān).
**koum*, stick put into the outlet hole of a pond to stop it up (Joushaqān).
**kuchar*, the grain harvest after it has been threshed and winnowed (Ḥasano).
**kūchīn va māli khudā*, deduction made from the harvest for the religious classes (Khwār and Varāmīn).
kūd, manure; see *kūt*.
**kulash*, stubble (Kurdistān and Tehrān).
**kulisī*, wooden implement shaped like the letter T used to flatten earth after it has been sown (Simnān).
kulūkh, clod of earth; land the soil of which has not been broken up by a harrow; (Gaz) land dug and prepared for cultivation but not sown.
**kumur* (Khurāsān), sown late (of crops).
**kunār*, some kind of tree growing in the *garmsīr* of Fārs and Khūzistān (? the nettle tree).
**kund*, the stays at the side of a dam in an irrigation channel (Gaz).
kundeh, coulter.
**kūneh sang*, 4 *manni tabrīz* per *kharman* given to the man who looks after the landlord's livestock (Joushaqān).
**kupayn*, hoe (Shūshtar).
kupeh, grain harvest after threshing and winnowing.
**kurā* (Nayrīz), see *katar*.
**kurāz* (Balūchistān), see *katar*.
kūreh, tax-district (obs.); seed-bed or plot smaller than a *kardū* (Joushaqān).
**kūreh* (Sīstān), see *gūreh*.
**kurpeh*, sown late (of crops; Khurāsān and Dārāb); heap of rice ready for threshing (Māzandarān).
**kurq*, underground cache especially for grain, constructed with brushwood or reed-matting and covered by sand (Sīstān; cf. *Tārīkhi Sīstān*, p. 12).
kursī, low table covered by a quilt placed over a charcoal brazier used for heating in winter.
**kurt*, land from which the rice harvest has been reaped and which is to be sown the following year (ʿAqīlī); plot of land (Kirmān; cf. *kard* and *kardū*).
**kurteh*, area taking 50–70 *manni tabrīz* (approximately 2 cwt., 103 lb.–4 cwt., 10 lb.) seed (Shūshtar); lot forming part of a plough-land (ʿAqīlī).
**kurūsheh*, rough heads which remain on the threshing-floor after the grain has been threshed and winnowed (Kirmān).
**kūshī*, 20–30 *manni tabrīz* (approximately 1 cwt., 19 lb.–1 cwt., 84 lb.) cotton which is given by the landlord to the crop-sharing peasant or his wife (Rafsinjān).
kusūr, (?) some kind of tax or levy made for broken coins (pre-Īlkhān period).
kūt, one of the five traditional shares into which the harvest is divided; *seh kūt*, the division according to which two shares go to the crop-sharing peasant and one to the landlord, or vice versa.
**kutal* (Kurdistān), see *kurūsheh*.
kūtālchī, (?) stockman (Īlkhān period).
**kūz*, (?) a *kārīz* or *qanāt* (*T.Q.*).
**kuzar* (Varzaqān), see *kurūsheh*.

**lābān*, *lābūn* (Nayrīz), see *lāvān*.
lārūbī, cleaning out irrigation channels.
**lāt*: *lāt kardan*, to divide water into shares for irrigation purposes (Iṣfahān); *lāt zadan*, to level land by breaking up the clods of earth preparatory to the sowing of rice (Māzandarān).
**lateh*, plot or field.
**latehkār*, peasant who cultivates *ṣayfī* crops (Joushaqān).
lavāḥiq (pl. of *lāḥiqeh*), see *tavābiʿ*.
**lāvān*, *lāvūn*, official under the *sar ṭāq* in charge of the distribution of the water of a *qanāt* (Nayrīz).
**lavār*, hot south wind (Balūchistān).
**lūdar*, shepherd who takes the village flocks to graze (Gaz).

**mādī*, main irrigation channel (Iṣfahān).
**mādī sālār*, official in charge of the distribution of the water of a *mādī* (Iṣfahān).
mafrūz, delimited (of property of which the shares of the joint holders are delimited).
maḥārim (obs.), (?) confidential reports.
majhūl al-maṣraf, said of a *vaqf* when the purposes for which it was constituted are unknown.
maks, see *mukūs*.
māl o jihāt, see *jihāt*.
**māl ullāhī*, deduction made from the harvest for the religious classes (Khurāsān).
māleh, harrow.

mālīāt, taxes.
mālik (pl. *mālikīn*), landowner.
malik, title given in the Seljūq period to minor members of the ruling house in contradistinction to *sulṭān*, which was the title of the ruling *khān*. In the Īlkhān and Ṣafavid periods the title was debased and used also by *amīrs* and governors.
**mālikbakhsh*, land which is not redistributed periodically but is permanently divided among the peasants (Fārs).
**malikīyi gāvbān*, small amount taken from the total harvest for the peasants attached to a plough-land for shoes (Khīr).
mamlakat (pl. *mamālik*), realm; (obs.) province.
manāfiʿ, chattels incorporeal.
manfaʿa, *manfaʿat*, usufruct.
manqūl, movable; *ghayri manqūl*, immovable.
marāʿī, pasture tax (*Mir'āt ul-Qāsān*, f. 64 *a*); tax paid on ewes and goats in milk.
**mard*, peasant working a plough-land who owns one ox and one ass (Kirmān).
**mardak*, upright shaft fixed at right angles to the beam or *rakht* near the front of the plough (Sīstān).
martaʿ, pasture.
marz, the bank of a river (*T.Q.*, p. 107); ridge dividing one plot of land from another.
marzbandī, dividing land into plots.
**marzū* (Joushaqān), see *marz*.
masāḥat, measurement; the assessment of the government tax by measurement of the land.
masjid, mosque; *khādimi masjid*, attendant of a mosque.
massāḥ, surveyor.
mavānīd, arrears of taxation (*T.Q.*, p. 102).
mavāsh, *mavāshī*, *mavāshīyeh*, cattle tax (*Mir'āt ul-Qāsān*, f. 64 *a*); tax paid on cows, mules, and asses.
mavāt, *arāẓīyi mavāt*, dead lands.
mavāẓiʿ (pl. of *mouẓiʿ*) places, villages (obs.).
**may*, *may rūz*, 12 hours' water; *nīm may*, 6 hours' water (Sīstān).
māzād, surplus.
mazraʿeh, grain land (obs.); hamlet belonging to a parent village (see also p. 4, n. 2, above).
**mīād*, coulter (Sīstān).
mihmāndār (obs.), official charged with the entertainment of foreign envoys, etc., whose duty it was to convey them through the country to their destination.
mihmānī, due levied for the entertainment of officials and travellers.
milk, landed property; private property in land, in contradistinction to crown lands or land assignments.
milkī (obs.), privately owned (of land).
**miʿmār*, person (other than the landowner) who rents draught animals to the peasant (Bihbahān).
miʿmāri arbāb, landowner's bailiff (*T.Q.*).
mināl, some kind of due (Īlkhān period); the state dues on *khāliṣeh*; (Kirmān) the landowner's share of the harvest in a crop-sharing agreement.
mīrāb, official in charge of the distribution of water for irrigation.
mouẓūʿāt, deductions made from the harvest for the payment of local officials, etc.
muʿābir, official sent by the government to see that a surveyor had carried out his duties properly (*T.Q.*, p. 108).
muʿāfī, (tax) exemption.
muʿāhad (obs.), member of a protected community who pays *jizya* according to a treaty of capitulation (*ṣulḥ*).
muʿāmaleh, transaction. The contract regulating the relations between the cultivators of Khaybar, Fadak, Tayma', and Wādī'l-Qurā with Muḥammad appears to have been called *muʿāmaleh*. It is possible that *muʿāmaleh* was used as synonymous with *muzāraʿeh* (cf. Abū Yūsuf (Bulāq, 1933), p. 91). At a later date the term appears to have been used for tenancy and public contraction (see Løkkegaard, p. 94). In Seljūq times there was a special *dīvāni muʿāmalāt va qismat*, which was presumably concerned with revenue derived from public contraction, i.e. revenue paid under agreements of the *muqāṭaʿeh* type.
mubāḥ, *res nullius*.
mubāshir, bailiff; (Kirmān) man who collects the landowner's share of the harvest.
muftī, member of the religious classes who issues *fatvās*.
**muhar* (? for *māhir*), man who looks after date palms and gathers the harvest therefrom (Jahrum).
muḥaṣṣil (obs.), tax-collector, usually of a relatively low rank.
**muḥavvaṭeh*, land immediately surrounding a village which is regularly

manured and cultivated every year (Khurāsān); land immediately surrounding a village, enclosed by walls and held by the peasants (Turbati Ḥaydarī).

muḥtasib (obs.), official whose duties were to see that the religious precepts of Islām were obeyed. In so far as he performed the duties of a magistrate his jurisdiction was limited to matters connected with commercial transactions, defective weights and measures, fraudulent sales, and non-payment of debts (see art. in *E.I.*).

mujtahid, member of the religious classes who has reached a degree of eminence which permits him to issue opinions on matters of faith.

mukūs (pl. of *maks*), irregular taxes and dues.

mullā, see *ākhund*.

mulūk, pl. of *malik*.

mumaiyiz, assessor.

muqannī, one who makes and repairs *qanāts*.

muqāsameh (obs.), the assessment of the government tax by way of a fixed proportion of the crop.

muqāṭaʿeh (obs.), the assessment of the tax of a district at a fixed sum; the farming of the revenue of a district by the inhabitants for a fixed sum.

murūj (pl. of *marj*; obs.) common lands where cattle graze and logs or brushwood can be gathered.

murūri zamān, lapse of time.

muṣaddiq, assessor; valuer.

muṣādireh, capricious expropriation.

muṣāʿideh, advance (in money or kind).

musallamī, (tax) exemption.

musāqāt, crop-sharing contract for trees.

muṣārafeh, *pro rata* levy on tax-payers to make good deficits (*T.Q.*, p. 190).

mushāʿ, jointly owned in undivided shares (of land, etc.).

mushrif, overseer; (Sīstān) see *dashtbān*.

musht, 12 *musht* weigh approximately $1\frac{1}{2}$ *manni tabrīz* (9 lb., 13 oz.).

mushtuluq (obs.), levy made on a special occasion such as the announcement of good news.

mustaghallāt, real estate such as shops, baths, caravanserais, etc.

mustamarrī (pl. *mustamarrīāt*; obs.), pension; allowance.

mustaqeh, measure of water (*T.Q.*, p. 43).

mustoufī (obs.), revenue accountant; the chief revenue officer of a district; *mustoufī ul-mamālik*, chief revenue officer of the kingdom.

mutaʿazzir, unrealizable (of taxes, owing to the absence or poverty of the tax-payers; obs.); *mutaʿazzir al-maṣraf*, said of a *vaqf* when its proceeds cannot be put to the purpose for which it was constituted.

muṭabbaq, said of a vine which is not trained on a trellis (*T.Q.*; see also *sābāṭ*).

muṭālibāti sulṭānī (obs.), requisitions on behalf of the ruler.

mutaṣaddī, overseer; person in charge of an office.

mutaṣarrif (obs.), district tax-collector.

mutavajjihāt (obs.), taxes levied in addition to the original assessment.

mutavallī, administrator of a *vaqf*.

muvaqqiʿ (obs.), person who issues an authorization.

muzāraʿ, person to whom the land is entrusted in return for a share of the crop under a crop-sharing contract.

muẓārabeh, contract for trade by which one partner provides the capital.

muzāraʿeh, crop-sharing contract.

muzāriʿ, the person who entrusts the land to another in return for a share of the crop under a crop-sharing contract; peasant.

muzd, wage.

**nafaqeh*, expenses in connexion with irrigation (Kirmān).

nahāleh, some kind of tax or due (Īlkhān period).

nahr, irrigation channel.

nāʾib, deputy. In the Seljūq period the *nāʾib* was an official representing the *sulṭān* in a 'reserved' area in the land assigned to a *malik* or *amīr*, the *nāʾib* not being under the jurisdiction of the assignee. In the Īlkhān period the *nāʾib* was an important provincial official, and in the Ṣafavid period provincial governors and the holders of *tuyūl* in some cases had the title *nāʾib*, which had become virtually synonymous with *malik* (in its debased sense).

najjārī, due paid to the village carpenter.

namad, felt; felt coat or cloak.

**namūneh*, *daym* land sown with grain by a *ballak* (Khurāsān).

**nān sufreh*, advance given to a peasant when he first comes to a village to cultivate a plough-land or when a new village is made (Kurdistān).

**nānāneh*, levy made on the peasants at harvest time for bread for the landowner (Kurdistān).

**narmeh*, grain which has been threshed but not winnowed (Kirmān).
nasab, consanguinity.
**nasaq*, capacity of a village in plough-lands (Arāk).
nassājī, weaving tax; *khumsi nassājī*, (?) tax of 20 per cent. levied on looms (obs.).
nāvaqeh, measure of water (*T.Q.*, p. 43).
navvāb (pl. of *nā'ib*), deputies. In the Ṣafavid and Qājār periods *navvāb* is used as a singular to mean the supreme ruler or prince.
nāy, see *kaval*.
nayzār, reed bed.
nāẓir, overseer.
nāzi shasht (obs.), commission levied by officials for duties performed.
**nāẓūr* (Iṣfahān and Kirmān), see *dashtbān*.
**nīm kār*, peasant who receives half the crop under a crop-sharing agreement in *daym* land (the peasant provides the draught animals and the landlord the seed; Bāvī).
**nīm mard* (Kirmān), peasant attached to a plough-land who has no ox (see also *mard*).
nimār, *nimārī*, extraordinary levies (Īlkhān period).
**nīmeh*, contract by which a man buys a part share in a cow, feeds and tends it, giving half the produce and progeny to the other partner (Jahrum and elsewhere).
**nirseh* (Āẓarbāyjān), see *kishāvar*.
niṣfī, used of a crop-sharing agreement under which the produce is divided equally between the two parties.
nishā', transplanting (rice, etc.).
**nou darār*, new irrigation channel made when flood-water has carried away the old channel (Dizfūl).
**nourūzeh kardan*, to plough the land just before the Persian New Year (Jahrum).
nourūzī (obs.), due levied at the Persian New Year.
**nouvar*, large irrigation channel (Sīstān).
**nūnī* (= *nānī*), small quantity of wheat or barley reaped in an emergency before the grain is ripe (Kāshmar).

oubeh, Turkomān tent; tribal group living in such a tent.
ouqāf, pl. of *vaqf*.
**oushīn*, wooden pronged fork used for winnowing (Kirmān).

pādarāneh, the sum paid month by month by a man whose name was entered in the list of those who formed the military contingent provided by a village to someone whom he sent as his substitute (Qājār period).
**pāft kardan*, to prune (trees; Iṣṭahbānāt).
**pāgāv*, six shares (or land-holdings) run together as a unit (Sīstān).
pākār, local official who is (*a*) a subordinate of the *kadkhudā*, (*b*) a subordinate of the *mīrāb*, or (*c*) charged with watching over the peasants' fields.
**pakhal*, stubble (Bīrjand); wheat and barley straw before it is cut up (Sīstān).
**pakhalī*, stubble (Kirmān).
**pakheh*, stubble (Joushaqān).
**pakhtār kardan*, to prune (trees; Shūshtar).
**pal*, see *marz* (Khurāsān); sheepcote (Simnān).
palgīrī (Khurāsān), see *marzbandī*.
paṃbehchīn, labourer who gathers the cotton harvest.
**pānzdah*: the village land of Varzaqān in Uzum Dil is divided into 93 *pānzdah*.
**paran* (Sīstān), see *marz* (cf. *Tārīkhi Sīstān*, p. 33).
pārchīn, ditch or fence dividing fields.
parvānehcheh (obs.), royal missive or order.
**pasht kardan*, to divide by lot among the peasants land available for cultivation (Iṣfahān).
**pātīnī*, sieve used for winnowing grain (Simnān).
**pāt kardan* (Nayrīz), to prune (trees); to weed.
**pattār kardan*, to prune (trees; Kirmān).
**pay dirou*, stubble (Khurāsān).
pāyish kardan, to prune (a tree).
**pāyisht*, weeding (Iṣfahān).
paymān, a measure of water.
**paynār*, 1 *chārak* (Bihbahān).
piāleh, hour-glass.
**pindūk*, levy or due paid to a *sardār* by virtue of his position (Balūchistān).
pīneh: *pīneh zadan*, *pīneh jilou burdan*, to deepen the channel of a *qanāt* if it dries up; to extend the channel of a *qanāt* deeper into the ground if water is not reached after the excavation of a trial shaft or *gamāneh*.
ping, hour-glass; (Sīstān) place where a water channel is partially blocked by brushwood in order to narrow it

so that a bridge can be built over the channel.
**pirsāneh*, levy made for mourning ceremonies (Kurdistān).
**pishi dirou* (*pisha dura*), second crop of lucerne (Āẕarbāyjān).
pishk, drawing lots for the redistribution of land.
pīshkār, chief financial official of a province (Qājār period); bailiff; sown early (crops).
pīshkash, present (from an inferior to a superior); due levied in the form of a 'present'.
pīshkharīd, buying (crops) in advance.
pīshkhidmat, servant.
pīshnamāz, prayer-leader.
plākkūbī, initial stages of registration when claims to land are filed in the registration office.
**pūk, pūkeh*, disused *qanāt* (Mūrchehkhvart).
pūlād, coulter.
pushteh, distance between two wells of a *qanāt*; (Kirmān) see *bāfeh*.
**pushti kharmanī*, 1 *manni tabrīz* (6 lb., 9 oz.) per *kharman* given to the poor (Joushaqān).
**pūt*, disused *qanāt* (Kirmān).

qa'ānchī, qā'ānchī, official in charge of the flocks of the Īlkhān rulers.
qabāleh, title-deed; (obs.) contract by which one member of a local tax community undertook to pay to the state a fixed sum, collecting himself the *kharāj* of the tax-payers (Løkkegaard, pp. 94 ff.; see also Aghnides, *Muhammadan Theories of Finance*, p. 377, n. 1).
qal'eh, walled enclosure or building.
**qalūn*, labour service (Kirmān).
**qalūnī*, man who performs labour service (Kirmān).
qanāt, underground water channel (see above, p. 217).
qappānī, due for weighing.
**qarāpishk*, some kind of occupancy right (Tehrān); drawing lots for land the distribution of which is to be permanent (Asadābād); periodic redistribution of land by lot (Bakhtīārī).
qarāsūr, road guard (Ṣafavid period).
qar'ī, coming from deep water-bearing strata (of *qanāt* water, etc.).
qarīeh, village (see also above, p. 4, n. 2).
qaṣabeh, township or small town.
**qasī* (= *qasīl*) (Dizfūl), see *khasīl*.
qaṭā'ī (pl. of *qaṭī'a*; obs.), crown lands, waste-lands, dead lands, and swamps assigned as heritable property.
**qaykhā, qaykhvā*, village headman (Kurdistān).
**qayyā*, outlet hole of a pond which is stopped with a stick (Joushaqān).
qāẕī, judge who decided all cases involving questions of civil and criminal law according to the *sharī'a*. In the course of time the hearing of cases in the *sharī'a* courts became restricted until finally only cases of personal status were heard in them, other cases being heard by the temporal authorities, who were not limited in their procedure or decisions by the rules laid down for the *sharī'a* courts.
qāẕī ul-quẕāt (obs.), chief *qāẕī*.
qīās, analogy.
qilān, labour service (Īlkhān period).
qishlāq, winter quarters; (Kurdistān) hamlet.
qismat (obs.), see *mu'āmaleh*. The term *qismat* may possibly have been used for a levy made for extraordinary purposes, or for the payment of the expenses of the administration, etc.
**qubbeh*, threshing-floor (Kāzirūn).
qubchūr, qūbchūr, tax, levy; cattle-tax (Īlkhān period).
qubchurmeh, (?) cattle-tax (Ṣafavid period).
**qukhil* (Kurdistān), see *dashtbān*.
qūmush, see *muqannī* (*T.Q.*, p. 42).
**qumushkan* (Kurdistān), see *muqannī*.
qunāghliq, qunughla (obs.), tax for the entertainment of officials, etc.
quruq, royal hunting reserves.
qurūt, (?) curds (Īlkhān period).
quẕāt, pl. of *qāẕī*.
**qwaykhāh*, see *qaykhā*.

ra'āyā, (pl. of *ra'īyat*) peasants.
rāhdār, road guard (Īlkhān to Qājār periods).
ra'īs, chief, leader, head of a village, quarter, etc. In Seljūq times the *ra'īs* was an important local official.
ra'īyat, subjects of a ruler (obs.); peasants; a peasant.
**ra'īyatbaksh*, land redistributed annually among the peasants (Fārs).
rakht, beam of a plough.
rameh, flock; (Turbati Ḥaydarī) flock of 600 head.
**raneh kardan*, to plough land for fallow (Khūzistān).
raqabat, raqabeh (pl. *raqabāt*): *raqabat ul-arẕ*, the soil and also proprietary rights over the soil (see van Berchem, *La propriété territoriale*, p. 32, n. 1).

In Persian usage (from the Ṣafavid period onwards) *raqabeh* is used to denote a group of villages in a *bulūk* or district and especially of villages forming *vaqf* or *khāliṣeh* property.

rasad, tax-quota (*T.Q.*, p. 143); share of the harvest under a crop-sharing agreement (Ṣafavid period); (Iṣṭahbānāt), unit of water.

**rash*, *rashn*, rotation period of water used for irrigation (Gaz and Central Persia).

**rashteh*, group of 10–12 oxen yoked together to tread out grain (Sīstān).

rasm (obs.), due, commission; *rasm ul-ḥarz*, commission paid for the valuation of the crop; *rasm ul-masāḥat*, commission paid to a surveyor who measures the land; *rasm ul-vizāreh*, due paid to the *vazīr*.

**ravāl*, territory through which a tribe migrates along traditional routes (Fārs).

ray' kardan, to swell, set (grain).

rayyā', assessor of crops (Ṣafavid period).

rīsh safīd, elders, grey-beards.

**rīūn kardan*, to break through from one channel to another (water; Joushaqān).

roughan, clarified butter, ghee.

rouẓeh khwānī, recitation of some incident in a passion play, etc.

ru'asā, pl. of *ra'īs*.

**ruhn*, small receptacle into which grain is put (Qashqā'ī).

**rung*, submerged rut or water channel; water channel between reed-beds (Sīstān).

ruqbā, usufruct for life.

rusūmāt (pl. of *rasm*), dues; deductions made from the harvest for the payment of local officials, etc.

sabab, special cause (giving hereditary right).

sabad, box; (Varzaqān) receptacle holding approximately 10 *manni ahar* (approx. 1 cwt., 95 lb.).

sābāṭ, said of a vine trained on a trellis or wooden frame (Qumm).

sabzbān (Bīrjand), see *dashtbān*.

sāchūq, entertainment dues (Āq Qoyunlū period).

**ṣadaqa* (obs.), legal obligatory alms (see *zakāt*); voluntary almsgiving.

sādāt, pl. of *sayyid*.

ṣādir (pl. *ṣādirāt*, *ṣādirīāt*), extraordinary tax (Ṣafavid to Qājār periods).

ṣadr, official in the religious hierarchy corresponding in some respects to a *muftī* (Ṣafavid period; see *T.M.*, p. 111); *ṣadri a'ẓam*, chief minister, prime minister (Qājār period).

ṣāfīyeh, see *ṣavāfī*.

ṣaḥārī, pl. of *ṣaḥrā*.

ṣaḥib jam' (obs.), revenue assessment officer.

**ṣāḥib kār*, bailiff (Turbati Ḥaydarī).

**sahm*, share, portion; (Bīrjand) 24 hours' water.

ṣaḥrā, open country; (Khurāsān) several plough-lands grouped together and worked as a unit.

**ṣaḥradār*, peasant who cultivates part of the land in a *ṣaḥrā* (Khurāsān).

sakhlū (obs.), protection money paid by the settled population to the Yamūt.

salaf, *salam*, sale by which the purchaser pays the purchase money in advance while the seller is required to deliver the article purchased after the expiry of a definite period.

**salāmāneh*, levy made for the *mubāshir* or lessee on his first visit to a village (Kurdistān).

salāmāneh, *salāmī* (obs.), due paid for royal audiences and on receipt of news of the ruler's well-being.

**sālār* (Khurāsān), peasant attached to a *ṣaḥrā* whose duties include irrigating, weeding, and manuring the land; *sar sālār*, head of a group of *sālārs*.

salmānī, barber; due paid to the village barber.

**sanaghī*, due amounting to 1 *manni tabrīz* (approx. 6 lb., 9 ozs.) per cow paid to the *khān* (Mamasanī).

**sangajī*, constructing terraces on a hill-side for cultivation purposes (Bīrjand).

sar ābyār, see *ābyār*.

**sar buneh*, holder of a plough-land (Tehrān).

sar dihqān, see *dihqān*.

**sar dihqānī*, one day's free labour per annum performed by the *dihqāns* of a *ṣaḥrā* for the *sar dihqān* (Khurāsān).

sar juftī, due levied per plough-land by the landlord (apart from and in addition to a share of the crop).

**sar marzī*, crops sown round the edges of melon fields (Burkhwār).

sar mīrāb, head *mīrāb*.

sar quflī, goodwill of a business; occupation right (Kāzirūn).

sar sālār, see *sālār*.

**sar sālārī*, one day's free labour per annum performed by the *sālārs* of a *ṣaḥrā* for the *sar sālār* (Khurāsān).

sar shumār, *sar shumārī*, poll tax.

**sar ṭāq*, official in charge of the distribution of the water of a *qanāt* (Nayrīz).

sar zaʿīm, man who owns an ox and cultivates a plough-land (Balūchistān).

**sarak*, opening made in a water channel to let water into the land which it irrigates (Sīstān).

sarāneh, poll tax.

**sarband*, chief shepherd (Central Persia).

sarcharkhī, tax levied on wells (Qājār period; south Persia).

**sardār*, tribal leader, landowner (Balūchistān and Sīstān; cf. Bartholomae, *Zum Sasanidischen Recht*, ii. 23, 24).

sardsīr, temperate regions (as opposed to *garmsīr*).

sarghū, some kind of due (Āq Qoyunlū period).

sarḥadd, frontier; used also of those regions to which the tribes go in summer, i.e. the cool upland regions on the frontier of their tribal territory (Qashqā'ī and Khamseh).

sarijeh, round copper bowl with a hole in the bottom, which is placed in a larger bowl filled with water and used as a water-glass; unit of water (see Appendix II).

sarkār (Ṣafavid period), administrative department; account, fund.

sarkardeh, leader of a tribal group.

sarkāri intiqālī, department in charge of administering *khāliṣeh* lands and those *vaqf* lands of which the ruler was the *mutavallī* (Ṣafavid period; see *T.M.*, ff. 74 ff.).

sarkhānegī, house tax (Qājār period).

sarparast, man placed in charge of a tribal group by the government.

**sarūk*, cloth used for collecting stooks of wheat or barley and carrying them to the threshing-floor (Sīstān).

ṣavāfī (pl. of *ṣāfīyeh*; obs.), that part of the booty which went to the *imām* as distinct from that which was divided among the fighters; crown lands (cf. Ibn Wāẓiḥ, *Ta'rīkh*, ii. 258; Balāẕurī, p. 272).

savāqī (obs.), streamlets; irrigation channels; *qanāts*.

sāvarī, dues levied by way of 'presents' (Īlkhān to Ṣafavid periods).

ṣayfī, summer crops and vegetables (i.e. crops sown in summer and reaped for the most part in autumn).

ṣayfī kārī, the cultivation of summer crops and vegetables.

sayyid, descendant of the Prophet Muḥammad through his daughter Fāṭimeh.

seh bikār, threefold crop rotation.

shafīʿ, pre-emptor.

shahristān, district dependent upon a town.

shaʿīr, one-third of a *ḥabbeh* (obs.); (Kurdistān) 8 *khardal* or one-sixteenth of a *dāng*; (Zarand and Sāveh) a water measure.

**shākhāneh*, levy made on cattle (Kurdistān).

**shākh shumārī*, cattle and sheep tax (Bakhtīārī).

**shaligah*, *shalkah*, place where water is let into cultivated land from an irrigation channel (Kurdistān).

**shan* (Kurdistān), see *chahār shākh*.

**shana* (Ḥasano), see *chahār shākh*.

sharīʿa, the canon law of Islām.

shatvī, winter crops (wheat, barley, etc.).

shaykh, leader of an Arab tribal group; leader of a religious order.

shīʿah, the party of ʿAlī, the son-in-law of the Prophet Muḥammad. Sunnī Muhammadans recognize the succession of caliphs as the legitimate successors of Muḥammad. The Shīʿah on the other hand hold that the leadership of the community passed on the death of Muḥammad to ʿAlī, whom they consider the first *imām*, and after him by hereditary succession to his heirs. Shīʿīs of the Ithnā ʿAsharī rite recognize twelve *imāms*, the last of whom, Muḥammad al-Mahdī, disappeared in A.H. 260/A.D. 873–4; those of the Ismāʿīlī rite recognize seven *imāms* only.

**shīb*: *shīb kardan* (Khurāsān), see *pīneh zadan*.

shihneh (obs.), military governor; official placed in charge of or attached to a tribal group on behalf of the ruler.

shikār, hunting; (obs.) hunting dues (or possibly the provision of beaters for hunting).

**shikarteh*, grain sown, reaped, and threshed free for the landlord (Arab areas of Khūzistān).

shilān bahā (obs.), levies made for assemblies on feast-days.

**shīleh*, furrow on a hillside made by rain-water (Kirmān).

**shīmīsh*, plough (Sīvand).

shīreh, grape syrup; preparation for smoking made from the waste product of opium.

shufʿeh, pre-emption.

shūlāt, soft soil.

**shūmī*, armful of grain taken at harvest-time before threshing begins containing 5–6 *manni tabrīz* (approx. 32 lb., 12 oz.–39 lb. grain) by the *chāhkhū* and *dashtbān* (Kirmān).
**sīāhbakhsh*, land divided permanently among the crop-sharing peasants of a village (Fārs).
**sīfāl*, straw before it is cut up (Joushaqān and Kirmān).
**sifīd barg* (Sīstān), see *shatvī*.
sirishtehdār, minor revenue official (Qājār period).
**soum*, rice in the husk (Māzandarān).
**souz barg* (Sīstān), see *ṣayfī*.
soyūrghāl, grant of land or its revenue in lieu of salary or by way of a pension (Qarā Qoyunlū to Qājār periods).
suds, one-sixth; some kind of tax or due (obs.).
ṣudūr, pl. of *ṣadr*.
**sufāl* (Kirmān), see *sīfāl*.
sufreh bahā, levies made for those who prepared banquets (Āq Qoyunlū and Ṣafavid periods).
suknā, right of residence.
ṣulḥ, (in law) a contract by which a dispute is obviated, conciliation (see above, p. 200); (obs.) treaty of capitulation.
sulṭān, ruler. In the Qur'ān *sulṭān* means 'power', and in the Ḥadīth it is used exclusively in the sense of power. It is first used in the fourth/eleventh century in the sense of a powerful ruler or an independent ruler of a certain territory (see art. on *sulṭān* in *E.I.*). In the Ṣafavid period the term *sulṭān* was used to designate an army commander. Subsequently the term was further debased and in the late Qājār period it was used to designate an officer whose rank corresponded approximately to that of a captain.
**sumkār*, one of a number of peasants (usually four) attached to a plough-land, among whom one-eighth of the harvest is divided (ʿAqīlī).
**sūrāneh*, payment made by the peasant to the landlord for permission to marry (Kurdistān).
sūrsāt, purveyance (Qājār period).
suvar, river banks (*T.Q.*).
suvayn, sown late (of crops; Fasā).

taʿaddī, transgressing beyond the bounds of what is allowed or customary with regard to the property or right of another.
**taʿāruf*, payment made by the peasant to the landlord for permission to cultivate a piece of land when he first takes over (Kirmān).
tabar tarāshī: *ḥaqqi tabar tarāshī*, right acquired to a piece of forest land by virtue of having cleared it.
tafāvuti ʿamal, dues levied by government officials for their expenses over and above the revenue assessment (Qājār period).
**tāfīeh*: *tāfīeh shudan*, to be out of order, fall into disuse (a *qanāt*; Kirmān).
tafrīṭ, the abandoning of an action which by virtue of an agreement or custom is necessary for the preservation of the property of another.
**taghal*, 30 *kurdistāni mann* (approx. 1 cwt., 45 lb.).
**tahi bāfeh jamʿ kun*, gleaner (Kirmān).
**tahi qubbeh*, due amounting to 2½ per cent of the harvest paid to the peasants attached to a plough-land (but not to the owner of the draught animals; Iṣṭahbānāt).
taḥjīr, marking out dead land preparatory to reclaiming it.
taḥṣīldār, revenue collector, accountant.
**taḥvīldār*, receiver who helps the landowner's bailiff (Bīrjand).
ṭā'ifeh, group, clan.
tājīk, non-Turk, Persian.
takālīf, pl. of *taklīf*.
takhfīf (pl. *takhfīfāt*), reduction.
**takhtak*, platform made of reeds and earth upon which huts are built (Sīstān).
**takhteh*, group of plots of land or *kart* (Joushaqān).
**takhti pal*, method of cultivating melons, etc., by which the plants are sown on a flat surface and covered with earth (Khurāsān).
taklīf (obs.), extraordinary tax, requisition.
taklīfāti dīvānī (obs.), requisitions by the *dīvān*.
takmileh (obs.), additional tax imposed upon the tax-payers of a district to make good deficits occurring as a result of defaulting tax-payers or because tax-payers have left the district or died.
**talak*, the peasant's house and its surroundings (Māzandarān).
**taleh*, the taking of a share from the harvest by way of *salmānī*, *ḥaddādī*, and *najjārī* (Fīrūzābād, Fārs).
taljī'a, see *iltijā'*.
tanbūsheh, drainage pipe.
tamghā (Īlkhān period), dues on mer-

chandise; capital levy; town levies, octrois.

tamlīk, ownership.

**ṭannāb*, area of land equivalent to 2 ac., 4,672 sq. yds. (Riẓā'īyeh).

**ṭannābdār*, holder of a *ṭannāb*.

ṭāq, young tree without branches (*T.Q.*, p. 110); unit of water (see Appendix II).

taqabbul, (?) some kind of levy made when a tax-payer agrees to the assessment fixed by the revenue officer (Āq Qoyunlū).

ṭāqat, the tax-bearing capacity of land, etc.

**taqāvī*, advance given to a peasant when he first cultivates the land (Jahrum); advance made to a peasant when he first cultivates the land which he returns only if he leaves the land (Turbati Ḥaydarī); advance (Kurdistān).

taqdimeh, taxes demanded before they fall due (Īlkhān period); (Kirmān) advance of a fixed amount given under a contract by the landlord to the peasant at the beginning of the year to be returned at harvest time (cf. Muḥammad b. Maḥmūd Āmulī, *Nafā'is ul-Funūn*, i. 88, which defines *taqdimeh* as 'that which is taken [by a cultivator] in advance').

**ṭāqeh*, 12 hours' water (Bīrjand).

taqqovī (Jahrum), see *taqāvī*.

tarāz, contract between the owner of sheep and goats and a person to whom he entrusts these for a fixed period, the produce of the flock being shared between the two parties.

tarkhān, Mongol prince enjoying certain hereditary privileges including exemption from various taxes and dues (Juvaynī, *Ta'rīkh-i-Jahān-Gushā*, i. 27); other persons, including divines, were also given this rank (see Mīnovī and Minorsky, *B.S.O.A.S.*, x. 783 and 789). In the *yāsā* of Chinghīz Khān *tarkhān* was the appellation given to a person immune from general state service (Poliak, 'The General Organization of the Mamlūk State', ibid. 870).

tarkhānī, pension, hereditary grant of land carrying with it certain immunities (Īlkhān period and occasionally post-Īlkhān).

**ṭās*, 6 hours' water (Bīrjand).

tasabbub (obs.), see *tasbīb*.

taṣarruf, possession; *taṣarrufi 'āmm*, constructive possession; *taṣarrufi khāṣṣ*, actual possession.

tasbīb (obs.), making a charge on a fund or district.

**tāseh*, rough heads of barley and wheat left on the threshing-floor after the grain and straw have been separated from them (Joushaqān).

tash shumārī, hearth tax (Bakhtīārī).

tas'īr (obs.), conversion rate by which the tax assessed in gold *dīnārs* or in kind was converted into currency *dīnārs* or into cash.

ṭasq, tax schedule (*T.Q.*); quota laid upon cereals per *jarīb* (Khwārazmī, p. 59).

ṭassūj (obs.), one twenty-fourth of a *miṣqāl* (Khwārazmī, p. 62); weight of two grains of barley; (Īlkhān period) a coin (?).

tāsūj, *tasūj*, measure of water; see also *ṭassūj*.

tavābi': *tavābi' va lavāḥiq*, supplementary dues (*T.Q.*); dependencies.

ṭayyārāt, (?) some kind of extraordinary tax or possibly tolls levied at city gates (Seljūq period); revenue derived from property which escheats to the state, property belonging to the king which has been appropriated by others, lost things, and the property of those who are absent (Īlkhān period, see Mīnovī and Minorsky, *B.S.O.A.S.*, x. 774).

ta'zīeh, Shī'ī passion play.

tikīeh, kind of hall in which *ta'zīehs* are held.

**ting* (Sīstān), barrier made of brushwood to prevent the advance of drifting sand; lean-to made of reeds for cattle.

**tinzeh*, hire paid by one village which has more water than land to a neighbouring village for the use of its land (Rafsinjān).

tīr, beam of a plough.

**tīr māhī*, crops sown in autumn (Sīstān).

**tīreh*, portion or lot of land (Kirmān).

**tīrkār*, group of fields (the size of which varies) into which the village land is divided for cultivation (Bīrjand).

ṭisq, see *ṭasq*.

toujīh: *tavāmīri toujīh*, rolls of summons (Ṣafavid period).

**toujīh sari kharman*, levy made by the *kadkhudā* on the peasants (Qahdrījān).

toulīat, the function of a *mutavallī*.

touqī' (obs.), an authorization; *ṣāḥib ut-touqī'*, person in whose favour an authorization is issued.

touqīf, arrest, seizure; confiscation.

tufangchī, rifleman.
tukhm, seed.
**tukhmrīz*, peasant charged with sowing (Kirmān).
**tūlakī*, transplantation of rice (Iṣfahān; in Joushaqān the term is used for the transplantation of other crops).
tuʿma, assignment on state domains (pre-Seljūq times).
tūmān, monetary unit introduced by the Mongols in the thirteenth century A.D.
tūmār, roll, register.
tuyūl, land assignment (Īlkhān to Qājār periods).
tuyūldār, holder of a *tuyūl*.
tuyūl nāmeh, tuyūl nāmehcheh, document granting a *tuyūl*.

**ūkh*, beam of a plough (Ḥasano).
ūlāgh, ulāgh, levy for postal couriers or for animals for the post (Īlkhān to Qājār periods).
ulām, guide forced without pay into the service of an official to show him the way from one village to another (Qarā Qoyunlū to Qājār periods).
ʿulamā (pl. of *ʿālim*, 'learned man'), those learned in the religious sciences.
ʿulūfeh, levy of fodder for the horses of officials as they travelled through the country (Īlkhān to Qājār times).
umarā, pl. of *amīr*.
ʿumdeh mālik (pl. *ʿumdeh mālikīn*), large landed proprietor.
ʿummāl, pl. of *ʿāmil*.
ʿumrā, life grant.
ʿumrān, making flourishing or populous; development and maintenance of land.
ʿurf, customary law.
ʿurfī, customary.
ʿushr, tithe. *ʿUshr* was, broadly speaking, levied on all produce of the earth, but the jurists differ in exempting from it certain crops and fruits and in fixing the taxable minimum. The rates at which it was levied varied, and were half tenth, single tenth, one and a half, and double tenth. In general in early Islamic times lands which were irrigated by running water paid the single rate and lands artificially irrigated the half tenth. Sanction for this is found in Muḥammad's treatment of the people of Bīsha (see J. Wellhausen, *Skizzen und Vorarbeiten*, Berlin, 1884–9, iv. 130). *ʿUshr* was normally paid by Muslims (but see above, pp. 17 ff.). *ʿUshr* land was land which paid *ʿushr*, in contradistinction to *kharāj* land which paid *kharāj* (see pp. 20 ff., above, and Løkkegaard, pp. 72 ff., for a discussion of the differences between them). The term *ʿushr* is also used in the sense of *zakāt* and *ṣadaqa*.
ustān, province, governorate-general.
ustāndār, governor-general (of a province or *ustān*).

**vākār*, preparing the land for sowing rice (Māzandarān).
vakīl, representative; advocate.
**val* (Ḥasano), threshing-machine consisting of a board with stones attached to the bottom (which is drawn by an ox or ass, a man standing on it).
vālī (obs.), governor.
**vaqeh*, a weight of approx. 23 lb. (Khūzistān).
vaqf, land immobilized for some purpose; *vaqfi ʿāmm*, charitable *vaqf*; *vaqfi amvāt*, *vaqf* the revenue of which is devoted to purposes such as the holding of *rouẓeh khwānīs* for the dead, etc.; *vaqfi khāṣṣ*, personal *vaqf* (see above, p. 230).
vaqf nāmeh, deed constituting a *vaqf*.
vāqif, person who constitutes property into a *vaqf*.
**vār*, place in an irrigation channel where water is let through into cultivated land (Joushaqān, Maymeh, Gaz, and Abīāneh).
**varayn*, sown early (of crops; Fasā).
**vāreh*, see *vār*.
**vargeh*, sown late (of crops; Khurāsān).
**varzāv*, draught ox (Joushaqān).
**vashan*, rain, moisture (Kāshān).
**vaz*, implement used to divide water for irrigation purposes (*T.Q.*, p. 33); (Joushaqān) see *katar*.
vaẓā'if (obs., pl. of *vaẓīfeh*), tax schedules.
vaẓīʿat, vaẓīʿeh (obs.), tax schedule.
vaẓīfeh, see *vaẓā'if*.
vazīr, minister. The relative importance of the *vazīr* varied at different times. Under the Abbasid caliphs the *vazīr* was first the head of the chancellery; under Hārūn ar-Rashīd the office increased in importance. Under the Seljūqs the *vazīr* was the chief official in the bureaucracy but the office of *vazīr* declined in importance towards the end of the period. In the Ṣafavid period the *vazīr* was merely a minister.

**vīhir*, land dug after a crop has been harvested and left to lie fallow (Joushaqān).

vijīn kardan, to weed.

**vīl*, spade (Vafsī).

**vilgār* (Bīrjand), see *ṣayfī*.

vujūhāt, see *jihāt*.

vujūhi havā'ī (obs.), casual imposts (cf. the modern expression *pūli havā'ī*, a 'windfall').

vujūh ul-'ayn (obs.), (?) taxes levied by way of a proportion of the produce and converted into cash before payment.

**vūsh*, the upright shaft of a plough at right-angles to the beam (Kirmān).

yāftajeh, deed of quittance (*T.Q.*, p. 149).

**yak kār*, method of dividing the share of *daym* crops between the owner of the draught animals and the peasant by which the latter gets one-fifth (Jahrum).

yām, post station, postal service (Īlkhān and Āq Qoyunlū periods).

yāmbardār, levies for the post (Āq Qoyunlū period).

yārghūchī, investigator, prosecutor (Īlkhān period; see Mīnovī and Minorsky, *B.S.O.A.S.*, x. 771).

yarlīgh, yarlīgh khānī, royal order (Īlkhān period and also in later periods).

yāsāma, taxes other than *qilān* and *qubchūr* which were levied on nomads and peasants (see Hinz, 'Steuerinschriften', *Belleten*, xiii. 52, p. 743, n. 11).

**yāvarī* (Khurāsān), see *bīgārī*.

yaylāq, summer quarters.

yirghū, levy for the investigation of crimes (Īlkhān period).

yirlīgh, see *yarlīgh*.

**yūch*, ox-yoke (Vafsī).

yūgh, ox-yoke.

yurt, yūrt, tribal pasture.

yūshin, see *chahār shākh* (Joushaqān).

ẓābiṭ, revenue collector, controller; bailiff.

**za'īm*, peasant (Balūchistān and Kirmān).

zakāt, legal obligatory alms paid by Muslims on fruits of the field planted for food, fruits (especially grapes and dates), camels, oxen, flocks and domestic animals, gold and silver, and merchandise. A taxable minimum (*niṣāb*) for each of these categories was fixed. The yield from *zakāt* was destined for certain special classes (excluding the family of Muḥammad in contradistinction to *fay'* and *ghanīma*) as set out in the Qur'an, Sūra, ix. 60. In Kurdistān at the present day the term *zakāt* is used to denote a due paid by the peasants to the local *mullā*.

zakāt ul-fiṭr, obligatory gift of provisions for the poor at the end of the month of Ramaẓān.

zāri' (pl. *zāri'īn*), cultivator; (Hashtrūd) crop-sharing peasant.

ẓarībeh, premium or special levy made in connexion with the conversion of taxes assessed in one currency but paid in another (*T.Q.*, pp. 142–4; the term also occurs in Seljūq documents possibly with the same meaning).

zar kharīd: when the *a'yān* of *khāliṣeh* were bought (as distinct from the land itself which remained *khāliṣeh*) they were thenceforward known as *zar kharīd* (late Qājār period).

ẓī'ā (obs.; pl. of *ẓī'at*), landed estates.

zih kashī, draining (land).

ẕimmī (obs.), member of a protected community, i.e. a Jew, Christian, or Sabaean. Zoroastrians were not, properly speaking, *ẕimmīs*, but the term at an early date was extended to include them also.

**zīneh*, winter crops (Bīrjand).

**zinjī* (Bīrjand), see *kurūsheh*.

ẕirā', a measure of length, approx. 1 *gaz*.

**zouj* (Khurāsān), yoke of oxen; plough-land; measure of water.

**zū'ī* (Kirmān), pipe through which an irrigation channel flows; see also *kaval*.

**zung* (Sīstān), see *kurūsheh*.

ẕurratshikan, one who reaps maize.

INDEX